The political will of the business elite of nineteenth-century Brazil was expressed most clearly and forcefully through its organized interest groups (also known as pressure groups). Traditional advisory and regulatory prerogatives, lack of competing interest groups, and unexcelled access to government gave Brazilian business interest groups in the nineteenth century power unequaled by such organizations today. They affected development mainly by influencing the scope and direction of government support. This book examines their role in development and, through them, the business elite that they represented.

Business interest groups assumed much responsibility for the welfare of Brazilian agriculture. They tried to upgrade the quality of agricultural exports and helped market them, fought export taxation, and attempted to arrange cheap, ready rural credit. Several groups also tried to ensure agriculture's labor supply by defending slavery. Through their prerogative of advising on tariffs and through participation in the debate over economic liberalism, business interest groups strongly affected the pace of industrialization. By introducing new systems of communications, they helped determine Brazil's communications infrastructure. They also aided the young Brazilian state in economic and urban integration. Lastly, the most important of the business interest groups, the commercial associations, also may be seen as institutions through which ties of dependency to better-developed nations overseas were maintained.

CAMBRIDGE LATIN AMERICAN STUDIES

GENERAL EDITOR
SIMON COLLIER

ADVISORY COMMITTEE
MALCOLM DEAS, STUART SCHWARTZ, ARTURO VALENZUELA

78

BUSINESS INTEREST GROUPS IN NINETEENTH-CENTURY
BRAZIL

BUSINESS INTEREST GROUPS
IN NINETEENTH-CENTURY BRAZIL

EUGENE RIDINGS
Winona State University

CAMBRIDGE
UNIVERSITY PRESS

Published by the Press Syndicate of the University of Cambridge
The Pitt Building, Trumpington Street, Cambridge CB2 1RP
40 West 20th Street, New York, NY 10011-4211, USA
10 Stamford Road, Oakleigh, Melbourne 3166, Australia

First published in 1994

Printed in the United States of America

Library of Congress Cataloging-in-Publication Data
Ridings, Eugene.
Business interest groups in nineteenth-century Brazil / Eugene
Ridings
p.   cm. – (Cambridge Latin American studies ; 78)
Includes bibliographical references and index.
ISBN 0-521-45485-9
1. Pressure groups – Brazil – History – 19th century. 2. Commercial
associations – Brazil – History – 19th century. I. Title.
II. Series.
JL2481.R55   1994
322.4'3'098109034 – dc20   93-32152

A catalog record for this book is available from the British Library.

ISBN 0-521-45485-9 hardback

To Neill Macaulay

Contents

Acknowledgments

This work was made possible with the help of many individuals and institutions. Primary thanks must be given Neill Macaulay, not only for this book but for much of my scholarly work. His support and encouragement began with my dissertation at the University of Florida and has been constant in the many years since. This backing is all the more appreciated because we differ in many of our economic views. Kendrick Clements, Joan Meznar, Patricia Mulvey, Michael Trochim, and John Hoyt Williams also read the entire manuscript and improved it with their comments. Other scholars over the years have helped shape my ideas through criticism, suggestion, or discussion. They include Donald Barnhart, George Bates, Seymour Byman, R. Frank Colson, James Eddy, Richard Graham, the late Phil Brian Johnson, Kenneth Kiple, Eul-Soo Pang, José Gabriel da Costa Pinto, Thomas Skidmore, Sheldon Smith, and Joseph Sweigart. Responsibility for the interpretations and any errors of this work is, of course, mine alone. Research during numerous trips to Brazil was facilitated by the advice or the kindness of Roderick and Jean Barman, Rudy Bauss, Roberto da Cunha, Marc and Judith Hoffnagel, Martha Knisely Huggins, Margaret Wright Maia, Ron L. Seckinger, the late Olive Shaw, and José Luiz Werneck da Silva.

Institutions not only of research but of business are basic to a study such as this. Central places for my research were many of Brazil's commercial associations and other business interest groups whose leaders not only provided the indispensable right to use their archives but often valuable guidance as well. Special thanks is due the Associação Comercial da Bahia and Carlos Tôrres, the Associação Comercial de Pernambuco and Oscar Frederico Raposo Barbosa and Luís Moura, the Associação Comercial do Rio de Janeiro and Raul de Góes and Carlos Alberto Silva de Abreu, the Associação Comercial de Santos, the Associação Comercial de São Paulo and Marcel Domingos Solimeo, and the Centro Industrial do Rio de Janeiro and Edgard Lauria. As important were Brazilian institutions of research and their personnel. I am especially grateful to Raul de Lima and José Gabriel da Costa Pinto of the Arquivo Nacional, Maria Marta Gonçalves of the

Arquivo Histórico de Itamaratí, Adelaide Alba of the Instituto Histórico e Geográfico Brasileiro, and Aida Ortiz Cardim of the Arquivo do Estado de São Paulo, as well as to the staffs of the Arquivo Público Estadual de Pernambuco, and the Biblioteca Nacional, Rio de Janeiro. In Great Britain I was greatly aided by the staffs of the Adam Smith Record Store, the University, Glasgow, the Latin American Business Archives, University College Library, London, and the Manuscript Room, Sidney Jones Library, the University, Liverpool. Special thanks is due private mercantile and banking firms that generously granted access to their archives. I am particularly grateful to M. D. Thatcher of Churchill and Sim, Ltd., M. J. Orbell of Baring Brothers, P. K. Walker and Christopher Barrett of Norton, Megaw & Co., Ltd., London, and T. E. Kemp of Norton, Megaw & Co., Brazil, for permission and guidance. This by no means lists all the individuals who have helped my research. Over the years – too many – it took to complete this study I have lost or forgotten some of their names. To them I can offer only a heartfelt apology.

    Works like this are always made possible by generous financial support. I have benefited from two American Philosophical Society Research Grants, two Organization of American States Research Fellowships, a Fulbright-Hays Faculty Research Abroad Fellowship, and numerous research grants from Winona State University.

    In the preparation of this book for publication, particular thanks is owed to Simon Collier for his patience and assistance and to Frank Smith, Russell Hahn, and others of the editorial staff at Cambridge University Press. Finally, I owe a special debt of gratitude to my wife, Kristin, for her editorial help, patience, and support over many years.

Abbreviations and usage

AACB	Arquivo da Associação Comercial da Bahia, Salvador
AACP	Arquivo da Associação Comercial de Pernambuco, Recife
AACRJ	Arquivo da Associação Comercial do Rio de Janeiro
AACS	Arquivo da Associação Comercial de Santos
ABC	Arquivo do Barão de Cotegipe, AIHGB, Rio de Janeiro
ACD	*Anais da Câmera dos Deputados*
ACIRJ	Arquivo do Centro Industrial do Rio de Janeiro
AEB	Arquivo do Estado da Bahia, Salvador
AHI	Arquivo Histórico do Itamaraty, Rio de Janeiro
AIHGB	Arquivo do Instituto Histórico e Geográfico Brasileiro, Rio de Janeiro
BN	Biblioteca Nacional, Rio de Janeiro
HAHR	*Hispanic American Historical Review*
JLAS	*Journal of Latin American Studies*
LABA, UCL	Latin American Business Archives, University College, London
NA/DS	United States National Archives/Department of State
PRO/FO	Public Records Office/Foreign Office
RMACOP	Brazil, *Relatório do Ministério de Agricultura, Comércio, e Obras Públicas*
RMF	Brazil, *Relatório do Ministério da Fazenda*
SH/AN	Seção Histórico, Arquivo Nacional
SPE/AN	Seção do Poder Executivo, Arquivo Nacional
USRC	*United States Reports from Consuls*

Usage

Modern Brazilian Portuguese spelling is used in both text and citations. Date of actual publication is used when citing *relatórios* (annual reports), even when most of the events discussed in the reports took place the previous year.

Value of the *Mil-reis* against the Dollar and the Pound, 1834-1905

Year	Dollar	Pound (in pence, d)
	Exchange at 43 $\frac{1}{8}$ d	
1834	.79	38 $\frac{3}{4}$
1835	.80	39 $\frac{1}{4}$
1836	.78	38 $\frac{7}{16}$
1837	.60	29 $\frac{9}{16}$
1838	.57	28 $\frac{1}{16}$
1839	.64	31 $\frac{5}{8}$
1840	.63	31
1841	.61	30 $\frac{5}{16}$
1842	.54	26 $\frac{13}{16}$
1843	.52	25 $\frac{13}{16}$
1844	.51	25 $\frac{3}{16}$
1845	.52	25 $\frac{7}{16}$
1846	.55	26 $\frac{15}{16}$
	Exchange at 27 d	
1847	.57	28
1848	.51	25
1849	.52	25 $\frac{7}{8}$
1850	.58	28 $\frac{3}{4}$
1851	.59	29 $\frac{1}{8}$
1852	.56	27 $\frac{7}{16}$
1853	.58	28 $\frac{1}{2}$
1854	.56	27 $\frac{5}{8}$
1855	.56	27 $\frac{9}{16}$
1856	.56	27 $\frac{9}{16}$
1857	.54	26 $\frac{5}{8}$
1858	.52	25 $\frac{9}{16}$
1859	.51	25 $\frac{1}{16}$
1860	.52	25 $\frac{13}{16}$
1861	.52	25 $\frac{9}{16}$
1862	.53	26 $\frac{5}{16}$
1863	.55	27 $\frac{1}{4}$
1864	.54	26 $\frac{3}{4}$
1865	.51	25

Value of the Mil-reis

Year	Dollar	Pound (in pence, d)
	Exchange at 27 d	
1866	.49	$24\frac{1}{4}$
1867	.46	$22\frac{7}{16}$
1868	.34	17
1869	.38	$18\frac{13}{16}$
1870	.45	$22\frac{1}{16}$
1871	.49	$24\frac{1}{32}$
1872	.51	25
1873	.53	$26\frac{3}{32}$
1874	.52	$25\frac{25}{32}$
1875	.55	$26\frac{7}{32}$
1876	.51	$25\frac{11}{42}$
1877	.50	$24\frac{9}{16}$
1878	.47	$22\frac{15}{16}$
1879	.43	$21\frac{3}{4}$
1880	.45	$22\frac{3}{32}$
1881	.44	$21\frac{29}{32}$
1882	.43	$21\frac{5}{32}$
1883	.44	$21\frac{9}{16}$
1884	.42	$20\frac{11}{16}$
1885	.38	$18\frac{19}{32}$
1886	.38	$18\frac{11}{16}$
1887	.46	$22\frac{7}{16}$
1888	.51	$25\frac{1}{4}$
1889	.54	$26\frac{7}{16}$
1890	.46	$22\frac{9}{16}$
1891	.30	$14\frac{29}{32}$
1892	.24	$12\frac{1}{32}$
1893	.24	$11\frac{19}{32}$
1894	.20	$10\frac{3}{32}$
1895	.20	$9\frac{5}{16}$
1896	.18	$9\frac{1}{16}$
1897	.16	$7\frac{23}{32}$
1898	.15	$7\frac{3}{16}$
1899	.15	$7\frac{7}{16}$
1900	.19	$9\frac{1}{2}$
1901	.23	$11\frac{3}{8}$
1902	.24	$11\frac{31}{32}$
1903	.24	$12\frac{9}{32}$
1904	.25	$12\frac{7}{32}$
1905	.32	$15\frac{57}{64}$

Sources: Julian Smith Duncan, *Public and Private Operation of Railways in Brazil* (New York: Columbia University Press, 1932), p. 183; Centro Industrial do Brasil, *Brazil: Its Natural Riches and Industries* (Foreign Edition). *Volume I: Preface-Productive Industry* (Paris: Librarie Aillaud, 1910), p. 232.

Brazil, with cities. *Source:* C. H. Haring, *Empire in Brazil: A New World Experiment with Monarchy* (Cambridge, Mass.: Harvard University Press, 1958)

LEGEND:
1. RIO GRANDE DO NORTE
2. PARAÍBA
3. PERNAMBUCO
4. ALAGOAS
5. SERGIPE
6. RIO DE JANEIRO

Introduction

The idea of writing a history of Brazilian business interest groups came by accident. Many years ago I arrived in Salvador to undertake research, only to find that my topic had been taken. Desperate to find another, and aware that the Commercial Association of Bahia had played a role in regional politics, I obtained permission to leaf through its archival records. The dusty nineteenth-century annual reports (*relatórios*), minutes (*atas*) of its meetings, and other records stored in the attic of its historic headquarters were something of a revelation. They indicated that the Bahian association, and by inference other commercial associations, had rather quietly exercised great influence on all levels of government. The commercial associations today remain among the most powerful of organized interest groups (also called pressure groups) in Brazil, but their impact obviously had been much stronger in the nineteenth century, when other organized interest groups were few, great corporations had yet to appear in any number, and countervailing, or contrary, influences were rare.[1] As Philippe Schmitter has noted, "Until well into the twentieth century these commercial associations served as the sole aggregators of the interest of the conservative classes,"[2] that is, merchants, industrialists, and planters. Wider research showed that the influence of the commercial associations was sometimes enhanced and sometimes contradicted by two other types of potent, although usually less enduring, business interest organizations: the factor and industrial groups.

There is no book-length treatment of Brazilian business interest groups in the nineteenth century, although numerous histories of individual commercial associations have been written by members or employees of those organizations.[3] These treatments vary greatly in quality and often say

1. For advantages in the use of the term "interest group," now prevalent, rather than "pressure group," see Graham Wootton, *Interest Groups* (Englewood Cliffs, N.J.: Prentice Hall, 1970), p. 76. For the importance of countervailing power in interest group politics, see V. O. Key, *Politics, Parties, and Pressure Groups* (4th ed.; New York: Thomas Y. Crowell, 1958), pp. 112, 166–167.
2. *Interest Conflict and Political Change in Brazil* (Stanford, Calif.: Stanford University Press, 1971), p. 142.
3. For Rio de Janeiro, see Eudes Barros, *A Associação Comercial no Império e na República* (2d ed. rev.;

little about the central purpose of the groups: influencing government. With some exceptions, professional historians of Brazil have shown little interest in the subject.[4] In part, the power of business interest groups has been underestimated in both past and present because their leaders wished it so. They wanted to keep their success in moving government inconspicuous. They realized, as do most interest groups today, that continued strong influence on government depended on that influence being used judiciously and inconspicuously. Moreover, the organizations they led were objects of suspicion. As will be seen, businessmen were traditionally mistrusted in Luso-Brazilian culture and so by extension were their organizations. A further cause of suspicion of Brazil's business elite was that most of it was foreign, that is, composed of persons holding citizenship other than Brazilian. The commercial associations, often led by foreigners, were particularly liable to nationalist resentments. In general, business interest group leaders hoped that public perception of the power of their organizations would be less than its reality.

Business interest groups had strong bases for such power in the nineteenth century. One was the relative absence of other types of interest groups. Nor had the great corporation yet made a significant appearance. In a period when most firms were simple partnerships and necessarily of limited size, only collective representation could exert the pressures on government that corporations do today. Another asset for business interest groups were advisory and regulatory prerogatives inherited from the centuries-old traditions of Iberian corporatism. Finally, group leaders enjoyed numerous and varied personal relationships with government decision makers. These resources gave business interest groups unmatched

Rio de Janeiro: Gráfica Olímpica, 1975), and Heitor Beltrão, *Um Capítulo da História da Praça do Rio de Janeiro: Considerações de Ordem Histórica e Jurídica, 1820–1929* (Rio de Janeiro: Imprensa Nacional, 1929); for Pernambuco, Estevão Pinto, *A Associação Comercial de Pernambuco* (Recife: Jornal do Comércio, 1940); for Bahia, M. S. L. Valverde, *Subsídio para a História da Associação Comercial da Bahia* (Salvador: Duas Américas, 1917), and Waldemar Mattos, *Palácio da Associação Comercial da Bahia (Antiga Praça do Comércio)* (Salvador: Benditina, 1950); for Amazonas, Associação Comercial do Amazonas, *Documentário Comemorativo do Primeiro Centenário da Associação Comercial do Amazonas, 18 de Junho de 1971* (Manaus: Associação Comercial do Amazonas, 1971); for Ceará, José Bonifácio de Souza, *Associação Comercial do Ceará: Memória Histórica, 1868–1968* (Fortaleza: Associação Comercial do Ceará, 1969); for Maceió, Moacir Medeiros de Santa Ana, *Uma Associação Centenária* (Maceió: Arquivo Público de Alagôas, 1966). Much on the Maranhão organization is found in Jerônimo de Viveiros, *História do Comércio do Maranhão, 1612–1895* (2 vols.; São Luís: Associação Comercial do Maranhão, 1954).

4. Conspicuous exceptions are Barbara Weinstein, who used the annual reports of the Commercial Association of Pará in *The Amazon Rubber Boom, 1850–1920* (Stanford, Calif.: Stanford University Press, 1983), and Evaldo Cabral de Melo, who based much of *O Norte Agrário e o Império, 1871–1889* (Rio de Janeiro: Nova Fronteira, 1984) on annual reports and minutes of the Commercial Association of Pernambuco. Nícia Villela Luz has much material on the Industrial Association (*Associação Industrial*) in her *A Luta pela Industrialização do Brasil (1808 a 1930)* (2d ed.; São Paulo: Alfa-Omega, 1975).

access to a government smaller and less complex than is common today. Politicians and bureaucrats willingly accepted and responded to their counsel because it fulfilled a role traditional for business interest groups in Iberian culture and because of the pivotal position of group membership in the Brazilian economy. It also answered a lack of expertise in government circles about business, economics, and processes leading toward modernization. The "technocrat" had yet to make an appearance on the government stage. Even when government expertise was not lacking, it was considered advisable, as a Minister of Finance (*Ministro da Fazenda*) acknowledged to the Board of Directors of the Commercial Association of Rio de Janeiro in 1896, to hear the "opinion of experience" and the "concepts of knowledgeable men."[5]

The purpose of this book is to examine and evaluate the role of organized business interest groups in the development of Brazil from 1834, date of the founding of the first permanent organization, the Commercial Association of Rio de Janeiro, to 1900. Over the years the term "development" has given rise to considerable controversy. For my purposes, development includes economic growth in all its forms, industrial and agricultural, inward- and outward-oriented, and also modernization. Nor does my use of the term imply any judgment as to the direction or justice of the distribution of the wealth created. A second, somewhat subsidiary, aim of this study is to examine the characteristics and will of the business elite itself, as they are revealed through its groups. In both aims my focus is on the organized interest group itself. Business interest groups affected Brazilian development in the nineteenth century in a number of significant ways. My approach is to examine each, developing from them various subsidiary theoretical issues. At the same time, the choice of topics and the extent to which they are examined are determined by the groups themselves. Those not covered are topics in which Brazil's nineteenth-century business interest groups either had little interest or were unwilling to take a public stand.

A brief survey will indicate the scope of business interest group activity in development. Perhaps in no other area was this activity more central to development than in industrialization. Business interest groups mainly affected it by influencing the amount and direction of government aid, virtually indispensable for the growth of manufacturing in the context of nineteenth-century Brazil. Advisory prerogatives derived from corporate tradition and from the role of their membership in industrialization gave them a number of ways to do so. Business interest groups also affected industrialization by being main participants in the debate over economic

5. Minutes, meeting of March 15, 1896, Livro de Atas, 1890–1896, AACRJ, p. 112.

liberalism. Appeals to the public over economic philosophy also formed part of the public relations efforts of business interest groups, efforts in which they took a role similar to that of corporations today.

Commercial associations and factor groups assumed responsibility for the welfare of agriculture. The former did so specifically for the exports of the regions they represented, the latter for either the sugar or coffee industry. This responsibility was impelled partly by the relative absence and the lethargy of agricultural groups and by the landed interests of many of the business elite, but mainly by the realization that the prosperity of export agriculture was the base on which the entire Brazilian economy rested. Business interest groups worked to upgrade the quality and volume of export commodities. They tried through various means to provide abundant, cheap credit for planters. They also attempted to help agriculture by marketing exports abroad and by campaigning against export taxation. Finally, business interest groups tried to assure planters sufficient workers, through slavery, forced labor, and immigration.

Business interest groups helped determine Brazil's communications infrastructure, including ports and their approaches. Mainly through influencing government aid, but sometimes through their own initiative or funding, they helped introduce the railroad, steam navigation, and the telegraph to Brazil. They were able to influence the geographical patterns in which these innovations were laid out and also which harbors first would be cleared of geographical obstacles and modernized.

Also important to development was the integrating role of business interest groups in the economy and in urban areas. In some cases they substituted for private initiative, founding or helping found banks, insurance companies, railroads, and steamer lines that otherwise would have been lacking. More often they acted as a surrogate for government, performing services that today would be considered the responsibility of the state. They regulated business practices and business personnel and supplied otherwise unobtainable information, including statistics. They provided or helped set up vital urban services and dispensed charity and disaster relief. These services were particularly relevant, because the Brazilian state was administratively weak and other voluntary organizations with resources were few. The basis of many of these integrating functions was prerogatives derived from the Iberian corporate tradition. Business interest groups, especially the commercial associations, were a concrete expression of this tradition.

In addition to illuminating the key role of business interest groups in the development of Brazil during the nineteenth century, this book aims at examining its business elite through those groups. The business elite was certainly the most affluent segment of the urban middle class and probably the most dynamic in its claims on government. The commercial associations provide useful parameters for study of that elite, as well as insights into it. Membership in them may be said to define the business elite in major cities. The commercial associations were intended to represent that entire elite, and most prominent businessmen were members even though they might also have belonged to a factor or industrial group. Recruiting policies and high dues kept nonelite businessmen from joining. The leadership, or top echelon, of the business elite may be defined by membership on commercial association boards of directors. Boards were composed to reflect proportionately elite business interests, as well as the prestige of the individual chosen. Selection was made by those most knowledgeable of such criteria: the board member's peers in the business community. Commercial association boards of directors form particularly convenient and representational units for study of the economic and personal interests of the leaders of Brazil's business elite.

Equally important, the political role and the political will of the business elite logically may best be understood through the actions of its representative groups before government. Examination of such actions may clear up long-standing misconceptions. Contrary to supposition, for example, businessmen who were part of the export complex did not favor the depreciation of Brazilian exchange, which increased the remuneration of the export sector.[6] Except when shaken by agricultural distress, they supported a stable currency, preferably one based on precious metals (see Chapter 5). Nor was the restrictive 1860 law on incorporation, often blamed for inhibiting Brazilian development, forced by agrarian-minded legislators on a resisting business elite.[7] Business interest groups did not oppose it (see Chapter 11). An examination of group views not only serves to correct misconceptions about business elite attitudes, but to illuminate broader questions. Did overseas merchants in Brazil, for example, share with their counterparts in other nations a cosmopolitan ideology of radical liberalism and free trade?[8] The views of the business elite may best be understood through the organizations that expressed its will before government and the public. The business elite is commonly studied as part of often vaguely defined abstractions such as "middle class," "middle sectors," or "urban groups." Organized representative groups, acting in concrete situations, offer an attractive alternative means of examination of that elite.

6. Celso Furtado, *The Economic Growth of Brazil: A Survey from Colonial to Modern Times* (Berkeley: University of California Press, 1965), pp. 182–185; Nelson Werneck Sodré, *Formação Histórica do Brasil* (4th ed.; São Paulo: Brasiliense, 1967), pp. 264–265.

7. Nelson Werneck Sodré, *História da Burguesia Brasileira* (2d ed.; Rio de Janeiro: Civilização Brasileira, 1967), p. 161; Peter L. Eisenberg, *The Sugar Industry in Pernambuco, 1840–1910: Modernization without Change* (Berkeley: University of California Press, 1974), p. 75.

8. The concept of a worldwide "cosmopolitan bourgeoise," bound together by shared ideology as well as business and kinship ties, is found in Charles A. Jones, *International Business in the Nineteenth Century: The Rise and Fall of a Cosmopolitan Bourgeoise* (Brighton, Sussex: Wheatsheaf Books, 1987).

Finally, Brazilian business interest groups, particularly the commercial associations, also can be of interest to students of dependency. Studies of dependency have often been criticized for offering too much theory and too little empirical evidence to back their assertions (to be sure, an approach more common in the 1960s and 1970s). Here, no sweeping theoretical construct is offered, rather an insight into a viable mechanism for the transmission of foreign influence. Commercial associations were commonly led by the managers of foreign companies operating in Brazil and had foreign majorities among membership. Possessing access of the highest order to politicians and administrators, the commercial associations were an effective means by which foreigners, both in Brazil and in the headquarters of their firms at home, could exercise influence on the Brazilian government. Their actions also help answer a related question: What policies did foreigners favor? They would be the policies supported by the boards of directors of those associations most dominated by aliens. Some indication of foreign influence on economic development can be recorded through the commercial associations.

Some explanation should be offered about the parameters of this study. To begin at 1834, date of foundation of the first lasting business interest group, is logical, but what of 1900? It would be more conventional to end with the overthrow of the Empire in 1889. However, here conventionality would miss a key period of transition. Change is usually the most interesting part of history. While the year 1889 brought no marked change in the groups themselves, the decade 1890–1900 witnessed a notable, significant decline in the status of commercial associations. Of course, the associations did not cease to be influential after 1900. They continued strong during the Old Republic and remain today among the most important of Brazil's organized interest groups and among its best known institutions. But the great preponderance of power they had enjoyed during most of the nineteenth century weakened decisively during 1890–1900. It had been based on the paucity of other lasting interest groups, especially those with countervailing influence, and on the nearly unquestioned ascendancy of the export-import economy based on free trade that they represented. Both conditions ended around 1900.

The first agricultural interest group with national representation appeared in 1897. More significant as far as countervailing influence is concerned, around the turn of the century small industrial interest groups, usually organized around a single branch of manufacturing, arose for the first time. The first lasting group representing all national industry was founded in 1904. Similarly, during the decade 1890–1900 tariffs became increasingly protectionist. For the first time, commercial association objections were largely ineffective. Rate increases culminated in the Tariff of 1900, the first in Brazilian history that truly could be described as a protective tariff.[9] Perhaps equally significant as an indicator of diminished power, for the first time no commercial association was consulted by the Brazilian government when it fixed a tariff. The decade 1890–1900 was one of novel, decisive change in the status of Brazil's most important business interest groups. The year 1900 marked a major turning point in Brazilian development. It seems an appropriate date on which to end a study of groups that profoundly affected that development.

9. Stanley J. Stein, *The Brazilian Cotton Manufacture: Textile Enterprise in an Underdeveloped Area, 1850–1950* (Cambridge, Mass.: Harvard University Press, 1957), p. 85.

1

The genesis of Brazilian business interest groups

The rise of business interest organizations in the nineteenth century reflected first the increasing prosperity and complexity of Brazil's international trade and later the significant growth of manufacturing. These
organizations included commercial associations, industrial groups, and
factor groups. Factors acted as intermediaries between the overseas merchant and the export producer, not only marketing the latter's commodities but usually furnishing him with credit and consumer goods as well.
Commercial associations and factor groups were created to confront the
problems and grasp the opportunities of an expanding economy based on
foreign commerce. More specifically, commercial associations aimed at
promoting the economic development of the region tributary to the entrepôt they represented and defending the general interests of overseas
trade. Factor groups worked to bolster the prosperity of sugar and coffee
exportation. Industrial groups promoted the spread of manufacturing.
Realization of all such objectives required a favorable attitude from the
state or its outright aid. Government intervention in the economy was a
Brazilian tradition that even the fashion for economic liberalism in the
nineteenth century would do little to weaken. Business interest groups
would mainly affect Brazilian development by influencing the government's role in the economy.

Advancing the interests of overseas trade, local prosperity, industry, or a
specific commodity required collective representation. Large corporations
were few in nineteenth-century Brazil, and individual business firms, as
elsewhere, of limited size and economic impact. They usually consisted of
several partners operating on such capital as they could raise themselves.
Individually such partnerships, even those representing large overseas
trading companies, could exercise little influence on government. Complicating the problem of dealing with government was the fact that the
majority of Brazil's business elite, particularly its overseas trader and

manufacturer elements, was foreign, that is, holding citizenship other than Brazilian.[1] Collective representation was a practical necessity.

The technological advances of the nineteenth century offered opportunities, not only for manufacturing but for the expansion of overseas trade. Export volume and quality, for example, could be increased by new or improved agricultural machines, cultivation techniques, processing, and varieties of plants and animals. Such innovations were particularly important in Brazil in view of the notorious backwardness of its farming and agricultural processing methods (see Chapter 4). Commercial associations and factor groups were to assume much responsibility for the introduction of agricultural improvements, in addition to the general welfare of Brazilian agriculture. Other opportunities for economic expansion came from innovations in communications. The railroad, the steamship, and the telegraph would make overseas trade less risky, expand the frontiers of export plantation agriculture, cheapen the importation of consumer goods, and even widen the trade area tributary to an entrepôt. Trade rivalries between major entrepôts also impelled improvement in communications. But such improvements were expensive; most had to be introduced with government aid or sponsorship. To secure this vital backing for improvements benefiting its entrepôt would be a prime task of each commercial association.

Along with opportunities for expanded prosperity arose problems. Confronting them also required collective representation. Industrialists had the problem of convincing the nation that manufacturing was desirable or even feasible in nineteenth-century Brazil. Most influential Brazilians held the conviction that the nation's "natural" or "God-given" role was that of exporter of raw materials and importer of manufactured goods in a world economy governed by the principles of free trade.[2] Nearly all Brazilian manufactures lacked established markets and skilled labor and had to import much of their raw material and fuel and nearly all of their machinery. Without government aid in the form of subsidies, low-cost loans, tax exemptions, and especially tariff protection, the chances of industry for expansion, even survival, were precarious.

The long-dominant export-import economy also faced problems. Overseas competition and inefficient Brazilian production brought crises in cotton and sugar exportation, the former dating from the end of the Civil War in the United States, the latter from the early 1870s. Coffee and rubber prices fell in the 1880s and coffee again in the second half of the

1. Eugene W. Ridings, "Business, Nationality, and Dependency in Late Nineteenth Century Brazil," *JLAS*, 14 (May 1982): 55–96. This definition of the terms "foreign" and "foreigner" will be used throughout.
2. Heitor Ferreira Lima, *História do Pensamento Econômico no Brasil* (São Paulo: Editôra Nacional, 1976), pp. 80–82.

1890s. Factor groups were specifically created to confront the crises in sugar and coffee. They joined the commercial associations in searching for ways to improve the quality and the growing, processing, and marketing of faltering exports.

The most persistent of problems for business was taxes. Overseas commerce was the focal point of Brazil's taxation system: throughout the nineteenth century some seventy to seventy-five percent of national tax revenues were extracted in the customs house.[3] Merchants also bore the brunt of other forms of taxation. These included levies on business transactions, the urban real estate tax (*décima urbana*), and the Industries and Professions Tax (*Impôsto de Indústrias e Professões*), a sort of primitive income tax that fell almost entirely on businessmen, touching professionals but lightly and exempting landowners entirely.[4] Import duties, Brazil's main source of revenue, tended to rise during the nineteenth century, propelled first by revenue needs and later also by a desire to protect native industry. Protective tariffs by definition damaged importation and were thought to hurt exportation as well. The Alves Branco Tariff of 1844 put an end to an era of virtual free trade, but even in the 1830s, revenue demands had begun to push duties upward, whenever it could be done without violating treaty commitments.[5] This threat helped create Brazil's first lasting business interest groups, the commercial associations of Rio de Janeiro, Pernambuco, and Bahia, in 1834, 1839, and 1840. The tendency of import tariffs to climb increased during the 1880s and then accelerated with the coming of the Republic in 1889.

Taxes on export commodities, pushed by the same fiscal necessity as import tariffs, also rose during the second half of the nineteenth century. Commercial associations and factor groups blamed them for much of the difficulty of Brazilian exports in competing in world markets. Provincial (after 1889 state) customs duties also presented a serious threat to prosperity. National export or import levies could theoretically be passed on to the consumer, but provincial export or import duties, if higher than those of

---

3. Amaro Cavalcanti, *Resenha Financeira do Ex-Império do Brasil em 1889* (Rio de Janeiro: Imprensa Nacional, 1890), p. 11; Nathaniel H. Leff, "Economic Retardation in Nineteenth-Century Brazil," *Economic History Review*, 25 (Aug. 1972): 503; Anibal Villanova Villela and Wilson Suzigan, *Política do Govêrno e Crescimento da Economia Brasileira, 1889–1945* (Rio de Janeiro: IPEA/INPES, 1975), pp. 9–10.

4. For Industries and Professions Tax regulations, see Brazil, laws, statutes, etc., *Coleção das Leis do Império do Brasil de 1874* (Rio de Janeiro: Tipografia Nacional, 1875), XXXVII, Part 2, II: 735–773, and *Leis, 1888*, LI, Part 2, I: 117–143.

5. As early as 1834, the Brazilian government attempted to circumvent the fifteen percent ceiling on duties by increasing the number and size of handling fees. Parkinson to Foreign Office, Salvador, Jan. 31, 1834, PRO/FO Microfilm Series 13/113, fl. 168; Charge d'Affairs W. R. Gordon to Brazilian Foreign Ministry, Rio de Janeiro, March 10, 1838, AHI, Rio de Janeiro, 284/3/9. In 1839 duties on some goods not specifically covered by treaty provisions were raised as high as fifty percent. Porter to Foreign Office, Salvador, Dec. 31, 1841, PRO/FO 13/174, fl. 263.

neighboring provinces, served to deflect trade to those provinces.[6] Excessive provincial duties could seriously damage the trade of an entrepôt. Not the least vexatious aspect of taxation was its regulation. Tax regulations were bewildering in number and variety. In Salvador, in 1833, the passage of goods from ship to merchant's warehouse often took sixty days; in Rio de Janeiro, in the late 1880s, the signatures of sixteen officials were necessary to liberate merchandise from the customs house.[7] For men who held dearly the proverb "time is money," combatting tax regulations was a prime reason for having collective representation before government.

Another area of concern for Brazil's business elite was less concrete than taxes but also painful: the status of their profession. Disdain for businessmen and for business as a profession had deep roots in Luso-Brazilian culture.[8] Overseas merchants and other large-scale businessmen enjoyed greater prestige than retailers, but still lacked social standing commensurate with their wealth. An early twentieth-century Bahian legislator summed up the attitude of many Brazilians: "In the opinion of many good people commerce is generally correctly reputed to be a necessary evil, a parasitic worm with two mouths, one attached to the consumers and one stuck to the producers, sucking their blood simultaneously."[9] This negative image was reflected in the reluctance of Brazilians to enter business as a profession and in the hostility of government officials with whom merchants dealt.[10] The task of rectifying it, essentially one of public relations, was one of the most urgent undertaken by business interest groups.

Business interest groups also assumed a third objective: compensating for the administrative weaknesses of government in a variety of fields. All had the right and duty, inherited from the traditions of Iberian corporatism, to advise and aid government in their area of specialty. The commercial associations, for example, were consulted on all matters related to

6. For example, Commercial Association of Pernambuco to Provincial Legislative Assembly, Recife, May 20, 1879, *Relatório da Associação Comercial Beneficente Lido na Assembléia Geral de 8 de Julho de 1879* (Recife: Mercantil, 1879), pp. 38–42; Speech by Luís Tarqüínio in *Jornal de Notícias* (Salvador), Aug. 26, 1882, p. 1; Commercial Association of Pernambuco to Provincial Legislative Assembly, no date, 1880, *Relatório de 1880*, pp. 69–72; Commercial Association of Pernambuco to Governor of State, Recife, Dec. 3, 1889, *Relatório de 1890*, pp. 9–11.

7. Parkinson to Foreign Office, Salvador, Jan. 31, 1834, PRO/FO 13/113, fl. 168; Cavalcanti, *Resenha Financeira*, p. 303.

8. Charles R. Boxer, *The Portuguese Seaborne Empire, 1415–1825* (New York: Alfred A. Knopf, 1969), pp. 318–319; A. J. R. Russell-Wood, *Fidalgos and Philanthropists: The Santa Casa da Misericórdia of Bahia, 1550–1755* (London: Macmillan, 1968), p. 125; Stuart B. Schwartz, *Sovereignty and Society in Colonial Brazil: The High Court of Bahia and Its Judges, 1609–1751* (Berkeley: University of California Press, 1973), p. 288.

9. Wenceslau Guimarães, May 11, 1928, Estado da Bahia, Assembléia Legislativa, *Diário da Assembléia* (Salvador: Imprensa Oficial do Estado, 1928), p. 285.

10. C. F. Van Delden Laërne, *Brazil and Java: Report on Coffee Culture in America, Asia, and Africa* (London: W. H. Allen, 1885), p. 189; James Wetherell, *Stray Notes from Bahia* (Liverpool: Webb and Hunt, 1860), p. 75; Associação Comercial do Maranhão, *Relatório da Diretoria da Associação Comercial do Maranhão, 1879* (São Luís: Frias, 1879), pp. 2–5.

economics, regulated business practices and business personnel, set weights and measures, helped supervise harbors, waterfronts, and adjacent urban areas, and dispensed charity and relief. Such functions, today usually the province of government, were not performed by private agencies simply because of fiscal and organizational deficiencies of the young Brazilian state.[11] Business interest organizations substituted for government in even the most economically and socially advanced nations, such as the United States, during the nineteenth century and had done so in Europe since late medieval times.[12] It was a burden that Brazilian business interest groups readily accepted, despite the time and expense involved. Eventually the Brazilian state would take over nearly all such activities, but it would do so later than in more developed nations.

A final objective of Brazilian business interest organizations was to provide a place for business activities, a function legally assigned the commercial associations and the factor group Commercial Agricultural Association (*Associação Comercial Agrícola*) of Pernambuco. Most of the business elite belonged to their local commercial association, even if they were also members of factor or industrial groups. The *praça do comércio* was the traditional name for the location, originally a *praça* or town square, of mercantile transactions and meetings. It became a synonym for commercial association and was in fact the original title that many took. The *praça do comércio* legally meant both the representative group before government of those engaged in commerce and their meeting place.[13] This double meaning was emphasized by an 1861 law that declared commercial associations to be the only legal place for market transactions and thus the location of the nation's incipient stock and commodity exchanges.[14]

For their members, commercial associations provided a repository of information essential to business: current price quotations, ship movements, tax regulations, trade statistics, and newspapers and journals from Brazil and overseas centers of commerce. In nineteenth-century Brazil such information usually could be had nowhere else. Finally, the commer-

11. On the weakness of the Brazilian state until mid-century, see Nelson Werneck Sodré, *Formação Histórica do Brasil* (4th ed.; São Paulo: Brasiliense, 1967), pp. 223–225. Fernando Uricoechea, *O Minotauro Imperial: A Burocratização do Estado Patrimonial Brasileiro no Século XIX* (Rio de Janeiro, São Paulo: DIFEL, 1978), discusses the gradual replacement of patriarchal by bureaucratic authority.

12. For an overview of business interest group activities in the United States, see Kenneth Sturges, *American Chambers of Commerce* (New York: Moffat Bard, 1915), Robert Sidney Smith, *The Spanish Guild Merchant: A History of the Consulado, 1250–1700* (Durham, N.C.: Duke University Press, 1940), pp. 60–85, and "A Research Report on Consulado History," *Journal of Interamerican Studies*, 3 (Jan. 1961): 41.

13. Brazil, laws, statutes, etc., *Código Comercial do Império do Brasil, Anotado . . . pelo Bacharel Salustiano Orlando de Araújo Costa* (2d ed.; Rio de Janeiro: Eduardo & Henrique Laemmert, 1869), p. 17.

14. Bernardino José Borges, *O Comerciante, ou Completo Manual Instrutivo* (2d ed. rev.; Rio de Janeiro: Eduardo & Henrique Laemmert, 1878), p. 142.

cial association building gave the businessman a place to relax and socialize with his peers in comfortable surroundings. In the days before the introduction of the social club to Brazil, this was no inconsiderable benefit.

The origins of business interest groups

The business interest groups of nineteenth-century Brazil were shaped by centuries-old tradition and by contemporary models. They were by no means unique. In organization, powers, and range of activities, they followed both the traditions of Iberian corporatism and the example of the nineteenth-century chambers of commerce of Great Britain and the United States.

The traditions of Iberian corporatism were fundamental in determining the relationship of the commercial associations with the state. From medieval times Portuguese and Spanish functional interest groups – guilds, corporations, or societies – enjoyed special legal privileges and direct access to the decision-making levels of government.[15] They had the right to have their opinion heard by the state on matters affecting their membership and in turn were expected to aid the state in administration, as advisers or supervisors.[16] Such corporations were closely linked to the government, whose official recognition endowed them with a juridical personality. Nevertheless, they retained considerable autonomy, together with claims to customary privilege, because of the recognized special interest of their membership.[17]

The Iberian corporate tradition was represented more strongly in the Spanish merchant guilds, or *consulados,* than in the short-lived medieval Portuguese business interest groups. Arising in the late thirteenth century, the *consulados* appeared in the New World first in Mexico City in the late sixteenth century, then in Lima in the early seventeenth. But only in the last decade of the eighteenth century did the Spanish crown create eight more.[18] These new *consulados* were expressly ordered to promote economic development and included landowners in number equal to busi-

15. Ronald C. Newton, "On 'Functional Groups,' 'Fragmentation,' and 'Pluralism' in Spanish American Political Society," *HAHR,* 50 (Feb. 1970): 9, 14, 25; Philippe C. Schmitter, "Still the Century of Corporatism?" in *The New Corporatism: Social-Political Structures in the Iberian World,* eds. Frederick B. Pike and Thomas Stritch (Notre Dame, Ind.: University of Notre Dame Press, 1974), p. 86.
16. Ronald C. Newton, "Natural Corporatism and the Passing of Populism in Spanish America," in Pike and Stritch, eds., *New Corporatism,* p. 46.
17. Ibid.; Howard J. Wiarda, "Corporatism and Development in the Iberic-Latin World: Persistent Strains and New Variations," in ibid., p. 18.
18. Robert Sidney Smith, "The Institution of the Consulado in the New World," *Hispanic American Historical Review,* 24 (Feb. 1944): 61, 73. The Consulado of Valencia was founded in 1283.

nessmen.[19] With some notable exceptions, the *consulados* of the New World did not long survive independence, most expiring before the end of the 1820s.[20] But they were well known to merchants in Brazil. Their orientation toward promoting development and the participation of landowners probably influenced similar policies in the commercial associations.

The *consulados* aided government by regulating business activities and business personnel, helping administer taxes and planning or even carrying out road, harbor, and navigational improvements.[21] These services were similar not only to many carried out later by Brazilian business interest groups, but by chambers of commerce. *Consulados* were also much like nineteenth-century business interest groups in organization. Both were led by an executive council elected by membership, were often housed in a merchants' exchange building, specifically intended for the transaction of business, and had a tribunal of merchant judges elected by membership, with original jurisdiction in mercantile disputes.[22] Only in their extremely close ties to the state and in their wider range of quasi-governmental administrative and regulatory activities did the *consulados* differ greatly from nineteenth-century business interest groups.

Portuguese business interest groups lacked the continuity of their Spanish counterparts. The first recorded Portuguese business organization was the Fund of Porto (*Bôlsa do Porto*), dating from 1293.[23] A similar group arose in Lisbon in the early fourteenth century.[24] The Fund of Porto was reconstituted in 1402 after apparently having been inactive. Its purposes were to furnish shipwreck insurance to membership by means of a common tax, to offer relief for members who fell into poverty, and to provide

19. Eduardo Arcila Farías, *El Real Consulado de Caracas* (Caracas: Universidad Central de Venezuela, 1957), pp. 11–12, 25–26; Ralph Lee Woodward, *Class Privilege and Economic Development: The Consulado de Comercio of Guatemala, 1793–1871* (Chapel Hill: University of North Carolina Press, 1966), pp. 7–9.

20. The Consulado of Guatemala lasted ·until 1871 and the Consulado of Lima into the 1850s. Woodward, *Class Privilege*, pp. 31, 33; Jorge Basadre, *Historia da la Cámera de Comercio de Lima* (Lima: Cámera de Comercio de Lima, 1963), p. 12; Paul Gootenberg, "The Social Origins of Protectionism and Free Trade in Nineteenth-Century Lima," *JLAS*, 14 (Nov. 1982): 333, 337. In 1832 the Consulado of Havana split, separating judicial and developmental functions, into the Junta de Comercio and Junta de Fomento. Julio Le Riverend, *Historia Económica de Cuba* (4th ed.; Havana: Instituto Cubano del Libro, 1974), p. 266.

21. Smith, *Spanish Guild Merchant*, pp. 55–56, 60–61, 76–83; Woodward, *Class Privilege*, pp. 25–26; Arcila Farías, *Consulado de Caracas*, pp. 38–41.

22. Arcila Farías, *Consulado de Caracas*, pp. 59, 64; Smith, "Research Report," 41; Basadre, *Cámera de Comercio de Lima*, p. 11.

23. Associação Comercial do Porto, *Associação Comercial do Porto: Resumo Histórico de sua Atividade desde a Fundação até ao Ano das Comemorações Centenárias* (Porto: Associação Comercial do Porto, 1942), p. 7.

24. Joaquim Roque Fonseca, *Cem Anos em Defesa da Economia Nacional, 1834–1934* (Lisbon: Associação Comercial de LIsboa, 1934), pp. 9–10.

an organization where the interests of commerce could be discussed.[25] But there is no evidence of the Fund of Porto or similar organizations surviving after the early fifteenth century. Not until 1722, when the General Welfare Board (*Mesa do Bem Comum*) was founded in Lisbon, did another representative group of businessmen appear.

The establishment of the General Welfare Board led to the foundation of Brazil's first formal group representing business. In 1726 Salvador merchants won the right to an organization known as both the General Welfare Board of Bahia and the Board of Commerce (*Mesa do Comércio*).[26] It consisted of twelve men elected by the overseas and wholesale merchants (*homens de negócio*) of the city. Its appearance expressed traditions of corporatism strong in Brazil. Since at least the 1620s in Salvador and the 1720s in Rio de Janeiro, merchants had assembled informal groups to present business opinion on key issues and to file protests.[27] Later, the right of businessmen to band together to voice their interests before government was confirmed by a 1755 edict defining twenty of them as constituting a representative *praça do comércio*.[28] The formation, beginning in the 1770s, of militia units in which merchants served as officers and their employees as enlisted men further increased the corporate consciousness of overseas merchants.[29]

The General Welfare Boards of both Bahia and Lisbon were short-lived. They made the mistake of offending Marquis Pombal (Sebastião José de Carvalho e Melo), autocratic and all-powerful chief minister of Portugal. Both openly protested one of Pombal's favorite projects, the creation in 1756 of a monopoly trading company for northern Brazil. Opposition to the Maranhão Company (*Companhia Mercantil do Grão Pará e Maranhão*) was at least partially instigated by the Jesuit order, whose economic interests in the region would also be damaged by the competing company. Pombal reacted fiercely. He ordered the General Welfare Board of Lisbon dissolved and sent several of its members to prison or into exile.[30] He then

25. Associação Comercial do Porto, *Associação Comercial do Porto*, p. 10.
26. Viceroy Conde dos Arcos to Thomé Joaquim da Costa Corte Real, Salvador, Aug. 24, 1757, Eduardo de Castro e Almeida, ed., *Inventário dos Documentos Relativos ao Brasil Existentes no Arquivo da Marinha e Ultramar de Lisboa*, Vol. 1: *Bahia, 1613–1752* (Rio de Janeiro: Biblioteca Nacional, 1913), p. 171; Catherine Lugar, "The Merchant Community of Salvador, Bahia, 1780–1830" (Ph.D. Diss., State University of New York at Stony Brook Press, 1980), pp. 23–24.
27. Rae Flory and David Grant Smith, "Bahian Merchants and Planters in the Seventeenth and Early Eighteenth Centuries," *HAHR*, 54 (Nov. 1978): 589; Luís Lisanti, "Estudos: Cenário e Personagens," in *Negócios Coloniais (uma Correspondência Comercial do Século XVIII)*, ed. Luís Lisanti (Rio de Janeiro: Ministério da Fazenda, 1973), I: cxxix, cxlvii.
28. Alfredo Pujol, "Consultas e Pareceres: LXXXVI, Associações Comerciaes," *Revista de Comércio e Indústria: Publicação Mensal do Centro do Comércio e Indústria de São Paulo*, 3 (Jan.-Dec. 1917): 388.
29. Lugar, "Merchant Community," pp. 218–220.
30. Kenneth R. Maxwell, *Conflicts and Conspiracies: Brazil and Portugal, 1750–1808* (Cambridge: Cambridge University Press, 1973), p. 24; Lugar, "Merchant Community," p. 27.

abolished the General Welfare Board of Bahia on the grounds that it had never been formally authorized by the Portuguese crown.[31]

The abolition of the General Welfare Board of Bahia in 1757 channeled business functional representation in Brazil into organizations sponsored and controlled by the Portuguese crown. Although lacking the independence that would make them true business interest groups, they foreshadowed areas of future commercial association activity. In them merchants worked with leading planters, assuming general responsibility for the welfare of agriculture and specific accountability for the quality of the area's exports. These bodies were also supposed to promote and guide economic development, much in the manner of the eighteenth-century Spanish-American *consulados*.

Perhaps the most important of these government-sponsored groups were the Boards of Inspection of Sugar and Tobacco (*Mesa de Inspeção de Açúcar e Tabaco*) established in Salvador, Rio de Janeiro, Recife, and São Luís in 1751. In Salvador this organization replaced the Superintendency of Tobacco (*Intendência de Tabaco*), which had been founded in 1698, expanding its activities to sugar and after 1798 to cotton.[32] The Boards of Inspection were designed to represent all groups involved in exportation. After 1757 the Salvador Board consisted of a tobacco planter, a sugar planter, and two merchants who shipped those commodities. The official responsibilities of the Boards of Inspection were to examine and price the colony's chief exports, maintaining their reputation in European markets, and to advise on local agricultural development.[33]

The Board of Inspection of Sugar and Tobacco survived in Salvador until 1827, although apparently disappearing elsewhere earlier. The Salvador Board never functioned as a representative business interest group despite devoting most of its attention to commerce and sometimes acting as the "coordinator" of the city's merchants on ceremonial occasions. Reflecting its government sponsorship, it remained silent on important issues affecting business.[34] The Boards of Inspection, however, served to accustom merchants to working in the areas of economic development and agricultural improvement. The practice of inspecting exports to ensure quality would be revived later in the nineteenth century by the commercial associations of the Northeast.

Later government-sponsored organizations with merchant membership

31. Viceroy Conde dos Arcos to Thomé Joaquim da Costa Corte Real, Salvador, Aug. 24, 1757, Castro e Almeida, ed., *Documentos Relativos ao Brasil, Vol. I*, p. 172.
32. Catherine Lugar, "The Portuguese Tobacco Trade and Tobacco Growers of Bahia in the Late Colonial Period," in *Essays Concerning the Socioeconomic History of Brazil and Portuguese India*, eds. Dauril Alden and Warren Dean (Gainesville, Fla.: University of Florida Press, 1977), p. 42.
33. Lugar, "Merchant Community," pp. 259–260.   34. Ibid., pp. 263–264.

were the Royal Boards of Commerce, Agriculture, Manufactures, and Navigation (*Real Junta do Comércio, Agricultura, Fábricas e Navegação*), instituted in 1809 in Rio de Janeiro and 1811 in São Luís.[35] Created by an order of the Prince Regent, the future Dom João VI, they were intended to stimulate the economy of a Brazil now cut off from its mother country by the French occupation. They were to improve roads and canals, introduce useful plants and machines, award prizes for new products, and serve as a consultant on agricultural policy for the Council of State. They helped integrate business by registering merchants, keeping information on navigation, supporting schools of business education, and building *praças*, or meeting places, for each business community.[36] A moderate tax on exports and shipping financed such activities. The Royal Board in Rio de Janeiro lasted until 1849 and in São Luís until at least 1822, but there is little evidence of effectiveness in carrying out their aims.[37] However, they provided a strong model for the commercial associations. The associations also introduced useful plants and machines, served as consultants on agriculture for government, and performed all Royal Board functions related to the integration of business.

The construction of meeting places for merchants, or *praças do comércio*, was central to the Prince Regent's program for economic development.[38] It signified not only concern for the prosperity of the business communities of Brazil's entrepôts, but recognition of their growing size and corporate consciousness in the wake of the freeing of trade in 1808. The Portuguese crown supported the construction or renovation of such buildings not only with government funds but with the services of royal officials. In Salvador, Belém, and Rio de Janeiro, the provision of a center for business transactions preceded the foundation of a representative group. This has led to misconceptions about the dates of foundation of their commercial associations, especially that of Bahia.

The most notable of the buildings constructed under João VI was the palace of the Commercial Association of Bahia, completed in 1817. It remains the headquarters of that organization and one of Brazil's architec-

35. "Alvará Creando a Real Junta de Comércio, da Agricutura, das Fábricas, e da Navegação," SH/AN, Rio de Janeiro, cod. 440, doc. 7; Eulália Maria Lahmeyer Lobo, *História Político-Administrativa da Agricultura Brasileira, 1808–1889* (Rio de Janeiro: Ministério da Agricultura, 1980), p. 16; Jerônimo de Viveiros, *História do Comércio do Maranhão, 1612–1895* (São Luís: Associação Comercial do Maranhão, 1954), I: 118–119.

36. Viveiros, *Comércio do Maranhão*, I: 118–119.; Lahmeyer Lobo, *Agricultura Brasileira*, p. 17.

37. Lahmeyer Lobo, *Agricultura Brasileira*, p. 21; Viveiros, *Comércio do Maranhão*, I: 119.

38. The desired model was the Lisbon *Praça do Comércio*, established in 1758; construction of such a building for Salvador had been suggested to the Portuguese crown by local officials and merchants in 1802 and 1807. João Rodrigues de Brito, *Cartas Econômico-Políticas sôbre a Agricultura e Comércio da Bahia* (Salvador: Imprensa Oficial do Estado, 1924), pp. 53–54; Waldemar Mattos, *Palácio da Associação Comercial da Bahia (Antiga Praça do Comércio)* (Salvador: Beneditina, 1950), pp. 13, 17.

tural monuments. The provincial governor, Count dos Arcos, initiated construction with the support of Salvador's merchant community.[39] More than two-thirds of the funds for building construction came from merchant donations and guarantees for a bank loan, but the government contributed the balance, as well as the land and the free services of the governor's adjutant as architect.[40] Thus began a tradition of generous government support for the construction of commercial association headquarters. Less happily, this support later gave rise, in Salvador and elsewhere, to long and bitter disputes between commercial associations and government over the legal ownership of such property.

The existence of the palace and of a board of administrators composed of three merchants led the Commercial Association of Bahia to claim to be the oldest of Brazil's business interest organizations. In 1900 it selected July 15, 1811, date of the appointment of the first administrators by Count dos Arcos, as its foundation date and in 1961 formally observed its sesquicentennial.[41] This claim has been honored by other commercial associations and by some historians. However, the Administrators of the Commerce Building (*Administradores da Casa do Comércio*), as they were known, were little more than caretakers, appointed by and rendering accounts to the presidents of the province (a title equivalent to governor).[42] They engaged in no representative group activity. The prior existence of the commercial associations of Rio de Janeiro and Pernambuco, created in 1834 and 1839, was acknowledged by the founders of the Commercial Association of Bahia in 1840, when they explained their intention to create a business interest organization "in the manner of others now established in the Capital of the Empire and in Pernambuco."[43]

Government authorities in Belém and in Rio de Janeiro also provided buildings for the convenience of business. In 1819 the Governor of Pará awarded merchants of Belém part of the local customs house, a site later abandoned either because of insufficient business activity or because of

39. J. Caetano Tourinho, "Associação Comercial da Bahia: Apontamentos para sua História, sua Fundação, seu Desenvolvimento," *Jornal de Notícias* (Salvador), July 15, 1911, p. 2.
40. Eugene W. Ridings, "The Bahian Commercial Association, 1840–1889: A Pressure Group in an Underdeveloped Area" (Ph.D. Diss., University of Florida, 1970), p. 31.
41. Minutes, meeting of Sept. 3, 1900, Livro 7 de Atas, AACB. The claim was perhaps first made forcefully in Tourinho, "Associação Comercial da Bahia," p. 2, and often repeated. See, for example, Antônio Osmar Gomes, "Associação Comercial da Bahia é a Mais Antiga do Brasil. É a Primaz," *Boletim da Associação Comercial da Bahia*, 45 (Jan. 1954): 2–6.
42. *O Monarchista* (Salvador), May 8, 1841, p. 1; Administrator Pedro Pires Gomes to President of Province, Salvador, Jan. 18, 1833, Presidência da Província ao Associação Comercial, 1828–1889, AEB.
43. Commercial Association of Bahia to Treasury Supervisor (*Inspetor da Tesouraria*) Joaquim Bento Pires de Figueiredo, Salvador, May 11, 1841, Presidência da Província ao Associação Comercial, 1828–1889, AEB.

damage suffered in an 1835 uprising.[44] In Rio de Janeiro an imposing building was constructed, like its predecessor in Salvador, on land ceded by the government and with a combination of business donations and public funding.[45] It was inaugurated in the presence of Dom João VI in July 1820.

Rio's merchants did not use the building long. According to the traditions of the Commercial Association of Rio de Janeiro, they abandoned it to protest the use of troops to clear a merchant-dominated meeting held to select Rio de Janeiro delegates to the newly constituted Portuguese *Côrtes* in 1822, an action resulting in at least one death and many injuries. It was ordered by the King's son, the future Pedro I, because radicals dominated the meeting and made far-reaching demands, including adoption of the liberal Spanish Constitution of 1812.[46] Tradition has it that the defiant merchants scrawled on the empty building the sarcastic notation "Royal Slaughterhouse." This explanation for the abandonment of the building does not ring true. Those who dominated the meeting were not leaders of Rio's merchant community or in some cases even merchants, nor was the community itself, then or later, politically radical.[47] Whatever the reason for abandonment, the empty edifice was turned over to the customs house in 1824 by a royal order.

The early *praças do comércio* of Salvador, Belém, and Rio de Janeiro were typical colonial-period manifestations of the Iberian corporate tradition because they were sponsored and controlled by government. They could not serve as models for true interest group activity. But the Iberian corporate tradition was basic in defining the role of commercial associations and later business interest organizations. It helped determine the parameters of their regulatory and advisory activities and, perhaps most important, their relationship with the state.

The more immediate inspiration and model for the commercial associations was the chambers of commerce of Great Britain and the United States. Early Brazilian business interest organizations might have adopted the title "chamber of commerce," as did their Spanish-American counterparts later.[48] The influence of chambers of commerce stemmed not only

44. Ernesto Cruz, *História da Belém* (Belém: Universidade Federal do Pará, 1973), II: 316, 319, 322–323.

45. José Vieira Fazenda, "Notas Históricas sôbre a Praça do Comércio e Associação Comercial do Rio de Janeiro," *Revista do Instituto Histórico e Geográfico Brasileiro*, 73, Part II (1910): 90, 93.

46. José Domingues de Ataíde Moncorvo, "Memória sôbre os Acontecementos dos Dias 21 e 22 de Abril de 1821 na Praça do Comércio do Rio de Janeiro Escrita em Maio do Mesmo Ano, uma Testimunha Presencial," AIHGB, lata 17, doc. 10; Neill Macaulay, *Dom Pedro: The Struggle for Liberty in Brazil and Portugal, 1798–1834* (Durham, N.C.: Duke University Press, 1986), pp. 84–85.

47. Macaulay, *Dom Pedro*, pp. 82–83; Eudes Barros, *A Associação Comercial no Império e na República* (2d ed. rev.; Rio de Janeiro: Gráfica Olímpica, 1975), pp. 60–66.

48. The Commercial Association of Pernambuco, first Brazilian organization to take that title,

from close trade relations between Brazil and the English-speaking world, but from the strong role of citizens of Great Britain and the United States in Brazilian mercantile communities and in the foundation of most early commercial associations.[49] The commercial associations may be seen as part of a world wide proliferation of chamber of commerce-type organizations during the nineteenth century.

Chambers of commerce in modern form arose in Great Britain and the United States in the last third of the eighteenth century. That of New York, dating from 1767, appears to have the most solid claim to being the oldest, although a number of British chambers of commerce, not all of which adopted that title initially, arose at virtually the same time.[50] The term "chamber of commerce" is itself much older, first being used in France in the fifteenth century.[51] But French chambers of commerce, like those of Germany arising during the nineteenth century and the British business organizations known as boards of trade, were largely controlled by government.[52] The chambers of commerce of the Anglo-Saxon world, though enjoying government support, were autonomous.

As noted, chambers of commerce differed surprisingly little from the more ancient Spanish *consulados* in purpose, organization, and range of activities. Like the older business interest groups, chambers of commerce promoted the interests of overseas trade and local prosperity, governed themselves through an annually elected executive council, judged commercial litigation, and regulated business practices.[53] They differed from the *consulados* in that they were not as a matter of course subsidized by the government and did not monopolize mercantile jurisprudence. Nor did they directly manage public works, although they often assisted in plan-

initially pondered calling itself chamber of commerce (*câmera de comércio*) or mercantile association (*associação mercantil*). Minutes, meeting of Preparatory Committee of the Commercial Association of Pernambuco, June 18, 1839, Livro 1 de Atas, AACP, p. 1. Some United States business interest groups, on the other hand, were known as commercial associations. Sturges, *American Chambers*, p. 47.

49. The Commercial Association of Bahia, however, was an exception in having neither nationality on its organizing committee nor first board of directors. Ridings, "Bahian Commercial Association," pp. 55–56.

50. "History of the New York Chamber of Commerce," *Harper's Weekly*, 46 (Nov. 15, 1902): 1720; Alfred Roman Ilersic, *Parliament of Commerce: The Story of the Association of British Chambers of Commerce, 1820–1960* (London: Association of British Chambers of Commerce, 1960), p. 3.

51. L. H. Bisbee and J. C. Simonds, *The Board of Trade and the Produce Exchange: Their History, Methods, and Law* (Chicago: Callaghan, 1884), p. 10.

52. Lorenzo Sabine, "The Origin of Boards of Trade," *The Banker's Magazine and Statistical Register*, 13 (March 1859): 678–692; United States Bureau of Foreign and Domestic Commerce, *Commercial Organizations in Germany: Special Agent Series No. 78* (Washington, D.C.: Government Printing Office, 1914), pp. 96–99; Sturges, *American Chambers*, pp. 5–6.

53. Sturges, *American Chambers*, pp. 20–32; Bisbee and Simonds, *Board of Trade*, pp. 24, 27; Sabine, "Origin of Boards," 687–691.

ning them.[54] Their slightly weakened prerogatives in comparison with *consulados* reflected the expanded range of government responsibilities in the late eighteenth and early nineteenth centuries.

Parallels in policies and areas of activity indicate the strong influence of chambers of commerce on the commercial associations of Brazil. Both opened membership to much the same occupations, rewarded influential supporters outside business with honorary membership, and usually avoided identification with a political party or other open political partisanship.[55] Both helped government regulate port and waterfront activities, aided in standardizing weights and measures, tried to upgrade the quality of export commodities, and collected economic statistics.[56] Chambers of commerce became a conspicuous model in the first half of the nineteenth century. By 1825, twelve chambers of commerce or similar organizations under different names had been founded in Great Britain, and by 1858, thirty in the United States.[57] They spread to Portugal, where, preceded by several temporary business interest groups, the commercial associations of Lisbon and Porto were founded in 1834.[58] The Portuguese groups probably led Brazilian organizations to adopt the label "commercial association." The Portuguese were the most numerous of all nationalities, including Brazilian, in the commercial associations of Brazil. In sum, the commercial associations and other Brazilian business interest groups may be seen as the product of influences of the English-speaking world grafted on a solid foundation of Iberian corporate tradition. It was a combination with strong potential to influence government and public opinion.

The first business interest groups

The first representative business interest group of nineteenth-century Brazil was an organization of British merchants in Rio de Janeiro known as the Committee. The opening of Brazilian ports to world trade in 1808 brought an influx of British merchants. Within nine months probably more than one hundred had taken up residence in Rio.[59] The creation of the Committee late in 1808 or early 1809 was their means of confronting unaccustomed

54. Sabine, "Origin of Boards," 686–691; Sturges, *American Chambers*, pp. 49–51; Franklin Mathews, "The Organized Conscience of the Rich," *The World's Work*, 4 (Oct. 1902): 2629–2630.
55. Mathews, "Conscience of the Rich," 2627; Richard Wheatley, "The New York Chamber of Commerce, " *Harper's Magazine*, 83 (Sept. 1891): 502; Sturges, *American Chambers*, p. 33.
56. Sturges, *American Chambers*, pp. 33–34; Mathews, "Organized Conscience," 2628–2630; Sabine, "Origin of Boards," 688–690.
57. Ilersic, *Parliament of Commerce*, pp. 3–4; Bisbee and Simonds, *Board of Trade*, p. 13.
58. Fonseca, *Cem Anos*, p. 23; Associação Comercial do Porto, *Associação Comercial*, p. 19.
59. Herbert Heaton, "A Merchant Adventurer in Brazil," *Journal of Economic History*, 6 (May 1946): 6.

and sometimes difficult conditions of trade.[60] Elected by all resident British merchants, its twelve-man board petitioned the Brazilian government both directly and through the British consul. The latter's zeal led the Committee to reward him with a percentage of the value of all imports arriving in British vessels.[61] The concerns of the Committee were largely those of the later commercial associations. Like them it petitioned for improved cargo-handling and customs-house facilities, demanded more equitable price evaluations of imports by customs officials, and even regulated commissions charges.[62]

The Committee, according to available evidence, lasted only about a year.[63] There was then no real need for it. The powerful influence of British diplomatic representatives and a privileged position reinforced by treaty until 1844, which included special courts of law, made any organization of British merchants to pressure the Brazilian government superfluous.[64] But even if short-lived, the Committee provided an example of true interest organization activity by economically powerful foreigners whose business methods and even life-style were often emulated by Brazilians. This example was reinforced by the creation of similar organizations for British merchants in Buenos Aires in 1810 and in Lima in 1821.[65] The former eventually evolved into a wider based group, admitting other foreigners in 1829 and Argentines in 1854.[66]

The commercial associations, Brazil's first enduring business interest groups, did not appear until the second third of the nineteenth century. They were preceded by other organizations that, like the Committee,

60. The Committee, already functioning, is first mentioned on Feb. 7, 1809. John Wylie to John Hancock, Rio de Janeiro, Feb. 7, 1809, Letter Book, John Wylie & Co., Ltd., Feb. 1809 to Dec. 1809, Adam Smith Record Store (hereafter cited as ASRS), University of Glasgow, UGD 28–1/1, p. 8.
61. John Wylie to John Hancock, Rio de Janeiro, April 26, 1809, ibid., p. 32.
62. John Wylie to John Hancock, Rio de Janeiro, Feb. 7, 1809, ibid., p. 8; Committee to Brazilian Foreign Ministry, Rio de Janeiro, no date, AHI, 239/1/5.
63. John Wylie, a contentious member of the Committee, does not mention it in his correspondence after December 1809. John Wylie to Edward Murphy, Buenos Aires, Dec. 8, 1809, Letter Book, John Wylie & Co., Ltd., Dec. 1809 to June 1810, ASRS, UGD 28–1/2, p. 1.
64. For law courts see Antônio Paulino Limpo de Abreu, *Memória Acerca da Jurisdição do Juiz Conservador dos Inglêses no Brasil*, Oct. 11, 1844, AHI, 257/1/1. For the special position given British merchants, see John Mawe, *Travels in the Interior of Brazil, Particularly in the Gold and Diamond Districts of That Country, by Authority of the Prince Regent of Portugal* (London: Longman, Hurst, Rees, Orme, and Brown, 1812), p. 331.
65. George Thomas Love, *A Five Years' Residence in Buenos Aires During the Years 1820 to 1825; Containing Remarks on the Country and Inhabitants and a Visit to Colonia del Sacramento* (London: G. Herbert, 1825), pp. 37–38; John Arthur Gibbs, *The History of Antony and Dorothea Gibbs and of Their Contemporary Relatives, Including the History of the Origin and Early Years of the House of Antony Gibbs and Sons* (London: Saint Catherine, 1922), p. 400; Vera Blinn Reber, *British Mercantile Houses in Buenos Aires, 1810–1880* (Cambridge, Mass.: Harvard University Press, 1979), p. 41.
66. Reber, *British Mercantile Houses*, p. 43; Jorge Navarro Viola, *El Club de Residentes Estranjeros: Breve Reseña Histórica en Homenaje a sus Fundadores* (Buenos Aires: Coni, 1941), pp. 12–13, 80.

failed to last. Most of these were informal and organized on an ad hoc basis to promote improvements in communications or to present business opinion to government. Merchants of the city of São Paulo, for example, working through the city council, built the first viable road connecting that city and the port of Santos between 1780 and 1826.[67] Rio de Janeiro merchants formed a committee to advise the Prince Regent on the organization of a university in 1816.[68] Similar temporary informal business organizations continued to appear throughout the nineteenth century in locations where no commercial association yet existed. They lacked official recognition by government, the key ingredient in the Iberian corporate tradition, and usually disbanded once their objectives had been achieved.

The first permanent interest organization of an independent Brazil was also created to meet immediate needs, but offered a union of business with other economic sectors. The Agricultural, Commercial, and Industrial Society of the Province of Bahia (*Sociedade de Agricultura, Comércio e Indústria da Província da Bahia*) was founded in Sergipe do Conde in Bahia's prime sugar-producing *Recôncavo* region in March 1832.[69] The power and prestige of its founding members gave it an auspicious start. Its principal organizer was Miguel Calmon du Pin e Almeida, later Marquis Abrantes and several times minister of Foreign Affairs and of Finance; its ranks included an Imperial Senator, four later provincial presidents of Bahia, most of the great names of the province's sugar-planting aristocracy, and leading merchants.[70] By its second year membership rose to 279 and it began to publish a journal.[71]

According to its statutes, the Agricultural, Commercial, and Industrial Society had two main aims. The first was "to promote, by all possible and permissible means, the growth and improvement of different branches of provincial Agriculture, Commerce, and Industry."[72] This meant bettering the quality and volume of export production, a subject on which Miguel Calmon wrote several books. The other aim was to provide "security in case of disturbance of order." It was likely the stronger motive for forming the society.

67. Elizabeth Anne Kuznesof, "The Role of the Merchants in the Economic Development of São Paulo, 1765–1850," *HAHR*, 60 (Nov. 1980): 585–589.
68. J. F. de Almeida Prado, *Dom João VI e o Início da Classe Dirigente do Brasil, 1815–1889* (São Paulo: Editora Nacional, 1968), p. 153.
69. Sociedade de Agricultura, Comércio, e Indústria da Província da Bahia, Ata de Instalação (1832), Arquivo do Instituto Geográfico e Histórico da Bahia (hereafter cited as AIGHB), Salvador.
70. Ibid., pp. 3–10; Braz do Amaral, *História da Bahia do Império a República* (Salvador: Imprensa Oficial do Estado, 1923), p. 80.
71. Francisco Marques do Góes Calmon, "Ensaio de Retrospeto sôbre o Comércio e a Vida Econômica e Comercial na Bahia de 1823 a 1900," in *Diário Oficial: Edição Especial do Centenário*, 8 (July 2, 1923): 380.
72. Sociedade de Agricultura, Comércio, e Indústria da Província da Bahia, Ata de Instalação (1832), AIGHB, p. 11.

In the federalist movement of postindependence Bahia, leading planters and merchants faced an implicit threat of social revolution. Since 1823 Bahian federalism had manifested itself in sporadic barracks revolts and street riots, the most serious upheaval resulting in the removal of the president of the province in 1831. Ostensibly aimed at various degrees of local autonomy or at expulsion of Portuguese merchants and shopkeepers, such uprisings were fueled by the hostility of the black and mulatto lower and lower-middle classes toward white planters and businessmen.[73] The federalist agitation also was suspected of aiming at the abolition of slavery and at universal manhood suffrage, two blows that would have shaken the traditional oligarchic social order.[74] Particularly threatening from the standpoint of security was the insubordinate attitude of Bahia's predominantly mulatto military units, one of which successfully demanded a "man of color" as its commander.[75] The Agricultural, Commercial, and Industrial Society was consequently an instrument for defense of the province's white upper class, as well as an organ for economic improvement: it featured a Committee for Security (*Comissão de Segurança*) composed of planters with military training.[76]

The dual-purpose Agricultural, Commercial, and Industrial Society of Bahia did not last. It probably died out in 1836, as indicated by the cessation of its correspondence with the Auxiliary Society for National Industry (*Sociedade Auxiliadora da Indústria Nacional*), Brazil's foremost learned society.[77] The reason for its demise was not the end of the threat of federalist revolution, which in fact climaxed in Bahia in 1837–1838 with a major upheaval, the "Sabinada." Rather, it was probably the difficulty of pursuing the divergent aims of export improvement and mutual defense and, judging from later attempts to organize a representative body for Bahian agriculture, indifferent support on the part of the planters.

The Society was also patently inadequate as a vehicle for business interests. The location of its headquarters in a rural sugar-producing area was indicative of domination by sugar planters, as was their monopoly of its high offices. Although most of Bahia's leading merchants were members, including João Gonçalves Cezimbra, recently acting president of the

73. Private letter, Consul Parkinson to Consul-General Bidwell, Salvador, July 14, 1831, PRO/FO 13/88, fl. 123; Kátia M. de Queirós Mattoso, *Bahia: A Cidade do Salvador e seu Mercado no Século XIX* (São Paulo: Hucitec, 1978), pp. 233–235.
74. Consul Parkinson to Foreign Office, Salvador, April 30, 1831, PRO/FO 13/88, fl. 94.
75. Consul Parkinson to Foreign Office, Salvador, Aug. 24, 1831, PRO/FO 13/88, fl. 137.
76. Arnold Wildberger, *Os Presidentes da Província da Bahia, Efetivos e Interinos, 1824–1889* (Salvador: Beneditina, 1949), pp. 217, 221. For the convergence of planter and merchant elites against threatened social upheaval, see John Norman Kennedy, "Bahian Elites, 1750–1822," *HAHR*, 53 (Aug. 1973): 435–438.
77. Noted in "Relatório," *O Auxiliador da Indústria Nacional*, 5 (Aug. 6, 1837): 295.

province, their services were confined to a Committee on Commerce.[78] Furthermore, foreigners were not given full membership but only the status of "corresponding members."[79] This disenfranchised the probable majority of the province's business elite. Merchants in Brazil were more than willing to work with planters in matters of common interest, but they would not do so from a subordinate position.

Brazil's first lasting business interest group appeared even before the demise of the Agricultural, Commercial, and Industrial Society of Bahia. The Commercial Association of Rio de Janeiro was founded in September 1834. It originally styled itself the Society of Subscribers to the *Praça* (*Sociedade dos Assinantes da Praça*), taking its present name only in 1867. The moving spirit in its formation was the Brazilian Felipe Nery de Carvalho, who also became its first president.[80] Brazil's first lasting business interest group would also, because Rio was Brazil's capital and dominant trade center, be its most powerful.

The creation of the Rio de Janeiro organization showed features that would also highlight most later commercial associations: the financial and ceremonial support of government and the strong participation of foreigners, especially from Great Britain and the United States. Through the Director of the Treasury and the Minister of Finance, Nery de Carvalho arranged the concession of a customs building for use as association headquarters.[81] The future Emperor Pedro II, then nine years of age, was the largest contributor among many donating funds for the remodeling of the building and attended its inauguration, seated on an especially prepared throne. The little boy dutifully listened to the ceremonial speeches, thanked all, and then promised that he would always try to defend commerce.[82] Foreign participation was equally manifest. Exclusive of the Emperor, the eight leading contributors to its building fund were foreign firms or individuals.[83] That at least six of them were British or American shows the probable influence of chambers of commerce in inspiring the Rio group. Eight of the nine authors of the organization's statutes were also foreigners.[84] Finally, its policies would be from the first controlled by

78. Wildberger, *Presidentes da Bahia*, pp. 217, 221.
79. Sociedade de Agricultura, Comércio, e Indústria da Província da Bahia, Primeira Ata, no date, 1832, AIGHB, pp. 22–23.
80. Heitor Beltrão, "A Ansia de Brasildade, os Comerciantes e a sua Agremiação Mater: A Propósito do Cento Nono Aniversário da Associação Comercial do Rio de Janeiro," *Mensário do Jornal do Comércio*, 24 (Oct. 1943): 30.
81. Ibid. 82. Ibid., 31; *Jornal do Comércio* (Rio de Janeiro), Sept. 2, 1834, p. 2.
83. *Jornal do Comércio*, Sept. 2, 1834, p. 2.
84. Associação Comercial do Rio de Janeiro, "Regulamento para a Praça do Comércio do Rio de Janeiro," in José Vieira Fazenda, *Notas Históricas sôbre a Praça do Comércio e Associação Comercial do Rio de Janeiro* (Rio de Janeiro: Jornal do Comércio, 1915), p. 22.

aliens. Only two of the seats on its nine-man Board of Directors, including that of president, were reserved for Brazilians.[85] Strong foreign influence would equally typify later commercial associations.

Brazil's second oldest lasting business interest group, the Commercial Association of Pernambuco, dates from 1839. It was unlike the Rio de Janeiro organization in adopting the title "commercial association" from the first, but like it in foreign participation. The surnames of its twenty-six organizers reveal that at least half were probably non-Portuguese foreigners.[86] Another Recife organization, the factor-controlled Commercial Agricultural Association (*Associação Comercial Agrícola*) of Pernambuco, appeared even earlier, in 1836. However, it functioned initially as a commodity exchange for sugar and apparently did not begin true interest group activity until 1878.[87] Third among lasting business interest groups was the Commercial Association of Bahia, established in 1840. Other early lasting organizations included the commercial associations of Maranhão (1854), Pôrto Alegre (1858), Paraíba (1858), Pará (1864), Rio Grande (1865), Ceará (1866), Maceió (1866), Amazonas (1871), Santos (1871), Sergipe (1872), and Pelotas (1873). By 1900 twenty-five existed. Those founded in the last quarter of the nineteenth century usually represented smaller communities, although the powerful Commercial Association of São Paulo was not established until 1894, reflecting that city's inland location and relatively late development as a major trade center.

Opportunity, challenge, and adversity

Why did representative business interest groups arise at certain times in specific localities? A viable interest organization presupposed either a mercantile community or a local industrial base of a certain size and wealth. The emergence of most business interest groups hinged on economic growth. Typical was the 1834 creation of the Commercial Association of Rio de Janeiro, in what was for most of the nineteenth century the world's greatest coffee port. It was precisely during the 1830s that coffee became Brazil's chief export and its shipment volume doubled.[88] The

85. Eudes Barros, *A Associação Comercial no Império e na República* (1st ed.; Rio de Janeiro: Associação Comercial do Rio de Janeiro, 1959), p. 32. Interestingly, this information does not appear in the revised edition of this work.
86. Estevão Pinto, *A Associação Comercial de Pernambuco* (Recife: Jornal do Comércio, 1940), p. 7.
87. See Livro de Atas da Diretoria da Associação Comercial Agrícola de Pernambuco (hereafter cited as ACAP), Aug. 10, 1877 to Aug. 8, 1892, AACP. The organization itself may have been revived in 1873 after having been inactive. Reference is made to repairs that year on the headquarters of the "new" association. Minutes, meeting of July 10, 1882, ibid., p. 70.
88. Brazil, Instituto Brasileiro de Geografia e Estatística, *Anuário Estatístico, 1939–40* (Rio de Janeiro: Imprensa Nacional, 1941), pp. 1374, 1379.

birth of the Commercial Association of Pernambuco in 1839 came in a five-year period witnessing the virtual doubling of Recife's sugar exportation.[89] Similarly, the creation of the Commercial Association of Pará in 1864 signaled the emergence of rubber as a major export; production had nearly doubled the previous decade.[90] The birth of the Industrial Association (*Associação Industrial*) and the Engineering Club (*Clube de Engenharia*) in Rio de Janeiro in 1880 followed a decade in which both Brazil's textile plants and the rate of imports of industrial machinery from Britain more than doubled.[91] But if prosperity created Brazilian business interest groups, its absence could kill them. The Commercial Association of Ceará, founded in 1866, folded after the celebrated Northeastern drought of 1878 and was not permanently reestablished until 1897.[92]

The stimulus of prosperity in giving rise to business interest organizations often was strengthened by an accompanying challenge to that prosperity. For example, the linking of Santos with the coffee-producing highlands of the Province of São Paulo by rail in 1867 made possible the birth of the Commercial Association of Santos in 1871. But that organization's leaders had as a main objective the freeing of their city from the commercial domination of Rio de Janeiro.[93] Creation of the Commercial Association of São Paulo, in turn, was stimulated not only by spectacular economic growth but by a desire to bypass Santos as gateway for the province's trade by establishing a customs house in São Paulo.[94] Foundation of the Industrial Association followed the lowering of Brazilian tariff levels and a pronounced fall in the price of imported goods.[95] The mercantile commu-

89. Peter L. Eisenberg, *The Sugar Industry in Pernambuco: Modernization without Change, 1840–1910* (Berkeley: University of California Press, 1974), p. 16.

90. Centro Industrial do Brasil, *Brazil: Its Natural Riches and Industries (Foreign Edition). Volume I: Preface – Productive Industry* (Paris: Librarie Aillaud, 1910), p. 248.

91. Flávio Rabelo Versiani, "Industrial Investment in an 'Export' Economy: The Brazilian Experience Before 1914," *Journal of Development Economics*, 7 (Sept. 1980): 310, 312.

92. José Bonifácio de Sousa, *Associação Comercial do Ceará: Memória Histórica, 1868–1968* (Fortaleza: Associação Comercial do Ceará, 1969), pp. 22, 93–94.

93. For this rivalry, see, for example, Associação Comercial de Santos, *Relatório da Associação Comercial de Santos Apresentado em Sessão Extraordinária da Assembléia Geral em 29 de Janeiro de 1876 e Parecer da Commissão de Exame de Contas* (Rio de Janeiro: Perseverança, 1876), pp. 20–21, and *Relatório de 1881*, p. 16.

94. "Relatório do Presidente da Junta Comercial," in Estado de São Paulo, Secretário da Justiça, *Relatório Apresentado ao Senhor Doutor Vice-Presidente do Estado de São Paulo pelo Secretário dos Negócios da Justiça Manoel Pessoa de Siqueira Campos em 31 de Março de 1894* (São Paulo: Espíndola, Siqueira, 1894), Anexo no. 5, p. 5; Minutes, meeting of Sept. 11, 1894, Livro de Atas, 1874–1894, AACS, pp. 194–196; Associação Comercial de São Paulo, *Relatório da Associação Comercial de São Paulo, Ano de 1895* (São Paulo: Industrial, 1896), pp. 43–45.

95. Associação Industrial, *Relatório Apresentado à Assembléia Geral da Associação Industrial em Sessão de 10 de Junho de 1882 pela Diretoria da Mesma Associação* (Rio de Janeiro: G. Leuzinger & Filhos, 1882), p. 14. The period 1873–1881 marked a significant decline in the international price of manufactures. Reinaldo Gonçalves and Amir Coelho Barros, "Tendências dos Termos-de-Troca: A

nities of Pôrto Alegre, Pelotas, and Rio Grande in the flourishing Province of Rio Grande do Sul faced a common challenge: each other. Led by its commercial association, each strove for economic dominance within the province.

Finally, the factor-dominated groups were born of adversity. The declining prosperity of sugar in the Northeast brought about the entry into interest group activity of the Commercial Agricultural Association of Pernambuco in 1878. Falling coffee prices and the threatened abolition of slavery brought forth the Center for Coffee Agriculture and Commerce (*Centro da Lavoura e Comércio do Café*) of Rio de Janeiro in 1880 and probably the Commercial and Agricultural Association (*Associação Comercial e Agrícola*) of São Paulo in 1884.[96] A nadir in sugar prices, combined with a high exchange rate, gave rise to the Center for Sugar Industry and Commerce (*Centro da Indústria e Comércio do Açúcar*) in Rio de Janeiro in 1887.[97] The adversity stimulating the rise of business interest groups, however, was not always wholly economic. Another factor-dominated group, the Commercial Center (*Centro Comercial*) of Rio de Janeiro, appearing in 1897, responded not only to a crisis in the coffee industry but to the control of the Commercial Association of Rio de Janeiro by an unrepresentative clique.

Business interest groups whose rise was stimulated by adversity were likely to disappear once their problems eased. The Commercial and Agricultural Association of São Paulo did so when coffee prices began to rise after 1886. Improved coffee and sugar prices and a fall in the exchange rate, which increased the remuneration of exportation, brought about the disappearance of both the Center for Coffee Agriculture and Commerce and the Center for Sugar Industry and Commerce in the early 1890s.[98] The Commercial Center merged with the Commercial Association of Rio de Janeiro in 1905, after a more representative and dynamic leadership had gained control of the latter.[99]

The business interest groups of nineteenth-century Brazil, then, arose

Tese de Prebisch e a Economia Brasileira, 1850–1979," *Pesquisa e Planejamento Econômico*, 12 (April 1982): 124.

96. *Gazeta da Tarde* (Rio de Janeiro), Nov. 15, 1880, p. 2, and Dec. 12, 1880, p. 2; Associação Comercial de São Paulo, *Relatório de 1895*, pp. 106–108.

97. Since export producers were usually paid in hard currency, the fall of Brazilian exchange acted as a bonus or premium and its rise actually decreased remuneration. J. P. Wileman, *Brazilian Exchange: The Study of an Incontrovertible Currency* (1896; reprint ed., New York: Greenwood Press, 1969), p. 13.

98. *RMF, 1897*, p. 151; Henri Raffard, *O Centro da Indústria e Comércio de Açúcar no Rio de Janeiro* (Rio de Janeiro: Brasil, 1892), pp. 78–79.

99. Associação Comercial do Rio de Janeiro, *Relatório da Associação Comercial do Rio de Janeiro, Apresentado à Assembléia Geral dos Sócios em 1906* (Rio de Janeiro: Leuzinger, 1906), pp. 6–8. Factors had meanwhile founded the Center for Coffee Commerce (*Centro do Comércio do Café*) of Rio de Janeiro in December 1901. Antônio Maria Cardozo Cortés, *Homens e Instituições no Rio* (Rio de Janeiro: Instituto Brasileiro de Geografia e Estatística, 1957), p. 235.

to confront specific challenges as well as to grapple with the general opportunities and problems of economic development. Their emergence also presupposed a certain level of prosperity. No isolated phenomenon, they had deep roots in Iberian tradition, but at the same time followed the contemporary example of the Anglo-Saxon chambers of commerce. They also had, as will be seen, a strong potential to influence development.

2

Leadership and organization

The business interest groups of nineteenth-century Brazil were oligarchic institutions. Theoretically responsive to the majority of membership through democratic elections and other devices, the organizations were in effect guided by a small number of their wealthiest and most influential businessmen. However, the ordinary membership, with infrequent exceptions, accepted this domination.

Virtually all power in business interest groups was vested in the board of directors, whose numbers ranged from four, in the Commercial Agricultural Association of Pernambuco prior to 1880, to twenty-five in the Engineering Club.[1] Commercial associations sat from five directors, in the Commercial Association of Amazonas before 1880, to as many as seventeen, in the Commercial Association of Rio de Janeiro from 1877 to 1883.[2] The authority of a board of directors was neatly summed up by the 1883 statutes of the Rio organization: "The mandate of the directorate is ample and unlimited . . . with no reservations of powers."[3] Membership as a whole had few chances to challenge the authority of the board of directors. General assemblies were held no more than once or twice a year, whereas most boards met weekly or biweekly and would do so even more frequently if conditions warranted.

Theoretically, group membership could still exercise control through periodic election of the board. This was often true in theory only; elections for boards of directors were frequently contrived. The Commercial Association of Bahia, for example, customarily presented the general assembly of the membership with a slate (*pauta*) of candidates selected by the

1. Livro de Atas da Associação Comercial Agrícola de Pernambuco (hereafter cited as ACAP), 1877–1892, AACP; *Revista do Clube de Engenharia*, Ano I, 2 (Jan. 1887): 135.
2. Associação Comercial do Rio de Janeiro, *Estatutos da Associação Comercial do Rio de Janeiro Aprovados por Decreto n. 6494 em 1 de Março de 1877* (Rio de Janeiro: Carioca, 1877), p. 20; Associação Comercial do Amazonas, *Documentário Comemorativo do Primeiro Centenário da Associação Comercial do Amazonas, 18 de Junho de 1971* (Manaus: Umberto Calderaro, 1971), p. 5.
3. Associação Comercial do Rio de Janeiro, *Estatutos da Associação Comercial do Rio de Janeiro Aprovados pela Assembléia Geral Extraordinária de 12 de Junho de 1883* (Rio de Janeiro: Montenegro, 1884), p. 18.

outgoing directorate.[4] Occasional uniformity of voting results in the Commercial Association of Pernambuco indicates that its elections also were sometimes managed.[5] Where management of elections was practiced, group rank-and-file rarely objected. In commercial associations, although not factor or industrial groups, it was an acknowledged necessity that the composition of a board reflect a business community's distribution of economic power, by individual, by firm, and by nationality. Businessmen also had a tendency to defer to the wealthiest and most successful of their peers, those most likely to be on the board. The rare rebellions against boards of directors by rank-and file usually stemmed from objection to policies, not resentment of domination. A gadfly member of the Commercial Association of Bahia who tried to oust its board in 1878 on the grounds that it was unrepresentative found himself virtually unsupported.[6]

Duty on the board of directors of a business interest group was time consuming, had heavy responsibilities, and subjected the server to recriminations from membership. Yet it might not only bring personal prestige but substantial business advantages. One was the opportunity to sway public policy so as to benefit one's own enterprises. Through group influence taxes might be lowered or raised, freights or handling fees cut, and bureaucratic obstacles overcome. Government aid could be mobilized for companies a director led or invested in. On the other hand, the presence of a company head on a group board of directors usually shielded his company from criticism. The complaints of the Commercial Association of Bahia about the Bahian Navigation Company (*Companhia de Navegação Bahiana*), for example, ceased after its president became a director of the company in 1879 and its attacks on British banks ended after the Salvador manager of the London and Brazilian Bank joined its board.[7] Defending the interests of one's firm or firms was the primary reason for service as a board member.

In the commercial associations, which served as clearinghouses for business information, opportunities for investment could be readily recognized and grasped by board members. In the early years, opportunities were created by the boards themselves when they sponsored enterprises essential to the business community they represented. The commercial

4. This practice began in 1851. Minutes, general assembly of Sept. 22, 1851, Livro 1 de Atas, AACB, pp. 344–345.
5. For example, Minutes, general assemblies of Nov. 26, 1867, and Aug. 4, 1871, Livro 3 de Atas, AACP, pp. 1, 79.
6. His attempt to force the board's resignation was answered by a vote of commendation (*louvor*) for the latter by membership. Minutes, general assembly of Jan. 22, 1878, Livro 4 de Atas, AACB, p. 301.
7. Eugene W. Ridings, "The Bahian Commercial Association, 1840–1889: A Pressure Group in an Underdeveloped Area" (Ph.D. Diss., University of Florida, 1970), pp. 78–79, 145.

associations of Rio de Janeiro, Bahia, and Pernambuco fostered three of Brazil's earliest banks, in 1838, 1844, and 1851, respectively.[8] The Bahian association organized in 1841 a maritime insurance and in 1850 a fire insurance company.[9] In 1840 the Commercial Association of Rio de Janeiro initiated one of Brazil's earliest coastal steamer enterprises and in 1854 helped organize the nation's first rail line, the Petrópolis or Mauá, headed by the group's president, Ireneu Evangelista de Sousa (later Baron and Viscount Mauá).[10] The boards of directors of the new enterprises were largely or entirely drawn from the boards of their sponsoring commercial associations.

Who sat on the boards of directors of business interest groups? A knowledge of the economic and personal interests of the men who served is a key to understanding their impact on development. It also has intrinsic interest: just as membership in a commercial association may serve to define the business elite, the directors of commercial associations represent the leadership of that elite.

Boards of directors of commercial associations – a foreign complexion

Perhaps the most salient characteristic of the boards of directors of commercial associations was foreign predominance. The most extreme cases were the Commercial Association of Pôrto Alegre, whose rules reserved only three of fifteen seats for Brazilians, and the Commercial Association of Rio de Janeiro, whose 1877 statutes allotted natives but three of seventeen.[11] The statutes of the commercial associations of Santos and Campos also specified a foreign majority.[12] Other associations did not set foreign numerical dominance by statute, perhaps in deference to local nationalist sentiment, but nevertheless practiced it. The principal exceptions were the Commercial Association of Bahia, where foreigners were usually about a third of board members, and possibly the Commercial Association of Pará, where nativist sentiment predominated. Alien domination of commercial association boards of directors sometimes led to

8. Minutes, meeting of Oct. 2, 1844, Livro 1 de Atas, AACB, p. 151; Heitor Beltrão, "O Civismo da Praça num Século de Labor," in Associação Comercial do Rio de Janeiro, *Aspetos Colegidos a Propósito do Centenário da Associação Comercial* (Rio de Janeiro: Associação Comercial do Rio de Janeiro, 1935), p. 75; Estevão Pinto, *A Associação Comercial de Pernambuco* (Recife: Jornal do Comércio, 1940), p. 230.
9. Minutes, meetings of Nov. 22, 1841, and Dec. 23, 1850, Livro 1 de Atas, AACB, pp. 58, 330.
10. Beltrão, "Civismo da Praça," pp. 74–75.
11. Associação Comercial do Rio de Janeiro, *Estatutos de 1877*, p. 20; Brazil, laws, statutes, etc., *Coleção das Leis do Império do Brasil de 1871* (Rio de Janeiro: Tipografia Nacional, 1871), Parts 1 & 2, II: 349.
12. Brazil, laws, statutes, etc., *Leis, 1871*, 364; Brazil, laws, statutes, etc., *Leis, 1873*, Part 2, II: 977.

awkward situations. The Brazilian vice-president of the newly elected board of the Commercial Association of Pernambuco in 1854 was forced to take instead the post of secretary, because no other eligible board members were capable in written Portuguese.[13]

Most punctilious in the matter of nationalities was the Commercial Association of Rio de Janeiro. Between 1877 and 1883, it allotted its seventeen board seats to three Brazilians (including the president), two Portuguese, two British, two French, one German, one North American, one Austrian, one Belgian, one Spaniard, one Italian, one representative either Danish or Swedish, and another either Argentine or Uruguayan.[14] At other times during the century the proportion of foreigners was less, but Brazilians never numbered more than three. Other associations, less precise, usually designated two seats for Portuguese and British merchants and two or one for French or Germans. Nationality representation reflected economic power, not numbers, for the Portuguese commonly outnumbered all other foreigners combined in the business elite.

It was apparently the strength of foreign representation on commercial association boards of directors, rather than specific nationalities, that was important. Foreign members forced the Commercial Association of Bahia in 1873 and the Commercial Association of Santos in 1874 to allot more board seats to aliens by threatening to boycott those organizations. They showed no concern over which nationalities got the seats.[15] Foreign rivalries over Brazilian commerce were rarely evidenced in commercial associations, and nationality lines were often blurred when merchants of one nationality served as partners in a firm of another. The prime interest appears to have been preservation of foreign influence per se, as guarantee for the continuation of policies favoring Brazil's traditional export-import economy within a framework of free trade. It might be supposed that the Portuguese would, for cultural reasons, be more favorably inclined toward Brazilian interests, in a sense much less foreign. This apparently was not the case. The Portuguese were, in fact, more resistant than most other nationalities to Brazilian pressures toward naturalization.[16] Hostility between Portuguese and Brazilians, erupting at times into mob violence, characterized the nineteenth century.

13. Minutes, meeting of Aug. 9, 1854, Livro 2 de Atas, AACP, p. 36.
14. Associação Comercial do Rio de Janeiro, *Projeto de Reforma de Estatutos da Associação Comercial do Rio de Janeiro, Apresentado à Apreciação dos Srs. Sócios, pela sua Diretoria* (Rio de Janeiro: Apóstolo, 1875), p. 15. The allotments proposed were not specified in the final draft of the group's 1877 statutes but were followed nevertheless.
15. Minutes, meeting of Jan. 17, 1873, Livro 4 de Atas, AACB, p. 148; Minutes, meeting of Oct. 14, 1874, Livro de Atas, 1874–1894, AACS, p. 1.
16. José Murilo de Carvalho, *Os Bestializados: O Rio de Janeiro e a República que não Foi* (São Paulo: Letras, 1987), pp. 81–83; Mathews to Department of State, Belém, Dec. 12, 1894, *USRC*, XLVII, no. 175 (April 1894): 527.

Restriction of commercial association presidency to Brazilians would have seemed a minimum concession to nationalism, but many organizations did not even do that. The associations of Amazonas, Ceará, Maceió, Maranhão, Pernambuco, and Sergipe all had one or more foreign presidents.[17] The first four presidents of the Commercial Association of Ceará were aliens, as were seven out of the first nine of the Commercial Association of Amazonas. At any rate nationalism was not strong among Brazilian merchants. Most worked in cooperation, sometimes in partnership, with foreigners. Successful foreign businessmen, especially British, often served as role models for Brazilians in business methods and even in style of living.[18] In 1894 organizers of the Commercial Association of São Paulo heatedly argued over whether its presidency should be restricted to Brazilians. It was the Brazilians among them, however, who wanted the post open to aliens; the foreigners, more prudent, urged that it be confined to nationals.[19]

Did the foreign majorities on commercial association boards of directors reflect their proportions among the business elite of nineteenth-century Brazil? There is little doubt that it did. Returns for the Industries and Professions Tax and other government records indicate that foreigners constituted from three-fifths to four-fifths of the business elite in Brazil's major commercial centers from 1871 to 1898.[20] The more dynamic the city's economy, the greater this foreign preponderance tended to be; it was greater in booming Rio de Janeiro and Belém, for example, than in relatively stagnant Salvador and São Luís.[21] The oft-repeated notion that Brazil was singular in that natives managed exportation, unlike the case in other tropical nations, is quite wrong.[22]

17. Associação Comercial do Amazonas, *Primeiro Centenário*, pp. 37–38, 45–47; José Bonafácio de Souza, *Associação Comercial do Ceará: Memória Histórica, 1868–1968* (Fortaleza: Associação Comercial do Ceará, 1969), p. 29; Moacir Medeiros de Santa Ana, *Uma Associação Centenária* (Maceió: Arquivo Público de Alagôas, 1966), pp. 69–80; Jerônimo de Viveiros, *História do Comércio do Maranhão, 1612–1895* (São Luís: Associação Comercial do Maranhão, 1954), II: 449–475; Pinto, *Associação Comercial de Pernambuco*, p. 14; Associação Comercial de Sergipe, *Associação Comercial de Sergipe, 1872–1972* (Aracaju: Regina, 1972), p. 19.
18. Richard Graham, *Britain and the Onset of Modernization in Brazil* (Cambridge: Cambridge University Press, 1968), pp. 187–215 and passim; Gilberto Freyre, *Inglêses no Brasil: Aspectos da Influência Britânica sôbre a Vida, a Paisagem e a Cultura do Brasil* (Rio de Janeiro: José Olympio, 1940), pp. 132–133.
19. Associação Comercial de São Paulo, *Relatório da Associação Comercial de São Paulo, Ano de 1895* (São Paulo: Industrial, 1896), pp. 7–8.
20. Eugene W. Ridings, "Business, Nationality, and Dependency in Late Nineteenth Century Brazil," *Journal of Latin American Studies*, 14 (May 1982): 55–85.
21. Brazilians were sixteen percent of registered businessmen in Pará and thirty-nine percent in Maranhão, 1855–74. They ranged, according to year, from seventeen to thirty percent of all contributors to the Industries and Professions Tax in Rio de Janeiro, 1871–98, and totaled thirty-six percent of business elite contributors in the Province of Bahia, 1873–74. Ibid., pp. 78, 80, 76. For other correlations see ibid., pp. 64–84.
22. As claimed in, for example, Nathaniel H. Leff, *Underdevelopment and Development in Brazil. Volume*

Since the proportion of Brazilians in the business elite tended to increase slightly during the last three decades of the nineteenth century, it may be inferred that the foreign majority was probably even larger previously.[23] Furthermore, foreigners were a large majority of all businessmen, not just the elite, in Brazil's principal centers of trade.[24] Foreign domination of business had roots deep in the colonial period. More than four-fifths of Salvador's merchants between 1600 and 1700 were born in Portugal.[25] Foreigners also numerically dominated the business elites of most other Latin American nations in the nineteenth century and were prominent in other parts of the world where foreign trade was economically important.[26] That they should dominate commercial association boards of directors must have seemed natural in the context of business in nineteenth-century Brazil. The foreign preponderance seems to have aroused little resentment among educated Brazilians, nor did it damage association influence. That so many foreign businessmen, however, should have refused to become Brazilian citizens when naturalization was convenient and easy indicates that much of the orientation and sympathies of the business elite lay abroad.[27]

No precise statistics on the various nationalities in overseas trade are available, but it is clear that the Portuguese were the most numerous. In Rio de Janeiro from 1871 to 1898 they usually were more than half of all overseas merchants, with other foreigners numbering between thirteen and twenty-four percent.[28] Among the latter, British, French, and Germans shared predominance, with the British particularly numerous in the cloth trade. There were few geographical patterns in the location of foreign merchants. Portuguese were found in unusually large proportion in

II: Reassessing the Obstacles to Economic Development (London: George Allen & Unwin, 1982), p. 43. Eulália Maria Lahmeyer Lobo sees native dominance replaced in Amazonia, Maranhão, and much of the Northeast, but persisting in Recife, Salvador, Rio de Janeiro, and Santos. *História Político-Administrativa da Agricultura Brasileira, 1808–1889* (Rio de Janeiro: Ministério da Agricultura, 1980), p. 172. According to Celso Furtado, natives controlled coffee exportation but not sugar. *The Economic Growth of Brazil*, trans. Ricardo W. de Aguiar and Eric Charles Drysdale (Berkeley: University of California Press, 1965), pp. 125–126.

23. Ridings, "Business, Nationality, and Dependency," 70. 24. Ibid., 79–84.

25. Rae Flory and David Grant Smith, "Bahian Merchants and Planters in the Seventeenth and Early Eighteenth Centuries," *Hispanic American Historical Review*, 54 (Nov. 1978): 575.

26. Eugene W. Ridings, "Foreign Predominance Among Overseas Traders in Nineteenth-Century Latin America," *Latin American Research Review*, 20, no. 2 (1985). For the strong presence of foreign merchants in Great Britain and other trading nations, see Stanley Chapman, *Merchant Enterprise in Britain: From the Industrial Revolution to World War I* (Cambridge: Cambridge University Press, 1992); and Charles A. Jones, *International Business in the Nineteenth Century: The Rise and Fall of a Cosmopolitan Bourgeoisie* (Brighton, Sussex: Wheatsheaf Books, 1987).

27. The only impediment to naturalization, a two-year waiting period, could be waived for such vague reasons as "talent," "learning," or "professional aptitude." Brazil, Exposição Universal, *The Empire of Brazil at the Universal Exhibition of 1876 in Philadelphia* (Rio de Janeiro: Imperial Instituto Artístico, 1876), p. 384.

28. Ridings, "Business, Nationality, and Dependency," 64–68, 70.

the Amazon region and Germans in the Province of Rio Grande do Sul, an area of heavy immigration from that nation. But the nation whose merchants were most numerous was not necessarily dominant economically. Brazil's largest overseas trading firms were most often British, although this supremacy was increasingly challenged after 1870.[29]

The nations apparently exerting the most influence within business interest groups were Great Britain and Portugal, reflecting respectively economic and numerical strength among membership. The power of the former was illustrated by the case of the Brazilian-United States reciprocity treaty of 1891, ironically an idea urged by the factor-led Center for Sugar Industry and Commerce and the commercial associations of Rio de Janeiro and Pernambuco.[30] However, as signed, it gave the United States duty exemption for many basic foodstuffs, most fuels, agricultural and mining machinery, machine tools, and railroad equipment, and a twenty-five percent reduction in rates for most other products, in exchange for continued duty-free importation of Brazilian commodities.[31] It would have meant the end of Great Britain's long-standing commercial supremacy in Brazil. Adverse reaction followed a telegram (oddly but appropriately not translated into Portuguese) from the London Chamber of Commerce to the Commercial Association of Rio de Janeiro, urging Brazil's commercial associations to oppose the treaty.[32] The Rio organization published the telegram in major newspapers, as well as circulating it to other associations. Led by *Jornal do Comércio,* a paper with close ties to the Rio association, most of Brazil's press joined in the attack. The commercial associations of Pernambuco, Bahia, and Pôrto Alegre denounced the treaty on the grounds that it left without tariff protection Brazil's fledgling manufactures.[33] This objection was most curious in view of those organizations' customary opposition to tariffs (see Chapter 8). Attacks

---

29. Their decline in the dress goods trade has been attributed to the establishment of direct cable communication with Europe, enabling manufacturers to communicate directly with their Brazilian customers, thus bypassing the British importer middleman. Stanley J. Stein, *The Brazilian Cotton Manufacture: Textile Enterprise in an Underdeveloped Area, 1850–1950* (Cambridge, Mass.: Harvard University Press, 1957), p. 71; White to Department of State, London, Feb. 18, 1899, *USRC,* LX, no. 224 (May 1899): 2.

30. Consul-General Armstrong to Department of State, Rio de Janeiro, Feb. 26, 1887, *USRC,* XXII, no. 78 (May 1887): 450–451; Commercial Association of Rio de Janeiro to Viscount Ouro Preto, President, Council of Ministers, Rio de Janeiro, Aug. 31, 1889, *Relatório da Associação Comercial do Rio de Janeiro do Ano de 1890* (Rio de Janeiro: Montenegro, 1891), p. 37; Associação Comercial de Pernambuco, *Relatório da Associação Comercial Beneficente de Pernambuco, Lido em Sessão da Assembléia Geral de 9 de Agôsto de 1889* (Recife: O Norte, 1889), pp. 7–8.

31. Brazil, laws, statutes, etc., *Leis, 1891: Segundo Fascículo,* pp. 382–383.

32. Minutes, meeting of March 28, 1891, Livro de Atas, 1890–1896, AACRJ, p. 40.

33. Associação Comercial de Pernambuco, *Relatório de 1891,* pp. 20–22; Minutes, meeting of Aug. 8, 1891, Livro 5 de Atas, AACB, p. 375; Joseph L. Love, *Rio Grande do Sul and Brazilian Regionalism, 1882–1937* (Stanford, Calif.: Stanford University Press, 1971), p. 47.

from commercial associations and press did not cease until Brazil renounced the treaty in 1894, following the imposition of duty on Brazilian sugar by the United States.[34] The vehemence of opposition to the treaty, which might well have proved advantageous to Brazil, was testimony to the strength of British influences in the commercial associations and in Brazil's economy.[35]

Portugal's ties to Brazil were based on heritage and constant migration and, given its small population and commerce, were more of sentimental than of economic importance. Nevertheless, commercial associations illogically often suggested expanded trade with Portugal as an answer to Brazilian economic problems. The commercial associations took a prominent part in centennial celebrations honoring the birthday of Portuguese poet Luís de Camões and the epic voyage to India of Vasco da Gama, with the Pernambuco group even arranging the unprecedented honor of a total closedown of Recife business for the former.[36] Such sentimental attachments, as well as their large representation of Portuguese nationals, earned them their lingering popular nickname of "the old Portuguese associations."[37]

Boards of directors of business interest groups – diversity and wealth

Aside from nationality, what did the leadership of the commercial associations represent? Primarily, association boards held the wealthiest and most influential of each business community. The Brazilians among them included most of the nation's famous businessmen. Viscount Mauá, most celebrated of Brazilian entrepreneurs, Teofilo Ottoni, liberal statesman and entrepreneur, and Francisco de Paula Mayrink, a financier of such scope as to be termed "a tropical J. P. Morgan," all served as President of the Commercial Association of Rio de Janeiro.[38] Viscount Guaí (Joaquim Elísio Pereira Marinho), dominant figure in the Salvador business community, long presided over the Commercial Association of Bahia. Francisco

34. *RMF, 1895*, pp. 121–123.
35. Minister of Finance Inocêncio Serzedelo Correia credited it with significantly increasing Brazilian trade. *RMF 1893*, pp. 120–122.
36. Minutes, meeting of May 31, 1880, Livro 5 de Atas, AACP, p. 24.
37. Corwin D. Edwards, "Associações Comerciais Brasileiras," in *A Missão Cooke no Brasil* (Rio de Janeiro: Fundação Getúlio Vargas, 1949), p. 350.
38. Eudes Barros, *A Associação Comercial no Império e na República* (2d ed. rev.; Rio de Janeiro: Gráfica Olímpica, 1975), pp. 88, 106, 157. Mayrink's label is from Steven Topik, "Francisco de Paula Mayrink of Brazil: A Bourgeois Aristocrat," in *The Human Tradition in Latin America: The Nineteenth Century*, eds. Judith Ewell and William H. Beezley (Wilmington, Del.: Scholarly Resources, 1989), p. 250.

Matarazzo (later Count Matarazzo), an outstanding industrialist, served on the board of the Commercial Association of São Paulo.[39]

Foreigners on commercial association boards commonly served not as individual entrepreneurs but as representatives of large overseas trading firms. The leading British coffee exporter, Edward Johnston & Co., for example, placed two partners on the board of the Commercial Association of Rio de Janeiro and two on that of the Commercial Association of Santos.[40] The foremost companies of each business community expected to be represented, at least periodically, on association boards, with partners often alternating as directors. In practice, the nationality interests of foreign companies and their representatives on association boards were often blurred. In the Commercial Association of Rio de Janeiro, for example, German representative Ferdinand Schmidt was a partner in the large British import firm Edward Ashworth & Co., and Brazilian representative Antônio Gomes Netto led a Swiss-owned firm headquartered in Paris.[41]

Wide diversity of economic and personal interests characterized commercial association directors, particularly the Brazilians. Perhaps typical was Antônio de Lacerda, a director of the Commercial Association of Bahia from 1871 to 1876. Lacerda headed an export firm, directed two shipping companies, invested in sugar mills, founded the local streetcar utility, and built the Lacerda elevator, Salvador's most famous landmark. He was also an agent for three steamship companies and served as consul for Belgium, Chile, and Costa Rica.[42] An even more celebrated example was Francisco de Paula Mayrink, President of the Commercial Association of Rio de Janeiro. This immensely wealthy and energetic financier at one time or another directed or held financial interest in eight banks, nine streetcar lines in various cities, five factories, four railroads, three shipping lines, two insurance firms, two newspapers, a hotel, and companies dealing in sanitation, immigrant colonization, sugar refining, and gold mining, and he owned extensive urban property and a plantation! He also found time to serve as a member of the National Chamber of Deputies and of a commercial court, to found a theater and a preparatory school, and to help direct some nine charitable organizations or learned societies.[43] The

39. Minutes, meeting of July 2, 1898, Livro de Atas, 1894–1906, Arquivo da Associação Comercial de São Paulo, São Paulo, p. 5.
40. John Hollocombe and Edward Tootal served on the Rio board. Associação Comercial do Rio de Janeiro, *Relatório de 1868*, p. 17, and *Relatório de 1882–1883*, p. 37. John Holden Ford and Edward Greene were Santos directors. Minutes, meetings of Dec. 7, 1895, and Aug. 16, 1898, Livro de Atas, 1894–1904, AACS, pp. 17, 31.
41. *Almanak Administrativo, Mercantil, e Industrial da Corte e Província do Rio de Janeiro para o Ano de 1855 {Almanak Laemmert}* (Rio de Janeiro: Eduardo e Henrique Laemmert, 1855), p. 435; *Almanak Laemmert, 1851*, p. 311.
42. Ridings, "Bahian Commercial Association," p. 77.
43. Francisco de Paula Mayrink Lessa, *Vida e Obra do Conselheiro Mayrink (Completada por uma*

business interests of foreigners on commercial association boards were not as varied as those of their Brazilian counterparts, but by century's end, foreign export-import firms had begun to diversify into banking and even into manufacturing.[44] This tendency would increase after 1900. Diversity of interests occasionally led to conflicts. In 1871 Manuel Antônio Pimenta Bueno, a founder and first President of the Commercial Association of Pará, invaded that organization's boardroom, theatrically scratched his name and those of his business partners from the list of membership, and insulted the assembled directors. The Pará board had just recommended to the Provincial Assembly that a lucrative contract for a river steamer line be taken from his company and given to a rival.[45] In 1900 Manuel José Bastos, acting President of the Commercial Association of Bahia, strode angrily from that organization's boardroom, never to return. His fellow directors had just voted to recommend higher taxes on manganese export as an answer to Bahia's fiscal crisis.[46] Bastos had invested heavily in manganese.

Which of the diverse interests of commercial association leaders predominated on boards of directors? Logically, these would be the interests that guided association policies. Light may be shed on the question by examining the business and personal activities of 111 men on the Board of Directors of the Commercial Association of Rio de Janeiro in 1834 and between 1844 and 1902 and ninety-one who were directors or had leadership roles in the Commercial Association of Bahia between 1840 and 1900.[47] Although data are incomplete, the trends shown were probably

*Genealogia da Família) (Rio de Janeiro: Pongetti, 1975); Topik, "Mayrink of Brazil." Other sources for Mayrink's activities are indicated in note 47.

44. An example is Theodor Wille & Co. See Theodor Wille & Co., Dec. 14, 1898, SPE/AN, Contratos, Lo. 358, Reg. 46,795; Reginald Lloyd et al., *Twentieth Century Impressions of Brazil: Its History, People, Commerce, Industries, and Resources* (London: Lloyd's Greater Britain Publishing, 1913), p. 710. Such diversification was part of a worldwide trend. Chapman, *Merchant Enterprise;* Jones, *International Business,* passim.

45. Associação Comercial do Pará, *Relatório da Comissão da Praça do Comércio do Pará, Apresentado em Sessão da Assembléia Geral dos Srs. Assinantes em 2 de Janeiro de 1871* (Belém: Diário de Belém, 1871), pp. 18–27.

46. Minutes, meeting of Aug. 6, 1900, Livro 7 de Atas, AACB, p. 97.

47. Directors of the Rio organization who served between 1834 and 1844 are not included because of lack of data. Directors, 1834 and 1844–1902, actually numbered 117, but six were eliminated from the sample because of insufficient data. The Bahia sample includes eight nonboard members who exercised appreciable leadership in the group's affairs. That group's directors totaled ninety between 1840 and 1900, but seven were eliminated because of lack of data. Information on leadership of the Rio and Bahian associations was compiled mainly, although not exclusively, from the following sources. Archival: Atas da Associação Comercial da Bahia, 1840–1900, AACB; Atas da Diretoria da Associação Comercial do Rio de Janeiro, 1881–1902, AACRJ; AIHGB; Pedido de Matrícula de Comerciante, 1809–1850, AN, caixa 444; SPE/AN; Associações e Sociedades . . . 1831 a 1899, Arquivo do Estado de Guanabara (hereafter cited as AEG), código 39-4-4; Estrangeiros Naturalizados, 1833–1858, AEG; Baring Brothers & Co., Ltd., "Proposals for Credit or Business," Guildhall Library (hereafter cited as GL), London, Ms.

fairly typical of other commercial association boards of directors as well. Rio de Janeiro, the world's chief coffee port during most of the nineteenth century, was Brazil's main center of commerce, while sugar-exporting Salvador was less dynamic and more traditional.

Among board members of both commercial associations, ownership or investment in overseas trade was almost universal. Export-import interests were usually retained, even when the businessman achieved success in other fields.[48] In the two organizations, only three managers of British banks and an uncertain number of factors never participated directly in overseas trade. Of course, British banks lent extensively to overseas trading houses, and factors were an integral part of the export-import complex. Thus, virtually all leaders of commercial associations based their prosperity in some degree on overseas trade. Such ties were intensified among those, numbering at least twenty-four in the Commercial Association of Rio de Janeiro, who led houses with headquarters or branches overseas. Advancement of foreign trade was the obvious chief aim of Brazil's nineteenth-century commercial associations.

Participation in exportation and importation was well balanced. Importers slightly outnumbered exporters, one hundred and two to eighty-

18,321, HC 17; Baring Brothers and Co., Ltd., "Brazil, from 1824," GL, Ms. 18,321, HC 4.2; British Bank of South America, Letter Books, Packets, Private Letters and Reports on Firms, Rio de Janeiro and São Paulo to/from London and Santos, 1886–1918, LABA, UCLL; London and Brazilian Bank, Letter Books, Packets, and Cable Books, Rio de Janeiro, Pernambuco, and São Paulo to/from London and Various, 1868–1924, LABA/UCLL; London and River Plate Bank, Letter Books and Packets, Rio de Janeiro and Pará to/from London and Branches, 1891–1930, LABA, UCLL. Printed: João Dunshee de Abranches Moura, *Govêrnos e Congressos da República dos Estados Unidos do Brasil* (2 vols.; São Paulo: M. Abranches, 1918); *Almanach Civil, Político, e Comercial da Cidade da Bahia para o Ano 1845* (Salvador: M. A. da Silva Serva, 1844); *Almanak Laemmert, 1844–1904* (Rio de Janeiro: Laemmert, 1843–1903); Associação Comercial da Bahia, *Relatórios,* 1867–1900; Associação Comercial do Rio de Janeiro, *Relatórios,* 1868–1902; Augusto Vitorino Sacramento Blake, *Dicionário Bibliográfico Brasileiro* (7 vols.; Rio de Janeiro: Imprensa Nacional, 1883–1902); Brazil, Ministério da Justiça e Negócios Interiores, Arquivo Nacional, *Registro de Estrangeiros,* 1808–1842 (4 vols.; Rio de Janeiro: Arquivo Nacional, 1960–1964); R. Frank Colson, "The Destruction of a Revolution: Polity, Economy, and Society in Brazil, 1870–1891" (2 vols.; Ph.D. Diss., Princeton University Press, 1979); Antônio Freire, ed., *Almanak da Província da Bahia, 1881* (Salvador: João Gonçalves Tourinho, 1881); International Bureau of the American Republics, *Commercial Directory of Brazil* (Washington, D.C.: Government Printing Office, 1891); Lloyd, *Twentieth Century Impressions;* Pan American Union, *Brazil* (Washington, D.C.: Pan American Union, 1891); Altino Rodrigues Pimenta, ed., *Almanaque Administrativo, Comercial, e Industrial da Província da Bahia para o Ano de 1873* (Salvador: Oliveira Mendes, 1872); Antônio Alexandre Borges dos Reis, ed., *Almanak do Estado da Bahia, 1898–1909* (Salvador: Reis, 1898–1909); Inocêncio Francisco da Silva, *Dicionário Bibliográfico Português. Estudos de Inocêncio Francisco da Silva, Aplicaveis a Portugal e ao Brasil* (23 vols.; Coimbra: Biblioteca da Universidade; Lisbon: Imprensa Nacional, 1858–1958); J. P. Wileman, ed., *The Brazilian Year Book* (2 vols.; New York: G. R. Fairbanks, 1908–1909).

48. Eugene W. Ridings, "The Foreign Connection: A Look at the Business Elite of Rio de Janeiro in the Nineteenth Century," *New Scholar,* 7 1/2 (1979): 173; Warren Dean, "A Industrialização Durante a República Velha," in *Estructura de Poder e Economia,* Vol. I of *O Brasil Republicano,* ed. Boris Fausto, Tomo III of *História Geral da Civilização Brasileira,* ed. Sérgio Buarque de Holanda (São Paulo: Difusão Editorial, 1975): 270.

six in the Commercial Association of Rio de Janeiro and fifty-eight to forty-five in that of Bahia. Most of the directors of both groups obviously practiced both. The larger and more prosperous trading houses were particularly likely to engage in both exportation and importation.[49] Expansion from one field to another was relatively easy, a logical first step toward diversification, and a great convenience in arranging transmission of assets from one country to another. A surprising number of directors, forty-two in the case of the Rio de Janeiro organization, belonged to houses that also exported or imported on commission. Trading on commission, rather than outright purchase of goods for resale, was noted as a familiar means of starting a career in overseas commerce; apparently it was also common to well-established firms. Specialization in only one type of overseas commerce was much more characteristic of smaller, weaker houses. There was, then, little rivalry related to fields of overseas trade in commercial association boards of directors.

Exporters on commercial association boards naturally tended to concentrate in the produce of their region. Fifty-one (and possibly more) of the directors of the Rio de Janeiro association shipped coffee. Among importers on the Rio board, the greatest number, thirty-three, dealt in the cloth trade, but a surprising thirty, as well as seventeen leaders of the Commercial Association of Bahia, brought in food. Food importation was particularly important in the Northeast. In 1874, the only year for which evidence is available, sixty-three of the Commercial Association of Pernambuco's 182 members and six of its eight directors imported food.[50] Brazilian dependency on overseas for basic necessities was widespread and deep.

The export-import business or factorage also appear to have been the earliest or most basic economic activities for virtually all commercial association board members examined. Capital and business skills were usually accumulated first in overseas trade or factorage and then invested in other fields.[51] The most important of these was banking. In the Commercial Association of Rio de Janeiro, 42 of the 111 directors led banks, had large investments in them, or belonged to merchant firms engaged

49. Typical was Edward Johnston & Co., a large-scale importer before becoming a major coffee exporting firm. Edward Johnston & Co., Rio de Janeiro, *Um Século de Café* (Rio de Janeiro: Edward Johnston & Co., 1942), pp. 13–14. In Santos, eight of eleven firms and thirteen of eighteen firms signing importers' petitions in 1895 and 1887, respectively, were also major export houses. Associação Comercial de Santos, *Relatório da Associação Comercial de Santos, Apresentado em Sessão Ordinária da Assembléia Geral em 14 de Outubro de 1895 e Parecer da Comissão de Contas* (São Paulo: Carlos Zanchi, 1896), Anexo no. 24, unpaginated, and *Relatório de 1887*, Anexo no. 10, p. 45.
50. Associação Comercial de Pernambuco, *Relatório de 1874*, pp. 13–19, Anexos, pp. 40–43.
51. Ridings, "Foreign Connection," 173; Joseph E. Sweigart, "Financing and Marketing Brazilian Export Agriculture: The Coffee Factors of Rio de Janeiro, 1850–1888" (Ph.D. Diss., University of Texas, 1980), p. 164.

in banking. In the Bahian organization, thirty-four of ninety-one leaders had banking interests. The movement from export-import commerce into banking, upon accumulation of large amounts of capital, seems to have been a natural one, common in other areas and times.[52] Another field where large accumulations of capital might be used to advantage was insurance. Twenty-five of the Rio de Janeiro board members and twenty-four of Bahia's leaders directed insurance companies or had heavy investments in them. Transportation also absorbed the capital and energies of commercial association leaders. Twenty-one directors of the Commercial Association of Rio de Janeiro and six Bahia leaders guided railway companies. Fifteen Rio directors and three Bahians headed coastal or river steamer lines. Personal economic interests help explain much of the enthusiasm of Brazil's commercial associations for improvements in transportation.

The enterprises that attracted commercial association leadership were by no means exclusively urban. Seven of the board members of the Commercial Association of Rio de Janeiro and four leaders of the Bahian group directed sugar mills. Another eight Rio directors headed companies for large-scale agricultural development. Although data are lacking, it is likely that most of the Brazilians and even some of the foreigners on the boards of the two organizations were landowners or belonged to landowning families.[53] Landowning traditionally was a source of prestige, as well as profit, in Luso-Brazilian culture.[54] The involvement of commercial association leaders in agriculture, as well as a realization that the prosperity of all Brazilian enterprise largely rested upon it, meant that there would be no major conflict between businessman and planter.

Other interests of commercial association boards of directors underline their strong ties to foreign nations. Thirteen of the Rio board and eight Bahians served as agents for foreign shipping companies; eight Rio and eight Bahia leaders represented non-Brazilian insurance companies, usually maritime or fire. But the ties of commercial association leaders to other nations were emotional as well as economic. Twenty of the Rio de

---

52. For example, John Mayo, "Before the Nitrate Era: British Commission Houses and the Chilean Economy, 1851–80," *Journal of Latin American Studies*, 11 (Nov. 1979): 299–300; Susan Migden Socolow, "Economic Activities of the Porteño Merchants: The Viceregal Period," *HAHR*, 55 (Feb. 1975): 18; José Raimundo Sojo, *El Comercio en la Historia de Colombia* (Bogotá: Cámera de Comercio de Bogotá, 1970), p. 131.

53. Only ten Brazilians were identified as landowners or members of landowning families, but they included all for whom biographical data were most complete. Foreign firms took over many plantations in the last decade of the nineteenth century. Robert Greenhill, "The Brazilian Coffee Trade," in *Business Imperialism, 1840–1930: An Inquiry Based on British Experience in Latin America*, ed. D. C. M. Platt (Oxford: Oxford University Press, 1977), pp. 208–209; Graham, *Britain and the Onset*, p. 78.

54. Gilberto Freyre, *The Mansions and the Shanties (Sobrados e Mucambos): The Making of Modern Brazil*, trans. and ed. Harriet de Onís (New York: Alfred A. Knopf, 1966), pp. 8–9; John Norman Kennedy, "Bahian Elites, 1750–1822," *HAHR*, 53 (Aug. 1973): 424.

Janeiro directors helped lead cultural or welfare organizations representing their nationality. Twenty-five of Rio's directors, including Brazilians, proudly wore foreign decorations. Finally, service as an unpaid foreign consul was a favorite avocation of business leaders.[55] Twenty-six Commercial Association of Bahia leaders and fifteen of Rio were consuls of foreign nations. It was not simply nationality or the nature of overseas trade that bound commercial association leaders to foreign interests.

As significant as the economic interests predominating on the boards of directors of Brazil's commercial associations were those overshadowed. Conspicuously missing were retailers, most numerous by far of nineteenth-century businessmen. Ten of the Commercial Association of Bahia's leaders and one of Rio's operated retail stores, but they did so as a branch of an import house. Small-scale retailers traditionally were considered socially inferior to overseas traders and factors.[56] They were not invited to membership in most commercial associations, and their welfare was for the most part ignored. Retailers were forced to organize their own interest groups.[57] Other economic interests were represented on association boards by only a minority of the directors. This meant they could be outvoted on issues vital to their prosperity. Perhaps most adversely affected was industry. The board of the Commercial Association of Rio de Janeiro sat only fifteen men who directed manufacturing enterprises and the Commercial Association of Bahia but eight during the nineteenth century. Small as industrial representation was on the commercial associations of Rio de Janeiro and Bahia, it was probably even less elsewhere. Rio was Brazil's main locus of manufacturing during the nineteenth century and Salvador and its environs the early center of textile production.[58]

A key element in nineteenth-century Brazil's economy also was weakly represented: the factors. In coffee production these intermediaries between overseas merchant and export producer were known as *comissários*, in sugar

55. Service as a consul might bring concrete advantages as well as prestige. It gave advance information on market conditions and on the activities of competitors. J. Orton Kerbey, *An American Consul in Amazonia* (New York: W. E. Rudge, 1911), pp. 167–168.

56. Charles R. Boxer, *The Portuguese Seaborne Empire, 1415–1825* (New York: Alfred A. Knopf, 1969), p. 333; Stuart B. Schwartz, *Sovereignty and Society in Colonial Brazil: The High Court of Bahia and Its Judges, 1609–1751* (Berkeley: University of California Press, 1973), pp. 288–289.

57. Rio's Commercial Union of Retailers Society (*Sociedade União Comercial dos Varegistas*) dated from 1880. Sociedade União Comercial dos Varegistas, *Relatório Apresentado à Assembléia Geral dos Varegistas de Sêcos e Molhados em 10 de Agôsto de 1881 pela Diretoria da Mesma Sociedade* (Rio de Janeiro: Central, 1881), p. 4.

58. Stanley J. Stein, *The Brazilian Cotton Manufacture: Textile Enterprise in an Underdeveloped Area, 1850–1950* (Cambridge, Mass.: Harvard University, 1957), pp. 20–21; Roberto Simonsen, *Evolução Industrial do Brasil e Outros Estudos*, ed. Edgard Carone (São Paulo: Editôra Nacional e Universidade de São Paulo, 1973), p. 17. The Provinces of Pernambuco and Alagôas, by contrast, had only one small textile mill each as late as 1889. Williams to Foreign Office, Recife, March 29, 1895, Great Britain, Foreign Office, *Annual Series of Diplomatic and Consular Reports*, no. 1547 (1895): 8.

as *correspondentes*, and in rubber as *aviadores*.[59] Many factors were wealthy and politically influential; the occupation attracted ambitious Brazilians and its ranks had a larger proportion of natives than perhaps any other major business profession.[60] Yet only in the case of the Commercial Association of Pará did factors, *aviadores* in this case, dominate an association's board of directors.[61] The importance of the factor's role in the wild rubber trade, unequaled in plantation commodity production, and also sharp local resentment over alleged price manipulation by foreign exporters aided the supremacy of the *aviador* there.

On other commercial association boards of directors factors were usually a minority, although Brazilian factors often served as commercial association presidents. Provisions for foreign majorities on boards, by statute or by custom, promoted the underrepresentation of factors, for virtually all were either Brazilians or Portuguese.[62] Factors totaled only seventeen of the Commercial Association of Rio de Janeiro's 111 directors during 1834 and 1844–1902. Furthermore, it was common for large and successful factorage firms to expand into overseas trade; sixteen of the Rio de Janeiro organization's factors were also overseas traders at one time or another. Consequently the few factors on commercial association boards were often of divided loyalties. It was not only the problems facing sugar and coffee that gave rise to the factor groups but also the realization that the commercial associations were unresponsive to the special problems of *comissários* and *correspondentes*.

Factor interest organizations were oligarchic, as were the commercial associations, with power concentrated in their boards of directors. But the representation of economic interests on their boards was simple: nearly all board members were primarily factors although, typical of the business elite, they had other diverse economic holdings.[63] Planters were invited as

59. For a detailed examination of *comissários*, see Sweigart, "Coffee Factors." For *correspondentes*, see Peter L. Eisenberg, *The Sugar Industry in Pernambuco, 1840–1910: Modernization Without Change* (Berkeley: University of California Press, 1974), pp. 63–79. Much information on *aviadores* is contained in Barbara Weinstein, *The Amazon Rubber Boom, 1850–1920* (Stanford, Calif.: Stanford University Press, 1983).

60. Ridings, "Business, Nationality, and Dependency," 63–68, finds Brazilians to have been a slight minority among *comissários*, 1871–1898. Sweigart, "Coffee Factors," pp. 59n., 70, reaches the same conclusion for 1870–1888, although Brazilians constituted fifty-seven percent of the partners in *comissário* firms.

61. As indicated by that association's support of *aviadores* in conflict with exporters. Commercial Association of Pará to Members of the Provisional Government of Pará, Belém, Dec. 7, 1889, *Relatório de 1890*, pp. 17–19. For *aviador*-exporter conflict, see Weinstein, *Rubber Boom*, pp. 137–164.

62. Ridings, "Business, Nationality, and Dependency," 63–68; Sweigart, "Coffee Factors," pp. 59n., 70; Weinstein, *Rubber Boom*, pp. 72–75.

63. For membership of the Commercial Agricultural Association of Pernambuco, see Sociedade Auxiliadora da Agricultura de Pernambuco, *Relatório Anual Apresentado na Sessão de 4 de Julho de*

members, and many if not most of the factor organizations' directors were also landholders.[64] Neither landholdings nor other varied interests, of course, kept those directors from aggressively defending factor welfare. Unlike the commercial associations, factor groups were not dominated by foreigners. Brazilians were a large plurality, if not a majority, of their membership, and the wish to exert a maximum of political influence dictated a largely native board.

The factor groups shared personnel, as well as many policy aims, with the commercial associations. Probably all directors of the Center for Coffee Agriculture and Commerce and of the Center for Sugar Industry and Commerce were also members of the Commercial Association of Rio de Janeiro. Two Rio association directors served on the board of the former factor organization and four on the latter.[65] The Commercial Agricultural Association of Pernambuco shared leaders with the Commercial Association of Pernambuco. Usually at least one member of the former's five-man board of directors was a sometime director of the latter, as was the Commercial Agricultural Association's president during approximately half of its years of interest group activity. That the factor organizations drew much of their leadership from commercial associations meant there would be cooperation, not rivalry, between them. But it also underlined the factors' perception that the commercial associations were not responding to their needs.

The representation of economic interests on the boards of directors of industrial interest organizations was also simple. The Industrial Association, located in Rio de Janeiro, and the Agricultural Industrial Center of Pelotas were directed by the leading manufacturers of those communities. The Engineering Club was composed of men with formal engineering training, allowing them to call themselves "engineer," and of "industrialists," with the former a majority among membership and on the board of directors. But many styling themselves engineer had industrial interests and many of those who did not also favored industrial development. Like the commercial associations, most directors of the Industrial Association and Agricultural Industrial Center of Pelotas were probably foreign. Industrialists during the late nineteenth century tended to be alien even more than overseas merchants.[66] Since the aim of industrial groups was to

1878 da Assembléia Geral, pelo Gerente Inácio de Barros Barreto em Ata da Mesma Sessão (Recife: Jornal do Recife, 1878), p. 17. For the Center for Coffee Agriculture and Commerce, see Sweigart, "Coffee Factors," pp. 196, 286–293.

64. All members of the first board of the Center for Coffee Agriculture and Commerce were landowners as well as factors. Sweigart, "Coffee Factors," pp. 286–293.

65. All members of the former's first board also belonged to the Rio association. Ibid., pp. 286–293; Henri Raffard, *O Centro da Indústria e Comércio de Açúcar no Rio de Janeiro* (Rio de Janeiro: Brasil, 1892), p. 11.

66. Ridings, "Business, Nationality, and Dependency," 71–77. A survey of Brazilian industrial firms

promote autonomous development, such foreign predominance was probably irrelevant. Manufacturers, whether Brazilian or foreign, had staked their hopes and capital on native industry. Also perhaps because of this aim, industrial groups shared relatively few leaders with the commercial associations. Although formal relations between industrial groups and commercial associations were usually cordial, the two types of business interest group were working at cross purposes, particularly regarding government aid for manufactures (see Chapter 8). The traditional export-import economy presupposed a lack of autonomous industrial development.

The commercial associations claimed to represent all business. But this was a hollow assertion, as the need for the formation of retail, factor, and industrial interest groups during the nineteenth century would indicate. Commercial associations were the vehicle of overseas trading firms, especially, it would seem, the foreign ones.

The rank-and-file of business interest groups

Ordinary members of business interest groups rarely challenged the overwhelming authority vested in their boards of directors. They were not expected or encouraged to concern themselves with the day-by-day affairs of administration. The likelihood that the policies of the board would deviate from the wishes of membership was much smaller in factor and industrial groups, created for a single purpose, than in commercial associations, which purported to represent all business interests in a community. The Industrial Association, for example, allowed ordinary members to attend board meetings and to speak.[67] Although some commercial associations occasionally published in newspapers minutes of the meetings of the board as a public relations device, more typical was the attitude of the Commercial Association of Rio de Janeiro, which barred ordinary members from access to those minutes.[68]

Ordinary group members had three statutory means of control of policy in addition to the election of boards of directors. First, their approval was required for the *relatório*, or annual report, of the organization. This

in São Paulo in 1962 showed roughly half to be owned by foreign-born and thirty-five percent by sons or grandsons of immigrants. Luís Carlos Bresser Pereira, "Origens Étnicas e Sociais do Empresário Paulista," *Revista de Administração de Emprêsas*, 4 (June 1964): 93–94. Foreign-born industrialists were also preponderant in Argentina, Chile, Peru, and Uruguay from 1870 to 1930. Colin M. Lewis, "Industry in Latin America before 1930," in *The Cambridge History of Latin America. Volume IV: c. 1870 to 1930*, ed. Leslie Bethell (Cambridge: Cambridge University Press, 1986), p. 311.

67. This concession admittedly was made possible by small membership. Associação Industrial, *Relatório Apresentado 'a Assembléia Geral da Associação Industrial em Sessão de 10 de Junho de 1882 pela Diretoria da Mesma Associação* (Rio de Janeiro: G. Leuzinger & Filhos, 1882), p. 32.

68. Minutes, meeting of April 16, 1881, Livro de Atas, 1881–1890, AACRJ, p. 6.

document, consisting of a narrative of the board's actions, and usually published with accompanying correspondence and other documentation, was commonly approved unanimously by the general assembly. A second means of control for ordinary membership was the election of an "accounts committee." It met before every periodic general assembly to review not only the finances but the leadership of the board of directors. However, the effectiveness of this body as a check on the directors was often dubious. Accounts committee members, if not former directors themselves, were usually heads of the same leading firms from which a board was chosen. Their review tended to be perfunctory. An accounts committee of the Commercial Association of Rio de Janeiro in 1902 not only failed to notice massive embezzlement of organization funds but even that its financial ledgers had been so altered as to be rendered "incomprehensible."[69]

A third means of control was the "extraordinary general assembly." This convocation of the membership could be called by the board itself or by petition of a minimum number of members, usually twenty or thirty. Commonly called to determine emergency policy, extraordinary general assemblies, unlike ordinary ones, were usually well attended, vociferous, and discordant. They were also the occasions when the membership as a whole wrested policy from the board of directors. In 1882, for example, an extraordinary general assembly of the Commercial Association of Bahia, led by importers, voted against the wishes of the board to give the organization's highest honors to a provincial president who had annulled a rigorous provincial import tariff bill.[70] Such revolts were rare. They were dreaded by all because they made the organization involved appear to be divided in its pursuit of objectives.

The autocratic control of commercial association boards of directors led to occasional abuses. The most flagrant took place in the Commercial Association of Rio de Janeiro late in the century. The Rio Board of Directors did not hold an election between 1892 and 1902. It did not publish a *relatório* between 1890 and 1901. Power became further concentrated when directors gradually dropped out, and by 1902 only three survivors were present to hand over authority to a new board. "In truth," the latter stated, "the association was directed during this long period by a veritable dictatorship, which little by little concentrated all power in its hands and apparently felt it unnecessary to continue to present the required accounts of its administration."[71] The Commercial Association of

69. Minutes, general assembly of May 2, 1902, Livro de Atas da Assembléia Geral, 1902–1904, AACRJ, p. 6; Minutes, meeting of May 28, 1902, Livro de Atas, 1902–1906, AACRJ, pp. 34–35.
70. Minutes, meeting of Feb. 22, 1883, Livro 5 de Atas, AACB, p. 57; Minutes, extraordinary general assembly of March 1, 1883, Livro 5 de Atas, AACB, p. 61.
71. Associação Comercial do Rio de Janeiro, *Relatório de 1902*, p. 7.

Rio de Janeiro paid heavily for its long years of autocratic leadership. Its records and information services for members were in chaos or missing, its lack of response to the business community helped give rise to a rival interest group, the Commercial Center and, most embarrassing, much of its treasury was looted.[72]

With considerable difficulty, auditors determined that a total of Rs. 213:048$047 (approximately U.S. $ 51,131. 53) was missing.[73] Responsibility was laid on a surviving member of the old board, Treasurer Hermano Joppert, who, when confronted, expressed over time surprise, outraged innocence, and eventually deep remorse. He had given most of the money, he confessed, as loans to firms in financial need owned by friends. But Rs. 56:000$000 also had been borrowed by the Association's acting president, the late Honório Augusto Ribeiro, and never repaid.[74] A further Rs. 10:909$890 wound up in the pocket of the organization's head bookkeeper. The new board of directors was understandably unreceptive when the latter, fired and consequently jobless, requested a pension.[75] Embarrassed by the revelations of cupidity and carelessness, and with little hope of recovering its money, the Commercial Association of Rio de Janeiro decided to let the matter drop. Both the abuses of the period 1892–1902 and Hermano Joppert himself, once one of Brazil's leading entrepreneurs, faded from public notice.

Perhaps one reason ordinary members of business interest groups willingly entrusted power to their boards of directors is that their economic interests were much the same. The Industrial Association ensured this by restricting membership to manufacturers. The factor groups were more open, soliciting the membership of planters and overseas merchants as well as factors, in fact any profession connected with the commodity in question. Factors, however, were by far the majority in every factor group. Commercial association membership, despite being drawn from nearly every facet of the business world, also was dominated by the same interests as were its boards of directors:

Membership in the commercial association served to define the business elite of each community. The leading overseas trading houses were the backbone of membership. In Santos in 1892–1893, for example, the twenty-four leading coffee exporting firms (of a total of twenty-nine exporters) were members.[76] Most associations gave membership to both

72. Ibid., p. 3. Including many former Commercial Association of Rio de Janeiro members among its organizers, the Commercial Center was formed in June 1897. *Jornal do Brasil* (Rio de Janeiro), June 9, 1897. pp. 2–3.
73. Associação Comercial do Rio de Janeiro, *Relatório de 1902*, p. 21.
74. Minutes, meetings of March 18 to May 28, 1902, Livro de Atas, 1902–1906, AACRJ, pp. 1–37; Associação Comercial do Rio de Janeiro, *Relatório de 1902*, p. 114.
75. Minutes, meeting of Dec. 12, 1902, Livro de Atas, 1902–1906, AACRJ, pp. 88–89.
76. Associação Comercial de Santos, *Relatório da Associação Comercial de Santos, Apresentado em Sessão*

individuals and firms. This practice, specifically outlawed by a few organizations, gave greater voting weight to the larger houses that could afford dual membership. Factors were also important, although apparently they outnumbered overseas merchants only in the Commercial Association of Pará. Nonmercantile interests usually were a minority among association membership. Of the 185 founding members of the Commercial Association of São Paulo, for example, only fourteen had no obvious stake in foreign trade.[77]

In addition to overseas traders and factors, commercial association statutes usually specifically welcomed industrialists, bankers, and capitalists as members. Most also enlisted what Brazilian law defined as the "auxiliary branches of commerce": brokers (*corretores*), warehouse owners, shipfitters, auctioneers, and commercial translators.[78] The auxiliary branches of commerce, however, ranked lower in hierarchy. Non-elite businessmen were rare. Few associations opened their ranks to *caixeiros* (merchant house clerks) and none welcomed retailers. Association initiation fees and dues, at any rate, were high enough to discourage socially "inferior" occupations from joining. Commercial associations all claimed to speak for agriculture, but differed on admitting planters to membership. The associations of Campos, Maranhão, Pelotas, Rio de Janeiro (from 1877), and São Paulo specifically welcomed them.[79] However, no planters (unless also businessmen) were elected to commercial association boards.

No matter what occupations were admitted, business interest groups varied greatly in size of membership. The most important determinant was the size and prosperity of the community from which it drew its members. The Commercial Association of Rio de Janeiro reached a high of 851 in 1881, the Engineering Club 572 in 1888, and the Commercial Center of Rio de Janeiro 815 at the century's end.[80] Most commercial associations had between one hundred and three hundred members, but

---

Ordinária da Assembléia Geral em 10 de Julho de 1893 e Parecer da Comissão de Exame de Contas (Santos: W. Kraemer, 1893), Anexo no. 30, unpaginated.

77. They were seven capitalists, four industrialists, two engineers, and one planter. Both overseas traders and factors were listed as "negotiante." *O Estado de São Paulo* (São Paulo), Nov. 24, 1894, p. 3.

78. Commodity brokers or *corretores* (literally "runners") *de mercadorias* served as intermediaries between factor and exporter or, in the case of Rio coffee, between sacker and exporter. For their origin in the Luso-Brazilian historical context, see Maria Bárbara Levy, *História da Bolsa de Valores do Rio de Janeiro* (Rio de Janeiro: Instituto Brasileiro de Mercado de Capitais, 1977), pp. 21–28.

79. Brazil, laws, statutes, etc., *Leis, 1873*, Part 2, II: 833, 975; Associação Comercial do Maranhão, *Estatutos da Associação Comercial do Maranhão* (São Luís: Frias, 1878), p. 4; Associação Comercial do Rio de Janeiro, *Estatutos de 1877*, p. 8; Associação Comercial de São Paulo, *Estatutos da Associação Comercial de São Paulo, Aprovados pela Assembléia Geral dos Sócios em 7 Dezembro de 1894* (São Paulo: Industrial de São Paulo, 1895), p. 5.

80. Associação Comercial do Rio de Janeiro, *Relatório de 1881*, p. 31; *Revista do Club de Engenharia*, ano II, vol. 7 (1888); Centro Comercial do Rio de Janeiro, *Relatório dos Atos da Terceira Direção, desde 17 de Julho de 1900 a 17 de Julho de 1901* (Porto: Comércio do Porto, 1901), pp. 111–121.

totals fluctuated greatly depending on the energy of the directors in recruiting and especially on the prosperity of overseas trade. Bad market conditions often simply bankrupted many eligible members. Membership in the commercial associations of Pernambuco and Pará, for example, varied by more than one hundred percent within seven- and five-year periods.[81]

Many businessmen and others wished to use commercial association headquarters for transacting business, for information services, or for relaxation but could not or would not pay the initiation fees and annual dues of regular members. For them most associations provided the status of "subscriber" (*assinante*). This gave, for an annual fee usually about half regular dues, the same access to headquarters facilities enjoyed by regular members but not the right to vote or otherwise influence policy. Other individuals, for whom access to headquarters was a convenience to regular members and an asset to public relations, were admitted free. The Commercial Association of Rio de Janeiro, for example, welcomed to the use of its headquarters all foreign diplomats, high-ranking bureaucrats and legislators, and all newspaper editors.[82] Most associations also opened their doors to visiting sea captains, who often owned and sold the cargoes they carried.

Finances – government aid and private problems

Finances were a major preoccupation of most business interest groups. Several were deeply in debt, despite being guided by the best business minds in Brazil and aided by the state with direct or indirect funding. The Industrial Association received subsidies and the free use of government property for exhibitions of Brazilian manufactures in Rio de Janeiro and abroad.[83] The centers for Coffee Agriculture and Commerce and Sugar Industry and Commerce received yearly stipends as well as funding for exhibitions.[84]

Government aided the acquisition of nearly all commercial association headquarters with money, property, or services. The Commercial Association of Pernambuco boasted in 1866 that it was the only one in Brazil with a headquarters acquired from its own resources.[85] Various associa-

81. Associação Comercial de Pernambuco, *Relatório de 1889*, p. 34, and *Relatório de 1896*, p. 7; Associação Comercial do Pará, *Relatório de 1870*, p. 6, and *Relatório de 1875*, p. 3.
82. Associação Comercial do Rio de Janeiro, *Estatutos de 1883*, pp. 43–44.
83. Associação Industrial, *Relatório de 1882*, pp. 33, 76–77.
84. Center for Coffee Agriculture and Commerce to Baron Cotegipe, Rio de Janeiro, July 10, 1885, ABC, AIHGB, lata 90, doc. 19; Centro da Indústria e Comércio de Açúcar, *Crise do Açúcar: Representação e Memorial Apresentado ao Corpo Legislativo da Nação Brasileira pelo Centro da Indústria e Comércio de Açúcar do Rio de Janeiro* (Rio de Janeiro: Imprensa Nacional, 1887), p. 43.
85. *Relatório de 1866*, p. 16.

tions demanded assistance for construction from national or provincial governments in the form of concessions of land, low-interest, long-term loans, guarantees for loans from private banks, exemptions from import taxes for all materials used in construction, or official authorization for a tax on exports, imports, or both, a tax on the dividends of local banks and companies, or a direct tax on local business. Most succeeded in getting some form of aid, although their own membership sometimes balked at special levies on trade or on business firms.

Government help for the construction of a commercial association headquarters often became in effect a continuous indirect subsidy. All associations with adequate headquarters rented office space to government bureaus or to private firms. Such rents could be a major source of funding. Rents exceeded income from initiation fees and dues as much as threefold for the Commercial Association of Bahia and equaled it for the Commercial Association of Rio de Janeiro by the 1890s.[86] Both organizations nevertheless wrestled with debt problems during the last third of the century.

Most serious, and eventually souring its relations with government, was the debt of the Commercial Association of Rio de Janeiro. Demanding a building "worthy of the premier capital of South America," the organization began construction of a new headquarters in 1872.[87] As it was part of a three-building complex housing a new main post office and another government bureau, the imperial government contributed one-third of the cost.[88] Unfortunately, the association's aspirations overreached its resources. Disagreement over details of construction prevented completion, and in 1889 the organization was forced to appeal for government help in the form of a guarantee for a major loan from a Portuguese bank. Most of this sum went to repay past construction debts. Then further construction halted in 1891 when the new Republican government refused to hand over the roughly one-seventh of the Portuguese loan still in its hands.[89] Republican leaders were irritated by the association's professed inability to service the loan from its own resources and also probably by its close ties with the recently overthrown Empire.[90] Although partially occupied, the headquarters remained gapingly unfinished until

86. Ridings, "Bahian Commercial Association," pp. 68–69; Commercial Association of Rio de Janeiro to Minister of Finance Francisco de Paula Rodrigues Alves, Rio de Janeiro, Jan. 21, 1896, *Relatório de 1901*, pp. 3–4.

87. Associação Comercial do Rio de Janeiro, *Relatório de 1868*, p. 6; Commercial Association of Rio de Janeiro to National Chamber of Deputies, Rio de Janeiro, April 21, 1886, *Relatório de 1884–1885*, p. 44.

88. *RMF, 1874*, pp. 137–140.

89. Associação Comercial do Rio de Janeiro, *Relatório de 1890*, pp. 6–18; Associação Comercial do Rio de Janeiro, *Relatório de 1901*, Anexos, 1892, pp. 17–19; *RMF, 1892*, pp. 34–39.

90. Minister of Finance Francisco de Paula Rodrigues Alves to Commercial Association of Rio de Janeiro, Rio de Janeiro, Jan. 11, 1896, *RMF, 1896*, pp. 141–142.

1902, when the first of a new series of government loans permitted construction to resume.[91] Not until far into the twentieth century would the Commercial Association of Rio de Janeiro's huge debt to the government be settled.[92]

Whether kept low or not by rental income, most business interest group initiation fees and dues were affordable by prosperous businessmen and firms. An exception was the Industrial Association, whose high costs were probably a factor in its early demise. Commercial association costs were more moderate. Between 1842 and 1889, when the value of the *milreis* was relatively constant, both annual dues and initiation fees ranged generally from Rs. 20$000 (about U.S. $10.00) to Rs. 50$000. The Commercial Association of Rio de Janeiro offered lifetime membership (*sócio remido*) for a sum roughly equal to ten years of annual dues.[93] However, commercial association initiation fees and dues could rarely be raised without threats of resignation from membership.

While income could be increased only with difficulty, business interest group expenses tended to be greater than foreseen. Thus most experienced financial problems, especially during periods of falling membership. The cost of influencing government was surprisingly small, except for hired lobbyists and subsidies paid to newspapers for favorable articles. For commercial associations, the greatest constant expense was the salaries of employees. They might include a lawyer, a bookkeeper and his assistant, an archivist, persons who furnished statistics on shipping and commodity movement, and a number of servants and janitors. Information was usually the next heaviest expense. Costly by modern standards, it usually included foreign and domestic newspaper and journal subscriptions and eventually telegraph and undersea cable service.

For most commercial associations one expense was conspicuous by its absence: pensions. Virtually all of Brazil's commercial associations had statutory provisions for a pension fund to support impoverished members or their survivors. Given the risks of international commerce, such help was most apt. Yet only the Commercial Association of Rio de Janeiro, wealthiest of all, succeeded in setting up a viable pension system. Other associations were strongly reluctant to undertake the expense of regular pension payments. Even the endowment by a wealthy member of the basis for a fund failed to loosen the purse strings of the Commercial Association of Bahia.[94] The Commercial Association of Pernambuco, which began a

91. Associação Comercial do Rio de Janeiro, *Relatório de 1903*, p. 12.
92. Terms of settlement were not arranged until 1920. Barros, *Associação Comercial*, pp. 199–201.
93. Associação Comercial do Rio de Janeiro, *Estatutos de 1877*, p. 14.
94. Minutes, meeting of Aug. 2, 1883, Livro 5 de Atas, AACB, pp. 73–74; Ridings, "Bahian Commercial Association," pp. 69–70.

pension fund in 1879 after a number of destitute widows had appealed for aid, eventually used it to repair its headquarters.[95]

The functioning pension system of the Commercial Association of Rio de Janeiro was close-fisted. Prior to the onset of inflation in 1890 monthly payments usually ranged from Rs. 20$000 (roughly U.S. $10.00) to Rs. 60$000, depending on size of family and other need. Association financial problems brought about a temporary reduction in these modest sums in 1887.[96] By the 1890s pensioners totaled but forty, a number nearly double that of the previous decade and made possible only through voluntary contributions to the pension fund by philanthropists.[97] The uncertainties of overseas commerce and the need for some type of social security for merchants were illustrated by the names of the Rio association's pensioners. Among them were six former members of the board of directors or their survivors, including the widow of Felipe Nery de Carvalho, founder of the Commercial Association of Rio de Janeiro.[98]

The neglect of pensions perhaps reflected the dominance of business interest group leadership by their wealthiest and most successful members. All were oligarchic institutions with power concentrated in their boards of directors. Ordinary members, probably because they shared goals with their directors, rarely objected to this subordination. As membership in the commercial associations served to define the business elite, their directors represented the leaders of that elite. The associations claimed to represent all business but, consonant with their leadership, mainly answered the interests of large foreign overseas trading companies. The creation of factor and industrial groups was thus made necessary. The foreign predominance on the boards of most commercial associations and industrial groups reflected the composition of nineteenth-century Brazil's business elite, also preponderantly alien save for factors. There is little to indicate that Brazilian members of business interest groups resented this foreign leadership. Nor did Brazilian governments, which directly or indirectly funded virtually all such groups.

95. Minutes, meeting of June 1, 1892, Livro 7 de Atas, AACP, pp. 67–68.
96. Minutes, meeting of Feb. 11, 1887, Livro de Atas, 1881–1890, AACRJ, p. 165.
97. Associação Comercial do Rio de Janeiro, *Relatório de 1890*, pp. 58–59.
98. Associação Comercial do Rio de Janeiro, *Relatório de 1868*, p. 15.

3

Influence, ideology, and public relations

Most business interest groups in nineteenth-century Brazil enjoyed a notable potential for influence. It rested on the relative scarcity of other interest groups and on the advisory and regulatory prerogatives inherited from Iberian corporatism. Enhancing it were the personal contacts of group leaders with Brazilian government heads. Group members had economic and business expertise that the government needed and overseas ties that gave them access to technology and modernizing influences from abroad. Finally, the central position of overseas merchants in Brazil's economy even enabled the commercial associations to coerce government if conditions warranted. Although commercial associations and factor groups enjoyed access of the highest order to government decision makers, industrial groups did not. Despite influential leaders, they faced a government largely unreceptive to the idea of industrialization. They were forced to appeal more than commercial associations and factor groups to the educated public. All business interest groups also broadcast images and themes intended to legitimate enterprise and enhance the image of the business elite with that public.

The commercial associations benefited most from the relative lack of other interest organizations competing for the attention and favor of government. Although primarily responding to the interests of overseas commerce, the associations had no real rivals as business interest organizations. Factor groups shared with commercial associations most policy objectives, membership, and even leadership. Retailer interest groups had virtually no impact on national policy. First appearing in the 1880s, they usually concerned themselves with limited problems such as licensing, labeling, or municipal taxation.[1] Their impotence in part reflected the small scale of operations and the low social standing of most retailers in nineteenth-century Brazil.

The interest organizations that most formed a countervailing or con-

1. For example, Sociedade União Comercial dos Varegistas, *Relatório Apresentado à Assembléia Geral da Sociedade União Comercial dos Varegistas de Sêcos e Molhados em 10 de Agôsto de 1881 pela Diretoria da Mesma Sociedade* (Rio de Janeiro: Central, 1881), and *Relatório de 1897*.

trary influence to the commercial associations were industrial groups. However, they were few in the nineteenth century and tended to be short-lived. Brazil's first true industrial interest group, the Industrial Association, was not founded until 1880 and became inactive by 1885, reviving briefly in 1887, while the Agricultural Industrial Center of Pelotas, Rio Grande do Sul, was active only from 1887 to 1889. Other short-lived industrial groups were formed to petition the government briefly on specific issues. The only lasting advocate for Brazilian industry was a professional association, the Engineering Club of Rio de Janeiro, founded in 1880. Despite the ephemeral nature of most industrial interest organizations, their propaganda efforts probably were influential in swinging Brazilian public opinion toward aid for industrialization.

Sometimes thought to have been an active spokesman for industry, the prestigious Auxiliary Society for National Industry (*Sociedade Auxiliadora da Indústria Nacional*) was in fact a learned society, not an interest group. Most of its activity was devoted to the improvement of agricultural technology, and its public support of manufacturing was sporadic and tentative.[2] There was no continuity of leadership and little of purpose between the Auxiliary Society for National Industry, defunct after 1896, and the new manufacturing interest group that took over its headquarters in 1904, the Industrial Center of Brazil (*Centro Industrial do Brasil*).[3]

The commercial associations and factor organizations were spokesmen for agriculture by default as well as by intent. Surprisingly, there were few lasting and effective interest groups representing Brazil's basic economic activity, agriculture, during the nineteenth century. The first organized interest group of an independent Brazil, the Agricultural, Commercial, and Industrial Society of the Province of Bahia, primarily a spokesman for planters, lasted less than five years. A second agricultural group from that province was an official advisory body to the provincial government. The Farming Council (*Junta da Lavoura*) was installed in the *Recôncavo* town of Santo Amaro in 1844 and continued for at least ten years.[4]

The nation's first nongovernmental interest organizations created spe-

---

2. *O Auxiliador da Indústria Nacional: Periódico da Sociedade Auxiliadora da Indústria Nacional*, 1833–1896; Edgard Carone, *O Centro Industrial do Rio de Janeiro e a sua Importante Participação na Economia Nacional (1827–1977)* (Rio de Janeiro: Centro Industrial do Rio de Janeiro, 1978), p. 53.

3. Its subsidy from the nation ended, the Auxiliary Society for National Industry expired after publishing its last journal in 1896. *O Auxiliador da Indústria Nacional*, 61, no. 1 (1896): 1–55. There was no carryover of directors or other leaders to the Industrial Center of Brazil in 1904. Minutes, meeting of the Board of Directors, Industrial Center of Brazil, Aug. 18, 1904, Livro de Atas, 1904–1923, ACIRJ, pp. 1–2.

4. Minutes, meeting of May 14, 1844, Livro 1 de Atas, AACB, p. 174; Bahia, Presidente da Província, *Fala Recitada na Abertura da Assembléia Legislativa da Bahia pelo Presidente da Província, o Doutor João Maurício Wanderley, no Primeiro de Março de 1854* (Salvador: Antônio Olavo da França Guerra, 1854), pp. 26–28.

cifically to represent agriculture were the Imperial Agricultural Institutes of Rio de Janeiro (*Fluminense*), Bahia, Pernambuco, Sergipe, and Rio Grande do Sul. They were founded in 1859–1860 on the initiative of Emperor Pedro II. But neither the Emperor's support, national and provincial subsidies, nor a membership composed of the Empire's landed aristocracy made them effective spokesmen for agriculture. The Rio Grande do Sul and Sergipe organizations were stillborn, and the Pernambuco Institute lapsed into dormancy within a few years. Only the Bahia and Rio de Janeiro groups proved lasting, and only the latter was vigorous.[5] It worked mainly at improving agricultural technology and maintaining the National Botanical Gardens, rather than promoting agricultural legislation.[6] The Imperial Agricultural Institute of Rio de Janeiro expired two years after the coming of the Republic, although its Bahian counterpart, dropping the word "Imperial" from its title, continued lethargically into the early twentieth century.[7]

More solid interest group activity on behalf of planters was carried on by a number of agricultural societies and clubs organized principally in the provinces of Rio de Janeiro, São Paulo, and Pernambuco. Appearing as early as 1860, they proliferated during the 1880s when planters faced the threatened abolition of slavery, scarce agricultural credit, and low commodity prices. By 1884, forty-nine were in operation in southeastern Brazil alone, as well as in most of Pernambuco's *municípios* (an administrative unit roughly equivalent to a county in the United States).[8] However, most were created to find immediate solutions to specific planter problems; once the issue had been resolved one way or another, they had little reason to continue. Few lasted longer than a year or two. The most important exception was the Agriculture Club (*Clube da Lavoura*) of Campinas, São Paulo, active from 1876 to 1889.[9]

Only one organization combined true planter interest group activity with permanence. The Recife-based Agriculture Auxiliary Society of Pernambuco, which shared many aims and much membership with the Commercial Association of Pernambuco and the factor group Commercial

5. Miguel Antônio da Silva, "Agricultura Nacional: Estudos Agrícolas," *Revista Agrícola*, 9 (March 1878): 17–18; "Extratos," *Revista Agrícola*, 13 (March 1882): 37–38. For the Bahian Institute see Bahia, Presidente da Província, *Relatório de 1889*, pp. 163–164; Arlindo Fragôso, *Ensino Agrícola: Escola Agrícola da Bahia, Série de Artigos Publicados no "Jornal de Notícias," sôbre a Urgência e Bases de Reforma dêsse Estabelecimento* (Salvador: Dois Mundos, 1893), pp. 98–99.
6. See minutes of meetings in Imperial Instituto Fluminense de Agricultura, Atas, Ofícios, Etc., 1860–1862, ACIRJ, and in *Revista Agrícola*, 1869–1891.
7. Bahia, Governador do Estado, *Relatório de 1904*, p. 52.
8. Laura Jarnagin Pang, "The State and Agricultural Clubs of Imperial Brazil, 1860–1889" (Ph.D. Diss., Vanderbilt University, 1981), pp. 24–81, 338; Marc Hoffnagel, "From Monarchy to Republic in Northeast Brazil: The Case of Pernambuco, 1868–1895" (Ph.D. Diss., University of Indiana, 1975), pp. 75–76.
9. Pang, "State and Agricultural Clubs," pp. 185–237.

Agricultural Association of Pernambuco, worked to aid Brazil's sugar industry from 1872 until well into the twentieth century. Even this bellwether for agricultural interests suffered from planter indifference. Although roughly 2000 *engenhos* were dependent on the Recife market, the Agriculture Auxiliary Society never had more than 160 members and could not gather a quorum for its general assemblies in 1884 and 1885.[10] It was increasingly dominated by urban members, mainly factors and exporters. Not until 1897 did there emerge a planter interest group with national scope, the National Society of Agriculture (*Sociedade Nacional de Agricultura*).

It is not clear why planter interest groups were short-lived. The zealousness of commercial associations and factor groups in defending agriculture perhaps lessened the need for them. Planters may have felt that their political strength and their family influence in government also diminished the need for interest organizations, despite manifest agricultural discontent.[11] They also controlled the municipal councils of rural towns, which actively petitioned on their behalf, particularly during the abolition struggle.[12] Furthermore, it has been suggested that the Imperial Agricultural Institutes represented an attempt, perhaps partially successful, to defuse planter interest group activity by channeling it into organizations under governmental tutelage.[13] Finally, blame also must be placed on the planters themselves. As noted, many planter interest groups suffered, sometimes fatally, from inertia and indifference.

Other interest groups were few. Among the most active were those organized around a single issue, such as the emancipation of slaves or the promotion of immigration. Professional associations, appearing in the last two decades of the nineteenth century, commonly devoted themselves to technical matters. Only the Engineering Club made significant attempts to influence public policy. Occupational associations were more numerous but were created for mutual aid, not for interest group activity.[14] Labor unions were few, purely local, and had almost no access to government.[15]

10. Evaldo Cabral de Melo, *O Norte Agrário e o Império, 1871–1889* (Rio de Janeiro: Nova Fronteira, 1984), pp. 178–179.
11. Men of landowner origin overwhelmingly dominated imperial cabinet positions. José Murilo de Carvalho, *A Construção da Ordem: A Elite Política Imperial* (Rio de Janeiro: Campus, 1980), p. 165.
12. I am indebted for this observation to Michael Trochim.
13. Pang, "State and Agricultural Clubs," p. 76.
14. For information on the associations of the nineteenth century, see Manuel Duarte Moreira de Azevedo, "Sociedades Fundadas no Brasil Desde os Tempos Coloniais até o Começo do Atual Reinado," *Revista do Instituto Histórico e Geográfico Brasileiro*, 48, part 2 (1885): 265–322, and Antônio Maria Cardozo Cortés, *Homens e Instituições no Rio* (Rio de Janeiro: Instituto Brasileiro de Geografia e Estatística, 1957).
15. Philippe C. Schmitter, *Interest Conflict and Political Change in Brazil* (Stanford, Calif.: Stanford University Press, 1971), pp. 139–140.

The relative dearth of other interest organizations magnified the power of business interest groups, especially the commercial associations. During the nineteenth century no business interest groups with true nationwide representation or organization existed. The Industrial Association claimed to represent all manufacturers, the Center for Coffee Agriculture and Commerce the coffee industry, and the Center for Sugar Industry and Commerce all sugar interests, but most of their members resided in the city or province of Rio de Janeiro. The establishment of interest groups with real nationwide representation, so-called peak organizations, was retarded by Brazil's lack of economic integration. However, the problems of making contact with officials and an increasing need for common effort slowly impelled the commercial associations toward federation. But the larger associations were wary of the creation of a peak interest organization under the Rio group, while Rio would not support any independent national organization.[16] No compromise was reached until 1912, when the Federation of Commercial Associations, led by the president of the Rio association, was formed.

Corporate tradition and personal influence

A second major source of power for business interest groups was their advisory and regulatory powers. As noted, they performed many of the present-day activities of national, provincial, and local government. In part these powers derived from the rich inheritance of Iberian corporatism, in part from functional necessity. Reliance on interest groups for specialized information characterizes even well-organized modern states; where administration is weak such reliance may be nearly unavoidable.[17] An overall lack of technical expertise forced the Brazilian government to depend heavily on private organizations for advice and aid in regulation. The Auxiliary Society for National Industry, for example, officially evaluated applications for patents, while the Imperial Agricultural Institute of Bahia administered the Northeast's only agricultural school.[18]

Government relied on no other private organizations as much as the commercial associations. Until the rise of the academically trained economist (some would say afterward as well), businessmen, especially overseas

16. Commercial Association of Rio de Janeiro to Commercial and Industrial Center (*Centro de Comércio e Indústria*) of Santos, Rio de Janeiro, Nov. [no date] 1903, *Relatório da Associação Comercial do Rio de Janeiro, Apresentado 'a Assembléia Geral em Março de 1904* (Rio de Janeiro: Jornal do Comércio, 1904), pp. 60–61.

17. V. O. Key, *Politics, Parties, and Pressure Groups* (4th ed.; New York: Thomas Y. Crowell, 1958), p. 165; Reinhard Bendix, *Max Weber: An Intellectual Portrait* (New York: Anchor Books, 1962), pp. 336–337.

18. See, for example, "Indústria Nacional, Lista das Patentes de Invenção," *O Auxiliador da Indústria Nacional*, 52, no. 4 (1884): 75–79; Fragôso, *Ensino Agrícola*.

traders, were the best sources of economic knowledge. The Brazilian state also extracted the vast bulk of its tax revenue from the operations of commercial association membership, making its advisory and regulatory help almost indispensable. As noted the commercial associations aided government in a surprising breadth of activities. During the nineteenth century they enjoyed what has been termed a "quasi-official" relationship with the state.[19]

The Brazilian state depended heavily on commercial associations as adjuncts to administration. Yet the latter's advisory and regulatory prerogatives were based more on custom than on statute law. Except for Brazil's Commercial Code of 1850, the legal position and privileges of commercial associations were spelled out only in scattered laws, regulations, and executive decrees. A Brazilian legal scholar notes: "No special disposition concerning the duties, prerogatives, and rights of commercial associations exists in our legislation after 1850."[20] Much of the relationship between the organizations and government followed tradition and necessity, not formal law. No legislation, for example, required national government approval of commercial association statutes, yet neither party would have thought of forgoing this formality, which implied a special relationship to the state.

Legal definition of the special position of the commercial associations came late. National decrees in 1916 and 1917 recognized individual associations as "institutions of public utility."[21] However, formal acknowledgment of the long-standing special relationship between the groups and government came only after that relationship had lost much of its significance. In a series of decrees beginning in 1940, President Getúlio Vargas conceded to individual associations formal status as technical and consultative organs to government and specified their rights and duties.[22] By then the commercial associations had been drained of much of their importance by the multiplication of competing interest organizations and by the weakening of the traditional export-import economy. Even more significant, by 1940 government itself had taken over many of the advisory and regulatory functions the associations once performed.

19. Heitor Beltrão, *Um Capítulo da História da Praça do Rio de Janeiro: Considerações de Ordem Histórica e Jurídica, 1820–1929* (Rio de Janeiro: Imprensa Nacional, 1929), p. 3.
20. Alfredo Pujol, "Consultas e Pareceres: LXXVI, Associações Comerciaes," *Revista do Comércio e Indústria: Publicação Mensal do Centro do Comércio e Indústria de São Paulo*, 3 (Jan.-Dec. 1917): 388.
21. For example, Associação Comercial do Amazonas, *Documentário Comemorativo do Primeiro Centenário da Associação Comercial do Amazonas, 18 de Junho de 1971* (Manaus: Associação Comercial do Amazonas, 1971), p. 85; Estevão Pinto, *A Associação Comercial de Pernambuco* (Recife: Jornal do Comércio, 1940), p. 66.
22. "A Mentalidade Econômica e as Associações Comerciais," *Revista do Direito Comercial*, 40, vol. 10 (1940): 338; João da Costa e Silva Sobrinho, *Santos Noutros Tempos* (São Paulo: Revista dos Tribunais, 1953), p. 251.

Their prerogatives had shrunk to but a fraction of their nineteenth-century importance.

The personal relationships of business interest group leaders were a major source of influence. Access to centers of power in Brazil in the nineteenth century was facilitated by the structure of government itself. Smaller and much less complex than in modern states, its key decision makers were fewer, making personal contacts and friendships much more important. The small size of the educated elite in nineteenth-century Brazil also heightened the significance of personal relationships as well as increasing their likelihood. As of 1890, a bare fifteen percent of the population was literate.[23] It is likely that business interest group directors were chosen as much for their personal ties to government heads as for their prominence in their field.

The relationships of group leaders with government officials were based on kinship, social contacts, business affairs, or politics. Family ties by blood or marriage, always important in Brazilian culture, could be valuable in propagating the influence of business interest groups.[24] But they were not of universal significance. Much of the leadership of business interest groups was foreign; some Brazilians among leadership were from relatively poor or obscure families. However, certain commercial association heads enjoyed powerful kinship connections. Perhaps most directly useful was that of Count Tocantins (José Joaquim de Lima e Silva Sobrinho), President of the Commercial Association of Rio de Janeiro for twenty-four years. He was the brother of the Duke of Caxias (Luís Alves de Lima e Silva), greatest military leader of the Empire and three times its prime minister.

Personal relationships between business interest group leaders and government heads deriving from social contacts were more widespread than those stemming from kinship. While these friendships were made primarily to advance the business affairs of such leaders, they obviously also were of advantage to the interest organizations as well. Friends in high places could facilitate the granting to companies of privileges of exclusivity, financial aid, or tax exemptions. And such friendships could be valuable sources of inside knowledge of government policy. "By constantly presenting yourself to the Minister," advised a manager of the London and

23. Joseph L. Love, "Political Participation in Brazil, 1881–1969," *Luso-Brazilian Review*, 7 (Dec. 1970): 8.
24. Two recent studies of the significance of family ties are Linda Lewin, "Some Historical Implications of Kinship Organization for Family-Based Politics in the Brazilian Northeast," *Comparative Studies in Society and History*, 21 (April 1979): 262–292, and *Politics and Parentela in Paraíba: A Case Study of Family-Based Oligarchy in Brazil* (Princeton, N.J.: Princeton University Press, 1987).

Brazilian Bank, "you will often, even if you do no business, pick up very valuable information."[25]

Many valuable contacts were made in the high social circles of nineteenth-century Brazil. The stereotype of the dour and reclusive merchant, often held by Brazilians, does not ring true. Overseas traders had the money and sophistication to entertain lavishly and well. Count Figueiredo (Francisco de Figueiredo), a leader of the Rio association, hosted as many as 2,000 guests at a time.[26] Among the centers where the "society" of the Empire gathered were the houses of Marquis Bom Fim (José Francisco de Mesquita), his son Count Mesquita (Jerônimo José de Mesquita), Count São Clemente (Antônio Clemente Pinto), and Count Estrêla (Joaquim Manuel Monteiro), also Rio organization leaders.[27] Rio association heads were also especially prominent in the Casino Fluminense, the most noted social club in the imperial capital.[28]

Other valuable contacts were made in the voluntary societies – religious, charitable, learned, or mutual aid – which were conspicuous in the late nineteenth century.[29] Because of their financial experience, business interest group leaders often served as treasurer in such groups. Most important from the social standing of their leadership were the lay religious brotherhoods, ceremonial and charitable organizations that enrolled much of the nation's educated male population. They offered prime opportunities for making valuable personal contacts. In the Imperial Brotherhood of Senhor dos Passos in 1872, for example, five Commercial Association of Rio de Janeiro leaders shared board duties with the prime minister, his successor, and two prominent senators.[30]

Personal relationships with government heads that derived from business may have been the most significant of all for business interest group leaders, because of mutual financial benefits. If friendship with government officials could advance the business interests of association leaders,

25. John Gordon to Manager, London and Brazilian Bank, Rio de Janeiro, London, Sept. 19, 1887, Letters, London to Rio, 1885–89, LABA, UCLL, G.2., p. 7.
26. José Wanderley de Araújo Pinho, *Salões e Damas do Segundo Reinado* (São Paulo: Martins, 1945), p. 286.
27. Ibid., p. 244; Heitor Lyra, *História de Dom Pedro II, 1825–1891* (São Paulo: Editôra Nacional, 1939), III: 45–77: Jeffrey Needell, "The Origins of the Carioca Belle Epoque: The Emergence of the Elite Culture and Society of Turn-of-the-Century Rio de Janeiro" (Ph.D. Diss., Stanford University, 1982), p. 222.
28. Needell, "Carioca Belle Epoque", pp. 100–117.
29. Michael L. Conniff, "Voluntary Associations in Rio, 1870–1945: A New Approach to Urban Social Dynamics," *JLAS*, 17 (Feb. 1975): 64–81. See also June E. Hahner, *Poverty and Politics: The Urban Poor in Brazil, 1870–1920* (Albuquerque: University of New Mexico Press, 1986), pp. 75–84.
30. *Almanak Administrativo, Mercantil e Industrial da Corte e da Capital da Província do Rio de Janeiro com os Municípios de Campos e de Santos para o Ano de 1872 {Almanak Laemmert}* (Rio de Janeiro: E.&H. Laemmert, 1872), p. 388.

the latter had the financial resources, knowledge, and business connections to help expand the fortunes of their friends in government through advice or partnership. Banking was a prime point of business contact between government and business interest group leaders. The most important of the institutions where they worked together during the Empire was the government-sponsored but privately organized Bank of Brazil. Ten leaders of the Commercial Association of Rio de Janeiro served among its directors, together with sometime prime ministers Angelo Muniz da Silva Ferraz, Manuel Pinto de Sousa Dantas, and Baron Cotegipe (João Maurício Wanderley) and many lesser officials.[31] Dantas and Cotegipe also worked with directors of the Commercial Association of Bahia, the former on the Board of the *Caixa Econômica* bank and Cotegipe as a founder and officer of the Bank of Bahia.[32]

Business interest group leaders sometimes helped manage the personal financial affairs of high government officials. Prime minister Viscount Rio Branco (José Maria da Silva Paranhos) and his son Baron Rio Branco (also José Maria da Silva Paranhos), later a celebrated Minister of Foreign Affairs in the early Republic, deposited much of their family fortune in the merchant firm of Count Mesquita, President of the Commercial Association of Rio de Janeiro.[33] Some of the business affairs of Conservative Party head Baron Cotegipe were handled by Count Figueiredo of the Rio association and by Aristedes Novis, a director of the Bahian group.[34] Perhaps more significant as far as influence was concerned, Cotegipe was at the time of his death in 1889 deeply in debt to the firm of his friend Viscount Guaí, longtime President of the Commercial Association of Bahia.[35]

In sum, in a political situation in which personal relationships were of primary importance, those of business interest group leaders with government decision makers were numerous and close. Customary Brazilian reliance on personal and family loyalties to influence government, rather than handicapping business interest groups, was readily converted into an asset. The groups concentrated the impact of such ties. It might be argued that personal associations, together with traditional advisory and regula-

31. *Almanak Laemmert, 1892*, p. 1113.
32. Thales de Azevedo and E. Q. Vieira Lins, *História do Banco da Bahia, 1858–1958* (Rio de Janeiro: J. Olympio, 1969), pp. 68–69; Arnold Wildberger, *Os Presidentes da Província da Bahia, Efetivos e Interinos* (Salvador: Beneditina, 1949), p. 507.
33. José Maria da Silva Paranhos to Baron Mesquita, Rio de Janeiro, July 16, 1881, Coleção Instituto Histórico, AIHGB, lata 311, pasta 92.
34. For example, Viscount Figueiredo to Baron Cotegipe, Rio de Janeiro, Dec. 26, 1879, ABC, AIHGB, lata 23, doc. 111; Aristedes Novis to Baron Cotegipe, Salvador, Mar. 21, 1882, ABC, AIHGB, lata 49, doc. 13.
35. Cotegipe owed Marinhos & Co. 84:374$170 out of his total assets of 106:748$065. Other creditors, mainly firms, were owed 5:059$976. "Inventário dos Bens do Barão de Cotegipe, 28 Aug., 1890," ABC, AIHGB, lata 95, doc. 25.

tory prerogatives and a relative absence of competing organizations, gave nineteenth-century business interest groups, especially the commercial associations, a potential for influence rarely matched by modern interest groups.

Targets of influence

Business interest groups confronted a framework of government much smaller and less complex than in modern states, one whose key decision-making individuals were consequently fewer. Who were they? The most powerful man in the Empire was the Emperor, Pedro II. Although a constitutional monarch, he was no mere figurehead. His "Moderating Power" and his great eminence gave him the ability to bring about indirectly most legislative or administrative measures that he wanted. But, like the creator god in a pagan pantheon, he seemed somewhat remote. Business interest groups appealed to him only in the most important matters. After 1889 his position was filled by the president of the Republic, less remote but equally powerful.

Second to Pedro II under the Empire was the president of the Council of Ministers, commonly referred to as the prime minister. He had the wide powers that informal title implied, although he could be replaced upon the will of the Emperor. Next in importance was the Minister of Finance (*Ministro da Fazenda*), who governed the nation's financial affairs, including taxation. The president of the Council of Ministers often assumed the portfolio of finance, making this official doubly significant to business interest group leaders. The Minister of Agriculture, Commerce, and Public Works, heading a ministry created in 1860, was also a natural focus of attention. Other cabinet members were appealed to less frequently and as circumstances warranted.

Important petitions were sent to the Imperial Parliament as well as to the Emperor. To ensure their favorable reception, it was necessary to work through individual parliamentarians. Much of the lobbying efforts of business interest groups were aimed at cultivating these politicians. Business interest groups directed most of their attention toward members of the elected Chamber of Deputies rather than the appointed Senate, perhaps because the former was more active in initiating legislation. Following the Republican takeover, Congress assumed the importance of the Parliament in the eyes of petitioners, with the change that the Senate now carried weight equal to the Chamber of Deputies. Some business interest groups were fortunate enough to be led by men who were themselves national deputies. During the nineteenth century, at least eight men who served in the Chamber of Deputies headed commercial associations and the Industrial Association at various times, including four presidents of the Commercial Association of Rio de Janeiro.[36] The latter were men of some national prominence: Viscount Mauá, Teofilo Benedito Ottoni, a notable Liberal Party statesman, the well-connected Count Tocantins, and Francisco de Paula Mayrink.

The individual most commonly dealt with by business interest groups outside of Rio was the provincial president. Appointed by the Emperor, he was easily the most powerful figure in a province. He could recommend legislation to the provincial assembly, force the withdrawal of bills under discussion, and veto legislation. He was also an invaluable intermediary in dealing with national bureaucrats or administrations of other provinces. The authority of the provincial president was such that the groups directed most of their appeals for both executive and legislative action at provincial level to him and only rarely to the elected provincial assembly. This situation did not change greatly with the Republic. Although the new state assembly gained in importance, the elected governor inherited much of the de facto power of the provincial president.

Under the Empire, a bonus in influence might come from gaining the friendship of a provincial president. The imperial government used a principle of circulation of elites similar to the mandarin system employed in imperial China.[37] Although rarely serving for more than two years, provincial presidents often moved on to other influential posts: national deputy or senator, cabinet minister, member of the Council of State, or the prime ministership. Relations formed with a talented provincial president could pay important future dividends. The Commercial Association of Bahia, for example, formed strong ties with Baron Cotegipe and Manuel Pinto de Sousa Dantas, later prime ministers and heads, respectively, of the Conservative and Liberal parties, when each served as President of the Province of Bahia.

There were also a number of minor officials and government bodies whose goodwill was useful to the commercial associations, although less so to factor and industrial groups. The local chief of customs (*inspetor da alfândega*) figured in trade profitability, since he strongly influenced the severity of duty exaction on goods, their speed of passage through customs, and their safety. The municipal council (*câmara municipal*) could impose annoying minor taxes. Under the Republic its power to levy direct taxes was increased and consequently its demands on commerce grew.

36. They were Antônio Felício dos Santos of the Industrial Association, Manuel Gomes de Matos of the Commercial Association of Pernambuco, and José Alves da Cruz Rios and Viscount Guaí of Bahia, in addition to the four from Rio.

37. Eul-Soo Pang and Ron L. Seckinger, "The Mandarins of Imperial Brazil," *Comparative Studies in Society and History*, 14 (March 1972): 215–244.

Means of influence

The number of individuals and groups whose decisions affected the prosperity of business interest group membership was relatively limited. How did the groups attempt to influence them? The means were varied and to a degree different from those used by modern organized interest groups. First, open support for political parties was usually avoided. The statutes of most business interest groups specifically forbade political activity; all tried to avoid the appearance of a partisan stance.

Forthright identification with one political party would have been dangerous during the Empire, for Conservative and Liberal parties alternated frequently in power. It would have been difficult during the Republic, characterized by shifting, impermanent political alignments. Ideological differences between the Empire's parties were not such as to impel partisanship on the part of interest groups. The Conservatives favored administrative centralization and were more skeptical of democratic institutions but did not differ greatly from the Liberals in their economic views.[38] Nor were there clear-cut differences in the personnel of the two parties. Contrary to what is often believed, landowners were no more predominant in the Conservative than in the Liberal Party, and leaders of business background were actually more numerous among the Conservatives.[39] Support for one party, furthermore, would necessarily offend part of the membership, many of whom were linked to the other by family, friendships, or political enthusiasm. Interestingly, preference for political nonpartisanship has continued in Brazilian interest groups down to the present.[40] But theoretical nonpartisanship did not mean the avoidance of political activity; business interest groups were willing to support those who backed their objectives in whatever party they might be found.

In contrast to interest groups in the modern United States, electoral support was not central to business interest group activity. This may seem surprising. Although provincial legislatures and municipal councils were of secondary importance, having favorable representatives in the National Chamber of Deputies or, later, in Congress was central to interest group influence. Furthermore the potential for success was great, because of

---

38. João Camillo de Oliveira Torres, "Paraná e a Conciliação," *Revista Brasileira de Estudos Políticos*, I (Dec. 1956): 95–96. See also Emília Viotti da Costa, "Brazil: The Age of Reform, 1870–1889," in *The Cambridge History of Latin America. Volume V, c. 1870–1930*, ed. Leslie Bethell (Cambridge: Cambridge University Press, 1986), pp. 761–762; and Richard Graham, *Patronage and Politics in Nineteenth-Century Brazil* (Stanford, Calif.: Stanford University Press, 1990), pp. 169–180.
39. Murilo de Carvalho, *Construção da Ordem*, p. 165.
40. Schmitter, *Interest Conflict*, pp. 259, 272, 275.

membership size relative to the small number of eligible voters. Slavery, minimum income requirements, male-only suffrage, and exclusion of opposition by the party in power meant that less than one percent of the population cast direct ballots during the Empire.[41] The electoral power of group membership also was increased in 1881 with the Saraiva voting reform law. It provided for direct elections, but also increased the power of monied urban groups by doubling income qualifications and making proof of income much more difficult.[42] Only 1,391 persons cast ballots, for example, in the 1881 election of Commercial Association of Bahia President Viscount Guaí to the Chamber of Deputies, and most elections had even fewer voters.[43] The coming of the Republic, which granted suffrage to all literate adult males, did not immediately much widen voter participation. Only 2.7 percent of the population, the largest proportion of the nineteenth century, voted in the 1898 election.[44]

Despite such favorable prospects, open participation in political campaigns by business interest groups was rare and done amid affirmations of "nonpartisanship." The Commercial Association of Rio de Janeiro worked to enroll merchants on the voting lists, and the Bahian association urged its membership to support the three successful campaigns for National Deputy of Viscount Guaí, but only the Commercial Association of Pernambuco officially participated in an election. Emboldened by the electoral reforms and supported by the Commercial Agricultural Association of Pernambuco, it selected and ran two candidates for national deputy in 1881.[45] Both nonpartisan "candidates of commerce" were badly beaten. The commercial association blamed membership indifference, but it is also likely that, given the unpopularity of merchants among the public, the endorsement simply backfired.[46] The experiment was not repeated.

Such experiences illustrated the problems of electoral participation. Given the dubious popularity of merchants, any endorsement might be counterproductive. Because of the rancors of Brazilian politics, gaining the united support of membership was virtually impossible. Even the

---

41. Love, "Political Participation," 6–7. However, prior to the 1881 reform indirect voters were much more numerous. Registered voters comprised about half the nation's free males above twenty-one in the 1870s. Graham, *Patronage and Politics,* pp. 108–109.

42. Graham, *Patronage and Politics,* pp. 198–199. Graham estimates the 1881 law reduced the number of voters from over 1,000,000 to roughly 150,000.

43. Jorge João Dodsworth, Barão de Javari, *Organizações e Programas Ministeriais: Regime Parlamentar no Império* (2d ed.; Rio de Janeiro: Estado de Guanabara, 1962), p. 375.

44. Love, "Political Participation," 7.

45. Associação Comercial de Pernambuco, *Relatório da Associação Comercial Beneficente Lido na Assembléia Geral de 4 de Agôsto de 1881* (Recife: Industrial, 1881), pp. 12–14; Minutes, meeting of Feb. 28, 1881, Livro de Atas da Associação Comercial Agrícola de Pernambuco (hereafter cited as ACAP), 1877–1892, AACP, p. 46.

46. Associação Comercial de Pernambuco, *Relatório de 1882,* p. 12.

campaigns of Viscount Guaí did not have the backing of all the directors of the Commercial Association of Bahia. It is hardly surprising that electoral activity by business interest groups was rare.

There were safer means of gaining the favor of government leaders. Very common was the public granting of honors and respect. The most important honorific gesture was the awarding of honorary membership, an event usually marked by solemn ceremonies. It was sometimes conferred upon men distinguished for their military or intellectual contributions or upon those who had given a group nonpolitical aid. But its usual purpose, in the words of a director of the Commercial Association of Pernambuco, was to recognize government "authorities of high rank, after they had rendered valuable services to commerce and the association."[47] Implicit in the award was the expectation that the honorary member would continue to provide assistance. Honorary membership symbolized a special relationship of mutual respect and support between the business interest group and the person honored. It encompassed a large number of high officials. Eight, and possibly more, of the Empire's twenty-three prime ministers were honorary members of commercial associations, as was Count D'Eu, the Emperor's son-in-law.

Ceremonial public hospitality was another means used, principally by commercial associations, to honor those who were, or whom they wished to make, their friends. Visiting notables, Brazilian and foreign, were invariably entertained at association headquarters. Although the goodwill of Brazilian war heroes or North American industrialists was of little direct value, their presence conferred distinction. The most elaborate hospitality was reserved for leading national figures. Ceremonies often began with the association chartering a boat to meet their guest's ship at sea. Similarly, the Commercial Association of São Paulo greeted arriving President-elect Manuel Ferraz de Campos Sales in 1898 in two chartered railway trains after having decorated the city.[48]

A peak of eulogy was reached by the Commercial Association of Rio de Janeiro in receiving Viscount Ouro Preto, last prime minister of the Empire. The group renamed the main room of its headquarters after him, formally installed his bust, and pledged to commission his statue for the city, to engrave on a wall in gold and precious stones his legislative decrees that it most appreciated, and to mint and distribute gold and silver coins commemorating his administration.[49] The tribute was a masterpiece of bad timing. It took place on November 7, 1889, a scant eight days before

47. Minutes, meeting of Oct. 7, 1876, Livro 4 de Atas, AACP, p. 66.
48. *O Estado de São Paulo* (São Paulo), Aug. 31, 1898, p. 1.
49. *Novedades* (Rio de Janeiro), Nov. 8, 1889, p. 1, and Nov. 14, 1889, p. 1; Associação Comercial do Rio de Janeiro, *Relatório de 1890*, pp. 44–45.

the overthrow of the Empire by military leaders who considered Ouro Preto their chief enemy. It obviously contributed to the mistrust with which the new Republic regarded the Rio association.

Finally, business interest groups would sometimes break their vows of political neutrality to demonstrate solidarity with government figures whom they considered particularly valuable friends. In 1877, for example, the Commercial Association of Bahia publicly congratulated Baron Cotegipe on his successful defense against grave charges of malfeasance made against him in the Chamber of Deputies and, in 1887, the Commercial Association of Rio de Janeiro openly defended him when, as prime minister, he was widely denounced for using troops to break up antislavery demonstrations.[50]

Although the ceremonial granting of honors and respect were basic to business interest group efforts to ingratiate themselves with those they wished to influence, perhaps no less important were the frequent informal contacts made by association leaders. The installation of an official in office or his leaving, his birthday or a death in the family, his triumphs or setbacks in performing his duties – all found association leaders present to offer congratulations or condolences. This style of personal interaction, often used by lobbyists elsewhere, was particularly important in the Brazilian cultural context.[51] As the manager of a British bank noted, "These small attentions are much appreciated in Brazil, and often bear good fruit."[52]

The art of lobbying

Business interest groups used varied and effective means to win the friendship of high government officials, and as noted, they enjoyed access of the highest order. How were actual lobbying operations conducted? Most lobbying was direct, that is, done through personal contact with the targeted official. Although requests were spelled out in detail in a formal written petition, they were usually delivered face-to-face. Their impact was intensified by being presented where possible not by represen-

50. Cotegipe was exonerated by a vote of 70 to 16 of charges of being the partner of a well-known smuggler, refusing to pay a huge debt, and exercising undue influence on the Empress through an illicit gift. *Diário da Bahia* (Salvador), July 21, 1877, p. 2; Minutes, meeting of July 21, 1877, Livro 4 de Atas, AACB, p. 281; Cotegipe sent telegrams to all presidents of province announcing the Rio association's support for his actions. *The Rio News* (Rio de Janeiro), Sept. 15, 1887, p. 4.

51. On the importance of frequent informal contacts in modern lobbying, see Norman J. Ornstein and Shirley Elder, *Interest Groups, Lobbying, and Policymaking* (Washington, D.C.: Congressional Quarterly, 1978), pp. 83–84.

52. John Gordon to Manager, London and Brazilian Bank, Rio de Janeiro, London, May 6, 1886, Letters, London to Rio, 1885–89, LABA, UCLL, G.2., p. 2.

tatives, but by business interest group leaders themselves. Particularly important petitions were delivered by the group's board of directors as a body.

Of course, personal meetings with central government officials were rarely feasible for groups not based in Rio de Janeiro. Such groups often employed agents, usually politically influential figures who themselves had held or were to hold national political office. Differing little from modern professional lobbyists, they either received an annual stipend or were paid by the task.[53] Commercial associations based outside Rio sometimes were able to use the unpaid services of prominent Rio businessmen as go-betweens.[54] And the Commercial Association of Rio de Janeiro itself increasingly acted as an intermediary before government, especially for newer and smaller commercial associations. To appeals for lobbying services the Rio group commonly responded with enthusiasm, having the petition handed over by a board member and often adding its own written support. But larger and longer established associations rarely used the Rio organization as an intermediary because of an undercurrent of jealousy and, in the case of the Bahia and Santos organizations, competition with Rio over commercial territory.

The most effective of business interest group representatives were themselves high government officials. Most leading groups had several deputies or, more rarely, a senator who spoke for them in legislative and administrative circles. Some of these champions volunteered their services.[55] Often the friendly relationship leading to these arrangements had been established during the legislator's tenure as president of a province. The Industrial Association and Agricultural Industrial Association of Pelotas were helped by legislators sympathetic to manufacturing, in some cases because they held industrial interests.[56] Some lucky groups could count on outstanding political figures to push forward their interests. The Commercial Association of Pernambuco could often entrust petitions to João Alfredo Correia de Oliveira, Conservative prime minister and holder at various times of four cabinet posts. The Commercial Association of Bahia relied on, during at least part of his career, Manuel Pinto de Sousa Dantas,

53. For example, Minutes, meetings of June 20, 1879, and Jan. 17, 1882, Livro 5 de Atas, AACP, pp. 5, 52.
54. For example, Minutes, meeting of May 26, 1877, Livro 4 de Atas, AACP, p. 88; Minutes meeting of Sept. 17, 1861, Livro 3 de Atas, AACB, p. 3.
55. For example, Associação Comercial de Pernambuco, *Relatório de 1866*, p. 12; Minutes, meeting of Sept. 23, 1879, Livro 5 de Atas, AACP, pp. 17–18.
56. This was true for two senators, João José de Oliveira Junqueira and Manuel Francisco Correia, who were honorary members of the Industrial Association. Associação Industrial, *Relatório Apresentado 'a Assembléia Geral da Associação Industrial em Sessão de 9 de Junho de 1884 pela Diretoria da Mesma Associação* (Rio de Janeiro, Leuzinger & Filhos, 1884), p. 89; R. Frank Colson, "The Destruction of a Revolution: Polity, Economy, and Society in Brazil, 1870–1891" (Ph.D. Diss., Princeton University, 1979), II: 510, 586.

Liberal prime minister and sometime occupant of five cabinet positions.[57] All such relationships were likely to be formalized by honorary membership.

Business interest groups had well-defined techniques of lobbying. What of a less ethical means of gaining the favor of government officials: bribery? Nineteenth-century Brazilian customs officials and even judges were considered by foreigners, at least in certain periods and locations, to be venal.[58] However, there is no evidence that business interest groups resorted to open bribery as a means of influence. On the other hand, the giving of expensive gifts to government figures was not unknown. The Commercial Association of Rio de Janeiro, for example, gave Princess Isabel, heir to the throne, Rs. 2:120$000 (approximately U.S. $1,144.80) and President Prudente de Morais a jewel-studded gold plaque and his bust in bronze to adorn the Presidential Palace.[59] The largest and most questionable of such gifts went to José Mariano Carneiro da Cunha, longtime Deputy and champion of the Commercial Association of Pernambuco. Under the auspices of the latter, overseas trading firms of Recife contributed in 1882 to purchase him a luxurious town house.[60] But there is no record of comparable gifts being offered to government officials by business interest groups. The honesty of the relationship between the two was probably no worse than that between lobbyists and officials of the U.S. government during the nineteenth century.[61]

Indirect lobbying – an appeal to the general public or to the constituents of an elected official through a public relations campaign – was of secondary importance to the direct approach with most business interest groups. This is in marked contrast to the priorities of modern interest groups.[62] Most commercial associations and factor groups had an access to high government officials that usually made appeal to the public superfluous. And, as noted, the literate and politically aware population of

57. Dantas offered the organization "all his assistance" upon being appointed Minister of Agriculture, Commerce, and Public Works in 1866. Minutes, meeting of Aug. 21, 1866, Livro 3 de Atas, AACB, p. 89. The association relied less upon Dantas in the last years of the Empire, probably because of his advocacy of abolition and other causes the organization disliked.
58. For example, John Gordon to Manager, London and Brazilian Bank, Rio de Janeiro, London, Sept. 2, 1887, Letters, London to Rio, 1885–89, LABA, UCLL, G.2., p. 3; T. M. Farrell to Manager, Wilson Sons & Co., Rio de Janeiro, London, May 11, 1900, Manager's Letter Book, 1899–1900, LABA, UCLL, p. 386; James C. Fletcher and D. P. Kidder, *Brazil and the Brazilians* (8th ed. rev.; Boston: Little, Brown and Company, 1868), pp. 31–32.
59. Associação Comercial do Rio de Janeiro, *Relatório de 1902*, p. 45; Associação Comercial do Rio de Janeiro, *Relatório de 1901*, p. 42.
60. Associação Comercial de Pernambuco, *Relatório de 1883*, pp. 115–123.
61. For the nineteenth-century United States, see Karl Schriftgiesser, *The Lobbyists: The Art and Business of Influencing Lawmakers* (Boston: Little, Brown and Company, 1951), pp. 3–21.
62. Key, *Politics*, p. 103; David Truman, *The Governmental Process: Political Interests and Public Opinion* (New York: Alfred A. Knopf, 1962), pp. 213–214.

nineteenth-century Brazil was tiny. Nevertheless, all groups were eager to have the favorable opinion of this small minority.

Newspapers, used mainly by the commercial associations, were the usual means of reaching the literate public. Commercial association appeals consisted of news stories with a slant favorable to overseas commerce or to the group, correspondence with high government officials, formal policy statements by the organization, and the minutes of general assemblies. Space in newspapers had to be bought by fee, by stock purchase, or by taking a large number of subscriptions, unless the local publisher was a member of the association. The services of individual writers, who usually published anonymously, also usually required purchase, either for a yearly stipend or on a piece basis. Many such writers were leading local intellectuals. The Commercial Association of Pernambuco enlisted Manuel Buarque de Macedo, later Deputy and Minister of Agriculture, Commerce, and Public Works, who also refused payment for his services.[63]

Business interest groups also made their causes known through publication. The Industrial Association and the Engineering Club issued journals, the former giving it special emphasis in view of the formidable task of changing public opinion on industrialization. Detailed petitions to Parliament or the Emperor were often published in booklet form simultaneous with presentation to government. In addition, the groups issued more general books promoting their ideas on economic policy issues. The commercial associations and the Industrial Association also broadcast their views through publication of their annual reports (*relatórios*). The Commercial Association of Pernambuco was the first to do so, beginning in 1857.[64] Usually appearing in well-bound book form, annual reports were mailed to all other commercial associations, to foreign chambers of commerce concerned with Brazilian trade, to national and provincial legislative bodies, and to all government leaders the associations wished to influence. They were considered comprehensive enough to be sent in reply to government requests for information on the needs of overseas commerce.

Another effective way of gaining the attention of the educated public was the staging of expositions. Most were opened abroad for the purpose of promoting Brazilian exports, but when put on at home they served not only to display the products dealt with by the sponsoring group but to broadcast its views. They commonly were attended by government officials, and if held in Rio de Janeiro, by the royal family as well. A related means of broadcasting group views was through participation in congresses. These were convened to discuss the problems of a particular

---

63. Minutes, meeting of Feb. 21, 1871, Livro 3 de Atas, AACP, p. 71.
64. The Commercial Association of Bahia began publication of *relatórios* in 1863 and the Rio association in 1867.

economic field. Because of their economic implications, government representatives were present, and when the congress was held in Rio usually the Emperor as well. The Engineering Club organized a Brazilian Railway Congress in 1881 and in 1900 a Congress of Engineering·and Industry, but all others concerned agriculture and were usually staged by the government itself.[65] Commercial associations and factor groups were central participants in the agricultural meetings, using the opportunity to air their views on agricultural problems and to stress the importance of their membership in Brazil's commodity export complex.

A final means of influencing government was one largely unavailable to modern interest groups: coercion. Done by interrupting trade, it was made possible by the pivotal position of the overseas merchant in Brazil's export-import economy and was employable only by the commercial associations. Coercion was applied through the collective refusal of importers to despatch (pay duty on and remove) goods from the customs house. Termed a "commercial strike," it had the effect of creating an immediate revenue shortage. The national government during the nineteenth century usually derived half or more of its income from import duties.[66] Although forbidden by the constitution to tax imports, the provinces also did so through a number of subterfuges. The second effect of a commercial strike was to send the price of food, much of which was imported, shooting upward. This often brought angry mobs into the street, especially in the impoverished Northeast. Because the motive for a commercial strike was usually to protest a tax increase on imports, certain in itself to increase prices, the wrath of the poor was more likely to be directed against the government than against overseas commerce.

Coercion was rarely applied, but could be potent. In August of 1882 the Commercial Association of Pernambuco declared a commercial strike, followed by the Commercial Association of Bahia in November of that year, to force their respective provinces to suspend new provincial import taxes. The Province of Pernambuco yielded after three days and Bahia after six.[67] Expressing the general outrage of overseas merchants at an 1891 decree that import duties be paid in gold, the Commercial Association of Bahia tried to organize a nationwide commercial strike. The attempt

65. For two of the best-known agricultural congresses, see Congresso Agrícola, *Coleção de Documentos* (Rio de Janeiro: Tipografia Nacional, 1878); and Sociedade Auxiliadora da Agricultura de Pernambuco, *Trabalhos do Congresso Agrícola do Recife em Outubro de 1878* (Recife: Manuel Figueiroa de Faria e Filhos, 1879).
66. Luís Aureliano Gama de Andrade, "Dez Anos de Orçamento Imperial, 1867–1877," *Revista Brasileira de Estudos Políticos*, 31 (May 1971): 188; H. Schlitter Silva, "Tendências e Características Gerais do Comércio Exterior no Século XIX," *Revista de História da Economia Brasileira*, 1 (June 1953): 6.
67. Associação Comercial de Pernambuco, *Relatório de 1882*, pp. 19–22; Bahia, Presidente da Província, *Relatório de 1882*, pp. 1–7.

aborted because other associations could not enforce unanimity among importers, feared the unpredictable response of the affected masses, or were simply timid.[68] Nevertheless, the mere threat of the strike, or perhaps the volume of protest, forced the national government to end the collection of duties in gold.[69]

Other drastic forms of protest, partly coercive and partly symbolic, were used by business interest groups under what they considered extreme provocation. Members of the Commercial Association of Bahia voted to shut down their commercial firms in November of 1899 to protest the use of troops and gunfire to break up a demonstration against the state government by businessmen and *caixeiros* (merchant-house clerks). Most firms remained closed until the last arrested *caixeiros* were freed nearly a week later.[70] Outraged by repeated state tax increases and rejection of petitions, Pernambuco's two business interest groups tried in 1895 to embarrass Governor Alexandre José Barbosa Lima and to deprive his administration of economic advice. The Commercial Association closed down for ten months and the Commercial Agricultural Association for two.[71] The action apparently neither shamed nor inconvenienced Barbosa Lima. Coercive tactics implied difficulty for the users as well as for government, and the groups resorted to them only when other means of persuasion had failed. Such was the power of business interest groups that there was rarely need for force.

Evaluating influence

A final question remains: How influential were the business interest groups of nineteenth-century Brazil? That is, to what extent were bases of power and varied techniques of persuasion translated into success? Evidence of effectiveness may be gauged in the chapters that follow, which outline group policies in detail. However, it is difficult to give an overall evaluation. One problem is the classic one in studies of interest organizations: finding clear proof that a certain measure is the result of the particular pressure of a specific group or groups. Interest group theorists note that definitive demonstration of such a causal relationship is almost

68. For example, Associação Comercial do Maranhão, *Relatório, Janeiro a Dezembro de 1891* (São Luís: Frias, 1892), p. 4; Minutes, meeting of May 12, 1891, Livro 7 de Atas, AACP, p. 53.
69. Burke to Department of State, Salvador, June 8, 1891, NA/DS Microfilm Series T-331, Despatches from United States Consuls in Bahia, 1850–1906, Vol. 6, unpaginated.
70. *Jornal de Notícias* (Salvador), Nov. 18, 1899, p. 1.
71. Associação Comercial de Pernambuco, *Relatório de Abril de 1896*, pp. 80–93; Minutes, general assembly of Sept. 9, 1895, Livro de Atas da ACAP, 1895–1903, AACB, p. 1. Probable cause of the latter's early reopening was the approaching sugar harvest and the need to use the building as a commodity exchange.

impossible.[72] Another complication was the reluctance of group leaders to acknowledge their triumphs publicly. In the words of D. C. M. Platt: "Businessmen are reticent about success. They can see no point in calling attention to an opportunity for future profit."[73]

Factor groups had a strong potential for influence because of the importance of the sugar and coffee export crises which gave them birth. Government concern was shown by subsidies and other official support. But when the crises eased so did attention, most importantly that of group membership. As noted, only the Commercial Agricultural Association of Pernambuco lasted much longer than a decade. With the exception of the Engineering Club, industrial groups were on the scene even more briefly. The Engineering Club, however, as a professional association had a prestige and a seeming disinterest that gave its petitions and proclamations a force beyond that of most interest groups.

Given their number and longevity, the commercial associations were easily the most influential of Brazil's business interest groups. The extent of influence depended greatly on the association in question. Probably most successful and undoubtedly strongest was the Commercial Association of Rio de Janeiro. It was situated in the capital, boasted the largest and wealthiest membership, and was led by men connected to the highest ranks of government. Its president could inform membership in 1874 that every one of its petitions had a favorable outcome.[74] Such power led to a certain arrogance. In 1881 an indignant director, noting that no reply to a request had yet been received from the Minister of Finance, proposed "that it be insisted upon that His Excellency respond to this or any other letters he may have received from the commercial association."[75] "His Excellency" apologized.[76] Similarly, in the infrequent but significant conflicts over policy with other commercial associations, especially those of the Northeast, the Rio association usually had its way. Less powerful associations also enjoyed periods of outstanding success. The Commercial Association of Pará acknowledged an overwhelmingly favorable response from government in 1888, 1889, and 1890.[77]

72. S. E. Finer in "Discussion: The Over-All Effects of Pressure Groups on Political Consensus and Decision-Making – Results of a Comparative Study of Pressure Groups for the Advancement of Political Theory," in *Interest Groups on Four Continents*, ed. Henry W. Ehrmann (Pittsburgh: University of Pittsburgh Press, 1958), p. 295; Betty H. Zisk, "Interest Groups and the Political Process," in *American Political Interest Groups: Readings in Theory and Research*, ed. Betty H. Zisk (Belmont, Calif.: Wadsworth, 1969), p. 158.
73. *Latin America and British Trade, 1806–1914* (New York: Barnes & Noble, 1972), p. 308.
74. *Relatório de 1874*, p. 3.
75. Minutes, meeting of Oct. 26, 1881, Livro de Atas, 1881–1890, AACRJ, p. 30.
76. Minutes, meeting of Nov. 11, 1881, Livro de Atas, 1881–1890, AACRJ, p. 31.
77. Associação Comercial do Pará, *Relatório da Comissão da Praça do Comércio do Pará, Apresentado em Sessão da Assembléia Geral de 10 de Janeiro de 1889* (Belém: Tavares Cardoso, 1889), p. 5, *Relatório de 1890*, p. 4, and *Relatório de 1891*, p. 5.

On the other hand, some associations, even taking into account the tendency of leadership to paint all situations in somber colors, never seemed to enjoy the favor of government. The President of the Commercial Association of Maranhão noted in 1864 that in an important appeal to the Provincial Legislature, "not one voice was raised in our behalf," and that newly elected local representatives to Parliament had not even bothered to acknowledge congratulations sent by the association.[78] In 1878 the same group lamented that it had been "largely ignored" by government in the past and that recent changes of title and organization had brought no improvement.[79]

How may differences in the influence of commercial associations be explained? Obviously, the size and wealth of their merchant communities was a key factor. Also important, as indicated by the problems of the Maranhão association, was the local strength of traditional Luso-Brazilian values that deprecated the occupation of businessman. These values were usually strongest where the economy was least prosperous and dynamic. The Province of Maranhão, known for its traditional outlook, experienced relative economic stagnation during the second half of the nineteenth century.[80] "The years run by, the annual reports follow one another," lamented its commercial association, "but the apathy, the lifelessness continue in Maranhão society, one noticing only the worsening of public problems."[81] By contrast, the Commercial Association of Pará, set in an area experiencing its celebrated rubber boom and whose landed aristocracy was increasingly attracted by business, enjoyed much greater local power and acceptance.[82] The same was true of the Commercial Association of Santos, located in a province of dynamic and enterprising coffee agriculture. But traditional attitudes and economic stagnation could be overcome. The Commercial Association of Bahia, representing a culturally conservative area whose prosperity foundered from the 1870s on, remained one of Brazil's most powerful business interest groups.

Time brought changes in the favor of government. The overall power of commercial associations to influence provincial and national legislation, particularly tariffs, may have begun to wane by the late 1880s. Disillusionment with exportation as Brazil's sole economic base and the appeals of industrial groups on behalf of manufacturing apparently had an effect.

---

78. *O País* (São Luís), Dec. 3, 1864, p. 2.   79. *O País*, Jan. 21, 1878, p. 2.

80. Maranhão had lost the domination of the trade of neighboring provinces it had enjoyed in the early nineteenth century. Associação Comercial do Maranhão, *Relatório de 1867*, p. 11, and *Relatório de 1872*, pp. 34–35. Agricultural depression became especially serious by the late 1870s. Jerônimo de Viveiros, *História do Comércio do Maranhão, 1612–1895* (São Luís: Associação Comercial do Maranhão, 1954), II: 455–458.

81. *Relatório de 1872*, p. 10.

82. On the commercial orientation of Pará's landed elite see Barbara Weinstein, *The Amazon Rubber Boom, 1850–1920* (Stanford, Calif.: Stanford University Press, 1983), p. 258.

Revenue demands, reaching critical levels in the Northeastern provinces, blunted the campaigns of commercial associations against taxation. These tendencies accentuated with the coming of the Republic. The gospel of industrialization, now spread by the Engineering Club and some short-lived industrial groups and committees, found a more willing reception.

Despite fluctuations, the potential for influence of Brazil's nineteenth-century business interest groups was unusually strong by modern standards. They enjoyed most of the assets used in evaluating the strength of modern interest groups: prestige, financial resources, control over votes, leadership skills, members in influential positions, and, especially in the case of regulatory and advisory prerogatives, a privileged status related to expert knowledge.[83] That influence could be weakened when the groups were divided in aims or facing the financial imperatives of the state. And, as will be seen, nineteenth-century Brazil's business elite had serious problems of public image. But group influence remained on extremely strong bases. Individually, the ability of the leading business interest groups to affect development was arguably greater than that of virtually any interest organization today.

Public relations and ideology

While the business elite of nineteenth-century Brazil had a strong potential for influence through its interest groups, it also had an unfavorable public image. The improvement of this image before the public, essentially one of public relations, was entrusted to business interest groups. In their public relations campaigns, business interest groups utilized, as noted above, public proclamations, petitions, newspaper articles, annual reports, expositions, honorific awards, and demonstrations, together with charitable, religious, and patriotic public gestures. Contrary to what has been written by many authorities, the practice of business public relations did not develop only at the beginning of the twentieth century as part of the rise of large-scale corporate enterprise.[84] As noted, large corporations were few in Brazil in the nineteenth century. Since the resources of even the largest of ordinary partnerships were necessarily limited, the task of molding public opinion was left to business interest groups. It was one of their essential objectives.

83. Harry Eckstein, *Pressure Group Politics: The Case of the British Medical Association* (Stanford, Calif.: Stanford University Press, 1960), pp. 34–35; Graham Wootton, *Interest Groups* (Englewood Cliffs, N.J.: Prentice Hall, 1970), p. 83.

84. For example, Thomas C. Cochran, *Business in American Life: A History* (New York: McGraw-Hill, 1974), pp. 151–152; Key, *Politics*, pp. 103–106. For an analytical definition of public relations, see Rex F. Harlow, "Building a Public Relations Definition," *Public Relations Review*, 2 (Winter 1976): 34–42.

A favorable image was important to the business elite as a means of promoting economic expansion. The close connection between private enterprise and the state was traditional and government intervention common.[85] The nineteenth-century vogue for economic liberalism little affected this role for the state. Even Viscount Mauá, foremost entrepreneur of the nineteenth century and a symbol of rugged individualism in Brazilian historiography, depended in "all his important enterprises, to a greater or lesser degree, upon government backing in the form of privileges and subsidies."[86] Overseas merchants and factors, Brazil's most zealous defenders of economic liberalism, rarely hesitated to demand government intervention in the economy when it would benefit their interests. Government support was even more vital to manufacturers. They not only faced the long-standing and entrenched competition of foreign imports, but were handicapped by a lack of skilled workers and by the need to import most of their fuel and raw materials and virtually all of their equipment. To expand, even to survive, Brazilian industrialists needed aid from government in the form of subsidies, tax exemptions, and particularly tariff protection.

Those wishing the support of the state aimed much of their appeal to Brazil's small literate and politically aware minority. Not only did it wield political power through the electoral process, but its small numbers increased the likelihood of personal influence upon government leaders in legislatures and bureaucracy. On the other hand, neither could the vast majority which was denied political participation be ignored. When provoked, or manipulated by clever agitators, Brazil's urban poor were capable of violent demonstrations, often aimed at businessmen or their property. The overriding purpose of business public relations in nineteenth-century Brazil was to avoid the political consequences (including mob violence) of a hostile public opinion.

Brazil's business elite faced formidable obstacles in creating a favorable public image. The profession of businessman was traditionally lowly regarded in Luso-Brazilian culture, in part because of its association with "New Christians" (converted Jews or their descendants) during the colonial period.[87] "There are no hereditary merchant houses among us," remarked a newspaper in 1821, "the rich merchant who has sons gives them a more honorable occupation."[88] While the prestige of the business pro-

85. José Arthur Rios, "A Tradição Mercantilista na Formação Brasileira," *Revista Brasileira da Economia*, 26 (July-Sept. 1972): 255–272; Steven Topik, "The Evolution of the Economic Role of the Brazilian State, 1889–1930," *JLAS*, 11 (Nov. 1979): 325–342.
86. Roderick Barman, "Business and Government in Imperial Brazil: The Experience of Viscount Mauá," *JLAS*, 13 (Nov. 1981): 242.
87. Charles R. Boxer, *The Portuguese Seaborne Empire, 1415–1825* (New York: Alfred A. Knopf, 1969), pp. 333–334.
88. Quoted in José Wanderley de Araújo Pinho, *História de um Engenho do Recôncavo, 1553–1944* (Rio de Janeiro: Zélio Valverde, 1946), p. 316n.

fession rose during the nineteenth century, traditional disdain did not entirely disappear. Speaking of the attitudes of government leaders, the prominent entrepreneur Luís Tarqüínio remarked in 1891: "The business community for these gentlemen is a heap of ignoramuses, the businessman a soulless person, a thief: that's the way the worthy saviors of the nation express themselves."[89] Businessmen were stereotyped as being habitually dishonest, especially in dealing with government. Customs house employees, complained a Commercial Association of Santos leader in 1881, "seem to profess as an article of faith that all [merchants] wish to defraud the treasury."[90] Scorn and rudeness were common. The President of the Commercial Association of Maranhão noted that in tax offices merchants were treated "with little consideration, or rather, with complete disrespect."[91] A Salvador customs chief summed up the prejudices of many Brazilians when, echoing the French anarchist Proudhon, he characterized the property of the merchant as "theft."[92]

Several areas of dispute with planters complicated the business elite's task of shaping a favorable image. The good opinion of planters was crucial because of their political power and domination of government leadership posts. Planters complained of low prices or arbitrary measurement set by overseas traders for the purchase of commodities. During periods of falling prices they accused exporters of conspiring to depress the market. Factors, in even closer economic contact with planters, were also a target of animosity. Planters accused them of charging exorbitant interest for credit and of levying excessive marketing costs (about one quarter of the export price in the case of coffee) on the producer.[93] Resentful of overseas traders and factors, but unable to do without them. many planters accorded them only a grudging tolerance and mocked t. _ir professed concern for agriculture.

If many planters harbored resentment toward nineteenth-century Brazil's business elite, so did the urban working class. This animosity mainly stemmed from the suspicion that periodic shortages and price increases in

89. Minutes, extraordinary meeting of Nov. 17, 1891, Livro 5 de Atas, AACB, p. 386.
90. Associação Comercial de Santos, *Relatório da Associação Comercial de Santos, Apresentado em Sessão Ordinária da Assembléia Geral em Março de 1881* (Rio de Janeiro: G. Leuzinger & Filhos, 1881), p. 14.
91. Associação Comercial de Maranhão, *Relatório de 1879*, p. 4.
92. Chief of Customs H. de Rego Barros to Commercial Association of Bahia, Salvador, Oct. 9, 1877, Associação Comercial da Bahia, *Relatório da Associação Comercial da Bahia de 22 de Janeiro de 1878* (Salvador: Dois Mundos, 1878), p. 38.
93. Sociedade Auxiliadora da Agricultura de Pernambuco, *Relatório Annual Apresentado na Sessão de 4 de Julho de 1878 da Assembléia Geral pelo Gerente Inácio de Barros Barreto e a Ata da Mesma Sessão* (Recife: Jornal do Recife, 1878), pp. 15–16; Pang, "State and Agricultural Clubs," pp. 64–68. For marketing costs, see Joseph E. Sweigart, "Financing and Marketing Brazilian Export Agriculture: The Coffee Factors of Rio de Janeiro, 1850–1888" (Ph.D. Diss., University of Texas, 1980), pp. 47, 62.

basic foodstuffs were the result of manipulation by merchants. In the Northeast, where poverty was deep and staples such as jerked beef and manioc flour often were brought in by sea, resentment might erupt into violence. It was sometimes inflamed when commercial associations opposed municipal council regulation of the price and movement of food. Salvador's celebrated 1858 "Uprising of Meat without Bone and Manioc Flour without Stone" (*Motim da Carne sem Osso e Farinha sem Carôco*) expressed the anger of the urban poor not only at the shortage of foodstuffs but at the blocking by the president of province and the Commercial Association of Bahia of efforts by the Municipal Council to lower prices.[94] The rioting had to be put down by cavalry. Furthermore, antimerchant violence in the Northeast could be triggered not only by genuine want but by the manipulation of agitators for political purposes.[95] Commercial associations could by no means aim their public relations efforts solely at the nation's educated minority.

The industrialists of nineteenth-century Brazil faced a different problem: convincing the nation of their right to exist. As noted, most influential Brazilians firmly believed that Brazil's "natural" role was that of exporter of raw materials and importer of manufactured goods in an economy governed by the principles of free trade. Upon asking Emperor Pedro II to become the honorary president of their organization, officials of the protectionist Industrial Association were dismayed to hear that "August Gentleman" declare himself opposed to the idea of tariff protection for industry.[96] Further impeding attempts of industrialists to spread their views was the opposition of their fellow businessmen in the commercial associations and factor groups.

The role of the business elite in Brazil's economy and society was all the more suspect because that elite was largely foreign. The alien nature of big business was most notorious in overseas trade. "No one is unaware," commented Minister of Finance Rui Barbosa in 1891, "that commerce, especially large-scale commerce, in our most important trade centers resides in greatest part, not to say in its near entirety, in the hands of foreigners."[97] The stigma of being foreign did not attach itself as easily to factors and industrialists. Factors rallied political support in their disputes

94. Morgan to Foreign Office, Salvador, March 16, 1858, PRO/FO 13/365, fl. 54; *Diário da Bahia*, March 6, 1858, p. 1.

95. Chief of Police, State of Bahia to Commercial Association of Bahia, Salvador, March 20, 1895, *Relatório de 1896*, p. 65; Commercial Association of Bahia to Chief of Police, State of Bahia, Salvador, April 26, 1899, *Relatório de 1900*, p. 27.

96. Associação Industrial, *Relatório Apresentado à Assembléia Geral da Associação Industrial em Sessão de 10 de Junho de 1882 pela Diretoria da Mesma Associação* (Rio de Janeiro: G. Leuzinger & Filhos, 1882), p. 27. Despite such philosophical differences, the Emperor did become honorary President of the organization.

97. *RMF, 1891*, p. 317.

with exporters by denouncing "foreign manipulation" of commodity prices and alleging that alien exporters and buyers in their homelands conspired to exploit Brazilian producers. Probably about half the factors, however, were also foreign, mainly Portuguese.[98] Industrialists were even more hypocritical. Assuming the mantle of Brazilian nationalism, they denounced the influence of foreigners in the traditional export-import economy and characterized free trade as an alien, principally British, device to keep Brazil agricultural and underdeveloped. But industrialists probably were themselves more overwhelmingly foreign than were overseas traders.[99]

Continual foreign numerical domination of overseas trade derived mainly from the practice of foreign merchants of recruiting their *caixeiros*, many of whom would rise to control merchant houses themselves, from among their own countrymen. They correspondingly regarded most Brazilians as unsuited for mercantile employment. Nationalists noted and resented the absence of opportunity for Brazilian youth. Imperial budgets for 1838–1839 and 1839–1840 mandated a tax on merchant houses employing more than one foreign *caixeiro*, and the budget for 1843–1846 taxed houses with more than two.[100] Fear of foreign reaction apparently kept these laws from being enforced.[101] Provincial governments also confronted the foreign domination. Bahia in 1863 placed a heavy impost on all businesses not having a Brazilian *caixeiro*, and Pernambuco in 1868 gave tax exemptions to merchant houses employing all Brazilian *caixeiros*.[102] The Pernambuco law admittedly was not put into effect and the Bahian tax apparently unenforced, again most likely for fear of foreign protest.[103] But such laws indicated that preponderant foreign numbers in overseas trade disturbed educated Brazilians.

In the case of the Portuguese, resentment over the foreign presence in business turned violent. Portuguese businessmen were killed and beaten,

98. Sweigart, "Coffee Factors," pp. 59ñ., 70. Eugene W. Ridings, "Business, Nationality, and Dependency in Late Nineteenth Century Brazil," *JLAS*, 14 (May 1982): 63–68.
99. Ridings, "Business, Nationality, and Dependency, 72–73.
100. Brazil, laws, statutes, etc., *Coleção das Leis do Império do Brasil de 1838* (Rio de Janeiro: Tipografia Nacional, 1863 [sic]), Part I, I: 40; Liberato de Castro Carreira, *História Financeira e Orçamentária do Império do Brasil* (2d ed.; Brasília: Fundação Casa de Rui Barbosa/MEC, 1980), I: 256–257, 300.
101. The British charge d' affaires, who protested passage of the first tax, said he had been assured it would not be enforced. W. G. Ousely to Brazilian Ministry of Foreign Relations, Rio de Janeiro, Sept. 8, 1840, AHI, 284/3/11, and Jan. 4, 1841, AHI 284/3/12.
102. Bahia, Presidente da Província, *Relatório de 1863*, "Orçamento da Receita da Tesouria Provincial da Bahia para o Ano de 1864," unpaginated; Pernambuco, Presidente da Província, *Relatório Apresentado à Assembléia Legislativa Provincial de Pernambuco pelo Exm. Sr. Conde de Baependy, Presidente da Província, na Sessão de Instalação em 10 de Abril de 1869* (Recife: M. Figueiroa de Faria & Filhos, 1869), p. 65.
103. Pernambuco, Presidente da Província, *Relatório de 1869*, p. 65. Neither the Commercial Association of Bahia nor British authorities protested the Bahia regulation.

and their property destroyed, in nationalist revolts and riots in the cities of the North and Northeast during the first half of the nineteenth century. At the same time, the persons and property of non-Portuguese foreigners, especially British, generally seem to have been respected.[104] The marked antagonism to the Portuguese appeared to derive from memories of colonial rule, from their alleged refusal to hire Brazilians, and from their domination of retail trade, which put them in personal contact with the urban masses.[105] During the last third of the nineteenth century, Portuguese probably constituted roughly two-thirds of the retailers in large urban centers.[106] Commercial associations were particularly disturbed by the unpopularity of the Portuguese, easily the most numerous nationality among membership. Uprisings directed against the Portuguese ceased from the mid-nineteenth century until the early Republic, but antagonism did not. They were the target of ridicule or abuse in the press, and brawls between Brazilian students and Portuguese *caixeiros* punctuated the weekends in major cities.[107]

Making enterprise respectable

The business elite of nineteenth-century Brazil clearly faced formidable obstacles to the creation of a favorable public image. How were they to be overcome? The most fundamental barrier was the traditional low prestige of business as a profession. But if the Luso-Brazilian inheritance presented this problem, it also suggested a defense. Business interest groups, in particular the commercial associations, evoked the ancient Iberian concept of corporation, characterizing the business elite in petitions and public pronouncements as "our class" and urging a spirit of solidarity in defense of traditional rights and prerogatives.[108] This concept envisioned busi-

---

104. Envoy Extraordinary and Minister Plenipotentiary Hamilton to Brazilian Foreign Office, Rio de Janeiro, Sept. 25, 1841, AHI 284/3/13; William Lewis Herndon, *Exploration of the Valley of the Amazon, Made Under Direction of the Navy Department by William Lewis Herndon and Lardner Gibbon, Part 1* (Washington, D.C.: Robert Armstrong, 1854), p. 341; Eugene W. Ridings, "The Bahian Commercial Association, 1840–1889: A Pressure Group in an Underdeveloped Area" (Ph.D. Diss., University of Florida, 1970), p. 26.

105. Amaro Quintas, *O Sentido Social da Revolução Praieira* (Rio de Janeiro: Civilização Brasileira, 1967), pp. 7, 21–24; João José Reis, "A Elite Baiana Face aos Movimentos Sociais: Bahia, 1824–1840," *Revista de História*, 54 (Oct.–Dec. 1976): 342–367.

106. Ridings, "Business, Nationality, and Dependency," 80–85.

107. Verediano Carvalho, *A Praça do Rio, 1890–1891: Série de Artigos do Jornal Fluminense 'O Tempo' com o Pseudonymo Zeferino* (Rio de Janeiro: Laemmert, 1892), p. 28; Associação Comercial do Pará, *Relatório de 1875*, p. 4; Gilberto Freyre, *The Mansions and the Shanties (Sobrados e Mucambos): The Making of Modern Brazil*, trans. and ed. Harriet de Onís (New York: Alfred A. Knopf, 1966), pp. 177–178; Richard Morse, *From Community to Metropolis: A Biography of São Paulo* (Gainesville, Fla.: University of Florida Press, 1958), pp. 135–136.

108. For Iberian traditions, see Ronald C. Newton, "On 'Functional Groups,' 'Fragmentation,' and 'Pluralism' in Spanish American Political Society," *HAHR*, 50 (Feb. 1970): 1–29; Howard J.

nessmen as a distinct group with an officially recognized function in society and claims to traditional privilege. Typically, on the occasion of its centennial celebration, an editor hailed the Commercial Association of Bahia as the embodiment of "the old spirit of class of medieval times."[109]

Part of the tradition of corporation was an emphasis on solidarity. Business interest groups usually insisted on replying to any injury or slight to their members or to the business elite as a class. The Commercial Association of Santos, for example, threatened in 1891 to refuse all services to the government and to publish protests in all major newspapers of the nation until an insulting customs official was fired. He was.[110] For years the Commercial Association of Bahia staged solemn public ceremonies to mark the anniversary of the use of troops to break up a political demonstration by businessmen and their clerks.

Business interest groups were particularly sensitive to matters involving arrest or imprisonment. They were determined that members of their organization or even members of their "class" not be treated as ordinary criminals. Arrested merchants, argued the Commercial Association of Pernambuco in 1854, should be pardoned or freed on bail, otherwise both their business and their reputation might suffer.[111] An example of aggressive class solidarity occurred in Recife in 1900 with the arrest of Delmiro Gouveia, later a noted industrialist. He was apprehended following a suspicious fire in his heavily insured property that resulted in injuries to eight persons, including Recife's fire chief. All businesses, including banks, closed down until Gouveia was freed.[112] The Commercial Association of Pernambuco (of which Gouveia apparently was not a member) formally protested to the governor and to the president of the republic. A mob of angry businessmen damaged the headquarters of the factor group Commercial Agricultural Association because it did not close its doors in protest quickly enough.[113] The fierceness of the reaction was provoked not so much by the arrest but, as the commercial association put it, by the

Wiarda, "Corporatism and Development in the Iberic-Latin World: Persistent Strains and New Variations," in *The New Corporatism: Social-Political Structures in the Iberian World*, eds. Frederick B. Pike and Thomas Stritch (Notre Dame, Ind., 1974).

109. *Jornal de Notícias*, June 5, 1911, p. 1.

110. Associação Comercial de Santos, *Relatório de 1893*, pp. 75–77.

111. Minutes, meeting of June 16, 1854, Livro 2 de Atas, AACP, pp. 75–77.

112. *Jornal do Recife*, Jan. 3, 1900, p.1, and Jan. 4, 1900, p. 1. Recife historian José da Costa Pôrto states that the fire was set by government agents in retaliation for a physical or verbal street attack by Gouveia on Pernambuco political boss Francisco de Assis Rosa e Silva. *Os Tempos de Rosa e Silva* (Recife: Universidad Federal de Pernambuco, 1970), pp. 119–121. This intepretation of events is not mentioned in the records of the Commercial Association or Commercial Agricultural Association.

113. Minutes, meeting of Jan. 3, 1900, Livro de Atas da ACAP, 1877–1892, AACP, pp. 51–52.

spectacle of Gouveia being led publicly through the streets "in contempt of our local business community, belittled by such audacity."[114]

This emphasis on the concept of class solidarity helped stifle clashes between overseas traders, factors, and manufacturers until the last two decades of the century, when crises in exportation and rivalry for government aid made harmony increasingly difficult. Even then, open attacks by one business interest group on another were rare, as were open policy struggles within organizations. The commercial associations, claiming to represent all business, reaped most of the benefit from this spirit of business elite solidarity. Factor groups did not pursue their own aims as persistently or aggressively as they might have. The concept of class harmony also may have blunted the initiative of manufacturers in forming industrial groups.

In striking contrast to the concept of traditional corporate solidarity was another self-image used by members of the business elite, principally overseas traders and factors, to elevate themselves in public esteem. It was that of the competitive and self-reliant entrepreneur of the age of laissez-faire, his role promoting Brazilian progress and prosperity. Merchants constituted, according to a typical commercial association pronouncement, a "class essentially active and fighting for all the improvements and progress of society."[115] Commerce and its agents were the sources of development and civilization, and free competition was their mainspring. Merchants saw themselves as, in the words of Brazilian liberal essayist Aureliano Cândido Tavares Bastos, "called by the cosmopolitan spirit, which is distinctive in the human genius, to apportion and to compete fraternally for the world's production, that is for the riches, for the well-being of peoples."[116]

This competition-induced march toward progress and prosperity could be impeded only by government interference with business or the free labor market. "In no country, in no period," the Center for Coffee Agriculture and Commerce informed the prime minister, "can the regulation of [economic] activities produce anything but the weakening of the energy and the lulling of the impetus of those who toil."[117] Opposition to government economic regulation let merchants pose as protectors of the common man. Commercial associations maintained that their insistence on low tariffs and open cabotage (letting foreign ships engage in coastal

114. Commercial Association of Pernambuco to President of Republic, Recife, Jan. 2, 1900, *Relatório de 1900*, anexo 23, unpaginated.
115. Minutes, meeting of March 9, 1904, in Pinto, *Associação Comercial*, p. 177.
116. *Cartas do Solitário* (3d ed.; São Paulo: Editôra Nacional, 1938), p. 357.
117. Center for Coffee Agriculture and Commerce to Viscount Ouro Preto, Rio de Janeiro, June 27, 1885, Coleção Ouro Preto, AIHGB, lata 427, doc. 10.

trade) kept goods of prime necessity, especially foodstuffs, affordable to all. The merchant, stated the president of the Commercial Association of Rio de Janeiro in 1867, was "the most dedicated and zealous protector of the common people."[118] The Bahian Association claimed in 1891 to be opposing a tariff increase "in defense of the rights of all the proletariat."[119] But such posturing was strained at best in light of the commercial associations' usual opposition to government regulation of food prices and their hard line in labor disputes.

In the commercial associations, advocacy of economic liberalism did not stem simply from its utility. It also reflected the influence of British merchants, whose homeland (together with France) was the main source of such ideas. Britons were prominent on commercial association boards and were admired by other businessmen.[120] A particular center of British influence was Recife, whose Commercial Association of Pernambuco was twice headed by Englishmen.[121] No business interest group promoted economic liberalism more vociferously in its communications with government.

Commercial associations and factor groups also tried to promote laissez-faire and free trade doctrines by presenting them as the most modern of economic theories (as they were until late in the century). This was an effective approach to an educated Brazilian public always anxious to consume things up-to-date and foreign, whether goods or ideas.[122] Industrialists and their interest groups tried in public statements and petitions to combat such argument by characterizing protectionism as the wave of the future and citing nations such as the United States (from the 1860s) and Germany (from 1879) which had adopted it. Given the sway of economic liberalism in Brazil, they faced an uphill battle. Commercial associations and factor groups, however, hurt their own cause by being notably inconsistent in condemning government economic interference. Whenever such intervention benefited overseas trade they enthusiastically backed it. "Commerce in young nations cannot do without the tutelage of government, if not direct, at least indirect," rationalized the Commercial

118. Associação Comercial do Rio de Janeiro, *Relatório de 1867*, p. 12.
119. Commercial Association of Bahia to President of Republic and Governor of State of Bahia, Salvador, March 31, 1891, *Relatório de 1892*, p. 51.
120. Most notably in the cases of Viscount Mauá and Luís Tarqüínio. Anyda Marchant, *Viscount Mauá and the Empire of Brazil: A Biography of Irineu Evangelista de Sousa (1813–1889)* (Berkeley: University of California Press, 1965), pp. 22–32; Pericles Madureira de Pinho, *Luiz Tarqüínio: Pioneiro da Justiça Social no Brasil* (Salvador: Vitória, 1944), pp. 4–5.
121. Philip F. Needham headed the group in 1865–1868 and 1871–1872 and Theodore Christiansen in 1881–1883. Pinto, *Associação Comercial*, pp. 284–285.
122. Richard Graham, "Sepoys and Imperialists: Techniques of British Power in Nineteenth-Century Brazil," *Inter-American Economic Affairs* 23, no. 1 (1969): 25; Gilberto Freyre, *Ordem e Progresso* (2d ed.; Rio de Janeiro: José Olympio, 1962), I: 102.

Association of Bahia.[123] Even the Commercial Association of Pernambuco, arch-exponent of economic liberalism, proposed that the national government build a long-delayed Pernambucan railway line and that its province erect certain barriers to trade with other provinces.[124] "The protectionist system," a director remarked characteristically while discussing the latter proposition, "however much condemned in theory, cannot entirely be dispensed with in practice."[125]

Commercial associations and factor groups also promoted free trade by attacking trade barriers erected by foreign nations. They vigorously protested foreign quarantine regulations that impeded the importation of Brazilian commodities and sometimes prompted negotiations that would reduce foreign tariffs. In 1899, for example, the Commercial Association of Rio de Janeiro involved both the Foreign Office and President Manuel Ferraz de Campos Sales in a successful campaign to persuade France to lower its tariff on Brazilian coffee.[126] Commercial associations and factor groups frequently petitioned for reciprocal trade treaties to lower foreign trade barriers.

Along with their vocal, if selective, advocacy of laissez-faire and free trade doctrines, business interest organizations espoused other economically useful elements of middle-class ideology of mainly British origin. The gospel of work was naturally emphasized. Industrial groups promised manufacturing would bring an improved, tractable citizenry, because the worker would be "subject to a rigorous discipline, which would progressively inoculate in his spirit ideas of order and the habit of obedience and respect toward superiors."[127] Punctuality also was felt to be a trait worth spreading. The Commercial Association of Pernambuco awarded honorary membership to an Englishman who set up a cannon to mark the precise noon hour in Recife. It paid the expense of operating this weapon, arranged for the synchronization of all of Recife's clocks, and hired a man to walk the city to see that their time was properly set.[128]

Gambling, on the other hand, was seen as economically harmful. Com-

123. Minutes, general assembly of Feb. 21, 1881, Livro 4 de Atas, AACB, p. 376.
124. Associação Comercial de Pernambuco, *Relatório de 1877*, pp. 63–64; Minutes, meeting of Sept. 12, 1877, Livro 4 de Atas, AACB, p. 111.
125. Minutes, meeting of Sept. 12, 1877, Livro 4 de Atas, AACB, p. 111.
126. Commercial Association of Rio de Janeiro to President of Republic, Rio de Janeiro, May 20, 1899, AHI, 313/1/29; *Jornal do Comércio* (Rio de Janeiro), Oct. 2, 1899, p. 1.
127. Associação Industrial, *O Trabalho Nacional e seus Adversários* (Rio de Janeiro: G. Leuzinger & Filhos, 1881), pp. 165–166. For further claims of moral uplift through factory labor, see Associação Industrial, *Representação Dirigida ao Exm. Sr. Ministro da Fazenda pela Associação Industrial, Relativamente ao Projeto da Tarifa da Alfândegas, e de Conformidade com os Relatórios dos Representantes de Diversas Indústrias* (Rio de Janeiro: Central, 1881), p. 18.
128. Associação Comercial de Pernambuco, *Relatório de 1875*, p. 16; Minutes, meetings of April 6 and April 20, 1874, Livro 4 de Atas, AACP, pp. 7–8.

mercial associations were among the first to demand suppression of Brazil's famous numbers game, the "jôgo do bicho."[129] Ironically, this gambling passion, still popular today, was invented by a president of the Commercial Association of Rio de Janeiro, Baron Drummond (João Batista Viana Drummond).[130] The associations also denounced public lotteries. The embrace of British middle-class ideas by the business elite, however, was selective. Other causes, such as expansion of the suffrage, were ignored or, like abolition, for the most part opposed. Like other Latin American elites of the period, Brazil's business elite took from liberalism what was useful and discarded the rest.[131]

As noted, the business elite promoted two contrasting images of the businessman. One was that of a member of a tight-knit traditional corporation, entitled to distinct rights and privileges and demanding government confirmation of them. The other image was that of the dynamic, self-reliant individualist, promoting progress and prosperity and demanding from government only nonintervention. To these images the various elements of the business elite added themes stressing the importance of their roles. Industrialists portrayed themselves as leading the way to the future. Manufacturing would bring power and prosperity to Brazil, and even ensure political stability: "Suppress toil and you will have revolution. The spirit of the common people is restless; it needs, in order to be calmed, something constantly before its eyes which will seize its attention."[132] Overseas traders and factors called attention to the economic and social value of commerce. Such claims were rarely modest. According to the president of the Commercial Association of Santos, the merchant community was "the most important base of the prosperity of the Empire."[133] The president of the Commercial Association of Rio de Janeiro saw that community as "doubtless, the most powerful prop of the equilibrium of the nation."[134] To merchants, asserted the president of the Commercial Association of Maranhão, were owed "the greatest share of the present improvement in the human species and the major part of the discoveries that mankind has made."[135]

Linked to asserting the importance of the business elite was calling

129. Associação Comercial da Bahia, *Relatório de 1899*, pp. 51–53; José Bonifácio de Souza, *Associação Comercial do Ceará: Memória Histórica, 1868–1968* (Fortaleza: Associação Comercial do Ceará, 1969), p. 24.

130. Eudes Barros, *A Associação Comercial no Império e na República* (2d ed. rev.; Rio de Janeiro: Gráfica Olímpica, 1975), p. 107.

131. Florencia E. Mallon, "Economic Liberalism: Where We Are and Where We Need to Go," in *Guiding the Invisible Hand: Economic Liberalism and the State in Latin American History*, eds. Joseph L. Love and Nils Jacobsen (New York: Praeger, 1988), pp. 183–185.

132. Associação Industrial, *Trabalho Nacional*, p. 167.

133. Associação Comercial de Santos, *Relatório de 1880*, p. 8.

134. Associação Comercial do Rio de Janeiro, *Relatório de 1867*, p. 12.

135. Associação Comercial do Maranhão, *Relatório de 1879*, 5.

attention to its vital public services, performed through interest groups. For this there was much justification, for such organizations performed many functions today done by the state. The most conspicuous from a public relations standpoint were the commercial associations' organizing and dispensing of charity and of disaster relief. Their importance, in light of the administrative weaknesses of the Brazilian state, led some commercial associations to portray themselves in newspapers and petitions as public service organizations rather than as interest groups. Government gave this dubious assertion partial ratification. In 1854 the Province of Pernambuco awarded the Commercial Association of Pernambuco the right to style itself "beneficent," an adjective it dropped from its official title early in the twentieth century.[136] The imperial government also endorsed the commercial associations' self-portrayal as public service organizations by exempting the headquarters of the Commercial Association of Bahia from urban property taxes in 1866 and that of Pernambuco in 1868.[137] It reneged on this privilege, however, less than a decade later.[138] The services given by business interest organizations received more concrete acknowledgment from the state in the form of direct or indirect aid. As noted, the imperial government subsidized, regularly or occasionally, the Industrial Association and the centers for Coffee Agriculture and Commerce and Sugar Industry and Commerce and aided the acquisition of nearly all commercial association headquarters. Business interest groups could take comfort that at least one aspect of their public relations efforts brought material rewards.

In addition to more concrete ideas, the business elite also tried to disseminate a general image of piety and patriotism. Commercial associations and factor groups tried to be officially represented at all celebratory masses, religious processions, and Church festivals. Manifesting respect for the Catholic Church was considered important because of the largely foreign composition of the business elite, which included many Protestants. This same foreignness made patriotism an even more important sentiment to project. A crisis for Brazil's commercial associations, strongly British-influenced, erupted in 1863. Tension between the two nations culminated in the blockade of Rio de Janeiro by the British Navy and the breaking of diplomatic relations following incidents of Brazilian abuse of British sailors and ships.[139] The commercial associations of Rio de Janeiro

---

136. Minutes, meeting of Sept. 25, 1854, Livro 2 de Atas, AACP, p. 38.
137. Minutes, meeting of June 19, 1866, Livro 3 de Atas, AACB, p. 87; Pinto, *Associação Comercial*, p. 12.
138. Minutes, meeting of Nov. 30, 1875, Livro 4 de Atas, AACP, p. 50.
139. This was the well-known "Christie Affair," in which long-standing bad feeling between Great Britain and Brazil came to a head when some British sailors said to be drunk and disorderly were jailed and mistreated in Rio de Janeiro and a beached British ship looted and several of its crew allegedly murdered in Rio Grande do Sul. British Minister William D. Christie, no admirer of

and Pernambuco immediately pledged total support to the Brazilian government.[140] The Rio organization also awarded honorary membership to Brazil's prime minister and foreign minister, central figures in the dispute.[141] The displays of adherence came not despite British influences in these associations, but rather because such influences were widely known. In the Pernambuco group, British directors and ordinary members were conveniently absent when support was voted.[142] Among the three Rio association leaders delivering its resolution to the Emperor was Viscount Mauá, well known for his British impress and sympathies.[143]

The war with Paraguay (1864–1870) provided the maximum opportunity for patriotic display. The commercial associations (the only type of business interest group then in existence) launched a number of public contributions to aid the war effort and the families of volunteers. They put a perhaps equal effort into celebrating the successful conclusion of the war, with receptions for war heroes, public festivals, and the building of monuments. The Commercial Association of Maranhão spent more than half its 1870 income in commemoration, while erection of a towering pedestal and statue celebrating a naval victory forced the Commercial Association of Bahia into long-term debt.[144]

Elite conflict and changing perceptions

Displays of piety and patriotism could not, in the long run, overcome foreignness. By the 1880s a change had begun in public perceptions of the business elite, especially its overseas trader component. It was signaled by increasing awareness and resentment of the dominance of foreigners in overseas trade. Ironically, the proportion of foreigners in overseas commerce actually decreased slightly in the last two decades of the century.[145]

Brazil, backed his demands for apologies and reparations by blockading Rio, leading to the suspension of diplomatic relations in 1863–1865. Alan K. Manchester, *British Preëminence in Brazil, Its Rise and Decline: A Study in European Expansion* (New York: Octagon, 1964), pp. 274–282.

140. Associação Comercial de Pernambuco, *Relatório de 1863*, p. 5; Commercial Association of Rio de Janeiro to Marquis Olinda, President, Council of Ministers, Rio de Janeiro, Jan. 27, 1863, Coleção Marquês de Olinda, AIHGB, lata 215, doc. 39.
141. Commercial Association of Rio de Janeiro to Marquis Abrantes, Foreign Minister, Rio de Janeiro, Jan. 27, 1863, AHI, 313/1/29; Commercial Association of Rio de Janeiro to Marquis Olinda, President, Council of Ministers, Rio de Janeiro, Jan. 27, 1863, Coleção Marquês de Olinda, AIHGB, lata 215, doc. 39.
142. Minutes, meeting of Jan. 22, 1863, and general assembly of Jan. 24, 1863, Livro 2 de Atas, AACP, pp. 164–165.
143. Associação Comercial de Pernambuco, *Relatório de 1863*, p. 5.
144. Associação Comercial do Maranhão, *Relatório de 1870*, pp. 5–6; Associação Comercial da Bahia, *Relatório de 1871*, p. 7; Minutes, general assembly of Jan. 20, 1874, Livro 4 de Atas, AACB, p. 172.
145. Ridings, "Business, Nationality and Dependency," 70, 87–88.

Awakening resentment of foreign economic domination coincided with growing interest in industrialization and increasing disenchantment with Brazil's export-import economy. For these changes in the attitudes of educated Brazilians, the public relations efforts of industrialists and factors were at least partially responsible.

The traditional economy and the role of foreigners in it began to be seriously questioned in the 1880s. The questioning was impelled first by disillusionment with exportation as Brazil's sole economic base and then by conflicts within the export sector itself. In 1880 coffee prices and in 1884 rubber prices experienced a downturn, as had sugar since 1872 and cotton since the end of the United States Civil War. The squeeze on profits inflamed issues of credit and remuneration. It pitted coffee planters against factors and exporters and *aviadores* (rubber factors) against exporters. Coffee planters, heavily burdened by debt, blamed low income and high interest rates on the coffee factor and the exporter and discussed ways to circumvent their role. The sharp decline in rubber prices aroused nationalist resentment of the foreign role in Brazilian commerce. *Aviadores,* using the Commercial Association of Pará as their spokesman, blamed the fall on the machinations of overseas buyers, supposedly in collusion with foreign exporters in Belém.

A return to export prosperity eased tensions between sectors of the export economy and weakened the resolution of factors. By the early 1890s prices for sugar, coffee, and rubber had risen and their remuneration further increased by a weak exchange rate. The factor groups created to deal with the 1880s export crises lapsed into dormancy. *Aviadores* eased their demand for economic independence from foreign buyers. But the commodity crises had increased doubts about reliance on an exclusively export economy and the struggle between exporters, factors, and planters had sharpened mistrust of the role of overseas merchants, particularly foreigners, in it (see Chapter 4).

The industrial interest groups which emerged in the 1880s strongly contributed to such doubts and mistrust (see Chapter 8). To garner support for industrial development manufacturers tried to discredit the ideas that justified Brazil's export-import economy and those who supported it.[146] In publications and petitions, they appealed skillfully to nationalist aspirations and fears. The struggle of industrialists for public and govern-

146. The aggressive public relations activities of industrial groups and industrialists contradict the idea, at least for Brazil, that spokesmen for industry in Latin America rarely challenged traditional export activities and made little headway against theses of comparative advantage (see also Chapter XI). Joseph L. Love, "Structural Change and Conceptual Response in Latin America and Romania, 1860–1950," in *Guiding the Invisible Hand: Economic Liberalism and the State in Latin American History,* eds. Joseph L. Love and Nils Jacobsen (New York: Praeger, 1988), pp. 23–27.

ment support, the rivalries between sectors of the export economy, and the export crises had a cumulative effect. The 1880s saw changes in the attitudes of Brazil's literate public and its government. Symptomatic of growing nationalism and support for industrialization (and of increased revenue needs), tariffs rose in the second half of the decade. The trend of the 1880s became a firm direction with the advent of the Republic in 1889. The new military government was nationalistic and sympathetic to industry. After the end of military rule in 1894 the commitment of Brazilian leaders to foster industrialization lessened, but public support for industry and nationalistic resentment of foreign control of commerce remained high.

Events during the 1890s further inflamed nationalistic passions. Portuguese shopkeepers were blamed for high food prices, and, as in the 1830s and 1840s, there were demands for nationalization of retail commerce and sporadic violence.[147] The plunge of coffee prices beginning in 1895 revived conflict within the export sector. Facing intense pressure on profits, exporters began to send agents into the interior to buy directly from planters, thus bypassing factors.[148] Coffee factors now faced not only the loss of profits but of their very livelihood. In public pronouncements and meetings they made the same accusations of conspiracy between foreign buyers and exporters that *aviadores* had made in the 1880s.[149] Obtaining no support from major commercial associations, coffee factors in 1897 helped organize the Commercial Center of Rio de Janeiro to act as their spokesman. When Brazil's currency was strengthened after 1898, the coffee crisis worsened and antiforeign sentiment intensified.

Growing nationalism and support for industrial development found concrete form in the legislation of the 1890s. Aided by fiscal necessity, tariffs rose rapidly. The protests of commercial associations or their importer members had decreasing impact. In 1899, for the first time, the government neglected to seek commercial association opinion in drawing up a tariff; a result was Brazil's first "markedly protective" tariff.[150] It remained in effect, with minor revisions, for the next three decades.

---

147. June E. Hahner, "Jacobinos Versus Gallegos: Urban Radicals Versus Portuguese Immigrants in Rio de Janeiro in the 1890s," *JLAS*, 18 (May 1976): 128–131.
148. Associação Comercial de São Paulo, *Relatório da Associação Comercial de São Paulo, Ano de 1895* (São Paulo: Industrial, 1896), pp. 54–55. On the profit squeeze, see Edward Greene to John Gordon, Santos, July 18, 1899, Personal Copy Book, Edward Greene, E. Johnson & Co., LABA, UCLL, pp. 321–322.
149. For example, "Coffee Speculation and Trade," *USRC*, LVII, no. 215 (Aug. 1898): 498–501; *Gazeta de Notícias* (Rio de Janeiro), Jan. 28, 1902, p. 1.
150. *ACD*, 1899, V: 421; Stanley J. Stein, *The Brazilian Cotton Manufacture: Textile Enterprise in an Underdeveloped Area, 1850–1950* (Cambridge, Mass.: Harvard University Press, 1957), p. 85.

Business public relations and its results

Brazil's nineteenth-century business interest groups had used public relations to create a favorable image for business. What did they achieve? The prestige of the business profession rose markedly. Public relations efforts were aided by the increasing sophistication of mercantile operations and by the dignified example of the British merchant.[151] Nevertheless, by century's end the business elite was more divided than ever before, and suspicion and resentment of its overseas trader element had reached new heights. The efforts of factors and industrialists to defend their economic interests and obtain government aid helped focus public attention on that element's foreignness. The same efforts, combined with falling export prices, highlighted the explosive question of foreign economic domination.

Overseas traders now were increasingly unable to convince the public of the utility of their role or the value of the economy they represented. The disparate images they offered – of traditional corporate solidarity and of contemporary self-reliant dynamism – were difficult to reconcile. Faith in economic liberalism was undermined by the inconsistency of the commercial associations in applying its principles and by the success of the industrialists in portraying free trade as a foreign ideological ploy to arrest Brazilian development. Aided by disillusionment with exportation as the nation's sole economic basis, manufacturers and their groups also made significant progress in selling the idea of an industrialized Brazil to the educated public. Although support for the traditional economy remained powerful and would weaken only slowly in the twentieth century, by 1900 Brazilian development had taken a new direction.

The use of public relations by Brazilian business interest groups preceded its employment in the United States. It had been aimed at overcoming the traditional unpopularity of businessmen in Luso-Brazilian culture and of the visible foreign predominance in the business elite. Efforts to create a favorable public image had been necessary for economic expansion because of the dynamic role of the state in the Brazilian economy, for smooth day-to-day business operations, and even for security. Like modern practitioners of public relations, members of Brazil's business elite worked to avoid the consequences of a hostile public opinion. As evidenced by Brazilian business interest groups in the nineteenth century, the use of business public relations emerged long before the twentieth century and the rise of the large corporation.

151. Gilberto Freyre, *Inglêses no Brasil: Aspectos da Influência Britânica sôbre a Vida, a Paisagem, e a Cultura do Brasil* (Rio de Janeiro, 1948), pp. 132–133; Verediano Carvalho, *Praça do Rio*, pp. 30–31.

Brazil's regions. *Source:* Stefan H. Robock, *Brazil's Developing Northeast: a Study of Regional Planning and Foreign Aid* (Washington, D.C.: Brookings Institution, 1963)

4

The export economy: agricultural quality, markets, and profits

"The greatest or almost the only economic strength in Brazil resides in agriculture," remarked the President of the Commercial Association of Pernambuco in 1888. "This is a truth so well-known that it seems pure idleness to repeat it."[1] This was how the commercial associations and factor groups saw agriculture. The phrase "our only source of wealth" is a leitmotiv in their statements on the subject. As a high customs official explained: "In this country . . . where manufacturing industry barely struggles to get out of infancy, agriculture is the principal base of private and public fortune, and [being] the thermometer which regulates importation, commerce finds itself tightly linked with it and above all dependent on it."[2] Business interest groups tried to develop agriculture by improving the quality of exports, expanding export markets, reducing export taxes, arranging cheap credit, and ensuring abundant labor.

As noted, the absence or weakness of agricultural interest groups promoted the role of business interest groups as advocates for agriculture. Commercial associations presumed to speak on behalf of the agriculture of their region, while factor groups represented the sugar or coffee industries. Government ratified the claim of business interest groups to speak for agriculture. National and provincial authorities commonly called on them for suggestions on agricultural development, evaluations of the crop situation in their areas, and remedies for crises. In addition, commercial association and factor group leaders were often appointed to special government committees dealing with agricultural problems. In one case, a committee chosen by the Minister of Finance to evaluate agriculture in the Province of Bahia in 1874 consisted entirely, except for its chairman, of directors of the Commercial Association of Bahia.[3]

Far from feeling any rivalry with planter interest organizations, busi-

---

1. Associação Comercial de Pernambuco, *Relatório da Associação Comercial de Pernambuco, Lido em Sessão da Assembléia Geral de 6 de Agôsto de 1883* (Recife: Homeopatha, 1883), p. 24.
2. Bernardo José Borges, *O Comerciante, ou Completo Manual Instrutivo* (2d ed. rev.; Rio de Janeiro: Eduardo & Henrique Laemmert, 1878), p. 77.
3. *RMF*, 1874, p. 47.

ness interest groups leaders tried to foster them and participate in them. They were particularly active in founding and leading the various Imperial Institutes of Agriculture.[4] Viscount Mauá, former President of the Commercial Association of Rio de Janeiro, was the first Vice-President of the Imperial Institute of Agriculture of Rio de Janeiro and also donated a plantation to serve as its experimental farm.[5] At the end of the Empire, the Vice-President, Secretary, and Treasurer of the Imperial Institute of Agriculture of Bahia were directors of the Commercial Association of Bahia.[6] Commercial Association of Pernambuco leaders probably sat on all the boards of the Agriculture Auxiliary Society of Pernambuco, nineteenth-century Brazil's most lasting planter interest group.[7]

Commercial associations and factor groups often lobbied in conjunction with agricultural organizations. Business and agricultural groups also worked together in the agricultural congresses convened during the last quarter of the century to deal with commodity problems. The Commercial Association of Pernambuco, for example, aided the Agriculture Auxiliary Society of Pernambuco in organizing the well-known Recife Agricultural Congress of 1878, which defined its geographical scope by inviting all landowners whose commodities were traded by Recife merchants.[8] Finally, commercial associations and factor groups tried to characterize businessmen and landowners as a unified class. They spoke of them as the "useful class," or the "productive class," settling by the twentieth century on the label "conservative class."

This convergence of major sectors of Brazil's elite was not without problems. In fact, businessmen showed considerably more enthusiasm for the concept of unity than did planters. Economic relations were the areas of contention. Landowners complained about the low prices merchants offered for their products and about the arbitrary determination by the latter of the tares, deductions from the price paid to compensate for containers and wrappings. The issue of credit most aroused planter resentment. Because of the reluctance of banks to lend to planters, most credit was furnished by factors, at relatively high rates of interest. By the mid-

---

4. For example, receipt for 4:000$000 from Visconde de Ipanema to Visconde de Bomfim, Rio de Janeiro, Aug. 8,1860, Coleção Instituto Histórico, AIHGB, lata 328, doc. 38; Minutes, meeting of Jan. 7, 1860, Livro 2 de Atas, AACP, p. 120.
5. Minutes, meeting of Aug. 1, 1862, Atas do Imperial Instituto Fluminense de Agricultura, 1860–1862, ACIRJ, p. 23.
6. "Imperial Instituto Bahiano de Agricultura," *Revista Agrícola*, 18 (March 1887): 151.
7. Three sometime directors of that association served on the 1877–1878 board. Sociedade Auxiliadora da Agricultura de Penambuco, *Relatório Anual Apresentado na Sessão de 4 de Julho de 1878 da Assembléia Geral pelo Gerente Inácio de Barros Barreto e a Ata da Mesma Sessão* (Recife: Jornal do Recife, 1878), pp. 21, 50. Data on commercial association leaders serving on this group's board in other years are not available.
8. Sociedade Auxiliadora da Agricultura de Pernambuco, *Trabalhos do Congresso Agrícola do Recife em Outubro de 1878* (Recife: Manuel Figueiroa de Faria & Filhos, 1879), p. 31.

1880s two-thirds of the plantation mortgages in the southern coffee zone were held by factors.[9] Their economic grip was such, according to planter spokesmen, as to turn agriculture into "the submissive slave of commerce," or into "a docile and obedient automaton."[10] In 1860 and 1887, planter members of coffee zone agricultural clubs proposed to eliminate factors by selling produce directly to the exporter or the overseas buyer.[11] São Paulo planters, meeting in 1896, demanded creation of a state agricultural credit bank in order to end the need to borrow from factors.[12] Such hostility was the more noteworthy because factors, the only element in Brazil's nineteenth-century business elite not largely foreign, were often linked to planters by rural origin, social background, or kinship.

Given difficulties of organization and lack of capital, plans to bypass the factor had little prospect of success. Nor, for the same reasons, did schemes to eliminate or control the exporter through direct sale to overseas buyers or formation of monopoly purchasing companies. Most planters were reconciled to the role of factors and exporters in the Brazilian economy because they could see no alternative. Throughout the nineteenth century, planter and business elites usually displayed at least a surface amicability toward one another, and open conflict was rare.[13]

A reason for convergence between planters and businessmen was that their personal interests touched at many points. When planters entered business they usually did so in partnership with members of the business elite. The latter's expertise and business connections made such ventures much more likely to succeed. A prime point of the entry of planters into business was factorage. One out of six partners of Rio de Janeiro coffee factor firms during the period 1870–1888 lived in rural areas, usually as a coffee planter.[14] Among factors, business and agricultural interests often mixed. Each of the twelve founders of the factor-spokesman Center for Coffee Agriculture and Commerce in 1880 was either a coffee planter, had married into a prominent coffee planter family, or was a partner with a

9. Laura Jarnagin Pang, "The State and Agricultural Clubs of Imperial Brazil, 1860–1889" (Ph.D. Diss., Vanderbilt University, 1981), p. 363.
10. Miguel Antônio da Silva, "Agricultura Nacional: Estudos Agrícolas," *Revista Agrícola*, 8 (Dec. 1877): 141; Pang, "State and Agricultural Clubs," p. 362.
11. Pang, "State and Agricultural Clubs," pp. 65–67, 362–363.
12. *O Estado de São Paulo* (São Paulo), Sept. 2, 1892, p. 1.
13. For convergence of Brazilian elites, see Emilia Viotti da Costa, *The Brazilian Empire: Myths and Histories* (Chicago: University of Chicago Press, 1986), p. 200; Peter L. Eisenberg, *The Sugar Industry in Pernambuco: Modernization Without Change, 1840–1910* (Berkeley: University of California Press, 1974), p. 140; Richard Graham, "Brazil from the Middle of the Nineteenth Century to the Paraguayan War," in *The Cambridge History of Latin America, Vol. III: From Independence to c. 1870*, ed. Leslie Bethell (Cambridge: Cambridge University Press, 1985), p. 772; and Joseph L. Love, *São Paulo in the Brazilian Federation, 1889–1937* (Stanford, Calif.: Stanford University Press, 1980), p. 268.
14. Joseph E. Sweigart, "Financing and Marketing Brazilian Export Agriculture: The Coffee Factors of Rio de Janeiro, 1850–1888" (Ph.D. Diss., University of Texas, 1980), pp. 84–85.

coffee planter in his factor firm.[15] The movement of business elite members into agriculture was even more common. It was encouraged by traditional Luso-Brazilian values, which honored the landowner but deprecated the businessman. During the colonial period, the movement of business elite members into land ownership, through foreclosure, purchase, or marriage with landowning families, was notable.[16] It continued in the nineteenth century, by the 1880s including investment in large corporate farms and in the central sugar mills (*engenhos centrais*) designed to revive Brazil's sugar industry through large-scale processing. Finally, in the last five years of the century a number of British export firms bought and operated coffee plantations.

Clearly the business and personal interests of business and landowning elites were often intermixed. But this was not the prime reason for the concern of the business elite for agriculture. British, North American, and German merchants, whatever may have been the case in their homelands, had much less enthusiasm than their Brazilian and Portuguese fellows for landowning as a means of increasing social status. Marriage ties between business and landowning families were frequent but far from predominant. In fact, business interest group leaders who had no ties to the land were no less solicitous for agricultural welfare than those who did. The overriding reason for the unity of outlook of business and landowning elites in nineteenth-century Brazil was their mutual dependence on export agriculture. Defending the Commercial Association of Pernambuco before a skeptical audience of planters, one of its leaders stated that "the interests of commerce find themselves tightly linked to those of agriculture." "Because commerce lives off agriculture and without agriculture it will die," shouted back a planter.[17] He could hardly have put it better.

A basic problem: technological backwardness

In defending and developing Brazilian agriculture, commercial associations and factor groups assumed a task that was herculean as well as vital. Agriculture's problems included technological backwardness, low export prices, lack of credit, heavy export taxes, shortage or uncertain supply of labor, and high transportation costs. Most of these problems were significantly worse in the Northeast, which during the course of the nineteenth

15. Ibid., p. 196.
16. Stuart B. Schwartz, "Free Labor in a Slave Economy: The *Lavradores de Cana* of Colonial Bahia," in *The Colonial Roots of Modern Brazil: Papers of the Newberry Library Conference*, ed. Dauril Alden (Berkeley: University of California Press, 1973), p. 188; Rae Flory and David Grant Smith, "Bahian Merchants and Planters in the Seventeenth and Early Eighteenth Centuries," *HAHR*, 54 (Nov. 1978): 577.
17. Sociedade Auxiliadora da Agricultura de Pernambuco, *Congresso Agrícola*, p. 423.

century declined from the nation's economic hub to its economic embarrassment.[18] Between 1872 and 1900 the Northeast's share of the Brazilian gross internal product declined by nearly half.[19]

Technological backwardness contributed to other agricultural problems. It meant low agricultural productivity, thus a reduced volume of exports, a slim profit margin for the planter, and little generation of capital. It contributed to the poor quality of exports, thus low prices and the loss of overseas markets. Its source lay, according to the prestigious Auxiliary Society for National Industry, in "the inertia with which the greatest part of our planters and farmers resist the introduction of improvements that threaten the routine inherited from their elders and preserved by them with all of their traditions."[20] Planters ignored not only up-to-date agricultural machinery but basic implements. Even in the prosperous provinces of Rio de Janeiro and São Paulo the hoe remained the mainstay of cultivation; as of the mid-1880s less than two thousand plows were sold in Rio de Janeiro yearly.[21] Farming in the southernmost province of Rio Grande do Sul, except for that done by German immigrants, likewise remained "crude and primitive," and complex machinery found no purchasers.[22] In the North as of 1847 an immigrant plantation owner was noted as having the only plow in the Province of Pará, an area then encompassing approximately forty percent of Brazil's territory.[23]

In the Northeast indifference to efficient farming and to technological improvement was a tradition brought down from the colonial period.[24] According to the President of the Province of Bahia in 1871, the hoe reigned unchallenged among agricultural devices, together with "the conviction that it is neither necessary to prepare the soil, nor manure it, nor prepare roads for the transportation of crops."[25] With some notable excep-

---

18. For the Northeast's decline, see Nathaniel H. Leff, "Economic Development and Regional Inequality: Origins of the Brazilian Case," *The Quarterly Journal of Economics*, 86 (May 1972): 243–262; and David Denslow, "As Origens da Desigualdade Regional no Brasil," in *Formação Econômica do Brasil: A Experiência da Industrialização*, eds. Flávio Rabelo Versiani and José Roberto Mendonça de Barros (São Paulo: Saraiva, 1977), pp. 41–61.
19. From 24.5% to 13.5%. Raymond W. Goldsmith, *Brasil, 1850–1984: Desenvolvimento Financeiro sob um Século de Inflação* (São Paulo: Harper & Row do Brasil, 1986), p. 13.
20. *O Auxiliador da Indústria Nacional*, 8 (Feb. 1860): 48.
21. Andrews to Department of State, Rio de Janeiro, June 27, 1884, and Wright to Department of State, São Paulo, July 17, 1884, *USRC*, XIII, no. 48 (Dec. 1884): 685–688.
22. Mackey to Department of State, Rio Grande, May 20, 1884; ibid., pp. 690–691.
23. William H. Edwards, *A Voyage Up the River Amazon, Including a Residence at Pará* (London: John Murray, 1861), p. 15.
24. Stuart B. Schwartz, *Sovereignty and Society in Colonial Brazil: The High Court of Bahia and Its Judges, 1609–1751* (Berkeley: University of California Press, 1973), p. 117. However, Schwartz in *Sugar Plantations in the Formation of Brazilian Society: Bahia, 1550–1835* (Cambridge: Cambridge University Press, 1985), pp. 431–433, notes the "progressive attitudes" of some Bahian planters in the late eighteenth and early nineteenth centuries.
25. Bahia, Presidente da Província, *Relatório Apresentado 'a Assembléia Legislativa da Bahia pelo Excelentissimo Senhor Barão de S. Lourenço em 1 de Março de 1871* (Salvador: Jornal da Bahia, 1871), p. 15.

tions (for example, a Bahian planter introduced Brazil's first cane-grinding machine in 1813), the planters of the Northeast displayed, in the words of a president of the Province of Pernambuco, "a cursed spirit of routine, always ready to condemn totally any attempted improvement."[26] Economic and social conditions contributed to this attitude. Labor was cheap, performed by slaves and by the increasingly numerous and poor landless. Capital was especially dear. The Northeast's technological backwardness was highlighted by the decline of that region's two basic exports, sugar and cotton.

During the nineteenth century sugar suffered a pronounced fall in importance as an export. In the five-year period 1826–1830 it produced an average thirty-eight percent of the nation's export revenue, but by 1896–1900 only five percent.[27] The drop was especially noteworthy because sugar had been the nation's agricultural export staple from early colonial times until overtaken by coffee in the 1830s. The predicament lay not in quantity but in revenue generated. Revenue climbed at an average annual rate of 1.5 percent until the 1883–1884 harvest.[28] Then it fell from 3,514,000 British pounds sterling in 1883–1884 to a low of 642,000 in 1899.[29] Part of the reason for declining export revenue was price. Despite a rapid increase in world sugar consumption, its price fell steadily from 1872 to 1902.[30] But price decline was by no means solely responsible for the falling value of Brazilian sugar exportation. Much was due to the loss of markets to formidable competitors. From midcentury on, Brazil progressively lost its European markets to European beet sugar. It lost its North American market, particularly important to the Northeast, to Cuba in the 1890s.[31] The long decline of sugar prices squeezed the profits from the Northeast's sugar industry because of its low productivity, but not the Cuban sugar industry, which had successfully modernized during the nineteenth century.[32] But Brazilian productivity com-

26. *Fala com que o Exm. Sr. Comendador Henrique Pereira de Lucena Abriu a Sessão da Assembléia Legislativa Provincial de Pernambuco em 1 de Março de 1874* (Recife: M. Figueiroa de Faria & Filhos, 1874), p. 60.

27. Brazil, Instituto Brasileiro de Geografia e Estatística, *Anuário Estatístico, 1939–40* (Rio de Janeiro: Imprensa Nacional, 1941), p. 1379.

28. Nathaniel H. Leff, *Underdevelopment and Development in Brazil, Volume I: Economic Structure and Change, 1822–1947* (London: George Allen & Unwin, 1982), p. 85.

29. Brazil, Instituto Brasileiro de Geografia e Estatística, *Anuário Estatístico, 1939–40*, p. 1375.

30. Noel Deerr, *The History of Sugar* (London: Chapman and Hall, 1949), II: 505.

31. Eisenberg, *Sugar in Pernambuco*, p. 23; Stevens to Department of State, Recife, Jan., 1893, *USRC*, XLI, no. 148 (Jan. 1893): p. 80.

32. In part this was because Cuba's soils were superior and its terrain better suited than Brazil's for the use of railroads to haul sugar and the employment of large machinery. Eisenberg, *Sugar in Pernambuco*, p. 218; David Denslow, "Sugar Production in Northeastern Brazil and Cuba, 1858–1908" (Ph.D. Diss., Yale University, 1974), pp. 118–119. Denslow also sees economic problems and social structure as inhibiting sugar industry modernization. "As Exportações e a Origem do Padrão de Industrialização Regional do Brasil," in *Dimensões do Desenvolvimento Brasileiro*, eds.

pared badly with that of Cuba even before the widespread use of railroads and large machinery in sugar production.[33]

Poor quality was as damaging as low productivity in international competition. Cuban sugars fetched higher prices than Brazilian of the same type during most years of the first half of the nineteenth century; after 1862 they did so without fail and by progressively wider margins.[34] The exportation of high-quality Northeastern sugar became increasingly difficult. The port of Salvador, for example, shipped 5,730,908 kilograms of white sugar in 1865–1866, but only 1,048 in 1884–1885.[35] Contemporary observers usually blamed the problem on poor preparation. "In some localities," a customs official in 1873 remarked of Bahian sugar, "preparation has degenerated to such a point as to bring about complete discredit in consumer markets."[36]

Cotton exportation, also primarily associated with the Northeast, experienced not one but two periods of painful decline during the nineteenth century. Like sugar it suffered from falling export revenue, low international prices, and the loss of European markets, but its international competition consisted mainly of the United States. Most Brazilian cotton was the long-fiber variety whose price advantage disappeared with the invention of the cotton gin and machinery to produce high-quality thread from short fibers. The amount of cotton exported also fluctuated because the acreage planted varied greatly with its price. Grown largely in areas removed from major seaports, high transportation costs made cotton unremunerative if prices dipped too low. Few navigable rivers crossed the interior of the Northeast, and railroads generally only skirted the cotton zone; most cotton was hauled on mule trains, at high cost. Freight from the São Francisco River region to the port of Salvador in the 1850s, for example, nearly equaled the market price.[37] From providing twenty percent of Brazil's export revenue in 1820–1830, cotton's share fell to only six percent by 1851–1860.[38]

Werner Baer, Pedro Pinchas Geiger, and Paulo Roberto Haddad (Rio de Janeiro: Campus, 1978), pp. 38–39.

33. For example, Bahia, Presidente da Província, *Relatório de 1852*, pp. 60–61; Denslow, "Northeastern Brazil and Cuba," pp. 77, 89.

34. Denslow, "Northeastern Brazil and Cuba," pp. 19–21.

35. Eugene W. Ridings, "Elite Conflict and Cooperation in the Brazilian Empire: The Case of Bahia's Businessmen and Planters," *Luso-Brazilian Review*, 12 (Summer 1975): 87. In part the rejection of Northeastern white sugar stemmed from tariffs on refined sugar by Great Britain and the United States. Eisenberg, *Sugar in Pernambuco*, pp. 24–25.

36. Bernardino José Borges to Baron Cotegipe, Salvador, Dec. 27, 1873, ABC, AIHGB, lata 85, pasta 24. See also Bahia, Presidente da Província, *Relatório de 1869*, pp. 106–107; Commercial Agricultural Association of Pernambuco to Minister of Finance, Recife, no date, 1874, *RMF*, 1874, pp. 45–47; *RMF*, 1875, pp. 30–31.

37. Morgan to Foreign Office, Salvador, April 17, 1857, PRO/FO 13/354, fl. 118–120.

38. "Evolução da Cotonicultura Brasileira," *Conjuntura Econômica*, 24 , no. 5 (1970): 43–44.

What revived Brazilian cotton exportation was the United States Civil War. By the harvest of 1862–1863 prices in *mil-reis* were more than double, and by 1863–1864 more than triple, their average during the 1850s.[39] Export volume in 1865–1866 was more than four times greater than in 1860–1861 and export revenue in *mil-reis* ten times greater.[40] But the Civil War's end ended prosperity. By 1868 prices were roughly a third of their 1863–1864 level.[41] Fortunately for planters, factors, and exporters, the financial demands of war with Paraguay pulled the *mil-reis* to a low of seventeen pence (par was twenty-seven pence) in 1868. Currency depreciation mitigated the effect of falling cotton prices and benefited the export sector because its members were remunerated in the hard currencies of the developed nations to which Brazil exported. Such currencies could purchase more vis-a-vis the weak Brazilian *mil-reis*. Production continued high. Brazilian cotton exportation in 1871–1872 reached an all-time peak in volume and its second highest total in revenue.[42] But the recovery of the *mil-reis* to the value of twenty-six pence by 1873 ended cotton's second period of prosperity.

The technology of cotton in the Northeast was even more backward than that of sugar. Most cotton was grown by small farmers who lacked capital and knowledge for improvement. A North American expert visiting the Northeast in the 1880s found "substantially the same system of cultivation . . . that was in vogue three hundred years ago."[43] He noted that once fields were burnt and seed planted, "this is the whole story. There is no uprooting of stumps, no digging out of sprouts, no breaking up with the plow, no penetration of the soil, no laying out of furrows, no cultivation other than the occasional chopping out with the hoe of weeds or sprouts."[44] In keeping with the spirit of the rest of the process, a type of gin speedy but damaging to fiber was used, further lowering the value of export. In addition to bad preparation, inferior wrapping and outright falsification were common. Thus, like sugar, cotton from the Brazilian

39. Brazil, Instituto Brasileiro de Geografia e Estatística, *Anuário*, 1939–40, p. 1378.
40. Ibid., pp. 1376, 1378. Large-scale production in the provinces of Rio de Janeiro and São Paulo also began. Associação Comercial de Santos, *Relatório da Associação Comercial de Santos Apresentado em Sessão Extraordinária da Assembléia Geral em 29 de Janeiro de 1876 e Parecer da Comissão de Contas* (Rio de Janeiro: Perseverança, 1876), Anexo, unpaginated; John Casper Branner, *Cotton in the Empire of Brazil*, Department of Agriculture Special Report no. 8 (Washington, D.C.: Government Printing Office, 1885), pp. 47–48.
41. Associação Comercial de Pernambuco, *Relatório de 1865*, p. 3; Associação Comercial do Maranhão, *Relatório da Comissão da Praça do Comércio do Maranhão, Lido pelo Respectivo Presidente na Sessão de 22 de Dezembro de 1870* (São Luís: Mattos, 1871), pp. 10–11.
42. Brazil, Instituto Brasileiro de Geografia e Estatística, *Anuário*, 1939–40, p. 1376.
43. John Casper Branner, "The Cotton Industry in Brazil," *Popular Science Monthly*, 40 (March 1892): 669.
44. Branner, *Cotton in Brazil*, p. 33.

Northeast was frequently quoted below similar varieties in European markets or actually discounted.[45]

The business interest groups of the Northeast realized early that only a thorough improvement of growing and preparation would ensure the viability of its sugar and cotton in world markets. They played the role of Cassandra. Planters were usually indifferent to the effects of technological backwardness as long as prices tended to rise, but exporters, in contact with overseas customers, could anticipate trouble. As early as 1852 the Commercial Association of Bahia warned that local sugar was already fetching ten percent less than similar types in Europe and urged a campaign to upgrade quality.[46] In 1862 and again in 1865 the Commercial Association of Pernambuco noted the progressive loss of European and even River Plate markets and predicted the eventual collapse of the sugar industry unless the "fatal routine and debility in which cultivation rests" was ended.[47] After the fall of cotton prices in the late 1860s and sugar in the early 1870s, warnings of impending ruin as a result of careless preparation and outmoded technology became virtually routine.

Business interest groups intervene — export inspection
and imposed standards

What brought the first intervention of business interest groups to upgrade export quality was outright fraud. Both sugar and cotton planters frequently falsified the weight and quality of their shipments. They adulterated sugar with sand or gravel and increased the weight of cotton shipments by packing them with "rocks, bricks, pieces of iron, and nails."[48] Like indifference to technology, the habit of fraud also had roots deep in the colonial period, as an investigating committee of the Province of Bahia noted ruefully in 1873.[49] The logical means to counteract it was inspection.

The issue of export inspection brought merchants and planters into conflict. Soon after its foundation in 1839 the Commercial Association of Pernambuco began to warn the provincial president that European buyers

45. Associação Comercial do Maranhão, *Relatório de 1872*, p. 31; Minutes, meeting of Feb. 3, 1870, Livro 4 de Atas, AACB, pp. 8–9
46. Minutes, meetings of Jan. 22, Sept. 20, and Oct. 7, 1852, Livro 2 de Atas, AACB, pp. 12–13, 30–32, 44.
47. Associação Comercial de Pernambuco, *Relatório de 1862*, p. 5, and *Relatório de 1865*, pp. 5–6.
48. Minutes, meeting of Sept. 9, 1889, Livro 7 de Atas, AACP, p. 39. For other notice of falsification, see, for example, Minutes, meeting of Aug. 4, 1839, Livro 1 de Atas, AACP, p. 7; Minutes, meeting of March 22, 1883, Livro 5 de Atas, AACB, pp. 64–65; "Comissão de Inquérito da Lavoura da Bahia," ABC, AIBHG, lata 85, doc. 24.
49. "Comissão de Inquérito da Lavoura da Bahia," ABC, AIBHG, lata 85, doc. 24. See also Schwartz, *Sugar Plantations*, pp. 122–123.

were complaining of short weight in the province's sugar and cotton and were giving them a discounted price.[50] By 1843 it had persuaded the provincial government to begin official inspection of cotton. But it was unable to promote the same for sugar, even after trying to mobilize the support of the province's planters.[51] The Commercial Association of Pernambuco consequently decided to create its own inspection service. Planters were invited to participate in its organization and permitted to select one of its two-man inspection team. The association's private inspection of sugar began early in 1846 but lasted less than two years, primarily because of heavy expenses.[52] In the meantime, the province allowed its official cotton inspection begun in 1843 to lapse.

In 1846 Pernambuco's provincial assembly legislated official inspection of sugar. Although previously advocating such inspection, the Commercial Association of Pernambuco sharply reversed itself. It appealed first to the president of province and then to the imperial government to block the law, without success.[53] The new provincial inspection system was a blow to merchants. Not only were they billed for its cost, but provincial inspection was considered to relieve the seller of all responsibility for fraud or inferior quality. Perhaps worse, the weight and quality of a shipment as determined by the official inspector were binding on the purchaser.[54] By implication, the provincial inspector would usually place a greater value on a shipment than would the merchant. Obviously, Pernambuco's inspection legislation was the fruit of pressure by planters.

Similar inspection systems would be enacted or proposed in other Northeastern provinces. Merchants and planters saw quite different purposes in inspection of exports. For merchants it was a means of blocking fraud and bad quality; for planters it was a way to avoid being cheated by merchants.[55] The issue implied fundamental conflict between planters and merchants, although as in most such situations, both sides kept the debate at a subdued level. Since the influence of planters in provincial legislatures usually produced inspection legislation that reflected their interests, business interest groups would attempt to block such legislation.

The struggle over official inspection in the Northeast was lengthy and widespread. Business interest groups, or ad hoc committees of local busi-

50. Minutes, meetings of Aug. 4, 1839 and Nov. 3, 1841, Livro 1 de Atas, AACP, pp. 7, 40.
51. Minutes, meetings of July 5 and July 24, 1844, Livro 1 de Atas, AACP, pp. 75–77.
52. Minutes, meeting of Oct. 4, 1847, Livro 1 de Atas, AACP, pp. 155–156.
53. Minutes, meetings of Dec. 17, 1846 and Feb. 11, 1847, Livro 1 de Atas, AACP, pp. 143, 148.
54. Minutes, extraordinary general assembly of May 18, 1863, Livro 2 de Atas, AACP, pp. 170–171; Commercial Association of Pernambuco to Vice-President of Province, Recife, June 5, 1866, *Relatório de 1866*, pp. 47–49; Commercial Association of Pernambuco to President of Province, no date, 1867, *Relatório de 1867*, pp. 19–21.
55. Pernambuco, Presidente da Província, *Relatório de 1865*, p. 38.

nessmen where no formal organization existed, were successful in blocking most, but not all, official inspection.[56] Occasionally they were able to bend legislation to make sellers responsible for bad quality or fraud in exports, as did the Commercial Association of Bahia in 1845.[57] But even then constant vigilance was needed to keep provincial inspectors from favoring the planter. Pernambuco witnessed the fiercest struggle against provincial inspection. Lobbying and petitioning doggedly, the Commercial Association of Pernambuco in 1864, 1865, twice in 1866, and in 1867, 1870, 1872, 1873, 1880, and 1882 was able to convince presidents of province either to reject or to refuse to enforce legislation imposing inspection of cotton.[58] The association rewarded obliging presidents of province with effusive thanks and in one case with immediate honorary membership.

For the business interest groups of the Northeast, provincial inspection of exports was unpalatable. Yet fraud and poor quality continued to threaten overseas markets and to be punished by painful discounts. The answer was private inspection by the groups themselves. Unlike the sugar inspection tried by the Commercial Association of Pernambuco in 1846–1847, the new system would not seek the cooperation of planters but would be enforced by pledges by exporters to buy no shipments not previously inspected. The way was shown by forty-three cotton exporters of the Province of Alagôas who signed a pact for private inspection in July 1866 and then organized themselves as the Commercial Association of Maceió.[59]

The planters of Alagôas fumed at the unilateral imposition, but for merchants private inspection worked wonderfully, uncovering numerous attempts at fraud and even forcing on sellers the uniform sacking of their product.[60] Success led the Commercial Association of Maceió to attempt similar private inspection of sugar in July 1872, but resistance by the more politically powerful sugar planters forced its abandonment within

56. As of 1865, no provincial cotton inspection remained in Brazil. Ibid., p. 37.
57. Commercial Association of Bahia to Inspector, Tesouraria da Fazenda, Salvador, Nov. 3, 1845, Registro de Ofícios, 1840–1850, AACB, unpaginated.
58. Associação Comercial de Pernambuco, *Relatório de 1864*, p. 7; *Relatório de 1865*, pp. 4–5; Commercial Association of Pernambuco to Vice-President of Province, Recife, June 5, 1866, *Relatório de 1866*, pp. 47–49; *Relatorio de 1867*, pp. 19–27; Commercial Association of Pernambuco to President of Province, Recife, July 27, 1870, *Relatório de 1870*, pp. 38–39; *Relatório de 1872*, p. 5; *Relatório de 1882*, p. 6; Minutes, meeting of Dec. 5, 1866, Livro 2 de Atas, AACP, p. 274; Minutes, meeting of May 5, 1873, Livro 4 de Atas, AACP, p. 112; Commercial Association of Pernambuco to President of Province, Recife, March 12, 1880, Arquivo Público Estadual de Pernambuco, Recife, "Associação Comercial, 1878–81," doc. 226.
59. Moacir Medeiros de Santa Ana, *Uma Associação Centenária* (Maceió: Arquivo Público de Alagôas, 1966), pp. 59–60, 66–67.
60. Associação Comercial de Maceió, *Relatório da Direção da Associação Comercial de Maceió, Apresentado à Assembléia Geral da Mesma em 22 de Julho de 1871* (Maceió: Jornal de Alagôas, 1871), pp. 5–6, and *Relatório de 1872*, p. 9.

months.[61] Other pressures from planters probably led the membership of the Maceió organization to vote to end cotton inspection late in 1872. The group's Board of Directors and cotton exporter members resigned in protest. Styling themselves the Cotton Covenant (*Convénio de Algodão*) Maceió cotton exporters vowed to continue the struggle and appealed to the nation's other commercial associations for support.[62] Within five months, peace had been made and private inspection of cotton resumed.[63]

Petitions of complaint signed by hundreds of cotton growers bombarded Alagôas's provincial president after the reestablishment of private inspection in 1873. Planters had reason to denounce the system. Without their consent they were charged the cost of inspection. Worse, it was done by the *caixeiros* of cotton export houses, who, planters claimed, regularly downgraded the quality of cotton brought before them in order to establish a cheap purchase price for their employers.[64] The Commercial Association of Maceió refused to bow to pressure, although apparently no longer charging planters for the inspection after 1877.[65] The success of the Maceió group inspired emulation. Cotton exporters working within their commercial associations organized similar compulsory private inspection systems in Bahia in 1872, Pernambuco in 1874, and Parahyba in 1875.[66] Merchants were rarely able to impose inspection of sugar, but were more successful with cotton, grown by poorer, more isolated, and politically weaker planters.

There is no information on how long these private inspection systems lasted. It is probable that they were quietly discontinued by at least the mid-1880s, because of planter resentment and, perhaps more important, because of lessening interest by merchants. Both volume and value of cotton exportation generally declined after the mid-1870s. Lower exportation in part reflected an increasing consumption by domestic textile mills. Much of Pernambuco's cotton went to other Brazilian states by the 1890s; consumption of cotton by Bahian mills outran supply by 1889.[67] The need for inspection lessened as domestic consumption grew. Because of

61. Associação Comercial de Maceió, *Relatório de 1872*, p. 10; Moacir Medeiros de Santa Ana, *Contribuição à História do Açúcar em Alagôas* (Recife: Instituto do Açúcar e do Alcool, 1970), p. 272.
62. Minutes, meetings of Nov. 20, 1872 and Jan. 20, 1873, Livro 3 de Atas, AACP, pp. 109, 112; Associação Comercial do Rio de Janeiro, *Relatório da Associação Comercial do Rio de Janeiro no Ano de 1872* (Rio de Janeiro: Apóstolo, 1873), p. 8.
63. Minutes, meeting of Feb. 5, 1873, Livro 3 de Atas, AACP, p. 113.
64. Santa Ana, *Açúcar em Alagôas*, pp. 60–61.
65. Minutes, meeting of Sept. 12, 1877, Livro 4 de Atas, AACP, p. 110.
66. Sixty cotton export firms to Commercial Association of Bahia, Salvador, Dec. 6, 1872, *Relatório de 1874*, pp. 17–18; Minutes, meetings of Jan. 20 and Feb. 5, 1875, Livro 4 de Atas, AACP, pp. 30–31.
67. Associação Comercial de Pernambuco, *Relatório de 1896*, p. 14; Bahia, Presidente da Província, *Relatório de 1889*, pp. 160–162.

high tariffs, there was no foreign competition for Brazilian cotton in the domestic market. Furthermore, unless the cotton was shipped to factories through a major seaport, it rarely passed through the hands of business interest group members, thus arousing little concern for its quality.

Connected with countering fraud and poor preparation was the establishment by business interest groups of uniform standards of quality, volume, weight, and means of shipment for exports. Uniform standards also were usually imposed unilaterally, but in this case with more permanent effect. Like inspection, the move to establish standards began early. In 1852 the Commercial Association of Bahia began to promote shipment of sugar in sacks, rather than the traditional cases (*caixos*), boxes (*feixos*), and barrels (*barricas*), in order to inhibit falsification of weight and quality.[68] The campaign was successful. By 1856 the use of sacks had become general in the province, and complaints from overseas buyers had diminished.[69] In 1852 that group also began a drive, repeated in 1864 and 1870, to force cotton planters to declare precisely the tares, or weight, of the vines used to wrap cotton for shipment.[70] Overuse of these bindings was a favorite method of extracting payment above the true value of the cotton sold.

Establishing standards for quality was more difficult. After an unsuccessful attempt at standardization in 1845, the Commercial Association of Pernambuco, working in conjunction with that province's Commercial Agricultural Association, was able in 1858 to force the adoption of Dutch standard sugar types for classification.[71] The Commercial Association of Bahia took the same action in 1870.[72] The Commercial Association of Maceió, originator of private cotton inspection, also pioneered in the establishment of quality norms for that commodity. It attempted to make its standards general throughout Brazil by sending samples to other commercial associations in 1866, 1867, 1872, 1873, and 1874.[73] These quality samples were widely displayed and apparently adopted elsewhere, although it is difficult to gauge the extent.[74]

---

68. Bahia, Presidente da Província, *Relatório de 1852*, pp. 61–62.
69. Morgan to Foreign Office, Salvador, March 15, 1856, PRO/FO 13/344, fl. 136; Minutes, general assembly of Oct. 24, 1856, Livro 2 de Atas, AACB, p. 109.
70. Minutes, meeting of Nov. 30, 1852, Livro 2 de Atas, AACB, p. 48; Minutes, meeting of Feb. 3, 1864, Livro 3 de Atas, AACB, p. 44; Minutes, meeting of Feb. 3, 1870, Livro 4 de Atas, AACB, pp. 8–9.
71. Minutes, meeting of Dec. 22, 1845, Livro 1 de Atas, AACP, p. 117; Associação Comercial de Pernambuco, *Relatório de 1858*, p. 6. The Commercial Agricultural Association, founded in 1836, functioned at this time as a sugar exchange, not beginning true interest group activity until 1878.
72. Minutes, meeting of March 21, 1870, Livro 4 de Atas, AACB, p. 17.
73. Minutes, meetings of Sept. 4, 1866 and April 3, 1867, Livro 2 de Atas, AACP, pp. 264, 281; Associação Comercial do Rio de Janeiro, *Relatório de 1872*, p. 8; Minutes, meeting of Jan. 5, 1874, Livro 4 de Atas, AACP, p. 1.
74. The commercial associations of Pernambuco and Bahia apparently adopted Maceió quality norms

By the 1880s business interest groups had made progress in improving shipment and quality of sugar and cotton. Standards in volume and weight were established as part of their campaign to impose the metric system (see Chapter 11). The quality of the Northeast's exports was aided temporarily by private inspection and more permanently by the establishment of uniform standards. But neither measure struck at a root cause of low productivity and quality: technological backwardness.

Modernizing Northeastern agricultural technology

Merchants were convinced that only modernization of Northeastern sugar and cotton growing and preparation would enable these products to compete in world markets. But who was to promote it? In the absence of other effective government or private agencies, business interest groups had to do it themselves. Happily, the close ties of their membership to technologically advanced nations made them apt for such a role.

To gather, evaluate, and transmit to Brazil the many innovations in agriculture coming out of Europe a knowledgeable and energetic agent was needed. The ideal man appeared in João Diego Sturz, a naturalized Brazilian serving as consul in Prussia. A native of Prussia married to an Englishwoman, Sturz spoke and wrote in three languages and had been a merchant in Rio de Janeiro and Salvador.[75] From 1843 to at least 1857 he sent a stream of information, statistics, lithographs, and blueprints to Brazil's three major commercial associations, usually dispatching them first to the Commercial Association of Pernambuco, thence to Bahia and finally to Rio de Janeiro. On the recommendation of the three associations, he was made Brazilian delegate to the London Great Exhibition of 1851.[76] In addition to shipping quantities of models and blueprints from London, Sturz used imperial government funds to purchase agricultural and sugar processing machines, which were displayed at the headquarters of the Commercial Association of Bahia.[77] The energetic Sturz was also from 1836 European contact for the Auxiliary Society for National Industry and for the Farming Council, an agricultural organization sponsored by the Province of Bahia, as well as serving as purchasing agent for wealthy individual planters.[78]

      at least temporarily. Minutes, meeting of Jan. 5, 1874, Livro 4 de Atas, AACP, p. 1; Minutes, meetings of Nov. 13, 1874, and Oct. 14, 1875, Livro 4 de Atas, AACB, pp. 195, 226.
75. "Estrangeiros Naturalizados," Arquivo do Estado de Guanabara, Rio de Janeiro, cod. 43-1-78, unpaginated; Augusto Vitorino Alves Sacramento Blake, *Dicionário Bibliográfico Brasileiro*, (Rio de Janeiro: Tipografia Nacional, 1883-1902), III: 414.
76. Minutes, meetings of Nov. 5 and Dec. 1, 1850, Livro 1 de Atas, AACP, pp. 239-240, 248.
77. Minutes, general assembly of Sept. 20, 1852, Livro 2 de Atas, AACB, p. 30.
78. Ibid.; Bahia, Presidente da Província, *Relatório de 1848*, p. 48; O Auxiliador da Indústria Nacional, 4, no. 12 (1836): 359.

The commercial associations of Bahia and Pernambuco supplemented the work of Sturz. At the request of its provincial president in 1846, the Bahian group nominated a committee to study means to better sugar and other local products. The association published and distributed widely its report, as well as translating and distributing a new French work on sugar in 1849.[79] The Commercial Association of Pernambuco evaluated agricultural machines or blueprints for its province to see if they merited support in the form of tax exemptions or subsidies to their inventors.[80]

Despite the efforts of business interest groups to diffuse technology, modernization of agriculture in the Northeast remained piecemeal. Yet just as sugar prices and prosperity began a decline in the 1870s, hope for technological redemption of that industry appeared. Central sugar mills, tried with success in the West Indies and Egypt, promised to revolutionize the industry. Instead of processing their own cane, as was traditional, planters would send it to large, modern mills, each serving a given locality. As advocates put it, this would free planters from the bother of processing sugar, so that they could devote themselves to perfecting its cultivation.[81] Central mills promised both efficiency and profit. They allegedly extracted from thirteen to twenty percent of the cane's sugar content, in contrast to the seven or less usual in the Northeast, and offered from seventeen to forty-three percent return on capital.[82] In 1874 the provinces of Bahia and Pernambuco passed laws guaranteeing proposed mills seven percent return on capital investment, as did the imperial government the following year.[83]

Northeastern business interest groups initially were fervent supporters of central mills. Typically, the Commercial Association of Maranhão proclaimed: "We do not believe there is a single person of half-way clear intelligence who does not have faith that central mills will *invariably* [italics theirs] give great profits," and predicted its province's first central mill would end the traditional inferiority of Maranhão sugar.[84] The Com-

---

79. Minutes, meeting of Jan. 20, 1846, Livro 1 de Atas, AACB, pp. 197–198; Commercial Association of Bahia to President of Province, Salvador, May 14, 1846, Registro dos Ofícios, 1840–1850, AACB, unpaginated; Minutes, meeting of Nov. 27, 1849, Livro 1 de Atas, AACB, p. 303.
80. Minutes, meeting of Oct. 2, 1848, Livro 1 de Atas, AACP, p. 165; Minutes, meeting of Aug. 10, 1852, Livro 2 de Atas, AACP, p. 9.
81. Bahia, Presidente da Província, *Relatório de 1889*, p. 157; Borges, *O Comerciante*, pp. 81–82.
82. Associação Comercial do Maranhão, "Economia Rural," *Revista Agrícola*, 15 (1884): 74; Brazil, Congresso, Câmara dos Deputados, *Parecer e Projeto sôbre a Creação de Bancos de Crédito Territorial e Fábricas Centraes de Açúcar Apresentados à Câmera dos Deputados na Sessão de 20 de Julho de 1875, pelas Comissões de Fazenda e Especial Nomeada em 16 de Abril de 1873* (Rio de Janeiro: Tipografia Nacional, 1875), p. 27.
83. Brazil, Congresso, Câmara dos Deputados, *Parecer e Projeto*, pp. 34, 48–49; Borges, *O Comerciante*, pp. 78–80; Eisenberg, *Sugar in Pernambuco*, p. 88.
84. Associação Comercial do Maranhão, "Engenhos Centrais," 74; Jerônimo de Viveiros, *História do Comércio do Maranhão, 1612–1895* (São Luís: Associação Comercial do Maranhão, 1954), II: 530.

mercial Association of Pernambuco helped the Swiss company that had obtained the first concession to sell its stock.[85] Such enthusiasm was not solely due to the expectation that central mills would revitalize the sugar industry. Business interest group leaders had invested heavily in them. Nine sometime directors of the Commercial Association of Bahia, for example, took shares in that province's first concession.[86]

Planters did not share the enthusiasm. In 1876 and 1878 the Agriculture Auxiliary Society of Pernambuco called for the distribution of guaranteed interest and other benefits to "smaller mills," presumably the traditional *engenho,* rather than only to large central mills and voiced fears that the latter would monopolize sugar processing.[87] Planters were not only jealous of the benefits going to investors in central mills, but feared being reduced to mere furnishers of cane.

The performance of the mills themselves soon reinforced misgivings. Not until the 1880s were any successfully mounted. Many persons who acquired concessions lacked capital or experience in sugar refining; some procured them only for speculation.[88] Once in operation, the heralded profitability of the mills proved an illusion. The system demanded long-term contracts between central mills and planters furnishing cane. Mill companies thus frequently had to pay far above market price for their raw material in a period when the price of sugar was declining. Planters, on the other hand, could continue to grind cane in their own *engenhos* if the central mill price was not to their liking. Much of the difficulty lay with the foreign, mainly British, companies that undertook the concessions. The mills were badly equipped and incompetently run, often by persons who spoke no Portuguese. Especially notorious was the mounting of mills by a British company with machinery that had been rusting in Egypt for years.[89]

Eventually the business interest groups of the Northeast turned against the central mills. In 1884, the Commercial Association of Pernambuco blamed the fiasco on government guarantee of interest on capital, the following year reiterating that the central mills were "only profitable for the stockholders, lenders of capital, through the receipt of a certain and guaranteed income."[90] In 1887 it pronounced the central mills experi-

85. Minutes, meeting of July 6, 1875, Livro 4 de Atas, AACP, p. 43.
86. *Particular Contrato de Sociedade em Comandita para o Estabelecimento de uma Fábrica Central de Açúcar no Município de Santo Amaro em Ponto Fixado de Acordo com o Govêrno pela Sistema Adotada nas Colônias Francêzas de Martinica e Guadeloupe* (Salvador: J. G. Tourinho, 1875), unpaginated.
87. Sociedade Auxiliadora da Agricultura de Pernambuco, *Relatório de 1878,* pp. 26–30.
88. *RMACOP, 1880,* I: 132; Evaldo Cabral de Melo, *O Norte Agrário e o Império, 1871–1889* (Rio de Janeiro: Nova Fronteira, 1984), pp. 170–172.
89. Great Britain, Foreign Office, *Diplomatic and Consular Reports,* no. 1547 (1895): 7.
90. Associação Comercial de Pernambuco, *Relatório de 1884,* p. 8; Commercial Association of Pernambuco to Chief of Customs, Recife, March 14, 1885, *Relatório de 1885,* p. 36.

ment "a failure."[91] Group leaders also began to support the demand that benefits be given smaller, planter-owned mills. In its 1884 attack the Commercial Association of Pernambuco recommended the formation of companies by planters, and in 1888 the Commercial Association of Bahia made a joint proclamation with the planters of its province calling for expansion of local ownership and more widespread government aid.[92] Business interest groups did not swing to the planter's point of view solely to restore harmony. Central mills were an obvious failure and a drain on tax revenue, most of which was extracted from commerce. The smaller, locally owned mills demanded by planters also provided opportunities for investment or for furnishing credit.[93]

The drive of planters and Northeastern business interest groups to diffuse ownership of mills locally prevailed in legislation. The Province of Pernambuco, in bills of 1885 and 1889, gave aid to new sugar mills in the form of loans rather than guaranteed interest, placed a ceiling on the sum given any one mill, and required that concession holders be local planters.[94] In 1888 the imperial government passed legislation awarding guaranteed interest only to planters or other natives and redistributing to Brazilian companies central mills funds already appropriated.[95] Meanwhile, the cost of mounting a mill was lowered when petitions by Pernambuco's Commercial Association, Commercial Agricultural Association, and Agriculture Auxiliary Society and by the Center for Sugar Industry and Commerce of Rio de Janeiro successfully exempted sugar mill machinery and equipment from import duties and other taxation.[96]

The Republic brought decentralization and an end to national aid, but state governments appropriated funds for modern, planter-owned mills with increasing generosity. This legislation, and the lessons learned from the failure of the central mills experiment, enabled the rapid spread of a more successful type of mill, the *usina*. Although a large, modern processing unit like the central mill, the *usina* differed in growing its own cane in addition to buying it from local planters, thus lessening dependence on them. Hailed nearly everywhere, it was credited by Bahian officials in 1896 with saving the state's sugar industry.[97] By 1910 *usinas* produced a

91. Associação Comercial de Pernambuco, *Relatório de 1887*, p. 37.
92. Representação Dirigida pela Comissão da Lavoura e Comércio a sua Alteza Imperial Regente, Salvador, July 5, 1888, Presidência da Província/Govêrno ao Associação Comercial, 1846–1889, AEB.
93. Indebtedness of producers to Recife merchants greatly increased as modernization progressed. Gadiel Perruci, *A República das Usinas: Um Estudo de História Social e Econômica do Nordeste, 1889–1930* (Rio de Janeiro: Paz e Terra, 1978), p. 125.
94. Eisenberg, *Sugar in Pernambuco*, p. 299; Singer, *Desenvolvimento Econômico*, p. 102.
95. Cabral de Melo, *Norte Agrário*, pp. 175–176.
96. Ibid.; McCall to Department of State, Rio de Janeiro, Nov. 1887, *USRC*, XXIV, no. 86 (Nov. 1887): 235.
97. Bahia, Secretaria da Agricultura, *Relatório Apresentado ao Dr. Governador do Estado da Bahia pelo*

third of Brazil's refined sugar, but the traditional *engenho*, inefficient but with low expenditure, remained important until after 1930.[98]

The exchange crisis and recovery

Although the *usina* would eventually modernize Brazil's sugar industry, it would not do so until well into the twentieth century. Production processes remained little changed while prices continued their post-1872 fall. Fortunately, the low exchange rate for Brazilian currency mitigated their impact. In 1887 the Agriculture Auxiliary Society of Pernambuco credited the survival of Brazil's sugar industry since the early 1860s to the exchange rate usually having been below par.[99] However, financial orthodoxy demanded that the *mil-reis* be maintained at par. This was the policy of Conservative governments during the last three years of the Empire, a policy made easier by high coffee export revenues, which brought in foreign exchange. From 1886 on, the *mil-reis* made a rapid climb in unfortunate conjunction with a steep plunge in sugar prices, which reached an all-time low in 1886–1887. The combination of high exchange rate and low price squeezed virtually all profit from the sugar industry.

The crisis gave birth in February 1887 to a new business interest group: the Center for Sugar Industry and Commerce. Founded by leading Rio de Janeiro sugar factors, it invited to membership planters and in fact any profession connected with sugar production. The circular announcing its creation sounded the tocsin: "The growing of sugar cane and the products that come from it are presently undergoing a general crisis, which threatens to annihilate this ancient industry."[100] Other reasons for the foundation of the center included the impending abolition of slavery, the examples of effective interest group activity provided by Rio's Center for Coffee Agriculture and Commerce and by a Russian sugar industry group, and probably the disinclination of the coffee-oriented Commercial Association of Rio de Janeiro to act as a spokesman for sugar interests.[101]

Engenheiro Civil José Antônio Costa, Secretário da Agricultura, Indústria, Viação e Obras Públicas no Ano de 1896 (Salvador: Correio de Notícias, 1897), p. 12.

98. Robert M. Levine, *Pernambuco in the Brazilian Federation, 1889–1937* (Stanford, Calif.: Stanford University Press, 1978), p. 29; Perruci, *República das Usinas*, pp. 114, 126.

99. Agriculture Auxiliary Society of Pernambuco to Center for Sugar Industry and Commerce, Recife, June 13, 1887, in Henri Raffard, *O Centro da Indústria e Comércio de Açúcar no Rio de Janeiro* (Rio de Janeiro: Brasil, 1892), p. 23.

100. Center for Sugar Industry and Commerce to Imperial Institute of Agriculture of Rio de Janeiro, Rio de Janeiro, March 8, 1887, *Revista Agrícola*, 18 (1887): 99, 102.

101. Centro da Indústria e Comércio de Açúcar, *Crise do Açúcar: Representação e Memorial Apresentados ao Corpo Legislativo da Nação Brasileira pelo Centro da Indústria e Comércio de Açúcar do Rio de Janeiro* (Rio de Janeiro: Imprensa Nacional, 1887), pp. 17, 24.

The Center for Sugar Industry and Commerce quickly received numerous pledges of cooperation and support. They came not only from the commercial associations of Bahia and Pernambuco, heretofore considered the chief spokesmen for the sugar industry, but from the Minister of Agriculture, nine presidents of sugar-producing provinces, and numerous city councils located in sugar-growing areas.[102] The center saw the crisis as stemming from loss of overseas markets to subsidized sugar beets and to Cuban and Puerto Rican sugar cane. To make Brazil competitive it advocated abolition of export duties on sugar, lower railway freights, government premiums for production and exportation, expositions of cane products in Rio de Janeiro and abroad, special favors for mills established without government aid (planter-owned mills), reciprocal trade treaties, and establishment of agricultural laboratories and schools.[103]

For roughly three years the Center for Sugar Industry and Commerce pursued its program with energy and considerable success. It succeeded in lowering sugar freights on government-owned railways, staged an exhibition of sugar products in Rio de Janeiro, and was particularly active in promoting scientific improvement of Brazilian sugar by analyzing diverse sugar types, experimenting with new varieties of cane, and surveying Brazilian growing and processing methods.[104] But the center could not withstand prosperity. After 1890 it lapsed into dormancy. The reasons appear to have been a temporary rise in sugar prices (nearly double the 1886–1887 nadir) and a rapid drop in the value of the *mil-reis*. By 1892 the exchange rate was less than half its 1889 level. This combination induced near-euphoria among sugar producers and even temporarily revived the prosperity of such a long-depressed area as Pernambuco.[105]

By the mid-1890s it became evident that the Center for Sugar Industry and Commerce had quit too soon. Its drive to improve the quality of Brazilian sugar and mobilize various types of government aid had not continued long enough to have much permanent effect. In 1895–1897 prices dipped, then recovered, but after 1900 sugar exportation was again caught in the vise of falling prices and a rising exchange rate. By then it mattered little, because foreign markets had largely vanished.

The last nineteenth-century intervention by business interest groups in sugar production was an attempt by the Commercial Association and Commercial Agricultural Association of Pernambuco, supported by the state governor, to manipulate the now-dominant domestic market. In 1896, they urged planters and mills to limit production of fine-quality

102. Ibid., p. 6; Raffard, *O Centro*, pp. 16–21.
103. Centro da Indústria e Comércio de Açúcar, *Crise do Açúcar*, pp. 5, 21–31; McCall to Department of State, Rio de Janeiro, Nov., 1887, *USRC*, XXIV, no. 86 (Nov. 1887): 233–234.
104. Raffard, *O Centro*, pp. 14–15, 77–78, 97–120.
105. Great Britain, Foreign Office, *Diplomatic and Consular Reports*, no. 1547 (1895): 2–3.

white sugar for the first sixty days of harvest in favor of low-quality sugar, more easily marketed abroad during this period.[106] This would force domestic prices to rise. The scheme failed because producers in the Brazilian Southeast filled the gap and reaped the benefit of higher prices. The two Pernambuco business interest groups tried it again in 1901, with the same result.[107]

Brazil's sugar industry entered the twentieth century with dismal prospects. International prices remained low, and only a small proportion of the nation's production could be exported. By the period 1901–1905 sugar provided but 1.6 percent of Brazils export revenue.[108] Only the domestic market remained to keep the industry afloat.

The bellwether – coffee

The history of coffee as an export during the nineteenth century was in happy contrast to that of sugar and cotton. In the 1830s coffee became Brazil's leading export, constituting by the last two decades of the century more than sixty percent of Brazilian export value.[109] Sheer volume of exportation rose dramatically from an average two and one-half million bags in 1857–1860 to nine and one-half by 1897–1900.[110] During most of that period, Brazil was producing roughly half the world's coffee. Perhaps most important, export revenues also rose, forming three distinct, increasingly higher levels in 1858–1872, 1872–1888, and 1888–1905.[111] Fortunately, coffee prices were little influenced by the early 1870s to mid-1890s depression that damaged other international commodities.[112] Coffee benefited from growing demand in its major markets, especially the United States. As an export, its main weakness was the inability of production to respond quickly to changes in price. Coffee trees only begin to bear in quantity five years after planting. The five-year lag between planting and maturity meant danger of overproduction when the market was weak. Luckily, such periods often corresponded with those of low exchange rate, thus mitigating the effect of low price.

106. Minutes, meetings of Sept. 5 and Sept. 30, 1896, Livro de Atas da ACAP 1895–1903, AACP, pp. 15, 17–18.
107. Minutes, meeting of Aug. 26, 1901, Livro de Atas da ACAP, 1895–1903, AACP, p. 66; Eisenberg, *Sugar in Pernambuco*, p. 26;
108. Eisenberg, *Sugar in Pernambuco*, p. 10.
109. José Ribeiro de Araújo Filho, "O Café, Riqueza Paulista," *Boletim Paulista de Geografia*, 23 (July 1956): 81.
110. Antônio Delfim Netto, "Foundations for the Analysis of Brazilian Coffee Problems," in *Essays on Coffee and Economic Development*, ed. Carlos Manuel Peláez (Rio de Janeiro: Instituto Brasileiro do Café, 1973), p. 46.
111. Ibid., p. 62.
112. W. Arthur Lewis, *Growth and Fluctuations, 1870–1913* (London: George Allen & Unwin, 1978), p. 72.

In contrast to sugar and cotton, then, the efforts of business interest groups on behalf of coffee were less often a response to crisis. On the other hand, the position of coffee in Brazil's economy made its welfare of immense importance. Six nineteenth-century interest groups were the product of coffee: the commercial associations of Rio de Janeiro, Santos, and São Paulo, and the Center for Coffee Agriculture and Commerce, the Commercial and Agricultural Association of São Paulo (created in 1884, but lasting less than two years), and the Commercial Center of Rio de Janeiro. The policies of these groups would be influenced not only by concern for coffee prosperity, but by occasional conflict between exporters and factors and by rivalry between the world's two leading coffee ports, Rio de Janeiro and Santos.

Coffee exportation encountered two major crises. The first occurred in the early 1880s and was the more painful for following nearly a decade of record high prices. By 1882–1883, average price had dropped nearly sixty percent from its 1879–1880 level.[113] However, an exchange rate that remained low until 1887 and vastly increased production kept coffee export revenue in *mil-reis* rising. High revenue meant that the crisis did not bear heavily on exporters, but for planters and factors it produced deep anxiety. Planters were not only caught between low market prices and high expenses, but threatened with the loss of their labor force by rising support for abolition. Coffee factors, as chief creditors of planters, also faced ruin if the latter went under. The early 1880s witnessed the proliferation, encouraged by the factor-dominated Center for Coffee Agriculture and Commerce (founded in 1880), of planter societies and clubs in the coffee zone, organized to combat abolition and promote government aid for agriculture.

Recovery from the crisis of the early 1880s was decisive and lucrative. A combination of smaller harvests and growing demand brought prices in 1886–1887 to eighty percent above their 1882–1883 low.[114] The situation got even better when the coming of the Republic in 1889 brought a steep fall in the exchange rate, greatly increasing the remuneration of the export sector. The Commercial Association of Santos boasted in 1891: "It would be difficult to encounter a business community in such a state of joy and prosperity as ours finds itself in – for two years now."[115] In this euphoric atmosphere, the Center for Coffee Agriculture and Commerce and the planter societies and clubs lapsed into dormancy. Exchange rate depreciation continued while prices remained strong. By 1895–1896 the average price of coffee in *mil-reis* was more than twice what it had been in

---

113. Brazil, Instituto Brasileiro de Geografia e Estatística, *Anuário, 1939–40*, p. 1378.
114. Associação Comercial de Santos, *Relatório de 1903*, Anexo no. 9, unpaginated; Great Britain, Foreign Office, *Diplomatic and Consular Reports*, no. 168 (1886): 1.
115. *Relatório de 1891*, p. 6.

the recovery harvest year of 1886–1887.[116] Coffee revenues, even in hard currency, reached their nineteenth-century peak in 1895.[117] The Commercial Association of Santos noted that year: "At present, it may be affirmed, everyone who comes to the State of São Paulo to do something has only one idea: to dedicate himself to anything that has to do with coffee."[118]

The flush times ended emphatically with the second coffee crisis. In 1896 prices began a steep drop, one that not even a low exchange rate could soften. After 1897, export revenue also fell; for the first time expanded volume did not compensate for price decline. Coffee supply had overtaken demand, also for the first time.[119] Edward Greene, a well-known British exporter, complained in 1898 that it was now "next to impossible" to make money.[120] The squeeze on profits led export firms, including Greene's, to try to cut costs by purchasing coffee directly from planters, thus eliminating the factor.[121] In 1898 the government took drastic measures to strengthen the exchange rate, and coffee prices in *milreis* soon fell to little over one-third of their previous high. The worsening situation would lead to the first large-scale intervention of the government in the export marketplace, the 1906 coffee valorization.[122]

The coffee industry clearly had problems, but technological backwardness was not a major one. Although coffee growing still relied on the hoe, preparation had been modernized.[123] By the 1880s Brazilian coffee, in the words of a contemporary expert, had "on the whole acquired a better and well-deserved reputation, the result of careful preparation by machinery."[124] Only in the case of coffee from the Province of Bahia, exported in relatively small quantity, did careless preparation lower international prices and threaten markets. Business interest groups occasionally evaluated coffee processing machines as a service to their inventors, but saw no

116. Associação Comercial de Santos, *Relatório de 1903*, Anexo no. 9, unpaginated.
117. Associação Comercial do Rio de Janeiro, *Relatório de 1901*, p. 104.
118. *Relatório de 1895*, p. 18.
119. Edgard Carone, *A República Velha (Instituições e Classes Sociais)* (São Paulo: Difusão Européia do Livro, 1970), pp. 34–35; Araújo Filho, "Café, Riqueza," 125.
120. Edward Greene to John Gordon, Rio de Janeiro, Santos, Oct. 22, 1898, "Private Copy Book, E. Greene," Edward Johnston & Co., LABA, UCLL, p. 187.
121. Edward Greene to Charles Edward Johnston, London, Santos, Aug. 30, 1897, and to Reginald E. Johnston, London, Santos, Dec. 19, 1898, ibid., pp. 152, 202.
122. Carlos Manuel Peláez, "Uma Análise Econômica da História do Café Brasileiro," in *Economia Brasileira: Uma Visão Histórica* ed. Paulo Neuhaus (Rio de Janeiro: Campus, 1980), p. 345. For valorization itself, see Thomas Holloway, *The Brazilian Coffee Valorization of 1906: Regional Politics and Economic Dependence* (Madison, Wis.: Department of History, University of Wisconsin, 1975).
123. Stanley J. Stein, *Vassouras: A Brazilian Coffee County, 1850–1900* (Cambridge, Mass.: Harvard University Press, 1957), pp. 48–50, 214–216.
124. C. F. Van Delden Laërne, *Brazil and Java: Report on Coffee Culture in America, Asia, and Africa* (London: W. H. Allen, 1885), p. 520.

urgent need to push modernization. Ironically, despite the general excellence of Brazilian coffee, much continued to be sold as "Java" or "Mocha," a legacy of its early reputation as inferior.

Business interest groups helped raise and maintain the quality of Brazilian coffee by imposing standards. The Commercial Association of Rio de Janeiro, as part of a drive to convert Brazil to the metric system, established the sixty-kilogram bag as standard for coffee in meetings with exporters, factors, and sackers in 1872–1873.[125] The sixty-kilo bag was subsequently adopted world-wide. In 1885 the Commercial Association of Santos, aroused by complaints from overseas buyers, began to campaign for improvement of the bagging itself. Noting that coffee tended to absorb the odor of whatever it came in contact with, exporters urged that factors not ship it in old and dirty bags.[126] Resolutions supporting these measures were passed in the association's general assembly, but factors complied with reluctance. They cited instances in which good cotton bags for shipment had been loaned to planters, only to have the bags, with the names of factor firms on them, wind up as clothing for slaves![127] Finally, in 1894 the Commercial Association of Santos organized the replacement of burlap, easily torn or chewed by rodents, by cotton sacking, arranging an agreement between factors and exporters by which the latter would absorb part of the extra expense.[128] The association also canvassed Brazilian cotton textile manufacturers for samples and prices and campaigned for a reduction of tariffs on cotton bagging.[129]

More controversial was the establishment of quality norms. Careless or imprecise classification had been blamed for damaging the early reputation of Brazilian coffee. In 1883, following a harvest in which poor quality due to overplanting allegedly reduced prices, the Commercial Association of Rio de Janeiro faced organizing standard coffee types. Many merchants were quite willing to let sleeping dogs lie. Voted down by the Board of Directors and by a committee of major coffee exporters, the organizing of standard types was undertaken only after being twice approved by association membership in general assembly.[130] Even then coffee brokers (*corretores*), who served as middlemen between factor and exporter, refused to take part.[131] Nevertheless, the association sent samples of its standard

125. *O Jornal* (Rio de Janeiro), Oct. 15, 1927, "Quarta Seção," p. 6.
126. *Diário de Santos,* Dec. 11, 1885, "Seção Comercial," p. 2; Associação Comercial de Santos, *Relatório de 1887,* pp. 10–11.
127. Associação Comercial de Santos, *Relatório de 1887,* Anexo no. 22, pp. 75–76; *Diário de Santos,* Dec. 11, 1885, "Seção Comercial," p. 2.
128. Minutes, meeting of July 9, 1894, Livro de Atas, 1874–1894, AACS, pp. 192–193.
129. Associação Comercial de Santos, *Relatório de 1900,* pp. 9–10, 49–50.
130. Minutes, meetings of April 3, April 12 and April 21, Livro de Atas, 1881–1890, AACRJ, pp. 76–81.
131. Associação Comercial do Rio de Janeiro, *Relatório de 1882–1883,* pp. 26–31.

types to all major coffee markets and did so again in 1884, this time with the cooperation of the brokers. The association's standards eventually became binding.[132] Customs officials then applied Rio standards to Santos coffee for tax purposes, much to the annoyance of the latter's merchants, who claimed Santos types were generally superior in quality. In 1890 the Commercial Association of Santos organized its own quality standards.[133] Similarly, in 1894 the Commercial Association of Bahia brought together all local coffee merchants to set standards, classify Bahian coffee by place of origin, and establish price gradations.[134]

Since the quality of Brazilian coffee was not a major issue, most business interest group activity on its behalf was to ensure the survival of its planters. This, of course, also ensured that of factors, their chief creditors. The best way to help planters survive was to cut the costs of coffee exportation. In the early 1880s there were twenty-three separate items of expense, roughly half of which were charged to the planter, in exporting a bag of coffee from Rio de Janeiro.[135] In 1882 the Commercial Association of Santos estimated that average charges, commissions, taxes, and freight to Santos totaled roughly forty percent of the export price. That association also calculated that the average planter, even with low prices, could make a profit of eight percent. Unfortunately, it noted, most planters were paying ten to twelve percent interest on capital.[136] Without government aid they faced ruin. Business interest groups thus worked to cheapen agricultural credit, to lower railway freights on coffee and improve service, and to reduce or eliminate taxes on exportation. They also tried to ensure abundant plantation labor and to expand foreign markets for coffee. Unlike the case with sugar and cotton it was in these areas, rather than modernization of technology, that most business interest activity took place.

Since coffee's viability as an export was rarely questioned, it is not surprising that business interest groups in the impoverished Northeast would try to expand cultivation in their own provinces. From 1867 the Commercial Association of Ceará worked to increase that province's small-scale production by assembling quality samples as models for growers and by distributing planting and processing information. The effort ultimately helped enlarge Ceará's exportation several fold.[137] The Commer-

---

132. Associação Comercial do Rio de Janeiro, *Relatório de 1884–1885*, p. 33.

133. Minutes, meeting of Aug. 23, 1890, Livro de Atas, 1874–1894, AACS, pp. 142–143.

134. Minutes, meeting of Aug. 20, 1894, Livro 6 de Atas, AACB, pp. 119–120.

135. Van Delden Laërne, *Brazil and Java*, pp. 248–250. Using his figures, a modern scholar has calculated the average total marketing cost to planters shipping through Rio de Janeiro at roughly twenty-three percent. Sweigart, "Coffee Factors," pp. 47, 62.

136. *Relatório de 1882*, pp. 14–16.

137. Associação Comercial do Ceará, *Relatório da Associação Comercial do Ceará, 1867* (Fortaleza: Cearense, 1867), pp. 5–6; Van Delden Laërne, *Brazil and Java*, p. 388.

cial Association of Pernambuco, located in a province where coffee growing was practically nil, saw its exportation as a means of compensating for
the decline of sugar and cotton. Stimulated by a visionary landowner and
by one of its directors, it began in 1875 to display coffee samples and to
publish and distribute information on production methods (including a
booklet by the director).[138] The following year it used modern publicity
techniques to spread the message of economic redemption through coffee.
The association arranged to greet the mule train bringing the first cargo of
coffee from the interior with massed bands, prizes, flowers, hymns, fire-
works, speeches by politicians, and thousands of spectators. "It was sub-
lime to witness!" enthused the association's official description.[139] Coffee
tree plantings vastly increased, and in 1878–1879 the Commercial Agricultural Association and Agriculture Auxiliary Society of Pernambuco
combined with Brazil's Minister of Agriculture to acquire and distribute
coffee seed from Liberia.[140] All was in vain. In the late 1880s Pernambuco
was still importing coffee from the Southeast, perhaps because the local
product tasted "base and harsh."[141] Even the most herculean of efforts
could not overcome handicaps of climate or soil.

Other crops – missed opportunities

Business interest groups made little effort to modernize the technology,
upgrade the quality, or expand the growing of products other than Brazil's
traditional staples – sugar, cotton, and coffee. This probably was a mistake. The Commercial Association of Bahia made a limited effort to
enhance the quality of Bahian tobacco, an important export since colonial
times. In 1858 it moved to halt the falsification of tares and the mixing of
inferior with fine quality tobacco by planters and rejected a petition that
tobacco in the hands of exporters be exempted from examination by
customs.[142] But the interest of the association in tobacco soon waned. In
1871 it voted down a proposal to set up its own private tobacco inspection
service and gave the commodity little attention thereafter.[143] Favored by
Bahian tobacco's somewhat unique taste and by good growing conditions,
exportation climbed steadily, more than doubling in tonnage between

138. Minutes, meeting of Dec. 21, 1875, Livro 4 de Atas, AACP, p. 51; Associação Comercial de
  Pernambuco, *Descrição dos Festejos Promovidos pela Associação Comercial Beneficente para Receber o
  Comboio de Café Vindo da Vila do Bonito* (Recife: Jornal do Recife, 1876), p. 23.
139. Associação Comercial de Pernambuco, *Descrição dos Festejos*, p. 1.
140. Sociedade Auxiliadora da Agricultura de Penambuco, *Relatório de 1878*, pp. 63–64; Minutes,
  meeting of May 12, 1879, Livro de Atas da ACAP, 1877–1892, AACP, p. 25.
141. "Coffee in South America," *USRC*, XXVIII, no. 98 (Oct. 1888): 14; Carlos Pinheiro da
  Fonseca, *O Ciclo do Café* (Rio de Janeiro: Departamento Nacional do Café, 1934), p. 92.
142. Minutes, meetings of June 28, July 1, and Oct. 15, 1858, Livro 2 de Atas, AACB, pp. 130–
  131, 137.
143. Minutes, meeting of Nov. 30, 1871, Livro 4 de Atas, AACB, p. 105.

1865–1866 and 1897.[144] But cultivation and selection of leaf remained extremely primitive.

The Commercial Association of Bahia also paid little attention to two other promising local exports that could have profited from an upgrading of quality. In the early nineteenth century Bahian coffee was considered by many to be better than that of Rio de Janeiro, and its "inherent superior flavor" was widely acknowledged.[145] Its low market price came from careless preparation and drying. Shipments full of husks, dust, and broken bean left an unclean taste in the mouths of drinkers.[146] Cacao exportation expanded from 103,105 kilos in 1840 to 3,502,478 in 1890, and it became the state's leading source of revenue during the first decade of the Republic.[147] Such growth reflected superb natural conditions, not careful cultivation. Ignored by the state as a partial consequence of its neglect by the Commercial Association, cacao exportation suffered from poor quality and lack of transportation facilities.[148] The Commercial Association of Bahia's disdain for tobacco, coffee, and cacao may have at least partially reflected the social status and location of their growers. Tobacco was grown by small farmers, most of them descended from slaves, coffee by small planters and squatters of the interior, and cacao by a new group of planters in a geographically detached area.[149]

Another group to neglect opportunity was the Commercial Association of Pará, chief representative of the rubber industry. During the nineteenth century, Brazil was easily the world's main source of rubber, then only gathered from the wild. The invention of vulcanization in 1839 and the development of new uses, including tires, took demand to ever-increasing heights. By 1899 rubber provided twenty-four percent of Brazil's export revenue.[150] Its fall was more sudden and devastating than that of any other Brazilian export. In 1900 plantation rubber from Southeast Asia, cheaper than the gathered Amazon variety, began to appear in quantity in

144. Bahia, Diretoria do Serviço de Estatística do Estado, *Anuário Estatístico da Bahia*, 1923 (Salvador: Imprensa Oficial do Estado, 1924), p. 37.
145. Parkinson to Foreign Office, Salvador, Jan. 31, 1834, PRO/FO 13/113, fl. 169; Manuel Jesuino Ferreira, *A Província da Bahia, Apontamentos* (Rio de Janeiro: Tipografia Nacional, 1875), p. 82; Morgan to Foreign Office, Salvador, April 8, 1859, PRO/FO 13/374, fl. 257.
146. Morgan to Foreign Office, Salvador, April 8, 1859, PRO/FO 13/374, fl. 257.
147. Joaquim Wanderley de Araújo Pinho, "A Cultura do Cacaoeiro na Bahia," in *Diário Oficial: Edição Especial do Centenário*, 8 (July 2, 1923): 234; Joaquim da Silva Tavares, *O Comércio do Cacau, Particularmente no Estado da Bahia* (Salvador: By the Author, 1913), pp. 15–17.
148. Rómulo Almeida, *Traços da História Econômica da Bahia no Ultimo Sêculo e Meio* (Salvador: Instituto de Economia e Finanças da Bahia, 1951), pp. 9–10.
149. Ibid., pp. 9–11; "Cultivation of, and Trade in, Coffee in Central and South America," *USRC*, XXVIII, no. 98 (Oct. 1888): 14; Eugene W. Ridings, "The Bahian Commercial Association, 1840–1889: A Pressure Group in an Underdeveloped Area" (Ph.D. Diss., University of Florida, 1970), p. 244.
150. Brazil, Instituto Brasileiro de Geografia e Estatística, *Anuário*, 1939–40, p. 1379.

world markets; in 1910 rubber prices broke drastically and stayed low. By 1915 Asian plantations were producing two-thirds of the world's supply.[151] By 1920 Brazil's share of world rubber export was insignificant, and the economy of the Amazon region was stagnant.

A nineteenth-century visitor to the Amazon commented with little exaggeration that "the rubber industry is still in the primitive state it was received from the . . . Indians."[152] Gatherers used crude methods of tapping wild rubber that not only were wasteful but killed trees by the millions. They cured the rubber primitively over an open fire. By 1900 not only were many stands of rubber trees exhausted, but Brazilian rubber was notably inferior in quality to the new Asian rubber reaching the market.[153] Nevertheless, the Commercial Association of Pará showed little interest in improving gathering or processing techniques. Nor did it promote or even suggest a later undertaking to revive prosperity, the cultivation of rubber in plantations.[154]

An important part of agriculture neglected by all business interest groups was food production for domestic consumption. The groups seldom mentioned, much less encouraged, food growing. Economist Nathaniel Leff has pointed to the poor performance of the domestic agricultural sector as "the main reason for Brazil's slow overall economic development in the nineteenth century."[155] One reason Brazil's domestic agricultural sector was notably unproductive was because it increasingly yielded its best lands for the growing of export crops.[156] Food that could not be grown locally had to be imported or brought in from other parts of Brazil at high cost. Almost all export-producing areas had to bring in at least some basic foodstuffs, the most absurd extreme being the Amazon region, which freighted in virtually everything.

Business interest groups were more likely to obstruct than encourage domestic food production. Their membership ordinarily did not handle food grown and consumed locally, thus did not profit from it. Even

---

151. Barbara Weinstein, *The Amazon Rubber Boom, 1850–1920* (Stanford, Calif.: Stanford University Press, 1983), p. 219.

152. José Vieira Couto Magalhães, "Estado Atual da Extração e Comércio da Borracha na Província do Pará," *O Auxiliador da Indústria Nacional,* 6 (June 1865): 219.

153. Kennedy to Department of State, Belém, May 25, 1899, *USRC,* LXI, no. 228 (Sept. 1899): 31; Randolph R. Resor, "Rubber in Brazil: Dominance and Collapse, 1876–1945," *Business History Review,* 51 (Autumn 1977): 349.

154. The viability of this expedient is disputed by Warren Dean, who lays the failure of attempts to grow rubber on Brazilian plantations to the "South American Leaf Blight," spread by plantation conditions. *Brazil and the Struggle for Rubber: A Study in Environmental History* (New York: Cambridge University Press, 1987).

155. *Economic Structure and Change,* p. 227.

156. Sebastião Ferreira Soares, *Notas Estatísticas sôbre a Produção Agrícola e Carestia dos Gêneros Alimentícios no Império do Brasil* (Rio de Janeiro: J. Villeneuve, 1860), pp. 122–137; Buescu, *Evolução Econômica,* p. 137; Delfim Netto, "Foundations for Analysis," pp. 56–58.

more important, importing food, which may have comprised forty percent of total importation by the 1880s, and bringing it in from other parts of Brazil was a large-scale and lucrative enterprise.[157] Food importation was a large part of the export-import economy whose preservation and expansion were a major goal of commercial associations and factor groups.

The business interest groups of nineteenth-century Brazil shouldered the task of developing Brazilian export agriculture because it was fundamental to the economy and because there were no other agencies for the task. But their achievements were uneven. They helped raise and maintain the quality of Brazilian coffee, but were less successful in reviving the agriculture of the Northeast. Imposition of standards and private inspection improved sugar and cotton exportation, but much betterment was only temporary. Business interest groups helped introduce the *usina,* but its use would not become general until well into the twentieth century. In the late 1890s, knowledgeable observers could still describe cultivation in the Northeast as "rudimentary" and defined by "the entire absence of modern agricultural implements."[158] Despite improvement, the Brazilian Northeast slipped further behind its rivals. In 1858 it took 114 days of labor to produce a ton of sugar in the Northeast and 111 days in Cuba. In 1908 the respective days were fifty-three in the Northeast and thirteen in Cuba.[159] But planters, not business interest groups, must take most of the blame for the primitiveness of Northeastern agriculture. Planter inertia and lack of receptivity to new technology, amply recorded by contemporaries and historians alike, were too much to overcome.

More blameworthy for business interest groups were the missed opportunities to improve or spread the cultivation of other, less prominent, exports. Brazil's export base could have been diversified and its agricultural development enhanced. Business interest groups were apparently complacent when prosperity continued or influenced by the social status of the export producers. Or perhaps they simply lacked imagination. As for the encouragement of domestic food production, that policy seems precluded by the nature of nineteenth-century Brazil's economy and the role of business interest members in it. It would have been too much to expect men who lived from overseas trade to encourage a type of agriculture that, at least in the short run, tended to diminish it. The task of

---

157. Wilson Cano, *Raizes da Concentração Industrial em Saõ Paulo* (Rio de Janeiro, São Paulo: DIFEL, 1977), pp. 57–58. This proportion declined to thirty percent in 1901–1920.
158. Henri Diamanti, "Nota sôbre a Indústria Açucareira no Brasil [1898]," trans. Gadiel Perruci, in Perruci, *República das Usinas,* p. 222; Furniss to Department of State, Salvador, Jan. 17, 1900, *USRC,* LXIII, no. 236 (May 1900): 7–8.
159. Denslow, "Northeastern Brazil and Cuba," p. 58.

realizing the full potential of Brazilian agriculture was perhaps too herculean for the energy and inventiveness of Brazil's business elite.

Marketing

Business interest groups also worked to develop Brazilian agriculture by marketing its products. Business interest group marketing of exports, like many other group activities, answered a need not otherwise satisfied. Marketing was not a function of government in the nineteenth century, and most Brazilian agricultural interest groups, to whom the task more properly belonged, were lethargic or short-lived. A popular means of marketing in the second half of the nineteenth century was to display products at special expositions or international fairs. Publicity and wide renown came to those products considered outstanding and awarded medals or prizes.

Business interest groups were well aware of the significance of international expositions or fairs for the marketing of Brazilian exports. They usually took over, often at the request of government, the task of gathering, preparing, and shipping exhibits of local products. Group leaders occasionally accompanied these exhibits as official delegates. Since national and provincial governments rarely offered aid, except for paying shipping fees, participation could be expensive as well as time-consuming. Expositions and fairs were frequent. The Commercial Association and Commercial Agricultural Association of Pernambuco between them took part in seven in Brazil and abroad from 1881 to 1890.[160] It is indicative of the leanings of commercial associations and factor groups that of the dozens of exhibits they prepared, only one, by the Commercial Association of São Paulo, was for an industrial exposition, arranged in Rio de Janeiro in 1895 by the government.[161] None participated in the industrial expositions staged in Rio by the Industrial Association in 1881 and the Engineering Club in 1900.

If other opportunities were lacking, business interest groups could stage their own expositions. This was particularly costly in time and money, although government usually provided some support, and only eight business interest groups tried it.[162] By far the most active was the

160. Livros 5 and 6 de Atas, AACP; Livro de Atas da ACAP, 1877–1892, AACP.
161. Associação Comercial de São Paulo, *Relatório da Associação Comercial de São Paulo, Ano de 1895* (São Paulo: Industrial, 1896), pp. 40–41.
162. In addition to the Commercial Association of São Paulo, the Center for Coffee Agriculture and Commerce, the Industrial Association, and the Engineering Club, they were the Commercial and Agricultural Association of São Paulo (1885), the Center for Sugar Industry and Commerce (1889), and the commercial associations of Maranhão (1883) and Pernambuco (1885). Ibid., p. 42; Raffard, *O Centro*, pp. 35–45; Associação Industrial, *Relatório Apresentado à Assembléia Geral*

Center for Coffee Agriculture and Commerce. More than simply an anti-abolition organization, as sometimes pictured, it was spurred by the coffee crisis of the early 1880s to expand overseas markets through staging expositions of Brazilian coffee. The Center's first exposition, in Rio de Janeiro in 1881, indicated that it would enjoy unusually wide government and private support. The royal family attended the exposition and Brazilian diplomatic representatives abroad publicized it. The government provided subsidies, free transportation and tax exemptions for exhibits, and reduced railroad passenger fares during the period of the event. The Center also mobilized the help of the Rio and Santos commercial associations, all willing planters, and the European and North American branches of foreign merchant houses.[163]

That was only a start. By 1885 the Center had organized two more expositions in Rio and claimed to have staged or participated in thirty-nine in foreign countries.[164] Three took place in Russia, where the Center also distributed free samples to military barracks, hospitals, asylums, and schools in an attempt to convert that huge nation of tea drinkers into consumers of coffee.[165] In its publicity, the Center portrayed coffee as a refresher and as an alternative to the evils of liquor. It also occasionally exhibited other Brazilian products. The Brazilian government subsidized most of the Center's staging of expositions or participation in them but, as its leaders complained, not all. Nor did the subsidies always cover expenses.[166]

How effective was the campaign of the Center for Coffee Agriculture and Commerce? Precise cause and effect are hard to gauge, but it is likely that it contributed to a rise in world coffee consumption recorded for the late 1880s.[167] It is also difficult to judge the worth of the frequent participation of other business interest groups in expositions and fairs. Such efforts probably expanded Brazilian overseas markets to some degree, and

da *Associação Industrial em Sessão de 16 de Junho de 1882 pela Diretoria da Mesma Associação* (Rio de Janeiro: G. Leuzinger & Filhos, 1882), pp. 66–75; Associação Comercial do Maranhão, *Exposição do Açúcar e Algodão Feita pela Associação Comercial do Maranhão, 1883* (São Luís: País, 1883); Associação Comercial de Pernambuco, *Relatório de 1885*, p. 18; Reginald Lloyd et al., *Twentieth Century Impressions of Brazil: Its History, People, Commerce, Industries, and Resources* (London: Lloyd's Greater Britain Publishing, 1913), p. 513.

163. Centro da Lavoura e Comércio do Café, *Breve Notícia sôbre a Primeira Exposição de Café do Brasil* (Rio de Janeiro: Moreira, Maximino, 1882), pp. 5–19, 51–52; Commercial Association of Rio de Janeiro to Commercial Association of Santos, Rio de Janeiro, Aug. 19, 1881, *Relatório da Associação Comercial de Santos de 1882*, pp. 49–50.

164. Center for Coffee Agriculture and Commerce to Baron Cotegipe, Rio de Janeiro, July 10, 1885, ABC, AIHGB, lata 90, doc. 19.

165. Ibid.; *O Auxiliador da Indústria Nacional*, 52 (May 1884): 104–105.

166. Center for Coffee Agriculture and Commerce to Baron Cotegipe, Rio de Janeiro, July 10, 1885, ABC, AIHGB, lata 90, doc. 19; Karl von Koseritz, *Imagens do Brasil* [1883], trans. Afonso Arinos de Melo Franco (São Paulo: Martins, 1943), pp. 182–183, 208.

167. Delfim Netto, "Foundations for the Analysis," p. 53.

in the case of the three industrial expositions held in Rio de Janeiro, undoubtedly helped implant in Brazilians themselves the desire for future industrialization.

Conflict within the export sector: exporters versus factors

Business interest groups also affected economic development by their central role in struggles between exporters and factors. Potential conflict between factor and exporter was implicit in their roles. A United States consul described the latter as "the natural business enemy" of the factor, "as he represents foreign interests who are desirous of buying as cheaply as possible, and he wishes to obtain a margin."[168] Contests between factors and exporters were usually touched off by export crises, and were bitter because fought not just for dominance and profits but, or so many thought, for sheer survival. Strife centered on exporters' relations with coffee and rubber factors; there was no serious conflict between exporters and sugar factors. It took place in public, as well as within the groups, violating the prized concepts of unity of membership and of the business community. Because most were foreigners, exporters tried to keep the strife inconspicuous. On the other hand, factors, much less alien in nationality, appealed to the public as defenders of Brazilian economic sovereignty. Such appeals, made by rubber factors in the 1880s and by coffee factors in the last five years of the century, combined with the public relations efforts of industrial interest groups helped to call attention to foreign domination of the nation's economy and to heighten Brazilian nationalism.

The likelihood of conflict between coffee factor and exporter was greater in Santos than in Rio de Janeiro. In Rio the factor sold plantation coffee to an intermediary, the sacker (*ensacador*) who sorted and rebagged it and sold it to exporters through a broker. In Santos the factor sold directly to the exporter, sometimes through the intermediary of a broker, sometimes not.[169] In Rio the broker worked for the exporter and could usually procure the exact number of bags he had been instructed to purchase. In Santos the broker worked for the factor, so that the exporter often had to buy in excess of his needs to get the quantity and quality desired.[170] This not only increased the potential for friction, but the temptation to try to eliminate the factor middleman.

168. Hill to Department of State, Santos, Jan. 11, 1898, *USRC*, LVII, no. 215 (Aug. 1898): 483.
169. McCall to Department of State, Santos, Dec. 1, 1887, *USRC*, XXVIII, no. 98 (Oct. 1888): 79; Afonso de Escragnolle Taunay, *História do Café no Brasil* (Rio de Janeiro: Departamento Nacional do Café, 1939–1943), VII: 67–68, 74–75.
170. Hill to Department of State, Santos, Jan. 11, 1898, *USRC*, LVII, no. 215 (Aug. 1898): 483–484.

In a contest with coffee factors, exporters had the advantage of numbers, that is, a smaller number of export houses controlled the bulk of exportation. Some ten firms, for example, shipped more than two-thirds of Santos's coffee during the last fifteen years of the century, and an average of seven firms exported roughly half of Rio de Janeiro's coffee in the period 1857–1888.[171] Although there were a number of giant coffee factor houses, economic power among factors was more diffuse. Between 1850 and 1890, Rio's coffee factor and sacker houses (some performed both functions) numbered roughly one hundred to two hundred.[172] It was much easier for exporters to combine forces effectively against factors. On the other hand, factors had the advantage of being perceived as native. Factorage was popularly considered the only branch of business left to Brazilians, although probably only about half the factors were natives. Coffee exporters, by contrast, were overwhelmingly foreign; Brazilian firms were few and shipped an insignificant proportion of total export.[173] The characterization by Gilberto Freyre of coffee exportation as "an economic activity dominated, oriented, and directed from its beginnings to its apogee principally by Brazilians" is quite wrong.[174] Any conflict between coffee factors and exporters was likely to be seen by the public as a struggle between Brazilians and foreigners.

Two minor disputes between coffee factors and exporters preceded the major conflict at century's end. The first came during the Commercial Association of Santos's 1885 campaign to improve the quality of bagging. The issue had arisen not only because old bagging harmed the taste of the coffee, but because factors were charging the price for new sacks while furnishing used ones. Noting that it was necessary to "proceed with caution in this matter in order to avoid serious conflict," association directors arranged a general assembly of membership that mandated fines for those selling coffee in old sacks.[175] The slow and reluctant acquiescence of factors, however, was more likely due to a concerted refusal of major export firms to accept old bagging than to the general assembly resolution.[176] In 1887, directors of the Commercial Association of Santos offered a table of regulations governing transactions between factors and exporters. The most important issue was legal responsibility for damages

171. *Diário de Santos*, Dec. 11, 1885, p. 2; Holloway, *Coffee Valorization*, p. 39; Sweigart, "Coffee Factors," p. 33.

172. Sweigart, "Coffee Factors," p. 31.

173. Robert Greenhill, "The Brazilian Coffee Trade," in *Business Imperialism, 1840–1930: An Inquiry Based on British Experience in Latin America*, ed. D. C. M. Platt (Oxford: Oxford University Press, 1977), p. 208; Holloway, *Coffee Valorization*, p. 39.

174. *Ordem e Progresso* (2d ed.; Rio de Janeiro: José Olympio, 1962), II: 441.

175. Minutes, meeting of Oct. 24, 1885, Livro de Atas, 1874–1894, AACS, p. 104; Associação Comercial de Santos, *Relatório de 1887*, Anexo 22, pp. 75–76.

176. *Diário de Santos*, Dec. 11, 1885, p. 2.

to coffee purchased by the exporter but not yet handed over by the factor.[177] Because of inability to summon a quorum for a general assembly, however, the regulations could neither be discussed nor ratified. Factors had learned to stay away from general assemblies that might vote against their interests, thus preventing a quorum. Not until 1890 were new regulations, which made concessions to factors, approved in general assembly.[178]

The major clash between factors and exporters occurred during the coffee crisis of the last five years of the century. The end of slavery had already weakened coffee factors, because planter demands for funds for salary and other new expenses strained their financial resources. They could no longer stockpile coffee to wait for a better price, but had to market it immediately. In 1895 a squeeze on exporters' profits began, sending eight Santos coffee firms into bankruptcy by the first quarter of 1896.[179] Several major houses started to send agents into the interior to buy coffee directly from planters, paying in advance for future shipment. As prices continued to fall, many large houses, including Edward Johnston & Co., set up permanent agencies in the interior. Its Santos manager, Edward Greene, spoke for most exporters when he declared: "Our hope for the future lies entirely in the interior business and unless we go on steadily developing it, we may as well shut up shop," adding, as would most, "Personally, I am heartily sick of shipping coffee at an everlasting loss."[180]

The reaction of coffee factors was to appeal to antiforeign sentiments and speak of conspiracy. In lectures at the Commercial Association of São Paulo and in interviews in 1897, prominent factor J. F. Lacerda accused United States export houses of conspiring to drive down coffee prices and of taking advantage of planters by purchasing directly from them.[181] A series of public meetings on the crisis was held that year at the Commercial Association of Rio de Janeiro, led by its acting president, factor Honório Ribeiro.[182] Denying that overproduction was a cause of low prices, factor spokesmen demanded the creation of an overall agency, ideally government-sponsored, to control coffee exportation. Their views found some echo in government. Minister of Finance Bernardino de Campos repeated many of their arguments before Congress. Significantly, however, he called merely for easier credit, better statistical services to

177. Associação Comercial de Santos, *Relatório de 1887*, pp. 13–15.
178. Associação Comercial de Santos, *Relatório de 1891*, pp. 20–21.
179. Greene to R. E. Johnston, London, Santos, March 23, 1896, Private Copy Book, E. Greene, Edward Johnston & Co., LABA, UCLL, p. 53.
180. Greene to John Gordon, Rio de Janeiro, Santos, July 18, 1899, Private Copy Book, E. Greene, Edward Johnston & Co., LABA, UCLL, pp. 321–322.
181. *Jornal do Comércio*, Sept. 6, 1897, p. 1; Hill to Department of State, Santos, Jan. 11, 1898, USRC, LVII, no. 215 (Aug. 1898): 498–501.
182. *Jornal do Comércio*, Sept. 6, 1897, "Folhetim," p. 1.

forecast price trends, and the creation of more and stronger native export houses, rather than a government-sponsored coffee export monopoly.[183] This was a blow to factor hopes. Without government aid such an organization would be extremely hard to establish.

As the coffee crisis deepened in 1898, a national measure to aid hard-pressed planters brought factors and exporters together temporarily in defense of mutual interests. It authorized the Santos Dock Company, then completing its reconstruction of Santos harbor (see Chapter 10), to open "General Warehouses" (*Armazens Gerais*), enabling planters to deal directly with exporters. For a small storage fee and sales commission, General Warehouses would hold the planter's coffee until he wished to sell and, demonstrating samples, vend it directly to the exporter. By promising to complete the circumvention already begun by exporters, General Warehouses threatened a definitive end to coffee factorage. Nor did it spare exporters. They would lose the extra profit made through payment in advance to planters and be forced to bid competitively for the latter's coffee. Coordinating its action with the Commercial Association of Santos, the Commercial Association of São Paulo called an open meeting to reinforce its views and then protested to its representatives in Congress, while the Santos group petitioned the President of Brazil.[184] Hypocritically, the Santos association attacked the "odious monopoly" of the General Warehouses plan for threatening to do to factors what its exporter members already had been doing for several years.

The campaign of the two commercial associations, backed by the state's leading newspapers, defeated the proposed law.[185] The idea of general warehouses persisted, however, eventually being regulated in 1903 in a form that gave no monopoly to the Santos Dock Company. Two warehousing operations organized by the Edward Johnston Company's Edward Greene arose in 1905–1906, received guaranteed interest on capital from the state government, and consolidated in 1909 into the Brazilian Warrant Company.[186] Meanwhile, continuing direct purchase from planters by export firms greatly cut the number of coffee factors in the State of São Paulo, although it did not eliminate them. A consequent demand for credit from other sources led to twice as many banks being established

---

183. *RMF, 1897*, pp. 14, 134–138.
184. Minutes, meeting of Dec. 20, 1898, Livro de Atas, 1894–1906, Arquivo da Associação Comercial de São Paulo, São Paulo, pp. 15–16; Associação Comercial de Santos, *Relatório de 1900*, Anexos 7 and 8, unpaginated; Minutes, meeting of Dec. 20, 1898, Livro de Atas, 1894–1904, AACS, pp. 39–40.
185. Minutes, meeting of Jan. 24, 1899, Livro de Atas, 1894–1904, AACS, p. 41; Hélio Lobo, *Docas de Santos: Suas Origens, Lutas, e Realizações* (Rio de Janeiro: Jornal do Comércio, 1936), p. 123.
186. Edward Johnston & Co., Rio de Janeiro, *Um Século de Café* (Rio de Janeiro: Edward Johnston & Co., 1942), p. 27; Love, *São Paulo*, p. 42.

there in 1896–1900 as in any previous five-year period.[187] In Rio the circumvention of factors by export firms had helped reduce them by 1900 to perhaps half their 1888 total.[188] Attacks on price manipulation by foreign interests, especially North American, multiplied, as did calls for a government-controlled export monopoly.

Significantly, the commercial associations of Rio de Janeiro, Santos, and São Paulo did not defend factor interests. Despite large factor membership, which had led the Rio and São Paulo organizations to lend their headquarters as meeting places for those attacking conspiracies by foreign buyers, the boards of all three were dominated by exporters and foreigners. Virtually the only comment on the crisis from the three organizations was an irritatingly bland statement from the Commercial Association of Santos in 1900, blaming no one and recommending only the flaccid remedies of more credit for planters and a reduction of coffee import duties by France and Italy.[189]

This absence of organizational support for factors led to the formation in June of 1897 of a new, large business interest group, the Commercial Center of Rio de Janeiro. Its rise also was fueled by the anger of members of the Commercial Association of Rio de Janeiro at its failure since 1892 to hold an election for Board of Directors. The Center's founders included many coffee factors formerly active in the Rio association. Backed by more than five hundred firms, the new organization declared its intention to be constituted mainly by "houses which represent middleman commerce" and promised to repair a "lack of unity" in Rio business.[190] At the same time it expressly disavowed any intention of being a rival to the Commercial Association. Although the Center dealt with matters of general interest to commerce, its major early move was to meet with President Campos Sales about "the present crisis" and to offer remedies for it.[191]

By early 1901 the Center was campaigning actively for creation of a government-sponsored coffee marketing monopoly. Spurred on by a special committee of factors, it presented to Campos Sales a detailed plan for a self-financing organization.[192] Like earlier spokesmen for factor interests, the Center denied that supply and demand was affecting prices, asserted that exporters were only dealing directly with planters in order to

187. José de Souza Martins, *Empresário e Emprêsa na Biografia do Conde Matarazzo* (Rio de Janeiro: Instituto de Ciências Sociais, 1967), p. 74.
188. Sweigart, "Coffee Factors," p. 221.
189. *Relatório de 1900*, p. 11.
190. *Jornal do Comércio*, June 9, 1897, p. 1; Minutes, general assembly of June 12, 1897, Livro de Atas, Centro Comercial do Rio de Janeiro, AACRJ, p. 3.
191. Minutes, meeting of July 22, 1898, Livro de Atas, Centro Comercial, AACRJ, p. 26.
192. Commercial Center of Rio de Janeiro to President Campos Sales, Rio de Janeiro, Feb. 6, 1901, *Relatório das Atas da Terceira Direção, Desde 17 de Julho de 1900 a 17 de Julho de 1901* (Porto: Comércio do Porto, 1901), pp. 218–223.

cheat them, and accused foreign export firms of a vast conspiracy to defraud Brazilians.[193] The Center's demands had little effect, perhaps because only the obscure Commercial Association of Campos backed them. Late in 1901, a new group, including men who had helped found the Commercial Center, seized control of the Commercial Association of Rio de Janeiro.[194] The return of the Rio association to its membership and the continued frustration of the Commercial Center's demand for government management of coffee exportation weakened the latter's reasons for existence. In 1905, recommending that its remaining members join the Commercial Association, it voted its own dissolution.[195]

The popularization of the idea of government control of marketing no doubt aided the enactment of the Coffee Valorization plan in 1906. Coffee exporters did not find it objectionable, since it was not aimed at them. The three original commercial associations representing coffee, together with the recently created Commercial Association of Minas Gerais, participated in the 1906 and subsequent valorization programs. In the first they promoted sales of surplus stock in Europe and in a second in 1917 advised government on the amount and timing of purchase. In the 1925 program, group members were appointed to the provincial boards which oversaw its application in São Paulo and Minas Gerais.[196]

Conflict in the Amazon: exporters versus aviadores

A second major clash between exporters and factors took place in the Amazon region. The struggle differed from that in the coffee area in that the issue was profit margins, not circumvention, and the comparative power of *aviadores,* rubber factors, was much greater. They also were able to mandate the support of the region's principal business interest group, the Commercial Association of Pará. The outcome of the struggle was similar, however, in that the *aviadores* could not wrest permanent advantage from powerfully backed exporters.

The *aviador* was a more dominant figure than the coffee factor. The *Aviador* received rubber from the owners of groves (*seringueiros*) for sale to exporters, usually on commission, and contracted with import houses for

193. Commercial Center of Rio de Janeiro to President Campos Sales, Rio de Janeiro, Jan. 22, 1901, ibid., pp. 67–71, 81–83, 215–216.
194. Júlio Cesar de Oliveira and João Vieira da Silva Borges, for example, served on both the association's new directorate and the first directorate of the Commercial Center. *Jornal do Brasil* (Rio de Janeiro), June 14, 1897, p. 3; Associação Comercial do Rio de Janeiro, *Relatório de 1902*, p. 15.
195. Minutes, meeting of Oct. 13, 1905, Livro de Atas, 1902–1906, AACRJ, p. 173.
196. Steven Topik, "The Old Republic," in *Modern Brazil: Elites and Masses in Historical Perspective*, eds. Michael L. Conniff and Frank D. McCann (Lincoln, Neb.: University of Nebraska Press, 1989), p. 98.

goods for grove owners, roving peddlers, or small-town merchants. He customarily extended long-term credit to these customers.[197] *Aviadores* also played a major role in sending out agents with tools, goods, and manpower to open up new rubber districts or to set up commercial contacts with those beginning to develop. Exporters, as in the coffee trade, were few and foreign. In 1884 they were "divided between, not without struggle, a dozen houses, among which are counted five of the first order."[198] *Aviadores* were also mostly foreign, in this case Portuguese, but with a sizable Brazilian minority in their ranks. The potential for friction between *aviador* and exporter was great. Despite the strength of several large *aviador* houses, prices were largely determined by powerful overseas buyers in London and New York.[199] Adding to the price squeeze were export taxes, maintained at the high level of twenty-two percent since 1868.

The idea of some sort of combination to force rubber prices higher was natural, since the Amazon region produced the vast bulk of the world's raw rubber. Attempts to control the market were all associated with a Portuguese merchant, João Caetano Gonçalves Vianna, awarded the Portuguese title Baron Gondoriz. In 1877–1879 he attempted to corner the rubber market by purchasing through private firms, financed by loans from Brazilian banks. The venture collapsed when the banks recalled their loans.[200] Baron Gondoriz then organized a shareholding corporation of *aviadores*, the Commercial Union Company (*Companhia União Comercial*) in 1883. The Commercial Association of Pará gave it a ringing endorsement, asserting that it would reverse currently declining prices and foil the "machinations of the American bears," New York buyers allegedly in collusion to keep rubber prices low.[201] Either because the company was unable to impose an unprecedented high price after cornering two-thirds of the rubber supply, could not attract the business of several of the most important factor houses, or simply could not obtain the desired capital, it failed in mid-1884.[202] The Baron's answer was to form a new corporation,

197. Ellis to Managing Director at London, Belém, Nov. 3, 1883, Pará Branch, English Bank of Rio de Janeiro to London and Various, 1883–1887, LABA, UCLL, p. 67; Associação Comercial do Pará, *Relatório da Comissão da Praça do Comércio do Pará do Ano de 1897, Apresentado e Aprovado em Sessão da Assembléia Geral de 25 de Janeiro de 1898* (Belém: Tavares, Cardoso, 1898), p. 21; Weinstein, *Rubber Boom*, pp. 18–19.
198. "Indústria Extrativa: A Borracha," *O Auxiliador da Indústria Nacional*, 52 (Aug. 1884): 182.
199. Ibid.; Weinstein, *Rubber Boom*, pp. 19–20.   200. Weinstein, *Rubber Boom*, p. 140.
201. Associação Comercial do Pará, *Relatório de 1884*, p. 20.
202. The first premise is from Howard Wolf and Ralph Wolf, *Rubber: A Story of Glory and Greed* (New York: Covici, Friede, 1936), p. 214, followed by Roberto Santos, *História Econômica de Amazônia, 1800–1920* (São Paulo: T. A. Queiroz, 1980), p. 219, and Weinstein, *Rubber Boom*, p. 142. It states that the attempt took place in 1881 and that British buyers gave in to Gondoriz's demands, but North Americans, with excess stocks on hand, held out, inflicting heavy losses on the company. But both the Commercial Association (*Relatório de 1884*, p. 20) and the Manager

with many of the original shareholders, under the name New Union Company. It too received the enthusiastic endorsement of the Commercial Association.

With a relatively small capital, the new company had little impact on declining prices, although the Commercial Association credited it with acting as a brake on "short-selling manipulation."[203] Troubled by the removal of Baron Gondoriz by stockholders for mismanagement, the New Union Company went bankrupt in 1888. The ousted Baron had already organized a successor, the Mercantile Company (*Companhia Mercantil*) of Pará. This third enterprise of the Baron also received the blessing of the Commercial Association.[204] Gondoriz had learned from failure. The new Mercantile Company of Pará would enroll the support of government. It first requested a three percent rebate on export duties, which would have enabled it to undersell the competition without paying any less to *aviadores*. Fearing that export houses might respond by moving their operations to rival entrepôt Manaus, the Commercial Association of Pará kept silent and the company's proposal foundered.[205]

The Mercantile Company's prospects dramatically brightened with the coming of the Republic. Appointed governor was Justo Chermont, former officer and major shareholder in the Mercantile Company. The Pará association staged a rally for Chermont and then threw its strength behind a new proposal. A petition representing virtually all *aviador* houses demanded a twenty *reis* per kilo tax on rubber, to be given the Mercantile Company (exempt from the tax) to build up its capital to the point where it could truly dominate the market. In forwarding the petition to the governor, the association repeated its blasts at "short-selling overseas speculators."[206] Belém's seven leading exporters countered with their own petition, denouncing the proposed monopoly and claiming that their own commissions were now down to one percent.[207] Only one of the seven firms did not resign from the Commercial Association. The group retali-

---

of the English Bank of Rio de Janeiro in Pará (Ellis to Managing Director at London, Belém, Jan. 9, 1884, Pará Branch, English Bank of Rio de Janeiro to London and Various, 1883–1887, LABA, UCLL, p. 91) describe the Commercial Union Company as being organized in late 1883 and early 1884. For the second premise, see Ellis to Managing Director at London, Belém, April 17, 1884, ibid., p. 163. For the third, see Moacir Fecury Fereira da Silva, "O Desenvolvimento Comercial do Pará no Período da Borracha (1870–1914)" (Master's Thesis, Universidade Federal Fluminense, Instituto de Ciências Humanas e Filosofia, 1978), p. 64.

203. Associação Comercial do Pará, *Relatório de 1889*, p. 4.
204. Ibid.   205. Weinstein, *Rubber Boom*, p. 149.
206. Commercial Association of Pará to Provisional Government, Pará, Belém, Dec. 7, 1889, and *Aviador* commerce to State Government, Pará, Belém, Nov. 30, 1889, *Relatório de 1890*, pp. 17–20.
207. Seven export firms to Governor of State, Belém, Nov. 28, 1889, *Relatório de 1890*, p. 20.

ated by condemning their later petition that the tax be collected from *aviadores* rather than exporters.[208]

With the governor and the Commercial Association arrayed against them, exporters had no choice but to look outside Brazil for help. They complained to their native governments. Diplomatic force exerted on the new Republican government soon was felt. A reproving "letter of inquiry" from Minister of Finance Rui Barbosa arrived after the tax was promulgated in December, and other pressures from Rio officials followed. By mid-January 1890, the tax was repealed.[209] Without government aid the Mercantile Company of Pará went the way of its predecessors, hastened by a sudden and steep upturn in rubber price, which removed the rationale for its existence. Baron Gondoriz made one more unsuccessful attempt to found a giant rubber export corporation, this time seeking investors in Rio de Janeiro and New York. He died poor and in debt in 1904.[210]

Contests between factors and exporters certified the dominance of the latter. Exporters controlled Brazil's commercial associations, with the exception of the Pará organization and the Commercial Center of Rio de Janeiro. Older and more prestigious groups nullified the influence of the Center, and foreign diplomatic pressure overcame the Commercial Association of Pará and its local political allies. The conflicts did have the effect of exacerbating Brazilian nationalism, increasingly expressed in support for industry (see Chapter 8). Finally, the outcome of struggles between factors, representing local enterprise, and exporters, representing overseas interests, highlighted foreign domination of nineteenth-century Brazil's export-import economy.

Contests between exporters and factors took place alongside the continuing efforts of business interest groups to develop agriculture. Because of the relative lack of other agencies, commercial associations and factor groups acted as agriculture's champions and spokesmen. They were particularly active in promoting technological improvement and in expanding markets for exports. Such campaigns complemented their efforts on behalf of agriculture in the fields of credit, manpower, and export taxation. Although the interests of planters and merchants converged at many points, the efforts of business interest groups in agricultural development mainly were based on a belief that the welfare of agriculture was the indispensable basis of Brazilian prosperity. Despite areas of sharp dispute, the prevalent relationship between businessmen and planters in the nineteenth century was one of cooperation rather than conflict.

208. Commercial Association of Pará to Governor of State, Belém, Dec. 31, 1889, ibid., pp. 21–23.
209. Weinstein, *Rubber Boom*, p. 152.   210. Ibid., pp. 153–154.

5

The export economy: banking, credit, and currency

Business interest group activities and advice to government had a particularly strong influence on banking, credit, and currency. Enrolling most of Brazil's bankers, many of them in positions of leadership, the groups were a prime source of knowledge on such complex matters.[1] Problems of banking, credit, and currency threatened Brazil's economic development in the second half of the nineteenth century. The most crucial was inexpensive credit for agriculture. Without it planters could not modernize their operations, as business interest groups urged, or in some cases even survive. Commerce itself also suffered from expensive credit and from periodic shortages of currency, which lifted interest rates and made ordinary business transactions difficult.

Shortages of credit and currency were interrelated. They were in large part attributable to the underdevelopment of Brazil's banking system and to a lesser extent to a flawed monetary policy.[2] Business interest groups worked hard to ameliorate both. Unfortunately, there often was no agreement among them on how best to do it. Differences of opinion appeared between the Commercial Association of Rio de Janeiro and the rest of Brazil's commercial associations, between overseas merchants and factors, between businessmen and planters, and finally, between Northeast and Southeast. For the elites who controlled Brazil's export economy, questions of banking, credit, and currency proved unusually divisive.

Interest rates reflected the scarcity of credit. Like much else connected with the export economy, they were a worse problem in the Northeast and North than in the Southeast. From midcentury through the 1880s in the Southeast they ranged from six to ten percent annually for merchant

---

1. Like other members of the business elite, businessmen who led banks, had large investments in them, or who directed merchant firms engaged in banking enrolled in local commercial associations as a matter of course, often serving as directors. Except for the commercial associations of Rio de Janeiro, where forty-two of 111 directors in 1834 and between 1844 and 1902 had banking interests, and Bahia, where thirty-four of ninety-one leaders between 1840 and 1900 also did (see Chapter II), participation as directors has not been quantified.
2. Gustavo Henrique Barroso Franco, *Reforma Monetária e Instabilidade Durante a Transição Republicana* (Rio de Janeiro: BNDES, 1983), p. 78.

houses and from eight to fourteen percent for planters, but in the North-east from nine to eighteen percent for merchant firms and from eighteen to twenty-four percent for planters.[3] Shortage of currency would send such rates temporarily higher. In certain localities, under especially unfavorable conditions, rates for planters climbed to more than seventy percent.[4] Interest rates fell significantly when effective credit institutions were created, but the improvement was usually local and temporary, rather than general and permanent. Overall, Brazil's agricultural credit problem remained unsolved during the nineteenth century.

Business interest groups and banking: filling the void

An early means by which business interest groups confronted credit problems was to encourage and, if necessary, create banks wherever they were needed. Brazil had few institutions of credit during most of the first half of the nineteenth century. Loans, usually short term and high interest, commonly were available only from merchant houses, wealthy planters, and private moneylenders. The creation of banks not only aided agriculture, the acknowledged base of business prosperity, but lowered interest rates for merchant houses. Banking was also a favorite enterprise for the successful merchant eager to expand or diversify. Business interest groups proved a handy base for the organization of banks, with the group's directors taking many, and in some cases all, of the seats on the bank's first board of directors.

Commercial associations founded the first two successfully established private banks in Brazil. The Rio organization created the Commercial Bank *(Banco Comercial)* of Rio de Janeiro in 1838.[5] The Commercial

3. Consul-General Andrews to Department of State, Rio de Janeiro, Sept. 6, 1883, *USRC*, XIII, no. 43 (July 1884): 446; C. F. Van Delden Laërne, *Brazil and Java: Report on Coffee Culture in America, Asia, and Africa* (London: W. H. Allen, 1885), p. 213; Joseph Sweigart, "Financing and Marketing Brazilian Export Agriculture: The Coffee Factors of Rio de Janeiro, 1850–1888" (Ph.D. Diss., University of Texas, 1980), p. 121; Bahia, Presidente da Província, *Fala que Recitou o Presidente da Província da Bahia, o Desembargador Conselheiro Francisco Gonçalves Martins, na Abertura da Assembléia Legislativa da Mesma Província no Primeiro de Março de 1852* (Salvador: Vicente Ribeiro Moreira, 1852), p. 64; Pernambuco, Presidente da Província, *Relatório com que Fez Entrega da Administração Provincial o Exm. Sr. Vitor de Oliveira, ao Exm. Sr. Francisco Antônio Ribeiro* (Recife: M. F. de Faria, 1852), p. 28; Sociedade Auxiliadora da Agricultura de Pernambuco, *Trabalhos do Congresso Agrícola do Recife em Outubro de 1878* (Recife: Manuel Figueiroa de Faria & Filhos, 1879), p. 169.

4. *RMACOP, 1880*, I: 39; Brazil, Câmara dos Deputados, Comissão da Fazenda, *Parecer e Projeto sôbre a Creação de Bancos de Crédito Territorial e Fábricas Centraes de Açúcar Apresentados à Câmara dos Deputdos na Sessão de 20 de Julho de 1875, pelas Comissões de Fazenda e Especial Nomeada em 16 de Abril de 1873* (Rio de Janeiro: Tipografia Nacional, 1875), p. 36.

5. Heitor Beltrão, "O Civismo da Praça num Século de Labor," in Associação Comercial do Rio de Janeiro, *Aspetos Coligidos a Propósito do Centenário da Associação Comercial* (Rio de Janeiro: Associação Comercial do Rio de Janeiro, 1935), p. 75; Carlos Manuel Peláez and Wilson Suzigan, *História Monetária do Brasil* (Rio de Janeiro: IPES, Instituto de Pesquisas, 1976), p. 66. The Banco do Ceará, founded in 1836, soon failed because of lack of resources. Ibid., p. 65. Salvador's Caixa

Association of Bahia, in conjunction with that province's government-sponsored Farming Council, founded the Commercial Bank of Bahia in 1845. Seven of the association's directors plus the President of the Farming Council formed its Board of Directors.[6] After individuals founded several other banks, the Commercial Association of Pernambuco, the nation's only other business interest group existing at that time, established the Commercial Bank of Pernambuco in 1851.[7]

Contemporaries described the three banks founded by commercial associations as well run and of great service to their business communities. The commercial banks of Bahia and Pernambuco were credited with reducing local mercantile interest rates from eighteen or twelve percent to nine or eight.[8] The three banks were forbidden to print banknotes, since the Royal Treasury retained monopoly of currency issue, so they issued vouchers (*vales*), redeemable within a short fixed period and bearing a low interest. The vouchers served as currency, helping to relieve a longstanding shortage in those communities.[9] None of the three banks retained its independence long, in part because the government wished to cement its policy of monopoly of issue. The Commercial Bank of Rio de Janeiro formed the basis for the second Bank of Brazil, created by act of Parliament in 1853. The commercial banks of Pernambuco and Bahia were converted into branches of the Bank of Brazil in 1855 and 1856, respectively. As government-controlled institutions, they seem to have offered poorer service, and both were discontinued on the grounds of unprofitability in 1868.[10]

Subsequent attempts by business interest groups to found banks were aimed more at aiding agriculture than commerce and were also less successful. The Commercial Association of Ceará failed in an attempt to

Econômica, founded in 1834, functioned as a savings and loan institution. Francisco Marques de Góes Calmon, *Vida Econômico-Financeira da Bahia: Elementos para a História, de 1808 a 1899 (Reimpressão)* (Salvador: Fundo de Pesquisas, CPE, 1978), p. 74.

6. Minutes, meeting of Oct. 2, 1844, Livro 1 de Atas, AACB, p. 151; Commercial Association of Bahia to President of Province, Salvador, April 3, 1845, Registro dos Ofícios, 1840–1850, AACB, p. 201.

7. Minutes, meeting of April 10, 1851, Livro 1 de Atas, AACP, p. 254.

8. Bahia, Presidente da Província, *Relatório de 1852*, p. 64; Pernambuco, Presidente da Província, *Relatório de 1852*, p. 28; Sebastião Ferreira Soares, *Elementos da Estatística* (Rio de Janeiro: J. Villenueve, 1865), I: 307.

9. Dorival Teixeira Vieira, *Evolução do Sistema Monetário Brasileiro* (São Paulo: Universidade de São Paulo, 1962), pp. 110–112; Maria Bárbara Levy, *História dos Bancos Comerciais no Brasil (Estudo Preliminar)* (Rio de Janeiro: IBMEC, 1972), pp. 17–18.

10. The Commercial Association of Pernambuco described the Recife branch as "more of an image than a real credit institution." Associação Comercial de Pernambuco, *Relatório da Direção da Associação Comercial Beneficente de Pernambuco, Apresentado à Assembléia Geral da Mesma em 26 de Novembre de 1867* (Recife: Jornal do Recife, 1868), p. 5. The Commercial Association of Bahia, however, protested the closure. Associação Comercial da Bahia, *Relatório da Junta Diretora da Associação Comercial da Praça da Bahia, Apresentado em Sessão Ordinária da Assembléia Geral de 29 de Outubro de 1868* (Salvador: J. G. Tourinho, 1868), pp. 72–79.

found that province's first lasting bank in 1869.[11] Both the Commercial Agricultural Association and the planter Agriculture Auxiliary Society of Pernambuco were unsuccessful in founding agricultural mortgage banks in 1883, the former because the imperial government refused to approve its statutes.[12] The Commercial Agricultural Association tried again in 1898, this time planning to finance its bank by a surtax on exports. The refusal of Pernambuco's Commercial Association to support any proposal that increased taxes killed the idea.[13] In 1888 the Center for Sugar Industry and Commerce launched the short-lived Agricultural Bank (*Banco Agrícola*) of Brazil in Rio de Janeiro, and in 1899 the Commercial Association of Rio de Janeiro joined the recently created National Society of Agriculture to draw up plans for a Central Bank of Agricultural Credit (*Banco Central de Crédito Agrícola*).[14]

As the many failed attempts indicate, acquiring capital, community support, and government approval to found new banks was not easy. It was more common for business interest groups to try to attract other banks to serve community needs. The efforts of the Commercial Association of Pernambuco within a short period of time are illustrative. In 1887 it encouraged two local capitalists to form a bank, only to have the project fail, urged the Bank of Brazil to establish a branch in Recife but was rejected, and finally attracted a branch of the Rio-based International Bank of Brazil.[15] In 1889 it assisted in setting up a branch of the Bank of South America (*Sul Americano*) and in 1893 and 1894 unsuccessfully petitioned the President of Brazil and other high officials for a branch of the government-sponsored Bank of the Republic.[16] Other business interest groups made similar attempts to attract or encourage new banks. That such efforts, together with the attempted creation of banks, continued throughout the nineteenth century indicates that Brazil's banking system remained deficient.

Frustrated by the general inadequacy of Brazil's banking system, busi-

---

11. Associação Comercial do Ceará, *Relatório da Direção da Associação Comercial da Praça do Ceará, Apresentado à Assembléia Geral da Mesma em 2 de Maio de 1870* (Fortaleza: Comércio, 1870), pp. 5, 11.
12. Minutes, meeting of Sept. 19, 1883, Livro de Atas da Associação Comercial Agrícola de Pernambuco (hereafter cited as ACAP), 1877–1892, AACP, p. 91; Associação Comercial de Pernambuco, *Relatório de1883*, p. 13 and *Relatório de 1884*, p. 13.
13. Associação Comercial de Pernambuco, *Relatório de 1898*, pp. 13–14.
14. Henri Raffard, *O Centro da Indústria e Comércio de Açúcar no Rio de Janeiro* (Rio de Janeiro: Brasil, 1892), p. 75; Sociedade Nacional de Agricultura, *Sociedade Nacional de Agricultura: Histórico dos Trabalhos da Sociedade Durante o Ano de 1899* (Rio de Janeiro: Imprensa Nacional, 1900), p. 18.
15. Associação Comercial de Pernambuco, *Relatório de 1887*, pp. 31–32.
16. Minutes, meeting of Dec. 11, 1889, Livro 7 de Atas, AACP, p. 42; Associação Comercial de Pernambuco, *Relatório de 1891*, pp. 33–34; Commercial Association of Pernambuco to President, Bank of the Republic of Brazil, Recife, Feb. 17, 1893, *Relatório de 1893*, pp. 72–73; Minutes, meeting of July 16, 1894, Livro 7 de Atas, AACP, p. 96.

ness interest groups resented banks that did not fulfill their expectations for aiding economic development. Resentment focused on the most successful of nineteenth-century Brazil's banking institutions, the British banks. Appearing in Brazil after 1862, British banks ignored manufacturing and, for the most part, direct aid to agriculture.[17] They granted a few rural mortgages in the 1870s, but otherwise only accepted landed mortgages as restitution from bankrupt merchants.[18] Their chosen activity was to service export-import trade and factorage along very conventional and conservative lines.

Resentment was tinged with jealousy. British banks were generally profitable, stable, and financially powerful. In Brazil as elsewhere in Latin America, "British banks were the place of deposit of last resort because it was believed that they would not fail, and that – even if they did – they would pay what they owed in good coin."[19] They also were often on close terms with high Brazilian officials, thus privy to "inside" information. This may have helped them in exchange speculations, which appear to have been a good source of profits.[20] Accusations that British banks were weakening the Brazilian exchange rate for their own advantage were common.

Occasionally business interest groups made their attitude toward British banks public. Answering a query presented by the Parliamentary Committee of Inquiry in 1883, the Commercial Association of Pôrto Alegre stated that British banks "undoubtedly" took advantage of the depreciation of Brazilian currency, and the Commercial Association of Bahia declared that British banks performed scarcely any useful service, dedicating themselves instead "almost exclusively to exchange speculation" and profiting from the depreciation of Brazilian currency. On the other hand, the commercial associations of Rio de Janeiro and Pernambuco defended the British banks, arguing that since they held large amounts of Brazilian currency, they could hardly profit from its depreciation.[21]

Such contradictory testimony reflected not so much differences in opinion as differences in the composition of the boards of directors of the

17. They were allegedly forbidden by home directors to invest in native industrial enterprise. Great Britain, Foreign Office, *Annual Series of Diplomatic and Consular Reports*, no. 1547 (1895): 3.
18. Sweigart, "Coffee Factors," p. 127; D. C. M. Platt, "Economic Imperialism and the Businessman: Britain and Latin America Before 1914," in *Studies in the Theory of Imperialism*, eds. Roger Owen and Bob Sutcliffe (London: Longman, 1972), p. 299.
19. Charles Jones, "Commercial Banks and Mortgage Companies," in *Business Imperialism, 1840– 1930: An Inquiry Based on British Experience in Latin America*, ed. D. C. M. Platt (Oxford: Clarendon, 1977), p. 27.
20. For example, this was allegedly the product of the relationship between Minister of Finance Joaquim Murtinho and the Manager of Rio's London and River Plate Bank. Manager, British Bank of South America, Rio de Janeiro, to Manager, London, Rio de Janeiro, July 25, 1900, Letter Book, 1895–1909, LABA, UCLL, E.9., pp. 186–187.
21. Brazil, Congresso, Comissão Parlamentar de Inquérito, *Informações Apresentadas pela Comissão Parlamentar de Inquérito ao Corpo Legislativo na Terceira Sessão da Décima Oitava Legislatura* (Rio de Janeiro: Tipografia Nacional, 1883), pp. 164, 204–207, 455, 482.

commercial associations in question. Two Englishmen served on the Rio board; an Englishman led the Pernambuco group. The attitude of the Commercial Association of Pernambuco reversed after its English president left. In 1885 it complained that the lending activities of British banks were "very scanty" and that credit was given to a limited number of merchants, and in 1890 it charged that British banks gave almost no support to commerce, rather "withdrawing [and] egotistically limiting themselves to exchange speculation."[22]

Accusations against British banks had a limited effect. The manager of the London & Brazilian Bank attributed to them the otherwise unexplained delay of an imperial decree authorizing the opening of its branch at Pôrto Alegre in 1887.[23] When the value of the *mil-reis* plummeted in 1893, the head of the London & Brazilian Bank's Rio branch felt compelled to personally assure the Minister of Finance that accusations of deliberate currency manipulation were untrue, to show him the bank's records, and to pledge to help the government raise the exchange rate, without any profit to the bank.[24] But no amount of criticism could make British banks forgo exchange speculation or expand their lending practices. They realized that their financial strength, close ties with Brazilian officials, and of course the prestige of the British government would keep resentment from taking concrete form. Native banks would take a much more active part in economic development, but would not enjoy the British banks' profitability or stability.

Another fierce debate in early Brazilian banking was whether currency should have one or a plurality of sources of issue. Business interest groups were at its center. In 1853 the second National Bank of Brazil was created by the merger of the Commercial Bank of Rio de Janeiro with a private bank headed by former President of the Commercial Association of Rio de Janeiro, Irineu Evangelista de Sousa, later Viscount Mauá. Like other national banks, the Bank of Brazil was a quasi-governmental institution. Its president and vice-president were appointed by the Emperor and its directors elected by stockholders. Not surprisingly, nineteen Commercial Association of Rio de Janeiro board members served as Bank of Brazil directors between 1853 and 1889.[25] This relationship, and the bank's role as a focus of Rio de Janeiro financial interests, established a strong identity of interest with the Rio association. It also led the latter's policies on

22. Associação Comercial de Pernambuco, *Relatório de 1885*, p. 15, and *Relatório de 1890*, p. 16.
23. J. Beaton, Manager, London & Brazilian Bank, to Rio de Janeiro Manager, London, May 2, 1887, Letters, London to Rio, 1885–89, LABA, UCLL, G.2., pp. 1–2.
24. Manager, London & Brazilian Bank, Rio de Janeiro to Inocêncio Serzedelo Correia, Rio de Janeiro, Dec. 23, 1892, Copy Book, 1892, LABA, UCLL, G.5., p. 62; Manager, London & Brazilian Bank, Rio de Janeiro to J. Beaton, London Manager, Rio de Janeiro, Feb. 9, 1893, Copy Book, 1892, LABA, UCLL, G.5., pp. 95–98.
25. Eugene W. Ridings, "The Foreign Connection: A Look at the Business Elite of Rio de Janeiro in the Nineteenth Century," *New Scholar*, 7: 1/2 (1979): 175.

banking questions to diverge often from those of other business interest groups.

Soon after the new Bank of Brazil, intended to monopolize currency issue, absorbed the commercial banks of the provinces, a cabinet change in 1857 brought in as Minister of Finance Bernardo de Sousa Franco, an advocate of plurality of issue as a stimulus to economic growth. He authorized establishment of five new banks, giving them and one already founded the right to issue banknotes. But fiscal conservatives regained control of the cabinet in 1859. Blaming overissue of banknotes for a panic in 1857, they presented legislation severely regulating and restricting the faculty.[26]

Brazil's three oldest business interest organizations struggled to influence this new legislation. By a unanimous vote of membership, the Commercial Association of Pernambuco strongly condemned it, as did the Commercial Association of Bahia, backed by that province's Farming Council.[27] In Rio de Janeiro, location of two of the new banks, the business elite split. The Commercial Association, wanting to keep financial power concentrated in Rio and seeing provincial banks of issue as rivals to the Bank of Brazil, backed the new restrictions, as did its spokesman, the newspaper *Jornal do Comércio*. Businessmen opposing the new legislation, backed by the paper *Correio Mercantil,* sent their own petition to Parliament.[28] Fiscal conservatives and the Rio association prevailed in 1860. Now much restricted in volume, plural issue continued until 1866, when the Treasury resumed its monopoly of issue. Business interest groups outside Rio de Janeiro would continue to advocate plurality of issue as an answer to scarce and expensive credit. The Commercial Association of Rio de Janeiro usually would oppose it.

Shortages of cash and monetary policy

Plurality of issue was also seen as a remedy for one of nineteenth-century Brazil's most vexing economic problems: periodic shortages of cash. Although occurring everywhere, this problem, like most others, was most frequent and severe in the North and Northeast. Almost all cash shortages had the same basic cause. Harvest time, when currency was used in great quantity to buy exports, was also the period of greatest expenditure for

26. Peláez and Suzigan, *Política do Govêrno.*, pp. 113–119. Legislators were also influenced by the example of monopoly of issue in Great Britain, France, and Belgium. Teixeira Vieira, *Evolução do Sistema,* pp. 112, 115.
27. Minutes, general assembly of July 5, 1859, Livro 2 de Atas, AACP, p. 105; Minutes, meeeting of June 30, 1959, Livro 2 de Atas, AACB, p. 58.
28. Evaldo Cabral de Melo, *O Norte Agrário e o Império, 1871–1889* (Rio de Janeiro: Nova Fronteira, 1984), p. 99; Afonso Arinos de Melo Franco and Cláudio Pacheco, *História do Banco do Brasil* (Rio de Janeiro: Artenova, 1973), I: 130.

importation. Consequently an abnormal proportion of currency went into public coffers as export and import duty.[29] The resulting cash shortage made business difficult, particularly at retail level. Occasionally small bills could only be had by paying a premium. In extreme cases, cash shortages even lifted regional exchange rates above the Rio de Janeiro level. Among their most aggravating effects was to raise interest rates, not only for agriculture but even for the soundest merchant houses.

Various expedients were used to combat periodic cash crises. One was the use of vouchers, sometimes backed by a deposit of specie, although this substitute was declared illegal.[30] The Commercial Association of Pernambuco, located in a frequently hit area, occasionally arranged for certain foreign coins or obsolete Brazilian coins to be accepted locally as legal tender. This left the thorny task of removing them from circulation once the crisis had ended.[31] The most common reaction of business interest groups was to request emergency shipments of currency from government coffers in Rio de Janeiro. This remedy, like the others mentioned, could only be temporary.

Business interest groups repeatedly petitioned for more permanent solutions. Most frequently suggested was the employment of government tax receipts locally to acquire bills of exchange from London or other European financial centers, rather than shipping them to Rio de Janeiro, where they were usually used for the very same purpose. The removal of tax receipts to Rio not only robbed regional centers of currency but their banks of the profit from exchange operations. Business interest groups also recommended that tax receipts be used to purchase money drafts from Rio de Janeiro or simply returned to circulation in the provinces where they had been gathered. The imperial government occasionally granted one of these three alternatives, but rarely permitted them to last more than one or two years. In view of the persistence of the problem, it is difficult to see why the imperial government did not adopt one of the remedies suggested. An answer might be the profits of Rio de Janeiro

---

29. Brazil, Congresso, Comissão Parlamentar de Inquérito, *Informações Apresentadas*, p. 481. Banks had difficulty expanding their funds because of a low propensity of the Brazilian public to retain money in the form of bank deposits. Gustavo Henrique Barroso Franco, "A Primeira Década Republicana," in *A Ordem do Progresso: Cem Anos de Política Econômica Republicana, 1889–1989*, ed. Marcelo Paiva Abreu (Rio de Janeiro: Campus, 1989), pp. 16–18.

30. Associação Comercial do Pará, *Relatório da Comissão da Praça do Comércio do Pará, Apresentado em Sessão Ordinária da Assembléia Geral em 2 de Janeiro de 1869* (Belém: Jornal do Amazonas, 1869), p. 13; Associação Comercial do Amazonas, *Documentário Comemorativo do Primeiro Centenário da Associação Comercial do Amazonas, 18 de Junho de 1871* (Manaus: Associação Comercial do Amazonas, 1971), p. 41; Jerônimo de Viveiros, *História do Comércio do Maranhão, 1612–1895* (São Luís: Associação Comercial do Maranhão, 1954), I: 196–199.

31. Minutes, meeting of Oct. 10, 1855, Livro 2 de Atas, AACP, pp. 49–50; Commercial Association of Pernambuco to Minister of Finance, Recife, July 10, 1878, *Relatório de 1878*, pp. 9, 45; Associação Comercial de Pernambuco, *Relatório de 1879*, p. 6.

banks from exchange operations and the influence of their interest group, the Rio Commercial Association. The latter officially recommended only that shortages of cash in outlying areas be met with the usual emergency shipment of currency from the Treasury.[32]

Business interest groups were less at odds on a related question, monetary policy. Debates on monetary policy during the nineteenth century revolved around two questions: Should Brazilian currency be convertible to precious metals and should it be cheap, that is, depreciated, or dear? As noted, depreciation of Brazilian exchange benefited the export sector, which was remunerated in the hard currencies of the more developed nations. Some historians, most notably Celso Furtado and Nelson Werneck Sodré, state that the export sector of the Brazilian economy, particularly the coffee industry, has traditionally encouraged exchange depreciation. They reason that planter, factor, and exporter benefit from a falling exchange rate, while the population as a whole bears the onus in the form of higher import prices.[33] This would be particularly true for the nineteenth century, when necessities such as basic foodstuffs and textiles made up a large part of importation. This thesis may be tested by examining the monetary policy recommendations of organizations that represented exporters and factors and claimed to speak for agriculture as well: commercial associations and factor groups.

In their attitudes toward exchange depreciation, commercial associations demonstrated some inconsistency. They complained about the harmful effect on exportation of high or rising exchange, but also grumbled about the damage to importation when it was low.[34] They often advocated policies with inflationary tendencies, such as plurality of issue and easy credit, but also manifested a fear of pronounced inflation. For example, the Commercial Association of Pernambuco complained in 1875 that the nation's money supply was not keeping pace with economic expansion, but at the Recife Agricultural Congress of 1878 denounced as inflationary a proposed issue of paper money to be used as loans for agriculture.[35]

The prospect of strong inflation and exchange depreciation frightened all commercial associations. None queried by the Parliamentary Committee of Inquiry in 1883 favored special issues of currency to overcome cash shortages or provide easier credit.[36] Monetary conservatism was strongest

32. Brazil, Congresso, Comissão Parlamentar de Inquérito, *Informações Apresentadas,* pp. 448, 453.
33. Celso Furtado, *The Economic Growth of Brazil: A Survey from Colonial to Modern Times* (Berkeley: University of California Press, 1965), pp. 182–185; Nelson Werneck Sodré, *Formação Histórica do Brasil* (4th ed.; São Paulo: Brasliense, 1967), pp. 264–265.
34. See, as examples of inconsistency, Associação Comercial de Pernambuco, *Relatório de 1871,* p. 6; *Relatório de 1885,* p. 15; *Relatório de 1899,* p. 7; and *Relatório de 1900,* p. 10.
35. *Relatório de 1875,* p. 9; Sociedade Auxiliadora da Agricultura de Pernambuco, *Congresso Agrícola,* pp. 118–119.
36. Brazil, Congresso, Comissão Parlamentar de Inquérito, *Informações Apresentadas,* pp. 163–164, 202–204, 453, 470, 480–481.

in two associations foreign-dominated and most closely associated with coffee exportation. The Commercial Association of Rio de Janeiro in 1878 strongly criticized the government for issuing additional paper money to help business recover from the panic of 1875, a crisis other commercial associations blamed at least partly on lack of currency.[37] In 1883, during a coffee crisis, the Commercial Association of Santos condemned a weakening of the exchange rate, maintaining somewhat illogically that weak exchange did not really help the planter.[38]

Business interest groups and planters, at least those of the Northeast, diverged on monetary policy. The Agriculture Auxiliary Society of Pernambuco in 1877 praised the effects of a low exchange rate and rebuked the government for having let it rise again.[39] In 1888 it called for a special issue of currency to indemnify planters for the abolition of slavery.[40] Similarly, at the Recife Agricultural Congress of 1878 most planters backed the idea of a special emission of currency to be lent to agriculture, even if inflationary. Planter spokesman Henrique Augusto Milet denied that inflation would harm commerce, maintaining rather that business would boom when planter prosperity was secured.[41] This contradicted the stand of the Commercial Association of Pernambuco and most of the businessmen present. Only agricultural distress led business interest groups to advocate radical measures. The Commercial Agricultural Association of Pernambuco backed the demands of planters at the 1878 Agricultural Congress for a new emission of paper money, stating that its bad effects were preferable to the impending ruin of agriculture.[42] A crisis of liquidity in its state's rural economy impelled the Commercial Association of São Paulo to demand an increase in money supply in 1896.[43] But these were exceptions; factor groups and commercial associations rarely strayed from orthodox views on currency.

What was the basis of this prevailing monetary conservatism? Even businessmen not in the export sector had reasons to favor a weak exchange rate and moderate inflation. Manufacturers often welcomed inflation be-

37. Associação Comercial do Rio de Janeiro, *Relatório da Associação Comercial do Rio de Janeiro do Ano de 1878* (Rio de Janeiro: Apóstolo, 1879), p. 4; Associação Comercial de Pernambuco, *Relatório de 1875*, p. 9; Associação Comercial do Pará, *Relatório de 1876*, pp. 40–41.
38. Associação Comercial de Santos, *Relatório da Associação Comercial de Santos Apresentado em Sessão Ordinária da Assembléia Geral em Março de 1883 e Parecer da Comissão de Exame de Contas* (Santos: Diário de Santos, 1883), pp. 10–13.
39. Sociedade Auxiliadora da Agricultura de Pernambuco, *Relatório Anual Apresentado na Sessão de 4 de Julho de 1878 da Assembléia Geral pelo Gerente Inácio de Barros Barreto e a Ata da Mesma Sessão* (Recife: Jornal do Recife, 1878), pp. 12–13.
40. *ACD, 1888*, IV: 236.
41. Sociedade Auxiliadora da Agricultura de Pernambuco, *Congresso Agrícola*, pp. 338–340.
42. Associação Comercial Agrícola de Pernambuco, *Congresso Agrícola do Recife* (Recife: M. Figueiroa de Faria & Filhos, 1878), pp. 18–19.
43. Associação Comercial de São Paulo, *Representação Dirigida ao Congresso Nacional sôbre as Medidas Financeiras Constantes do Aditivo Apresentado ao Projeto de Orçamento da União pelo Deputado Sr. Francisco Glycério em 26 de Setembro de 1896* (São Paulo: Indústrial de São Paulo, 1896), pp. 6–11.

cause prices could be raised much more rapidly than wages where labor was weak, as in nineteenth-century Brazil. Furthermore, Brazilian enterprises, as in most developing countries, were usually debtors. Domestic bankers, provided they had few foreign obligations, might participate profitably in measures that tended to be inflationary, such as plural bank issue or state-sponsored distribution of credit.[44] Finally, a low exchange rate was thought to aid the nation's economy as a whole by aiding its basis, export agriculture.

But there were equally good reasons for business interest groups to favor a strong exchange rate and stable prices. Commercial associations represented not only leading exporters, but powerful importers, hurt by exchange rate decline. Many, if not most, of the largest and most successful merchant houses engaged in both exportation and importation. They did so not only because it was profitable and relatively easy, but to protect themselves from, and to take advantage of, swings in the exchange rate. Moreover, the most powerful elements in business interest groups, large merchant houses, tended to be creditors and thus adverse to having their interest eaten away by inflation. In addition, inflation would hurt the many members of the business elite who invested heavily in government bonds at five or six percent.

Importantly, overseas obligations favored a high exchange rate. A strong Brazilian *mil-reis* facilitated the repayment of the nation's considerable foreign debt; overseas lenders considered maintenance of the exchange rate a show of good faith. Foreign investors also demanded it. They had to convert receipts in Brazilian currency into hard currency before repatriation; a weak *mil-reis* diminished their profits. It was no coincidence that the most determined resistance to exchange depreciation came from two of the commercial associations most dominated by foreigners, Rio de Janeiro and Santos. Above all, monetary stability represented the prevailing economic wisdom in the nineteenth century, no small consideration to men who believed themselves, and were considered by government and others to be, key sources of economic expertise.

In sum, business interest groups usually favored monetary conservatism and a strong and stable Brazilian currency. Judging from the representative interest groups of the export sector, the thesis of its support for exchange depreciation and inflation is only partly true for the nineteenth century. Only the planters of the Northeast openly demanded them. Factors favored them only in 1878, and with reluctance, while exporters were generally opposed. But some ambiguity remained, even among commercial associations, especially during periods of lack of liquidity and agricultural distress.

44. Steven Topik, "The State's Contribution to the Development of Brazil's Internal Economy, 1850–1930," *HAHR*, 65 (May 1985): 206.

If business interest groups retained some doubts concerning the ideal strength for Brazil's currency, they were virtually unanimous in condemning the inconvertible paper money that was the prevailing medium of exchange. They blamed it for the frequent and sometimes violent fluctuations of the exchange rate, which could be affected by the balance of payments, by foreign investment, by foreign loans, by the quantity of currency in circulation, and even by the money market activities of Rio's largest banks.[45] Between 1846 and 1889, the *mil-reis* wandered between twenty-nine and fourteen pence, varying by as much as six and one-half pence in a single year. Such fluctuations were not always harmful. Merchants could take advantage of them to buy cheaply either Brazilian or foreign currency as needed, and some of the larger merchant houses speculated in exchange with profit. But exchange fluctuations added more uncertainty to business and thus diminished confidence. Business interest groups unanimously decried them.

The groups also had little indecision about with what to replace inconvertible paper money. Nearly all commercial associations advocated a system of convertible currency based on gold or silver.[46] Several of them filed petitions demanding an end to inconvertible paper money, but the Rio group made it a special target, terming its elimination "perhaps the prime necessity of the country," and bombarding government during the 1880s with pleas to replace it with a currency based on precious metals.[47] The change would not only stabilize exchange and stimulate foreign investment, the association argued, but would encourage investment in agricultural mortgage banks. There was justification for the view that exchange fluctuations discouraged purchase of agricultural mortgage bonds. Only the bonds of Francisco de Paula Mayrink's Bank of Land Credit (*Banco de Crédito Real*) of Brazil, whose premiums were tied to the pound sterling, were popular with investors during the 1880s.[48] Significantly, in the case of the Rio group, steadiness of exchange also was greatly desired by British banks. As the head of one noted, "We rely, for our profits, on the margin existing between Bank and Merchant's paper. In the absence of fluctuations risk of loss is very small."[49]

Unfortunately, the obstacle in changing to a convertible currency based on precious metals was not in convincing Ministers of Finance, most of

45. Ibid., pp. 35–36. For the effect on exchange rate of "forcing tactics" by one British bank, see Manager, London & Brazilian Bank, Rio de Janeiro, to London Manager, Rio de Janeiro, Dec. 23, 1892, Copy Book, 1892, LABA, UCLL, G.5., pp. 65–66.
46. Brazil, Congresso, Comissão Parlamentar de Inquérito, *Informações Apresentadas*, pp. 164, 202–204, 453, 470, 480–481.
47. Associação Comercial do Rio de Janeiro, *Relatório de 1881*, p. 6, *Relatório de 1882–1883*, pp. 6–7, *Relatório de 1890*, pp. 20–21, 35, and *Resposta da Associação Comercial do Rio de Janeiro aos Quesitos da Comissão Parlamentar de Inquérito* (Rio de Janeiro: Montenegro, 1883), p. 15.
48. Sweigart, "Coffee Factors," p. 154.
49. John Gordon, Manager, London & Brazilian Bank, to Rio de Janeiro Manager, London, Aug. 3, 1889, Letters, London to Rio, 1885–89, LABA, UCLL, G.2., p. 3.

whom agreed with the Rio association, but in implementing the transformation. Brazil usually suffered from a shortage of precious metal reserves, which would have to be shipped abroad to maintain the currency at parity whenever the balance of payments was adverse. Nevertheless, the change remained a prime goal of most business interest groups.

The lingering problem: rural credit

Inadequate banking facilities, shortages of cash, and debates over monetary policy affected another serious weakness in Brazilian development: the lack of credit for agriculture. Despite expansion of the banking system, most planters continued to receive loans from the traditional source, their factors. It was the latter, and other merchants, who drew credit from the new banks. For short-term loans, factors charged two to four percent over the current bank discount rate.[50] Factors were reluctant to give long-term loans and usually charged very high interest on them. The early banks usually avoided direct lending to planters. The President of Province of Bahia noted in 1863 that "the province's institutions of credit, although numerous and possessing considerable funds, are almost of no use to agriculture."[51] Despite their names, neither Rio's Rural and Mortgage (*Rural e Hipotecário*) Bank, founded in 1854, nor its Commercial and Agricultural (*Comercial e Agrícola*) Bank, dating from 1857, gave much aid to planters. The latter granted few rural mortgages, the former, none.[52] Of the early banks, only the Commercial Bank of Bahia is recorded as providing a significant number of loans to planters before its absorption by the Bank of Brazil in 1856.[53]

Banks had good reasons to be wary of issuing rural mortgages. Mortgage registration and rural land demarcation were uncertain and foreclosure was difficult. Local mortgage registers, dating from 1846, indicated whether land was mortgaged but did not specify how many times; as a result two or three parties often ended up having a lien on the same property. In addition, landed interests had successfully blocked legislation requiring clear title registration or precise demarcation of boundaries, because few landholders held clear titles.[54] The true value of rural proper-

---

50. Sociedade Auxiliadora da Agricultura de Pernambuco, *Congresso Agrícola*, p. 318; Sweigart, "Coffee Factors," pp. 120–121.
51. Bahia, Presidente da Província, *Relatório de 1863*, p. 87.
52. Sweigart, "Coffee Factors," p. 126; Ruy Guilherme Granziera, *A Guerra do Paraguay e o Capitalismo no Brasil* (São Paulo: Hucitec, 1979), pp. 94–95.
53. Bahia, Presidente da Província, *Relatório de 1863*, p. 88; Imperial Institute of Agriculture of Bahia to Emperor Pedro II, Salvador, Feb. 3, 1860, Seção de Manuscritos, BN, Rio de Janeiro, II-33, 28, 68, p.12.
54. Emilia Viotti da Costa, *The Brazilian Empire: Myths and Histories* (Chicago: University of Chicago Press, 1985), pp. 78–93; Warren Dean, "Latifundia and Land Policy in Nineteenth-Century Brazil," *HAHR*, 51 (November 1971): 606–625.

ty thus rarely could be established. The difficulty of foreclosure was, if anything, an even more serious obstacle to rural credit. The legal disadvantages of the creditor in trying to attach rural property offered as security were notorious. A businessman remarked in 1878: "There can be no credit where there is no guarantee for the creditor; there can be no credit in a country where everyone has great compassion for the foreclosed-on debtor and no consideration for the deceived creditor."[55]

The formidable protection enjoyed by planters had roots in the colonial period, when *senhores de engenho* had received special legal privileges.[56] The legal device that vexed creditors most was forced adjudication, dating from 1774. To foreclose on landed rural property the creditor was required to call on a judge to establish an open auction. The judge then appointed appraisers, whose appraisal could not legally be less than the value of the original loan. If, after two attempted auctions, there were no bids high enough to cover the appraised value, the creditor had to buy the property at four-fifths of that value. Appraisals were often outrageously high. The supervising judge and the appraisers he appointed were liable to be landowners and debtors themselves, if not friends or relatives of the debtor. Landowners often came out ahead in the settlement, even after reimbursing the creditor for the original loan and any penalties for late payment. The creditor, meanwhile, suffered from extensive delays and high judicial costs and lost control of the foreclosure process after initiating it.[57] Not surprisingly, a foreign expert noted that foreclosure "is never resorted to if it can be helped," and that lenders were more likely to aid delinquent planters than to prosecute them.[58]

While anxious to eliminate forced adjudication, merchants also wished to legalize the practice of crop collateral (*penhor agrícola*). This made possible loans of up to two years on the security of the planter's crop alone or on the crop plus agricultural equipment. Lending on the basis of crops and equipment as security was common by the 1880s in the southern coffee zone, where it was embodied in private contracts between factors and their planter clients.[59] Elsewhere, particularly in the Northeast, it might present difficulties. Sugar planter spokesman Henrique Augusto Milet remarked at the Recife Agricultural Congress in 1878: "I, for my

55. Sociedade Auxiliadora da Agricultura de Pernambuco, *Congresso Agrícola*, p. 86.
56. José Wanderley de Araújo Pinho, *História de um Engenho do Recôncavo: Matoim-Novo Caboto-Freguezia, 1552–1944* (Rio de Janeiro: Zélio Valverde, 1946), pp. 181–182, 194, 308–309; Stuart B. Schwartz, "Free Labor in a Slave Economy: The *Lavradores de Cana* of Colonial Bahia," in *Colonial Roots of Modern Brazil: Papers of the Newberry Library Conference*, ed. Dauril Alden (Berkeley: University of California Press, 1973), p. 186.
57. Sociedade Auxiliadora da Agricultura de Pernambuco, *Congresso Agrícola*, p. 86; Sweigart, "Coffee Factors," pp. 194–195; Van Delden Laërne, *Brazil and Java*, pp. 227–228.
58. Van Delden Laërne, *Brazil and Java*, p. 228.
59. Van Delden Laërne, *Brazil and Java*, p. 216; Cabral de Melo, *Norte Agrário*, p. 131.

part, being a *senhor de engenho* and seeing someone, with any type of deed, coming to take my crop from me, can say with perfect conviction that if I did not consent he would not take it."[60] Another planter added ominously, "Maybe he would not even return with his hide intact."[61]

The business elite had long wanted to reform rural credit legislation. The commercial associations of Pernambuco and Bahia had complained during the 1860s about the injustice of mortgage laws, adding that in the Northeastern interior even the few legal safeguards for creditors were often ignored.[62] But pursuit of the issue implied a head-on clash with planters, something business interest groups always wanted to avoid. Most planters wanted no change in credit legislation. The Agriculture Auxiliary Society of Pernambuco even complained in 1877 about the "bondage of usury" and urged the reestablishment of certain colonial legislation protecting borrowers.[63] Conflict erupted during the Recife Agricultural Congress in 1878. Queried by the imperial government on the availability of rural credit, the Commercial Association and Commercial Agricultural Association of Pernambuco affirmed that there was plenty of capital in Brazil and that it would flow toward agricultural credit institutions once mortgages were clearly registered and mortgage law gave creditors a fair chance.[64] Planters testily denied that there was sufficient capital in the nation for agricultural needs or that credit legislation needed changing.[65] When the changes in land demarcation, registration of mortgages, and mortgage legislation wanted by the business elite were put before the congress as a resolution, they were voted down.[66]

Clearly, obstacles to rural lending were formidable. It was evident that without government intervention little bank credit would reach planters directly, no matter how many banks were founded. The government's first move was to make the Bank of Brazil a source of agricultural credit in 1866, but not until 1873, when the government appropriated a large sum to be lent at 6.2 percent interest, did it become a major furnisher of rural credit.[67] However, the benefits reached only the Southeastern coffee zone. In the Northeast bitter accusations of government favoritism toward the Southeast were heard again. The Commercial Association and the Com-

60. Sociedade Auxiliadora da Agricultura de Pernambuco, *Congresso Agrícola*, p. 125.
61. Ibid.
62. Associação Comercial de Pernambuco, *Relatório de 1861*, p. 4; Commercial Association of Bahia to President of Province, Salvador, Jan. 18, 1869, *Relatório de 1869*, p. 48.
63. Sociedade Auxiliadora da Agricultura de Pernambuco, *Relatório de 1878*, p. 15.
64. Sociedade Auxiliadora da Agricultura de Pernambuco, *Congresso Agrícola*, pp. 116–117, 332, 425–426.
65. Ibid., pp. 122, 133, 139–140, 434.
66. "Congresso Agrícola," *O Auxiliador da Indústria Nacional*, 46 (Dec. 1878): 276.
67. Sweigart, "Coffee Factors," p. 138–147; Cabral de Melo, *Norte Agrário*, pp. 107–108.

mercial Agricultural Association of Pernambuco demanded that the Northeast be included in the government's largesse.[68]

To mollify regional resentment, the imperial government proposed in 1874 to sponsor agricultural loans at six percent interest and five percent amortization yearly, attracting capital by a guarantee of two percent interest.[69] The Commercial Association of Rio de Janeiro denounced the guaranteed interest as government interference in the capital market.[70] The Northeast saw the proposal as a feeble gesture. Assemblies of planters and merchants convoked by the commercial associations of Pernambuco and Bahia derided the government's proposed interest rates as too high to aid planters but too low to entice capital.[71] Consequently, subsequent government proposals to stimulate rural credit would increase the guaranteed interest and look to Europe for financing. A cabinet change brought as Minister of Finance Baron Cotegipe, himself a *senhor de engenho* and closely linked to the Commercial Association of Bahia, which enthusiastically endorsed and helped promote his administration's plan.[72] Capital for agricultural banks offering mortgage loans at seven percent interest and two percent amortization would be raised in Europe by five percent guaranteed interest.[73]

Europe failed to respond to the 1875 law. The Continent was then in recession, the plan had some glaring weaknesses and, most significantly, Europeans found other Brazilian investments more attractive.[74] Several Brazilian railway securities were already offering seven percent guaranteed interest, but the most serious rivals of the 1875 law were Brazilian public debt bonds. These gave only five or six percent interest but were regarded as very secure. They attracted both foreign and Brazilian capital that might otherwise have gone into mortgage banks, communications, or industry. Business interest groups frequently blamed public debt bonds when capital was difficult to raise, but never proposed restricting their issue or lowering their interest rates. The bonds were also a favorite investment of group membership.   ·

68. *RMF, 1874*, pp. 45–47, 89.   69. Ibid., p. 50.

70. Cabral de Melo, *Norte Agrário*, p. 110.

71. Ibid., p. 111; Ninety-six planters and merchants to Minister of Agriculture, Commerce, and Public Works, Salvador, July 29, 1874, SH/AN, IA, 10.

72. Minutes, meeting of Oct. 14, 1875, Livro 4 de Atas, AACB, p. 226.

73. Bernardino José Borges, *O Comerciante, ou Completo Manual Instrutivo* (2d ed. rev.; Rio de Janeiro: Eduardo & Henrique Laemmert, 1878), pp. 220–222; Benedito Ribeiro and Mário Mazzei Guimarães, *História dos Bancos e do Desenvolvimento Financeiro do Brasil; History of Brazilian Banking and Financial Development*, trans. George Reed (Rio de Janeiro: Pro Service, 1967), p. 86.

74. Among its faults were offering as security insufficient lands and also property in the form of slaves, anathema to British investors. *RMF, 1878*, p. 29; Morgan to Foreign Office, Salvador, Dec. 17, 1875, PRO/FO 13/485, fl. 137–139; Cabral de Melo, *Norte Agrário*, pp. 117–119.

Subsequently, legislators made fresh proposals to establish mortgage banking on the basis of the 1875 law. None received government backing until the founding of the Bank of Land Credit by Rio financier Francisco de Paula Mayrink. Debate over the project revealed serious divergence within the business elite itself. The commercial associations of Santos and Bahia backed Mayrink with enthusiasm.[75] Surprisingly, the Commercial Association of Rio de Janeiro, of which Mayrink was a member, offered only tepid support.[76] Vested interests within that group had been affected. Rio's leading coffee factors apparently felt the proposal threatened their role as furnishers of credit to agriculture. In a series of meetings late in 1880 they drafted anti-Mayrink petitions to Parliament and offered as a substitute a rival mortgage bank project they had drawn up.[77] Even then, a number of coffee factors dissented, filing a petition favoring Mayrink's project.[78] Most of the dissenters headed smaller firms more dependent on bank credit, which Mayrink's project would facilitate. Once established, the Bank of Land Credit operated with fair success, but its scope was limited to the Southeast.

Despite the presence of the Bank of Land Credit and a few other effective mortgage banks, the agricultural credit situation began to worsen in the early 1880s. Lending was progressively curtailed because of falling coffee prices, because of declining land values due to soil exhaustion in the Paraíba Valley of the Province of Rio de Janeiro, and most significantly, because of realization that the end of slavery was near.[79] Slaves were the principal asset on which credit was given. The Bank of Brazil, major lender in the coffee zone, first restricted its credit, then in 1884 stopped granting rural mortgages altogether.[80] By 1888, only six rural mortgage banks were operating in Brazil.[81] In addition to Mayrink's Bank of Land Credit, apparently only the much-praised Bank of Land Credit of Pernambuco (founded in 1886) was aiding planters effectively.[82]

75. Commercial Association of Santos to Minister of Finance, Santos, Oct. 14, 1881, *Relatório de 1882*, pp. 55–58; Commercial Association of Bahia to Francisco P. Mayrink, Salvador, April 11, 1881, *Relatório de 1882*, pp. 15–18.
76. *Relatório de 1880*, p. 6.
77. *O Cruzeiro* (Rio de Janeiro), Dec. 19, 1880, p. 3, and. Dec. 25, 1880, p. 1.
78. *O Cruzeiro*, Dec. 16, p. 2, and Dec. 25, 1880, p. 3.
79. Sweigart, "Coffee Factors," pp. 187–188; Barroso Franco, *Reforma Monetária*, pp. 77–78.
80. Van Delden Laërne, *Brazil and Java*, p. 214.
81. Sweigart, "Coffee Factors," pp. 190–192; Manuel Paulo Vieira Pinto, "Quadro do Estado das Sociedades de Crédito Real do Império do Brasil, Rio de Janeiro, 18/10/1888," SM, BN, I-48, 17, 34, Mss; 332.1, P.
82. Associação Comercial de Pernambuco, *Relatório de 1887*, pp. 33–35; Peter L. Eisenberg, *The Sugar Industry in Pernambuco, 1840–1910: Modernization Without Change* (Berkeley: University of California Press, 1974), p. 78.

The liquidity crisis

A growing lack of liquidity in the economy further contracted credit. Brazil's per capita money supply declined by an estimated twenty-five percent between 1870 and 1888.[83] The situation worsened in the 1880s because the Empire virtually ended its traditional practice of issuing money to finance deficits.[84] Decreasing agricultural credit and growing planter distress provided a favorable atmosphere for business interest groups to campaign for credit legislation reform. To the weight of the commercial associations was added the factor group Center for Coffee Agriculture and Commerce, created late in 1880. Along with stopping abolition and expanding coffee markets, the Center made reform of credit legislation a main goal. It not only petitioned government and published a book specifying the changes it wanted, but staged public lectures on the subject during its coffee exhibitions.[85] Rejection of credit reform by Parliament in 1882 only brought renewed pressure by business interest groups. When queried by the government in 1883, every commercial association blamed retrograde laws for impeding the flow of credit to agriculture.[86] When reform was brought before Parliament again in 1885, the Commercial Association of Rio de Janeiro helped push it into law with two formal petitions, one of which also was signed by the heads of all Rio banks.[87]

Passage of the 1885 legislation ended forced adjudication, provided for speedier foreclosure on terms much more favorable to the creditor, and legalized crop collateral. But it did not provide for clear registration of mortgages. Landowners resisted such legislation with particular tenacity because it required them to present legal documents proving title, which few could do. Legislation establishing the Torrens Mortgage Register devised in Australia was finally passed in 1890, but proved very difficult to enforce because of landowner opposition.[88] Much of Brazil's rural land remained with unclear title and unknown encumbrances and creditors could still easily be swindled.[89] Capital continued to avoid agricultural

83. Topik, "State's Contribution," 208. 84. Barroso Franco, *Reforma Monetária*, p. 32.
85. Centro da Lavoura e Comércio do Café, *Representação Submetida ao Poder Legislativo sôbre Algumas das Necessidades da Lavoura e do Comércio* (Rio de Janeiro: Moreira, Maximino, 1882); Sweigart, "Coffee Factors," pp. 198–199.
86. Brazil, Congresso, Comissão Parlamentar de Inquérito, *Informações Apresentadas*, pp. 164, 204, 456, 471.
87. Associação Comercial do Rio de Janeiro, *Relatório de 1884–1885*, pp. 24–28.
88. *RMF, 1891*, p. 189, and *RMF, 1897*, pp. 122–127. Eulália Maria Lahmeyer Lobo, *História Político-Administrativa da Agricultura Brasileira* (Rio de Janeiro: Ministério da Agricultura, 1980), p. 127.
89. São Paulo, Governador do Estado, *Mensagens Apresentadas ao Congresso Legislativo de S. Paulo pelos*

mortgage institutions. Contrary to the repeated assurances made by business interest groups during their campaign, the 1885 legislation had no appreciable effect on the flow of rural credit.[90]

Far from improving, the agricultural credit situation deteriorated and shortages of cash became more widespread and frequent. The liquidity crisis worsened in 1885–1888 when the conservative cabinet withdrew money from circulation in order to strengthen the exchange rate. This was precisely when economic expansion and salaries for increased numbers of manumitted slaves and European immigrants brought an unprecedented demand for currency. These factors, noted the Commercial Association of Santos, had by November of 1886 forced the price of credit "extraordinarily high."[91] In the Northeast and North the lack of liquidity may have been worse. The Commercial Association of Bahia had to request two emergency shipments of bills from Rio to get its province through 1887.[92] The crisis reawakened calls for plurality of issue. Even the arch-conservative Commercial Association of Rio de Janeiro, which had heretofore refused to acknowledge shortages of cash in the Southeast, was swayed.[93] By April of 1887 that organization, noting that the discount rate for merchant firms had climbed above twelve percent, was calling for a return to plurality of issue.[94]

A final blow came in May of 1888, when the abolition of slavery without compensation took from planters both their property and their traditional security for loans. Banks and factors further restricted already scarce rural credit.[95] Leaders of the Empire worried about the loyalty of planters and with reason. Pressure for government-sponsored credit aid to agriculture and for a return to plural issue now became irresistible. Both were demanded in a petition to the Crown in July 1888 by a committee of planters and merchants of Bahia, chosen from that province's Commercial Association and Imperial Agricultural Institute.[96] Following initiatives

Presidentes do Estado e Vice-Presidentes em Exercício, desde a Proclamação da República até ao Ano de 1916 (São Paulo: Diário Oficial, 1916), p. 178.

90. Cabral de Melo, *Norte Agrário*, p. 132.

91. Associação Comercial do Santos, *Relatório de 1887*, p. 16.

92. Commercial Association of Bahia to President of Province, Salvador, May 4 and Oct. 5, 1887, Presidência da Província/Govêrno ao Associação Comercial, 1846–1889, AEB; Baron Guaí to Commercial Association of Bahia, Rio de Janeiro, Feb. 15, 1889, *Relatório de 1889*, p. 112.

93. The Rio association voted down a proposal to ask relief from the government in 1884. Minutes, meeting of March 7, 1884, Livro de Atas, 1881–1890, AACRJ, p. 101.

94. Commercial Association of Rio de Janeiro to Emperor Pedro II, Rio de Janeiro, April 13, 1887, *Relatório de 1890*, p. 21. Even then, this policy change aroused strong opposition, resulting in the resignation of a British director. Minutes, meetings of April 15 and May 11, 1887, Livro de Atas, 1881–1890, AACRJ, pp. 165–166.

95. John Gordon, Deputy Manager, London & Brazilian Bank, to Manager, Rio de Janeiro, London, July 17, 1888, Letters, London to Rio, 1885–1889, LABA, UCLL, G.2., p. 3.

96. Committee of Planters and Merchants to Princess Regent, Salvador, July 11, 1888, ABC, AIHGB, lata 79, doc. 78.

made by its predecessor, a new cabinet under Liberal prime minister Viscount Ouro Preto responded forcefully. In August 1888, the government appropriated interest-free funds to the Bank of Brazil to be lent to planters in the coffee-growing states at six percent interest. Protests from the commercial associations of Pernambuco and Pará forced extension of this so-called Aid to Agriculture (*Auxílios à Lavoura*) to the Northeast and to Pará.[97] Eventually administered through more than a dozen banks, the measure was popular. Even the factor Center for Coffee Agriculture and Commerce gave it strong support, as did the Commercial Association of Rio de Janeiro.[98] It provided significant relief to planters.

This type of aid was by nature only temporary. Ouro Preto contemplated founding on the basis of the 1875 law a large mortgage bank, which would primarily serve sugar planters. He entrusted the formulation of it to his friend, Commercial Association of Rio de Janeiro director Honório Augusto Ribeiro.[99] The Empire ended before the plan could be presented to Parliament. Then the new Republic, regarding "Aid to Agriculture" as a drain on the Treasury and as essentially a last-minute bid for planter support by the monarchy, suspended it with roughly a third of its funds still not disbursed.[100]

The Ouro Preto cabinet had also responded to the demand for a return to plurality of issue. Its November 1888 bill permitted the issue of banknotes backed by either gold and silver or by public debt bonds. However, through the first half of 1889 no banks agreed to become banks of issue.[101] Aware of weaknesses in the bill, the Commercial Association of Rio de Janeiro chose a three-man committee (including Honório Augusto Ribeiro) to recommend changes. Its recommendations, which centered on removing limits to the quantity of notes a bank could issue, were accepted and became law in July 1889.[102] They much increased the attractiveness of the measure, and thirteen banks soon became banks of issue.[103] Together with Aid to Agriculture, the return to plurality of issue more than doubled Brazil's total banking capital by the end of the Empire.[104] The Rio association's recommendations marked a radical departure from its traditional policy on currency. The reversal was not only due

97. Associação Comercial de Pernambuco, *Relatório de 1888*, p. 16; Associação Comercial do Pará, *Relatório de 1890*, pp. 4, 12.
98. Center for Coffee Agriculture and Commerce to Viscount Ouro Preto, Rio de Janeiro, July 17, 1889, Coleção Ouro Preto (hereafter cited as COP), AIHGB, lata 427, doc. 10.
99. Honório Augusto Ribeiro to Viscount Ouro Preto, Rio de Janeiro, Sept. 11, 1889, COP, AIHGB, lata 427, doc. 13.
100. *RMF, 1891*, pp. 151–152.   101. Barroso Franco, *Reforma Monetária*, p. 67.
102. Associação Comercial do Rio de Janeiro, *Relatório de 1890*, pp. 32–37.
103. Barroso Franco, *Reforma Monetária* pp. 67–68.
104. Steven Topik, *The Political Economy of the Brazilian State, 1889–1930* (Austin: University of Texas Press, 1987), pp. 28–29.

to pressures for greater liquidity, but to the prospective participation of influential members in the new banks of issue, and to the association's belief that the banking reforms were a step toward something it had long advocated: the conversion of Brazilian currency to the gold standard.[105]

The republic and the downfall of Brazilian currency

The overthrow of the Empire in November 1889 made Brazil's experience with a convertible currency backed by precious metals brief. Republican Minister of Finance Rui Barbosa in effect suspended convertibility before the year was over, as Brazilian exchange began what would be a spectacular plunge.[106] Barbosa and his three successors as Minister of Finance accelerated Ouro Preto's policy of expanding money supply. Led by banknotes, currency in circulation increased by 220 percent between 1889 and 1893, triggering the period of inflation and sometimes unbridled speculation known as the *Encilhamento*.[107] As inflation soared, the right of issue was progressively taken from private banks. It was made a monopoly of the government-sponsored Bank of the Republic (*Banco da República*) in 1893, then returned to the Treasury in 1896.

Accelerating inflation and a weakening exchange rate were particularly offensive to the Commercial Association of Rio de Janeiro, but it did not immediately protest. It was unpopular with Republican leaders because of its close ties with the Empire. However, knowing the heads of Rio de Janeiro's banks shared its views on monetary policy, it convoked them in April and November 1891 to discuss means of halting the decline of exchange, and presented their recommendations to the Minister of Finance.[108] The same year the Commercial Association of Maranhão pro-

105. Commercial Association of Rio de Janeiro to Emperor Pedro II, Rio de Janeiro, no date, 1889, *Relatório de 1890*, pp. 34–36.
106. Barroso Franco, *Reforma Monetária*, pp. 98–99. In addition to expansion of the money supply, an interruption of foreign capital inflow in 1890 and an unfavorable balance of trade promoted exchange depreciation. Ibid., pp. 139–141; Winston Fritsch, *External Constraints on Economic Policy in Brazil, 1889–1930* (Houndmills, Basingstoke, Hampshire: Macmillan, 1988), pp. 4–5.
107. Mircea Buescu, *Brasil: Problemas Econômicas e Experiência Histórica* (Rio de Janeiro: Forense-Universitária, 1985), p. 122; Raymond W. Goldsmith, *Brasil, 1850–1984: Desenvolvimento Financeiro sob um Século de Inflação* (São Paulo: Harper & Row do Brasil, 1986), pp. 93, 138. Maria Bárbara Levy and Luiz Antônio Tannuri blame the funds distributed through Aid to Agriculture for unleashing much of the speculation. Maria Bárbara Levy, "O Encilhamento," in *Economia Brasileira: Uma Visão Histórica*, ed. Paulo Neuhaus (Rio de Janeiro: Campus, 1980), p. 198; Luiz Antônio Tannuri, *O Encilhamento* (São Paulo: Hucitec/Fundação da Desenvolvimento da UNICAMP, 1981), pp. 46–47. Gustavo Henrique Barroso Franco blames balance of payments deficits, caused by a retraction of foreign investment, for most of the inflation (*Reforma Monetária*, pp. 139–141).
108. Minutes, meeting of April 30, 1891, Livro de Atas, 1890–1896, AACRJ, p. 42; Commercial Association of Rio de Janeiro to Director, Bank of Brazil, and ten other heads of banks, Rio de Janeiro, Nov. 18, 1891, *Relatório de 1901*, Anexos, 1891, pp. 5–6.

tested to the President of Brazil that exchange depreciation and inflation were creating worse economic disturbances than had abolition.[109] In 1892 the government took first steps against inflation, including curbing the expansion of the money supply, which was not increased again until 1896.[110]

The government's action stabilized the cost of living (although not the exchange rate) between 1893 and 1896, but also contributed to an economic contraction and a renewed lack of liquidity.[111] Meanwhile, neither the temporary return to plural issue nor the vast increase in money supply had overcome chronic shortages of cash. In 1891 several commercial associations complained that notes from the newly established banks of issue were being refused not only by other banks but even by government offices.[112] Early that year Rio de Janeiro underwent a worsening shortage of cash, which by 1892 virtually dried up credit and triggered bankruptcies. Taking care not to argue for increased money supply, the Commercial Association of Rio de Janeiro blamed the withdrawal of capital from use and the shipment of currency to satisfy the harvest needs of the Northeast.[113] Despite such aid the latter area and Pará continued to be plagued with cash shortages, as their commercial associations made plain. By 1896 lack of liquidity and resulting agricultural distress in its state brought the Commercial Association of São Paulo to publish in booklet form a petition demanding an immediate increase in money supply.[114] The government resumed expansion of the money supply that year.

Exchange depreciation and inflation worsened, and from 1896 plummeting coffee prices led to a large balance of payments deficit. The Commercial Association of Rio de Janeiro accelerated its push for a return to a conservative monetary policy. In late 1897 it apparently arranged meetings of businessmen and government officials to discuss halting currency depreciation and inflation.[115] In 1898, seconded by the commercial associations of Rio Grande and Bahia, the Rio group strongly endorsed the

---

109. Commercial Association of Maranhão to President of Republic, no date, 1891, *Relatório, Janeiro a Dezembro de 1891* (São Luís: Frias, 1892), pp. 19–21.

110. Carlos Manuel Peláez and Wilson Suzigan, *História Monetária do Brasil* (Rio de Janeiro: IPEA/INPES, 1976), pp. 180–181.

111. Ibid. A rapid reduction of money supply (11.3%, M-1, and 12.1%, M-2) resulted in 1892. Goldsmith, *Desenvolvimento Financeiro*, p. 101. The deflationary program was largely abandoned in 1894 because of the growth of public expenditure, accelerated by civil war. It was renewed, without success, in 1895. Fritsch, *External Constraints*, p. 6.

112. Minutes, meeting of Feb. 24, 1891, Livro de Atas, 1890–1896, AACRJ, p. 37; Associação Comercial do Maranhão, *Relatório de 1891*, p. 5.

113. Commercial Association of Rio de Janeiro to Minister of Finance, Rio de Janeiro, Feb. 22, 1892, *Relatório de 1901*, Anexos, 1892, pp. 5–6. The liquidity crisis of 1891 may have been triggered by demand for credit for market speculation, as well as for establishing or expanding enterprises. Tannuri, *Encilhamento*, pp. 63–67.

114. Associação Comercial de São Paulo, *Representação Dirigida ao Congresso*, pp. 6–11.

115. *Jornal do Comércio*, Oct. 22, 1897, pp. 1–2.

monetary stabilization efforts of new President Manuel Ferraz de Campos Sales and his Minister of Finance, Joaquim Murtinho.[116] It particularly praised the "Funding Loan," designed to finance a contraction of the money supply and other exchange-strengthening measures, and the decision to pay interest on national debt bonds in gold to holders abroad.[117] Part of the government's program to strengthen the exchange stipulated that merchants make partial payment (eventually twenty-five percent) of import duties in gold. Commercial associations had responded to the 1891 requirement that import duties be paid in gold with a nationwide commercial strike and to proposals to reestablish it in 1893, 1895, and 1896 with vehement protest. But there was now no objection. Their members were by 1898 quite willing to endure the financial burden and inconvenience of paying duties in gold in order to halt inflation and exchange depreciation.[118] In 1902 the Commercial Association of Rio de Janeiro rewarded Campos Sales with honorary membership.[119]

The economic changes that came with the Republic did not relieve the scarcity of agricultural credit. The Republic made several attempts to make low-cost loans available through the Bank of Brazil, but administrative defects kept the credit from reaching those who needed it most.[120] Calls from business interest groups and planters for credit relief and for effective mortgage banks continued. The situation now differed only in that the Southeastern coffee region shared fully in the deprivation.[121]

What had been the impact of business interest groups on nineteenth-century Brazilian banking, credit, and currency? Their individual influence had been strong, but often divided in opinion, they accomplished surprisingly little. The nation's banking system remained inadequate to spur economic development. The question of plurality of issue remained unsettled. Periodic shortages of cash persisted, becoming by the last decade of the nineteenth century more prevalent in the Southeast than before. Perhaps most serious, business interest groups failed to promote adequate credit for agriculture.

116. For the Bahian and Rio Grande associations, see Minutes, meetings of April 18 and Aug. 12, 1898, Livro 6 de Atas, AACB, pp. 295, 309.
117. *Relatório de 1901*, p. 44. For an unfavorable view of the Funding Loan and other fiscal policies of the period 1898–1902, see Carlos Manuel Peláez, "As Conseqüências Econômicas da Ortodoxia Monetária, Fiscal e Cambial no Brasil de 1889 a 1945," *Revista Brasileira de Economia*, 25 (July–Sept. 1971): 25–38.
118. The Funding Loan reduced both money supply and prices and strengthened Brazilian exchange. However, bank failures and a liquidity crisis resulted in September 1900. Paulo Neuhaus, *História Monetária do Brasil, 1900–45* (Rio de Janeiro: Instituto Brasileiro de Mercado de Capitais, 1975), pp. 17–18.
119. Minutes, meeting of Oct. 8, 1902, Livro de Atas, 1902–1906, AACRJ, p. 76.
120. *RMF, 1895*, pp. 112–117; Associação Comercial de Pernambuco, *Relatório de 1890*, p. 18.
121. *O Estado de São Paulo* (São Paulo), Sept. 2, 1896, p. 1; Associação Comercial de São Paulo, *Representação Dirigida ao Congresso* p. 17; [J.R.], *Auxílios à Lavoura* (Rio de Janeiro: C. G. da Silva, 1895); São Paulo, Governador do Estado, *Mensagens ao Congresso de São Paulo*, p. 130.

In part, lack of success was due to circumstances beyond group control. Brazilian economic weaknesses, for example, thwarted their near-unanimous support for a change to a convertible currency based on precious metals. The powerful opposition of planters blocked implementation of laws mandating precise registration of mortgages and demarcation of land. The 1885 changes in credit legislation and the legalization of crop collateral, therefore, were a triumph for merchants but could not increase agricultural lending. Disagreement between the powerful Commercial Association of Rio de Janeiro and most other business interest groups also hindered success. The former not only represented Rio financial interests, but was particularly foreign-dominated and attuned to the desires of overseas lenders and investors. It pushed Brazil's early repudiation of plurality of issue, refused to support permanent remedies for shortages of cash in the Northeast, and usually strongly opposed any weakening of Brazilian currency. Group influence in banking and currency was attenuated by disunity.

One demand of business interest groups had far-reaching consequences. The shortages of cash and credit that gathered force in the 1880s brought a nearly universal demand for greater liquidity. The resulting vast increase in currency supply, fueling the *encilhamento* and inflation, was hardly what the groups had envisioned. Rampant inflation also put an end to hopes of preserving plurality of issue or ending inconvertible currency. By the late 1890s, partially reflecting the interests of foreign lenders and investors, they strongly supported monetary stabilization. But inflation, although occasionally arrested, has continued to plague the Brazilian economy ever since.

Business interest groups had tried to help agricultural development by founding credit institutions or stimulating them and by promoting government support. But both private and government resources proved inadequate to create lasting, viable mortgage institutions. Business interest groups might have increased private funding by urging a reduction in the issue and the interest of public debt bonds, which competed so strongly for available capital. They also might have widened government resources to aid agriculture by supporting new, direct taxes which would have been better sources of revenue. They were willing to do neither. During the nineteenth century Brazilian agriculture enjoyed adequate credit only briefly and in certain parts of the country. Not until the 1920s, and in some areas the 1930s, would regular and sufficient credit for agriculture be established. [122]

122. Joseph L. Love, *São Paulo in the Brazilian Federation, 1889–1937* (Stanford, Calif.: Stanford University Press, 1980), p. 62; Peláez and Suzigan, *Política do Governo*, p. 12.

6

The export economy: manpower

In a plantation export economy cheap, abundant labor was essential. Business interest groups sought to guarantee it for Brazilian agriculture by variously defending slavery, urging that compulsory labor be imposed on rural Brazilians, promoting the influx of Asian or African contract workers, or urging that European immigrants be induced to fill the rural labor gap. In the end, planters and business interest group fears of agricultural labor shortage turned out to be greatly exaggerated.

Business interest groups for the most part helped planters to preserve slavery longer in Brazil than in any other Western nation. Its longevity in Brazil was more than simply an embarrassment to later generations. The presence of slavery and of other low-cost labor retarded economic development by leading landowners to maintain returns by increasing labor supply, rather than emphasizing capital formation and technical progress.[1] Slavery also retarded the growth of the mass market necessary for large-scale industrial development. In a more general sense, slavery was associated with ideological, political, and social patterns inimical to development.[2]

Slavery in Brazil was deeply entrenched. Shortly before independence an estimated 1,887,900 of Brazil's population of 3,817,900 were bondsmen.[3] They were concentrated in the first half of the century in the sugar-growing areas of the Northeast, the old gold-mining region of Minas Gerais, and the Province of Rio de Janeiro. As coffee plantations began to flourish in the Paraíba Valley, between the provinces of Rio de Janeiro and São Paulo, slaves from the economically stagnating Northeast were traded

1. Nathaniel H. Leff, "Economic Retardation in Nineteenth-Century Brazil," *Economic History Review*, 25 (Aug. 1972): 506.
2. Pedro Carvalho Mello and Robert W. Slenes, "Análise Econômica da Escravidão no Brasil," in *Economia Brasileira: Uma Visão Histórica*, ed. Paulo Neuhaus (Rio de Janeiro: Campus, 1980), p. 111; Warren Dean blames slavery for a roughly forty-year delay in the significant growth of Brazilian industry. "A Industrialização Durante a República Velha," in *Estrutura de Poder e Economia*, Vol. I of *O Brasil Republicano*, ed. Bóris Fausto, Tomo III of *História Geral da Civilização Brasileira*, ed. Sérgio Buarque de Holanda (São Paulo: Difusão Editorial, 1975): 251.
3. Robert Conrad, *The Destruction of Brazilian Slavery, 1850–1888* (Berkeley: University of California Press, 1972), p. 283.

there. In contrast to the United States, mortality among slaves was high and fertility low in Brazil, so that their numbers tended to decrease. Among the causes were harsh or careless treatment, generally poor sanitary conditions, a new disease environment for recent arrivals, and a low proportion of women among the slaves.[4] The situation was worsened by the preference of slaveowners for buying new slaves from Africa rather than encouraging their natural increase in Brazil. "If a slave died this worried [the slaveowner] little," noted the Commercial Association of Maranhão, "because with a few *arrobas* of cotton or *alqueires* of rice he could buy a substitute."[5] Although illegal from 1831 by international treaty and domestic legislation, the slave trade had wide support among Brazilians. The Brazilian government finally ended it after 1850, partly in response to British pressure. By 1864, slaves numbered an estimated 1,715,000 in a population of 10,245,000.[6]

Nearly all forms of economic endeavor relied on slave labor. Slaves were found not only in plantations and mines but even in Brazil's few manufactures. Of thirty-six factories in Rio de Janeiro examined between 1809 and 1847, only eleven did not use slaves.[7] Slaves were the sole sustenance of many Brazilians. An early nineteenth-century visitor recorded that "slaves are ordered out every day and must bring in a certain sum each night; and these are the boatmen, chairmen, porters, and weavers of mats and hats that are to be hired in the streets and markets and who thus support their masters."[8] Slavery was pervasive and ubiquitous in Brazilian life. Symbolic, perhaps, was the blind white beggar with a slave to lead him about noted by a visitor in 1882.[9]

At first glance the support of business interest groups for slavery seems surprising. Overseas trading and factorage houses employed few slaves, and slavery was anathema to the British-derived liberalism that business interest groups paraded as their ideology. It was also unpopular in many of the homelands of overseas merchants, Great Britain in particular. However, business interest group leaders often had direct connections to slavery. Some owned plantations that used slave labor; others took part in the

---

4. Ibid., pp. 24–27; Emilia Viotti da Costa, *The Brazilian Empire: Myths and Histories* (Chicago: University of Chicago Press, 1986), pp. 134–135.

5. Associação Comercial do Maranhão, *Exposição do Açúcar e Algodão Feita pela Associação Comercial do Maranhão, 1883* (São Luís: País, 1883), p. 6. For the slave trade question, see Leslie Bethell, *The Abolition of the Brazilian Slave Trade: Britain, Brazil, and the Slave Trade Question, 1807–1869* (Cambridge: Cambridge University Press, 1970).

6. Conrad, *Destruction of Slavery*, p. 283.

7. Eulalia Maria Lahmeyer Lobo, *História do Rio de Janeiro (do Capital Comercial ao Capital Industrial e Financeiro) (Rio de Janeiro: IBMEC, 1978)*, I: 120.

8. Maria Graham, Lady Callcott, *Journal of a Voyage to Brazil and Residence There During the Years 1821, 1822, 1823* (London: Longman, Hurst, Rees, Orme, Brown, and Green, 1824), p. 156.

9. Ulrick Ralph Burke and Robert Staples, Jr., *Business and Pleasure in Brazil* (London: Field and Tuer, 1884), p. 37.

slave trade. The trade was risky but profits were exceedingly high; it was a likely way for an ambitious businessman to start his fortune. James Birckhead, a North American and a founder and director of the Commercial Association of Rio de Janeiro, was involved in the trade, as were Commercial Association of Bahia directors José Alvarez da Cruz Rios, Antônio Francisco de Lacerda, and another North American, John S. Gillmer.[10] Lacerda and Gillmer also used some bondsmen in their textile factory "Todos os Santos" (largest in Brazil and perhaps in Latin America).[11] Also lucrative to overseas merchants, if less noticed, was the furnishing of trade goods for the African coast and slave-trade equipment to slavers. British and other foreign firms took the lead in that business.[12]

Nevertheless, business interest group leaders with a direct stake in slavery were probably a minority. Concern for the welfare of agriculture, seen as the irreplaceable source of Brazilian prosperity, was the overriding motive for support of slavery. The backing of individual groups for the institution tended to reflect its economic importance in the region they represented. Out-migration of slaves through the interprovincial trade and an early and relatively smooth transition from slave to free labor in the provinces of Ceará and Pernambuco meant their business interest groups would become increasingly hostile toward slavery. Conversely, growing numbers of slaves and their key role in economic expansion in the coffee-growing Southeast meant its groups would cling tightly to the institution, although that region was undoubtedly the most dynamic and least traditional. Business interest groups representing Northeastern provinces slow in making a transition from slave to free labor, such as Bahia and Maranhão, also defended slavery. Since all business interest groups contained both partisans and opponents of slavery, pronouncements on it depended largely on the opinions of the current directors. Statements on slavery also threatened group unity. They were carefully, sometimes ambiguously, worded and often issued with reluctance.

10. Antônia Fernanda Pacca de Almeida Wright, *Desafio Americano à Preponderância Britânica no Brasil, 1808–1850* (Rio de Janeiro: Imprensa Nacional, 1972), pp. 179, 233; chargé d'affairs at Rio de Janeiro to Foreign Office, Rio de Janeiro, Nov. 24, 1828, *British and Foreign State Papers*, 16 (1829): 341; Weiss to Foreign Office, Salvador, May 17, 1830, *British and Foreign State Papers*, 18 (1831): 564. Gillmer apparently had a change of heart after becoming United States Consul in 1850. By refusing to grant papers permitting North American vessels to proceed to the African coast he greatly aided suppression of the slave trade. Gillmer to Department of State, Salvador, May 6, 1850, NA/DS T-331, Vol. 1, unpaginated.

11. John Casper Branner, *Cotton in the Empire of Brazil*, Department of Agriculture Special Report no. 8 (Washington, D.C.: Government Printing Office, 1885), p. 42; Manuel Jesuino Ferreira, *A Província da Bahia, Apontamentos* (Rio de Janeiro: Tipografia Nacional, 1875), p. 75.

12. Luís Henrique Dias Tavares, *Comércio Proibido de Escravos* (São Paulo: Attica, 1988), pp. 120–141; See also Robert Conrad, *World of Sorrow: The African Slave Trade to Brazil* (Baton Rouge, La.: Louisiana State University Press, 1986).

Business interest groups and the abolitionist movement

Economic reliance on slavery, and its popularity, meant that abolitionist sentiment would make little impression in Brazil during the first half of the nineteenth century. The nation had virtually no antislavery organizations of consequence until the 1860s and little support for antislavery measures among business interest groups. The Commercial Association of Bahia in 1844 and 1857 condemned laws designed to inhibit slave smuggling on the grounds that they impeded commerce, and in 1845 it denounced British halting and searching of Africa-bound ships for slave-trade paraphernalia.[13] However, during the 1860s and particularly after the United States Civil War, Brazilians began to realize that slavery was a discredited institution among Western nations. Brazil's war with Paraguay (1865–1870) brought about the first tentative and oblique gesture of a business interest group against slavery. On the suggestion of its British president, the Commercial Association of Pernambuco in 1868 organized a committee and a fund to purchase able-bodied slaves for the Brazilian army.[14] Such slaves would become free upon induction. The project was suddenly canceled without explanation, probably because of pressure from planters.[15]

A strong abolitionist movement began to take shape in the late 1860s. Despite its urban and middle-class base, it found at first little support among business interest groups. Several felt obliged to openly defend slavery. The Commercial Association of Pernambuco declared in 1867 that "slavery considered as a whole is an evil; in relation to Brazil, however, it is an evil which must be preserved for some time, in order to avoid greater evils."[16] In 1871 the Maranhão association affirmed that slaves were the most productive workers, "as much because of their very condition as because of their lack of intelligence and education."[17] Nor did most business interest groups uphold government efforts to promote free labor. In 1870 the Commercial Association of Pernambuco protested a tax on slave port workers, and in 1871 the Bahian group denounced the transfer of waterfront employment from slaves to a company of free men as an

13. Commercial Association of Bahia to Chief of Police, Salvador, Dec. 5, 1844, Registro dos Ofícios, 1840–1850, AACB, pp. 179–180; Minutes, meeting of Feb. 17, 1857, Livro 2 de Atas, AACB, p. 116; Minutes, meeting of Dec. 2, 1845, Livro 1 de Atas, AACB, p. 196.
14. Minutes, meetings of Jan. 10 and Jan. 25, 1868, Livro 3 de Atas, AACP, p. 5.
15. Minutes, meeting of Feb. 25, 1868, Livro 3 de Atas, AACP, p. 7.
16. Associação Comercial de Pernambuco, *Relatório da Direção da Associação Comercial Beneficente de Pernambuco, Apresentado à Assembléia Geral da Mesma em 26 de Novembro de 1867* (Recife: Jornal do Recife, 1868), p. 6.
17. Associação Comercial do Maranhão, *Relatório da Comissão da Praça, Apresentado à Assembléia Geral dos Assinantes da Casa da Praça em 9 de Janeiro de 1872* (São Luís: País, 1872), p. 30.

assault on "freedom of work and rights of property."[18] The irony was quite unintentional.

Brazil's first major legislative blow against slavery came on September 28,1871 with the passage of the Law of Free Birth, also known as the Rio Branco Law. It provided that children born of slave mothers after the passage of the law were to be free. The owner could raise such slave children until the age of eight, when he could turn them over to the government for a small cash compensation or keep them and use their labor until the age of twenty-one. The law also created an emancipation fund for the liberation of a certain number of slaves each year. Promising the eventual, if gradual, elimination of slavery, the law had wide support among abolitionists. The Commercial Association of Ceará, which earlier in 1871 had stated disapproval of slavery, sent congratulations to Viscount Rio Branco.[19] The Commercial Association of Pernambuco, typically ambiguous in its actions, appointed a committee to deliver congratulations to the imperial government, but made no mention of doing so in its annual report.[20]

Few others of Brazil's business elite applauded the law. Opposition was strong among coffee factors, who could not visualize an agricultural system without slavery and who accepted slaves as collateral for loans. Between May and July 1871, while the Law of Free Birth was being debated, they organized the Rio-based Agriculture and Commerce Club to rally planters and factors against it. The Club marshaled an impressive array of the coffee region's planter aristocracy and political leadership. It set about creating anti–Free Birth Law groups in rural communities, encouraging legislative opposition to the law, and attacking it with unrestrained rhetoric.[21] One Club orator described blacks to be freed by the law as "illiterate, brute-like; those of peaceful disposition are nothing but crude instruments of labor; those with more spirit are ferocious animals, which the great reform is letting out of the cages to fall upon the peaceful population."[22] With the passage of the law in September the Agriculture and Commerce Club disbanded, but many of its organizers helped form the Center for Coffee Agriculture and Commerce in 1880. In the meantime, supporters of slavery found they could easily live with the Law of Free

---

18. Minutes, meeting of Sept. 5, 1870, Livro 3 de Atas, AACP, p. 60; Commercial Association of Bahia to President of Province, Salvador, March 17, 1871, Presidência da Província/Govêrno ao Associação Comercial, 1845–1889, AEB.

19. Commercial Association of Ceará to President of Province, Fortaleza, July 6, 1871, *Relatório da Associação Comercial da Praça do Ceará, Apresentado à Assembléia Geral dos Sócios pela Diretoria no Dia 1 de Maio de 1872* (Fortaleza: Odorico Colás, 1872), pp. 10, 19–20.

20. Minutes, meetings of Oct. 20 and Nov. 6, 1871, Livro 3 de Atas, AACP, pp. 84, 87.

21. *Diário do Rio de Janeiro*, July 17, 1871, p. l; *Diário de Notícias* (Rio de Janeiro), July 18, 1871, p. 2.

22. Cristiano Otoni in *Diário do Rio de Janeiro*, July 17, 1871, p. 1.

Birth. Nearly all slaveholders preferred to use the labor of those children of slaves born after the law, working them as slaves although they were legally free. Many owners did not register slave births; others recorded all as having occurred prior to September 28, 1871. Within a few years supporters of slavery came to regard the Law of Free Birth as a shield rather than as a threat.

Thus, opposition to those who "conspire against the solution made sacred by the law of September 28, 1871" was the stated chief purpose of the Center for Coffee Agriculture and Commerce upon its foundation in December 1880.[23] Its birth was a reaction against an upsurge of abolitionist activity in 1880; its growth in subsequent years was aided by falling coffee prices. Working through Rio de Janeiro coffee factorage houses, it moved to create local clubs in coffee-growing areas and adopted the newspaper *O Cruzeiro* as its spokesman.[24] By 1884 at least forty-nine agricultural clubs were in existence. Most, however, had either loose or no affiliation with the Center, and the ties that existed tended to weaken over time.[25] Planter mistrust of factor intentions was exacerbated by another activity of the Center: an intensive drive to reform credit legislation which had traditionally favored the planter borrower.

The antiabolition campaign of the Center for Coffee Agriculture and Commerce had backing from other business interest groups. The Commercial Association of Rio de Janeiro warned that any retreat from slavery might unleash an impending crisis, the Santos association applauded the creation of coffee-zone antiabolition groups, and the Maranhão organization denounced the idea of quick abolition as "sentimentality."[26] The support from the Commercial Association of Rio de Janeiro was natural, since all Center directors were members, if not leaders, of the latter organization.

Events of 1884 brought a renewed threat to slavery and an even greater mobilization of business interest groups in its defense. As antislavery agitation increased, the institution was shaken in March by abolition in the Province of Ceará. Some type of decisive move against slavery by the imperial government was widely expected. Emperor Pedro II called Senator Manuel Pinto de Sousa Dantas to head a reform ministry. The Dantas Project, read to Parliament early in June, called for an enlargement of the

23. "O Circular do Centro da Lavoura," in *O Cruzeiro* (Rio de Janeiro), Dec. 4, 1880, p. 3.
24. Ibid.; *O Cruzeiro*, Dec. 10, 1880, pp. 1–2; *Gazeta da Tarde* (Rio de Janeiro), Dec. 10, 1880, p. 2.
25. Laura Jarnagin Pang, "The State and Agricultural Clubs of Imperial Brazil, 1860–1889" (Ph.D. Diss., Vanderbilt University, 1981), pp. 311–312, 338, 359–361.
26. Associação Comercial do Rio de Janeiro, *Relatório da Associação Comercial do Rio de Janeiro do Ano de 1880* (Rio de Janeiro: Montenegro, 1881), p. 4; Associação Comercial de Santos, *Relatório da Associação Comercial de Santos, Apresentado em Sessão Ordinária da Assembléia Geral em Março de 1881* (Rio de Janeiro: G. Leuzinger & Filhos, 1881), p. 17; Associação Comercial do Maranhão, *Exposição do Açúcar e Algodão*, p. 13.

emancipation fund, the end of the interprovincial slave trade, and the liberation of all slaves upon reaching the age of sixty. The latter provision was potentially explosive – it would implicitly destroy the slaveowner's right to indemnification by the government.

Coyness in defense of slavery was thrown aside. Late in May, the Commercial Association of Bahia joined the Imperial Agricultural Institute of Bahia to demand "defense of the rights of property" and "faithful execution of the present law [of Free Birth]."[27] The joint proclamation, signed by most of Salvador's merchant firms and by all members of the Association's board then present, including an Englishman, was forwarded to the Brazilian Parliament and published in newspapers. It characterized the slave as "a social institution, an element of labor, a force of production; in sum . . . our national wealth," and predicted economic ruin, indigence, and crime in the wake of abolition.[28] The declaration marked a break with Dantas, an honorary member of the Bahian association and long one of its champions. The Center for Coffee Agriculture and Commerce took advantage of the charged atmosphere to attempt what it had been unable to do previously: unite the agricultural clubs of the interior under its leadership. Clubs adhered to the Center by the dozen, even from far-away Pernambuco and Maranhão.[29] It also convened an Agricultural Congress in Rio de Janeiro in July, which called for the organization of local defense forces and their liaison with sympathetic law-enforcement officials. But the congress also faced the reality that slavery was doomed. It demanded measures that would force freed slaves to continue working on the plantations and called for both increased European immigration and the importation of Chinese contract laborers.[30]

Given its close ties to the Center for Coffee Agriculture and Commerce, the Commercial Association of Rio de Janeiro could not hesitate to add its voice to the proslavery chorus. Its declaration, issued June 16, 1884, was signed by a special committee chosen in extraordinary general assembly rather than by its board of directors. Foreign directors, then twelve of fifteen, thus could avoid taking a stand. Like the Bahian association, the Rio group saw slavery as "rooted in the national economy, base of its riches, origin of its prosperity, and an indispensable factor in its productive activity."[31] It suggested an increase in the emancipation fund as a

27. Minutes, meeting of May 23, 1884, Livro 5 de Atas, AACB, p. 99.
28. Commercial Association of Bahia and Imperial Bahian Institute of Agriculture to Brazilian Parliament, Salvador, May 30, 1884, *Relatório da Junta Diretora da Associação Comercial da Praça da Bahia, Apresentado e Lido em Sessão da Assembléia Geral Ordinária em 23 de Janeiro de 1885* (Salvador: Dous Mundos, 1885), pp. 22–23, 26–29.
29. Evaristo de Morais, *A Campanha Abolicionista (1879–1888)* (Rio de Janeiro: Leite Ribeiro, 1924), p. 61.
30. Pang, "State and Agricultural Clubs," pp. 354–357.
31. Associação Comercial do Rio de Janeiro, *Elemento Servil: Primeira Representação da Comissão Especial*

harmless alternative to abolition. The Rio association's proclamation also had an ugly racist undertone. It warned that abolition would bring inevitable economic and social disaster, because "the freed slave is incompatible with any type of system of economy and order, of labor, and of morality," and it described freed slaves as individuals made "brute-like by their ignorance and by their moral and mental incapacity."[32]

In Pernambuco the reaction was less extreme. Prodded by agricultural clubs of the interior, the Agriculture Auxiliary Society of Pernambuco organized a "Second Agricultural Congress of Recife," its only purpose the defense of slavery. Still equivocal toward the institution, neither the Commercial Association nor the Commercial Agricultural Association took part as an organization, but both suggested their members attend as individuals.[33] The Commercial Association also implicitly endorsed the congress by letting its headquarters be used as the meeting place. However, the proclamation of the congress was restrained. It neither condemned abolition outright nor attacked the Dantas Project, but simply called for the restoration of order in rural areas disrupted by abolitionist activity.[34] Such moderation was due to a desire to present an appearance of unanimity and to the small proportion of planters at the congress compared to businessmen and professionals from Recife, long a center of British influence and by 1884 also one of abolitionist activity.[35]

The attack of business interest groups and their planter allies helped bring about the rejection of the Dantas Project, the fall of the Dantas cabinet, and the defeat in a bid for reelection as Deputy from Bahia of the bill's young author, Rui Barbosa. The new cabinet offered a substitute project, eventually known as the Saraiva-Cotegipe Bill. This "lame and odious caricature of Dantas' project," as one historian has termed it, required slaves freed upon reaching the age of sixty to give three more years of unpaid labor to their masters, specified that freed slaves live and work in the same rural locations for at least five years, set compensation for emancipated slaves at higher than market prices, and mandated fines and imprisonment for those who helped slaves flee.[36] Aimed at blocking

Nomeada em Assembléia Geral Extraordinária de 2 de Maio de 1884 (Rio de Janeiro: J. Villeneuve, 1884), p. 5.

32. Ibid., pp. 8, 12.
33. Associação Comercial de Pernambuco, *Relatório de 1884*, pp. 37–39; Minutes, meeting of June 14, 1884, Livro de Atas da Associação Comercial Agrícola de Pernambuco (hereafter cited as ACAP), 1877–1892, AACP, p. 107.
34. *ACD, 1884*, III: 394–395.
35. Evaldo Cabral de Melo, *O Norte Agrário e o Império, 1871–1889* (Rio de Janeiro: Nova Fronteira, 1984), pp. 181–182; Carolina Nabuco, *The Life of Joaquim Nabuco*, trans. and ed. Ronald Hilton (New York: Greenwood, 1968), pp. 126–127.
36. Quote from Nabuco, *Life of Joaquim Nabuco*, p. 61; Conrad, *Destruction of Slavery*, pp. 222–224; Robert Brent Toplin, *The Abolition of Slavery in Brazil* (New York: Athneum, 1975), pp. 105–107.

more radical reform, the Saraiva-Cotegipe Bill gained the support of all but the most recalcitrant defenders of slavery. The high compensation set for freeing slaves was also a boon to banks and factors who had lent to planters offering their slaves as security.[37] The Commercial Association of Rio de Janeiro, meeting in extraordinary general assembly, gave the bill a ringing endorsement.[38] The head manager of the London & Brazilian Bank perhaps spoke for foreign business interests in praising the measure, because "the value of property must, we opine, improve very considerably, as the fear of a sudden withdrawal of labor will disappear."[39] Saraiva's project became law in August 1885 under a cabinet led by the proslavery Baron Cotegipe.

The Saraiva-Cotegipe Law only postponed the inevitable. Abolitionist activity redoubled, much of it aimed at helping slaves to flee the plantations. Owners now began to free their bondsmen voluntarily, in order to retain them as free workers. In the Province of São Paulo, European immigrants began to successfully fill the labor needs of coffee plantations. The Cotegipe Ministry tried to stifle abolitionist activity by force, placing a ban on public meetings in Rio de Janeiro in August 1887. Sporadic violence erupted as rallies defying the ban were broken up by police with drawn swords. The Commercial Association of Rio de Janeiro abandoned neither its old friend Cotegipe nor his cause. In a declaration signed by its entire directorate, including the two English representatives, it congratulated him on effective suppression of a threat to public order.[40] Grateful, the beleaguered Cotegipe sent telegrams to all provincial presidents announcing the association's support.[41]

In Pernambuco the transition from slavery was relatively painless. As early as 1873 cotton cultivation was done "almost exclusively" with free labor, and decline in slave numbers on plantations was probably greater in the 1870s than in the late 1880s.[42] An abundance of rural poor made the

---

37. Especially the Bank of Brazil. John Gordon, Deputy Manager, London & Brazilian Bank to Rio de Janeiro Manager, London, July 4, 1888, Letters, London to Rio, 1885–1889, LABA, UCLL, G.2., p. 1.
38. Commercial Association of Rio de Janeiro to Brazilian Parliament, Rio de Janeiro, no date, 1885, *Relatório de 1884–1885*, p. 29.
39. J. Beaton, Manager, London & Brazilian Bank, to Rio de Janeiro Manager, London, June 19, 1885, Letters, London to Rio, 1885–89, LABA, UCLL, G.2., p. 2.
40. Commercial Association of Rio de Janeiro to Baron Cotegipe, Rio de Janeiro, Aug. 19, 1887, Arquivo do Barão de Cotegipe (hereafter cited as ABC), AIHGB, lata 77, doc. 14.
41. *The Rio de Janeiro News*, Sept. 15, 1887, p. 4.
42. *Diário de Pernambuco* (Recife), Jan. 10, 1874, in *O Diário de Pernambuco e a História Social do Nordeste*, ed. José Antônio Gonsalves de Mello (Recife: Diário de Pernambuco, 1975), I: 28; Peter L. Eisenberg, "Abolishing Slavery: The Process on Pernambuco's Sugar Plantations," *HAHR*, 52 (Nov. 1972): 588. For an opposing view of the decline of slavery in Pernambuco, see Jaime Reis, "Abolition and the Economics of Slavery in Northeastern Brazil," *Boletín de Estudios Latinoamericanos y del Caribe*, 17 (Dec. 1974): 3–20.

conversion from slavery easy for planters, as wages and living conditions fell steadily from the early 1870s to a level where free workers were, in a material sense, hardly better off than slaves.[43] The lessening dependence of its area on slavery affected the shifting attitudes of the Commercial Association of Pernambuco. In 1879 it protested that a tax destined for an emancipation fund was not actually being used to free slaves, and in 1882 it lent its headquarters "with pleasure" to an abolitionist society for the ceremonial freeing of slaves.[44] On the other hand, in 1884 it tepidly supported the Second Agricultural Congress of Recife and also refused to participate as a group or to recommend the participation of its members in festivities celebrating abolition in Ceará.[45] But after that year it came out more boldly against slavery. In 1885 it pointedly refused to blame the abolitionist movement when queried by government on the reasons for the decline in provincial exports, and it named to honorary membership the famed abolitionist Deputy Joaquim Nabuco.[46] For 1888 it chose as its president a noted abolitionist businessman, Manuel Gomes de Mattos.

On the eve of abolition, business interest groups variously showed eagerness, resignation, or dismay. The Commercial Association of Pernambuco's directors voted unanimously on April 2, 1888 to demand the immediate end of slavery.[47] The Commercial Association of Maranhão tried to prepare local agriculture for the blow. In 1887 and early in 1888 it invited planters to conferences on how to deal with the coming end of slavery, at the second offering a cash prize for the best plan to transform slave labor into free labor.[48] Its annual report, issued in March 1888, optimistically forecast that Maranhão could prosper without slavery.[49] There was no optimism in Bahia. An urgent plea for government aid issued jointly on May 5 by the directors of its Commercial Association and Imperial Institute of Agriculture spoke of slaves quitting the plantations in numbers and impending labor crisis.[50]

43. Eisenberg, "Abolishing Slavery," 590, 592; Jaime Reis, "From Bangüê to Usina: Pernambuco, 1850–1920," in *Land and Labour in Latin America*, eds. Kenneth Duncan and Ian Rutledge (Cambridge: Cambridge University Press, 1977), pp. 386–388; David A. Denslow, "Sugar Production in Northeastern Brazil and Cuba, 1858–1908" (Ph.D. Diss., Yale University, 1974), p. 56.

44. Associação Comercial de Pernambuco, *Relatório de 1879*, pp. 8–9; Minutes, meeting of Nov. 8, 1882, Livro 5 de Atas, AACP, p. 65.

45. Associação Comercial de Pernambuco, *Relatório de 1884*, pp. 35–36.

46. Minutes, meetings of March 13 and June 17, 1885, Livro 5 de Atas, AACP, pp. 116, 121.

47. Minutes, meeting of April 2, 1888, Livro 7 de Atas, AACP, p. 19.

48. Airlie to Foreign Office, São Luís, no date, 1888, Great Britain, Foreign Office, *Diplomatic and Consular Reports on Trade and Finance. Miscellaneous Series*, no. 441 (1888): 4; Jerônimo de Viveiros, *História do Comércio do Maranhão, 1612–1895* (São Luís: Associação Comercial do Maranhão, 1954), II: 556–557.

49. *Diário de Santos*, May 8, 1888, p. 1.

50. Commercial Association of Bahia and Imperial Institute of Agriculture of Bahia to Princess Regent, Salvador, May 5, 1888, *Relatório de 1889*, p. 29.

The longed-for and dreaded day fell on May 13, 1888. The Commercial Association of Pernambuco immediately sent congratulations to the Princess Regent (Pedro II was abroad) and to others involved in abolition and then joined and helped fund the public festivities and solemn masses staged in celebration.[51] Other business interest groups took the event in bad grace. Both the Bahia and Rio de Janeiro associations avoided taking part in the celebrations.[52] Nor, officially, did the Commercial Association of Santos, despite being situated in a city that was a noted hotbed of abolitionism and having, like Rio, a board of directors heavily dominated by foreigners.[53]

Mobilizing free labor

With the demise of slavery, business interest groups turned their full attention to mobilizing free labor. Facilitating use of free labor by planters had been a concern even while slavery was in bloom. During the Paraguayan War, the commercial associations of Pernambuco and Maranhão had complained to their presidents of province about the army's overly energetic recruitment of rural workers.[54] Pernambuco's Commercial Association and Commercial Agricultural Association advocated the building of railways not only for transportation, but to force some 20,000 mule skinners into "useful" agricultural work.[55] Most group leaders believed that freed slaves would not work without compulsion. At the Recife Agricultural Congress of 1878 a committee on labor composed of planters and businessmen emphasized the need for laws to fix the location of rural workers and also of drought refugees from the arid interior.[56] The report of the Commercial Agricultural Association was even more emphatic. Announcing a growing labor shortage, it called for "severe laws or police

51. Minutes, meeting of May 14, 1888, Livro 7 de Atas, AACP, p. 159; Associação Comercial de Pernambuco, *Relatório de 1888*, p. 14.
52. Directors of the Rio association made a decision not to participate; the Bahia group simply did not appear. Minutes, meeting of May 21, 1888, Livro de Atas, 1881–1890, AACRJ, p. 191; *Diário da Bahia* (Salvador), May 17–22, 1888, passim.
53. Minutes of meetings of the Board of the Santos association show no evidence of participation in festivities, nor is it listed among twenty-six committees officially celebrating emancipation. However, a "Praça do Comércio" committee, apparently composed of dissenting members acting on their own, appeared on May 16. Livro de Atas, 1874–1894, AACS, pp. 115–116. *Diário de Santos*, May 15, 1888, p. 1, and May 16, 1888, p. 1.
54. Commercial Association of Pernambuco to President of Province, Recife, Feb. 4, 1868, *Relatório de 1868*, p. 49; Associação Comercial do Maranhão, *Relatório de 1867*, p. 8.
55. Associação Comercial Agrícola de Recife [Pernambuco], *Congresso Agrícola do Recife* (Recife: M. Figueiroa de Faria & Filhos, 1878), p. 15; Associação Comercial de Pernambuco, *Relatório de 1883*, p. 12.
56. Sociedade Auxiliadora da Agricultura de Pernambuco, *Trabalhos do Congresso Agrícola do Recife em Outubro de 1878* (Recife: Manuel Figueiroa de Faria & Filhos, 1879), p. 331.

regulations [turning] labor obligatory, ending roaming, making standard a fixed location for service" and for putting young slaves freed under the Law of Free Birth into state institutions teaching "love of work, moral education, and advanced methods of cultivating the soil."[57] But, typically, the shortage of labor was exaggerated. During the discussions, several landowners reported no shortage of hands, but rather a surplus looking for work and not finding it.[58] Nevertheless, as slavery weakened, business interest groups increasingly called for forced labor, fixed locations of service, or binding labor contracts for ex-slaves, as well as government institutes to teach young freedmen discipline and love of agricultural labor. The Agricultural Industrial Center of Pelotas came into being in 1887 to protest the annulment by its province, Rio Grande do Sul, of binding labor contracts imposed on recently freed slaves to keep them working in jerked-beef processing plants.[59]

By the eve of abolition, slavery's hold had become feeble. Only an estimated four percent of Brazil's total population remained in bondage.[60] Nevertheless, abolition was painful in those localities unable or unwilling to have advanced the transition to free labor. Whereas plantations in the Province of São Paulo had made successful use of immigrant labor, the older plantations of the Province of Rio de Janeiro had not. The United States Consul attributed a drop of more than one-third in the latter's coffee crop to the effects of abolition.[61] In the Province of Bahia the transformation to free labor had been notably slower than in rival Pernambuco, and in neighboring Sergipe slaves had outnumbered free workers threefold as late as 1885.[62] A director of the Commercial Association of Bahia reported that freed slaves had quit the sugar fields to plant tobacco and cassava, that most *engenhos* had shut down, and that looting was "taking place on a grand scale."[63] The value of exports shipped from Bahia (which included those of Sergipe) dipped nearly forty percent in 1889, although part of the loss was due to a severe drought in the interior.[64] In Maranhão, another province laggard in changing to free labor, slaves abandoning work caused

57. Ibid., pp. 278–279.   58. Ibid., pp. 174–175, 382.
59. Agricultural Industrial Center of Pelotas to Baron Cotegipe, President, Council of Ministers, Pelotas, Feb. 18, 1888, ABC, IHGB, lata 77, doc. 19.
60. Nathaniel H. Leff, "Long-Term Brazilian Economic Development," *The Journal of Economic History*, 29 (September 1969): 103.
61. Consul-General Armstrong to Department of State, Rio de Janeiro, May, 1889, *USRC*, XXX, no. 105 (May 1889): 214.
62. Cabral de Melo, *Norte Agrário*, p. 23.
63. Aristides Novis to Baron Cotegipe, Salvador, May 30 and Aug. 25, 1888, ABC, AIHGB, lata 49, docs. 25 and 28.
64. From 15,434 *contos* in 1888 to 9,794. Bahia, Diretoria do Serviço de Estatística, *Anuário Estatística da Bahia, 1923* (Salvador: Imprensa Oficial do Estado, 1924), p. 19; Bahia, Presidente da Província, *Fala com que o Exm. Sr. Conselheiro Theodoro Machado Freire Pereira da Silva Abriu a Primeira Sessão da Vigésima Sexta Legislatura da Assembléia Legislativa Provincial no Dia 3 de Abril de 1886* (Salvador: Gazeta da Bahia, 1886), pp. 156–157.

a loss of perhaps half the sugar, cotton, and cereal crops, and closed some seventy percent of the sugar *engenhos* and thirty percent of the cotton plantations.[65] In other provinces, with the exception of small Rio Grande do Norte in the Northeast, the coffee zone of Minas Gerais, and Rio Grande do Sul where slaves had processed jerked beef, the impact of May 13, 1888 was much less.[66]

In affected areas business interest groups reacted to abolition with recriminations and demands for forced labor. Hyperbole was unrestrained. Typical was a July petition from a meeting of planters and merchants organized by the Commercial Association of Bahia. Addressed to the Princess Regent (Pedro II was abroad), its tone was indicated by its opening line: "Madame! This moment is more than grievous, it is desperate!"[67] The association insisted that free labor be organized so that it was "properly led and utilized," and loafing "energetically and forcefully repressed," otherwise, laborers, "ignored and handed over to the voracity of their own instincts, to sloth, to ignorance . . . will be the germ of constant strife and ruin for our nation."[68] The Commercial Association of Maranhão claimed that freed slaves were given over to "total laziness," and needed "laws [which] oppressed idleness and stimulated work."[69] The Maranhão association not only had discussed such laws but also a heavy tax on hunting and fishing to force workers back to the plantations.[70] The Center for Coffee Agriculture and Commerce informed the prime minister that emancipation had "swept away with dizzying speed the disciplined hosts of labor, leaving behind idleness and unrepressed turbulence, desolation, hunger, and misery to spread throughout the vastness of the nation," and hinted at the need for compulsory labor.[71] The demands of business interest groups generally echoed those of planters. On one of the latter's goals, however, most business groups were silent: financial compensation

65. Associação Comercial do Maranhão, "Relatório de 1888," in Viveiros, *Comércio do Maranhão*, II: 469, 557.
66. Great Britain, Foreign Office, *Diplomatic and Consular Reports*, no. 606 (1889): 12; João Pedro da Veiga Filho, *Estudo Econômico e Financeiro sôbre o Estado de São Paulo* (São Paulo: Diário Oficial, 1896), pp. 65–66; Joseph L. Love, *Rio Grande do Sul and Brazilian Regionalism, 1882–1937* (Stanford, Calif.: Stanford University Press, 1971), pp. 20, 54.
67. Representação Dirigida pela Comissão da Lavoura e Comércio a sua Alteza Imperial Regente, Salvador, July 5, 1888, Presidência da Província/Govêrno ao Associação Comercial, 1846–1889, AEB.
68. Ibid.
69. Quoted in Viveiros, *Comércio do Maranhão*, II: 469, 471.
70. João Dunshee de Abranches Moura, *Transformação do Trabalho: Memória Apresentada à Associação Comercial do Maranhão* (São Luís: Pacotilha, 1888), p. 49.
71. Center for Coffee Agriculture and Commerce to Viscount Ouro Preto, Rio de Janeiro, July 17, 1889, Coleção Ouro Preto, AIHGB, lata 427, doc. 10, pp. 1, 6. The Center did no more than hint because Ouro Preto was known to oppose forced labor. Michael R. Trochim, "Retreat from Reform: The Fall of the Brazilian Empire, 1888–1889" (Ph.D. Diss., University of Illinois at Chicago Circle, 1983), p. 141.

for slaveholders. It would have required increased taxation, most of which would have been levied on commerce.

Laws for fixed location of service and forced labor were discussed in Parliament but defeated. Thereafter, demands for regulation of rural labor lessened. After the initial exhilaration of freedom, most ex-slaves returned to the plantations; they had few alternative means of livelihood. Service tenure, sharecropping, wage labor (often seasonal), or gang labor run by local contractors replaced slavery, the importance of each varying according to locality. The alarming initial drop in production had occurred where planters had made little or no provision to substitute for slavery. When it ended, they found themselves without cash to pay salaries, thus usually unable to regain the services of their former slaves. They could not borrow, because of unsettled conditions and because slaves could no longer be offered as security.[72] These problems gradually ended, helped by loans through Viscount Ouro Preto's "Aid for Agriculture" program. With the exception of the Province (after 1889, State) of Rio de Janeiro, labor thenceforth appears to have been relatively plentiful and cheap.[73] Nevertheless, occasional grumbling about lack of hands and the laziness and undependability of ex-slaves continued. A British consul put his finger on the main reason for post-1888 rural labor problems:

Field hands are said to be scarce all over Brazil . . . but planters would find plenty of laborers at a fair wage if promptly and regularly paid. The mode of payment, frequent delays, and uncertainty of obtaining the full amount due, influence the upcountry laborers to work only when forced to do so by hunger. But whenever there is a good and honest system of payment labour is plentiful, and not too dear.[74]

A second alternative: immigration

A third means by which business interest groups tried to solve agriculture's manpower problems was through promoting immigration. They frequently urged government to escalate immigration, especially when discussing the inevitable end of slavery. Government occasionally consulted business interest groups on immigration problems, because of their strong foreign ties and economic knowledge necessary for the welfare of settlers. The Commercial Association of Santos, for example, was queried

---

72. For example, Aristedes Novis to Baron Cotegipe, Salvador, May 30 and July 11, 1888, ABC, AIHGB, lata 49, docs. 25 and 27; Great Britain, Foreign Office, *Diplomatic and Consular Reports,* no. 441 (1888): 4; Viveiros, *Comércio do Maranhão,* II, 470.
73. For wages in the State of Rio de Janeiro, see Great Britain, Foreign Office, *Diplomatic and Consular Reports,* no. 1136 (1892): 30, and Henri Diamanti, "Nota sôbre a Indústria Açucareira no Brasil," trans. Gadiel Perruci, in Gadiel Perruci, *A República das Usinas* (Rio de Janeiro: Paz e Terra, 1978), p. 233.
74. Williams to Foreign Office, Recife, March 29, 1895, Great Britain, Foreign Office, *Diplomatic and Consular Reports,* no. 1547 (1895): 10.

on the best crops for immigrant small farmers and the Bahian association on the best locations and methods of planting cotton for prospective settlement of Confederate refugees after the Civil War.[75] Some of the leaders of the Rio de Janeiro and Santos commercial associations also had a vested interest in promoting immigration. They headed companies that imported and settled immigrants for government or for landowners. Business interest group promotion of immigration before government also was important to its progress because it depended heavily on subsidies and other state support.

Business interest groups divided their efforts between promoting the entry of small farmers to settle the land and of rural workers to provide labor for the plantations. The first aim in a sense contradicted the groups' habitual concern for the landed aristocracy and the large landholding. But expansion of smallholdings did not necessarily threaten that institution. Large landholders in many parts of Brazil had traditionally drawn part of their labor force, especially for seasonal work, from nearby small farm communities. Most businessmen in the export sector also preferred to see land taken by small farmers rather than lie vacant. However, some group leaders apparently supported immigration of small farmers for the same reason as did many urban middle class Brazilians. They saw small farmer immigration as a counterweight to the power of the landed aristocracy and also as a means of whitening Brazil's racial composition. The result was occasional proposals out of line with the usual conservatism of business interest groups.

Until late in the nineteenth century Brazil attracted few immigrants. This was despite generally good private and government support and easy naturalization. Immigration was handicapped by the predominance of large estates and slavery, an uncertain land title system, and lack of systematic land surveys. Unclaimed land was not free; by an 1850 law it could only be purchased. Brazil also faced competition for immigrants from the United States, the British dominions, and, closer to home, Argentina. Until 1885, little more than 30,000 arrived in any one year, and most were Portuguese, as in colonial times.[76] Only in the southernmost Province of Rio Grande do Sul, where Germans had entered beginning in 1824, followed by Italians after 1875, were large numbers of immigrants settled before 1885.[77] In the Northeast and North the only

75. Associação Comercial de Santos, *Relatório de 1882*, pp. 20–21; Minutes, meeting of Dec. 19, 1865, Livro 3 de Atas, AACB, p. 79.
76. T. Lynn Smith, *Brazil: People and Institutions* (rev. ed.; Baton Rouge: Louisiana State University Press, 1963), p. 122.
77. Paul Singer, *Desenvolvimento Econômico e Evolução Urbana (Análise da Evolução Econômica de São Paulo, Blumenau, Pôrto Alegre, Belo Horizone e Recife* (2d ed.; São Paulo: Nacional, 1977), pp. 156, 164.

foreigners were businessmen, Portuguese predominating, and a handful of planters.

Business interest group attention to immigration began in the late 1860s. Conscription for the Paraguayan War reduced the supply of agricultural labor, and after the United States Civil War, group leaders could foresee the inevitable end of slavery. The Commercial Association of Rio de Janeiro created the International Immigration Society (*Sociedade Internacional de Imigração*), a major voluntary society supporting immigration, in January 1866. The society was housed initially in its headquarters and was led by its future vice-president. A hospice it established to receive newly arrived immigrants was supervised by another association director until taken over by the government.[78] Attempts to promote immigration of agricultural workers or settlers in the Northeast in 1866 found a much weaker response. The Commercial Association of Pernambuco, at the urging of an emissary from the International Immigration Society, and the Bahian association, at the request of its provincial government, held repeated meetings to gather support from membership and public for legislation or organizations furthering immigration.[79] The turnout was minimal. Public backing for increasing immigration in Bahia and in Pernambuco was clearly wanting.

Despite lack of public support, business interest groups in the Northeast and North kept urging immigration. They were well aware of the obstacles to the settlement of small farmers and sometimes offered solutions radical in the context of landowner-dominated Brazil. Noting that its province had spent much money with little success in settling immigrants, the Commercial Association of Pará in 1868 recommended selling public lands at minimal price to the local poor. They would undertake the formidable task of clearing the rain forest. Foreigners could then buy cleared land from them, avoiding the foremost difficulty encountered by settlers.[80] In 1867 the Pernambuco association asked its province to subsidize the introduction of European laborers.[81] However, queried by the imperial government in 1871, it put forth a sober assessment of the obstacles to immigration in the Northeast and a radical proposal for overcoming them. The association noted that immigrants faced monopoly by large landholdings, isolation due to lack of transportation, and, if agricultural workers, treatment like slaves by *senhores de engenho*. As solu-

---

78. Sociedade Internacional de Imigração, *Sociedade Internacional de Imigração, Relatório Anual da Diretoria . . . Numero 1* (Rio de Janeiro: J. Villeneuve, 1867), pp. 3–4.
79. Associação Comercial de Pernambuco, *Relatório de 1866*, p. 13; *Diário da Bahia* (Salvador), June 3, 1866, p. 2; Associação Comercial da Bahia, *Relatório de 1867*, p. 9.
80. Associação Comercial do Pará, *Relatório da Comissão da Praça do Comércio do Pará, Apresentado em Sessão Ordinária da Assembléia Geral em 2 de Janeiro de 1868* (Belém: Diário do Grão-Pará, 1868), pp. 11–12.
81. Associação Comercial de Pernambuco, *Relatório de 1867*, p. 7.

tions, it suggested support for railroads providing access to unclaimed lands and, surprisingly, a land reform law to force surrender to the government, albeit with compensation, of uncultivated landholdings.[82]

Business interest groups in the Southeast and South also called for the entry of small farmers. In 1872 the Commercial Association of Pôrto Alegre pleaded for a treaty restoring German immigration, prohibited at its source since 1859 because of alleged abuses.[83] In 1883 the Rio de Janeiro association called for stimulating immigration through a tax on land, apparently to force the breakup of large, uncultivated estates, as well as for civil marriage and unrestricted freedom of religion. The association emphasized that there would be little immigration without making it easy for immigrants to own land.[84] In 1885, urging Parliament to approve increased immigration funding, it repeated its recommendations of 1883, except the call for taxation of land.[85] Like the Commercial Association of Pernambuco earlier, the Rio group did not persist in urging the breakup of large, underutilized landholdings. To do so would have risked a split between Brazil's business elite and landed aristocracy.[86]

The approaching end of slavery reawakened calls for immigrant labor in the Northeast. In 1886 the Commercial Association of Bahia sponsored the Bahian Immigration Society (*Sociedade Bahiana de Imigração*), but found no money for its projects among planters or provincial government.[87] The President of Province of Pernambuco invited the Commercial Association and Commercial Agricultural Association to meetings in 1885 and in early 1888 to determine the best means of attracting immigrants.[88] The Commercial Association sent its 1888 counsel, which had been rejected by the province, on to Brazil's prime minister. It called for

82. Commercial Association of Pernambuco to President of Province, Recife, April 25, 1871, *Relatório de 1871*, pp. 39–42.
83. Commercial Association of Pôrto Alegre to President of Province, Pôrto Alegre, Sept. 23, 1872, *Relatório da Praça do Comércio de Pôrto Alegre dos Anos de 1872 e 1873* (Pôrto Alegre: Rio Grandense, 1873), pp. 5–6. Slowing rather than halting German immigration, the prohibition was not repealed until 1896. Smith, *Brazil*, p. 465.
84. Associação Comercial do Rio de Janeiro, *Relatório de 1882–1883*, pp. 5–6.
85. Commercial Association of Rio de Janeiro to Chamber of Deputies, Rio de Janeiro, July 2, 1885, *Relatório de 1884–1885*, pp. 30–32.
86. Fear of agrarian reform in the wake of abolition helped turn landowners against the Empire. Richard Graham, "Landowners and the Overthrow of the Empire," *Luso-Brazilian Review*, 7 (Dec. 1970): 44–56; Trochim, "Retreat from Reform," passim.
87. Minutes, meeting of March 17, 1886, Livro 5 de Atas, AACB, p. 246; it closed its doors a little over a year after its founding. Commercial Association of Bahia to President of Province, Salvador, July 21, 1887, Presidência da Província/Govêrno ao Associação Comercial, 1846–1889, AEB.
88. Minutes, meeting of Jan. 22, 1885, Livro 5 de Atas, AACP, p. 112; Minutes, meetings of March 9, 1885 and April 16, 1888, Livro de Atas da ACAP, 1877–1892, AACP, pp. 117, 159; Commercial Association of Pernambuco to President, Council of Ministers, Recife, April 2, 1888, *Relatório de 1888*, p. 61.

laws facilitating the acquisition of land by poor Brazilians, rather than spending public funds to settle foreigners.[89] The founding of settlements of native Brazilians was an alternative to immigration sometimes advocated by nationalists. The Commercial Association of Maranhão arranged a conference of planters and merchants in August 1887, which called on the imperial government to aid the introduction of immigrant agricultural workers into that province. The government responded with a plan (never fully implemented) to settle 6,000 foreigners there.[90] None of these proposals had much concrete result, and immigration continued to have little impact on the Northeast.

This was not the case in the Southeast and South. In 1885 planters in the Province of São Paulo began to import large numbers of immigrants as coffee plantation workers.[91] The successful use of nonslave labor multiplied the demand for immigrants. The influx was mainly to São Paulo and mostly Italian, and by 1900 foreigners constituted sixty-five percent of its rural work force.[92] Meanwhile, the settlement of small farmers had already provided great social and economic benefits to the Province of Rio Grande do Sul. Strong support for immigration would continue. After the coming of the Republic it would be financed mainly by the states rather than the federal government. São Paulo would emphasize the recruitment of agricultural laborers; the three southernmost states, Paraná, Santa Catarina, and Rio Grande do Sul, small farm homesteaders.

With the Republic, the interest of Northeastern and Northern business interest groups in European immigration lessened. Their states did not experience the predicted shortage of labor following abolition and were too impoverished, with the exception of Pará and Amazonas, to finance large-scale immigration. In the Southeast and South, conversely, the entry of both agricultural workers and small farmers accelerated. After abolition, the Commercial Association of Pôrto Alegre requested Parliament that the mostly unused funds collected in Rio Grande do Sul to emancipate slaves under the Saraiva-Cotegipe Law be turned over to the province to finance the immigration of small farmers.[93] The Commercial Associa-

89. Commercial Association of Pernambuco to President, Council of Ministers, Recife, April 2, 1888, *Relatório de 1888*, p. 61.
90. Viveiros, *Comércio do Maranhão*, II: 468, 470.
91. Earlier in 1885 a U.S. consul could still report that nothing was being done in the province to substitute free for slave labor. "Cultivation of, and Trade in, Coffee in Central and South America," *USRC*, XXVIII, no. 98 (Oct. 1888): 10. Pioneering efforts to use European immigrants took place around midcentury. Emília Viotti da Costa, *Da Senzala à Colônia* (São Paulo: Difusão Européia do Livro, 1966), pp. 79–83.
92. Martin T. Katzman, "São Paulo and Its Hinterland: Evolving Relationships and the Rise of an Industrial Power," in *Manchester and São Paulo: Problems of Rapid Urban Growth*, eds. John D. Wirth and Robert L. Jones (Stanford, Calif.: Stanford University Press, 1978), p. 11.
93. *ACD, 1888*, III: 370.

tion of Rio de Janeiro in 1891 praised immigration as a source of planta-tion labor and urged expanded national government support.[94] On the other hand, in 1895 the Commercial Association of Santos filed a curious objection to the successful importation of agricultural laborers by its province. It called for the immigration in volume of Europeans other than Italian and for the establishment in São Paulo of more small farm settle-ments such as characterized Rio Grande do Sul.[95] Support for smallholder occupation of the land emerged in unexpected places.

In the wake of slavery: Chinese contract labor

Despite the concern of business interest groups about agriculture's labor needs, they made relatively few calls for the immigration of European rural workers. Most group leaders probably believed that planters would treat Europeans like slaves, leading to either flight or violence, and that, at any rate, Europeans were unlikely to work for the wages Brazilian planters were willing to pay. Another solution, offered by the example of California and of British and French colonies in the Indian Ocean and elsewhere, was the labor of Asian contract workers. After abolition the idea of importing African contract labor, including repatriated former slaves, also arose.[96]

Proposals to import Chinese began even before abolition threatened. In 1854, João Maurício Wanderley, future Baron Cotegipe, recommended as substitutes for slaves, "the Chinese, men [who are] frugal, economical, used to suffering, and accustomed to rough labor."[97] Support for the introduction of Chinese grew as abolition drew nearer, but the idea re-mained controversial. Opponents of slavery saw importation of Chinese as an attempt to prolong the institution in another guise; proponents of white immigration saw their presence as blocking the entry of Europeans. The idea aroused misgivings even among those most dependent on slav-ery. A committee of Commercial Association of Maranhão and planter leaders formed by the government of that province in 1870 to confront threatened labor shortages declared itself against the introduction of

94. Commercial Association of Rio de Janeiro to Vice-President of Republic, Rio de Janeiro, Dec. 16, 1891, *Relatório de 1901*, Anexos, 1891, pp. 8–9.
95. Associação Comercial de Santos, *Relatório de 1895*, pp. 15–16.
96. Perhaps most seriously for Bahia. Stevens to Foreign Office, Salvador, Sept. 14, 1890, PRO/FO 13/670, fl. 196–199. For an overview of the Chinese labor question, see Robert Conrad, "The Planter Class and the Debate over Chinese Immigration to Brazil, 1850–1893," *International Migration Review*, 9 (Spring 1975): 41–55.
97. Bahia, Presidente da Província, *Relatório de 1854*, p. 34.

"those miserable coolies" and expressed the fear that in Brazil "they will come *to instruct* [italics theirs] and if it were in great numbers they might absorb us."[98]

The first business interest group to campaign for the importation of Chinese contract laborers was the Center for Coffee Agriculture and Commerce. In 1882 it declared the hope of large-scale immigration of Europeans to be unrealistic and proposed the Chinese as the future basis for plantation labor.[99] It then petitioned the government to establish a consulate in China and to grant a subsidy to a Chinese shipping company to facilitate immigration. In 1883 a company was formed to negotiate for the shipment of Chinese workers, but Chinese authorities, worried about possible mistreatment of the immigrants, would not cooperate.[100] When the Center for Coffee Agriculture and Commerce became inactive after 1890 the Commercial Association of Rio de Janeiro, probably motivated by labor costs in the State of Rio de Janeiro, took up the cause. In 1892 it asked for the repeal of an 1890 decree barring from Brazil natives of Asia and Africa and announced its support for the immigration of those races.[101] The decree was promptly revoked. Other business interest groups with labor problems also looked to Asian and African labor. In 1894 the directors of the Commercial Association of Santos voted unanimously to petition Congress in support of a proposal to introduce Liberians as waterfront labor.[102] That association had labor disputes with Santos longshoremen, which erupted with the coming of the Republic. The Commercial Association of Pará, complaining of a lack of manpower, petitioned the federal government in 1895 to aid the immigration of Chinese and Japanese labor as "most appropriate" for the region.[103]

The demands of business interest groups for Chinese labor had little effect and for African labor none. Only a little under 3,000 Chinese entered Brazil during the nineteenth century.[104] The frustration of large-scale immigration, however, was not primarily due to Brazilian opposition but to Chinese government mistrust of Brazilian working conditions and to the bad experiences of Chinese contract workers elsewhere, including Cuba and Peru.[105] The idea of using Asian labor on plantations remained, finally finding fruition after 1908 with the importation of

98. Associação Comercial do Maranhão, *Relatório de 1870*, pp. 13–14.
99. Centro da Lavoura e Comércio do Café, *Representação Submetida ao Poder Legislativo sôbre Algumas Necessidades da Lavoura e do Comércio* (Rio de Janeiro: Moreira, Maximínio, 1882), p. 14.
100. Conrad, "Chinese Immigration," 46–47.   101. *ACD, 1892*, V: 315–316.
102. Minutes, meeting of April 23, 1894, Livro de Atas, 1874–1894, AACS, p. 188.
103. Commercial Association of Pará to Minister of Finance, Belém, March 26, 1895, *Relatório de 1896*, pp. 11–12.
104. Conrad, "Chinese Immigration," 42.   105. Ibid., 55.

Japanese workers, whose descendants now constitute a numerous and prosperous element in the population of the State of São Paulo.

The manpower question: a variety of answers

The activities of business interest groups in the field of manpower were both retrograde and forward-looking in their effect on development. Many clung to the hope of preserving slavery as long as possible. The commercial associations of Ceará and Pernambuco were exceptions (the latter belatedly), but their influence was far outweighed by such groups as the Center for Coffee Agriculture and Commerce and the Commercial Association of Rio de Janeiro. The preponderance of foreign directors in the latter and in the Commercial Association of Santos did not make them hostile to the institution. The supposed antipathy of urban businessmen to slavery may have existed for individuals, but not for Brazil's business elite as a whole. Business interest group support was undoubtedly a factor in the longevity of Brazilian slavery.

Faced with its demise, many groups promoted, unsuccessfully, compulsory labor and fixed location of services as a substitute. Several of the most powerful business interest groups supported another ultimately untried substitute, the importation of Asian or African contract workers. Business interest groups made only sporadic demands for European rural workers, perhaps because of initial doubts that they could be used successfully. On the other hand, the groups showed surprising support for the settlement of small farmers, in some ways a contradiction to their attitudes on slavery, forced labor, and Chinese contract labor. This helped to ensure government support for the immigration and settlement of smallholders, a policy that spurred development of the South and that continued well into the twentieth century.[106] The complex and often contradictory attitudes of business interest groups toward manpower helped both restrain and advance Brazilian development.

106. Smith, *Brazil*, pp. 143, 411–427.

7

Taxation

The form and extent of taxation profoundly affected Brazilian development. As merchants were the axis of Brazil's export-import economy, so were they the focus of taxation. In addition to import and export tariffs, a host of minor taxes and fees were levied on the movement, handling, or storage of goods. Between 1831 and 1885, some seventy to seventy-five percent of the Empire's revenue came from the movement of external commerce.[1] The chief source was importation. Between 1850 and 1900 importation represented an average of ninety-four percent of the value of exportation, taking about thirty percent of national income.[2] During the Empire, import tariffs commonly accounted for half or more of the central government's revenue. With the Republic, export taxation was turned over to the states, and by 1896 import revenues furnished more than ninety percent of federal government income.[3]

In addition to taxes on the movement of trade, merchants also bore the brunt of several important noncommercial taxes, such as the urban real estate (*décima urbana*) tax and the industries and professions tax, which despite its title burdened physicians and lawyers little and landowners not at all. Their central position in the Brazilian taxation system not only encumbered merchants financially but complicated and slowed the conduct of business. Brazilian taxation was characterized by number and variety of levies and their frequent illogical application. As the president

---

1. Luís Aureliano Gama de Andrade, "Dez Anos de Orçamento Imperial: 1867–1877," *Revista Brasileira de Estudos Políticos*, 31 (May 1971):188; Nathaniel H Leff, *Underdevelopment and Development in Brazil, Volume II: Reassessing the Obstacles to Economic Development* (London: George Allen & Unwin, 1982), p. 84; Annibal Villanova Vilella and Wilson Suzigan, *Política do Govêrno e Crescimento da Economia Brasileira, 1889–1945* (Rio de Janeiro: IPEA/INPES, 1975), pp. 9–10. Overseas trade was as important a tax source in Spanish America. Colin M. Lewis, "Industry in Latin America Before 1930," in *The Cambridge History of Latin America, Volume IV: c. 1870 to 1930*, ed. Leslie Bethell (Cambridge: Cambridge University Press, 1986), p. 297.
2. Mircea Buescu, *História Econômica do Brasil: Pesquisas e Análises* (Rio de Janeiro: APEC, 1970), p. 256.
3. Vilella and Suzigan, *Política do Govêrno*, p. 16n. Sales (*consumo*) taxes reached ten percent only after 1900. Raymond W. Goldsmith, *Brasil, 1850–1984: Desenvolvimento Financeiro sob um Século de Inflação* (São Paulo: Harper & Row do Brasil, 1986), p. 123.

of a commercial association put it: "The tax office, that mysterious and terrible creature, well known to all, appears everywhere, takes part in all business, intervenes in everything, always for money, and unhappily everything gets damaged from its woeful intervention."[4] Of a total of 389 official letters and petitions sent to government by the Commercial Association of Pernambuco in the fiscal year 1883–1884, for example, 308 concerned taxation.[5]

The role of their membership in Brazil's revenue system entitled business interest groups, particularly the commercial associations, to strong regulatory and advisory prerogatives concerning taxation. In the hope of lowering taxes, business interest groups frequently preached fiscal economy in their communications with government and the public. They most often suggested a reduction in the number of government employees. The groups knew well that in Brazil government employment had the principal function of providing jobs for the educated elite.[6] Experience also had taught them the truth of the well-known dictum of an Imperial Senator that "the greater the number of employees in a department, the less the sum of services that they produce."[7] Because of the fundamental role of patronage in the Brazilian political system, however, business interest groups had scant hope of promoting this type of economy.

Although business interest groups might rail at taxes, they had to recognize them as a necessary evil, since so much went for the economic infrastructure improvements they urged. Nor could they legitimately complain about overseas trade bearing a disproportionate load. The groups usually opposed direct taxes on land or income, the only feasible alternatives to indirect taxes on commerce.[8] The Commercial Association of Pernambuco, the organization complaining most frequently about Brazil's revenue system, admitted in 1879 that direct taxes were "more just, proportional, and fair," but would be hard to collect and resented.[9] It candidly noted that an income tax would fall heavily upon businessmen,

4. Associação Comercial de Pernambuco, *Relatório da Associação Comercial Beneficente Lido na Assembléia Geral de 6 de Agôsto de 1874* (Recife: Jornal do Recife, 1874), Anexo 6, unpaginated.
5. Associação Comercial de Pernambuco, *Relatório de 1884*, p. 7.
6. Emilia Viotti da Costa, "Brazil: The Age of Reform, 1870–1889," in *The Cambridge History of Latin America, Volume V, c. 1870–1930*, ed. Leslie Bethell (Cambridge: Cambridge University Press, 1986), p. 742. See also José Murilo de Carvalho, *A Construção da Ordem: A Elite Política Imperial* (Rio de Janeiro: Campus, 1980), pp. 126–129; and Richard Graham, *Patronage and Politics in Nineteenth-Century Brazil* (Stanford, Calif.: Stanford University Press, 1990).
7. Liberato de Castro Carreira, *História Financeira e Orçamentária do Império do Brasil* (2d ed.; Brasília: Fundação Casa de Rui Barbosa/MEC, 1980), II: 667.
8. For example, Minutes, meeting of March 17, 1892, Livro 6 de Atas, AACB, p. 20; Minutes, meeting of April 5, 1877, Livro 4 de Atas, AACP, p. 83. Associação Comercial de Pernambuco, *Relatório de 1879*, pp. 36–37.
9. *Relatório de 1879*, pp. 33–35. For the difficulties of direct forms of taxation, see "Circular Acerca dos Impostos e Pareceres a Ela Concernentes," RMF, 1879, Anexo B.

but neglected to add that export and import tariffs did not, but usually could be passed on to producer and retail customer, respectively. Despite their habitual complaints, merchants could patiently accept national import tariffs.

This was not true, however, if tariffs were high enough to be protective of native industry. Such tariffs by definition damaged import trade and merchants fiercely opposed them. Equally feared were provincial import tariffs. If higher than those of neighboring provinces, they served to deflect imports to the chief ports of those provinces. If applied to goods from other provinces, they hurt not only overseas traders but Brazilian manufacturers. Export taxes, condemned by contemporary economic theory, were disliked on principle and thought to damage commodities facing competition in world markets. Nineteenth-century Brazil's business interest groups would spend much energy and time combating the protective tariff, provincial import taxation, and export taxes. Other tax-related issues, such as taxes that revealed business secrets, tax regulation, and smuggling, also seized their attention.

Taxation: irritants and smuggling

Business interest groups fought certain taxes not so much for financial reasons as because they violated business privacy. A 1900 stamp tax on goods (*selagem de stock*) not only required the stamping of all goods stocked or shipped, but gave tax agents the right to inspect goods on premises and even to examine account books.[10] This trespass of the "inviolability of bookkeeping," as opponents termed it, would reveal to authorities more about operations and profits than merchants or manufacturers wanted them to know. The indignation among business interest groups was general; a campaign to mobilize all of them against the tax was coordinated by the commercial associations of São Paulo, Ceará, and Maranhão.[11] The widespread protest succeeded in amending the law to preserve account books from the prying eyes of tax agents, although the tax remained.

As violating of privacy was an 1891 requirement for the purchase of duplicate consular invoices (*faturas consulares*) for all goods shipped to Brazil. It also laid bare a merchant's business operations, this time to Brazilian consuls who frequently also were merchants and thus business rivals. The Commercial Association of Rio de Janeiro took charge of the campaign against it, gaining the support of all the nation's other commer-

---

10. Associação Comercial da Bahia, *Relatório da Diretoria da Associação Comercial da Bahia, Apresentado na Sessão da Assembléia Geral Ordinária de 14 de Fevereiro de 1900* (Salvador: Reis, 1900), pp. 49–61.
11. Minutes, meeting of March 22, 1900, Livro 8 de Atas, AACP, pp. 17–18.

cial associations.[12] The federal government soon rescinded the measure. However, the requirement for consular invoices was common in other nations and useful for compiling trade statistics. It was revived in 1900. Again the Rio association led the fight against it, this time enlisting not only Brazilian business interest organizations but those abroad. The Fourth Congress of Chambers of Commerce of the Empire, held in 1900, denounced the requirement for consular invoices as damaging to trade with Brazil, complained to Britain's Foreign Office, and mobilized its membership in protest.[13] Now under diplomatic as well as domestic pressure, the Brazilian government again yielded. Taxes that revealed trade secrets were hated by all business interest groups and aroused resistance as determined as that against economically more burdensome taxes.

Tax regulation occupied nearly as much of the attention of business interest groups, particularly the commercial associations, as did the taxes themselves. The application of a tax, no less than its level, figured heavily in a firm's profit and loss. The associations usually could postpone the impact of a higher import tariff by demanding a stay before it was put into effect, on the grounds that new rates should not affect goods already ordered. During the Empire they came to expect a stay of from three to six months.[14] The Republic was somewhat less generous. Other common import regulation issues included overcharges on rates and improper classification of goods. With exportation, the most frequent causes of protest were the application of duties or fees to goods transshipped from provinces where they had already paid such charges and the overvaluation of exports. In all tax disputes, commercial associations defended the interests of their aggrieved merchant members. When officials were proven wrong, the associations had to wage protracted campaigns for restitution to their members of the overpayment of duty. All such wrongs to merchants had to be corrected through the petitioning and lobbying of government officials. Brazilian courts had no jurisdiction over violations committed by government officials in performing their jobs.[15]

The heavy financial burden and intricate regulations laid on importation not surprisingly encouraged smuggling and bribery. Merchants bribed customs officials to pass goods through the customs house without paying duty or to deliberately undervalue them. During the second half of the nineteenth century, scandals broke out periodically. In an investiga-

12. Commercial Association of Rio de Janeiro to Vice-President of Republic, Rio de Janeiro, Dec. 19, 1891, *Relatório da Associação Comercial do Rio de Janeiro do Ano de 1901* (Rio de Janeiro: Pereira Braga, 1902), Anexos 1891, p. 9.
13. George Henry Wright, *Chronicles of the Birmingham Chamber of Commerce, A.D. 1813–1913, and of the Birmingham Commercial Society, A.D. 1783–1812* (Birmingham: Birmingham Chamber of Commerce, 1913), p. 413.
14. Associação Comercial de Pernambuco, *Relatório de 1887*, p. 20.
15. Great Britain, Foreign Office, *Diplomatic and Consular Reports*, no. 504 (1884): 26.

tion into the customs house of Rio de Janeiro by a committee of Parliament in 1862, an imperial deputy alleged: "There are smugglers so protected that if someone steals their contraband, there are police who offer themselves to hastily look for the contraband object."[16] Scandals touched virtually all the nation's customs houses. Government investigators uncovered dishonesty by merchants and customs officials in 1872, 1879, 1887, 1894, 1895, and 1897, said to involve, among other things, the complete bypassing of the customs house, the substitution of goods within the customs house, the use of false documents, and even the alteration of documents by a secret ink-removing substance.[17]

Like all else concerned with the import economy, customs house dishonesty drew the attention of the commercial associations. Unless fraud involved large sums or unusual circumstances, merchants were usually fined or, together with their employees, barred from the customs house, rather than legally prosecuted. But such scandals were a severe embarrassment to the associations, particularly since they often involved their largest and most prestigious firms. Commercial associations occasionally denounced customs house smuggling to authorities and usually cooperated with officials in attempting to stamp it out. Association leaders held a great fear of having the entire merchant community discredited and also, doubtless, resentment of unfair competition by the violators. Cheating on customs duties appears to have occurred in many locations most of the century, but was rarely widespread or blatant.

This was not true, however, of Brazil's southernmost province of Rio Grande do Sul. Smuggling there was on a much greater scale, ultimately involving a large proportion of its merchants. It was facilitated by Rio Grande do Sul's common border with Uruguay and Argentina, by the lower import duties of those two countries, and also by the connivance of Uruguayan authorities.[18] Legitimate import commerce naturally suffered. A lengthy barrage of complaints from the province's three commercial associations, located in Pôrto Alegre, Pelotas, and the city of Rio Grande, resulted in 1879 in the granting of a special tariff for the province that more than halved rates on frequently smuggled goods.[19] But Uruguay then lowered its import duties and fees, and smugglers also adjusted by

16. Brazil, Congresso, Comissão de Inquérito na Alfândega da Corte, *Relatório da Comissão de Inquérito na Alfândega da Corte sôbre as Censuras e Acusações Feitas à Administração da Mesma Alfândega na Câmera dos Deputados e na Imprensa, em o Ano de 1862* (Rio de Janeiro: Tipografia Nacional, 1862), p. 26.
17. *RMF, 1872*, p. 72, *RMF, 1879*, Anexo B, p. 4, *RMF, 1894*, pp. 159–160, *RMF, 1895*, pp. 228–231, *RMF, 1897*, pp. 68–73, Anexo B, pp. 1–56; Baron Guaí to Baron Cotegipe, Salvador, March 25, 1887, ABC, AIHGB, lata 38, doc. 63.
18. *RMF, 1876*, Anexo E, unpaginated, and *RMF, 1883*, Anexo D, p. 9.
19. Bennington to Department of State, Rio Grande, July 12, 1888, *USRC*, XXVII, no. 96 (Aug. 1888): 282.

channeling their operations through the corrupt Brazilian customs house at Uruguayana. The commercial associations of Pôrto Alegre and Rio Grande now demanded, unsuccessfully, that the Uruguayana customs house be forbidden to issue bills of transit, which enabled smuggled merchandise to circulate freely through the province, and that the special tariff be lowered further and its scope broadened.[20] By 1885 trade, legal and otherwise, through Uruguayana was estimated at ten times the legitimate commerce of Rio Grande, and by mid-1888 the storage rooms of the latter's customs house were said to be completely bare.[21]

Earlier in 1888 the commercial associations of Rio Grande and Pôrto Alegre launched a flurry of angry petitions and complaints to Parliament and government ministries. Describing a turbulent open meeting of the Rio Grande association in February 1888, the British Consul noted that "it was evident that the patience of the commercial community was sorely tried, and there was reason to fear that as far as certain speakers were concerned, it was exhausted."[22] In June the Commercial Association of Pôrto Alegre called for a commercial strike unless its recommendations to control smuggling were immediately enacted, but backed down when the associations of Rio Grande and Pelotas withheld their support.[23] But a commercial strike proved unnecessary. The government was moved enough by the agitation of the three commercial associations to inaugurate a new, more generous special tariff for the Province of Rio Grande do Sul in March 1889.

The victory of the three commercial associations was fleeting. The coming of the Republic meant the end of the special tariff for Rio Grande do Sul. Meanwhile, the province's merchants had become tinged with the very corruption they denounced. An 1894 investigation uncovered widespread dishonesty in the customs houses of Rio Grande and Pôrto Alegre.[24] Thirteen merchant firms were barred from the latter. After some initial success by the Republic in repressing smuggling, the completion of several Uruguayan railway lines to the border enlarged the flow of contraband goods once again.[25] The remedy of a special tariff, however, was

20. Brazil, Congresso, Comissão Parlamentar de Inquérito, *Informações Apresentadas pela Comissão Parlamentar de Inquérito ao Corpo Legislativo na Terceira Sessão da Décima Oitava Legislatura* (Rio de Janeiro: Tipografia Nacional, 1883), pp. 161, 177, 466–467.
21. Great Britain, Foreign Office, *Diplomatic and Consular Reports*, no. 32 (1885): 5; *ACD, 1888*, III: 125.
22. Bennett to Foreign Office, Rio Grande, March 6, 1888, *Diplomatic and Consular Reports*, no. 323 (1888): 5.
23. Bennington to Department of State, Rio Grande, July 12, 1888, *USRC*, XXVII, no. 96 (Aug. 1888): 284.
24. *RMF, 1895*, Anexo M, pp. 3–13.
25. Great Britain, Foreign Office, *Diplomatic and Consular Reports*, no. 702 (1889–90): 4–5, and *Diplomatic and Consular Reports*, no. 1077 (1891): 12–14, 32; *RMF, 1891*, pp. 347–349; Joseph

dead. A flurry of new manufactures and the renewed prosperity of old ones in the wake of the tariff's abolition confirmed that it had damaged industrial development, and its importer proponents had been discredited by their own involvement in smuggling.[26] Smuggling continued into the twentieth century but diminished as the state achieved greater economic integration.

Smuggling, tax regulations, and taxes that revealed the secrets of business transactions were a recurring irritant to business interest groups. As threats to entrepôt prosperity, however, they were minor compared to provincial import taxes.

Provincial tariffs and financial crisis

Because the expense of national import tariffs could usually be passed on to the consumer, unless high enough to be protective, merchants could accept them grudgingly This was not the case with provincial import taxes. If higher than those of neighboring provinces, they tended to force imports to the chief ports of the latter. For example, a Salvador importer in 1882 credited the higher costs due to a Pernambucan provincial import tax with increasing sales by Salvador merchants in the intermediate provinces of Alagôas and Sergipe by fifty percent within a five-year period.[27] Having low or no provincial import taxes was particularly important to entrepôts, such as Rio de Janeiro, Recife, and Salvador, which served neighboring provinces as well as their own. If provincial import taxes applied to goods from other parts of Brazil, as was frequently the case, they served to stifle domestic trade. Such interprovincial taxes also were an important obstacle to industrial development since they impeded the entry into other provinces of manufactures from Rio de Janeiro and São Paulo.

The problem of provincial (later state) import tariffs has been generally overlooked in Brazilian economic history. But these imposts strongly affected the financial status and trade patterns of Northeastern states in the last three decades of the nineteenth century. They brought conflict between businessmen and provincial government, between business interest groups, and even occasionally between export and import commerce. Their impact was greatest in Pernambuco, where they changed political alignments and were a strong factor in the decline of Recife as an entrepôt.

L. Love, *Rio Grande do Sul and Brazilian Regionalism, 1882–1937* (Stanford, Calif.: Stanford University Press, 1971), p. 17.
26. Great Britain, Foreign Office, *Diplomatic and Consular Reports*, no. 1263 (1892): 3.
27. *Jornal de Notícias* (Salvador), Aug. 26, 1882, p. 1.

Perhaps no other question agitated the business interest groups of the Northeast more.

Legally, provincial tariffs should not have existed. National authorities usually considered them outlawed by the Additional Act of 1834. Violations were denounced first by Minister of Finance João Maurício Wanderley (later Baron Cotegipe) in 1857 and then frequently by his successors.[28] Despite the enmity of high officials and unfavorable judicial rulings, provincial import taxes persisted because substitute sources of revenue could not be arranged. During the 1870s they spread through the Northeast. They usually began as a substitute for provincial export taxes, reduced or eliminated as cotton prices collapsed following the United States Civil War and sugar prices began a long decline. Provincial tax receipts in the Northeast during that decade fell by roughly a third.[29] At the same time provincial revenue demands increased, usually to finance the building of railroads and other economic infrastructure. In a sense, business interest groups, which had both campaigned against export taxes and pushed infrastructure improvements, helped bring the problem down on their own heads. It worsened during the 1880s as returns from sugar and cotton exportation continued to decline.

By 1881 all provinces had import taxes or similar imposts except coffee-exporting Rio de Janeiro and São Paulo.[30] Provincial import taxes were not always impelled by budget needs. Pará, enjoying soaring revenue from rubber export, began such taxes (labeled disembarkation taxes) in 1871 and continued them through the rest of the century, over the repeated protests of its commercial association.[31] Provinces sometimes levied them to protect local commodities or manufactures as well as for revenue. In smaller provinces they often were designed to encourage direct importation from abroad, rather than the customary transshipment from a major entrepôt. The principal sufferer from this policy was Recife, which dominated or competed for trade in the provinces of Sergipe, Alagôas, Paraíba, Rio Grande do Norte, and Ceará.

28. *RMF, 1883,* pp. 9, 11–26; Guilherme Deveza, "Política Tributária no Período Imperial," in *Declínio e Queda do Império,* Vol. 4 of *O Brasil Monárquico,* Tomo 2 of *História Geral da Civilização Brasileira,* eds. Sérgio Buarque de Holanda and Pedro Moacyr Campos (São Paulo: Difusão Européia do Livro, 1971): 72–81.
29. Evaldo Cabral de Melo, *O Norte Agrário e o Império, 1871–1889* (Rio de Janeiro: Nova Fronteira, 1984), p. 258.
30. Brazil, Ministério da Fazenda, *Relatório e Projeto de Lei da Comissão Encarregada de Rever e Classificar as Rendas Gerais, Provinciais e Municipais do Império* (Rio de Janeiro: Tipografia Nacional, 1883), p. 72.
31. Commercial Association of Pará to President of Province, Belém, June 28, 1873, *Relatório da Comissão da Praça do Comércio do Pará, Apresentado em Assembléia Geral dos Srs. Assinantes em 4 de Janeiro de 1874* (Belém: Comércio do Pará, 1874), Anexo, pp. 9–10; Barbara Weinstein, *The Amazon Rubber Boom, 1850–1920* (Stanford, Calif.: Stanford University Press, 1983), p. 160.

The prerogatives of business interest groups with provincial tariffs were particularly strong. They derived not only from the central role of merchants in the tax process but often from a desire by provincial governments to mitigate the damage import tariffs were known to do to trade. At times the commercial associations of Pernambuco and Bahia enjoyed not only the right to written comment on provincial budgets but to have their board of directors or a committee aid in formulating those budgets.[32] The Commercial Association of Pernambuco made a practice of obtaining through other commercial associations a copy of the budgets of their provinces, to use in arguing its case. These prerogatives were sometimes effective, but fiscal necessity was usually the final word. It often led provinces to ignore the advice of business interest groups or throw out prior agreements between group and province. A less welcome prerogative resulted from the complexity of certain tax laws and the difficulty of just application by those not familiar with commerce. Business interest groups sometimes had to perform government's role in assessing taxes on the business community.

Provincial import tariffs under the empire: battles won, war lost

The struggle over provincial import taxation was most intense in Pernambuco. The Commercial Association of Pernambuco saw that province's import tariff, levied from 1874, as the main factor undermining Recife's entrepôt dominance. By 1877 it decried the loss of business even in Pernambuco's interior, as goods imported through other provinces could be sold more cheaply there.[33] The association struggled desperately to remove the tariff, petitioning repeatedly, appealing to the courts, lobbying with its directors en masse, and even arranging a march on the provincial president's palace by angry importers. But complicating this effort was its equally determined campaign to reduce or eliminate export taxes on faltering cotton and sugar exportation. Provincial export taxes on those two commodities were eliminated in 1875, but reimposed in 1877 after the association had obtained a reduction of the import tariff.[34] The province's fiscal straits made taxes like air in a balloon: pressed down in one spot they swelled in another. Meanwhile, the Commercial Association and Commercial Agricultural Association had to combat the province's attempt to tax goods from overseas and sugar from other provinces enter-

---

32. Associação Comercial de Pernambuco, *Relatório de 1878,* pp. 11–12; Minutes, meeting of July 31, 1900, Livro 8 de Atas, AACB, p. 92.
33. Commercial Association of Pernambuco to President of Province, Recife, no date, 1877, *Relatório de 1877,* pp. 13–14.
34. Associação Comercial de Pernambuco, *Relatório de 1877,* p. 11.

ing Recife for reexportation, a move that would have further undermined its position as an entrepôt.[35]

The stubborn campaign of the Commercial Association of Pernambuco against both provincial import and export taxation, the only existing large-scale sources of revenue, was by no means irrational. The association had formulated a plan to end dependence on both as well as relieve the budget crises of the Northeastern provinces. From 1875 on it championed the idea of eliminating provincial export and import taxes in exchange for a ten percent surtax on the national tariff, to be distributed to the provinces in the proportion it was collected in each.[36] Despite eventual support by the Commercial Association of Bahia, years of petitioning and lobbying, and publication of a book, the Pernambuco organization's plan was not debated nationally until 1882.

Meanwhile, the Commercial Association of Pernambuco's campaign against its province's import tariff made no headway. By 1882, the association's frustration had changed the face of provincial politics. Angry at the refusal of Pernambuco Conservative Party leaders to support its revenue-sharing proposal, the Commercial Association broke its ties with that party. It found a new political spokesman in the unlikely person of Liberal National Deputy José Mariano Carneiro da Cunha, also a champion of Recife's urban masses and one of Brazil's earliest populist leaders. The traditional Pernambuco alliance of merchants with landowners against the urban poor was reversed.

The budget difficulties of the 1870s in the Province of Pernambuco were echoed in Bahia. The success of the Commercial Association of Bahia in lowering provincial export taxes on sugar during that decade and in ending them on cotton in 1877 compounded the problem. The association was able to repel an attempt at provincial import taxation in that year by emphasizing its unconstitutionality, but the fiscal crisis grew. Neither protests from the association nor from the British consul could prevent import levies averaging some eighty percent of national duties from being included in the provincial budget for 1880–1881.[37] Salvador merchants agonized over the loss of business in the Bahian south and in the north of Minas Gerais to Rio de Janeiro, which had no import taxes, but could take

35. Minutes, meeting of Sept. 12, 1878, Atas, Associação Comercial Agrícola de Pernambuco (hereafter cited as ACAP), 1877–1892, AACP, p. 15; Associação Comercial de Pernambuco, *Relatório de 1878*, pp. 13–14.
36. Minutes, extraordinary meeting of March 23, 1875, in Estevão Pinto, *A Associação Comercial de Pernambuco* (Recife: Jornal do Comércio, 1940), pp. 167–180.
37. Commercial Association of Bahia to Provincial Assembly, Salvador, July 15, 1880, *Relatório de 1881*, pp. 41–44; Morgan to charge d'affairs at Rio de Janeiro, Salvador, Oct. 24, 1879, PRO/FO 13/564, fl. 87–88.

comfort that Pernambuco's equally high import tariff prevented a similar problem in the provinces that lay between them, Sergipe and Alagôas. The opportunity for both commercial associations to do away with provincial import tariffs came in 1882. Although numerous petitions had helped discredit such taxes, they were felled by the merchant's ultimate weapon, the commercial strike. Liberal prime minister Marquis Paranaguá (João Lustosa da Cunha Paranaguá) disliked provincial tariffs, although uncertain with what to replace them. On July 18, he ordered the national customs house in Recife to cease aiding the province in the collection of provincial import duties. Since Pernambuco did not have its own customs facility, this meant such duties could not be collected without the cooperation of importers. Meanwhile in Bahia, Provincial President Pedro Luís Pereira de Souza, under pressure from its Commercial Association, had refused to sanction a Provincial Assembly bill adding an extra duty of six percent to the import assessments in force since 1880. Taking advantage of the province's need for their cooperation and citing the act of the Provincial President of Bahia as precedent, Recife merchants mobilized by the Commercial Association of Pernambuco declared on August 15 that they would refuse to dispatch goods from the customs house until collection of the provincial import tariff was suspended.[38] As the price of basic necessities began to climb, Marquis Paranaguá considered apprehensively the likelihood of violence by Recife's notoriously volatile masses.[39] Within three days he ordered Pernambuco's provincial import tax suspended.

There remained the task of having Parliament revoke all provincial import taxes and award a ten percent national tariff surtax to the provinces. The Commercial Association of Pernambuco urged the nation's other commercial associations to support such a bill.[40] Submitted to Parliament by Marquis Paranaguá and pushed forward energetically by José Mariano, the measure passed the Chamber of Deputies, but stuck in the Senate. Marquis Paranaguá, meanwhile, ordered all provincial presidents to have their provincial assemblies repeal "illegal" import taxes. This was quickly done in Pernambuco and almost all Northeastern provinces, save Bahia.[41] The grateful Commercial Association of Pernambuco hung Paranaguá's portrait in the main salon of its headquarters. José Mariano's reward was more tangible. In a gesture unparalleled elsewhere,

---

38. *Diário de Pernambuco* (Recife), Aug. 15, 1882, p. 4, and Aug. 18, 1882, p. 3.
39. Cabral de Melo, *Norte Agrário*, p. 262.
40. Associação Comercial de Pernambuco, *Relatório de 1882*, p. 20. The Pernambuco association apparently received unqualified support only from the Rio Grande and Pelotas groups, in addition to Bahia. Minutes, meetings of Oct. 11 and Nov. 8, 1882, Livro 5 de Atas, AACP, pp. 63, 65.
41. Cabral de Melo, *Norte Agrário*, p. 274.

the association collected funds to buy him a town house. Large foreign import houses were the main contributors.[42]

What brought joy to Pernambuco brought consternation to Bahia. The latter's businessmen now faced the competition of Recife merchants unburdened by any provincial import tax. The Commercial Association of Bahia now demanded Pereira de Sousa abolish completely such duties. The provincial president refused on the grounds that such action went beyond his authority.[43] The provincial assembly, dominated by Conservatives unwilling to cooperate with the Liberal prime minister and his President of Province, also refused to comply. All entreaties failing, the Bahian association decided in November to organize a strike. Salvador merchants pledged not to despatch goods from the customs house until provincial import taxes were ended.[44] Again, the commercial strike worked. Cessation of tax revenue and the growing unrest of the urban poor as the price of foodstuffs soared brought the province to its knees within six days; Pereira de Sousa suspended collection of provincial import taxes.[45] Exhilarated, the Commercial Association's rank-and-file membership hung Pereira de Sousa's portrait with elaborate ceremony in its headquarters. At the same time it had to persuade association President Baron Guaí, a Conservative National Deputy, and other board members who disliked honoring the Liberal President of Province, not to resign.

The triumph of the Pernambuco and Bahian commercial associations was illusory. Provincial import tariffs were gone, but nothing had been provided to replace them. The Pernambuco association's 1882 campaign to enact its revenue-sharing plan demonstrated the difficulty of adjusting taxation to the diverse interests of groups and businessmen. The commercial associations of Rio de Janeiro, Santos, and Pará and the Center for Coffee Agriculture and Commerce vehemently opposed the measure. The surtax, they maintained, would burden the consumer, and its distribution to the provinces, whether according to revenue contribution or to population, would be inequitable.[46] The cruelest blow came from dissenting

---

42. Associação Comercial de Pernambuco, *Relatório de 1883*, pp. 22, 115–123. A total of 46:137$000 was collected, approximately U.S. $20,300.00 in 1883.
43. Pedro Luís Pereira de Sousa to Commercial Association of Bahia, Salvador, Sept. 28, 1882, *Relatório de 1883*, p. 42.
44. Minutes, extraordinary general assemby of Nov. 22, 1882, Livro 5 de Atas, AACB, pp. 26–32; *Jornal de Notícias* (Salvador), Nov. 24, 1882, p. 2.
45. *Jornal de Notícias*, Nov. 28, 1882, pp. 1–2.
46. Commercial Association of Rio de Janeiro to Brazilian Parliament, Rio de Janeiro, Sept. 11, 1882, *Relatório de 1882–1883*, pp. 23–25; Commercial Association of Santos to Brazilian Parliament, Santos, Sept. 9, 1882, *Relatório da Associação Comercial de Santos Apresentado em Sessão Ordinária da Assembléia Geral em Março de 1883 e Parecer da Comissão de Exame de Contas* (Santos: Diário de Santos, 1883), pp. 43–48; Minutes, meeting of Sept. 14, 1882, Livro 5 de Atas, AACP, p. 61; Laura Jarnagin Pang, "The State and Agricultural Clubs of Imperial Brazil, 1860–1889" (Ph.D. Diss., Vanderbilt University, 1981), p. 311.

petitions by importers and retailers in the Commercial Association of Pernambuco's own business community. They contradicted the association by asserting that the best means to eliminate the need for hated provincial import taxes was not to place a surtax on the national import tariff but to raise provincial export taxes![47]

The attitude of the dissenters should have surprised no one. Export taxes may have hurt the exportation of sugar and cotton, but little burdened products that dominated world markets, as did Brazilian coffee, represented by the Center for Coffee Agriculture and Commerce and the commercial associations of Rio de Janeiro and Santos, and rubber, represented by the Commercial Association of Pará. Those products also generated enough provincial export revenue to minimize the need for import taxation. The dissenting Rio and Santos commercial associations also knew that lack of provincial import taxes gave their business communities an advantage in competition for trade with entrepôts that had them, as illustrated by the success of Rio de Janeiro in taking trade from Salvador in southern Bahia and northern Minas Gerais. The protests also reflected the profitability of importation including, in the case of the Center for Coffee Agriculture and Commerce, the procuring of consumer goods for planters by their factors.[48] The measure became law, providing a two percent reduction of national export taxes but, most importantly, did not stipulate that the ten percent import tariff surtax be given to the provinces. It thus missed its main objective: relieving growing provincial revenue shortages. The Commercial Association of Pernambuco continued to advocate its revenue-sharing plan into the 1890s, without success. The failure to arrange an alternative source of revenue for the provinces was to vex and damage the poorer provinces of Brazil and their business communities through the Old Republic.

The elimination of provincial import taxes brought a general fiscal crisis to the Northeast. The provinces of that region were deprived of revenue just when their export crisis was deepening. During extended periods Pernambuco could not pay its police regularly, nor Maranhão for lighting the streets of its capital.[49] The situation was most critical in

---

47. [Large-scale importers] to Commercial Association of Pernambuco, Recife, May 7, 1883, and [retailers and commission houses] to Commercial Association of Pernambuco, Recife, May 4, 1883, *Relatório de 1883*, pp. 89–94.

48. Coffee factors did not charge planters for this service, but did exact interest on credit. Joseph E. Sweigart, "Financing and Marketing Brazilian Export Agriculture: The Coffee Factors of Rio de Janeiro, 1850–1888" (Ph.D. Diss., University of Texas, 1980), pp. 112–115.

49. Pernambuco, Presidente da Província, *Fala com que o Exm. Sr. Presidente Desembargador José Manuel de Freitas Abriu a Sessão da Assembléia Legislativa Provincial de Pernambuco no Dia 1 de Março de 1884* (Recife: Manuel Figueiroa de Faria & Filhos, 1884), p. 4; Brazil, Conselho de Ministros, *Breve Notícia do Estado Financeiro das Províncias, Organizada por Ordem do Barão de Cotegipe, Presidente do Conselho de Ministros* (Rio de Janeiro: Imprensa Nacional, 1887), "Informação no. 15," p. 1.

Bahia and Pernambuco, whose deficits by 1886 were, respectively, about five and two and one-half times larger than that of any other province.[50] Most Northeastern provinces also were spending heavily to improve economic infrastructure. This was especially true of Bahia, most of whose debt was for four railroads and other public works pushed by its Commercial Association, including a modern quay leading to its headquarters.[51] In Maranhão and Pernambuco, however, most spending was for the wages of public employees, whose excess numbers business interest groups had always decried.[52] This probably stiffened the resistance of Pernambuco's two business interest groups and the Commercial Association of Maranhão to provincial taxation.

Parliament discussed the transfer of imperial taxes to the provinces or the creation of new forms of taxation, but could agree on nothing. As a result, from 1884 provincial import taxes began to creep back under a variety of disguises such as "allotment" (*repartição*), "turnover" (*giro mercantil*), "statistics" (*estatística*), "commerce" (*comércio*), and "patent" (*patente*). By Empire's end the use of such subterfuges was general.[53] All had the impact of import tariffs. As a commercial association president explained, "Since the sum demanded from merchants cannot reasonably be deducted from their profits, call it sales, turnover or allotment tax, . . . it will enter into calculation of the price of sale, it will turn into a tax with repercussions, and it will damage the importation of goods."[54] Despite the crisis, provincial authorities rarely attempted to tap sources other than commercial. Speaking of the substitutes, the Manager of the New London & Brazilian Bank noted: "The inference from these expedients [is] that [provincial] governments share the helplessness of the Imperial Government to collect taxes, save at the ports or cities."[55] Provinces concocted clumsy substitutes for import tariffs, such as an 1886 Maranhão law that taxed the same goods at import, wholesale, and retail levels, and vastly increased the number of taxes.[56] Most new taxes fell on business transactions, complicating and delaying them more than ever. The commercial associations of Pernambuco and Bahia had opened a Pandora's box.

The severity of its fiscal crisis and the problem of loss of trade to

50. Brazil, Conselho de Ministros, *Estado Financeiro*, Tabella no. 1, unpaginated.
51. Bahia, Presidente da Província, *Fala com que o Exm. Sr. Des. Aurélio Ferreira Espineira, Primeiro Vice-Presidente da Província, Abriu a Segunda Sessão da Vigésima Sétima Legislatura da Assembléia Legislativa Provincial no Dia 3 de Abril de 1889* (Salvador: Gazeta da Bahia, 1889), p. 8.
52. Brazil, Conselho de Ministros, *Estado Financeiro*, pp. 43, 75.
53. *RMF, 1895*, p. 155.
54. Associação Comercial de Pernambuco, *Relatório de 1893*, p. 22.
55. J. Beaton to Rio de Janeiro Manager, London, July 18, 1885, New London & Brazilian Bank, Letters, London to Rio 1885–1889, LABA/UCL, G.2.
56. Great Britain, Foreign Office, *Diplomatic and Consular Reports*, no. 79 (1886): 2.

competing entrepôts compounded the struggle over substitutes for import taxation in Pernambuco. In 1884 that province levied an Allotment Tax on businessmen and professionals according to their specialization. The Commercial Association of Pernambuco charged angrily that it was "a true direct tax," the bête noire of business interest groups and the more unjust because levied on professionals at a much lower rate.[57] The crowning indignity was that the Commercial Association found itself, in its president's words, "converted into an auxiliary tax office," when told to classify all Recife businessmen for Allotment Tax assessments, members or not.[58] The association protested heatedly but complied in order to avoid bungling by government tax assessors.

Worse was to follow. Yielding to Commercial Association pressure to abolish the Allotment Tax in 1885, the Province of Pernambuco replaced it with a Turnover Tax. This was an assessment of three percent (later raised to five or more) on the value of all imports.[59] It differed (as initially formulated) from an import tax in that it fell uniformly on all goods regardless of their economic or social utility and was assessed on the market value of goods rather than the usually lower price set by tariff law. The dismayed Board of Directors of the association raised a special defense fund, fired petitions to provincial and national governments, paid for newspaper articles, pleaded before the acting President of Province as a body, and finally, when nothing succeeded, resigned. A renewed drive in Parliament by José Mariano for the distribution to the provinces of funds from the imperial government's ten percent surtax also failed. Recife importers proclaimed another commercial strike but backed down when the Commercial Association, still hoping the surtax might be distributed to the provinces, refused to sponsor it.[60] When the Turnover Tax was renewed in the provincial budget of the following year, desperation reigned. The association persuaded provincial legislators to replace it with the once-reviled import tariff! Accusing the group of calculating that the new import tariff would be declared unconstitutional, Pernambuco's President of Province refused to enact the budget.[61] The Turnover Tax remained until well into the Republic, although after 1887 the provincial government let the Commercial Association determine how its rates would be levied on specific goods.[62]

57. The province budgeted, for example, more from its five codfish importers than from its 52 physicians or 86 lawyers. Pernambuco, Presidente da Província, *Relatório de 1884*, pp. 27, 36.
58. Associação Comercial de Permanbuco, *Relatório de 1884*, pp. 23–26.
59. Great Britain, Foreign Office, *Diplomatic and Consular Reports*, no. 606 (1889): 3.
60. Minutes, meeting of Sept. 10 and Sept. 17, 1885, Livro 5 de Atas, AACP, pp. 131, 135.
61. Inácio Joaquim de Sousa Leão, President, Province of Pernambuco to Baron Cotegipe, Recife, Aug. 7, 1886, ABC, AIHGB, lata 33, doc. 5.
62. Associação Comercial de Pernambuco, *Relatório de 1887*, p. 16.

State import taxation under the republic: further variations,
same theme

The coming of the Republic did not relieve the financial crisis of the Northeast or stop the proliferation of provincial (now state) import tariffs and their substitutes. In 1893, Minister of Finance Inocêncio Serzedelo Correia, petitioned by several commercial associations, strongly condemned state taxation of imports and ordered customs houses to stop aiding their collection.[63] But revenue needs could not be resisted. Pleas from state governments soon forced Serzedelo Correia to reverse his order. Meanwhile, commercial associations and firms had challenged various forms of state import taxation in state or national courts with success. This forced the states to rely on taxation that also bore on importers but could not be challenged on legal grounds. Once more new taxes were invented or old ones reworked. Many required arbitrary decisions by tax officials, slowed business, or confused taxpayers. "Location" (*valor locativo*) imposts taxed a firm according to an officially assessed value of its buildings and their location, and stamp taxes on business documents duplicated a national tax, causing such bewilderment as to generate, in the words of a Minister of Finance, "a veritable anarchy."[64] Particularly hated were state "industries and professions" taxes, weighing mostly on businessmen. Bahia's industries and professions tax, for example, taxed by seven distinct economic criteria and could be applied to the same individual several times.[65]

As during the Empire, the struggle over state import taxation in the Republic was fiercest in Pernambuco, again affecting political alignments. It continued to be exacerbated by Recife's shrinking role as an entrepôt for smaller neighboring states. By 1896 the Commercial Association's president ruefully noted that all Northeastern states were now importing directly from overseas.[66] Ironically, Pernambuco's revenue needs continued to grow, largely because of efforts, promoted by the Commercial Association and Commercial Agricultural Association, to revive sugar production and improve transportation. By 1899 nearly two-thirds of Pernambuco's debt stemmed from guaranteed interest on capital for *usinas* and three railroads.[67]

The new state government revived the Allotment Tax, repealed in 1885 because of Commercial Association attacks. Both Commercial Association

---

63. *RMF, 1893*, pp. 131–134.   64. *RMF, 1899*, p. 27.
65. Bahia, laws, statutes, etc., *Constituição e Leis do Estado da Bahia, 1892* (Salvador: Diário da Bahia, 1892), pp. 70–84.
66. Minutes, meeting of May 11, 1896, Livro 7 de Atas, AACP, pp. 113–114.
67. Pernambuco, Presidente da Província, *Relatório de 1899*, p. 103.

and Commercial Agricultural Association were forced to classify their membership into occupational specialties for assessment.[68] By 1893 the burden of the Allotment Tax was such that the Commercial Association, long a crusader against export taxation, offered to have the export levy on cotton raised in exchange for reducing some of its rates. The provincial legislature accepted this offer and also struck the hated Turnover Tax from the new state budget, only to have Governor Alexandre José Barbosa Lima reinstate the budget from the previous year. Infuriated, the group urged Recife businessmen not to pay taxes stipulated in the "illegal" budget.[69] A head-on clash between Commercial Association and Governor was averted only by a more serious crisis, the outbreak of armed conflict when political enemies attempted to impeach the latter. Perhaps because Barbosa Lima emerged the winner, the association dropped its call for a tax rebellion.

Increasing doubts about the legality of the Turnover Tax and other variations on import tariffs excluded them from the budgets of Pernambuco after 1893. This meant the introduction of an Industries and Professions Tax (which the Commercial Association also had to help assess) and an increase in the Allotment Tax. When Allotment Tax rates were increased up to fourfold in 1895, the Commercial Agricultural Association and Commercial Association formulated a joint protest to the state legislature. The Commercial Association was now at the end of its tether. It had been unable to stem the fastening of increasingly vexatious taxes on its membership, and its petitions to Governor Barbosa Lima no longer received a courteous reply, much less assent. When its formal joint petition with the Commercial Agricultural Association was rejected in June 1895, members voted overwhelmingly to shut down its headquarters and operations as a gesture of protest.[70] The Commercial Agricultural Association also closed in protest, although remaining inactive less than two months.[71]

To the chagrin of Commercial Association leaders, the shutting of what most Pernambucans considered one of the state's key institutions had little effect. The reopening of the Commercial Association of Pernambuco in April 1896 was prompted only by the retirement of Barbosa Lima as governor. The tax burdens of Recife commerce continued when Pernambuco came under the control of Francisco de Assis Rosa e Silva. The two organizations enjoyed no more influence than under Barbosa Lima, that is, virtually none. Only the removal of Rosa e Silva from power by

68. Minutes, meeting of March 28, 1892, Livro de Atas da ACAP, 1877–1892, AACP, p. 193; Minutes, meeting of Aug. 23, 1897, Livro 7 de Atas, AACP, p. 134.
69. Associação Comercial de Pernambuco, *Relatório de 1893*, pp. 10, 21–26.
70. Minutes, meeting of June 26, 1895, Livro 7 de Atas, AACP, pp. 89–93.
71. Minutes, meeting of Sept. 9, 1895, Livro de Atas da ACAP, 1895–1903, AACP, p. 1.

enemies in the federal government in 1911 brought Pernambuco's business interest groups back from political oblivion.

Interstate tariffs were another response by states to challenges to the import tax and its variations. Appearing under the Empire, they increased in number and weight during the first years of the Republic. Because they restricted internal trade and the formation of a domestic market, they were anathema to manufacturers as well as to merchants. The commercial associations of Bahia, Pernambuco, Rio de Janeiro, and São Paulo fought them with particular determination. These organizations occasionally were able to force abolition of interstate tariffs in certain states – for example, Pará in 1893, by cooperation in lobbying and petitioning both state and national governments.[72] But the continued spread of such taxes (the commercial associations of Pernambuco and Bahia could not keep them from their own states) led the groups to try to end them through judicial decision or federal law. Apparent victory came in 1898 when the Federal Supreme Court declared interstate duties illegal. Unfortunately, legal loopholes and the possibility of delaying enforcement made the ruling ineffective. Spearheaded by the Commercial Center of Rio de Janeiro and the commercial associations of Rio de Janeiro, Pernambuco, and Bahia, the groups turned their efforts toward Congress. A bill by Serzedelo Correia abolishing interstate taxes became law in 1904, but its provisions were widely evaded. An obstacle to internal development, interstate taxation lasted through and well past the Old Republic, definitively ending only in 1944.[73]

The business interest group campaign against interstate tariffs, like that against state (earlier provincial) import tariffs in general, had been spurred by their bad economic effects. But both efforts were largely frustrated by fiscal necessity. The same was true of another target of business interest group wrath, export taxation.

The struggle against export taxation

Relief from export taxes was a help badly needed by Brazilian agriculture. Levied from 1835 on by both central government and provinces, export taxes were the major legal source of revenue for the provinces, forbidden by the Additional Act of 1834 to exact import duties. With the Republic they were given exclusively to the states. Most nineteenth-century economic theory rejected export taxation as harmful, as did many government leaders, at least in principle. Nevertheless, the imperial government

72. Associação Comercial de Pernambuco, *Relatório de 1893*, p. 14.
73. Joseph L. Love, *São Paulo in the Brazilian Federation, 1889–1937* (Stanford, Calif.: Stanford University Press, 1980), p. 195.

held fast to it, because it was considered indispensable. To eliminate this revenue source, stated a Minister of Finance, "would be to open in the national budget a breech impossible to repair."[74] Given the Empire's budget difficulties (only six years of surplus between 1835 and 1889) this was no disingenuous excuse. Export taxes never provided less than ten percent of the nation's yearly revenue between 1837 and 1887.[75]

A major argument for retaining or even increasing export taxation was that it was the only means by which rural landowners could be taxed. "As you well know, export taxes represent a tax on land," Minister of Finance Viscount Rio Branco informed Parliament in 1874, "and the more so because agriculture does not pay the urban real estate tax, the tax on industries and professions, the tax on slaves, or other levies to which are subject city proprietors and other industrious men."[76] Export taxation seemed all the more just to government leaders because much revenue was spent on the railroads, roads, and agricultural banks that large landowners often demanded.

Some experts maintained that the presence or size of export taxes did not affect the remuneration or demand for Brazilian exports, and that such taxes weighed only on the foreign consumer.[77] This was probably true for products that dominated world markets, such as rubber or coffee (as even the Commercial Association of Santos admitted).[78] Other authorities, however, cautioned that for exports facing sharp competition, such as sugar or cotton, export taxes weighed on the Brazilian producer and economically were "slow death."[79] The business interest groups most concerned with those exports strongly endorsed this view. Surprisingly, they also condemned the most reasonable alternative to export taxation, a direct tax on rural land. The commercial associations of Pernambuco and Bahia protested forcefully the few times it was discussed by government.[80] This opposition probably derived not so much from rural land-holding by some of their leaders, as from a belief that the large landholding was the indispensable foundation of the entire export economy.

Business interest group leaders were well aware that the tax revenue lost by eliminating export taxes would have to be made up elsewhere, almost surely by increased import tariffs. Despite the importance of importation to their membership, the commercial associations of Bahia, Maranhão,

74. *RMF, 1883*, p. 67.
75. Robert N. V. C. Nicol, "A Agricultura e a Industrialização no Brasil (1850–1930)" (Tese de Doutorado, Universidade de São Paulo, 1974), p. 229. See also Goldsmith, *Desenvolvimento Financeiro*, p. 74.
76. *RMF, 1874*, p. 48.   77. *RMF, 1872*, p. 75; *RMF, 1879*, Anexo B, pp. 5–6.
78. Associação Comercial de Santos, *Relatório de 1876*, Anexo no. 3, p. 3; *RMF, 1874*, p. 48.
79. "Inquérito da Lavoura da Bahia," ABC, AIHGB, lata 85, doc. 24, p. 15.
80. Minutes, meeting of April 5, 1877, Livro 4 de Atas, AACP, p. 83; Minutes, meeting of March 17, 1892, Livro 6 de Atas, AACB, p. 20.

and Pernambuco, concerned with the viability of sugar and cotton export, all proposed a trade-off of export for import taxes at one time or another.[81] This trade-off reflected their often-stated conviction that export agriculture was the base on which the entire economy rested.

The attack of business interest groups on national export taxation was impelled by the export crises of the 1870s. For nearly all of the period since 1835 national duties for most exports were seven percent, until raised to nine in 1867 to help finance the war with Paraguay. The Commercial Association of Pernambuco began the campaign in 1871 by demanding the progressive reduction and eventual abolition of export duties.[82] In 1872 the Commercial Association of Rio de Janeiro, soon backed by the Ceará, Maranhão, and Pará groups, began to mobilize all the nation's commercial associations and many municipal councils in export-growing areas in support of a general reduction in rates.[83] Also in 1872, the Commercial Association of Pernambuco, later echoed by Bahia, Pará, and Santos, began to campaign for relief for cotton.[84] Many of the petitioning commercial associations argued that revenue loss through reduction or elimination of export taxes would be more than compensated for by a renewed prosperity that would increase import levels and thus tariff receipts.

The imperial government was not convinced. It conceded no more than a reduction of the rate on sugar, cotton, and wool from nine to seven percent in 1875. Disappointment was widespread. The Commercial Association of Santos later blamed the government's stinginess for the ruin of cotton exportation in the Province of São Paulo.[85] However, the coffee

---

81. For example, Associação Comercial do Maranhão, *Relatório, Janeiro a Dezembro de 1891* (São Luís: Frias, 1892), p. 5; Minutes, meeting of Jan. 9, 1861, Livro 3 de Atas, AACB, p. 9. Minutes, meeting of Oct. 19, 1882, Livro 5 de Atas, AACB, p. 20. The Agriculture Auxiliary Society of Pernambuco favored a general suppression of export taxes, as did the Industrial Association, which hoped thus to have import tariffs increased. Sociedade Auxiliadora da Agricultura de Pernambuco, *Relatório Anual Apresentado na Sessão de 4 de Julho de 1878 da Assembléia Geral pelo Gerente Inácio de Barros Barreto e a Ata da Mesma Sessão* (Recife: Jornal do Recife, 1878), p. 15; Associação Industrial, *O Trabalho Nacional e Seus Adversários* (Rio de Janeiro: G. Leuzinger & Filhos, 1881), pp. 257–258.
82. Minutes, meeting of Aug. 12, 1871, Livro 3 de Atas, AACP, pp. 15–16; Associação Comercial de Pernambuco, *A Associação Comercial Beneficente de Pernambuco* (Recife: Carlos Eduardo Muhlert, 1871), pp. 3–4.
83. Commercial Association of Rio de Janeiro to various commercial associations and eleven municipal councils, Rio de Janeiro, Nov. 22, 1872, *Relatório de 1872*, p. 7; Associação Comercial de Ceará, *Relatório da Associação Comercial da Praça do Ceará Apresentado à Assembléia Geral dos Sócios pela Diretoria no Dia 1 de Março de 1872* (Fortaleza: Odorico Colás, 1872), p. 5; Associação Comercial do Maranhão, *Relatório de 1873*, p. 14; Commercial Association of Pará to Brazilian Parliament, Belém, Jan. 20, 1873, *Relatório de 1874*, Anexos, pp. 3–4.
84. Associação Comercial de Pernambuco, *Relatório de 1872*, p. 17; Minutes, meeting of April 30, 1875, Livro de Atas, 1874–1894, AACS, p. 9; Eugene W. Ridings, "The Bahian Commercial Association, 1840–1889: A Pressure Group in an Underdeveloped Area" (Ph.D. Diss., University of Florida, 1970), p. 238.
85. Associação Comercial de Santos, *Relatório de 1882*, pp. 16–17, 21.

crisis of the early 1880s soon followed the price declines in cotton and sugar. A product of that crisis, the Center for Coffee Agriculture and Commerce added a powerful voice to the struggle against export taxation. It broadcast its demands through public lectures, as well as through petitions and lobbying. But neither the center nor the commercial associations of Rio de Janeiro, Santos, or Pará wished, as did the Commercial Association of Pernambuco, to couple export tax reduction with distribution to the provinces of an import surtax. Parliament granted only the 1882 two percent reduction on export rates in return for a ten percent increase in import tariff.

For interest groups representing the faltering sugar industry only total abolition of its export duties would suffice. In September 1886, the directorates of Pernambuco's Commercial Association, Commercial Agricultural Association, and Agriculture Auxiliary Society held a protest meeting and successfully appealed for backing to other sugar-oriented commercial associations: Bahia, Maceió, and Sergipe.[86] In 1887 the newly created Center for Sugar Industry and Commerce added its weight to the struggle.[87] National export duties on sugar were abolished that year. The next year the Commercial Association of Pernambuco tried to arrange equal treatment for another foundering export, cotton, but failed.[88]

Provincial export rates were ordinarily much lower than national, but the combination of the two levies could be onerous. Only the provinces of Pará and Amazonas taxed their major export heavily. By 1868 Pará, which also marketed much of Amazonas's production, taxed rubber at thirteen percent (in addition to the nine percent levied by the Empire).[89] By contrast the three chief coffee-producing states taxed their staple at a modest four percent.[90] The repeated protests of the Commercial Association of Pará to provincial and national governments had little effect. Rubber export generally enjoyed a steep climb and the Province of Pará had become dependent on its tax revenue from it.

Until the early 1870s, business interest groups were content to request, with some success, only moderate reductions in provincial rates, because other sources of revenue were obviously lacking. Then the decline of cotton and sugar led them to demand elimination of all duty on those exports. In 1875, Pernambuco abolished duties on cotton and sugar and the Province of São Paulo on cotton.[91] In 1877 Bahia ended cotton duty

86. Minutes, meeting of Sept. 10, 1886, Livro 5 de Atas, AACP, p. 150.
87. The U.S. Consulate in Rio credited the Center and the Commercial Association of Pernambuco for the abolition of sugar duties. Consul-General Armstrong to Department of State, Rio de Janeiro, April 2, 1888, *USRC*, XXVI, no. 94 (June 1888): 529.
88. Minutes, meeting of June 4, 1886, Livro 7 de Atas, AACP, p. 21.
89. Associação Comercial do Pará, *Relatório de 1868*, p. 21.   90. *RMF, 1887*, p. 46.
91. Associação Comercial de Pernambuco, *Relatório de 1875*, p. 14; Associação Comercial de Santos, *Relatório de 1876*, Anexo no. 3, pp. 1–4.

and lowered its rate on sugar.[92] In 1887, the Center for Sugar Industry and Commerce campaigned against provincial duties on sugar, in conjunction with its drive against national duties, helping remove them in Bahia and Ceará.[93]

Northeastern provincial revenue needs in a period of fiscal crisis made such victories either fleeting or of dubious worth. In 1877, two years after abolishing export taxes on cotton and sugar, the Province of Pernambuco revived them and raised their rates in succeeding years.[94] In view of Pernambuco's budget problems, neither its Commercial Association nor Commercial Agricultural Association dared protest. In Bahia, the end of duty on cotton and sugar threw their revenue burden on other exports. By the end of the Empire, tobacco and cacao paid a combined national and provincial rate of sixteen percent, hides nineteen percent, piassava (a palm fiber used in brushes) twenty percent, and tropical woods twenty-three percent. Bahian coffee paid a combined fourteen percent, handicapping it in competition with coffee from Brazil's Southeastern provinces, which paid only eleven percent.[95] The level of taxation of exports in Bahia, and in other Brazilian provinces, reflected not only the vigor of the products in world markets but the influence of their producers with business interest groups and legislators. Sugar and, to a lesser extent, cotton were the supports of the traditional planter aristocracy. Other exports were raised by new planter groups, by smallholders, by squatters, or were simply gathered in the forest.

All Brazilian provinces also taxed exports to other provinces, although such taxes varied greatly in level and scope.[96] Since one of their purposes was to encourage exportation through that province's chief port, local business interest groups rarely protested them. The Province of Amazonas used provincial export rates to free itself from discriminatory taxation by Pará and from the commercial domination of Belém. The Province of Pará would heed neither a 1878 plea from the Commercial Association of Amazonas to end special taxes on goods to and from Amazonas nor a warning from the Commercial Association of Pará that such levies were encouraging direct shipment abroad from Manaus.[97] The Province of

92. Bahia, Presidente da Província, *Relatório de 1876*, p. 160; Ridings, "Bahian Commercial Association," p. 238.

93. President of Province of Ceará to Center for Sugar Industry and Commerce, Fortaleza, Sept. 1, 1887, *Jornal do Comércio* (Rio de Janeiro), Sept. 22, 1887, p. 2; Bahia, Presidente da Província, *Relatório de 1887*, p. 252.

94. Associação Comercial de Pernambuco, *Relatório de 1879*, p. 35, and *Relatório de 1883*, p. 84. Only the Agriculture Auxiliary Society protested their reestablishment. Agriculture Auxiliary Society of Pernambuco to Provincial Legislature, Recife, June 13, 1877, *Relatório de 1878*, pp. 23–24.

95. Ridings, "Bahian Commercial Association," p. 244; *RMF, 1887*, p. 46.

96. *RMF, 1887*, p. 46.

97. Commercial Association of Pará to President of Province, Belém, Jan. 18, 1878, *Relatório de 1879*, pp. 11–12.

Amazonas, prodded by its commercial association, retaliated by establishing a lower export rate, five percent lower by 1885, on rubber sent abroad directly than that transshipped through Pará. The Pará association's protest to the Emperor that the measure was unconstitutional had no effect. Together with subsidies granted to shipping lines for direct service overseas, the differential increased direct exportation from Manaus by more than fifty percent.[98]

Evaluating export taxation

The Republic magnified the importance of export taxes by giving them to the states as their principal source of revenue. Many states increased their export tax rates by simply adding on that part that previously had gone to the central government. Rubber in Pará, for example, continued to pay the same twenty-two percent as under the Empire, but now all went to the state. For states with booming export economies tax revenues increased dramatically; for the others revenue problems worsened. Pernambuco, for example, was forced to raise its duty on sugar and cotton year by year, despite the continuing malaise of those exports. Business interest groups now found they could do little to lower, much less eliminate, export duties. Because export taxes were indispensable to the states as revenue, complaints about them fell on deaf ears.

The imperial government and most provinces taxed exports by a *pauta,* or price schedule, calculated on the basis of overseas market prices determined weekly or at longer intervals. Business interest groups had a strong hand in this process. The imperial government *pauta* committee was legally required to have the advice of the local commercial association and commodity brokers and its decisions could be appealed.[99] In several provinces, commercial association representatives were a formal part of the provincial *pauta* committee and the price advised by the association usually was accepted without question.[100] The attitude of most business interest groups toward the intervals for setting the *pauta* depended on the direction of export prices. If prices were rising they favored longer intervals, less responsive to change. If prices were falling they dropped all demands for longer-lasting *pautas* and complained heatedly about the inability of weekly calculations to allow for rapid price declines.

98. Weinstein, *Rubber Boom,* p. 195.
99. Bernardino José Borges, *O Comerciante, ou Completo Manual Instrutivo* (2d ed. rev.; Rio de Janeiro: Eduardo & Henrique Laemmert, 1878), pp. 369–370.
100. For example, Commercial Association of Amazonas to Provincial Assembly, Manaus, April 18, 1873, Associação Comercial do Amazonas, *Primeiro Centenário,* pp. 22–23; Associação Comercial de Santos, *Relatório de 1882,* pp. 10–11; Minutes, meeting of April 17, 1893, Livro 6 de Atas, AACB, p. 59.

The campaigns against export taxes were central to business interest groups' defense of agriculture. In situations of great elasticity of international supply, such as sugar and cotton, they undoubtedly hurt Brazilian producers.[101] The struggle against export taxes, undertaken mainly to aid the planter, calls attention to a frequently debated question. Were planter interests, specifically those of coffee planters, dominant in Brazil in the late nineteenth and early twentieth centuries, or was the state relatively autonomous in its actions?[102] If the former, why did export taxation exist? But the question may be irrelevant. No state making a claim to a just fiscal policy could permit its most sizable group of wealthy to remain largely untaxed, nor is there evidence that planters felt they were entitled, solely by virtue of their status, to be free from taxation. Perhaps more to the point, export taxation was painful to cotton and sugar planters and to the Northeast, but borne with comparative ease by coffee interests. As noted, the conventional wisdom was that export taxes on commodities facing sharp international competition were borne by the producer, but those on commodities dominating world markets by the consumer. The persistence of export taxation, and its effects, may be a testimony to the growing hegemony of coffee and the Southeast.

Since business interest group membership was the focus of Brazilian taxation, the prerogatives of the groups concerning it were correspondingly strong. Unfortunately, their drives to suppress taxes that impeded development made little permanent headway. The fiscal needs of the increasingly impoverished Northeastern provinces and of the central government could not be overcome. Business interest groups had some success in eliminating or modifying taxes that unduly complicated business operations or violated business privacy. However, their struggle against provincial (later state) import tariffs and interstate taxation won only temporary successes, despite the illegality and economic prejudice of such taxes. Fiscal necessity was the last word. The struggle against export taxes, also harmful, was handicapped by a split between groups representing commodities that competed easily in world markets and groups repre-

---

101. David Denslow estimates for cotton a reduction in quantity offered equivalent to the percentage of tax. "As Exportações e a Origem do Padrão de Industrialização Regional do Brasil," in *Dimensões do Desenvolvimento Brasileiro*, eds. Werner Baer, Pedro Pinches Geiger, and Paulo Roberto Haddad (Rio de Janeiro: Campus, 1978), p. 45.

102. Recent contributions to the debate for this historical period include Joseph L. Love and Bert J. Barickman, "Rulers and Owners: A Brazilian Case Study in Comparative Perspective," *HAHR*, 66 (Nov. 1986):743–765; Steven Topik, "The State's Contribution to the Development of Brazil's Internal Economy, 1850–1930," *HAHR*, 65 (May 1985): 203–228, especially 226–228; and Winston Fritsch, *External Constraints on Economic Policy in Brazil, 1889–1930* (Houndmills, Basingstoke, Hampshire: Macmillan, 1988), especially pp. 161–164. The best-known case for the autonomy of the state throughout Brazilian history is Raymundo Faoro, *Os Donos do Poder: Formação do Patronato Político Brasileiro* (2 vols., 2d ed. rev.; Porto Alegre, São Paulo: Globo/Universidade de São Paulo, 1975).

senting those that did not. Despite notable victories, the revenue needs of central government and provinces impeded the drive against export taxation under the Empire, and the needs of the states defeated it entirely under the Republic. Continuing export taxation probably contributed to the declining fortunes of sugar and cotton. Together with interstate taxation, it slowed Brazil's overall economic development.

The revenue-sharing plan of the Commercial Association of Pernambuco presented some hope of alleviating provincial revenue needs and would have benefited both agriculture and the poorer states. The divergent interests of other business interest groups, located mainly in the Southeast, blocked it. Only a basic change in the Brazilian tax system in favor of direct taxes on land or income would have enabled business interest groups definitively to eliminate provincial tariffs, interprovincial taxes, and export taxation. These were measures offensive to the "conservative classes," wealthy businessmen and landowners, that the groups represented. They were measures business interest group leaders could not bring themselves to support.

8

Industrialization

Brazil's business interest groups played a major part on both sides of the struggle for industrialization. This reflected the central role of the Brazilian state in industrial development and the particularly strong advisory prerogatives on state aid to industry enjoyed by business interest groups. They derived from the presence in group ranks of both industrialists and importers, those businessmen most affected by government measures to foster manufacturing. Most contention was over the protective tariff, then considered the sine qua non for promoting industrial development. Although substitution for handicrafts was part of Brazilian industrialization, the core of that process, as in many underdeveloped nations, was import substitution theoretically promoted by tariffs.[1] Basic to the struggle over government aid was the battle for the minds of Brazil's educated elite. It would ultimately determine the state's role.

The strength and pervasiveness of Brazil's long-standing import economy implied a dearth of manufacturing. Imports included not only complex manufactures but basic goods otherwise readily producible at home. Bricks were brought in from Germany and salt from Portugal.[2] Travelers often remarked on the ubiquity of European consumer goods. They encountered English beverages deep in the Amazon region and in the west of the Province of Bahia, an area remote even today, "Tennant's Ale, Huntley and Palmer's biscuits, Swedish matches, pyretic saline, American and French

1. Recent scholarship has given increased importance to substitution for the products of domestic artisans. See Warren Dean, "The Brazilian Economy, 1870–1930," in *The Cambridge History of Latin America, Volume V: c. 1870 to 1930*, ed. Leslie Bethell (Cambridge: Cambridge University Press, 1986), p. 714; and José de Souza Martins, "Café e a Gênese da Industrialização em São Paulo," *Contexto*, 3 (July 1977): 1–17. For Minas Gerais, see Douglas Cole Libby, "Proto-Industrialization in a Slave Society: The Case of Minas Gerais," *JLAS*, 23 (Feb. 1991): 1–35. However, import substitution still seems central. Classic exponents of the import substitution thesis are Roberto Simonsen, *Evolução Industrial do Brasil e Outros Estudos*, ed. Edgard Carone (São Paulo: Editôra Nacional & Editôra da USP, 1973); and Celso Furtado, *The Economic Growth of Brazil: A Survey from Colonial to Modern Times* (Berkeley: University of California Press, 1963).
2. Eugene W. Ridings, "The Bahian Commercial Association, 1840–1889: A Pressure Group in an Underdeveloped Area" (Ph.D. Diss., University of Florida, 1970), p. 19.

patent medicine, Birmingham and Sheffield hardware, Staffordshire china ware, and Manchester's goods."[3]

As a colony, Brazil's economic relationship with its mother country had been determined by the mercantile system. Colonies functioned as exporters of primary goods to the mother country and importers of its consumer goods. The end of the mercantile system in 1808 did not spur industry. Brazilian manufacturing now faced the formidable competition of foreign imports, kept cheap from 1810 on by a treaty with Great Britain (later extended to other nations) that limited the import tariff to fifteen percent. At any rate, industrialization was not widely supported. Most Brazilian leaders apparently agreed with the observations of the early nineteenth-century German travelers Spix and Martius on Rio de Janeiro: "Hitherto no glass, china, cloth, or hat manufactories have been established in the capital; and the erection of them would hardly be advisable, in a country which can obtain the productions of European industry on such low terms, in exchange for the produce of its rich soil."[4] Free trade doctrines, mostly emanating from Great Britain, reinforced the idea that Brazil's "natural" or "God-given" role was that of exporter of food and raw materials and importer of finished products.

The first significant development of Brazilian industry came at mid-century. The treaty with Britain lapsed in 1844, enabling the passage of the Alves Branco Tariff, which provided some protection by raising rates to an average of forty-four percent. Industry also profited from suppression of the slave trade in 1850, which freed for investment the large amount of capital tied up in that illegal business. Most of the advance took place in the Province of Bahia, which by the 1860s had five of the nation's nine textile mills.[5] But industry remained of little real significance; national cotton textile production in 1866 was only six percent of cotton textile consumption.[6]

3. James W. Wells, *Exploring and Traveling Three Thousand Miles Through Brazil from Rio de Janeiro to Maranhão* (London: Low, Searle, and Rivington, 1886), II: 83.

4. Johann B. von Spix and Karl F. P. von Martius, *Travels in Brazil in the Years 1817–1820, Undertaken by Command of His Majesty the King of Bavaria* (London: Longman Hurst, Rees, Orme, Brown, and Green, 1824), I: 198. For the sway of free trade ideas among Brazil's governing elite, see Heitor Fereira Lima, *História do Pensamento Econômico no Brasil* (São Paulo: Editôra Nacional, 1976), pp. 80–82.

5. Stanley J. Stein, *The Brazilian Cotton Manufacture: Textile Enterprise in an Underdeveloped Area, 1850–1950* (Cambridge, Mass.: Harvard University Press, 1957), p. 20. Wilson Suzigan, *Indústria Brasileira: Origem e Desenvolvimento* (São Paulo: Brasiliense, 1986), pp. 127, 385, has Bahia with six of ten, but lists the mill São Carlos do Paraguassú as built in 1857, rather than in 1874, the correct date. Bahia, Presidente da Província, *Fala com que o Exm. Sr. Conselheiro Pedro Luís Pereira de Sousa Devia Abrir a Sessão Extraordinária da Assembléia Provincial Convocada para 10 de Dezembro de 1882, Precidida das Palavras com que o Exm. Sr. Dr. Augusto Alves Guimarães Abriu a Mesma Sessão* (Salvador: Diário da Bahia, 1882), p. 99.

6. Eulália Maria Lahmeyer Lobo, *História do Rio de Janeiro (do Capital Comercial ao Capital Industrial e Financeiro)* (Rio de Janeiro: IBMEC, 1978), I: 189.

Despite its tardy advance, the potential for manufacturing in Brazil in the nineteenth century was good. The nation possessed an outstanding quantity and variety of agricultural and mineral resources, lacking only good-quality coal.[7] Major handicaps existed, but they were often counterbalanced by assets. Internal communications were rudimentary, but population was concentrated near the coast and coastal transportation after the advent of the steamship was easy. The large proportion of slaves in the population and the low income of free workers precluded a wealthy internal market, but the slave-based economy provided good markets for crude textiles characteristic of early industrialization: bagging for exports and clothing for slaves. These needs stimulated early textile manufacture in the Province of Bahia.[8] Skilled labor was also wanting, but Brazilian industry partially overcame this by importing European and North American workers as cadres, and unskilled labor (including slaves) was abundant and cheap. Another problem was lack of capital. Interest rates were more than double those of Europe, and industry had to compete with commerce and with national debt bonds as an investment.[9] Government loans or other aid could help overcome this problem.

Government aid could ameliorate, if not overcome, other handicaps to industrial development. It could provide communications improvements, subsidies, loans, tax exemptions, guaranteed interest on investment, and, most important, tariff protection. In the words of W. W. Rostow, "the government has essential, major technical tasks to perform in the period of preconditions [for industrialization]."[10] As in many other nations, the attitude of government would be a key factor in the advance of Brazilian industry. However, the task of winning government support in Brazil was formidable. Because of tradition and the prevailing views of Brazil's proper role in the international division of labor, government leaders first had to be convinced that industrial development was desirable or even possible.

The views of business interest groups on industry had particular force because landowners and their groups tended to be ambiguous in their attitude toward it. They resented it as a competitor for labor supply and for capital that might otherwise go into agricultural mortgages. On the

7. Janet D. Henshall and R. P. Momsen, *A Geography of Brazilian Development* (London: G. Bell & Sons, 1974), p. 110.
8. Morgan to Foreign Office, Salvador, March 15, 1856, PRO/FO 13/344: fl. 140. As an institution, slavery was not incompatable with industrialization. See Richard Graham, "Slavery and Economic Development: Brazil and the United States' South in the Nineteenth Century," *Comparative Studies in Society and History*, 23 (Oct. 1981).
9. Brazil, Comissão de Inquérito Industrial, *Relatório Apresentado a S. Ex. o Sr. Ministro da Fazenda pela Comissão de Inquérito Industrial* (Rio de Janeiro: Tipografia Nacional, 1882), I: 59–60.
10. *The Stages of Economic Growth: A Non-Communist Manifesto* (2d. ed.; Cambridge: Cambridge University Press, 1971), p. 30.

other hand, they noticed that manufacturing provided markets for products increasingly uncompetitive in world markets, such as cotton, sugar, and hides. Nor were they immune to appeals to national pride. At the same time, they particularly disliked so-called "artificial" industry, which imported its raw materials, rather than using products from Brazilian agriculture, and they feared having tariffs raise their expenses.[11] For this reason, agricultural machines and tools were usually exempt from import duty or paid much lower rates than similar products. The ambivalent attitude of agriculture toward industry left business interest groups a nearly clear field on which to exercise their influence.

Until the rise of groups representing manufacturers, all business interest groups usually opposed industrialization. This resistance reflected the perceived interests of most commercial association and factor group members. Manufacturer members of commercial associations of course dissented, but they were invariably outnumbered on the associations' boards of directors. Furthermore, some manufacturers were not zealous in defending industrial interests because they also headed overseas trading firms or had heavy investments in them.[12] Importers had obvious reasons for opposing industry: they knew that tariffs designed to aid industrialization by definition restricted importation. Exporters and factors also opposed industry, although with less zeal. Many, if not most, large and successful export houses also engaged in importation, and factors profited from procuring imported goods for their clients. Furthermore, exporters and factors feared that high tariffs might result in retaliation against Brazilian commodities and believed that, even were there no retaliation, a decrease in importation always resulted in a corresponding drop in exportation.[13]

Less direct considerations reinforced merchant opposition. Industry was seen as a competitor for labor and capital to agriculture and for capital and government aid to transportation, which would expand the export econ-

11. Dean, "A Industrialização Durante a República Velha," in *Estructura de Poder e Economia*, vol. 1 of *O Brasil Republicano*, ed. Boris Fausto, tomo III of *História Geral da Civilização Brasileira*, ed. Sérgio Buarque de Holanda (São Paulo: Difusão Editorial, 1975), p. 275; Nícia Villela Luz, *A Luta pela Industrialização do Brasil (1808 a 1930)* (2d ed.; São Paulo: Alfa-Omega, 1975), pp. 55–56; Edgard Carone, "Prefácio," in *O Pensamento Industrial no Brasil (1880–1945)*, ed. Edgard Carone (Rio de Janeiro: Difel, 1977), p. 8.

12. Rômulo de Almeida, *Traços da História Econômica da Bahia no Ultimo Sêculo e Meio* (Salvador: Instituto de Economia e Finanças da Bahia, 1951), p. 14. A notable industrialist who long clung to his overseas trading interests was Count Francisco Matarazzo. José de Souza Martins, *Empresário e Emprêsa na Biografia do Conde Matarazzo* (Rio de Janeiro: Instituto de Ciências Sociais da UFRJ, 1967).

13. Commercial Association of Rio de Janeiro to Brazilian Parliament, Rio de Janeiro, Sept. 11, 1882, *Relatório da Associação Comercial do Rio de Janeiro dos Anos de 1882 e 1883* (Rio de Janeiro: Montenegro, 1884), p. 25; Associação Comercial de São Paulo, *Relatório da Associação Comercial de São Paulo, Ano de 1895* (São Paulo: Industrial, 1896), pp. 73–74; J. P. Wileman, *Brazilian Exchange: The Study of an Incontrovertible Currency* (Reprint of the 1896 Edition) (New York: Greenwood Press, 1969), p. 21.

omy. In any case, funds for government aid to industry would be, like most other government revenue, extracted from commerce. Finally, government aid for industry contradicted principles of economic liberalism and the precept that Brazil's correct role in the world division of labor was that of furnisher of raw materials and food.

Opposition to industrialization was rarely blatant or uncompromising. All commercial associations had at least a few manufacturer members, whom others were reluctant to offend openly. Significantly, one of the most overtly hostile proclamations on industrialization came from the Center for Coffee Agriculture and Commerce, which, like other factor groups, had few or no manufacturer members. In a published petition in 1882 it denounced the "vicious protectionist system," attacked "artificial" and "exotic" manufactures, and warned that a government attempt to push industrialization would bring about the ruin of the nation's agricultural economy.[14] Typically, commercial associations were milder in their rhetoric. They claimed that tariff increases fell most heavily on the poor and might bring a revenue crisis by throttling importation, and that a protective tariff kept manufactures from progressing by removing competition. They pronounced industrialization unnecessary for Brazil or feasible only in the very distant future. Furthermore, if Brazilian industry had not blossomed yet, it probably never would. To aid industrial development, most suggested only the innocuous measure of reducing import duty on raw materials.[15]

Some commercial associations applauded the abstract idea of industrialization, while opposing measures aimed at bringing it about. The Commercial Association of Rio de Janeiro occasionally demanded piecemeal tariff increases to help specific local manufactures. It recommended production of consumer goods in Brazil as the answer to the problem of balance of payments and predicted that the rise of a steel industry would make Brazilians "the richest people in the world."[16] But the Rio group consistently opposed a protective tariff, even suggesting in 1889 that the government award manufactures cash prizes for excellence instead of tariff protection.[17] The commercial associations of Santos and São Paulo, also in an industrializing area, were equally hostile to a protective tariff.[18] All

14. Centro da Lavoura e Comércio do Café, *Representação Submetida ao Poder Legislativo sôbre Algumas das Necessidades da Lavoura e do Comércio* (Rio de Janeiro: Moreira, Maximino, 1882), pp. 3–6.
15. Many of these attitudes are expressed in Brazil, Congresso, Comissão Parlamentar de Inquérito, *Informações Apresentadas pela Comissão Parlamentar de Inquérito ao Corpo Legislativo na Terceira Sessão da Décima Oitava Legislatura* (Rio de Janeiro: Tipografia Nacional, 1883), pp. 160, 166, 202, 446–447, 477.
16. Associação Comercial do Rio de Janeiro, *Relatório de 1880*, p. 5; Commercial Association of Rio de Janeiro to Minister of Finance, Rio de Janeiro, Aug. 31, 1889, *Relatório de 1890*, p. 41.
17. Commercial Association of Rio de Janeiro to Minister of Finance, Rio de Janeiro, Aug. 31, 1889, *Relatório de 1890*, p. 41.
18. Commercial Association of Santos to Brazilian Parliament, Santos, Sept. 9, 1883, *Relatório da Associação Comercial de Santos Apresentado em Sessão Ordinária da Assembléia Geral em Março de 1883 e*

commercial associations, in fact, opposed this most basic of aids to manufacturing. It was evident that, no matter how encouraging their statements, commercial associations were no friends of industry.

Stifling industry: government aid and free trade

Although tariff protection was the most basic form of government aid to industry, other help, usually awarded by the provinces, could also be vital. It included subsidies, low-cost loans, monopoly privileges, exemptions from taxation, and guaranteed interest on capital. The Province of Bahia offers an example of how denial of such aid could help throttle incipient manufactures. Despite the province's early lead in Brazilian textile production, the Commercial Association of Bahia was particularly negative toward help for industry. As early as 1843 it refused to endorse tax exemptions for a proposed hat factory, and when queried on financial aid to a paper factory in 1847 declared that no public money should be spent on enterprises that could not render a profit in competition with imported goods.[19] This statement became long-term policy; in 1891 the Bahian association was still publicly opposing government aid for manufactures.[20]

Particularly costly to local industry was the Commercial Association of Bahia's opposition to placing additional taxes on exports shipped in foreign-made bags. This was a common means to stimulate local manufacture of bagging, a mainstay of early industry. However, it not only raised the expense of exportation, but also hurt the lucrative importation of bags. In 1849, the association unsuccessfully fought the placing of a two percent additional duty on all commodities not shipped in locally made bagging, a measure that proved essential for the early survival of local textile plants.[21] In 1860, following the death of the lone manufacturer on its Board of Directors, the association renewed its attack on additional taxes on foreign-made bagging and succeeded in reducing, then repealing them. In the words of a provincial president, elimination of this stimulus to textile manufacture "damaged in no small way the existence of such factories."[22] Together with a steep rise in cotton prices due to the United States Civil War, it forced the shutdown of three of the province's five plants. The Commercial Association also successfully opposed new addi-

Parecer da Comissão de Contas (Santos: Diário de Santos, 1883), pp. 43–48; Associação Comercial de São Paulo, *Relatório de 1895*, pp. 73–75.

19. Minutes, meeting of May 11, 1843, Livro 1 de Atas, AACB, pp. 104–105; Commercial Association of Bahia to President of Province, Salvador, May 25, 1847, Registro de Ofícios, 1840–1850, AACB.
20. Minutes, meeting of Oct. 28, 1891, Livro 5 de Atas, AACB, pp. 381–382.
21. Minutes, meeting of Oct. 1, 1849, Livro 1 de Atas, AACB, p. 302; Morgan to Foreign Office, Salvador, March 18, 1858, PRO/FO 13/365, fl. 85.
22. Bahia, Presidente da Província, *Relatório de 1862*, p.70.

tional taxes on products shipped in foreign bagging in 1869.[23] Bahian textile manufactures had to survive on their own.

The bagging issue arose elsewhere. The Commercial Association of Pernambuco, for example, opposed an 1883 proposal to aid that province's first textile plant by the same means.[24] No attempt was made to stimulate the domestic bagging industry on a national scale until the coming of the Republic. In 1891 the administration of Floriano Peixoto raised the tariff on imported burlap bags by 900 percent. Citing alleged damage to the coffee industry, the Commercial Association of Santos, backed by Santos and Rio de Janeiro importers, succeeded in lowering the tariff almost to its former rate in 1897.[25] That same group, however, made a conspicuous exception in 1899 to commercial association opposition to stimulating manufacture of local bagging. It successfully petitioned for a two percent reduction in state export duty for coffee shipped in Brazilian-made cotton sacks.[26] The Santos association had long campaigned for the replacement of burlap bagging by cotton as a means of improving coffee quality.

In contrast to their usual opposition to provincial aid to manufactures, most commercial associations were open-handed in recommending help for transportation companies. All hoped to enlarge their tributary trade area. The commercial associations' policy of promoting government support for transportation while denying it to manufacturing slowed industrialization not only by withholding vital assistance from infant manufactures, but by making transportation companies a more attractive investment, thus enabling them to best industry in competition for scarce capital.

How much did the denial of aid by the provinces affect industrial development within them? In Bahia, five new cotton textile factories were added to the original five during the 1870s, but several acknowledged difficulty surviving without government help. Only seven of them were in operation in March 1882.[27] In Pernambuco and Maranhão, two provinces whose commercial associations were also cold toward industry, significant manufacturing had to await the favorable conditions of the early Republic.[28] In all three, declining export prosperity, which reduced capital for

23. Commercial Association of Bahia to President of Province, Salvador, Jan. 18, 1869, *Relatório da Junta Diretora da Associação Comercial da Praça da Bahia, Apresentado em Sessão Ordinária da Assembléia Geral de 17 de Novembro de 1869* (Salvador: Camillo de Lellis Masson, 1869), p. 53.
24. Associação Comercial de Pernambuco, *Relatório da Associação Comercial Beneficente de Pernambuco, Lido em Sessão de Assembléia Geral de 6 de Agôsto de 1883* (Recife: Homeopatha, 1883), pp. 4, 23–25.
25. Evaldo Sintoni, "A Indústria de Aniagem e o Café (1897–1899)," in *O Café: Anais do Segundo Congresso de História de São Paulo*, ed. Edgard Carone (São Paulo: Revista de História, 1975), pp. 328–332.
26. Minutes, meeting of June 18, 1899, Livro de Atas, 1894–1904, AACS, p. 48.
27. Bahia, Presidente da Província, *Relatório de 1877*, pp. 63–64, and *Relatório de 1882*, pp. 99–102.
28. For the Commercial Association of Maranhão, see *Relatório, Janeiro a Dezembro de 1891* (São Luís:

investment, and lack of a strong local market, because of widespread poverty, were also formidable obstacles to industry. Nevertheless, the denial of support by local business interest groups appears to have slowed, although it did not stop, industrialization.

There were other ways in which industrial development could be inhibited. In the case of Brazilian artificial wine, two commercial associations tried to discredit an entire industry. Artificial wine, a factory-made concoction whose basic ingredient was sugar, competed with natural wine, almost all of which was imported, and its demand for tariff protection attracted sugar planter support. The Rio de Janeiro and Pernambuco associations, both of which had a high proportion of beverage importers, made the artificial wine industry a special target. In 1877 the Pernambuco group declared the manufacture of artificial wine to be a "public menace."[29] Asked in 1879 by the Minister of Finance to evaluate a request by sugar factors for higher wine import duties, the Rio association denounced artificial wine manufacture as an unlawful industry, later describing it as "manifestly damaging to public health," and "slow poison," unless rigorously inspected.[30] The groups continued such attacks in the 1880s. The Rio and Pernambuco associations' portrayal of artificial wine as a menace to health generally frustrated that industry's demands for higher tariffs on imported wine.

Commercial associations and factor groups also inhibited the development of industry by insisting on tight legal protection for foreign patents, which made it difficult for Brazilian industries to turn out basic new products from abroad. They were perhaps Brazil's foremost disseminators, in communications with government and in newspapers and books, of doctrines of laissez-faire and free trade which provided a rationale for denying state aid to industry. However, business interest groups probably most affected the rise of industry by their ability to influence tariff levels.

Advisory prerogatives and the tariff

As representatives of manufacturers and other businessmen affected, commercial associations and the Industrial Association had the prerogative of advising on tariffs. The practice was regarded as wise, as well as just, because, as the Commercial Association of Rio de Janeiro put it, "the state

Frias, 1892) p. 8; and Jerônimo de Viveiros, *História do Comércio do Maranhão, 1612–1895* (São Luís: Associação Comercial do Maranhão, 1954), II: 565.

29. Commercial Association of Pernambuco to Brazilian Parliament, Recife, May 15, 1877, *Relatório de 1877*, p. 47.

30. Associação Comercial do Rio de Janeiro, *Relatório de 1879*, pp. 21–25; Commercial Association of Rio de Janeiro to Brazilian Parliament, Rio de Janeiro, May 21, 1884, *Relatório de 1884–1885*, p. 19.

has the men of theory, commerce the men who are practical and experienced."[31] The right of advising on tariffs, however, derived solely from custom, not law. There was no specified form in which the advice of the groups was to be tendered, nor, legally, did their advice even have to be solicited.

The ways in which business interest groups influenced tariffs were many and varied. The most direct means was by having group representatives aid in drawing them up. The President of the Commercial Association of Rio de Janeiro, for example, formed part of a three-man preparation committee in 1893.[32] A committee of business interest group representatives might serve as an advisory body in formulating a tariff or the group itself might furnish advice, channeling suggestions from members and other businessmen.[33] This was usually the role of the Commercial Association of Rio de Janeiro and, while it lasted, the Industrial Association, because of their location in Rio. However, in 1881 in addition to those two, representatives from six outside commercial associations helped put together a new tariff.[34] It was a practice, in all cases, for committees of import merchants to advise on the classification and costs of goods.

Once the draft of the tariff was completed, all commercial associations and the Industrial Association commonly enjoyed the right to make a formal critique. They gathered comments by having the draft reviewed systematically by all local import houses, by special committees representing each branch of the import trade, by a single specially chosen committee, or simply by any businessman who was interested.[35] When a tariff had been completed and put into operation for a period, business interest groups were often queried by the Ministry of Finance about its effects. Even this did not exhaust all means for business interest groups to influence tariffs. Once a tariff became law they could use ordinary lobbying and petitioning to force changes in its provisions or application. In sum, although the nature of their participation might vary, business interest groups were expected to play a strong part in the making of Brazilian tariffs.

How effective were Brazil's nineteenth-century tariffs? Their impact on industrialization remains controversial. Economic historians cannot even

---

31. Associação Comercial do Rio de Janeiro, *Relatório de 1878*, p. 33.
32. *RMF, 1893*, p. 10.
33. For example, Commercial Association of Rio de Janeiro to Viscount Ouro Preto, Rio de Janeiro, Sept. 18, 1889, Ofícios da Associação Comercial do Rio de Janeiro, 1887–1892, AACRJ, p. 51; *RMF, 1874*, p. 69, and *RMF, 1878*, p. 58.
34. *RMF, 1882*, p. 33.
35. For example, Minutes, meeting of July 18, 1850, Livro 1 de Atas, AACP, p. 217; Associação Comercial do Rio de Janeiro, *Relatório de 1890*, pp. 42–43; Associação Comercial de Pernambuco, *Relatório de 1860*, p. 13; Minutes, meeting of May 4, 1881, Livro de Atas, 1874–1894, AACS, pp. 63–64; Minutes, meeting of Aug. 27, 1890, Livro de Atas, 1890–1896, AACRJ, p. 10.

agree whether their purpose was to provide protection or merely necessary revenue. To many, the latter aim was paramount, with effective tariff protection denied until well into the twentieth century.[36] Others, to the contrary, see deliberate and effective protection provided in the nineteenth century, even as early as 1844.[37] Some deny that tariffs significantly aided manufactures. They maintain, rather, that inflation and currency depreciation alone accelerated industrialization by making imported goods more expensive.[38]

To offer true protection, tariffs needed to be much higher than, for example, the nineteenth-century protective tariffs of the United States.[39] Brazilian manufactures faced handicaps that made production more costly. Many raw materials and nearly all machinery had to be imported, credit was expensive, skilled labor was scarce and, unlike the United States, Brazil had no tradition of manufacturing enterprise or mechanical aptitude among its population. Moreover, the competition of foreign imports became increasingly formidable as the efficiency of manufacturing and transportation grew. According to one authoritative estimate, the average

36. Annibal Villela and Wilson Suzigan, in their authoritative *Política do Govêrno e Crescimento da Economia Brasileira, 1889–1945* (Rio de Janeiro: IPEA/INPES, 1975), pp. 218–219, argue that tariffs were never intentionally protective until 1945. Others who see revenue as the true purpose of tariffs and deny Brazilian industry had effective protection during the nineteenth century (and sometimes beyond) are Nícia Villela Luz, *Luta pela Industrialização*, p. 199; Hélio Jaguaribe, *Economic and Political Development: A Theoretical Approach and a Brazilian Case Study* (Cambridge, Mass.: Harvard University Press, 1968), p. 119; and Hélio Schlitter Silva, "Tendências e Características Gerais do Comércio Exterior no Século XIX," *Revista de História da Economia Brasileira*, 1 (June 1953): 7. Wilson Suzigan sees tariffs as helping mitigate declining import prices, but effectively protecting only certain industries. *Indústria Brasileira*, pp. 104–107, 120, 349.

37. Laura Randall, *A Comparative Economic History of Latin America, 1500–1914. Vol. 3: Brazil* (Ann Arbor, Mich.: University Microfilms International, 1977), pp. 95, 129, sees it beginning with the "strongly protective tariff legislation" of 1844, as does Mircea Buescu, *Evolução Econômica do Brasil* (2d ed.; Rio de Janeiro: APEC, 1974), p. 139. This is also asserted by Nathaniel Leff in "Economic Retardation in Nineteenth-Century Brazil," *Economic History Review*, 25 (Aug. 1972): 489, although his other analyses avoid the label "protective," such as "Long-Term Brazilian Economic Development," *The Journal of Economic History*, 29 (Sept. 1969): 478; *Underdevelopment and Development in Brazil. Volume I: Economic Structure and Change, 1822–1947* (London: George Allen & Unwin, 1982), pp. 174–175; and *Reassessing the Obstacles*, p. 74. Fábio Versiani, "Industrial Investment in an 'Export' Economy: The Brazilian Experience Before 1914," *Journal of Development Economics*, 7 (Sept. 1980): 321, finds "a definite and consistent pattern of protection" for Brazilian textiles from 1870 on, and D. C. M. Platt, *Latin America and British Trade, 1806–1914* (New York: Barnes & Noble, 1972), p. 82, terms the Brazilian government "extreme protectionists" concerning certain parts of the textile industry from the early 1870s. Roberto Simonsen, *Evolução Industrial*, p. 11, sees the tariff as protectionist by 1888, although more for revenue needs than for aiding industry.

38. Albert Fishlow, "Origins and Consequences of Import-Substitution in Brazil," in *International Economics and Development: Essays in Honor of Raul Prebisch*, ed. Luiz Eugenio di Marco (New York: Academic Press, 1972), pp. 311–365; Werner Baer and Annibal V. Villela, "Industrial Growth and Industrialization: Revisions in the Stages of Brazil's Economic Development," *The Journal of Developing Areas*, 7 (Jan. 1973): 221.

39. For a ratio of duty collected to total import value, see Jonathan J. Pincus, *Pressure Groups and Politics in Antebellum Tariffs* (New York: Columbia University Press, 1977), p. 9.

real cost of imports in Brazil fell faster than either tariffs, exchange depreciation, or inflation could raise it, declining to less than half of its 1855 level by 1900.[40] If so, much of the effect of the tariff was to mitigate, not overcome, the competition of foreign imports.

There was controversy over whether tariff rates were lower or higher than the true value of the import. Those who believed them too high pointed out that official values, which could be changed only by law, failed to reflect the ongoing reduction of import prices by more efficient manufacturing and transportation. A reason for believing them too low was that the same infrequent changes in official values did not accommodate price increases caused by inflation or exchange depreciation.[41] Another was that tariffs allegedly understated actual import price, even in years of price and exchange stability. Industrialists and Ministers of Finance alike denounced from the 1860s on the setting of official prices below market prices.[42] Estimates of average tariff levels by knowledgeable contemporaries were generally lower than those calculated by modern scholars.[43]

For such undervaluation, the role of overseas merchants in drawing up and criticizing tariffs and of committees of importers assisting customs officials in pricing goods, both exercised through the commercial associations, were largely to blame. Committees of importers also lowered duty requirements by putting goods into an inferior tax category. The Industrial Association denounced their role in 1881, adding that customs officials usually gave way to importers in close disputes over classification.[44] Prior to 1881, in fact, an especially chosen four-man committee, composed of equal numbers of customs officials and merchants, judged such

40. Suzigan, *Indústria Brasileira*, pp. 379–381. See also his "Investimento na Indústria de Transformação no Brasil, 1869–1939: Uma Visão Geral," *Pesquisa e Planejamento Econômico*, 15 (Aug. 1985): 383–397; and Carlos Manuel Peláez, "Uma Análise Econômica da História do Café Brasileiro," in *Economia Brasileira: Uma Visão Histórica*, ed. Paulo Neuhaus (Rio de Janeiro: Campus, 1980), pp. 332–334.

41. For the 1890s, see Suzigan, *Indústria Brasileira*, pp. 380–381; Nathaniel H. Leff, *Underdevelopment and Development in Brazil. Volume II: Reassessing the Obstacles to Economic Development* (London: George Allen & Unwin, 1982), p. 74; Great Britain, Foreign Office, *Diplomatic and Consular Reports*, no. 1321 (1890–93): 30–32.

42. Agostinho Vitor Borja Castro, "Relatório," in Antônio de Sousa Rego, *Relatório da Segunda Exposição Nacional de 1866* (Rio de Janeiro: Tipografia Nacional, 1869), pp. 14–15; Brazil, Congresso, Comissão Parlamentar de Inquérito, *Informações Apresentadas*, pp. 356–363; Sebastião Ferreira Soares, *Elementos de Estatística* (Rio de Janeiro: J. Villenueve, 1865), pp. 268–269; *RMF, 1872*, p. 75, and *RMF, 1886*, p. 50.

43. Ferreira Soares, *Elementos de Estatística*, pp. 268–269; Bernardino José Borges to Baron Cotegipe, Salvador, Dec. 27, 1873, Arquivo do Barão de Cotegipe (hereafter cited as ABC), AIHGB, lata 85, doc. 24; Associação Comercial de Santos, *Relatório de 1879*, p. 12. Compare Leff, *Reassessing the Obstacles*, p. 74, and *Economic Structure*, p. 175; Suzigan, *Indústria Brasileira*, pp. 379–381.

44. *O Trabalho Nacional e Seus Adversários* (Rio de Janeiro: G. Leuzinger & Filhos, 1881), pp. 90–100. See also "Relatório Apresentado ao Corpo Legislativo pela Comissão Parlamentar de Inquérito," *O Auxiliador da Indústria Nacional*, 53, no. 10 (1885): 227.

disputes.[45] The role of the commercial associations in shaping tariffs and the participation of their importer members in fixing values and classification suggest that imports were indeed undervalued.

Thus, the protection offered by nineteenth-century Brazilian tariffs was weaker than supposed. It should be remembered, however, that rates were higher on goods also made in Brazil, especially textiles. It should also be noted that much of the effect of Brazilian tariffs derived not from their level but from their rarely interrupted climb. Many importers probably turned to manufacturing not because the current tariff was damaging importation, but because they believed future ones surely would. The gradual expansion of Brazilian industry signaled the increasing effect, psychological or real, of the tariff, an effectiveness often enhanced by inflation and exchange depreciation.

Business interest groups and tariffs

Despite the opposition of most business interest groups, Brazilian tariffs tended to rise over time. The causes were two: revenue needs and growing sentiment in favor of industrialization. Revenue needs expanded as the economy expanded, one cause being the improvement in the economic infrastructure – railroads, steamer lines, and urban and port development – which business interest groups had taken the lead in demanding. Public backing for industrialization became a factor in the last quarter of the century, gathering momentum with the coming of the Republic.

The Alves Branco Tariff of 1844 aimed at ending the revenue starvation resulting from previous low rates, but also envisioned mild protection. Protests from importers, delivered through the commercial associations, brought lower rates in 1857.[46] The practice of having lower rates or no rates for agricultural tools and machinery, as well as for industrial raw materials and equipment, began early and generally continued. So did the placing of a surtax on tariff rates, as a means of increasing revenue without constructing a new tariff. War with Paraguay brought the first significant increase in rates. In 1867 levies on luxury goods were raised by twenty percent, with fifteen percent of import duties to be collected in gold. As a patriotic necessity and lasting only two years, the latter measure did not bring forth the storm of protest that greeted its reintroduction during the Republic. The war surtaxes were maintained afterward. This was done in

---

45. Minutes, meeting of Nov. 11, 1881, Livro de Atas, 1881–1890, AACRJ, pp. 31–32; Bernandino José Borges, *O Comerciante, ou Completo Manual Instrutivo* (2d ed. rev.; Rio de Janeiro: Eduardo & Henrique Laemmert, 1878), p. 335.
46. Guilherme Deveza, "Política Tributária no Período Imperial," in *História Geral da Civilização Brasileira,* eds. Sérgio Buarque de Holanda and Pedro Moacyr Campos (São Paulo: Difusão Européia do Livro, 1971), 2, no. 4: 70; H. Schlitter Silva, "Tendências e Caraterísticas," 6.

response to revenue needs, not to protect industry, but had "an involuntary protectionist result."[47] In the period 1869–1875, twenty new cotton mills were added to Brazil's previous twelve, and imports of industrial machinery were more than twice their 1860–1870 levels.[48]

As Brazil's modest industrial capacity grew, so did support for industrialization: the increasing number of manufacturers widened the demand for state aid.[49] But the turn toward industry also stemmed from disillusionment with agricultural exportation. Its instability was demonstrated by the rapid drop of cotton prices after the United States Civil War, the steady decline of sugar prices after 1872, and a tumble of coffee prices in 1881. Conveniently, the coffee industry's success to that date had generated much capital for potential investment in manufactures.[50] A growing spirit of nationalism, itself fed by dissatisfaction with Brazil's traditional role in the world division of labor, also heightened support for industrial development. Nationalist resentments were intensified by the sharp decline in rubber prices after 1884, which rubber factors blamed on collusion between overseas buyers and foreign exporters. The growing fascination of Brazilian intellectuals with the industrial might and prosperity of the United States also increased sentiment for industry. The impressive development of the United States, advocates of industry maintained, demonstrated the benefits of a protective tariff. As the nations of continental Europe also increasingly adopted protectionism, it became clear that free trade was no longer the most up-to-date of economic theories. Finally, the growth of manufactures and the realization that commercial associations were in no wise spokesmen for industry led to the rise of industrial interest organizations. Most were short-lived, but they were articulate and knew how to appeal to nationalism. To them is owed much of the increase in public support for industry.

The first organization to champion industry was not an interest group but Brazil's main learned society, the Auxiliary Society for National In-

---

47. Oscar Soto Lorenzo-Fernandes, *A Evolução da Economia Brasileira* (Rio de Janeiro: Zahar, 1976), p. 103.
48. Suzigan, *Indústria Brasileira*, pp. 355–356, 384–389. See also Versiani, "Industrial Investment," 310, 312.
49. A less influential group, artisans and workers who resented competing foreign products, often echoed the demands of industrialists. Emilia Viotti da Costa, "Brazil: The Age of Reform, 1870–1889," in *The Cambridge History of Latin America. Volume V: c. 1870–1930*, ed. Leslie Bethell (Cambridge: Cambridge University Press, 1986), p. 733.
50. For the interaction of coffee exportation and industrialization, see Wilson Cano, *Raízes da Concentração Industrial em São Paulo* (Rio de Janeiro, São Paulo: DIFEL, 1977); and Sérgio Silva, *Expansão Cafeeira e Origens da Indústria no Brasil* (São Paulo: Alfa Omega, 1976). The "Structuralist" school denies that exportation contributed greatly to industrial development, maintaining that more significant advances were made during periods of export crisis. For a refutation, see Carlos Manuel Peláez, *História Econômica do Brasil: Um Elo Entre a Teoria e a Realidade Econômica* (São Paulo: Atlas, 1979).

dustry (*Sociedade Auxiliadora da Indústria Nacional*). The society devoted most of its activity, from its beginning in 1828 until its demise in the 1890s, to promoting mechanization and other improvement of agriculture.[51] However, it also had an abstract interest in the advance of manufacturing, a concern increased by its role as an evaluator of patent applications for the imperial government. Its foray in 1877 as an advocate for industry stemmed from a dispute among hat manufacturers, many of whom were society members, over the raising or lowering of the tariff on hats and their raw materials and from the formal request of another member that the question of tariff protection be debated in the abstract.[52]

The three-month long debate was fervid. The society's Subcommittee on Manufacturing Industry pronounced a protective tariff vital for Brazilian development, while its Subcommittee on Commerce condemned it as a relic from a "semi-barbarian epoch," and a source of "want, nudity, and hunger."[53] By a vote of the society's membership, those favoring protection carried the day. Under the guidance of its President, former prime minister Viscount Rio Branco, the Auxiliary Society for National Industry submitted to the imperial government a twelve-point program for the development of industry, including significantly, "fair protection by means of a customs tariff."[54] From the Auxiliary Society for National Industry, such modest recommendations carried great weight. Despite periodic urging by pro-industry members, the society did not take up subsequently the role of an interest group representing industry. When queried by government, however, it continued to recommend "fair protection" and other measures designed to stimulate manufacturing.[55]

Another evidence of increasing support for industrial development was the tariff of 1879. Increasing rates on products also made in Brazil, it was widely criticized by economic liberals as being drawn up under the influence of protectionist ideology.[56] The Commercial Association of Rio de Janeiro assailed the government for ignoring the recommendations of its merchant members who had aided in the tariff's formulation.[57] Such pressures proved irresistible. Revision of the 1879 tariff was soon under-

51. Livros de Atas, Sociedade Auxiliadora da Indústria Nacional, 1827–1858, ACIRJ; *O Auxiliador da Indústria Nacional*, 1833–1896; Edgard Carone, *O Centro Industrial do Brasil e a sua Importante Participação na Economia Nacional (1827–1977)* (Rio de Janeiro: Centro Industrial do Rio de Janeiro, 1978), pp. 15–62.
52. Sociedade Auxiliadora da Indústria Nacional, *Números 5, 6 e 7, Maio, Junho e Julho de 1877; Sessão do Concelho Administrativo da Sociedade Auxilidora da Indústria Nacional em 21 de Junho de 1876* (Rio de Janeiro: Sociedade Auxiliadora da Indústria Nacional, 1877), pp. 177, 209–210.
53. *O Auxiliador do Indústria Nacional*, 45, nos. 5–7 (May-July 1877): 181–189.
54. Sociedade Auxiliadora da Indústria Nacional to Princess Isabel, Rio de Janeiro, July 5, 1877, *Números 5, 6 e 7*, pp. 348–353.
55. *O Auxiliador do Indústria Nacional*, 51, no. 2 (Feb. 1883): 25–26.
56. RMF, 1880, pp. 19–20.
57. Associação Comercial do Rio de Janeiro, *Relatório de 1879*, pp. 6–7, and *Relatório de 1880*, p. 9.

way, and it was replaced late in 1881 by another that significantly reduced the duties on imports also manufactured in Brazil. The participation of the Industrial Association, Brazil's first industrial interest group, in the preparation of the 1881 tariff was more than counterbalanced by that of seven commercial associations.

The first industrial interest groups

The debate over the 1879 tariff, by mobilizing pro-industry sentiment, helped give rise in September 1880 to the Industrial Association. A rapid fall of import prices also spurred its creation.[58] The organization specifically restricted its membership to manufacturers, probably to avoid domination by businessmen with contrary interests. It set to work with energy, repeatedly petitioning for tariff protection and organizing in 1881 an Industrial Exposition for Rio de Janeiro, which obtained the help of the imperial government. The products assembled were later shipped to a larger Continental Exposition in Buenos Aires. In May 1881, it began publication of a journal, *O Industrial*. Unlike most other business interest groups, the Industrial Association, admittedly swimming against the prevailing ideological tide, had little influence in high circles of government and thus was forced to take its views directly to the public.

In *O Industrial* and other publications and petitions, the Industrial Association appealed skillfully to national fears and aspirations. It denounced free trade doctrines ("the idolatrous cult of theory") as a ploy by industrialized nations, particularly Britain, to keep Brazil agricultural and dependent.[59] Foreshadowing another tenet of modern dependency theory, it maintained that in the economic sense the colonial system had "prolonged itself" into the present.[60] It cited the positive effects of protectionism in Europe and especially in the United States, whose prosperity and power were portrayed as the direct result of industrial development through tariff protection. The Industrial Association also emphasized the benefits of industrialization in the form of order and moral uplift: "Suppress work and you will have revolution. The spirit of the common people

58. Associação Industrial, *Relatório Apresentado à Assembléia Geral da Associação Industrial em Sessão de 10 de Junho de 1882 pela Diretoria da Mesma Associação* (Rio de Janeiro: G. Leuzinger & Filhos, 1882), p. 14. The price of British exports to Brazil diminished by more than twenty percent between 1870 and 1880. Raymond W. Goldsmith, *Brasil, 1850–1984: Desenvolvimento Financeiro sob um Século de Inflação* (São Paulo: Harper & Row do Brasil, 1986), p. 31.

59. Associação Industrial, *Representação Dirigida ao Exm. Sr. Ministro da Fazenda pela Associação Industrial, Relativamente ao Projeto da Tarifa das Alfândegas, e de Conformidade com os Relatórios dos Representantes de Diversas Indústrias* (Rio de Janeiro: Central, 1881), p. 4; and *O Trabalho Nacional*, pp. 20–21.

60. *O Trabalho Nacional*, pp. 21–22. This thesis has its best known expression in Stanley J. Stein and Barbara H. Stein, *The Colonial Heritage of Latin America: Essays on Economic Development in Perspective* (New York: Oxford University Press, 1970).

is restless; it needs, in order to be calmed, something constantly before its eyes which will seize its attention."[61] Industrialization would attract worthy immigrants, such as entered the United States, and provide for women and children an "honest means of subsistence, a healthy education in labor, and a precaution against disgrace, vice, and vagabondage in the streets."[62] In addition to its insistence on tariff protection, the Industrial Association contradicted the commercial associations by demanding lower export duty on commodities shipped in national bagging, less stringent protection of foreign patents, and the restriction of coastal shipping to Brazilian vessels.

On the surface, the Industrial Association's relations with the Commercial Association of Rio de Janeiro were excellent. The former was founded in the Commercial Association's headquarters, and the two organizations had prominent members in common. The Commercial Association of Rio de Janeiro hailed the creation of the Industrial Association and helped promote its 1881 Industrial Exposition.[63] However, the Industrial Association had no illusions about the Commercial Association's sympathies in the struggle for industrialization. It chided the latter for lauding industry while denouncing higher tariffs, and it made public the stratagems employed by the association's importer members to stifle debate on protection.[64]

Despite its initial vigor, the Industrial Association soon encountered troubles. Many of its members were not true manufacturers but proprietors of small artisan or handicraft shops, neither strongly interested in industrial development nor willing to pay high membership fees.[65] Such fees, because of the expense of disseminating the organization's uncommon point of view, were unusually steep. In addition to annual dues, which probably eventually reached Rs. 60$000, members were required to subscribe to the organization's journal at Rs. 12$000 per year.[66] By 1884, publication of *O Industrial* had ended, finances were in shambles, and membership, totaling 181 in 1882, had dwindled to 143.[67] Late that year the Industrial Association faded into inactivity.

It revived briefly in 1887, in an attempt to obtain government aid for a proposed second Industrial Exposition. Like the first, this was intended to assemble exhibits for Brazilian participation in a larger international expo-

61. Associação Industrial, *O Trabalho Nacional*, p. 167.
62. Associação Industrial, *Representação ao Ministro da Fazenda*, pp. 6, 18.
63. Commercial Association of Rio de Janeiro to Industrial Association, Rio de Janeiro, Aug. 21, 1881, *Relatório da Associação Comercial do Rio de Janeiro de 1881*, pp. 15–17.
64. Associação Industrial, *O Trabalho Nacional*, pp. 170–171, 317–334.
65. Luz, *Luta pela Industrialização*, p. 58.
66. Associação Industrial, *Relatório de 1882*, p. 40, and *Relatório de 1884*, p. 91.
67. Associação Industrial, *Relatório de 1882*, "Relação dos Sócios," pp. 1–4, and *Relatório de 1884*, pp. 8, 85–93, "Relação dos Sócios," pp. 1–3.

sition, this time in 1889 in France.[68] No government assistance was forthcoming, and the group once more disappeared. Although discouraged leaders in 1884 had described its propaganda efforts as "fruitless," this evaluation was much too pessimistic.[69] Together with similar appeals by other industrial interest groups and by individuals, the Industrial Association's endeavors contributed greatly toward changing the attitude of the literate public.[70]

Perhaps even more significant in such efforts, because it was lasting, was the Engineering Club, also founded in 1880. Although strictly speaking a professional association rather than an interest group, it recruited both engineers and manufacturers and campaigned vigorously for industrialization and for the expansion of Brazil's rail transportation system. Its membership numbered an impressive 572 by 1888, and its leadership was the more distinguished for overlapping somewhat with that of the Auxiliary Society for National Industry.[71] Following the tradition of exercising advisory prerogatives deriving from its members' role in society, the Engineering Club evaluated engineering and sanitary projects for Brazilian cities, and even helped plan such projects for Rio de Janeiro.[72] As did the commercial associations with agricultural devices, it evaluated new machines for their inventors.

The Engineering Club aimed at promoting autonomous economic development. In 1882 it organized Brazil's first Railway Congress, which discussed railway problems and evaluated progress, and in 1887 it staged the first Exposition of Brazilian Railways. In 1900 it organized a Congress of Engineering and Industry. In 1887 it began to publish a journal and in 1888 to offer medals and cash prizes for the best work by a Brazilian engineer.[73] While supporting a protective tariff and other measures toward industrialization, the Engineering Club avoided any wider attack on the Brazilian status quo. In 1885 and 1888 it emphatically rejected proposals by members that it advocate a tax on rural land.[74] But thus limiting its aims made it a more effective spokesman for industry. Its prestige as a professional association and its insistence that industrializa-

68. Associação Industrial, *Memorial Relativo a uma Exposição de Indústria Nacional em 1888 no Rio de Janeiro, Apresentada a S. Ex. o Sr. Conselheiro Rodrigo Antônio da Silva, DD. Ministro e Secretário de Estado dos Negócios da Agricultura, Comércio e Obras Públicas* (Rio de Janeiro: H. Lombaerts, 1887).
69. Associação Industrial, *Relatório de 1884,* p. 85.
70. Luz, "Tentativas de Industrialização," p. 40.
71. *Revista do Clube de Engenharia,* ano II, vol. 7 (1888): 31. As of 1892, three of the Engineering Club's six-person Directing Council (*Conselho Diretor*) were present or former Directors of the Auxiliary Society for National Industry. *O Auxiliador da Indústria Nacional,* 60, no. 7 (July 1892): 158.
72. *Revista do Clube de Engenharia,* ano II, vol. 1 (1888): 9–21, 38; ibid., ano I, vol. 3 (1887): 36; ibid., ano. II, vol. 7 (1888): 33–34.
73. Ibid., ano. II, vol. 6 (1888): 33–34.   74. Ibid., 8–22; ibid., ano II, vol. 7 (1888): 5–6.

tion was a necessary component of progress made the Engineering Club an especially strong factor in the gradual change of Brazilian opinion.

A third industrial interest group was in part an outgrowth of controversy over a Special Tariff for the Province of Rio Grande do Sul. As noted, the 1879 Special Tariff failed to halt smuggling. This led the province's three commercial associations to demand more drastic reductions, culminating in March 1889 in a new Special Tariff of lower rates and wider application. The province's manufactures, already allegedly damaged by the old Special Tariff, now faced the competition of imports made even cheaper. Opposition to the commercial associations' campaign was led by hatmakers and jerked-beef manufacturers in the town of Pelotas, the latter organized as the Agricultural Industrial Center. Both attacked commercial associations as vehicles for the malign influence of importers and castigated the Pôrto Alegre association as the instigator of the new Special Tariff.[75] The Agricultural Industrial Center accused it of "assuming the position of exclusively advocating the interests of the importer fraternity and foreign industry, which it makes a great show of defending."[76] In addition to being close to the truth, this statement was blunt. For the first time industrialists had openly condemned the role of commercial associations in industrial development.

The Agricultural Industrial Center demonstrated a strange mixture of conservative and radical attitudes. It had been created in 1887 not only to combat the Special Tariff, but to preserve a form of forced labor imposed on the eve of the abolition of slavery. Rio Grande do Sul's jerked-beef plants depended for labor on slaves and on recently freed former slaves made to continue working by binding contracts. The annulment of such contracts by provincial law in 1887 helped touch off the Agricultural Industrial Center's interest-group activity.[77] Once slavery was abolished in May 1888, it channeled its efforts into defense of industry.

The Agricultural Industrial Center demanded a protective tariff and lower taxes on Brazilian-made goods. To end smuggling it advocated severe penalties and giving law enforcement officials an unrestricted right to search mercantile firms. Like most business interest groups it urged the abolition of export taxes. Unlike most others, however, the Agricultural Industrial Center advocated an alternate source of revenue – a tax on rural land. Even more radical was its questioning of the social value of the large landed estate. Large landowners, it maintained, lived only from hereditary wealth and from the multiplication of "semi-savage cattle," contributing neither effort nor capital to industry nor to the improvement of

---

75. *ACD, 1888,* V: 223–225; ibid., IV: 153.   76. *ACD, 1888,* IV: 151.
77. Center for Agriculture and Industry to Baron Cotegipe, Pelotas, Feb. 18, 1888, ABC, IHGB, lata 77, doc. 19.

agriculture and paying no taxes.[78] Of all business interest groups, the Agricultural Industrial Center stood alone in refusing to defer to Brazil's dominant social group, the large landholders.

The Agricultural Industrial Center of Pelotas apparently became inactive after 1889. Its other reason for existence ended when the Republic abolished the Special Tariff for Rio Grande do Sul.[79] The Center had contributed significantly to industrial development by increasing public support and helping end the Special Tariff.

Gathering momentum: industry in the 1880s and 1890s

The expansion of industry during the 1880s marked a significant surge forward. It established a momentum that would continue for the next three decades.[80] At least seventeen new cotton mills were built in 1880–1884 and fourteen in 1885–1888.[81] The greatest development took place in the Southeast; by 1885 the city and Province of Rio de Janeiro had fifteen of Brazil's sixty-two cotton mills and the Province of São Paulo thirteen.[82] In the second half of the decade native industry began to compete effectively in cheaper textiles, underselling comparable imports by roughly ten percent and forcing a significant drop in the sales of imported cotton goods.[83]

Although some authorities give inflation and exchange depreciation principal credit for fostering Brazilian industrialization, they did not play a major part in early periods of advance. The *mil-reis* gradually weakened between 1876 and 1885, but the years 1870–1875 (in which fourteen textile mills were constructed) and 1886–1888 were ones of generally strengthening Brazilian exchange, making imported goods cheaper. Although periods of weakening exchange stimulated sales of local manufactures, rising exchange also aided industry by enabling cheaper importation of machinery and other production goods.[84] Thus periods of rising exchange also witnessed significant expansion.

78. *ACD, 1888*, IV: 143–148, 150.
79. The Special Tariff was reduced by stages and ended on January 1, 1891. Great Britain, Foreign Office, *Diplomatic and Consular Reports*, no. 702 (1889–90): 4.
80. Baer and Vilella, "Revisions in the Stages," 218; Simonsen, *Evolução Industrial*, p. 16.
81. Suzigan, *Indústria Brasileira*, pp. 384–389. See also Versiani, "Industrial Investment," 310.
82. Suzigan, *Indústria Brasileira*, p. 126; "Report by Consul Ricketts," *Parliamentary Papers 1886*, Vol. LXV, C 4657: 187.
83. "Report by Consul Ricketts," *Parliamentary Papers 1886*, Vol. LXV, C 4657: 188; Great Britain, Foreign Office, *Diplomatic and Consular Reports*, no. 179 (1886): 1; ibid., no. 217 (1887): 3.
84. Flávio Versiani and Maria Teresa R. O. Versiani, "A Industrialização Brasileira Antes de 1930: Uma Contribuição," in *Formação Econômica do Brasil: A Experiência da Industrialização*, eds. Flávio Versiani and José Roberto Mendonça de Barros (São Paulo: Saraiva, 1977). See also Vilella and Suzigan, *Política do Govêrno*, p. 219.

Part of the development of industry during the 1880s was a shift of merchants into manufacturing. Many coffee factors invested in industry as a response to impending abolition and other threats to their livelihood.[85] Even more conspicuous was the movement of importers.[86] Typically, of 117 directors of the Commercial Association of Rio de Janeiro during 1834 and 1844–1902, only fifteen were manufacturers, but all entered the field during the 1880s and thirteen started as importers.[87] The transition to manufacturing was relatively easy for importers: they had access to credit, knowledge of the market, and channels for distribution of the finished product. This movement toward manufacturing may have been in large part an anticipation of future changes. Although Brazil had not yet enacted a true protective tariff, growing support for industrialization indicated it might not be long in coming, and certain lines of textile importation were already hurt by the tendency to raise existing rates. Far sighted importers doubtless looked on a move to manufacturing as the logical means of meeting such a threat.

Thanks in part to the propaganda efforts of pro-industry interest groups, a subtle but perceptible change in attitude toward industrial development took place in government circles during the 1880s. While continuing to deny the necessity for a protective tariff, government officials now admitted that industrialization was a conceivable, even a desirable goal.[88] They were in effect abandoning the precept that Brazil's "natural" role was that of exporter of food and raw materials and importer of finished products. The tariff of 1887, the first overall revision since 1881, aimed at helping industry without being fully protectionist. It corrected official values of imports, established an overall ad valorum rate of forty-eight percent, and increased the levy on goods also produced in Brazil.[89] A volley of protests from commercial associations had little effect. They would find their ability to influence tariffs progressively waning.

The tendency to aid industry soon carried even further. The tariff of 1889 contained the first openly protectionist measure of any Brazilian tariff. A sliding scale of duties, which increased in percentage as the

---

85. Joseph E. Sweigart, "Financing and Marketing Brazilian Export Agriculture: The Coffee Factors of Rio de Janeiro, 1850–1888" (Ph.D. Diss., University of Texas, 1980), p. 206.
86. Stein, *Cotton Manufacture*, pp. 71–72; Warren Dean, *The Industrialization of São Paulo, 1880–1945* (Austin and London: University of Texas Press, 1969), pp. 19–33. Souza Martins, "Café e a Gênese," denies the central role of the importer in industrialization.
87. Eugene W. Ridings, "The Foreign Connection: A Look at the Business Elite of Rio de Janeiro in the Nineteenth Century," *New Scholar*, 7: 1/2 (1979): 176–177.
88. For example, Brazil, Comissão de Inquérito Industrial, *Relatório ao Ministro da Fazenda*, I: passim; "Relatório Apresentado ao Corpo Legislativo pela Comissão Parlamentar de Inquérito," in *O Auxiliador da Indústria Nacional*, 53, no. 10 (1885): 224–227.
89. *RMF, 1887*, pp. 23–29; Deveza, "Política Tributária," p. 82.

exchange rate rose, was placed on sixty-three items competing with those made in Brazil of native materials. The sliding scale aimed to compensate for the effect of rising exchange in making importation more profitable. "The persons interested in the manufacturing industry of Brazil are already beginning to assert their influence in shaping the legislation of the country," noted the United States Consul-General.[90] As usual, the Commercial Association of Rio de Janeiro reacted strongly. In August 1889, it called an extraordinary general assembly, recorded importers' complaints, and sent a lengthy petition of protest.[91] But with the coming of the Republic in November the association decided not to remonstrate further. It was unpopular with the new government because of its close ties with the monarchy, and it found protectionist sympathies surprisingly strong within its own ranks.[92]

The industrialization momentum of the 1880s accelerated with the Republic. It brought administrations more sympathetic to industry and favorable economic conditions. Textile plants, sixty-two in 1885, numbered 134 by 1895, while total factories increased from 636 in 1889 to 1,088 in 1895.[93] Much of the expansion was due to the policies of the new government. As a reaction to previous lack of liquidity, as well as to stimulate enterprise, it vastly increased the money supply, giving rise to the *encilhamento*. Industry was aided by easier credit and by a rapidly falling exchange rate that turned imported goods much more expensive. Exchange depreciation continued to plague importers through the decade. Although the *encilhamento* is often pictured as a time of frenzied and unsound economic activity that left little concrete result, far more lasting cotton mills were founded in 1890–1895 than during any previous period of similar length.[94] The propitiousness of conditions was shown by a resurgence of textile production in the State of Bahia and by its blossoming in Pernambuco, Alagôas, and Maranhão, areas virtually bereft of it previously.[95] The momentum given industrial development continued.

90. Consul-General Armstrong to Department of State, Rio de Janeiro, June 1, 1889, *USRC*, XXX, no. 105 (May 1889): 222.
91. Commercial Association of Rio de Janeiro to Viscount Ouro Preto, Rio de Janeiro, Aug. 31, 1889, *Relatório de 1890*, pp. 36–42.
92. Minutes, meeting of Dec. 6, 1889, Livro de Atas, 1881–1890, AACRJ, p. 226.
93. "Cotton Spinning and Weaving Industries in Brazil," *USRC*, LXIII, no. 236 (May 1900): 129; Werner Baer, *Industrialization and Economic Development in Brazil* (Homewood, Ill.: Irwin, 1965), p. 13.
94. On the number of textile plants built, see Fishlow, "Origins and Consequences," 315; Versiani, "Industrial Investment," 310. For the general solidity of enterprises founded then, see Maria Bárbara Levy, "O Encilhamento," in *Economia Brasileira: Uma Visão Histórica*, ed. Paulo Neuhaus (Rio de Janeiro: Campus, 1980), p. 226.
95. Great Britain, Foreign Office, *Diplomatic and Consular Reports*, no. 1290 (1892): 4–5; ibid., no. 1547 (1895): 8–9; ibid., no. 1486 (1892): 4–6.

The value of domestic cotton textile production, less than one-fifth that of importation in 1885, was twice the sum of the latter by 1907.[96]

Among the policies of the new Republic aimed at furthering industrialization was Brazil's first law for direct assistance to industry. The inflation and exchange depreciation unleashed by the *encilhamento*, although making imports expensive, were a mixed blessing for manufacturing. Many enterprises had ordered machinery from abroad in a period of strong exchange and by 1892 faced paying for it with weakened currency when credit, furthermore, was very scarce. To study the problem Minister of Finance Francisco de Paula Rodrigues Alves nominated a four-man committee including Honório Ribeiro, interim President of the Commercial Association of Rio de Janeiro, and Viscount Guaí, former President of the Bahian association. He accepted its recommendation that industry be aided with a special issue of low-interest government bonds.[97]

Aid to Industry (*Auxílios à Indústria*), as the project was named, was immediately controversial. Its very purpose antagonized import commerce. Despite the unpopularity of Aid to Industry among merchants, only the Commercial Association of Rio Grande voiced opposition. Many associations did not protest because the measure was vital to the survival of manufacturer members. In the case of the Rio group, moreover, its interim President was one of the authors of the project, and other members were connected with the government-sponsored Bank of the Republic of Brazil (*Banco da República do Brasil*), which had greatly extended itself in loans to manufacturers.[98] Protest had to be made outside the association's regular channels. Four hundred and twenty-eight Rio "industrialists and businessmen" signed an independent petition of protest to Brazil's Congress. Supporters of Aid to Industry alleged that many of the "industrialists" represented in reality merchant houses, and that only sixty-nine of the signers were Brazilians.[99] This petition and that from the Rio Grande association warned that the measure would further devalue the currency, that the bonds would drain federal revenue because they could be sold at discount while government honored them at face value, and, above all, that such aid was not a proper function of government.[100]

The protest was more than counteracted by partisans of industry. The Engineering Club backed the measure with a petition to Congress also broadcast in Rio de Janeiro newspapers, while a committee of industrialists pub-

96. Versiani, "Industrial Investment," 309. Imports of industrial machinery, however, fell to pre-*encilhamento* levels between 1897 and 1904. Suzigan, *Indústria Brasileira*, pp. 358–360.
97. *RMF, 1892*, pp. 54–56.   98. Luz, *Luta pela Industrialização*, pp. 113–114.
99. *ACD, 1892*, III: 152–153, 217; Steven Topik, *The Political Economy of the Brazilian State, 1889–1930* (Austin: University of Texas Press, 1987), p. 136.
100. Topik, *Political Economy*, p. 136; *ACD, 1892*, III: 2, 153.

lished in booklet form another such petition.[101] The latter repeated now-familiar appeals to nationalist fears and aspirations. It compared foreign merchants, aloof and parasitic, to Shakespeare's Shylock and stated that "the example of North America is demonstrating it: the solution to all economic and social problems for new nations is found in the encouragement of national [industry]."[102] Also helped by the interests of the Bank of the Republic of Brazil, Aid to Industry became law. It was more than a friendly gesture to manufacturers. Although about one quarter of the funds issued as bonds eventually went to agriculture and a lesser amount to other non-industrial pursuits, the measure's cost equaled about twelve percent of the 1893 budget and ten percent of the 1894 budget.[103] Aid to Industry represented a major and radical departure in Brazilian government spending.

Import duties in gold and the commercial associations

Despite increased money supply and Aid to Industry, the most important long-term help for industry came in the form of increasingly effective tariffs. The initial major advance in protection came under first Republican Minister of Finance Rui Barbosa. He decreed in May 1890 that twenty percent of import duty be paid in gold, then in October that all such duty be paid in gold.[104] Requiring a proportion of import duties in gold had been tried during the war with Paraguay and suggested during the 1880s as a means of stabilizing the exchange rate, slowing the flow of gold abroad, and compensating for the loss of revenue from payment of import duty in depreciated Brazilian currency.[105] Rui claimed that the latter loss amounted to fifty percent.[106] Manufacturers immediately realized the import of the measure. A new but short-lived Industrial Center (*Centro Industrial*) of Brazil supported it with a published petition, signed by several former leaders of the Industrial Association, including its first President, Antônio Felício dos Santos.[107] One historian has termed the requirements that import duty be paid in gold Brazil's "first effective mechanism for the protection of industrial development."[108]

The stipulations that import duties be paid in gold were a body blow to importation. They not only raised greatly the true value of duties paid, but confronted importers with the task of obtaining enough gold to clear

101. *Jornal do Brasil*, July 10, 1892, p. 2.
102. *Auxílios à Indústria: Representação dos Industriaes ao Congresso Nacional* (Rio de Janeiro: Luís Macedo, 1892), pp. 5–6.
103. Topik, *Political Economy*, p. 137.   104. *RMF, 1891*, pp. 301–304.
105. *RMF, 1883*, pp. 67–68; *O Auxiliador da Indústria Nacional*, 53, no. 10 (Oct. 1885): 233–234.
106. *RMF, 1891*, p. 329.
107. *Representação ao Sr. Ministro da Fazenda* (Rio de Janeiro: C. Gaspar da Silva, 1890). None of the signers led the group of the same name founded in 1904.
108. Lorenzo-Fernandes, *Evolução da Economia*, p. 121.

goods from customs. They aroused the strongest collective reaction ever from the commercial associations to a tax measure. It increased in fervor as the difficulty and expense in obtaining gold became apparent. Protest against the initial decree of May 1890, requiring twenty percent payment in gold, was led by the Commercial Association of Pernambuco, which telegraphed the nation's other major commercial associations for support. Support was forthcoming but tardy, most conspicuously in the case of the Rio association.[109] This enabled Rui Barbosa to declare that, among other reasons for his refusal to repeal the decree, "the commercial association here [Rio de Janeiro] does not agree with this agitation."[110]

The Commercial Association of Rio de Janeiro had temporarily abandoned leadership in defending overseas trade. By the advent of the Republic manufacturing and protectionist interests in its ranks were showing surprising strength. This, coupled with a desire to recover influence with the Republican government, brought about the election in 1891 of Francisco de Paula Mayrink as its President. Mayrink had been named by Rui Barbosa to head the government-sponsored Bank of the United States of Brazil (*Banco dos Estados Unidos do Brasil*). He numbered several manufactures among his far-flung interests, had helped found the Engineering Club, and was a former member of the Industrial Association. A man who in a speech before the Chamber of Deputies termed Brazil's heavy reliance on imports "this shame" and "this disgrace," he was reputed to be the author of the decrees requiring payment of import duties in gold.[111] Mayrink was too busy to assume active command of the Rio association during his two-year term of office and was substituted by an "interim president." However, his influence and that of his supporters among membership meant that the Rio association would not lead the attack on payment of import duties in gold.

The October 1890 decree requiring all import duty to be paid in gold magnified importers' costs and their difficulty in obtaining gold. In March 1891, the Commercial Association of Bahia convoked an open meeting of all merchants, formulated protests, and appealed to the nation's other commercial associations for support. Incongruously donning the mantle of friend of the poor in a petition to the President of the Republic, it declared itself to speak "in defense of the rights of all the proletariat," suffering from the high prices caused by payment of import duties in gold.[112] The Bahian association found the government unmoved by its posturing, but received encouragement from the nation's other commercial associations. It decided to organize,

109. Associação Comercial de Pernambuco, *Relatório de 1890*, pp. 14, 49, 53.
110. Rui Barbosa to Commercial Association of Pernambuco, Rio de Janeiro, no date, 1890, ibid., p. 50.
111. *ACD, 1893*, III: 525.
112. Commercial Association of Bahia to President of Republic and Governor, State of Bahia, Salvador, March 31, 1891, *Relatório de 1892*, pp. 50–51.

for the first time on a nationwide scale, a commercial strike. Its membership pledged to dispatch nothing from the customs house after May 15, unless the government repealed the October decree, and called on the nation's other commercial associations to do the same.[113]

The projected nationwide strike misfired badly, being effective only in Bahia. The Commercial Association of Maranhão, which actually had been first to suggest the action, struck but was unable or unwilling to force unanimous compliance by its importers.[114] The Commercial Association of Pernambuco retreated in face of possible mob violence by an "impassioned" populace.[115] The Commercial Association of Santos excused itself on the grounds that lack of customs house storage facilities kept its merchants from refusing to dispatch.[116] Other associations offered polite encouragement but promised only to continue written protests.

Nevertheless, the mere threat of a commercial strike, or perhaps the volume of protest, was effective. A new Minister of Finance first ordered the Bank of the United States of Brazil and the nation's customs houses to sell gold currency to merchants at a fixed price and then modified the law to permit payment of duties in paper currency, at a fixed rate of exchange.[117] Since importers no longer had to bid against one another for gold, driving its price upward, the worst effect of Rui Barbosa's decrees had been mitigated. Noting that most other commercial associations seemed satisfied with the government's action, the Bahian group called off its commercial strike. The United States Consul in Salvador stated in June that had the gold require- ment not been modified, "by this time the then black clouds of discontent would have grown blacker and huger and without doubt would have burst, scattering confusion, anarchy, and perhaps open revolt throughout the land."[118] The government had been forced to back down.

The commercial associations' fears revived briefly two months later when a new Minister of Finance revived enforcement of the October 1890 decree. A storm of protest again led by the Commercial Association of Bahia, together with fear of renewed increase in the cost of living, forced the suspension and eventual abolition of the decree.[119] But the commercial associations had won a costly victory: payment in gold was replaced by import surtaxes of fifty and sixty percent. Import tariffs had increased in fiscal importance, since the

113. Ibid., pp. 58–72.
114. Associação Comercial do Maranhão, *Relatório de 1891*, p. 4.
115. Minutes, meeting of May 12, 1891, Livro 7 de Atas, AACP, p. 53.
116. Commercial Association of Santos to Commercial Association of Bahia, Santos, May 12, 1891, *Relatório da Associação Comercial de Santos de 1891*, p. 123.
117. Great Britain, Foreign Office, *Diplomatic and Consular Reports*, no. 952 (1890–91): 11–12; Burke to Department of State, Salvador, June 8, 1891, NA/DS T-331, reel 6, unpaginated.
118. Ibid.
119. Great Britain, Foreign Office, *Diplomatic and Consular Reports*, no. 1321 (1890–91): 30; Asso- ciação Comercial da Bahia, *Relatório de 1892*, pp. 43–150, 171.

national government no longer taxed exports, and continued exchange depreciation reduced the true value of import duties paid. Tariff levels rose inexorably, continually subject to surtaxes and piecemeal increases. By 1894 their level was double that of 1890.[120] Meanwhile, support for requiring payment of import duties in gold was by no means dead. The idea continued to be advocated by men such as Mayrink, now a Federal Deputy, and new bills for that purpose were discussed in 1893, 1895, and 1896. Freed of the leadership of Mayrink after mid-1893, the Commercial Association of Rio de Janeiro now took the lead in combating revival of the measure, seconded by the Bahia and São Paulo groups.[121] They were able to prevent the return of payment of duties in gold, but no amount of protest could halt the tendency of rates to climb. Revenue needs could not be petitioned away.

These needs, together with continuing public support for industrialization, culminated in an even more protectionist tariff, that of 1896. In addition to raising rates some twenty to thirty percent, it stipulated an exchange rate that elevated duties a further twenty-five percent.[122] The reaction of committees of leading Rio and Santos importers mobilized by their commercial associations, plus renewed inflation, reversed the long tendency toward higher rates.[123] The tariff of 1897, drawn up by a committee advised by the Commercial Association of Rio de Janeiro and headed by its future President, José Leopoldo de Bulhões Jardim, reduced levels some twenty-five percent.[124]

It was the last victory of free trade sentiment. In 1898 was added a new and particularly pressing need for revenue. Newly elected President Manuel Ferraz de Campos Sales and his Minister of Finance Joaquim Murtinho contracted a ten-million pound "Funding Loan" from the banking house of Rothschild. It required not only the gradual retirement from circulation of paper *mil-reis* to an amount equal to the loan, but the mortgage of the revenue of the Rio customs house (and later other customs houses) as guarantee of repayment. It was designed to consolidate Brazil's foreign debt and to enable Campos Sales and Murtinho to curb inflation and exchange deprecia-

---

120. *RMF, 1894*, p. 58.
121. For example, Commercial Association of Rio de Janeiro to Brazilian Congress, Rio de Janeiro, Sept. 1, 1893, *Relatório de 1901*, Anexos, 1893, pp. 13–15; Minutes, meeting of Dec. 28, 1895, Livro de Atas, 1890–1896, AACRJ, p. 102; Commercial Association of Bahia to Commercial Association of Rio de Janeiro, Salvador, Nov. 14, 1896, *Relatório da Associação Comercial da Bahia de 1897*, p. 216; Minutes, meeting of July 21, 1896, Livro de Atas, 1894–1906, Arquivo da Associação Comercial de São Paulo (hereafter cited as AACSP), São Paulo, p. 4.
122. Luz, *Luta pela Industrialização*, p. 120; *RMF, 1896*, p. 44.
123. *RMF, 1896*, pp. 34–44; João Manuel Cardoso de Mello and Maria da Conceição Tavares, "The Capitalist Export Economy in Brazil, 1884–1930," in *The Latin American Economies: Growth and the Export Sector, 1880–1930*, eds. Roberto Cortés Conde and Shane J. Hunt (New York: Holmes & Meier, 1985), p. 99.
124. *RMF, 1897*, p. 38; Associação Comercial do Rio de Janeiro, *Relatório de 1906*, pp. 45–46.

tion, thus stabilizing Brazilian currency. The commercial associations now realized they had the unhappy choice of continued exchange depreciation and consequent increases in tariff rates, both raising the cost of importation, or the extra cost of partial payment of duties in gold, which would at least help arrest exchange depreciation. Exchange stabilization and an end to inflation were fervently desired by the commercial associations by the end of the chaotic 1890s. One reason was that they were also demanded by foreign holders of Brazilian debt and by foreign investors. A former British director of the Rio group, Edward Tootal, had originally drawn up the Funding Loan proposal and acted as emissary for the Rothschilds.[125] The commercial associations did not oppose the final, permanent, imposition of payment of a percentage of import duties in gold.

The Campos Sales government increased the required proportion of duty in gold to twenty-five percent in the tariff of 1900. This document underlined the declining influence of the commercial associations; for the first time the government neglected to consult them in tariff formulation.[126] The tariff of 1900 also raised rates to between fifty and eighty percent ad valorum. The combination of gold quota and higher rates was very effective. Ironically, Campos Sales and Murtinho, neither partisans of industry, had given Brazil its first strongly protective tariff.[127] The Commercial Association of Rio de Janeiro found itself in the contradiction of applauding Campos Sales's aim of strengthening the currency while condemning the tariff that helped bring it about. Neither its anguished protests against the rate increases nor those of some seven hundred businessmen mobilized by the Commercial Center could sway the government.[128] The tariff of 1900 remained in effect, with minor revisions, for three decades.[129]

During the 1890s, industrialization took its most emphatic leap forward. It would be a mistake, however, to characterize the advance of that decade, as does economist Albert Fishlow, "as a direct consequence of inflationary finances, and not influenced by tariff protection."[130] Although customs duties fell as a proportion of import price because of exchange depreciation and inflation, when added to general increases in the cost of imported goods they were especially painful. By 1899, thanks to exchange depreciation and inflation, the price level of imports was 335 percent above what it had been in 1889, while the general price level had increased only 229 percent.[131] Wages

---

125. Carlos Manuel Peláez, "As Conseqüências Econômicas de Ortodoxia Monetária, Fiscal e Cambial no Brasil de 1889 a 1945," *Revista Brasileira de Economia*, 25 (July-Sept. 1971): 34; Francisco de Assis Barbosa, "A Presidência Campos Sales," *Luso-Brazilian Review*, 5 (Summer 1968): 5.

126. *ACD, 1899*, V: 421.

127. Villela and Suzigan, *Política do Govêrno*, p. 331; Stein, *Cotton Manufacture*, p. 85.

128. *ACD, 1899*, V: 420–421; ibid., VI: 213–215; *Jornal do Comércio* (Rio de Janeiro), May 7, 1899, p. 1.

129. Stein, *Cotton Manufacture*, p. 85.   130. "Origins and Consequences," 311.

131. Goldsmith, *Desenvolvimento Financeiro*, p. 91.

lagged far behind such prices, particularly in the earlier years of the decade, and the volume of imports decreased.[132] The protective effect of tariffs during the 1890s was as much as, if not greater than, those taking a higher proportion of import price in conditions of monetary stability. Had tariffs been inconsequential, as Fishlow suggests, importers would not have fought against them with such desperation in the 1890s.

The imposition of the dreaded protective system did not bring the ruin to importation so long predicted. Despite their often-frenzied protests, importers had already learned that they could coexist with higher tariffs. If the competition of Brazilian industry lowered demand for certain consumer goods, it also greatly increased the need for machinery and other plant equipment, raw materials, and fuel. Such needs enabled the British consul in Santos to report in 1889 that "the trade between Great Britain and this province [São Paulo] continues to develop considerably. . . . [T]he importations from Great Britain steadily grow in bulk, variety, and value."[133] By the early twentieth century, steel and iron, and machinery and engines had replaced beverages and wool products as second and third, respectively, in value among Brazilian imports.[134] Although forced to change its nature, the import economy continued to thrive.

How important was the tariff to Brazilian industrial development? Because of a lack of essential statistics, the question is difficult to answer. Exchange depreciation and inflation aided industrialization by making imported goods more expensive but, as noted, significant progress also was made during periods of stable or strengthening exchange. Some indication of the utility of even modest protection comes from Rio Grande do Sul, an area bereft of it, because of the Special Tariff, from 1879 until the advent of the Republic. Removal of the Special Tariff brought forth a plethora of small consumer industries, cutting deeply into the state's import trade. Noting them, a British consul remarked that "the protective import duties have enabled all the above companies to start business and to compete successfully with goods manufactured abroad," and added that a reduction of the tariff would close them.[135] Finally, the rarely interrupted tendency of tariffs to rise encouraged apprehensive importers to diversify into manufacturing. Although not fully

132. Compared to 1889, urban wages in Rio de Janeiro lagged more than twenty percent behind prices in 1899 and nearly thirty-five percent in 1894. Between 1889 and 1901 import volume decreased fourteen percent. Ibid., pp. 92, 112.
133. Great Britain, Foreign Office, *Diplomatic and Consular Reports*, no. 498 (1889): 4.
134. Centro Industrial do Brasil, *Brazil: Its Natural Riches and Industries (Foreign Edition). Volume I: Preface, Productive Industry* (Paris: Aillaud, 1910), p. 170.
135. Great Britain, Foreign Office, *Diplomatic and Consular Reports*, no. 1263 (1892): 3. See also *Diplomatic and Consular Reports*, no. 1077 (1891): 5. A notable local exception would be the Rheingantz textile factory, which flourished even under the Special Tariff. However, Rheingantz enjoyed the advantages of an enlightened management, almost no Brazilian competition in woolen textiles, and an exclusive contract to supply all woolen goods for the Brazilian army. *Diplomatic and Consular Reports*, no. 32 (1885): 6.

protective until 1900, tariffs had a significant impact. It seems reasonable to assume that Brazil's industrial development during the nineteenth century would have been less significant under a regimen of free trade.

Business interest groups and industrialization: summing it up

Business interest groups were major role players in the struggle for Brazilian industrialization, a key component of economic development. Commercial associations had some success in impeding manufacturing outside the area of tariffs, but the issue of tariff protection was far more important. The influence of commercial associations (and secondarily factor groups) probably kept tariff levels lower than they otherwise would have been until the late 1880s. Until that time, thus, they probably retarded the march of industrialization. The commercial associations had formidable weapons with which to influence tariffs. These included traditional prerogatives in helping formulate tariffs, the role of importers in the classifying and evaluating goods, the right to review tariffs, the ability to affect legislation through petitioning and lobbying, and dissemination of doctrines of economic liberalism. But the effectiveness of these weapons decreased from the 1880s on.

Commercial association power was weakened partly by rising support for industrial development. Such support fed on itself. As tariff levels rose, industry expanded, leading to new claims for protection and other policies aiding industrialization. Industrial interest groups had success in selling to the literate public their vision of an industrialized Brazil. They were aided by the contemporary example of nations like the United States, whose power and wealth were portrayed as the result of protectionism. Problems of the export economy promoted desires for an economic autonomy that could only be gained through industrialization. They brought not only disillusionment with exportation as a sole economic base, but conflict between planters, factors, and exporters. Planters, factors, and factor-dominated business interest groups, the Commercial Association of Pará and the Commercial Center of Rio de Janeiro, fostered resentment against foreign economic domination. Nationalist fears and ambitions found expression in tariffs and legislation such as Aid to Industry. Public support for domestic manufactures solidified. This was indicated by an 1899 law, heatedly protested by the Commercial Association and the Commercial Center of Rio de Janeiro, prohibiting imported goods from having labels in Portuguese to make them appear Brazilian-made.[136]

But despite growing public backing for industrial development, the main thing overwhelming the commercial associations and factor groups in the

136. *ACD*, *1899*, VI: 214, and *ACD 1900*, II: 51, 124–125.

struggle over tariffs was the central government's ever-growing need for revenue. The tariff of 1900, for example, was the work of government leaders, Campos Sales and Murtinho, largely in sympathy with their aims.[137] And, once more, commercial associations and factor groups contributed to their own dilemma. Much of the increasing need of government for revenue came from the very infrastructure improvements they had demanded. The commercial associations also again helped preserve their own quandary by firmly opposing direct taxation, the only alternative to tariff increases.

The commercial associations had been a central force in resistance to industrialization. Despite appeals by all to the unity of the business classes and statements by some alleging support for manufacturing, it became evident to manufacturers and others favoring industry that they were an obstacle. As such, they would have to be bypassed or changed radically in leadership. Around the turn of the century small industrial interest groups began to be formed, usually representing a specific product. In 1904, Rio de Janeiro industrialists created the Industrial Center of Brazil, which until 1931 claimed to represent industry nationwide. In the city of São Paulo, the nation's other main center of manufacturing, the Commercial Association could not prevent its manufacturer members from leaving in 1928 to form the Industrial Center for the State of São Paulo, headed by the noted industrialists Roberto Simonsen and Francisco Matarazzo.[138] Eventually the commercial associations themselves changed. During the 1950s, industrialists and others less tied to the traditional economy and foreign commercial interests progressively took over their boards of directors.[139] The change in leadership effectively symbolized the end of the export-import economy the associations had so long represented.

Overseas merchants and industrialization

The policies of commercial associations and, to a lesser extent, factor groups in Brazilian industrialization are not only significant in themselves but clarify the role played by overseas merchants. In doing so they help to clear up some misconceptions by leading students of that industrialization. For example, it is obviously wrong to declare, as does Steven Topik, that merchants "as a group did not oppose protection, because many of them were also involved in production."[140] Warren Dean also errs in asserting that "the importing business was not an obstacle to the development of industry."[141] The state-

137. For Murtinho's views, see *RMF, 1899*, pp. xii-xiii.
138. Philippe C. Schmitter, *Interest Conflict and Political Change in Brazil* (Stanford, Calif.: Stanford University Press, 1971), pp. 147–148; Maurício A. Font, *Coffee, Contention, and Change in the Making of Modern Brazil* (Oxford: Basil Blackwell, 1990), pp. 110–111.
139. Schmitter, *Interest Conflict*, p. 195.
140. *Political Economy*, p. 139.   141. *Industrialization of São Paulo*, p. 20.

ment is correct in the sense that importers furnished most of the leadership for budding manufactures, but hardly true of importers as a political force. As seen, they were the core of resistance to tariff protection and other measures aiding industry. Finally, it is wrong to point to lack of a powerful merchant class as a factor retarding industrialization in Brazil, as does Hélio Jaguaribe.[142] To the contrary, if our reading of the evidence is correct, it was the presence and political influence of such a class that helped delay industrialization.

The influence and actions of commercial associations also illuminate the specific role of foreign merchants. They confirm the observation of Sir Arthur Lewis that control of overseas trade by foreign merchants can be an important obstacle to industrialization.[143] They refute the contention of Nathaniel Leff that the use of political power by foreign traders was not a relevant factor slowing Brazilian industrialization.[144] Finally, the varied ways available to the commercial associations to influence tariffs show it wrong to affirm, as does D. C. M. Platt, that the views of foreign importers on such matters "carried little weight."[145] As in other fields of economic endeavor, commercial associations gave foreigners a powerful means to affect Brazilian industrial development.

The aggressive and ultimately effective advocacy of manufacturing by industrial groups demonstrates that, at least in Brazil, Latin American manufacturers and their ideologues were by no means, in the words of Joseph Love, "apologetic, timid, and accommodationist."[146] At the same time, the statements of commercial associations and factor groups show that neither is it entirely correct to deny any Brazilian ideological dependency on the precepts of laissez-faire and free trade.[147] The reliance on such precepts existed, but was curiously twisted. They were repeatedly invoked by those groups as a weapon against government support for industrial development. It is true that the Brazilian government frequently violated laissez-faire, but it often did so at the urging of commercial associations and factor groups in order to strengthen the traditional export-import economy, whose supremacy the groups justified by the concept of free trade. Frequently asking government aid for the traditional economy also made it philosophically inconsistent to oppose government intervention on behalf of industry.

The struggle over industrialization, a cornerstone of economic development, by business interest groups was long and turbulent. The resistance of

142. *Economic and Political Development*, p. 136.
143. *The Evolution of the International Economic Order* (Princeton, N.J.: Princeton University Press, 1978), p. 22.
144. *Reassessing the Obstacles*, p. 88.   145. *Latin America and British Trade*, p. 81.
146. "Structural Change and Conceptual Response in Latin America and Romania, 1860–1950," in *Guiding the Invisible Hand: Economic Liberalism and the State in Latin American History*, eds. Joseph L. Love and Nils Jacobsen (New York: Praeger, 1988), p. 23.
147. As in Leff, *Reassessing the Obstacles*, p. 82.

commercial associations and factor groups to aid for manufacturing slowed its progress but was ultimately unsuccessful. A shift in Brazilian public opinion toward industrial development, promoted by business interest groups representing industry, aided their defeat. The most important factor, however, was that which overcame them in other struggles over taxation: the ever-increasing need of government for revenue. The year 1900 marked an important milestone, Brazil's first true protective tariff. From then on there would be pauses, but no turning back, on the road to industrialization.

9

Communications: regionalism perpetuated

The nineteenth century was an age of basic innovations in communications, including the railroad, the steamboat, the telegraph, and improved harbor construction. Business interest groups helped to introduce them, to determine their infrastructure, and to regulate them. In some cases they acted on their own or encouraged private endeavor, but more often they used prerogatives to influence the scope and form of government aid. Business interest group prerogatives in communications stemmed from a long historical tradition; they were reinforced by weaknesses of the Brazilian state and by the special expertise and the acknowledged self-interest of group membership. The new means of communications and their infrastructure, which the groups helped shape, would greatly affect the patterns and extent of future Brazilian economic development.

The support of the state was fundamental in the introduction of new communications to Brazil. It aided communications companies with guaranteed interest, subsidies, and tax exemptions and even built or managed communications facilities itself. Contrary to what is often supposed, the support of the Empire for development was ready and generous, particularly in light of the contemporary concept of the limited role of the state. In the period 1867–1877, for example, developmental expenditures, mainly for communications, were several times those of Mexico during the same period and even higher as a proportion of national budget than those of Mexico during the first two decades of the twentieth century.[1] The Republic did not significantly increase this support for development.[2] The developmental expenditures of the Empire, however, were aimed overwhelmingly at the expansion of Brazil's traditional export-import economy.

The prerogatives of business interest groups in shaping and regulating communications were for the most part customary, rather than written in

1. Luís Aureliano Gama de Andrade, "Dez Anos de Orçamento Imperial: 1867–1877," *Revista Brasileira de Estudos Políticos*, 31 (May 1971): 197–199.
2. Richard Graham, "Government Expenditures and Political Change in Brazil, 1880–1899: Who Got What," *Journal of Interamerican Studies and World Affairs*, 19 (Aug. 1977): 347.

law. Their tradition stretched back to medieval Portuguese and Spanish functional interest groups. The Spanish-American consulados of the eighteenth century partially were created to stimulate and guide the development of communications. In Brazil prior to the rise of commercial associations, this task had been entrusted to government-sponsored groups with merchant members. Finally, the contemporary example of the chambers of commerce of the United States and Great Britain in introducing and regulating communications reinforced these prerogatives.[3]

Traditional business interest group activity in communications was necessitated by weaknesses of the state. Academically trained economists, engineers, and technicians were uncommon in the nineteenth century even in the most educationally advanced nations. In Brazil, dependence upon business interest groups was heightened by a rarity of scientific or technical training. As of 1864, for example, not more than 150 students were enrolled in Brazil's few technical and commercial schools.[4] This weakness was compounded by an inert and inefficient bureaucracy usually chosen by patronage rather than by ability. Business interest groups could compensate somewhat for these deficiencies. The Engineering Club of Rio de Janeiro enrolled a large proportion of the nation's trained engineers. Virtually all the leaders of commercial associations and factor groups directed large export-import or factorage firms, whose effective functioning depended much upon knowledge of communications. These businessmen also maintained close contact with Europe and North America, the sources of innovations in communications in the nineteenth century. Government recognized the vital interests of business interest groups in communications, especially those of the commercial associations, each of which represented an entrepôt and its economic region.

Commercial associations, and to a lesser extent factor groups, customarily worked to preserve or expand the trade area of their entrepôt. This area was defined as the region from which exports were sent to the entrepôt for shipment abroad and into which it distributed imports. Occasionally a trade area was used as a unit of geographic measurement. The Agricultural Congress of Recife in 1878 invited all planters "whose export goods are sold in large part on the *praça* of Recife," an invitation encompassing a six-province area.[5] The concern of commercial associations with their ports' trading area was by no means abstract: the profits of

3. For activities of chambers of commerce in communications, see Kenneth Sturges, *American Chambers of Commerce* (New York: Moffat Bard and Co., 1915); and Alfred Roman Ilersic, *Parliament of Commerce: The Story of the Association of British Chambers of Commerce, 1820–1960* (London: Association of British Chambers of Commerce, 1960).

4. Robert J. Havighurst and J. Roberto Moreira, *Society and Education in Brazil* (Pittsburgh: University of Pittsburgh Press, 1965), p. 75.

5. Sociedade Auxiliadora da Agricultura de Pernambuco, *Trabalhos do Congresso Agrícola do Recife em Outubro de 1878* (Recife: Manuel Figueiroa de Faria & Filhos, 1879), p. 31.

their members' firms depended somewhat on its size. A major entrepôt with a large trade area also was an asset to the government of its province. Such a province was able to exploit commercially subordinate provinces by taxing their goods in transit across its borders.

Not surprisingly, the interest of commercial associations and factor groups in communications was fueled by competition with other entrepôts. Preserving or enlarging a port's trading area required keeping its costs lower than those of rivals. Although recognizing differentials in provincial taxes and the efficiency of individual firms as important, most merchants saw superior communications, including port facilities, as the dominant factor in lowering costs. Business interest groups not only tried to obtain improved communications for their entrepôt but to deny them to rivals.

Trade areas changed greatly during the course of the nineteenth century. At the beginning of the nineteenth century Brazil's major entrepôts were Rio de Janeiro, Salvador, Recife, and São Luís.[6] Rio's trade area was vast. It included the provinces of São Paulo, Paraná, Santa Caterina, Rio Grande do Sul, Mato Grosso (via the La Plata river system), Minas Gerais, and the southwestern interior and southern panhandle of Bahia.[7] Rio's economic grip on much of this area weakened or ended during the century. Guided by aggressive commercial associations, rival entrepôts such as Santos and Pôrto Alegre arose as their hinterlands prospered. Rio's hold on the trade of Rio Grande do Sul and Mato Grosso was damaged after 1878 by special lower tariffs to reduce smuggling in those provinces. The introduction of coastal steamer service in the 1850s took the trade of the panhandle of Bahia from Rio and sent it north to Salvador. Previously, produce from the area was shipped to Rio for export because of prevailing northerly winds.[8]

In the early decades of the century, Salvador controlled most of the trade of its own province and contended with Recife for that of Sergipe and Alagôas. Recife also disputed or controlled the commerce of Paraíba, Rio Grande do Norte, and Ceará, as well as that of Pernambuco. São Luís dominated the trade of Maranhão, and Pará, Amazonas, and Piauí, and contended for that of Ceará. These trade areas changed radically during the century. By the 1860s, Belém had established itself as an entrepôt and taken from São Luís the trade of both Pará and Amazonas. By the early 1870s São Luís had lost to Recife the commerce of Ceará and was losing that of Piauí. The Commercial Association of Maranhão blamed much of

6. Paul Singer, *Desenvolvimento Econômico e Evolução Urbana (Análise da Evolução Econômica de São Paulo, Blumenau, Pôrto Alegre, Belo Horizonte e Recife)* (2d ed.; São Paulo: Editôra Nacional, 1977), p. 282.
7. Eugene W. Ridings, "The Bahian Commercial Association, 1840–1889: A Pressure Group in an Underdeveloped Area" (Ph.D. Diss., University of Florida, 1970), p. 175; *RMF, 1882*, p. 5.
8. Morgan to Foreign Office, Salvador, March 18, 1856, PRO/FO 13/344, fl. 142–143.

the shrinkage on the imperial government for refusing to support communications improvements for the province, accusing it in 1873 of giving São Luís commerce "bastardly" treatment.[9] The trade hegemony of Recife also faded. The need of Pernambuco to increase taxes by the mid-1870s and the desire of its smaller neighbor provinces for commercial independence progressively weakened Recife's economic grip. Fierce contention also took place between Rio Grande, Pelotas, and Pôrto Alegre for the trade of Rio Grande do Sul, and between Rio de Janeiro and Santos, and Belém and Manaus. There was also a general belief among businessmen and their groups in the North and Northeast that the imperial government was discriminating against their regions in favor of the Southeast and South. The alleged discrimination occurred in financial policy, immigration, and agricultural improvement, but was felt to be most manifest in communications.[10] Rivalries over trade areas and communications would produce more discord between business interest groups than any other issue.

Queen of communications: the railroad

Of the many fundamental innovations in communications of the nineteenth century, none aroused greater interest or higher expectations than the railroad. Business interest groups most influenced it by helping determine the type and extent of government support. Government aid was central to its spread. By 1897, a little less than ninety percent of Brazil's rail mileage was either nationally or state-owned or enjoyed subsidies or guaranteed interest.[11] Even most of the remainder had been built with the aid of tax exemptions on installations and equipment. Accusations that the Brazilian government, unlike that of the United States, did not shoulder the burden of propagating the railroad are quite unfair. Brazil took a much larger part in constructing and operating railroads, private and public, than did most other South American nations.[12] Nor were the efforts of the Empire in this field much inferior to those of the supposedly

9. Associação Comercial do Maranhão, *Relatório da Comissão da Praça, Apresentado 'a Assembléia Geral dos Assinantes da Casa da Praça em 9 de Janeiro de 1872* (São Luís: País, 1872), pp. 34–35; *Relatório de 1870*, pp. 11–12, 19, *Relatório de 1873*, p. 11, and *Relatório de 1874*, p. 12.
10. For example, Associação Comercial de Ceará, *Relatório da Associação Comercial da Praça do Ceará, Apresentado 'a Assembléia Geral dos Sócios pela Diretoria no Dia 1 de Maio de 1872* (Fortaleza: Odorico Colás, 1872), p. 7; Associação Comercial de Pernambuco, *Relatório da Associação Comercial Beneficente Lido na Assembléia Geral de 5 de Agôsto de 1878* (Recife: Jornal do Recife, 1878), p. 20; and *Relatório de 1891*, p. 26. For imperial policy toward the North and Northeast, see Evaldo Cabral de Melo, *O Norte Agrário e o Império, 1871–1889* (Rio de Janeiro: Nova Fronteira, 1984), especially pp. 191–243.
11. Hill to Department of State, Santos, Dec. 20, 1897, *USRC*, LVI, no. 210 (March 1898): 387.
12. Steven Topik, *The Political Economy of the Brazilian State, 1889–1930* (Austin: University of Texas Press, 1987), p. 94.

more capitalist-minded Republic.[13] Business interest groups influenced the nature of much of this large-scale government activity.

Before the coming of the railroad, roads held the attention of business interest groups. The first commercial associations commonly urged government to construct and keep in repair highways from the entrepôt they represented to the export-producing areas of the interior. Symptomatic of this interest was the 1853 request of the President of the Province of Pernambuco that its commercial association fund a loan for road construction.[14] But after the onset of a veritable "railroad fever" in Brazil in the 1850s, commercial associations and other business interest groups rarely emphasized roads in their petitions and proclamations on communications. An exception was the Commercial Association of Maranhão, perhaps because it hoped to offset loss of its once-vast trade area by opening up its province's forested interior.[15] Implicit in the usual silence of business interest groups on the building of roads was the assumption that railroad development would make them unnecessary and the fear that they would divert scarce resources from railroad construction.

Brazil's business elite assumed the railroad would bring soaring prosperity by vastly expanding the trade area of their entrepôts. A projected line from Salvador to the São Francisco River, for example, was expected to enable that port to dominate or share the trade of nine of the Empire's twenty provinces.[16] By reducing transportation costs the railroad also was counted on to enlarge the zone of export plantation agriculture. An indirect benefit to export agriculture in the form of lowered labor costs was eagerly awaited. Railroads would replace mule transport, thereby releasing mule skinners – an estimated 20,000 in the Province of Pernambuco alone – for "useful" agricultural labor.[17] Finally, business interest group leaders also would profit directly. They were conspicuous among the directors and stockholders of railroad companies, although most relied on predominantly foreign capital and technology.

Business interest groups pushed railroad construction in Brazil from its beginning. In 1854 the Commercial Association of Rio de Janeiro helped organize the nation's first line, the Petrópolis or Mauá, headed by the

---

13. Graham, "Government Expenditures," 347.
14. Minutes, meeting of Jan. 10, 1853, Livro 2 de Atas, AACP, p. 12.
15. Associação Comercial do Maranhão, *Relatório de 1867*, pp. 11, 37–47, *Relatório de 1870*, pp. 9, 23–25; and *Exposição do Açúcar e Algodão Feita pela Associação Comercial do Maranhão, 1883* (São Luís: País, 1883), p. 10. At century's end, Maranhão's only line was of approximately seventy kilometers and had but one train. "Railways in Brazil," Consul-General Dawson to Department of State, Rio de Janeiro, no date, *USRC*, LVIII, no. 239 (Aug. 1900): 410.
16. John Morgan, *The Railroad Between the City of Bahia and the River Saint Francisco in the Empire of Brazil: Its Geographic Superiority and Commercial Advantage to Be Derived Therefrom* (London: Smith, Elder & Co., 1853), pp. 11–13.
17. Associação Comercial Agrícola do Recife [Pernambuco], *Congresso Agrícola do Recife* (Recife: M. Figueiroa de Faria & Filhos, 1878), p. 15; Associação Comercial de Pernambuco, *Relatório de 1883*, p. 12.

group's President, the future Viscount Mauá.[18] Business interest groups also aided private initiative by assuring entrepreneurs of the profitability of proposed lines or by recommending certain companies to government for the awarding of concessions.[19] Their greatest impact, however, came in urging generous government support for proposed construction. The core of such support was guaranteed interest on capital, usually amounting to seven percent, five from the imperial government and the rest from the province. After this stimulant proved more expensive than effective, government authorities replaced it by a fixed subsidy per kilometer of track. Railroads also were awarded options to buy up to thirty kilometers of land on both sides of the track, with timber and mineral rights, tax exemptions, including import taxes on equipment, and freedom from the competition of other lines over a vast area.[20] Business interest groups did not acknowledge that such government action violated a simple reading of liberal economic tenets. When private companies failed to undertake greatly desired construction, two commercial associations even demanded the national government build the lines itself.[21]

Nearly all business interest groups at one time or another urged government support for railroad construction within their trade area. Even the Commercial Association of Pará, whose members depended overwhelmingly on water transportation, pushed lines calculated to let Belém capture the trade of the Province of Goiás and the nation of Bolivia.[22] Certain lines were promoted with special intensity because it was believed the economic stakes were particularly large. The Commercial Association of Maranhão looked to a railroad connecting that province with the capital of Piauí not only to regain lost trade area, but to revitalize the very society of São Luís, now admittedly lifeless.[23] The commercial associations of Pernambuco and Bahia urged railroads, Brazil's second and third, de-

18. Heitor Beltrão, "O Civismo da Praça num Século de Labor," in Associação Comercial do Rio de Janeiro, *Aspectos Coligidos a Propósito do Centenário da Associação Comercial* (Rio de Janeiro: Associação Comercial do Rio de Janeiro, 1935), p. 75.
19. Associação Comercial do Pôrto Alegre, *Relatório da Praça do Comércio de Pôrto Alegre do Ano de 1870* (Pôrto Alegre: Jornal do Comércio, 1871), pp. 4–5, document no. 7, pp. 1–2; Commercial Association of Bahia to Hugh Wilson, Salvador, Jan. 19, 1871, *Relatório da Associação Comercial da Praça da Bahia, Apresentado em Sessão Ordinária da Assembléia Geral de 13 de Novembro de 1871* (Salvador: J. G. Tourinho, 1872), p. 18.
20. Ana Célia Castro, *As Empresas Estrangeiras no Brasil, 1860–1913* (Rio de Janeiro: Zahar, 1979), pp. 47–48. For individual awards, see Francisco Barreto Picanço da Costa, *Dicionário de Estradas de Ferro* (Rio de Janeiro: H. Lombaerts, 1891–1892), II: 85–89.
21. Associação Comercial do Maranhão, *Relatório de 1874*, p. 7; Associação Comercial de Pernambuco, *Relatório de 1877*, pp. 63–64.
22. Commercial Association of Pará to Minister of Finance, Belém, March 26, 1895, *Relatório da Praça do Comércio do Pará, Apresentado e Aprovado em Sessão da Assembléia Geral de 31 de Janeiro de 1896* (Belém: Pinheiro & Loyola, 1896), p. 12; Associação Comercial do Pará, *Relatório de 1873*, p. 4.
23. Commercial Association of Maranhão to Emperor Pedro II, São Luís, no date, 1873, *Relatório de 1873*, pp. 19–25; Associação Comercial do Maranhão, *Relatório de 1880*, pp. 8–9.

signed to connect Recife and Salvador, respectively, with the São Francisco River. Both associations were impelled by rivalry. That line reaching the river first was expected to tap for its entrepôt the vast wealth of the São Francisco basin, heretofore largely unexploited because rapids impeded navigation of the river to the sea.

Despite or, more likely, because of guaranteed interest and other generous aid, construction of both railroads proceeded slowly and with extraordinary expense. The Bahian line reached the São Francisco only in 1896; the one from Recife never did. Eventually both commercial associations became disillusioned. In 1871 the Pernambuco association denounced the bountiful concessions made by the province as "retrograde and highly noxious dispositions," which wasted tax revenue and actually slowed progress, and in 1872 and 1880 urged that resources intended for the São Francisco line be used for railroads to other parts of Pernambuco.[24] Similarly, in 1882 the Commercial Association of Bahia denounced the formulation of the Salvador-São Francisco railroad as a scientific and financial "disaster."[25]

There were other particularly determined railroad construction campaigns. The Commercial Association and the factor group Commercial Agricultural Association of Pernambuco, acting in concert, forced the completion of a long-postponed line running from Recife northwest to Limoeiro and by century's end its connection with another in the Province of Paraíba.[26] This enabled Recife to tap the commerce of Paraíba and Rio Grande do Norte. The Commercial Association of Bahia, urging guaranteed interest and other support, threw its weight behind a line from Salvador to the diamond-mining area in the center of its province.[27] As in the case of the São Francisco line, its income did not approach expenses and construction lagged.[28] It never reached the diamond area.

24. Commercial Association of Pernambuco to Provincial Assembly, Recife, March 22, 1871, *Relatório de 1871*, p. 14; Commercial Association of Pernambuco to Emperor Pedro II, Recife, March 25, 1872, *Relatório de 1872*, pp. 15–16. Associação Comercial de Pernambuco, *Relatório de 1880*, p. 7. In 1885, however, the group urged that the São Francisco and other unfinished lines in the province be completed. Commercial Association of Pernambuco to Brazilian Parliament, Recife, June 8, 1885, *Relatório de 1885*, pp. 43–44.

25. Brazil, Congresso, Comissão Parlamentar de Inquérito, *Informações Apresentadas pela Comissão Parlamentar de Inquérito ao Corpo Legislativo na Terceira Sessão de Décima Oitava Legislatura* (Rio de Janeiro: Tipografia Nacional, 1883), p. 205.

26. For example, Commercial Agricultural Association of Pernambuco to President of Province, Recife, Nov. 11, 1878, Associação Comercial, 1878–1881, Arquivo Público do Estado de Pernambuco, Recife, Mss. A.C-1, Doc. 64; Minutes, meeting of Aug. 20, 1877, Livro 4 de Atas, AACP, p. 109; Associação Comercial de Pernambuco, *Relatório de 1899*, pp. 8–10.

27. Commercial Association of Bahia to Emperor Pedro II, Salvador, Dec. 31, 1874, *Relatório de 1875*, p. 39; Minutes, meeting of Feb. 9, 1881, Livro 4 de Atas, AACB, p. 374.

28. Bahia, Governador do Estado, *Mensagem Apresentada 'a Assembléia Geral Legislativa pelo Exm. Sr. Dr. Luís Vianna, Governador da Bahia, em 10 de Abril de 1899* (Salvador: Correio de Notícias, 1899), 17.

Acerbic conflict accompanied one of the most intensive lobbying campaigns waged by a commercial association during the nineteenth century. The demand of the Commercial Association of Santos for additional railroad lines between that port and the province's coffee-growing upland brought it into confrontation with the British-owned San [sic] Paulo Railway Company, Limited. It is little exaggeration to state that Santos owed its entrepôt status to completion of that railroad to São Paulo's uplands in 1867, which halved transportation costs.[29] By the 1890s, however, Santos was overtaking Rio de Janeiro as the world's leading coffee port, and the company's single track, grossly inadequate for its volume of traffic, had become a major bottleneck. Both coffee and imports were piled up in warehouses and on docks, vulnerable to spoilage, weather damage, theft, and exaggerated handling and storage fees. Most alarming was the danger that yellow fever posed to the crews of ships, delayed up to six months.[30] Less mentioned, but very much on the minds of Santos merchants, was the handicap presented by the bottleneck in competition with Rio de Janeiro for upland São Paulo's trade.

The Commercial Association of Santos made its case against the "English Line," as it was unaffectionately known, in newspaper articles, numerous petitions, and two books, one of which was published in Great Britain by a returned Santos director and apparently was intended to sway public opinion in that country.[31] The association was unable to force the English Line to double its track, which, as the "most profitable British railway enterprise in Brazil or anywhere else in Latin America," it could easily have done.[32] Consequently, the group tried to promote the entry of competition. It obtained for two São Paulo railroads, the Sorocabana and Mogyana, government authorization to extend their lines to Santos and generous aid.[33] The San Paulo Railway Company, citing privileges of monopoly conceded in its original contract and backed by the formidable diplomatic power of Britain, forced the Brazilian government to retreat. Not until 1937 did the English Line face competition, although it relieved some of the pressure on itself and on the port of Santos by doubling its line in 1898–1899.[34] Again a business interest group found, as in the

29. Joseph L. Love, *São Paulo in the Brazilian Federation, 1889–1937* (Stanford, Calif.: Stanford University Press, 1980), pp. 41, 64.
30. Associação Comercial de Santos, *A Crise de Transportes no Estado de S. Paulo* (São Paulo: Industrial de São Paulo, 1892), pp. 10–15; Walter Wright, *A Few Facts About Brazil, by a Twenty Years' Resident in That Country* (Birmingham: Cornish Brothers, 1892), p. 27.
31. See Wright, *A Few Facts*, and Associação Comercial de Santos, *Crise de Transportes*.
32. J. Fred Rippy, *British Investments in Latin America, 1822–1949: A Case Study in the Operations of Private Enterprise in Retarded Regions* (Hamden, Conn.: Anchor Books, 1966), p. 154.
33. Associação Comercial de Santos, *Relatório da Associação Comercial de Santos, Apresentado em Sessão Ordinária da Assembléia Geral de 10 de Julho de 1893, e Parecer da Comissão de Exame de Contas* (Santos: W. Kraemer, 1893), p. 11.
34. Joseph L. Love, "External Financing and Domestic Politics: The Case of São Paulo, Brazil, 1889–

case of the Commercial Association of Pará's promotion of a government-sponsored monopoly marketing company for rubber, foreign diplomatic influence too powerful.

The support of most business interest groups for railway construction had a common flaw. Only the Engineering Club, which staged a Railroad Congress in 1882 and a Brazilian Railroad Exposition in 1887 and urged linkages with Brazil's neighbors, promoted railway construction with overall national development as a goal.[35] The others viewed it through the lens of localism and rivalry. Discussing three railroads being built in neighboring provinces in 1884, the Commercial Association of Pernambuco saw the true purpose of each as taking from Recife the trade of the province's interior.[36] Later that association waged a protracted campaign that delayed the linkage of Pernambuco's rail network with the port of Maceió, Alagôas. The group candidly admitted that its motive was to prevent drainage of Pernambuco's trade to Maceió, situated closer to much of that province's interior than Recife.[37] Fear of losing trade also led the Commercial Association of Pará to oppose the building of a line between its city of Belém and the rival port of Bragança.[38] Business interest groups worked hard to promote railroad construction, but usually with only the welfare of their own entrepôt in mind.

Railroad regulation: prerogatives and conflict

In regulating Brazilian railroads, business interest groups enjoyed prerogatives that somewhat resembled those with tariffs. For lines terminating in their entrepôts, group representatives usually formed part of government committees advising on or setting freights and fares. The presidents of the Commercial Association and Commercial Agricultural Association of Pernambuco, for example, formed part of an 1882 provincial committee recommending rates for the new Great Western of Brazil Limited and the president of the Commercial Association of Rio de Janeiro part of a three-man team in 1888 revising the rates of the government-owned Dom Pedro II.[39] Government also commonly asked business in-

1937," in *Latin American Modernization Problems*, ed. Robert E. Scott (Urbana, Ill.: University of Illinois Press, 1973), p. 243; Richard Graham, *Britain and the Onset of Modernization in Brazil, 1850–1914* (Cambridge: Cambridge University Press, 1968), p. 64.

35. *Jornal do Brasil* (Rio de Janeiro), July 10, 1892, p. 2; *ACD, 1898*, III: 209–210.
36. Associação Comercial de Pernambuco, *Relatório de 1884*, p. 48.
37. Commercial Association of Pernambuco to Minister of Agriculture, Commerce, and Public Works, Recife, June 19, 1890, *Relatório de 1890*, pp. 57–61; Associação Comercial de Pernambuco, *Relatório de 1891*, pp. 28–29.
38. Associação Comercial do Pará, *Relatório de 1884*, pp. 12–13.
39. Minutes, meeting of July 10, 1882, Livro de Atas da Associação Comercial Agrícola de Pernam-

terest group opinion on proposed changes in freights and fares affecting their membership. Of course the groups often did not wait to be consulted, but forced rate reductions directly from the railroad company or through government. Rail regulation, like construction, was strongly affected by localism and questions of entrepôt dominance, but differed in that it brought business interest groups and companies into frequent conflict, usually over rates.

Business interest groups also attempted to regulate railroad service. They were able to alter methods of assessing, carrying, and handling freight, to change schedules for passenger and freight trains, and to improve treatment of passengers. Despite quarreling with the San [sic] Paulo Railway Company over the bottleneck formed by its single-track line, the Commercial Association of Santos functioned as an intermediary between that corporation and other companies seeking to improve its service.[40] When equipment and service on the Central of Brazil Railroad (*Estrada de Ferro Central do Brazil*), formerly the Dom Pedro II, deteriorated badly in 1892, the Engineering Club arrested the attention of the government by holding a series of public conferences on the problem.[41]

Conflict over freight charges most often arose when the commodity hauled declined in prosperity. Reducing freights was an important component of business interest group campaigns to revive sugar and cotton export. The groups tended to be disillusioned, in any case, because freight rates generally remained much higher than anticipated, even on lines heavily subsidized by government. In Pernambuco in the 1880s, for example, rail freight represented between twenty and fifty percent of the value of sugar, depending on variety, international price, and exchange rate.[42] In that same province in the late 1870s and early 1880s, rail transportation from major growing areas for cotton was twenty-five to thirty percent of price.[43] Even relatively low charges could be crucial.

buco (hereafter cited as ACAP), 1877–1892, AACP, p. 68; Associação Comercial do Rio de Janeiro, *Relatório da Associação Comercial do Rio de Janeiro do Ano de 1890* (Rio de Janeiro: Montenegro, 1891), p. 25.

40. For example, Santos Transport Company (*Companhia Santista de Transportes*) to Commercial Association of Santos, Santos, no date, 1890, *Relatório de 1891*, Anexo 48, p. 149; Central Paulista [Railroad] Company (*Companhia Central Paulista*) to Commercial Association of Santos, São Paulo, Nov. 8, 1894, *Relatório de 1895*, pp. 157–158.

41. Commercial Association of Rio de Janeiro to Minister of Agriculture, Commerce, and Public Works, Rio de Janeiro, April 2, 1892, *Relatório de 1901*, Anexos, 1892, pp. 9–10.

42. Henrique Augusto Milet, *A Lavoura da Cana de Açúcar* (Recife: By the Author, 1881), p. 33; Associação Comercial de Pernambuco, *Relatório de 1887*, p. 36.

43. Pernambuco, Presidente da Província, *Fala Com Que o Exm. Sr. Dr. Adolfo de Barros Cavalcante de Lacerda, Presidente da Província, Abriu a Sessão da Assembléia Legislativa em 19 de Dezembro de 1878* (Recife: Manuel Figueiroa de Faria & Filhos, 1879), pp. 58–59; John Casper Branner, *Cotton in the Empire of Brazil*, Department of Agriculture, Special Report No. 8 (Washington, D.C.: Government Printing Office, 1885), p. 25.

Freight for cotton from the furthest large growing area in São Paulo in 1882 was only thirteen percent of value, but the Commercial Association of Santos declared that it must be halved if cotton growing in the province were to survive periods of high exchange.[44]

Reduction of freight for coffee was key to the program of business interest groups to combat the coffee crises of the early 1880s and late 1890s. Freight was estimated to constitute twenty-five percent of the average sale price in 1882.[45] Knowledge that by the 1880s the cost of shipping coffee from Brazil to New York was but a third to a tenth that of getting it from plantation to port also inflamed dissatisfaction.[46] During the first crisis, the Center for Coffee Agriculture and Commerce and the commercial associations of Rio de Janeiro and Santos obtained reductions of from ten to twenty-five percent.[47] The campaign of the latter two groups had less success during the second. In that crisis the Santos organization also attempted unsuccessfully through the governor of São Paulo to require that coffee freights be pegged to market prices.[48] Although usually forcing railroad companies to make at least compromise concessions, business interest groups were rarely satisfied and often renewed the struggle.[49]

Freight rates were as crucial to entrepôt dominance as to the viability of exports. This was particularly true in the long struggle between Rio de Janeiro and its fast-growing rival Santos. As coffee cultivation spread westward through the Paraíba Valley from the Province of Rio de Janeiro into São Paulo and then north and west, geographical advantage would seem to lie increasingly with Santos. But coffee was carried to the latter by the San Paulo Railway Company, and that powerful and extremely profitable British line had little inclination to lower its high rates. Most of Rio's São Paulo coffee came over the Dom Pedro II, a government line subject to political pressure. Rio needed coffee from the west of São Paulo not only to maintain a high volume of exportation, but to ensure the reputation of its product. Higher quality São Paulo coffees were blended in Rio with poorer varieties coming from the middle and lower Paraíba Valley.[50]

44. Associação Comercial de Santos, *Relatório de 1882*, p. 21.
45. Wright to Department of State, Santos, March 25, 1882, *USRC*, VI, no. 20 (June 1882): 242.
46. "Cultivation of, and Trade in, Coffee in Central and South America," *USRC*, XXVIII, no. 98 (Oct. 1888): 7; Consul-General Andrews to Department of State, Rio de Janeiro, Dec. 31, 1882, *USRC*, IX, no. 28 (Feb. 1883): 222.
47. Joseph Sweigart, "Financing and Marketing Brazilian Export Agriculture: The Coffee Factors of Rio de Janeiro, 1850–1888" (Ph.D. Diss., University of Texas, 1980), p. 197.
48. Associação Comercial de Santos, *Relatório de 1901*, pp. 9–10.
49. For example, following freight reductions of twenty and fifty percent on Pernambucan and Bahian lines, respectively. Associação Comercial de Pernambuco, *Relatório de 1883*, p. 12; Associação Comercial da Bahia, *Relatório de 1901*, pp. 293–294.
50. R. Frank Colson, "On Expectations-Perspectives on the Crisis of 1889 in Brazil," *JLAS*, 13 (Nov. 1981): 281.

The imperial government rejected the pleas of the Commercial Association of Santos and provincial officials that the English Line be forced to lower its freights. Worse, it permitted the Dom Pedro II to put into effect from 1879 to 1889 a "special rate," designed to attract coffee from São Paulo. Coffee shipped from the City of São Paulo paid less freight for the 497 kilometers to Rio de Janeiro than for the ninety to Santos.[51] In 1884 the Rio-based Center for Coffee Agriculture and Commerce protested to the government voluntary rate reductions made by the English Line. Replying that the cuts made by the latter were only in response to new reductions forced on the Dom Pedro II by the Center, the Commercial Association of Santos acidly noted that "unfortunately the zeal which the illustrious Center manifests for national agriculture seems to be limited to the agriculture tributary to Rio de Janeiro and [seeks] to block its drainage toward other markets."[52] Desperate for a means to equalize rates with the Dom Pedro II, the Santos group also proposed that the imperial government expropriate the English Line.[53]

The administrations of the new Republic were more in sympathy with the interests of São Paulo. Consequently they established rates on the Rio-based former Dom Pedro II, now known as the Central of Brazil, more in line with actual distances of shipment. In 1894, however, the Commercial Association of Santos had to ask the intervention of the state governor to cancel drastic new rate cuts made by the Central of Brazil.[54] After 1898 a rising exchange rate added to low prices intensified pressures for cuts. In June of that year, Rio de Janeiro coffee factorage houses successfully petitioned the Central to equal the price of the English Line for coffee transported from the northern regions of São Paulo. The reduction resulted in a threefold increase in coffee shipments from that area to Rio by March of 1899, but Rio factors demanded and received even greater cuts.[55] These new reductions, claimed the Commercial Association of Santos, amounted to seventy percent and ensured that the Central could make no profit.[56] In effect taxpayers, including the membership of the Santos organization, were subsidizing Rio and its coffee factors. Fortunately for the Commercial Association of Santos, the state of São Paulo's power was at a height. That group eventually forced the Central of Brazil to raise its rates by appealing to state authorities and to President Prudente de Morais, a Paulista.

51. *Jornal do Comércio* (Rio de Janeiro), Oct. 10, 1899, p. 2; Associação Comercial de Santos, *Relatório de 1883*, pp. 19–20.
52. Associação Comercial de Santos, *Relatório de 1884*, Anexo no. 5, pp. 26–27.
53. Ibid., p. 26.
54. Minutes, meeting of Feb. 14, 1894, Livro de Atas, 1874–1894, AACS, p. 185.
55. *Jornal do Comércio*, May 6, 1899, p. 1.
56. Commercial Association of Santos to President of Republic, Santos, Sept. 6, 1899, *Relatório de 1900*, Anexo no. 21, unpaginated.

The coming of the railroad to Brazil aroused great enthusiasm among business interest groups, but its developmental benefits generally fell short of expectations. This, and concern about local interests, brought conflict between the groups and the railroads over regulation. Entrepôt rivalry would also affect group attitudes toward other communications systems, including steam navigation.

Steam navigation: integration and localism

Steam navigation was as revolutionary in its potential as the railroad and probably less disappointing in its results. In Brazil, as in much of the world, the application of steam to ships revolutionized overseas, coastal, river, and harbor transportation. It also affected patterns of economic development. Steam enabled for the first time an easy passage around Brazil's eastern bulge for coastal shipping, binding its northern coast more tightly to the rest of the nation and contributing to the decline of São Luís as an entrepôt. River steamers made possible the rubber-based prosperity of the Amazon Basin. "It is not superfluous to repeat," stated the Commercial Association of Pará in 1869, "that from the establishment of steam navigation dates the extraordinary development of the public wealth of Pará."[57] Steam navigation became and long remained the communications system which bound Brazil together. Brazilians relied overwhelmingly on coastal steamers for interregional transportation until the end of World War II and on river steamers within the Amazon basin to the present.

Business interest groups, as in the case of the railroads, made their greatest impact in using advisory prerogatives to shape government support. They evaluated first the awarding of government aid or privilege to shipping companies and then its continuation, based on performance. As with railroads, government support came from both nation and provinces, and was enjoyed, in some form, by most steamer companies, river, coastal, or overseas. It consisted, among other things, of annual subsidies, low-interest loans, exemptions from a variety of taxes, concessions of land, the privilege of cutting wood on the public domain, and the right to a monopoly on certain routes.[58] In return for national subsidies, shipping companies had to provide free or cut-rate passage for government officials and cargos, immigrants, and troops.

The regulatory prerogatives of business interest groups with steam navigation were also extensive. They evaluated fees, schedules, and service, approved the awarding of contracts, and even ratified company

57. *Relatório de 1869*, p. 14.
58. *RMACOP 1867*, II: "Quadro das Emprêsas de Navegação por Vapor . . . ," unpaginated.

mergers. One regulatory prerogative vitally affected geographical patterns of development. This was the recommendation of ports of call. Selection or elimination as a port of call often determined the prosperity or decay of Brazilian towns during the nineteenth century.

River steamers: binding together the Amazon

Steam navigation had its greatest immediate impact on river shipping. Most of Brazil's coastal provinces did not rely heavily on river transportation, nor did their business interest groups much concern themselves with it. An exception was the Commercial Association of Maranhão, which prodded government to keep the province's rivers dredged. They were the main means of communication between São Luís and the interior. Another was the Commercial Association of Rio de Janeiro, which insisted steam navigation of the Mucuri River, pioneered by association President Teófilo Ottoni, be kept functioning.[59] The Mucuri, which met the sea in the southern panhandle of Bahia, was Rio's main means of communication with its trade area in northern Minas Gerais.

On the other hand, river transportation was of all-encompassing importance to the commercial associations of Pará and Amazonas. Their trade area was by the 1890s as large as the United States east of the Rocky Mountains, with some rubber traveling further to reach Belém than from Belém to New York City.[60] Belém even traded with coastal Peru, whose goods were carried over the Andes on the backs of Indians.[61] The provincial governments of Pará and Amazonas conceded the two associations widespread prerogatives. The groups recommended the awarding of subsidies to open service to new ports or increase it to established ones and evaluated schedules, passenger fares, and freights for new lines or any changes in them for lines in operation. This advisory work was complex; by 1898 the State of Pará alone subsidized twenty-three separate routes.[62] Foreign overseas lines, likewise subsidized, also plied the Amazon system. Legislation of 1866, pushed by Manaus merchants soon to organize themselves as the Commercial Association of Amazonas, opened the Amazon waterways to international shipping.[63]

Steam navigation first came to the region in 1853 with the Amazon Navigation and Commerce Company (*Companhia de Navegação e Comércio do*

---

59. Commercial Association of Rio de Janeiro to Minister of Agriculture, Commerce, and Public Works, Rio de Janeiro, Nov. 5, 1872, *Relatório de 1872*, Doc. 4, unpaginated.
60. United States, Bureau of Foreign Commerce, "India Rubber," *Special Consular Reports* (Washington, D.C.: Government Printing Office, 1892), VI: 383
61. Associação Comercial do Pará, *Relatório de 1869*, pp. 4–5.
62. Associação Comercial do Pará, *Relatório de 1898*, Anexo no. 11, p. 37.
63. Carlos Pontes, *Tavares Bastos (Aureliano Cândido), 1839–1875*, Brasiliana, 136 (São Paulo: Editôra Nacional, 1939), pp. 228–229n.

Amazonas), founded by that seemingly ubiquitous pioneer entrepreneur, Viscount Mauá. Relations between this powerful company and the commercial associations of Pará and Amazonas were sometimes strained and in the case of the former group complicated by the presence of past or present directors among the managers of the company or its competitors. In 1870, the Commercial Association of Pará endorsed the bid of a rival, the Pará River Company (*Companhia Fluvial Paraense*), to take over a route and its provincial subsidy already awarded to the Amazon Navigation and Commerce Company.[64] This provoked the stormy resignation from the association of its first President, Manuel Antônio Pimenta Bueno, Manager of the Amazon company. In 1871 the Pará association approved the company's proposal to sell itself to a London-based corporation, the Amazon Steam Navigation Company.[65] Like most other Brazilian business interest groups in the nineteenth century, the Commercial Association of Pará had little aversion to foreign economic control. In 1874, maintaining that a current economic slump obviated the need for competition, it endorsed the Amazon Steam Navigation Company's establishment of a near monopoly through the purchase of its two major competitors.[66]

The Amazon Steam Navigation Company enjoyed national and provincial subsidies, extensive routes, and dominance. A traveler remarked, "There are several smaller companies, but they are all thrown into the shade by this rich Amazonian line, with its numerous branches. It has a large subsidy from the government – too much, probably, for its wants."[67] In 1879 the Commercial Association of Amazonas, blaming the company's subsidies for smothering competition, called on the Imperial Parliament to reduce them.[68] In 1885 the Commercial Association of Pará demanded cutting of the company's provincial subsidies.[69] The reversal of the Pará association's attitude probably did not stem from second thoughts about foreign economic domination or need for competition, but rather from the formation in 1884 of a rival, the Pará and Amazonas Company, whose five directors were all past or present board members of that association.[70] As in the case of railroads, vested interests played a secluded but

---

64. Commercial Association of Pará to Provincial Assembly, Belém, Aug. 26, 1870, *Relatório de 1871*, pp. 24–25.
65. Ibid., pp. 10–11.
66. Commercial Association of Pará to Manager, Amazon Steam Navigation Company, Belém, July 25, 1874, *Relatório de 1875*, pp. 5–6, Anexo 6, unpaginated.
67. H. H. Smith, *Brazil: The Amazons and the Coast* (London: Sampson Low, Marston, Searle, and Rivington, 1879), p. 47.
68. Associação Comercial do Amazonas, *Documentário Comemorativo do Primeiro Centenário da Associação Comercial do Amazonas, 18 de Junho de 1971* (Manaus: Umberto Calderaro, 1971), pp. 27–28.
69. Barbara Weinstein, *The Amazon Rubber Boom, 1850–1920* (Stanford, Calif.: Stanford University Press, 1983), p. 289.
70. They were Domingos José Dias, João Gualberto da Costa e Cunha, João Lúcio de Azevedo, Francisco Guadéncio da Costa, and Emílio Adolfo de Castro Martins. Kerby to Department of State, Belém, Oct. 4, 1890, *USRC*, XXXIV, no. 122 (Nov. 1890): 493.

important role in the policies of business interest groups toward steam navigation.

Coastal steamers: integration and rivalry

Coastal shipping was nearly as important to Brazil's seaboard provinces and business interest groups as was river transportation to the Amazon. It would remain their most effective link with the rest of the nation until well into the twentieth century and was almost as vital as the railroad in holding or expanding trade territory. As in other transportation systems, business interest groups principally affected coastal navigation by influencing government aid. And, as with the railroad, the Commercial Association of Rio de Janeiro in 1840 helped organize one of Brazil's first coastal shipping lines.[71] Virtually all coastal shipping companies were subsidized by central government or provinces (those they called at as well as those in which they were located) and often by both. For companies based in their entrepôt, the groups were expected to critique fares, freights, and schedules and to recommend ports of call. The Commercial Association of Rio de Janeiro did so for the nation's longest and most important coastal line, the government-owned Brazilian Steam Navigation Company (*Companhia Brasileira de Navegação 'a Vapor*). Smaller commercial associations often solicited the intercession of the Rio group with that company to improve service.

Stopovers were a matter of highest concern. Business interest groups demanded they be scheduled to coordinate with the movement of overseas lines. Any irregularity or uncertainty interfered with the movement of mail or cargo and obstructed business. The groups also demanded stopovers be as long as possible and in daylight, to expedite cargo handling and passenger movement. They protested early departures, which happened when ships were trying to make up time, and called on mail pouches to be officially closed as near to time of departure as possible, to enable the completion of last-minute business correspondence. As with other aspects of communications, rivalry fueled concern with stopovers. It was considered vital that their conditions be equal to those in rival entrepôts, otherwise local firms would be disadvantaged.

Entrepôt rivalry also made it important to have a coastal shipping company headquartered in the group's own entrepôt, as did Bahia, Pernambuco, and Maranhão. Commercial associations occasionally asked provincial or even national government for aid in financing such a company. If coastal steamer companies based elsewhere were derelict in their service, the groups sometimes threatened them with cancellation of their provincial subsidy or monopoly privileges, but halting service usually hurt local

71. Beltrão, "Civismo da Praça," 74.

merchants much more than the company. Business interest groups were suspicious of lines headquartered in rival entrepôts. The Commercial Association of Ceará accused Maranhão's coastal shipping company of charging discriminatory rates to Fortaleza, Ceará's capital, of demanding extra charges when no competing ships were available, and of making fewer voyages than called for in its contract, all presumably for the purpose of choking Fortaleza's development as an entrepôt.[72] That group also accused Recife authorities of deliberately disrupting the forwarding of overseas mail to Fortaleza.[73] Similarly, the Commercial Association of Maranhão complained that cargos destined for São Luís had been left unloaded (perhaps deliberately) in Salvador and Recife.[74] Business interest groups could also reciprocate suspected ill will. When queried by government on means to improve steamer service, they often suggested reducing or eliminating stopovers in rival ports. Present in nearly all aspects of nineteenth-century communications, localism was particularly visible in coastal shipping.

The importance of coastal shipping for business interest groups led most to oppose an early movement of Brazilian nationalism: the attempt to restrict such transportation to Brazilian vessels. They maintained that the service provided by foreign ships was more efficient and that wider competition kept down freight rates and repeated the precepts of economic liberalism. "In the era we are passing through, it is idleness to demonstrate how much privilege or monopoly retards the progress of societies," went a typical argument.[75] On the other hand the groups were sensitive to accusations by nationalists that open coastal shipping thwarted the formation of a Brazilian merchant marine. While rejecting restricted coastal shipping, most were careful to suggest alternative aid for the merchant marine, such as the reduction of taxes on ship construction or purchase and the exemption of seamen from military service.

Coastal shipping was restricted to Brazilian vessels, preferably manned by native crews, from independence. During the 1850s, commercial associations protested regulations making difficult the hiring of foreigners on Brazilian coastal ships.[76] In the 1860s they turned their fire, with the Maranhão group dissenting, against restrictions on foreign ships in the coastal trade.[77] These restrictions were gradually lifted and ended defini-

72. *Relatório de 1867*, pp. 8–9; Commercial Association of Ceará to Minister of Agriculture, Commerce and Public Works, Fortaleza, June 20, 1868, *Relatório de 1869*, pp. 31–32.
73. *Relatório de 1870*, p. 6.   74. *O País* (São Luís), Dec. 30, 1865, p. 2.
75. Associação Comercial de Pernambuco, *Relatório de 1871*, p. 9.
76. For example, Minutes, meeting of Aug. 11, 1854, Livro 2 de Atas, AACP, p. 26; Commercial Association of Bahia to Vice-President of Province, Salvador, Jan. 14, 1856, Presidência da Província/Govêrno ao Associação Comercial, 1828–1889, AEB.
77. For commercial association opinion, see Minutes, meeting of Jan. 2, 1863, Livro 3 de Atas, AACB, p. 31; Commercial Association of Bahia to President of Province, Salvador, Jan. 18, 1869, *Relatório de 1869*, p. 50; Associação Comercial do Pará, *Relatório de 1868*, pp. 19–20;

tively in 1869. The result, according to a Minister of Finance of the early Republic, was the virtual disappearance of the Brazilian merchant marine by 1875.[78] Queried by the government in 1870, the commercial associations strongly reiterated their support of open coastal shipping.[79] With the exception of the associations of Maranhão and Bahia, they did so again when questioned in the early 1880s.[80] The dissent of the Commercial Association of Bahia probably stemmed from something less than patriotism. Its president had become a director of the province's coastal navigation company. That association, ignoring its more than twenty years of previous support, announced in 1882 that "freedom of navigation was an error."[81]

A return to restricted coastal shipping was high on the agenda of the new Republic and stipulated in the Constitution of 1891. Business interest groups, many of them out of favor with the new regime, dared not oppose it openly. Instead, led by the commercial associations of the Northeast and North and the Commercial Association of Rio de Janeiro, they petitioned repeatedly to have its enforcement delayed.[82] They succeeded in keeping the coastal trade open until December 1897.[83] Even afterward, Pernambuco's Commercial Agricultural Association and Commercial Association, citing increased transportation costs, worked together to have restricted coastal shipping suspended.[84]

Overseas shipping: foreign trade and local prosperity

An economy oriented toward exportation and importation hinged on overseas shipping. The introduction of the steamer greatly cut sailing time to Brazil and, perhaps even more important, made possible regularly scheduled service. It contributed greatly to the impressive growth of Brazilian trade in the 1850s and its steady increase thenceforth. Once

---

Associação Comercial de Pernambuco, *Relatório de 1868*, p. 9; Associação Comercial do Maranhão, *Relatório de 1867*, p. 14.

78. *RMF, 1898*, p. 270.

79. Commercial Association of Pará to President of Province, Belém, Oct. 31, 1870, *Relatório de 1871*, Anexos, pp. 5–8; Commercial Association of Pernambuco to President of Province, Recife, Nov. 17, 1870, *Relatório de 1871*, pp. 29–32; Associação Comercial do Rio de Janeiro, *Relatório de 1871*, p. 4; Associação Comercial da Bahia, *Relatório de 1870*, pp. 6–7, 76–78.

80. Associação Comercial do Rio de Janeiro, *Resposta da Associação Comercial do Rio de Janeiro aos Quesitos da Comissão Parlamentar de Inquérito* (Rio de Janeiro: Montenegro, 1883), p. 23; Jerônimo de Viveiros, *História do Comércio do Maranhão, 1612–1895* (São Luís: Associação Comercial do Maranhão, 1954), II: 462; Brazil, Congresso, Comissão Parlamentar de Inquérito, *Informações Apresentadas*, pp. 166, 206, 458, 472, 485.

81. Ibid., p. 206.

82. Minutes, meeting of Feb. 24, 1891, Livro de Atas, 1890–1896, AACRJ, p. 37; *RMF, 1895*, p. 37.

83. *RMF, 1898*, p. 271.

84. Minutes, meeting of Nov. 7, 1899, Livro de Atas da ACAP, 1895–1903, AACP, p. 48; Commercial Association of Pernambuco to Brazilian Congress, Sept. 28, 1898, *Relatório de 1899*, pp. 102–105.

more the Commercial Association of Rio de Janeiro helped introduce a communications innovation, persuading the British Royal Mail Line to establish regular voyages to Rio in 1851.[85] Even before the first steam-powered voyage to Brazil in 1846, the commercial associations of Rio de Janeiro, Pernambuco, and Bahia (then Brazil's only business interest groups) had been making tentative scheduling arrangements with prospective steamship lines.[86] The pioneer 1851 voyage established another pattern as well: it was subsidized by both Brazilian and British governments.[87] Subsidies for regularly scheduled routes would, as in many countries, become common. Brazil's business interest groups attempted to attract new steamer lines, to persuade existing lines to make their entrepôt a port of call, and to regulate stopovers and other aspects of service, again using their prerogative of recommending government subsidies and other privileges. In such recommendations, the groups tried to be even-handed, hoping to maintain a situation of balanced competition.

Being a port of call for major steamer lines was obviously essential for any port that aspired to be an entrepôt. Business interest groups tried to attract lines to their port by emphasizing the importance of its trade, pledging the support of their membership, and promising government subsidies. The Commercial Association of Maceió, for example, made possible in 1878 the first direct communication between that obscure port and Europe through the entreaties of a member before the Royal Mail Line in London and the arrangement of a bountiful subsidy from its province.[88] The groups commonly were generous in their recommendations for subsidies or other aid. The Commercial Association of Pôrto Alegre urged the imperial government to award a line between Germany and the Province of Rio Grande do Sul "any aid the enterprise happens to request."[89] State funding for a line to the Mediterranean promoted by the Commercial Association of Pará in 1890 amounted to more than a third of the total the province spent to support twenty-three separate shipping routes.[90] The groups were equally resolute that established service to their entrepôt be maintained. Taking away a subsidy, like its awarding, could be used as a motivation. The Commercial Association of Pará reversed the decision of a

85. Beltrão, "Civismo da Praça," 75.
86. Minutes, meeting of Sept. 22, 1845, Livro 1 de Atas, AACB, p. 186. The Liverpool vessel *Antelope* made the first steam-powered voyage to Brazil in 1846. Porter to Foreign Office, Salvador, Nov. 11, 1846, PRO/FO 13/239, fl. 223.
87. Alan K. Manchester, *British Preëminence in Brazil: Its Rise and Decline. A Study in European Expansion* (Chapel Hill: University of North Carolina Press, 1938), p. 320.
88. Moacir Medeiros de Santa Ana, *Contribuição 'a História do Açúcar em Alagôas* (Recife: Instituto do Açúcar e do Alcool, 1970), p. 319.
89. Commercial Association of Pôrto Alegre to President of Province, Pôrto Alegre, Sept. 23, 1872, *Relatório de 1872–1873*, p. 9.
90. Commercial Association of Pará to Governor of State, Belém, July 23, 1890, *Relatório de 1891*, pp. 12–15; Associação Comercial do Pará, *Relatório de 1898*, Anexo 11, p. 37.

United States line to reduce service to Belém in 1871 by appealing for withdrawal of the company's imperial government subsidy.[91]

Business interest groups were instrumental in establishing regular steamer connections between Brazil and the United States. They were intrigued by the growing importance of the latter as a market for Brazilian exports and perhaps seeking an alternative to British economic preponderance. Regular service was impossible without government subsidies because competition kept freights low, passengers were few, and coffee export, the bulk of trade between the two nations, was important only half the year.[92] Petitions from the commercial associations of Rio de Janeiro and Bahia led to a healthy subsidy enabling a United States line to begin service in 1866.[93] Other associations urged their provinces at various times to add subsidies. But regular steamer connections were to be frequently interrupted because of the marginal profitability of the route and the failure of the U.S. government, unlike Brazil's other trading partners, to subsidize a national line.[94] A halt in service between 1881 and 1883 resulted from the successful campaign of the Commercial Association of Maranhão to make São Luís a mandatory port of call.[95] When the steamer line objected to stopping there, citing the difficulty of large ships using the port, the imperial government cut off its subsidy.[96] Steamer connection between the two countries was neither solidly established nor economically important during the nineteenth century, but the efforts of business interest groups to promote it paved the way for the large-scale direct trade of the twentieth century.

The regulation of scheduled overseas shipping by business interest groups presented problems not found with other communications. It was carried on almost exclusively by well-established foreign companies whose business in any one entrepôt was not of central importance. Only where a local subsidy was vital to a company's transatlantic operations, as with the line between Belém and the Mediterranean, did a business interest group (in this case the Commercial Association of Pará) evaluate freights and passenger fares for local authorities.[97] As in coastal shipping, the prob-

91. Commercial Association of Pará to President of Province, Belém, Aug. 6, 1870, *Relatório de 1871*, p. 10, Anexo, pp. 1–4.
92. Smith, *Brazil, Amazons and Coast*, p. 503.
93. Minutes, meeting of May 18, 1865, Livro 3 de Atas, AACB, p. 63; Aureliano Cândido Tavares Bastos, *Discursos Parliamentares* (Brasília: Senado Federal, 1977), p. 319; Brazil, laws, statutes, etc., *Leis, 1866*, Part 2: 93–97.
94. Dockery to Department of State, Rio de Janeiro, March 15, 1890, *USRC*, XXXIII, no. 116 (May 1890): 36–37; William Eleroy Curtis, *Trade and Transportation Between the United States and Spanish America* (Washington: Government Printing Office, 1889), p. 200.
95. For early lobbying efforts, see *O País*, Aug. 31, 1865, p. 2; Commercial Association of Maranhão to C. J. Harrah, São Luís, July 4, 1865, *Relatório de 1867*, pp. 55–60. By 1880 the stop at São Luís had been made compulsory.
96. *RMACOP, Anexos ao Relatório de 1881*, p. 13.
97. Associação Comercial do Pará, *Relatório de 1898*, p. 15.

lems of cutting stopover time and closing mail pouches complicated overseas service. Business interest groups petitioned variously a company's local agents or headquarters abroad, provincial or national authorities if the line was subsidized, and in one case the Director General of British Mail.[98] The commercial associations of Rio de Janeiro and Bahia had to petition both the company and the Emperor to compel the French line Messageries Imperiales to set a fixed schedule of departures in 1870 and again in 1888.[99]

As in the case with the railroad, the encouragement and regulation of steam navigation by business interest groups significantly helped shape its operations in Brazil. And as in the introduction of the railroad, entrepôt rivalry very much affected the attitudes of the groups. In this case, however, viable shipping networks were established, and there was less harm to the process of national integration and development.

The importance of information: telegraph, underseas cable, telephone, and mail

For Brazil's business elite, transmission of information was scarcely less important than transmission of goods. The invention of the telegraph and its development into the underseas cable had a revolutionary impact on business. It meant that information no longer traveled at the slow pace of surface transportation. Business interest groups were quick to see the implications of the new invention. They helped introduce and regulate the telegraph and the underseas cable, even aiding in funding the former. They also helped standardize ordinary mail service.

One of the first uses to which the telegraph was put in Brazil was to send news of incoming shipping to the headquarters of commercial associations, where interested merchants were gathered. It usually replaced systems of semaphores, whose maintenance also had been a concern of the associations. In 1862 the Commercial Association of Rio de Janeiro welcomed the government's suggestion that a telegraph station be placed on top of its headquarters to receive shipping news transmitted from nearby hills and the following year itself proposed extending a line further up the coast for earlier notice.[100] By 1871, the association was connected with the Cabo Frio telegraph station, some one hundred kilometers to the east on Rio's seaward approaches, and had devised, with the help of the

98. For the last, Associação Comercial de Pernambuco, *Relatório de 1869*, p. 11.
99. Associação Comercial do Rio de Janeiro, *Relatório de 1870*, p. 8, and *Relatório de 1890*, pp. 21–23; Minutes, meeting of Jan. 10, 1868, Livro 3 de Atas, AACB, p. 119; Commercial Association of Bahia to Emperor Pedro II, Salvador, Jan. 29, 1870, *Relatório de 1870*, pp. 45–47.
100. Manuel Duarte Moreira de Azevedo, "A Praça do Comércio: Écos de um Pasado Glorioso," *Boletim Semanal da Associação Comercial do Rio de Janeiro*, I, no. 5 (Nov. 8, 1935):15–16.

Royal Mail Line, a system of flag signals for ships to transmit information.[101]

The eagerness of business interest groups to introduce the telegraph was indicated by a willingness to use their own funds, a willingness the more unusual because Brazil's telegraph lines were constructed by the imperial government. In 1867 the Commercial Association of Rio de Janeiro built its own telegraph station on land ceded by the Empire and opened it to the public.[102] Other participation by business interest groups in constructing telegraph facilities resulted from the effort of Brazil's Director General of Telegraphs, Dr. Guilherme S. Capanema, to compensate for inadequate government funding. In 1868 he requested the Commercial Association of Pernambuco to aid in constructing a line from Rio to Recife. The Pernambuco group, marshaling the resources of wealthy Pernambucans and the provincial government, swiftly organized a private company for the task.[103] Despite the endorsement of Pernambuco's president of province, the imperial government twice rejected the association's offer to undertake construction.[104] The government was determined that telegraph construction remain in the hands of the state and was uncertain of its legal right to acquire private lines. In 1871 the Pernambuco association loaned funds to the government, as did apparently the Commercial Association of Bahia, to be repaid from income from the line.[105]

Director General of Telegraphs Capanema had less success with a similar appeal in 1870 to the Rio Grande do Sul commercial associations of Pôrto Alegre, Pelotas, and Rio Grande. The latter two responded with funds, but the Pôrto Alegre group only with a curt refusal.[106] Given the virulence of entrepôt rivalry, Capanema should have known better than to request telegraph building funds from the Pôrto Alegre association. The line from Rio had already reached that port and its commercial association had no desire to see telegraph service extended southward to entrepôt rivals Pelotas and Rio Grande. Nor was entrepôt competition dormant

101. Associação Comercial do Rio de Janeiro, *Relatório de 1871*, p. 4.
102. Eudes Barros, *A Associação Comercial no Império e na República* (2d ed. rev.; Rio de Janeiro: Olímpica, 1975), pp. 100–101. The station and land were expropriated by the government in 1869 for urban remodeling.
103. Minutes, general assembly of April 15, 1868, Livro 3 de Atas, AACP, pp. 8–10.
104. Commercial Association of Pernambuco to Brazilian Parliament, Recife, no date, 1869, *Relatório de 1869*, Anexo, pp. 14; Commercial Association of Pernambuco to Interim Minister of Agriculture, Commerce, and Public Works, Recife, Jan. 25, 1871, *Relatório de 1871*, pp. 27–29.
105. Commercial Association of Pernambuco to Interim Minister of Agriculture, Commerce, and Public Works, Recife, Jan. 25, 1871, *Relatório de 1871*, p. 28; Minutes, meeting of Jan. 25, 1871, Livro 3 de Atas, AACB, p. 69; Commercial Association of Bahia to Minister of Agriculture, Commerce, and Public Works, Salvador, March 2, 1871, *Relatório de 1871*, p. 23.
106. Commercial Association of Bahia to Minister of Agriculture, Commerce, and Public Works, Salvador, March 2, 1871, *Relatório de 1871*, p. 23; Commercial Association of Pôrto Alegre to Guilherme S. de Capanema, Director General of Telegraphs, Pôrto Alegre, April 6, 1870, *Relatório de 1870*, Doc. no. 5, unpaginated.

elsewhere regarding the telegraph. Fearing further loss of trade in the Province of Piauí, the Commercial Association of Maranhão implored Pedro II in 1878 not to let the São Luís telegraph connection be built via rival entrepôt Fortaleza, although it is difficult to imagine what other route it could have taken.[107]

Unlike most other communications systems, business interest groups regulated telegraph service little. Only the Commercial Association of Rio de Janeiro was asked by the central government to assess its table of telegraph rates. The Rio group also suggested improvements in the government company's billing and record keeping, based on European models with which its members were familiar.[108] Long-distance business communications were threatened in 1893 by a revolt in Rio Grande do Sul and by Brazil's navy, which blockaded Rio de Janeiro and demanded President Floriano Peixoto resign. The commercial associations of Pernambuco and Rio de Janeiro, which sent a delegation to plead with the beleaguered Peixoto, were able to keep most of the country's telegraph lines open. To avoid all suspicion of using the telegraph to give information to the rebels, the associations offered to eliminate all use of abbreviations and have telegrams censored by their directors as well as by government officials.[109]

The telegraph was even more revolutionary under the ocean than on land. By putting merchants in almost immediate contact with markets and suppliers, the underseas cable revolutionized the pace of information in overseas commerce. News no longer came in the sudden bursts that could immediately alter the climate of business opinion and entail huge losses. Export-import commerce became less risky; if fewer windfall profits were made, fewer crippling losses were taken. In addition, business interest groups unhappy with the service of the government-owned land telegraph company looked forward to using the British-controlled underseas cable to communicate with other Brazilian coastal cities.

The establishment of underseas cable connections between Europe and the United States in the 1860s spurred desires for the same in Brazil. In 1870 the Commercial Association of Rio de Janeiro began to lobby for state action.[110] In 1872 the imperial government signed with a British-backed company organized by Viscount Mauá for a cable connecting

107. Commercial Association of Maranhão to Emperor Pedro II, São Luís, April 20, 1878, *Relatório de 1879*, pp. 34–37.
108. Commercial Association of Rio de Janeiro to Director General of Telegraphs, Rio de Janeiro, Aug. 4, 1882, *Relatório de 1882–1883*, p. 11.
109. Commercial Association of Rio de Janeiro to Floriano Peixoto, Vice-President of Republic, Rio de Janeiro, July 15, 1893, *Relatório de 1901*, Anexos, 1893, p. 9; Minutes, meeting of July 20, 1893, Livro de Atas, 1890–1896, AACRJ, p. 77; Governor of Pernambuco to Minister of Finance, Recife, Sept. 15, 1893, in Associação Comercial de Pernambuco, *Relatório de 1894*, p. 44.
110. Barros, *Associação Comercial*, p. 120.

Brazil and Europe via Recife. The laying of the cable proceeded quickly, and rarely did business interest groups need to act to ensure connections for their entrepôt. An exception was the Commercial Association of Maranhão, which had to apply pressure through government on the underseas cable company, by 1874 entirely British-owned, to prevent São Luís being bypassed.[111] To avoid the consequences of breakage, the Commercial Association of Rio de Janeiro in 1889 requested the Empire grant a concession for a second transatlantic cable to the Western and Brazilian Telegraph Company, as it was now called, and the Amazonas organization in 1899 urged its province to accept another British company's bid for a line alternate to the cable that had reached Manaus in 1896.[112] Well aware of the implications of wire contact with Europe, business interest groups made the underseas cable welcome. The Board of Directors and much of the membership of the Commercial Association of Bahia chartered a coastal liner to greet the cable-laying ship as it approached Salvador. That association also made its headquarters a cable terminus, Salvador's first. The Commercial Association of Rio de Janeiro celebrated the arrival of the cable with a ball attended by the Emperor, cabinet ministers, and foreign diplomatic corps.[113]

In attempting to regulate underseas cable service, generally unsubsidized, the prerogatives of business interest groups did not come into play. The groups, however, were usually able to petition the companies successfully about rates and service. If not, even the giant Western and Brazilian Company could be moved by invoking the intercession of the imperial government. Despite lapses in service, mostly during the initial years, the underseas cable and the telegraph generally fulfilled the high expectations of business interest groups and significantly changed overseas trade.

As in the rest of the world, telephone service in Brazil began on a local, rather than a long-distance basis and thus initially was not as important to the business elite as other communications systems. The commercial associations of Rio de Janeiro and Santos, however, were among the first institutions to enjoy its use. In 1881 and 1883, respectively, local companies installed telephones free of charge in the headquarters of both, in order to publicize the new device.[114] Mail was more vital. Business interest groups usually demanded their city's central post office be near

111. Associação Comercial do Maranhão, *Relatório de 1874*, p. 9.
112. Commercial Association of Rio de Janeiro to Minister of Agriculture, Commerce, and Public Works, Rio de Janeiro, Sept. 9, 1889, *Relatório de 1890*, p. 28; Commercial Association of Amazonas to Governor of State, Manaus, Jan. 10, 1899, Associação Comercial do Amazonas, *Primeiro Centenário*, p. 55.
113. Associação Comercial do Rio de Janeiro, *Relatório de 1874*, pp. 11–13.
114. Associação Comercial do Rio de Janeiro, *Relatório de 1881*, p. 13; Minutes, meeting of May 9, 1883, Livro de Atas, 1874–1894, AACS, p. 76.

their headquarters and that postal facilities be abundant wherever mercantile firms were located. By 1875, six of Salvador's ten mailmen worked in
its commercial district, despite the area's few permanent residents.[115] The
Commercial Association of Pôrto Alegre fought to retain that entrepôt's
extraordinary privilege of having mail from the La Plata area brought by
Brazilian warship from the port of Rio Grande as soon as it arrived.[116]

All business interest groups wanted mail service to be faster, cheaper,
and more punctual. They bombarded postal authorities with petitions and
suggestions to that end and protested regulations that slowed mail or
made it more costly. The Commercial Association of Santos had a particular interest in improving postal service because it mailed samples of coffee
to firms and to other business interest groups abroad and in Brazil.[117] It
campaigned for better salaries for postal employees and, having argued
successfully in 1898 for improvements in the Santos Post Office, which
the government refused to remunerate, paid for them, plus a bonus for the
postmaster, itself.[118]

Brazil's nineteenth-century business interest groups were as much absorbed by the movement of information as by the movement of goods.
Their realization of its importance was shown by a willingness to spend
their own funds on information facilities. The revolutionary improvements in overseas trade brought by the telegraph and underseas cable
justified their efforts.

Results: railroad problems and regionalism

The role of business interest groups in Brazilian communications in the
nineteenth century had a varying effect on development. The groups were
most successful in helping introduce and regulate the steamship in its
various forms and the land telegraph and underseas cable. These innovations revolutionized the conduct of business and greatly benefited the
Brazilian economy. Localism influenced group policies, but did not prevent effective national networks from being set up. It was with the railroad that business interest group policies on communications were least
fruitful. One consequence of their overenthusiasm for the railroad was the
neglect of road building. Brazilian roads remained notoriously few, poorly

115. Ferreira, *Província da Bahia*, p. 71; Commercial Association of Bahia to Administrator of Mails
    (Correio Geral), Salvador, Sept. 25, 1872, *Relatório de 1873*, p. 46.
116. Commercial Association of Pôrto Alegre to President of Province, Pôrto Alegre, Sept. 23, 1872,
    Relatório de 1872–1873, p. 8.
117. Associação Comercial de Santos, *Relatório de 1882*, pp. 8–9, and *Relatório de 1887*, pp. 7–8.
118. Commercial Association of Santos to Minister of Agriculture, Commerce, and Public Works,
    Santos, no date, 1876, *Relatório de 1876*, Anexo no. 2, p. 3; Commercial Association of Santos
    to Minister of Interior, Santos, May 11, 1893, *Relatório de 1893*, p. 149; Minutes, meeting of
    Nov. 24, 1898, Livro de Atas, 1894–1904, AACS, p. 36.

built, and badly maintained until well into the twentieth century. The railroad itself turned out to have an uneven geographical impact. It enabled the rapid spread of coffee cultivation in the Southeast and aided the rise of industry there and in the South.[119] In the Northeast and North, despite some notable benefits, freights and fares remained high, service a cause of continual complaint, and most lines unprofitable.[120] It was in those areas that the influence of business interest groups on construction had been strongest.

A basic problem of Brazilian railroads was an absence of overall planning, reflecting a vision of transportation development almost purely local. Signaling this lack of interest in integration, seven different gauges were in use in Brazil as of 1890, sometimes even mandating transfers of cargo on the same line.[121] Many lines penetrated regions of dubious economic potential. At fault for much of the inept planning of Brazil's railways was government payment of guaranteed interest on capital, which business interest groups had at first wholeheartedly backed. It encouraged overcapitalization and overconstruction, leading to the incongruous sight of ornamental stonework gracing railroad bridges in the nation's vacant interior.[122] Worse, guaranteed interest made a railroad's profitability, service, and role in economic development irrelevant. Most entrepreneurs receiving this largesse were foreign, usually British. An envious United States consul noted: "These capitalists . . . care or trouble themselves very little as to the practicability or success of these enterprises; all they care for is to build and equip them, with a sharp look-out for the guarantee. Have we no live men equal to the occasion?"[123] Later

119. São Paulo, Presidente da Província, *Relatório Apresentado à Assembléia Legislativa Provincial de S. Paulo pelo Presidente da Província o Exm. Sr. Dr. Sebastião José Pereira em 2 de Fevereiro de 1876* (São Paulo: Diário, 1876), p. 13. Robert H. Mattoon, Jr., "Railroads, Coffee, and Big Business in São Paulo, Brazil," *HAHR*, 57 (May 1977): 273–295. For industry, see Colin M. Lewis, "Railways and Industrialization: Argentina and Brazil, 1870–1929, " in *Latin America: Economic Imperialism and the State*, eds. Christopher Abel and Colin M. Lewis (London: Athlone, 1985), pp. 199–230.

120. As of 1897, only seven of nineteen lines in the Northeast and North were profitable. "Railways in Brazil," Dawson to Department of State, Rio de Janeiro, no date, *USRC*, LVIII, no. 239 (Aug. 1900): 437–439. For the role of the railroad in expanding sugar growing in Pernambuco, see Eisenberg, *Sugar in Pernambuco*, p. 125; Cabral de Melo, *Norte Agrário*, pp. 207–208; Jaime Reis, "From Banguê to Usina: Pernambuco, 1850–1920," in *Land and Labour in Latin America*, eds. Kenneth Duncan and Ian Rutledge (Cambridge: Cambridge University Press, 1977), p. 379.

121. Adams to Department of State, Rio de Janeiro, June 1, 1890, *USRC*, XXXIV, no. 120 (Sept. 1890): 9. For prolongations different from their trunk lines, see Francisco Barreto Picanço da Costa, *Estradas de Ferro: Vários Estudos* (Rio de Janeiro: Machado, 1887), p. 49, and *Viação Ferrea do Brasil: Descrição Técnica e Estatística de Todas as Nossas Estradas de Ferro* (Rio de Janeiro: Machado, 1884), p. 64.

122. Picanço da Costa, *Vários Estudos*, pp. 186–187.

123. Comstett to Department of State, Desterro, Sept. 10, 1882, *USRC*, VIII, no. 26 (Dec. 1882): 312.

attempts to counteract such abuses by awarding a fixed subsidy per kilometer also failed. Railroad companies built the longest possible line at the lowest possible cost; track snaked to its destination.[124] Another alternative, encouraged almost in desperation by some business interest groups, was central government building and operation of railroads. These lines were almost inevitably unprofitable.[125] Such railroad jobs, like other government employment, were rewards for political influence or political service; government lines were badly overstaffed.

Whether government-owned or receiving guaranteed interest and other support, Brazil's nineteenth-century railroads were a tremendous drain on public funds. As of 1897 only thirty of sixty-two railroads made a profit and some had expenditures up to three or more times their income.[126] The true extent of the railway burden is difficult to discern from budget information, but it may have reached one-quarter of general revenue during the last fifteen years of the Empire.[127] Railway expenses also were a major component of provincial debt.[128]

Because most guaranteed interest on capital was payable in gold, the depreciation of the *mil-reis* after 1889 vastly increased its burden. By 1898 such payments came to the staggering proportion of nearly one-third of annual central government expenditures.[129] In 1901 the Republic after negotiations expropriated the twelve foreign railways that enjoyed guaranteed interest on capital and then leased most to foreign companies rather than operating them itself. The phase of supporting railway expansion through guaranteed interest on capital had ended. Although concrete

124. Pierre Denis, *Brazil*, trans. Bernard Miall (London: T. Fisher Unwin, 1911), p. 109.
125. Of nine government lines in the mid-1880s, only the Dom Pedro II usually showed a profit. Picanço da Costa, *Vários Estudos*, p. 47; Consul-General Armstrong to Department of State, Rio de Janeiro, June 1, 1889, *USRC*, XXX, no. 105 (May 1889): 217.
126. "Railways in Brazil," Dawson to Department of State, Rio de Janeiro, no date, *USRC*, LVIII, no. 239 (Aug. 1900): 437–439. Two Northeastern lines had expenses three, and one four, times their income. Ibid., pp. 412–413, 427.
127. One calculation put all railway expenses (including the cost of government operation of lines) at one-quarter of general revenue between 1874 and 1884. Great Britain, Foreign Office, *Diplomatic and Consular Reports*, no. 504 (1888): 57. Another calculation showed this same proportion budgeted by the Empire for 1889. Amaro Cavalcanti, *Resenha Financeira do Ex-Império do Brasil em 1889* (Rio de Janeiro: Imprensa Nacional, 1890), p. 16. Roberto Fendt Júnior maintains guaranteeing interest on investment was cheaper in the long run than financing construction through a European loan. "Investimentos Inglêses no Brasil, 1870–1913: Uma Avaliação da Política Brasileira," *Revista Brasileira de Economia*, 31 (July–Sept. 1977): 535–536.
128. Guaranteed interest on a single line comprised seventy percent of São Paulo's public debt as of 1886. Brazil, Conselho de Ministros, *Breve Notícia do Estado Financeiro das Províncias, Organisada por Ordem do Barão de Cotegipe, Presidente do Conselho de Ministros* (Rio de Janeiro: Imprensa Nacional, 1887), Quadro no. 2, unpaginated. Railroad expenses were fifty-six percent of Bahia's total debt in 1888 and were earlier cited as the chief reason for the province's financial crisis. Bahia, Presidente da Província, *Relatório de 1889*, p. 8, and *Relatório de 1885*, p. 132.
129. Julian Smith Duncan, *Public and Private Operation of Railroads in Brazil*, (New York: Columbia University Press, 1932), p. 47.

benefits had come, the results were not proportionate to expenditure. The burden of guaranteed interest also diverted funds more profitably spent on other forms of transportation or even on more rational planning of railroad building itself. Part of the blame must fall on those business interest groups that relentlessly promoted the bestowal of guaranteed interest, subsidies, and other aid for lines within their trade area.

The groups' obsession with railroad construction had been fed by two expectations. One was personal gain by business interest group leaders who were directors and stockholders of railway companies. Four of six members of the Committee for Distribution of Stock of Bahia's woeful Salvador to São Francisco River line, for example, were present or future directors of the Commercial Association of Bahia.[130] Guaranteed interest on capital, subsidies, and loans minimized the entrepreneur's risk and protected the investor against loss. The other expectation was of grandiose local economic expansion. The business elites of Rio de Janeiro, Salvador, and Recife looked forward to transcontinental rail lines connecting their entrepôts with ports in Chile and Peru – absurdly ambitious projects never undertaken.[131] The Recife line, proclaimed the President of the Commercial Association of Pernambuco in 1891, would make that city the "commercial emporium" not only of South America, but perhaps "of the entire world in the future."[132]

There is little doubt that the localist vision of business interest groups contributed toward a persisting absence of national economic integration. It is common among historians to characterize Brazil in the nineteenth century and well into the twentieth as a conglomerate of separate regional economies depending on overseas trade and too poorly interconnected to stimulate internal commerce. Such divisions strengthened external dependency and impeded industrial development by blocking the creation of a true national market. Brazil's major rail and highway systems were not linked until after World War II. A 1974 survey of Brazilian geography noted: "For many the lights of opportunity are only now beginning to flicker on, as physical unity becomes a reality for the first time in Brazil's long history."[133]

The role of business interest groups in introducing the communications innovations of the nineteenth century into Brazil highlighted some of

130. *Diário da Bahia* (Salvador), April 14, 1856, p. 1.
131. André Przewodowski, "Comunicação Entre a Cidade da Bahia e a Vila de Juazeiro," *Revista do Instituto Histórico e Geográfico Brasileiro*, 10 (1848): 376; Irineo Evangelista de Souza, Visconde de Mauá, *Autobiografia (Exposição aos Credores e ao Público), Seguida de "O Meio Circulante no Brasil,"* ed. Cláudio Ganns (2d ed.; Rio de Janeiro: Zélio Valverde, 1942), p. 198n.; Associação Comercial de Pernambuco, *Relatório de 1889*, pp. 40–41.
132. Associação Comercial de Pernambuco, *Relatório de 1891*, p. 41.
133. Janet D. Henshall and R. P. Momsen, Jr., *A Geography of Brazilian Development* (London: G. Bell & Sons, 1974), p. 185.

their characteristics. Their strong foreign connections made them particularly aware of communications improvements and eager to introduce them. Their promotion of the government's role in communications illustrated how readily they could overlook the principles of nineteenth-century economic liberalism. Above all, the policies of business interest groups showed their strong local orientation. Much more focused on regional than on national prosperity and on overseas than on domestic commerce, they had scant interest in integrating communications networks. In general, they had little concern for nationalistic goals. As in agriculture, their role in communications was often one of missed opportunities to enhance national economic development.

10

Port areas and harbors: efficiency and rivalry

The traditional prerogatives of Brazilian business interest groups included a large measure of control over the harbors and the waterfront districts of their ports. Business interest groups had helped supervise these areas from medieval times with the Spanish consulados to the nineteenth century with the Anglo-Saxon chambers of commerce. Both central and provincial governments recognized their right to advise on and assess all matters relating to the waterfront and harbor of their entrepôt. Business interest groups could also offer the expertise of a membership familiar with water-borne trade. As with most other prerogatives, group authority over these areas was customary, not statutory. It was shared with two government agencies, the customs house (*alfândega*) and the Port Authority (*Capitania do Pôrto*, later *Inspetor do Arsenal*). The three did not always agree on the needs of the area, and conflicts were frequent. The general aim of business interest groups – the commercial associations in particular – was to make seaborne commerce in their entrepôts as cheap, efficient, and safe as possible. They were driven by rivalry with competing entrepôts to attract shipping and to procure a competitive edge that would expand their trade areas. Such policies helped determine geographical patterns of development.

Safe and easy access for ships was primary for ports and for their business interest groups. The groups recommended lanes of access and exit and anchorages for shipping, and helped draw up port regulations.[1] They supervised navigational safety, not only for their immediate harbors, but for distant approaches such as the mouths of the Amazon River and Patos Lake (*Lagôa dos Patos*) in Rio Grande do Sul. They recommended locations for lighthouses and buoys and notified authorities of the location of submerged wrecks and other navigational hazards.[2] They acted as

1. For example, Captain, Port of Fortaleza, to Commercial Association of Ceará, Fortaleza, March 29, 1867, *Relatório da Associação Comercial do Ceará, 1867* (Fortaleza: Cearense, 1867), p. 16; Minutes, meeting of Aug. 10, 1852, Livro 2 de Atas, AACP, p. 9; Minutes, meeting of Feb. 19, 1841, Livro 1 de Atas, AACB, p. 15.
2. For example, Associação Comercial do Pará, *Relatório da Comissão da Praça do Comércio do Pará,*

intermediaries when ship captains, especially foreign ones, complained to government about unsafe conditions. Finally, they worked with authorities to define the precise responsibilities of all in the case of vessels in trouble or shipwreck.[3] Situations such as that in Recife in 1880 when the tugboat service refused to aid a British vessel in distress unless its agent paid a fee beforehand were both infuriating and embarrassing to local business communities.

Docking and loading facilities were crucial to port efficiency and entrepôt competitiveness. Local business interest groups customarily were consulted on new construction or other waterfront changes by government or private companies and usually appear to have held de facto veto power. They also recommended locations for passenger movement. Business interest groups frequently petitioned for enlargement and improvement of docking facilities, as both trade and the size of vessels increased rapidly during the century. Occasionally when government action was delayed by lack of funds or bureaucratic sloth, business interest groups or business communities built or contributed to the building of quays.[4] The problem of inadequate docking facilities was particularly acute in some areas. The Commercial Association of Pará, for example, had to call for replacement of a new customs house wharf for which it had successfully petitioned, even before the wharf's completion in 1875. By the time the larger substitute was finished in 1884 it, too, was already inadequate for Belém's volume of trade, and the association resumed campaigning for another.[5]

Business interest groups also exercised control over port services. They assessed the charges for them and determined whether such fees were to be paid by merchants or by ships' agents. Much as they did for coastal and river steamer service, the groups recommended to provincial governments authorization and the awarding of subsidies and privileges for tugboat companies. Of even greater concern to business interest groups was lighterage. Most of Brazil's ports used lighters to move goods from ship to

Apresentado em Assembléia Geral de 8 de Janeiro de 1880 (Belém: Comércio do Pará, 1880), pp. 6–7; Commercial Association of Pôrto Alegre to President of Province, Pôrto Alegre, Feb. 5, 1870, *Relatório da Praça do Comércio de Pôrto Alegre do Ano de 1870* (Pôrto Alegre: Jornal do Comércio, 1871), Doc. no. 2, unpaginated.

3. Commercial Association of Santos to President of Province, Santos, Jan. 4, 1875, *Relatório da Associação Commercial de Santos Apresentado em Sessão Extraordinária da Assembléia Geral em 29 de Janeiro de 1876 e Parecer da Comissão de Exame de Contas* (Rio de Janeiro: Perseverança, 1876), Anexo no. 1, unpaginated; Minutes, meeting of Nov. 2, 1880, Livro 5 de Atas, AACP, p. 35.

4. Jerônimo de Viveiros, *História do Comércio do Maranhão, 1612–1895* (São Luís: Associação Comercial do Maranhão, 1954), II: 145; Ernesto Cruz, *História da Belém* (Belém: Universidade Federal do Pará, 1973), II: 330; Bahia, Presidente da Província, *Relatório com que o Exm. Senhor Dr. João Ferreira de Moura Passou a Administração da Província ao Exm. Senhor Dr. José Bonifácio Nascentes d' Azambuja no Dia 21 de Junho de 1867* (Salvador: Tourinho, 1867), p. 10.

5. Associação Comercial do Pará, *Relatório de 1874*, pp. 4–5; Associação Comercial do Pará, *Relatório de 1884*, p. 8; Commercial Association of Pará to Brazilian Parliament, Belém, Nov. 13, 1889, *Relatório de 1890*, p. 14.

dock because they lacked the depth or the facilities to tie up larger ships directly. The groups complained frequently about damage to merchandise in handling and exposure to weather in the lighters. Austrian flour sold for a consistently higher price than the United States variety in Salvador, for example, simply because it was more sturdily packaged and thus less likely to be spoiled in unloading.[6]

Delays caused by inefficient lighter service multiplied weather damage and gave opportunity for theft. At Salvador, where during the last two decades of the century, lighters might wait ten days for unloading, guards on them sometimes were overpowered by gangs of assailants boarding from small boats. The Commercial Association of Bahia had to establish a "safe area" for lighter anchorage at night and initiate police patrols by boat.[7] The use of lighters, and its attendant problems, would continue in most of Brazil's entrepôts until port remodeling enabled large ships to berth at dockside.

The control of business interest groups extended to the wharf warehouses (*trapiches*). This prerogative was one of the few that had specific legal foundation. The commercial associations shared with the chief of customs the responsibility of determining which warehouses were to be used for storage of goods cleared by customs (*alfandegado*).[8] The associations also enjoyed the right, although not in this case specified in law, to determine where explosive, inflammable, or other dangerous materials were to be stored. Gunpowder and other explosives were imported in large quantity into the Northeast for the well-armed and bellicose inhabitants of its interior. As in the case of other waterfront charges, business interest groups had the right to assess warehouse fees. Entrepôt competition dictated keeping them as low as possible. The Commercial Association of Bahia, perhaps because it believed the cost of using Salvador's port already to be uncompetitive, was especially zealous and generally successful in preventing increases in warehouse fees. In 1851 Salvador warehouse owners struck back by locking their facilities. The association responded first by demanding that the president of province use force to open them and then by trying to arrange that Bahian sugar be taken directly from plantation to ship, bypassing the warehouses.[9] Such conflicts were rarer else-

---

6. Prindle to Department of State, Salvador, Nov. 24, 1881, NA/DS T-331, Vol. 4, unpaginated.
7. Minutes, meeting of May 14, 1875, Livro 4 de Atas, AACB, p. 212; Commercial Association of Bahia to Chief of Customs, Salvador, June 21, 1875, *Relatório da Junta Diretora da Associação Comercial da Praça da Bahia, Apresentado em Sessão Ordinária da Assembléia Geral de 21 de Janeiro de 1876* (Salvador: Econômica, 1876), p. 16.
8. Bernardino José Borges, *O Comerciante, ou Completo Manual Instrutivo* (2d ed. rev.; Rio de Janeiro: Eduardo & Henrique Laemmert, 1878), p. 359.
9. Commercial Association of Bahia to President of Province, Salvador, Jan. 14, 1854, Presidência da Província/Govêrno ao Associação Comercial, 1846–1889, AEB, unpaginated; Minutes, meeting of Feb. 13, 1854, Livro 2 de Atas, AACB, pp. 72–73.

where, where warehouse owners had more influence within their local commercial associations.

Grappling with government: the customs house

Much of the expense of port usage consisted of taxes and fees on merchants for the handling of goods in the customs house and on ships for the use of port facilities. While usually not in themselves onerous, such charges could slow local development if they increased port costs in relation to those of competitors. Business interest groups were quick to denounce attempts to tax merchant vessels entering their port to investigate the local market, as well as attempts to tax merchandise already despatched and taxed at other ports. Some handling taxes figured heavily in entrepôt rivalry. An 1877 national "forwarding" (*expediente*) duty of one and one-half to three percent for merchandise already despatched in another port presented a special threat to Santos. Alone among major Brazilian entrepôts, Santos imported at that time four times as much via coastal shipping, almost all from Rio de Janeiro, as it did directly from overseas. The new tax neatly handicapped Santos, most of whose imports paid it, against Rio, none of whose imports did, in the contest for the trade of the Province of São Paulo.[10] Its elimination in 1880 at the repeated insistence of the Commercial Association of Santos represented a major victory for that entrepôt over Rio de Janeiro.

Potentially more expensive than handling taxes and fees was the cost to merchants and ships of customs house delays. Fundamental to them was the inadequate size and equipment of nearly all the nation's customs houses. Complaints from commercial associations were made more urgent by increasing trade even in those entrepôts, such as São Luís, which supposedly were decaying. Association replies to the Parliamentary Committee of Inquiry in 1882 and to a survey by the Minister of Finance in 1893 revealed a nearly universal deficiency in customs house facilities.[11]

Political change was necessary to replace the customs house at Santos. Although built in 1877, it was too small for an importation whose values tripled between 1876–1877 and 1883–1884.[12] Increased expenses reduced calls by steamers and lack of storage space forced the spillover of

10. Commercial Association of Santos to Brazilian Parliament, Santos, July 31, 1877, *Relatório de 1879*, pp. 35–37; Commercial Association of Santos to Brazilian Parliament, Santos, May 5, 1880, *Relatório de 1881*, pp. 51–52.
11. *RMF, 1893*, pp. 161, 167, 170, 175, 183–185, 190; Brazil, Congresso, Comissão Parlamentar de Inquérito, *Informações Apresentadas pela Comissão Parlamentar de Inquérito ao Corpo Legislativo na Terceira Sessão da Décima Oitava Legislatura* (Rio de Janeiro: Tipografia Nacional, 1883), pp. 162–163, 203, 449–451, 469, 478–480.
12. Commercial Association of Santos to Minister of Finance, Feb. 28, 1886, *Relatório de 1887*, p. 44.

merchandise to nearby open areas, with resulting spoilage. The Commercial Association of Santos passed to the Minister of Finance petitions from agents of steamer lines in 1880 and from Santos importers in 1886, as well as its own frequent entreaties, but without result.[13] The coming of the Republic changed the situation. The Commercial Association of Santos boasted directors long active in the Republican cause, whereas its rival, the Commercial Association of Rio de Janeiro, had been embarrassingly close to the monarchy. The first Republican Minister of Finance, Rui Barbosa, was entertained by the Santos association in February 1890. He was shown the customs house, verifying, in his words, "its state of desolation."[14] Rui appointed the President of the Santos group and a director to a four-man committee to plan and supervise the building of a new customs house, its pier, and other supporting construction.[15] Completion of the new facility removed a major obstacle to rapid port movement and marked another major step in Santos's struggle to surpass Rio de Janeiro.

If most of Brazil's customs houses were inadequate, so were their personnel. Business interest groups petitioned frequently for more workers for their customs house and protested vehemently if its staff were cut. Merchants sometimes had to hire their own workers to aid the movement of goods.[16] Entrepôt competition also colored questions of personnel. In 1888, the Commercial Association of Bahia laid much of Salvador's problem in competing with Rio de Janeiro to the latter having twice as many workers in its customs house.[17] Customs house workers were deficient in quality as well as quantity. The Commercial Association of Santos described them in 1880 as "for the most part disabled and unable to find employment elsewhere because of incompetence."[18] Commercial associations responding to the 1882 Parliamentary Committee of Inquiry were virtually unanimous on the necessity of better customs house workers, some even being willing to have worker numbers cut in order to offer better pay.[19] The Republic brought no improvement. Minister of Finance Joaquim Murtinho admitted in 1899 that the customs service was suffering "profound disorganization," as veteran officials had been fired after

13. Ibid., pp. 43–45; Associação Comercial de Santos, *Relatório de 1881*, pp. 11–14.
14. *RMF, 1891*, p. 429.   15. Ibid., pp. 429–430.
16. Associação Comercial de Pernambuco, *Relatório da Direçao da Associação Comercial Beneficente de Pernambuco, Apresentado à Assembléia Geral da Mesma em 7 de Agôsto de 1857* (Recife: Santos, 1857), p. 7; Commercial Association of Santos to Minister of Finance, Santos, Dec. 28, 1880, *Relatório de 1881*, p. 13.
17. Commercial Association of Bahia to Minister of Finance, Salvador, June 27, 1888, *Relatório de 1889*, pp. 46–49, 66–67.
18. Commercial Association of Santos to Minister of Finance, Santos, Dec. 28, 1880, *Relatório de 1881*, p. 13.
19. Brazil, Congresso, Comissão Parlamentar de Inquérito, *Informações Apresentadas*, pp. 162, 202, 449, 465, 478.

the revolution, apparently to make way for Republican political appointees.[20]

Customs regulations also were a universal cause of delay. During the reign of Pedro II customs procedures and severity of enforcement were progressively tightened, and by the 1850s knowledgeable authorities could describe customs officers as "exceedingly particular and frequently unjust."[21] By the end of the Empire, seventeen employee signatures and thirty-six from the despatcher were necessary to despatch an article from the customs house.[22] Merchants faced a host of regulations, some manifestly absurd, such as forbidding lighters with masts to load cargo and refusing payment of duty in banknotes from Brazil's own national bank.[23] The traditional prerogatives of business interest groups provided some control over customs house regulations and procedures. They occasionally were able to change them significantly, either by petition or by working in committee with customs house officers. Entrepôt rivalry also spurred protest against regulations; removal of an obstructive rule in one was felt to give it an edge over competitors still saddled with it. Customs officials, however, tended to see such protests as aimed at facilitating avoidance of duty.

Although frequently denouncing the severity of customs regulations and the difficulty of obtaining even the most justifiable amelioration, business interest groups exaggerated their predicament. They exercised considerable control over customs personnel. Customs officials, like other government employees, received appointments and promotions mainly through family or political influence.[24] Officials could be arbitrarily removed because of the hostility of influential figures or simply to make way for someone better connected. In other words, the influence of business interest groups could be brought to bear on customs officials in the same way as on legislation.

Head-on clashes between business interest groups and chiefs of customs, the most powerful of such officials, were few, but often resolved by the removal of the offending chief of customs.[25] The groups also had less harsh means of winning cooperation. It was customary for government

20. *RMF, 1899*, p. 16.
21. Gillmer to Department of State, Salvador, Oct. 23, 1854, NA/DS T-331, Vol. I, unpaginated.
22. Great Britain, Foreign Office, *Diplomatic and Consular Reports, Miscellaneous Series*, no. 139 (Aug. 1889): 3.
23. Commercial Association of Bahia to Chief of Customs, Salvador, Oct. 24, 1896, *Relatório de 1897*, pp. 207–209; Commercial Association of Santos to Minister of Finance, Santos, March 11, 1877, *Relatório de 1879*, pp. 27–28; Associação Comercial de Santos, *Relatório de 1893*, p. 61.
24. For a discussion of this situation, see Baron Guaí to Viscount Cotegipe, Salvador, Oct. 7, 1884, ABC, AIHGB, lata 38, doc. 12.
25. Minutes, meetings of March 20, 1890 and May 22, 1890, Livro 5 de Atas, AACB, pp. 307, 313; Associação Comercial de Santos, *Relatório de 1893*, pp. 75–77.

officials in contact with businessmen, particularly customs employees, to request from business interest groups a letter of testimony of good service. Such testimony could be valuable in career advancement. Similarly, the groups sometimes rescued customs officials in trouble by favorable public declarations or by a word with superiors. Merchants, through their representative groups, were by no means impotent in their relations with Brazil's customs bureaucracy.

Reducing rivalry to its basics: the right to a customs house

A customs house defined an entrepôt. Only ports with customs houses could engage in direct overseas trade. The policy of both Empire and Republic was to have at least one customs house in each province; more than one was seen as duplication of function and an unnecessary expense. Inferior ports were equipped with a Revenue Board (*Mesa de Rendas*), which collected noncommercial taxes and despatched goods brought from customs house–equipped entrepôts by coastal shipping.[26] The surest way to thwart a potential rival entrepôt was to deny it entrepôt status, that is, a customs house. The question of who was to have a customs house pitted ports and their representative business interest groups against one another in undisguised contention.

One of the bitterest of such contests took place in the last quarter of the century in the Province of Rio Grande do Sul, between the city of Rio Grande, long dominating trade in that province, and challenger Pelotas. The Commercial Association of Rio Grande had already waged a successful campaign to deprive nearby rival São José do Norte of its customs house and thereby its prosperity.[27] However, it was shaken by the upsurge of another entrepôt, Pôrto Alegre, 180 miles northeast, at the end of Patos Lake, whose waters met the sea at Rio Grande. Pôrto Alegre had a customs house but little trade until increased immigration and the dredging of the approaches to its port attracted shipping. During the 1870s, it took the trade of northern Rio Grande do Sul from Rio Grande.[28] A new and closer threat appeared in October 1878, when a Liberal cabinet awarded the Revenue Board of Pelotas the right to despatch goods imported directly from overseas. Having lost the trade of the northern part of its province, the Commercial Association of Rio Grande now faced having

26. Brazil, laws, statutes, etc., *Leis, 1876*, Part 2, II: 852.
27. Associação Comercial de Pelotas, *A Praça do Comércio da Cidade de Pelotas (Província de S. Pedro do Sul): Representação* (Pelotas: Correio Mercantil, 1880), Doc. no. 9, p. 1.
28. Great Britain, Foreign Office, *Diplomatic and Consular Reports*, no. 323 (1888): 3; *RMF, 1882*, p. 17. Between 1872–1873 and 1880–1881, Pôrto Alegre customs house revenue doubled, that of Rio Grande fell by a third, and both sums were nearly identical.

the southern portion go to Pelotas, a thriving meat and hide processing center located between Rio Grande and its hinterland.

Rio Grande found an ally in the Conservative Party and its head Baron Cotegipe, who attacked in Parliament the privilege granted Pelotas. In October 1880, the Commercial Association of Pelotas published a petition requesting its city not only retain its direct importation privilege but be granted a full-fledged customs house.[29] Simultaneously, the Commercial Association of Rio Grande printed a formal demand that Pelotas be stripped of any right to direct overseas trade.[30] The Pelotas association replied with a point-by-point refutation of its rival's arguments.[31] Together with numerous petitions, the three booklets were mailed to Members of Parliament, government officials, and other interest groups. Each association characterized the other's port as a haven for smugglers and unable to handle large ships. The Commercial Association of Pelotas emphasized its port's geographic and economic superiority, which merited Pelotas a customs house according to the principles of free trade and comparative advantage. The Rio Grande Association admitted that granting the right to direct overseas trade to Pelotas meant the "sentence of death" and the "coup de grace" for Rio Grande's prosperity.

Parliament revoked Pelotas's right to import directly from overseas in July 1881. For Cotegipe, leader of the anti-Pelotas movement, the most telling argument of the Rio Grande association was its admission that its port could not compete with Pelotas. The customs house question, he informed the Commercial Association of Pelotas in explaining his position, meant "advantage" for Pelotas, which could continue to rely on meat and hide processing, but "life or death" for Rio Grande.[32] Cotegipe and his supporters beat back new moves to grant Pelotas a customs house in 1882 and 1885.[33] Rio Grande survived as a major entrepôt. This survival demonstrated the importance of the right to a customs house and the key role of business interest groups in determining it. It also showed what little real weight the principles of nineteenth-century economic liberalism, greatly favoring Pelotas, had as a guide to Brazilian economic policy.

Seemingly laid to rest, the question of which ports in Rio Grande do Sul would have a customs house revived with the coming of the Republic.

29. *Praça do Comércio: Representação.*
30. *Representação Dirigida ao Govêrno Imperial pela Associação Comercial da Praça do Rio Grande, Pedindo a Revogação do Decreto N. 7,063 de 21 de Outubro de 1878* (Rio Grande: Echo do Sul, 1880).
31. *Análise 'a Representação que ao Govêrno Imperial Dirigiu à Associação Comercial do Rio Grande Pedindo a Extinção da Mesa de Rendas Alfandegada de Pelotas* (Pelotas: Correio Mercantil, 1880).
32. Baron Cotegipe to Commercial Association of Pelotas, Rio de Janeiro, no date, 1880, ABC, IHGB, lata 76, doc. 94.
33. Municipal Council of Rio Grande to Baron Cotegipe, Rio Grande, Oct. 2, 1882, ABC, AIHGB, lata 76, doc. 95; Commercial Association of Rio Grande to Baron Cotegipe, Rio Grande, Sept. 19, 1885, ABC, AIHGB, lata 76, doc. 97.

Alexandre Cassiano de Nacimento, a Pelotas native serving as interim Minister of Finance, took the opportunity in 1896 to bestow its long-desired customs house.[34] But in 1897 new Minister of Finance Bernardino de Campos, anxious to adhere to the principle of one customs house per state, abolished this facility and also the customs house at Pôrto Alegre.[35] Rio Grande now had its desired monopoly of the state's direct overseas trade, but rejoicing was brief. In 1898 Bernardino de Campos ordered its customs house transferred to decayed former rival São José do Norte, located on the opposite side of the mouth of Patos Lake.[36] Protest led by the Commercial Association of Rio Grande kept the transfer from being made. The Pôrto Alegre association succeeded in keeping the entrepôt status of its city, enlisting the support of Rio Grande do Sul's Governor. Its customs house was restored in October 1899.[37] Pôrto Alegre eventually overshadowed its two rivals in size and commerce, although Pelotas received its long-awaited customs house in 1907.

An equally harsh struggle over the creation of a customs house, led by commercial associations, took place between Santos and São Paulo. The issue divided the state, pitting coastal area against uplands and one of its Senators against the other.[38] São Paulo's drive for a customs house to end its commercial dependency on Santos began when sixty-seven business-men, among them the later founders of the Commercial Association of São Paulo, formally petitioned Parliament in 1888.[39] São Paulo's Commercial Court, on which four founders of the Commercial Association sat or had sat, repeated the 1888 arguments in petitions to Brazil's Congress in 1892.[40] Both groups cited the slow movement of goods in Santos, its recurring yellow fever, its problems with smuggling, and the size and expanding prosperity of São Paulo. The Commercial Association of Rio de Janeiro struck a blow at old rival Santos by endorsing São Paulo's bid.[41]

Congress authorized a customs house for São Paulo, which would enable the greater part of the state's trade to bypass Santos, in 1893. The Commercial Association of Santos resisted with undisguised resentment. In meetings with Treasury officials, in petitions, and in public statements, it blamed the slow movement of goods on its single-track railway connections, cited the improvements resulting from the remodeling of its port,

34. *ACD, 1897,* IV: 496–499.   35. *RMF, 1898,* pp. 478–479, 489–490.
36. *ACD, 1898,* VI: 174.
37. Ibid., III: 219–229; *ACD, 1899,* V: 181–186; *RMF, 1900,* p. 22.
38. Hélio Lobo, *Docas de Santos: Suas Origens, Lutas e Realizações* (Rio de Janeiro: Jornal do Comércio, 1936), p. 95.
39. *ACD, 1888,* VI: 58–59.
40. São Paulo, Secretaria da Justiça, *Relatório Apresentado ao Presidente do Estado de São Paulo pelo Secretário dos Negócios da Justiça Manuel Pessôa de Siqueira Campos em 31 de Março de 1894* (São Paulo: Espíndola, Siqueira, 1894), Anexo no. 5, p. 5; Associação Comercial de São Paulo, *Relatório da Associação Comercial de São Paulo de 1895* (São Paulo: Industrial, 1896), p. 6.
41. Lobo, *Docas de Santos,* p. 87.

and emphasized the waste and inefficiency of duplicating customs houses.[42] It pointedly refused to send representatives to the elaborate (four brass bands, dress coat) ceremonies opening the Commercial Association of São Paulo in 1895.[43] The latter enthusiastically joined the struggle, defending its views in meetings with the Minister of Finance and in petitions, and promoting subscriptions for the Rio newspaper *O País*, the only one in that city supporting São Paulo's customs house.[44]

The Commercial Association of Santos found allies in Bernardino de Campos, Governor of the state, two transatlantic shipping companies, and the Santos Dock Company (*Companhia Docas de Santos*), fearful of losing its handling and storage fees. Early in 1895 they presented an agreement requiring full payment in Santos of all fees for goods destined for São Paulo if despatched in Santos.[45] This neatly nullified the advantage of the new customs house. The Santos Dock Company, however, insisted on collecting storage and handling fees on all goods before the agreement became state law in May 1896. Its action provoked from the two commercial associations meetings with the Minister of Finance, petitions, and heated public statements, Santos in praise, São Paulo in condemnation. São Paulo's hard-won customs house was doomed once Bernardino de Campos became Minister of Finance. Always disliking its duplication with that of Santos, and eager to cut administrative expenses, he abolished it as of January 1898.[46] Santos, like Rio Grande, had met the challenge of a rival by denying it a customs house.

Disputes over customs houses showed entrepôt rivalry and the role of business interest groups in such rivalry at its most blatant. The technicality of having a customs house determined a city's entrepôt status and profoundly affected the prosperity of its neighbors. Both influenced geographical patterns of development.

Squeezing costs and people: port labor

The traditional authority of business interest groups over waterfront and port areas extended to their workers. As with other port expenses, entrepôt rivalry dictated keeping the cost of labor as low as possible. The groups rarely faced organized labor. Scant urbanization, vast geographical distances, and a relatively elastic supply of labor made union organization extremely difficult. Unions with firm organization and an ideological

---

42. *RMF, 1895*, Anexo 1, pp. 3–5; Minutes, meeting of Sept. 11, 1894, Livro de Atas, 1874–1894, AACS, pp. 194–196; Associação Comercial de Santos, *Relatório de 1895*, pp. 6–10.
43. Associação Comercial de São Paulo, *Relatório de 1895*, pp. 11–16.
44. Ibid., pp. 78–83; Minutes, meeting of July 21, 1896, Livro de Atas, 1894–1906, Arquivo da Associação Comercial de São Paulo (hereafter cited as AACSP), São Paulo, p. 4.
45. Associação Comercial de São Paulo, *Relatório de 1895*, pp. 79–80.
46. *RMF, 1898*, pp. 478–479.

stance began only after 1890, and no national labor group appeared until 1903.[47] The wages of urban unskilled workers were low in comparison with the cost of living. In Rio de Janeiro, in the 1880s, common laborers received an equivalent of U.S.$1.30 per day and in the ports of the Northeast probably about a third less.[48] In the Northeast a large reserve of rural poor and relative economic stagnation kept wages in decline during most of the second half of the nineteenth century. The median salary in that region was less than half in 1900 what it had been in 1860.[49]

A focus of labor relations in the ports was a skilled worker element, the pilots (*práticos*). Business interest groups tried to ensure adequate numbers of pilots, to speed their work, and to end the practice of soliciting or extorting gratuities. Pilots were particularly important in harbors of difficult access. In Recife, the harbor of most troublesome entry, the local group placed pilots under tightest control. One of the first acts of the newly created Commercial Association of Pernambuco was to submit regulations for pilotage. It also cut pilot fees, arranged for pilots to be chosen by ships' agents rather than serving in turn, and demanded the government-sponsored pilots' association be disbanded.[50] The Pernambuco association wanted workers to compete against one another and consistently opposed any organization of labor. It justified itself by invoking the precepts of nineteenth-century liberalism.

It applied the same precepts to other port workers. In 1859 it successfully protested a requirement that stevedores register with the Port Authority, because it might bar nonpermanent workers, who could be hired at half the wage.[51] By 1869, however, registration of stevedores was reinstated. In one of Brazil's rare labor disputes during the Empire, Recife stevedores struck that year, demanding a wage increase of fifty percent and the banning of unregistered workers. Appealing to Pernambuco's president of province, the Commercial Association not only broke the strike but succeeded in having stevedoring tasks thrown open to all comers.[52] Although the association kept the port of Recife's wage costs low, its prerogatives with labor were not always detrimental to workers. In 1884

---

47. Edgard Carone, *Movimento Operário no Brasil* (São Paulo: DIFEL, 1979), pp. 5, 17; Philippe C. Schmitter, *Interest Conflict and Political Change in Brazil* (Stanford, Calif.: Stanford University Press, 1971), p. 140.
48. Consul-General Andrews to Department of State, Rio de Janeiro, no date, 1884, *USRC*, XII, no. 40 (April 1884): 200. David Denslow, "As Exportações e a Origem do Padrão de Industrialização Regional do Brasil," in *Dimensões do Desenvolvimento Brasileiro*, eds. Werner Baer, Pedro Pinches Geiger, and Paulo Roberto Haddad (Rio de Janeiro: Campus, 1978), p. 25.
49. Denslow, "As Exportações e a Origem," p. 25.
50. For example, Minutes, meeting of Sept. 2, 1845, Livro 1 de Atas, AACP, p. 35; Associação Comercial de Pernambuco, *Relatório de 1857*, p. 4 and *Relatório de 1864*, pp. 5–6.
51. Minutes, meeting of July 2, 1859, Livro 2 de Atas, AACP, p. 105.
52. Commercial Association of Pernambuco to President of Province, Recife, Aug. 12, 1869, *Relatório de 1870*, pp. 7, 37.

it successfully appealed to the Emperor and to Parliament to pay customs house manual workers two months of overdue salary, and in 1888 it intervened to restore to them a pay cut.[53] Mixed with humanitarian motives was the fear that worker discontent would further slow an already laggard customs house.

The rarity of labor disputes in Brazilian ports ended with the coming of the Republic. Labor discontent increased dramatically, partly because of the socialist and anarchist ideas arriving with increasing immigration, but mainly because of Brazil's first accelerated and prolonged inflation. A United States consul noted in 1895: "In consequence of having been paid with a greatly depreciated currency, at a rate of wages but immaterially increased, and of having to pay increased prices for commodities consumed, all labor has experienced the greatest suffering, and no outlook for relief is yet apparent."[54] Strife was worst in Santos, where many port workers were European immigrants. The Commercial Association of Santos took charge of suppressing unrest. It broke stevedore strikes in December 1889 and in May 1891 by having the governor send state armed forces and in the latter case also remove the strike leader from Santos.[55] The association insisted that the workers were well paid and satisfied, but misled by "disorderly elements" (*desordeiros*). The group also prompted police to break an August 1900 strike of railroad warehouse workers and coffee wagon teamsters.[56]

More complex and puzzling were the Commercial Association's actions in a waterfront strike of October 1897. Santos's port by then had been remodeled and most of its operations were handled by the giant Santos Dock Company. Touched off by an accident that injured twelve stevedores, the walkout quickly spread to all port workers. The Commercial Association took charge of suppressing the strike, persuading Minister of Finance Bernardino de Campos to send federal troops and a warship when local police could not handle the situation.[57] Within five days, Santos wharf warehouse owners settled with the strikers, but the Santos Dock Company refused to negotiate. The attitude of the association underwent a curious change. Terming the demands of the workers "reasonable" and "just," it recommended the Dock Company be forced to negotiate.[58] A

53. Associação Comercial de Pernambuco, *Relatório de 1884*, pp. 22–23; Minutes, meeting of Nov. 8, 1888, Livro 7 de Atas, AACP, p. 28.
54. Townes to Department of State, Rio de Janeiro, May 23, 1895, *USRC*, XLVIII, no. 179 (Aug. 1895): 656.
55. Minutes, meetings of Dec. 21, 1889 and May 18, 1891, Livro de Atas, 1874–1894, AACS, pp. 131, 155; Associação Comercial de Santos, *Relatório de 1891*, pp. 24–26.
56. Associação Comercial de Santos, *Relatório de 1904*, pp. 33–34; *O Estado de São Paulo* (São Paulo), Aug. 30, 1900, p. 1.
57. *O Estado de São Paulo*, Oct. 19, 1897, p. 1.
58. Commercial Association of Santos to President of Republic, Santos, Oct. 26, 1897, *O Estado de São Paulo*, Oct. 27, 1897, p. 1; Associação Comercial de Santos, *Relatório de 1904*, p. 30; *O Estado de São Paulo*, Oct. 22, 1897, p. 2.

furor erupted. Rio's *Jornal do Comércio* accused wharf warehouse owners of fomenting the strike and the Commercial Association of Santos of supporting it in order to embarrass the Santos Dock Company and to facilitate smuggling, which the company was charged with controlling.[59] The association indignantly denied the charges and Bernardino de Campos refused to sustain them.[60] But the association's attitude toward the 1897 strike differed from that displayed toward all others. The Santos Dock Company's remodeling had impeded access to several wharf warehouses, including one owned by the association's Secretary, and its own new warehouses offered formidable competition to all.[61] Association members also resented the Dock Company's fees and domination of port activities. It showed plainly in statements terming the company, among other things, "a bloodsucker of Santos commerce."[62]

The association's actions were motivated more by dislike of the Santos Dock Company than by concern for the dock workers. Like other business interest groups, it ordinarily had little empathy for workers and was affronted by their attempts to organize. Labor had no friend among Brazil's nineteenth-century business interest groups.

Seeking the ultimate advantage: port modernization

For most Brazilian entrepôts, high port costs could be greatly lowered by large-scale modernization. All, with the possible exception of Rio, lacked adequate docking, cargo-handling, and storage facilities. Difficult access and other topographical problems often added to the expense and sometimes excluded large vessels altogether. Because nineteenth-century engineering technology could correct such problems by remodeling basin and waterfront areas, business interest groups zealously and persistently promoted port modernization. The traditional prerogatives of business interest groups that entitled them to evaluate plans for their ports were reinforced by a national law of 1869 conceding privileges, including by 1886 six percent guaranteed interest on capital, to companies undertaking modernization. It was to be financed by a surtax on the movement of commerce, thus taking in business interest group prerogatives on taxation as well. Although not stipulated by law, group decisions appear to have been binding. Occasionally they even presented their own plans.[63] Para-

59. *Jornal do Comércio*, Oct. 22, 1987, p. 2; Lobo, *Docas de Santos*, pp. 118–119.
60. Commercial Association of Santos to President of Republic, Santos, Oct. 26, 1897, *O Estado de São Paulo*, Oct. 27, 1897, p. 1; Associação Comercial de Santos, *Relatório de 1904*, p. 30; *RMF*, *1898*, p. 376.
61. Lobo, *Docas de Santos*, pp. 121, 128.   62. *O Estado de São Paulo*, Oct. 21, 1897, p. 2.
63. For example, Associação Comercial do Ceará, *Relatório de 1869*, pp. 8–9; Moacir Medeiros de Santa Ana, *Contribuição à História do Açúcar em Alagôas* (Recife: Instituto do Açúcar e do Alcool, 1970), p. 318.

doxically, by insisting that the remodeling cost membership little and protect waterfront property rights, they sometimes delayed the modernization they worked to promote. Once more, their actions helped shape geographic patterns of development

Major port modernizations were promoted by the commercial associations of Rio Grande, Pelotas, and Pôrto Alegre, located in Rio Grande do Sul. The passage between the ocean and Patos Lake, on which all were situated, was partially blocked by a shifting bar of sand and mud. Pôrto Alegre was also plagued by silting in its near approaches and shoals within Patos Lake. The Patos Lake bar was an obvious target for engineering. It prohibited entry by vessels of more than ten to eleven feet draft, thus excluding larger liners.[64] The associations of Rio Grande, Pelotas, and Pôrto Alegre laid aside their usual enmity to plead repeatedly for its removal, even endorsing one another's petitions. Unless large vessels could enter Patos Lake, they warned, trade would decline and a foreign capital, Montevideo, would become the entrepôt for Rio Grande do Sul. Most aggressive was the Commercial Association of Rio Grande, which published formal petitions in 1882 and 1888 and a book in 1886.[65] The accumulation of pressure eventually moved the Brazilian government. Operations by a French company began in 1891, but soon ended when the depreciation of Brazilian currency made the contract unprofitable. The government took over in 1894.[66] Work proceeded fitfully. Not until 1918 was a passageway through the bar completed.

The Commercial Association of Pôrto Alegre was aware that, even when the bar was opened, shoals within Patos Lake and harbor silting would continue to block access to its port by large ships. In 1888 it urged on Parliament a plan for construction of an artificial port at the village of Torres, to be connected by rail with Pôrto Alegre, some 170 kilometers southwest.[67] The Commercial Association eagerly offered to support with surtaxes on commerce not only that expensive project, but a simultaneous removal of the Patos Lake bar. But despite a 1891 national government guarantee of six percent interest on capital, concessionaires were unable to organize operations.[68] The artificial port at Torres remained an issue in

64. Bennington to Department of State, Rio Grande, Dec. 20, 1889, USRC, XXXIV, no. 121 (Oct. 1890): 213.
65. Commercial Association of Rio Grande to Imperial Government [sic], Rio Grande, Aug. 3, 1882, *Jornal do Comércio*, Sept. 17, 1882, p. 3; Bennet to Foreign Office, Rio Grande, March 6, 1888, Great Britain, Foreign Office, *Diplomatic and Consular Reports*, no. 323 (1888): 2–3; Associação Comercial do Rio Grande, *Representação da Associação Comercial do Rio Grande ao Govêrno Imperial Solicitando o Imediato Emprehendimento das Obras da Barra Geral da Província de S. Pedro do Rio Grande do Sul, Segundo o Projeto do Especialista Holandês, Sr. P. Caland* (Rio Grande: Artista, 1886).
66. Great Britain, Foreign Office, *Diplomatic and Consular Reports*, no. 1263 (1892): 22; ibid., no. 1425 (1894): 11–12.
67. *ACD*, 1888, III: 123–124.
68. "The Port of Torres, Brazil," *USRC*, XXXVI, no. 128 (May 1891): 119.

the state until the opening of the bar and the final modernization of Pôrto Alegre's harbor in 1921 removed the need for it.

Salvador also had an obvious need for hydraulic engineering. It was handicapped by congestion in its waterfront area known as the Lower City and by shallow water near shore, necessitating lighterage for nearly all cargo. By the mid-1890s, the Commercial Association of Bahia claimed that port expenses made freights from Europe to Salvador fifty percent higher than to Chilean ports.[69] Although it knew filling in Salvador's bay waterfront and constructing deep-water docks would eliminate the need for lighters and relieve congestion in the Lower City, the Commercial Association was anxious to protect waterfront property owners. They even included the association, with its own quay. In 1853 member João Gonsalves Ferreira presented a plan for radically remodeling the port area even beyond its present boundaries. The group avoided taking a stand, and Gonsalves Ferreira's proposal was predictably forgotten.[70] The same happened when the association refused to comment on remodeling projects presented in 1871 and 1876, the latter by Viscount Mauá. Both also threatened waterfront property owners.[71]

The Commercial Association of Bahia's attitude changed in the 1880s. Salvador's freight rates had risen above those of Rio, and with them the threat of losing its southern trade area. Association membership voted enthusiastic support to plans by José Antônio de Araújo in 1882 and by British engineer Edmund Penley Cox in 1887, promoting both simultaneously before government and steamship agents.[72] A response was slow in coming. Not until 1900 did the national government take the first steps toward modernizing Salvador's port.[73] Work, by a private company, was completed in 1913. Had the Commercial Association of Bahia backed earlier proposals for port modernization, reduction of Salvador's port expenses might have lessened a considerable loss of trade to Rio de Janeiro in the Bahian south.

If the Bahian group might be faulted for failing to push port modernization, the Commercial Association of Pernambuco might be faulted for obstructing it. Recife, dubbed "the worst port in the world" by Michael G. Mulhall, an author of descriptive works on South America, was blocked by the reef that gave it its name, whose only opening took

69. Commercial Association of Bahia to Chief of Customs, Salvador, Oct. 24, 1896, *Relatório de 1897*, pp. 207–209.

70. Minutes, general assembly of Sept. 15, 1854, Livro 2 de Atas, AACB, pp. 78–79.

71. Theodoro F. Sampaio, "A Engenharia e a sua Evolução no Século da Independência na Bahia," in *Diário Oficial: Edição Especial do Centenário*, VIII (July 2, 1923): 33; Evaldo Cabral de Melo, *O Norte Agrário e o Império, 1871–1889* (Rio de Janeiro: Nova Fronteira, 1984), p. 237.

72. Commercial Association of Bahia to President of Province, Salvador, June 2, 1882, *Relatório de 1883*, pp. 20–21; Minutes, general assembly of Feb. 24, 1887, Livro 5 de Atas, AACB, p. 179; Associação Comercial da Bahia, *Relatório de 1889*, pp. 10–11.

73. Celso Spínola, "Pôrtos do Estado da Bahia," in *Diário Oficial: Edição Especial do Centenário*, VIII (July 2, 1923): 165.

considerable skill to enter.[74] Large steamers could not enter at all, and lighters or open boats had to take in their cargo and passengers. For the latter, commented a traveler, "a thorough ducking with salt water is not at all uncommon in the attempt to reach the shore."[75] Using Recife's harbor was not only difficult, but its expenses by the 1850s, according to the Commercial Association, were twice that of Rio and other entrepôts.[76] On the other hand, the association saw the rewards of modernization as spectacular. Its President assured members in 1864: "As you all know, gentlemen, nature put us in such an advantageous geographical position that our city would be the commercial emporium of South America if an accessible port offered the thousands of ships, which traverse our coast, a spacious and secure anchorage."[77] The association's demands for port modernization were frequent and insistent. When decades passed without fulfillment, it increasingly blamed obstruction by the Southeast, especially the nation's capital.

But much of the obstruction came from the Commercial Association of Pernambuco itself. Added to the usual vested interest of warehouse proprietors and other owners of waterfront property was the desire of members to have remodeling done without cost to themselves, that is, without surtaxes or extra fees. In 1859 association directors examined plans by Brazilian and British engineers, but would recommend neither. In 1866, they examined and praised another plan by a Brazilian engineer, but did not promote it. The same year the group's general assembly strongly condemned a plan by British engineer Edward de Mornay, with whom the imperial government had already prepared a contract.[78] De Mornay's project called for moving the customs house, thus displacing the focus of commerce and changing real estate values. The association forestalled an 1868 attempt to revive De Mornay's plan by insisting that remodeling the dock area was unnecessary, and all that was needed was deepening of the harbor.[79]

The association greeted the 1869 law for the remodeling of Brazil's ports by a surtax on commerce by informing the Emperor of its opposition to any project that increased port expenses.[80] With the group's declaration in mind, a Pernambucan serving as Minister of Agriculture, Commerce, and Public Works, Manuel Buarque de Macedo, devised a means in 1880 to develop Recife's port without additional costs. A plan by the well-

74. Michael G. Mulhall and E. T. Mulhall, *Handbook of the River Plate Republics, Comprising Buenos Ayres and the Provinces of the Argentine Republic and the Republics of Uruguay and Paraguay* (London: Edward Stanford, 1875), p. 5.
75. Maturin M. Ballou, *Equatorial America* (New York: Houghton, Mifflin, 1892), p. 125.
76. *Relatório de 1859*, p. 6; *Relatório de 1860*, p. 10.   77. *Relatório de 1864*, p. 4.
78. Associação Comercial de Pernambuco, *Relatório de 1866*, p. 7.
79. Commercial Association of Pernambuco to Emperor Pedro II, Recife, July 15, 1868, *Relatório de 1868*, p. 41.
80. Commercial Association of Pernambuco to Emperor Pedro II, Recife, March 25, 1872, *Relatório de 1872*, p. 13.

known British engineer Sir John Hawkshaw would be financed by giving his company the port fees usually collected by the imperial government. While admiring Hawkshaw's plan, the group again objected. It wanted no monopoly company operating the port and refused to believe that expenses would not be increased.[81] The group in 1883–1884 rejected another proposal, this time along the lines of the 1869 law.[82]

It was increasingly evident that the Commercial Association of Pernambuco, of all Brazil's business interest groups the one that most voiced the tenets of economic liberalism, wanted its port remodeled by government or by no one. This it admitted openly in 1884 to another proposal to finance remodeling by a private company without increasing expenses.[83] The association apparently felt that only the state could provide costless modernization. In 1888 it reiterated opposition to a monopoly company or any increase of expense.[84] The following year, however, with another Pernambucan, Manuel Portella, in the post of Minister of Empire (*Império*), a contract was signed to deepen the port, financed by moderate ship tonnage fees, with remodeling of the dock area postponed. The company suspended work in 1892, when exchange depreciation cut its remuneration.[85] The association continued to call for modernization of its port, even confronting Brazilian President Campos Sales in 1899 as he passed through Recife, but it also continued to insist that it would tolerate little or no extra expense.[86]

This insistence obstructed numerous opportunities. Had the Commercial Association of Pernambuco backed modernization early on, an efficient and economical port would have helped ease the decline of provincial economic fortunes during the last three decades of the century. The wish of the association that the government undertake the task was impractical. Nineteenth-century Brazilian government was not inclined to take on a project of such magnitude, and other provinces still less inclined to use government revenues soley to benefit Pernambuco. The association had erred. Not until 1918 was Recife's port completely modernized.

The model modernization: Santos

In Santos more than in other cases, competitive realities pushed its Commercial Association to remodel its port. Its modernization was a final

---

81. Commercial Association of Pernambuco to Manuel Buarque de Macedo, Minister of Agriculture, Commerce, and Public Works, Recife, June 3, 1880, *Relatório de 1880*, pp. 38–41.

82. Cabral de Melo, *Norte Agrário*, p. 241.   83. *Relatório de 1884*, pp. 14–15.

84. Commercial Association of Pernambuco to Inspector of Subsidized Shipping Lines (*Linhas de Navegação Subvencionadas*), Recife, Nov. 10, 1888, *Relatório de 1889*, pp. 14–16.

85. Commercial Association of Pernambuco to Minister of Agriculture, Commerce and Public Works, Recife, Feb. 17, 1893, *Relatório de 1893*, pp. 69–71.

86. Minutes, meeting of April 6, 1899, Livro 8 de Atas, AACP, p. 7; Associação Comercial de Pernambuco, *Relatório de 1900*, pp. 7, 16, and *Relatório de 1901*, pp. 19–20.

chapter in a long struggle of that entrepôt to free itself from the commercial suzerainty of Rio de Janeiro. A latecomer among Brazil's major entrepôts, Santos did not possess strong overseas ties until British and German coffee exporters established themselves in 1848. However, it had an advantage in competition with Rio because in the latter, coffee factors sold to "sackers," who classified and sacked the coffee before selling it to exporters through a broker. In Santos, coffee factors sold directly to export houses, employing their own brokers; elimination of the sackers' commission shaved costs for Santos exporters.[87]

An important milestone in Santos's struggle to free itself from its rival's economic domination came in 1876, when the Commercial Association of Santos obtained from its members a resolution to reduce the traditional practice of drawing upon Rio for letters of exchange.[88] Done with initial misgivings by much of the membership, local financing of exportation replaced dependence on Rio by 1881.[89] Elimination of the commissions formerly paid Rio banks and merchants also strengthened Santos's export houses.[90] At Empire's end, however, Rio still had two advantages that enabled it to handle much of the trade of upland São Paulo. One was the differential in railroad rates between the English Line running to Santos and the cheaper Dom Pedro II connecting with Rio; the other was Santos's lack of wharves and warehouses and the topography of its harbor. It silted rapidly, requiring cargo movement by lighters; at low tide appeared black and fetid expanses of mud, studded with dead mules.[91] Since the strong position of the English Line, backed by British diplomacy, made the remedy of the first handicap difficult, the Commercial Association of Santos focused its energy on the second.

The association's board evaluated and rejected a port remodeling plan at its initial meeting in 1874, along with another dating from 1870.[92] In the double condemnation, the association stated some conditions that it would continue to apply. Contractors must not monopolize warehouse and storage facilities, and construction must be in a straight line of quays. As with other commercial associations, waterfront property owners exercised strong influence on the Santos group. It also rejected any port charges that were as high as those of the Rio de Janeiro Dock Company, dating from 1869. Since Rio's rail transportation was cheaper, the association reasoned that only lower port charges could give Santos parity. The association

87. Great Britain, Foreign Office, *Diplomatic and Consular Reports*, no. 1531 (1895): 3.
88. Associação Comercial de Santos, *Relatório de 1876*, pp. 14–17, Anexo no. 4, p. 1.
89. *Relatório de 1881*, p. 6.
90. Associação Comercial de Santos, *Relatório de 1883*, pp. 9–10.
91. Edward Johnston & Co., *Um Século de Café* (Rio de Janeiro: Edward Johnston & Co., 1942), p. 19.
92. Minutes, meeting of Nov. 5, 1874, Livro de Atas, 1874–1894, AACS, pp. 3–5; *Diário de Santos*, Oct. 30, 1885, p. 1.

pushed port remodeling hard, even escorting the Emperor on a tour of Santos facilities to demonstrate their inadequacy in 1879.[93] In 1880 the group rejected three plans, principally because of excessive charges and, feeling that the imperial government was getting nowhere, it arranged for the Province of São Paulo to take over the awarding of concessions.[94] In 1883 and 1885 it turned down plans for the province, because they did not call for a straight line of quays and because the capital resources of the bidders were dubious.[95]

The Commercial Association of Santos had become increasingly impatient with the projects it had been reviewing. Drawing up a plan in 1883, it offered to remodel the port of Santos itself. The province responded with a law of April 1885, giving the association an option over other bidders.[96] When the Province of São Paulo returned the problem of Santos's port to the imperial government in 1886, the association repeated its offer, at the same time roundly condemning a proposal submitted by its old adversary, the English Line.[97] The association did not object when the Empire refused its bid. The project was enormous, and it is probable that the association's remodeling proposal was offered mainly as a yardstick by which others should be judged.

Meanwhile, the need for modernization grew. Silting had become much worse, and the increasing lack of warehouse space left goods piled high on the quays, lying unprotected in the sun and eventually spilling into nearby streets. A local historian notes: "An occasional businessman, in a greater hurry to get rich, came to stuff his sack by the diversion of such merchandise."[98] Prodded by its membership, the association in 1887 begged Minister of Agriculture, Commerce, and Public Works Antônio da Silva Prado, a native of São Paulo, to accept quickly any of six proposals submitted after the imperial government reassumed responsibility for the port.[99] Unlike previous plans, the Commercial Association of Santos made no attempt to evaluate them, leaving the choice to Prado and the Minister of Finance. It reviewed and enthusiastically endorsed the winning plan in July 1888. Presented by a Brazilian company eventually

93. Associação Comercial de Santos, *Relatório de 1879*, pp. 6–7.

94. Commercial Association of Santos to Minister of Agriculture, Commerce, and Public Works, Santos, June 3, 1880, *Relatório de 1881*, Anexo no. 4, unpaginated, and pp. 31–35.

95. Commercial Association of Santos to President of Province, Santos, Sept. 19, 1883, *Relatório de 1883*, pp. 41–50; Minutes, meeting of July 21, 1885, Livro de Atas, 1874–1894, AACS, p. 101.

96. Commercial Association of Santos to President of Province, Santos, Sept. 19, 1883, *Relatório de 1883*, pp. 49–50; President of Province, São Paulo, *Relatório de 1884*, p. 43.

97. Commercial Association of Santos to Minister of Agriculture, Commerce, and Public Works, Santos, August 1, 1885, *Relatório de 1887*, Anexo no. 6, pp. 31–36.

98. Great Britain, Foreign Office, *Diplomatic and Consular Reports*, no. 168 (1886): 3; João da Costa e Silva Sobrinho, *Santos Noutros Tempos* (São Paulo: Revista dos Tribunais, 1953), p. 401.

99. Minutes, meeting of March 30, 1887, Livro de Atas, 1874–1894, AACS, p. 110.

organized as Gafree, Guinle & Co., it offered rates lower than those specified by the association and did not demand a monopoly of warehousing and storage.[100] The enterprise was also unusual in that it had no foreign investment, nor did it ever require public funds.

The Commercial Association of Santos kept its hand on the construction process. It obtained from the Dock Company a new wharf, widespread dredging, modification of the waterfront sewer system, and removal of certain fees. At one point it summoned the entrepreneurs, the chief engineer, and the editor of *Diário de Santos* to ask why the works were not progressing more rapidly.[101] The first stretch of new quay opened in February 1892. Changes were soon noticeable. Customs revenue more than doubled between 1891 and 1893, with only a moderate increase in tonnage, indicating that evasion of duties, whose collection the company now supervised, had been widespread. More to the association's liking, delays in cargo movement ended and freight charges for Santos fell below their level for Rio.[102] Despite resentment among its rank-and-file, which emerged during the 1897 strike, the association praised the Dock Company at every opportunity, and scornfully refused the invitation of the Commercial Association of São Paulo for joint complaints about fees and slow progress in construction.[103] In 1900 Minister of Finance Joaquim Murtinho characterized Santos as that Brazilian port which "best serves the interests of the Federal Treasury and most answers the demands of commerce and navigation."[104] In the period between 1890–1891 and 1894–1895 Santos passed Rio as a coffee exporter and has been ahead ever since.

In perhaps no other aspect of communications were business interest groups more intimately involved than in port modernization. Only the Commercial Association of Santos, however, attained that goal during the nineteenth century. Its drive and persistence played a major role in creating Brazil's first modern port, and it did so on its own terms. Later, the support of their commercial associations helped obtain remodeling for Manaus in 1903, Belém in 1909, and Rio in 1910. The associations of Bahia and Pernambuco missed opportunities for early modernization. As a result, the inefficiency of their ports during the nineteenth century contributed to the relative economic stagnation of both areas. The activities of business interest groups in port modernization did not always further local economic development.

100. *ACD, 1888*, IV: 131–132.
101. Minutes, meetings of Feb. 8, 1890, May 31, 1890, and Dec. 3, 1891, Livro de Atas, 1874–1894, AACS, pp. 133, 139, 166; Associação Comercial de Santos, *Relatório de 1895*, pp. 10–12; Minutes, meeting of March 4, 1895, Livro de Atas, 1894–1904, AACS, p. 5.
102. Lobo, *Docas de Santos*, pp. 34–35; Associação Comercial de Santos, *Relatório de 1895*, pp. 13–14.
103. Minutes, meeting of Nov. 28, 1896, Livro de Atas, 1894–1904, AACS, p. 24.
104. *RMF, 1900*, p. 187.

Port efficiency and safety were linked with good communications in ensuring the development of an entrepôt, and were of equal concern. The prerogatives of business interest groups in waterfront districts and harbors also were based on long tradition. Perhaps even more than other aspects of communications, the attitudes and actions of business interest groups in waterfront areas and harbors were shaped by rivalry with other entrepôts. Rivalry drove the groups repeatedly to demand remedy for the deficiencies of their ports, but not always with success. Sometimes the lethargy and impecuniousness of government was responsible for the slow progress in improving Brazilian ports; sometimes it was an unwillingness of business interest group membership to make necessary sacrifices.

11

Business interest groups and economic
and urban integration

The Brazilian state left services essential for economic or urban integration that it could not provide or manage to private institutions such as the Church or voluntary associations. Of these, business interest groups were the most important. As noted, in the nineteenth century private institutions performed, even in the most advanced nations, many of the services today undertaken by government. Because of the comparative weakness of the Brazilian state, the range of services provided by private agencies was correspondingly wider. Within their recognized spheres of activity, business interest groups performed them with a remarkable degree of autonomy.

Economic integration came to the forefront when Portuguese mercantile restrictions ended in 1808, widening the scope for economic development. To take full advantage, Brazil had to integrate its economic practices both nationally and with other countries in the Atlantic trading community. Business law, commercial usage, measurement, and other aspects of trade had to be made uniform throughout Brazil and made to conform to the standards of the nation's trading partners. Economic information and registry services also had to be provided. The problem of urban integration also loomed. Nineteenth-century economic development brought an even more rapid city growth. Most of Brazil's major cities more than tripled in size during the nineteenth century, with Rio de Janeiro, São Paulo, and Belém expanding at an even greater rate.[1] Since nearly all began the century as little more than small towns, they lacked not only physical facilities but essential urban services. Sanitation, charitable and relief agencies, and fire and police protection were often inadequate or absent. They had to be rapidly introduced, even when government initiative and resources were lacking.[2]

---

1. Michael L. Conniff, Melvin K. Hendrix, and Stephen Nolhgren, "Brazil," in *The Urban Development of Latin America, 1750–1920*, ed. Richard M. Morse (Stanford, Calif.: Stanford University Press, 1971), p. 37.
2. Merchants, mainly foreign, also founded or financed new urban facilities and institutions in Chile, Argentina, and Uruguay. John Mayo, *British Merchants and Chilean Development, 1851–1886*

Business interest group participation in economic and urban integration came mainly from necessity. As noted, the Brazilian state was inefficient in administration and lacking in technical expertise, because of deficient education.[3] Business interest group membership could compensate in large measure for such weaknesses. Many, perhaps most, of Brazil's trained engineers were members of the Engineering Club, which also enrolled industrialists with technical knowledge acquired from experience, as did the commercial associations.[4] All business interest group members had skills scarce in Brazilian government: accounting, organization, and manipulating large sums of money. Because of their strong foreign ties, they were also the element of Brazilian society most familiar with innovations and new standards in economic and urban development.

The autonomy of business interest groups in such activities was based on prerogatives inherited from Iberian corporatism. Functional interest groups had long enjoyed the right and duty to advise government on all matters concerning the livelihood of their membership and to regulate members' occupational activities. In addition, the implicit control of commercial associations over their port areas was considered to extend to adjacent business districts, particularly when such districts were detached geographically from the rest of the city, as in Salvador and Recife. Self-interest also dictated participation. Business interest group members needed the smooth functioning of business activities and the safety and convenience of urban areas vital to commerce. Above all, members had a stake in the economic development that economic and urban integration would foster.

Helping economic integration: rules, measurements, and information

Basic to economic integration was the regulation and standardization of business practice. It had to be facilitated, made uniform, and brought into line with that of the Atlantic trading community. The most compre-

(Boulder, Colo.: Westview Press, 1987), p. 45; James William Duffy, *A Hand-Book to Valparaíso* (Valparaíso: W. Helfmann's "Universo," 1862), p. 50; Clifton B. Kroeber, *The Growth of the Shipping Industry in the Rio de la Plata Region, 1794–1860* (Madison, Wis.: University of Wisconsin Press, 1957), pp. 41, 78–79; Michael G. Mulhall, *The English in South America* (Buenos Aires: Standard Office, 1878), p. 330; Thomas Sutcliffe, *Sixteen Years in Chile and Peru from 1822 to 1839* (London: Fisher, Son, 1841), p. 515; Jorge Viola Navarro, *El Club de Residentes Extranjeros: Breve Reseña Historica en Homenaje a sus Fundadores* (Buenos Aires: Coni, 1941), pp. 31–32, 35–36, 115.
3. Only in the last decade of the nineteenth century did literacy reach fifteen percent and, as late as 1889, Brazil's one school of engineering had only 161 students. Joseph L. Love, "Political Participation in Brazil, 1881–1969," *Luso-Brazilian Review,* 7 (Dec. 1970): 8; Robert J. Havighurst and J. Roberto Moreira, *Society and Education in Brazil* (Pittsburgh: University of Pittsburgh Press, 1965), p. 76.
4. For the membership claims of the Engineering Club, see *ACD, 1892,* III: 224.

hensive step toward that end was the Commercial Code of 1850. Previously commercial problems had been resolved by Portuguese law of 1789, which specified observance of the customs and laws of the "civilized nations" of Europe for the considerable material it did not itself cover.[5] Gaps in the law and the vague means prescribed to compensate for them left great confusion.

Formulation and enactment of a Commercial Code by Parliament owed much to Brazil's three earliest permanent business interest groups. Work began in 1833 under a five-man committee, which included a future president of the Commercial Association of Rio de Janeiro.[6] A joint committee of Parliament endorsed the finished product in 1835, but it did not become law until fifteen years later. Merchants and legislators amended and added material during that period, beginning with a committee of the Rio association in 1838.[7] The influence of the Rio group meant that the Commercial Code would entrust many regulatory powers to commercial associations. Its final enactment was the result of a figurative blizzard of petitions from the commercial associations of Rio de Janeiro, Bahia, and Pernambuco, the latter despatching at least six within seven years.[8] By standardizing business regulations, the Commercial Code of 1850 made business activity easier and less risky; together with the freeing of capital following the ending of the slave trade, it brought about a significant spurt of enterprise in the 1850s.[9]

Business interest groups were less unified in their attitude toward regulating incorporation. The 1860 law on formation of corporations was a reaction to the financial crisis of 1857, blamed on proliferation of banks of emission. It required that the statutes of proposed corporations be approved by the Council of State, to determine if the interests of public and stockholders were protected and if the company was liable to succeed. The 1860 law has been widely attacked over the years. Contemporaries blamed its restrictions for dampening the spirit of enterprise and associa-

5. Virgílio de Sa Pereira, " Os Códigos Criminal, de Processo e Comercial; Formação de Nosso Direito Civil; A Reforma Judiciária de 1871," in *Tomo Especial Consagrado ao Primeiro Congresso de História Nacional: Revista do Instituto Histórico e Geográfico Brasileiro* (Rio de Janeiro: Imprensa Nacional, 1916), IV: 479; W. R. Swartz, "Codification in Latin America: The Brazilian Commercial Code of 1850," *Texas International Law Journal*, 10 (1975): 349–350.
6. *Jornal do Comércio* (Rio de Janeiro), Aug. 16, 1834, p. 4.
7. Comissão da Praça do Comércio [Associação Comercial] do Rio de Janeiro, *Projeto de Emendas para a Terceira Parte do Código Comercial do Império do Brasil, Oferecido à Assembléia Geral Legislativa* (Rio de Janeiro: J. Villeneuve, 1838).
8. Minutes, meetings of March 4, 1839, May 7, 1840, July 1, 1841, April 2, 1842, Feb. 4, May 5, and June 10, 1846, Livro 1 de Atas, AACP, pp. 14–15, 16, 32, 45, 122, 128, 130.
9. Richard Graham, *Britain and the Onset of Modernization in Brazil, 1850–1914* (Cambridge: Cambridge University Press, 1969), p. 25; Leslie Bethell and José Murilo de Carvalho, "Brazil from Independence to the Middle of the Nineteenth Century," in *The Cambridge History of Latin America, Volume III: From Independence to c. 1870*, ed. Leslie Bethell (Cambridge: Cambridge University Press, 1985), pp. 744–745.

tion and modern historians for delaying industrialization.[10] However, as Steven Topik has pointed out, the legislation was intended to encourage investment in corporations by making it safer, and Brazilian want of a "spirit of association" was probably more due to lack of familiarity with corporations and to caution.[11] Perhaps taking this view, Brazil's major business interest groups, the commercial associations of Rio de Janeiro, Bahia, and Pernambuco, did not oppose the 1860 law.

The associations of Bahia and Pernambuco retained reservations about unregulated incorporation when presented with legislation for it in 1865. The former group disapproved the bill after nearly a year's study; the latter recommended that certain restrictions on incorporation be retained. Both claimed to have been influenced by a recent crisis in England blamed on the creation of too many corporations.[12] The Council of State endorsed their views, rejecting the bill. In 1879, however, the Commercial Association of Rio de Janeiro termed the 1860 law a reaction to abnormal circumstances and pushed a new bill liberalizing incorporation to enactment in 1882.[13] Since Rio possessed Brazil's greatest concentration of capital and industry, its business elite had the most interest in freer incorporation. The Republic decreed an even more unrestricted incorporation law early in 1890.

In addition to influencing legislation on business, the groups created business law themselves by determining the standard trade practices of every commercial center, known as the "usages and customs of the business community" (*usos e costumes da praça*). Usages and customs included such crucial matters as maximum commissions on transactions and responsibility for payment of fees and taxes. The Commercial Code of 1850 provided that usages and customs be determined by the local commercial association, whereupon they became law, duly registered by the commercial courts. In provinces without a commercial association, those of the

---

10. For example, Aureliano Cândido Tavares Bastos, *Cartas do Solitário* (3d ed.; São Paulo: Editôra Nacional, 1938), pp. 39–40, 46; Joaquim Nabuco, *Um Estadista do Império: Nabuco de Araújo, Sua Vida, Suas Opiniões, Sua Época* (São Paulo: Editôra Nacional, 1936), I: 335; Carlos Manuel Peláez, "Uma Análise Econômica da História do Café Brasileiro," in *Economia Brasileira: Uma Visão Histórica*, ed. Paulo Neuhaus (Rio de Janeiro: Campus, 1980), pp. 339–340; Warren Dean, "The Brazilian Economy, 1870–1930" in *The Cambridge History of Latin America, Volume V: c. 1870 to 1930*, ed. Leslie Bethell (Cambridge: Cambridge University Press, 1986), p. 668.

11. "State Autonomy in Economic Policy: Brazil's Experience, 1822–1930," *Journal of Interamerican Studies and World Affairs*, 26 (Nov. 1984): 463–464.

12. Minutes, general assembly of Oct. 5, 1866, Livro 3 de Atas, AACB, p. 94; Commercial Association of Pernambuco to President, Commercial Tribunal (*Tribunal do Comércio*), Salvador, Feb. 21, 1866, *Relatório da Direção da Associação Comercial Beneficente de Pernambuco, Apresentado à Assembléia Geral da Mesma em o Primeiro de Agôsto de 1866* (Recife: Jornal do Recife, 1866), pp. 9, 50–51.

13. Associação Comercial do Rio de Janeiro, *Relatório da Associação Comercial do Rio de Janeiro do Ano de 1879* (Rio de Janeiro: Montenegro, 1880), p. 30, *Relatório de 1880*, p. 7, and *Relatório de 1881*, p. 7.

nearest city with one prevailed.[14] Association boards of directors ruled on the interpretation of usages and customs, and general assemblies updated them periodically. Commercial associations' control over usages and customs could be used to effect valuable change. The Commercial Association of Maranhão used it in the late 1860s to force on its unprogressive business community the universal acceptance of bills of exchange, the Santos group at Empire's end to spread the custom of payment by check.[15]

In addition to formulating business law, the commercial associations indirectly controlled commercial jurisprudence. The 1850 Code provided for major entrepôts a three-man Commercial Tribunal (*Tribunal do Comércio*), elected by commercial association members of Brazilian citizenship from within their ranks. In 1876 the Commercial Tribunal was replaced by a six-man (eight in Rio) Commercial Board (*Junta do Comércio*). It differed from its predecessor only in that the imperial government appointed its secretary and chose its president from among three candidates elected by the commercial association, which continued to elect directly the other members.[16] Both courts were customarily staffed with past, present, or future commercial association directors and housed in association headquarters. Not surprisingly, Brazil's commercial courts and commercial associations rarely varied in outlook.

Commercial associations also had their own private tribunals. The right to judge commercial disputes was among the most ancient of prerogatives enjoyed by business interest groups. Either an association's board of directors or a committee judged all business disputes brought before them with the consent of the contending parties. This handy private arbitration provided an informed judgment and avoided both lawyers' fees and the delays of official courts. In 1852 their powers were challenged by the Minister of Finance, at the instigation of a disgruntled loser in one of the Commercial Association of Bahia's decisions, but that group ably defended the prerogative.[17] In 1867 and again in 1922, the commercial associations' arbitration received legal sanction.[18] Using their private tribunals and choosing the members of official commercial courts, business interest

---

14. Brazil, laws, statutes, etc. *Coleção das Leis do Império do Brasil de 1850*, (Rio de Janeiro: Imprensa Nacional, 1851), XIII, Part 2: 255–256.

15. *O País* (São Luís), Aug. 22, 1865, p. 3; Associação Comercial do Maranhão, *Relatório da Comissão da Praça do Comércio do Maranhão, Lido pelo Respetivo Presidente na Sessão de 22 de Dezembro de 1870* (São Luís: Mattos, 1871), pp. 12–13; Minutes, meetings of Oct. 12 and Oct. 19, 1889, Livro de Atas, 1874–1894, AACS, pp. 127–128.

16. Bernando José Borges, *O Comerciante, ou Completo Manual Instrutivo* (2d ed. rev.; Rio de Janeiro: Eduardo & Henrique Laemmert, 1878), pp. 105–106.

17. Minutes, meeting of Feb. 27, 1852, Livro 2 de Atas, AACB, p. 14.

18. Brazil, leis, decretos, etc., *Leis, 1867*, XXX, Part 2: 225–233; Heitor Beltrão, "O Civismo da Praça num Século de Labor," in Associação Comercial do Rio de Janeiro, *Aspetos Coligidos a Propósito do Centenário da Associação Comercial* (Rio de Janeiro: Associação Comercial do Rio de Janeiro, 1935), p. 75.

groups could control the interpretation of business law, as well as its making.

Credit, debt, and honesty

The business elite of nineteenth-century Brazil frequently complained about the tradition of granting long credit to retailers. Importers and commission houses customarily allowed them twelve months, sometimes even eighteen, on sales of dry goods.[19] Exports, by contrast, were sold for cash or for a maximum of three months' credit. Interest on overdue retail accounts could seldom be collected, particularly on goods sold to the interior.[20] Retailers' use of long-term credit was often habitual or addictive, not abandoned even though importers offered discounts of twelve to fourteen percent for cash. Brazilian retailers, a United States consul noted, "are doubtless quite able to pay and are quite willing to allow large interest for the delay, but they cannot emancipate themselves from the old habit of procrastination."[21] The risks in this system were compensated by higher prices and contributed greatly to the instability of business. Mercantile credit reform was high on the agenda of the business elite.

That elite was able to effect little change on the system. Modest in aims and ultimately successful was an 1848 agreement by British houses in Rio de Janeiro and Salvador to sell only for bills with a definite date for payment accepted by the purchaser.[22] Although arousing the wrath of retailers, the use of bills with a definite date of payment was taken up by other foreign merchants and eventually spread to the rest of Brazil.[23] It was difficult to impose further improvement. In the wake of a commercial crisis in 1860, the Commercial Association of Bahia prevailed upon membership to accept regulations for more explicit terms of payment and shorter time periods, but a year later admitted it could not enforce the

19. Consul-General Andrews to Department of State, Rio de Janeiro, Sept. 6, 1883, *USRC*, XIII, no. 43 (July 1884): 445–448; C. C. Andrews, *Brazil: Its Conditions and Prospects* (New York: D. Appleton, 1887), p. 63; Eulália Maria Lahmeyer Lobo, "Evolução dos Preços e do Padrão da Vida no Rio de Janeiro, 1820–1930 – Resultados Preliminares," *Revista Brasileira de Economia*, 25 (Oct.-Dec. 1971): 243.
20. Consul-General Andrews to Department of State, Rio de Janeiro, Sept. 6, 1883, and Atherton to Department of State, Recife, July 16, 1883, *USRC*, XIII, no. 43 (July 1884): 446, 448.
21. Edes to Department of State, Salvador, Dec. 1, 1879, NA/DS T-331, Vol. 4, unpaginated.
22. *Rio Mercantile Journal* (Rio de Janeiro), July 6, 1848, p. 1. According to Luís Henrique Dias Tavares, the Rio meeting was arranged by the British Consul and aimed at inhibiting the participation of British merchants in furnishing goods to the slave trade. *Comércio Proibido de Escravos* (São Paulo: Atica, 1988), pp. 132–133.
23. Bahia, Presidente da Província, *Fala que Receitou o Presidente da Província da Bahia, o Conselheiro Francisco Gonçalves Martins na Abertura da Assembléia Legislativa da Mesma Província em 1 de Março de 1850* (Salvador: Constitucional de V. R. Moreira, 1850), pp. 54–55; Porter to Foreign Office, Salvador, May 8, 1851, PRO/FO 13/288, fl. 81.

new rules.[24] The Bahian association made another unsuccessful attempt to limit mercantile credit in 1887, as had the Commercial Association of Rio de Janeiro in 1883.[25] An attempt to extend the time period within which overdue payment for commercial debt could be demanded (*prescrição*), five years in most cases, also failed. Petitions for that purpose by the Commercial Association of Pernambuco in 1852 and the Rio association in 1855 were rejected by the Council of State.[26] Changing credit practices proved extremely difficult. Doing it by means of government decree or legislation meant overcoming a lack of sympathy by officials or legislators of planter background, many debtors themselves. Doing it through uses and customs meant overcoming business habits of long duration. Extended periods for credit and short ones for recovery of debt remained standard.

Regulation of bankruptcy was a matter of special urgency. Bankruptcy was frequent, hitting overseas trading and factorage firms as well as retailers, and in all cases merchant houses were liable to be major creditors. Commercial associations, dominated by the bigger merchant firms, intervened primarily to speed and clarify bankruptcy procedure and to defend the interests of large creditors. The associations also successfully fought attempts to try bankruptcy litigation in regular courts rather than in commercial tribunals. Creditors found more sympathetic ears in the latter. The commercial associations of Rio de Janeiro, Bahia, and Pernambuco in 1855 joined in a protracted struggle against the attempt of the Imperial Treasury to claim primacy as a creditor of bankrupt firms, definitively repelling it only in 1864.[27]

Much of the regulatory activity of commercial associations aimed at enforcing business honesty. Fraudulent bankruptcy and arson were major preoccupations. Business interest groups constantly petitioned for legislation making the former more difficult. The debtor would arrange fictitious liabilities with accomplices, often arranging a composition or settlement with them making possible his legal discharge from further obligations.[28] Legitimate creditors were thus cheated of their share of the bankrupt firm's assets. The long-voiced complaints of commercial associa-

24. Minutes, general assembly of Oct. 2, 1861, Livro 3 de Atas, AACB, p. 15.
25. *Diário de Notícias* (Salvador), Sept. 19, 1887, p. 1; Associação Comercial do Rio de Janeiro, *Resposta da Associação Comercial do Rio de Janeiro aos Quesitos da Comissão Parlamentar de Inquérito* (Rio de Janeiro: Montenegro, 1883), p. 22.
26. "Representações da Associação Comercial de Pernambuco e da Praça do Comércio da Côrte sôbre o Prazo, Demasiado Curto, para a Prescrição de Dívidas no Comércio . . . ," Coleção Marquês de Olinda, AIHGB, lata 212, doc. 20.
27. Minutes, meetings of July 25, 1855 and Dec. 3, 1862, Livro 2 de Atas, AACB, pp. 87, 162; Minutes, meeting of July 14, 1855, Livro 2 de Atas, AACP, p. 45; Associação Comercial da Bahia, *Relatório da Junta Diretora da Associação Comercial da Praça da Bahia, Apresentado em Sessão Ordinária da Assembléia Geral de 29 de Setembro de 1864* (Salvador: C. L. Masson, 1964), p. 3.
28. Associação Comercial de Pernambuco, *Relatório de 1878*, p. 6; London *Times*, Sept. 25, 1901, p. 11.

tions were answered by an 1890 law that tightened bankruptcy procedure and increased association control over trials by having them under a judge and two members of the local Commercial Board or, where none existed, the commercial association.[29] But defects in the law and lax enforcement meant that fraudulent bankruptcy increased dramatically when the economy worsened after 1898. The Commercial Association of São Paulo formed investigating committees of businessmen and lawyers in 1898 and 1899 to analyze both the problem and the 1890 law, as a result demanding, backed by the Rio association, that the law be revised.[30] Congress failed to respond, and fraudulent bankruptcy continued frequent. Arson to collect insurance was also common. Commercial Association of Rio de Janeiro statistics revealed that from 1875 to 1880, for example, twenty-one percent of the fires in Rio with known cause had been set for insurance fraud (*especulação*).[31] Since management of insurance companies or investment in them was common among their leaders, business interest groups constantly urged tightening of laws on incendiaries and enjoyed some success in promoting legislation increasing punishment.

Other major business dishonesty, aside from smuggling, tended to be local in nature. The problem of counterfeit copper and paper currency, common throughout Brazil in the first half of the nineteenth century, was especially serious in the Province of Bahia. A president of province who moved aggressively against the counterfeiters was waylaid and murdered, and copper to make counterfeit coins (whose face value was worth several times their content) was a major import item.[32] Despite the probable involvement of some of its members in counterfeiting, the Commercial Association of Bahia worked zealously to eradicate it. It arranged public displays of false banknotes in circulation and alerted businessmen to new appearances of bogus notes or coins. The provincial leaders who finally succeeded in suppressing Bahian counterfeiting received honors and also more concrete rewards. The association awarded one president of province with honorary membership and another (already an honorary member) by commissioning his full-length portrait for the main salon of its headquar-

29. Brazil, leis, decretos, etc., *Decretos do Governo Provisório da República dos Estados Unidos do Brazil: Décimo Fascículo de 1 a 31 de Outubro de 1890* (Rio de Janeiro: Imprensa Nacional, 1890), pp. 3063–3064; Judgeship of the Santos District (*Juizado de Direito da Comarca de Santos*) to Commercial Association of Santos, Santos, Feb. 20, 1891, *Relatório da Associação Comercial de Santos, Apresentado em Sessão Ordinária da Assembléia Geral em 20 de Junho de 1891 e Parecer da Comissão de Exame de Contas* (Santos: Diário de Santos, 1891), p. 28.
30. Minutes, meetings of Aug. 18, 1898, Aug. 1, 1899, and Aug. 24, 1899, Livro de Atas, 1894–1906, Arquivo da Associação Comercial de São Paulo, São Paulo, pp. 12, 22, 23; Commercial Association of Rio de Janeiro to Brazilian Senate, Rio de Janeiro, June 19, 1901, *Relatório de 1901*, pp. 12–13.
31. *Relatório de 1880*, "Mapa dos Incêndios . . . 1875–1880," unpaginated.
32. Parkinson to Foreign Office, Salvador, Jan. 31, 1831, PRO/FO 13/88, fl. 29.

ters. The provincial Chief of Police received a money gift.[33] In a similar spirit, the Commercial Association of Santos moved against the widespread theft of coffee being transported and the sale of it to merchants, although some of the latter were its members. It demanded that stolen coffee when apprehended be sold at auction and the proceeds given to charity and that the Municipal Council of Santos remove the license of any merchant caught buying stolen coffee.[34] It funded the capture and prosecution of coffee thieves if the victims were association members or if the Santos Chief of Police requested financial aid.[35]

Enforcing business honesty, like regulating credit practices and bankruptcy proceedings, was essential to standardizing business in Brazil. The statutes of business interest groups invariably called for the expulsion by vote of members acting dishonestly, although this punishment was rarely invoked. In enforcing business honesty, the groups were moderately successful. They were less so in attempts to regulate credit practices and bankruptcy proceedings, which were partly motivated by a desire to help large-scale creditors.

Control over business personnel

Another traditional prerogative exercised by commercial associations was regulation of business personnel. They supervised those whom the Commercial Code referred to as "auxiliary agents of commerce," encompassing brokers (*corretores*), business auctioneers (*agentes de leilões*), managers (*feitores*), bookkeepers (*guarda-livros*), *caixeiros,* and customs warehouse owners (*trapicheros*).[36] Businessmen were legally responsible for the business actions of their managers, bookkeepers, and *caixeiros* and probably felt some compulsion to control the others. Brokers were included, since, as an authority explained, "[they] are not merchants [because] they do not deal in their own name and for their own account."[37] The profession, divided into the specialties of public funds, ships, and commodities, was barred to foreigners (and women, military, and priests), and its numbers in each city were legally limited. The Commercial Code of 1850 subordinated brokers to their local commercial court, whose decisions were

33. Minutes, extraordinary general assembly of Dec. 28, 1853, Livro 2 de Atas, AACB, p. 69.
34. Commercial Association of Santos to Provisional Government of São Paulo [sic], Santos, no date, 1891, *Relatório de 1891*, pp. 59–61; Minutes, meeting of Jan. 28, 1896, Livro de Atas, 1894–1904, AACS, p. 19.
35. Minutes, meetings of July 9, 1895 and Oct. 28, 1896, Livro de Atas, 1894–1904, AACS, pp. 14, 23.
36. Brazil, leis, decretos, etc., *Código Comercial do Império do Brasil, Anotado . . . pelo Bacharel Salustiano Orlando de Araújo Costa* (2d ed.; Rio de Janeiro: Eduardo & Henrique Laemmert, 1869), p. 18. Warehouse managers (*administradores de armazens de depósito*) and transportation brokers (*comissários de transporte*) were also included.
37. Borges, *O Comerciante*, p. 145.

strongly influenced by commercial associations. Commercial courts usually appear to have accepted the recommendations of local commercial associations on numbers of brokers and whether they were to be organized into a Brokers' Board (*Junta dos Corretores*) to furnish official price quotations.[38]

The permitted number of brokers often was insufficient, especially coffee brokers, and much work was performed by unlicensed interlopers, often foreigners, picturesquely termed *zangões* or drones. The Rio Brokers' Board complained to the Minister of Justice in 1873 that the Commercial Association of Rio de Janeiro permitted *zangões* free entry into its headquarters, the only legal place for public funds brokerage operations.[39] Posting no bond and paying no industries and professions tax, *zangões* could charge lower fees. In 1875 the Pernambuco association, always foremost in advocating economic liberalism, tried to enlist the nation's other commercial associations in an unsuccessful campaign to remove all restrictions on the number of brokers.[40]

A decree of 1876 increased local commercial association control over brokers. A committee composed of the group's president, two men elected by membership, and an inspector designated by the Minister of Finance supervised the actions and verified the price quotations of brokers.[41] This oversight was not necessarily disadvantageous. In 1877 the Commercial Association of Pernambuco obtained an increase in the fees of local brokers, and in 1882 the Rio association reversed a decree cutting the fees of Rio brokers, which had been promoted by the Center for Coffee Agriculture and Commerce.[42] In February 1891, with the *Encilhamento* under full steam, the government attempted to curb speculation by decreeing a three percent tax on stock transactions. Brokers of public funds replied with a three-day strike, which ended only after negotiations between the government, the Rio association, directors of leading banks, and the Brokers' Board resulted in revocation of the decree.[43] The Rio association had

---

38. For example, Associação Comercial de Maceió, *Relatório da Direção da Associação Comercial de Maceió, Apresentado à Assembléia Geral da Mesma em 22 de Julho de 1871* (Maceió: Jornal das Alagôas, 1871), p. 6; Minutes, meetings of June 27, 1885 and Sept. 21, 1889, Livro de Atas, 1874–1894, AACS, pp. 100, 126; Associação Comercial de Santos, *Relatório de 1877*, p. 8, and *Relatório de 1887*, p. 7.

39. Maria Bárbara Levy, *História da Bolsa de Valores do Rio de Janeiro* (Rio de Janeiro: IBMEC, 1977), pp. 101–102.

40. Minutes, meetings of Oct. 6, 1875 and Jan. 20, 1876, Livro 4 de Atas, AACP, pp. 47, 52.

41. Associação Comercial de Pernambuco, *Relatório de 1877*, p. 21; Levy, *Bolsa de Valores*, p. 103.

42. Commercial Association of Pernambuco to President of Province, Recife, June 24, 1877, *Relatório de 1877*, pp. 66–69; Commercial Association of Rio de Janeiro to President, Commercial Board of Rio de Janeiro, Rio de Janeiro, Aug. 2, 1882, *Relatório de 1882–1883*, p. 19; *O Jornal: Edição Comemorativa do Bi-Centenário do Cafeeiro no Brasil, 1727–1927* (São Paulo: Casa Duprat e Casa Mayença, 1927), Quarta Seção, p. 6.

43. Maria Bárbara Levy, "O Encilhamento," in *Economia Brasileira*, p. 205.

already blasted it with a petition accusing it of, among other things, "communistic tendencies."[44]

The increasing assertiveness of brokers of public funds, together with the growing importance of the stock market, led government to sever them from Commercial Board and commercial association control. Decrees of 1893 and 1895 affirmed the monopoly of licensed brokers in stock market operations, more closely regulated them and, most importantly, placed brokers of public funds under the control of a Syndical Chamber (*Câmara Sindical*) of Brokers of Public Funds, whose governing body was elected by the brokers themselves. To these changes the commercial associations made no objection. Like other aspects of standardizing business practice, regulation of brokers was consuming of time and effort and willingly discarded when feasible.

Connected with brokerage operations was the opening of Brazil's first stock exchanges. According to the Commercial Code of 1850, commercial association headquarters were the only locale where negotiations to determine prices of commodities, services, instruments of credit, and exchange could take place legally. The Rio group's headquarters took on the aspect of a modern exchange in 1875 when its directorate, at the urging of the Brokers' Board, obtained a ruling that stocks and bonds be sold openly by proclamation (*pregão*).[45] Banks and merchant houses, however, objected to having the value of their bills of exchange or other certificates of credit revealed openly. Transactions in such bills ceased for more than a year, until the Rio association could persuade the Minister of Justice to make them an exception to the requirement for sale by proclamation.[46] The Commercial Association of Bahia opened its own stock exchange in 1876 and the Pernambuco association the following year, while the São Paulo Stock Exchange began in 1896.[47] All exchanges were regulated by their commercial associations.

Commercial associations were given or assumed varying degrees of control over other minor business occupations, as well as acting as their advocate before government. Logically, in view of their foreign complexion, they examined and officially qualified commercial translators. As part of their supervision of minor business occupations, the commercial asso-

44. Eudes Barros, *A Associação Comercial no Império e na República* (2d ed. rev.; Rio de Janeiro: Gráfica Olímpica, 1975), pp. 162–163.
45. Commercial Association of Rio de Janeiro to President, Commercial Tribunal, Rio de Janeiro, July 9, 1875, *Relatório de 1875*, Doc. no. 2, unpaginated.
46. Commercial Association of Rio de Janeiro to Minister of Justice, Rio de Janeiro, May 1, 1876, *Relatório de 1876*, pp. 8–11; Associação Comercial do Rio de Janeiro, *Relatório de 1877*, pp. 3–4.
47. Commercial Association of Bahia to President of Province, Salvador, Nov. 20, 1876, *Relatório de 1877*, p. 32; Minutes, meeting of Dec. 20, 1877, Livro 4 de Atas, AACP, p. 116; Associação Comercial de São Paulo, *Relatório da Associação Comercial de São Paulo, Ano de 1895* (São Paulo: Industrial, 1896), pp. 33–34.

ciations of Pernambuco and Bahia succeeded in the mid-1880s in having a head tax placed on traveling salesmen and factory representatives from outside their provinces, many of them agents for European manufacturers. At 1:000$000 (U.S.$420.00 in 1884), the levies were intended to be prohibitive.[48] These individuals, not otherwise taxed by the province, circumvented importers in contacts with retailers. The Commercial Association of Rio de Janeiro also denounced the outsiders, but asked only that they be subject to ordinary taxes on businessmen.[49] Decreeing Pernambuco and Bahia's prohibitive tax was one thing; applying it another. The interlopers immediately fled the province when told to pay. Recife importers in 1885 begged the Pernambuco association to help its province collect the head tax, a plea the group could not satisfy.[50] By 1889, Bahia's president of province admitted that the tax was impossible to collect and advised its elimination.[51] Traveling salesmen and factory representatives continued to offer formidable competition to established importers through the rest of the century.

A basic aspect of the commercial associations' control over business personnel was determination of who was a merchant. By tradition derived from Portugal, merchants upon proof of habitual profession, funds to carry on their business, good reputation, and knowledge of double-entry bookkeeping and other mercantile practice could register with their local Commercial Tribunal.[52] Only those registered could officially style themselves "businessman" (*homen de negócios*) and enjoy the provisions in the Commercial Code in favor of commerce. From 1850 on, commercial associations informed the Commercial Tribunal whether the applicant had the "habitual profession of merchant."[53] From an association's decision there was no appeal. Despite the law, the benefits of the Commercial Code apparently were increasingly given to nonregistered businessmen as well, for the requirement was more and more ignored. By 1889, Laemmert's *Almanak* no longer bothered to identify "registered merchants."[54] Com-

---

48. Pernambuco, Presidente da Província, *Fala com que o Exm. Sr. Presidente Desembargador José Manuel de Freitas Abriu a Sessão da Assembléia Legislativa Provincial de Pernambuco no Dia 1 de Março de 1884* (Recife: Manuel Figueiroa de Faria & Filhos, 1884), p. 20.
49. Commercial Association of Rio de Janeiro to Minister of Finance, Rio de Janeiro, Aug. 31, 1889, *Relatório de 1890*, p. 39.
50. Associação Comercial de Pernambuco, *Relatório de 1886*, p. 6.
51. Bahia, Presidente da Província, *Relatório de 1889*, pp. 14–15.
52. For qualifications and sample applications, see "Pedido de Matrícula de Comerciante, 1809–1850," SH/AN, caixa 444. For Portuguese background, see John Norman Kennedy, "Bahian Elites, 1750–1822," *HAHR*, 53 (Aug. 1973): 420.
53. Brazil, leis, decretos, etc., *Leis, 1850*, Part 2, II: 235; After 1868 testimony was no longer obligatory. Brazil, leis, decretos, etc., *Coleção das Decisões do Govêrno do Império do Brasil de 1868* (Rio de Janeiro: Tipografia Nacional, 1868), XXXI: 296.
54. *Almanak Administrativo, Mercantil, e Industrial do Império do Brasil para 1889* (Rio de Janeiro: Laemmert, 1889), p. 738 n.

mercial associations, however, continued to certify the "habitual profession of merchant" of individuals upon request and in court cases.

Measures and the metric system

Commerce also had its physical side. If regulations for business and businessmen had to be standardized, so obviously did measurements. The situation in Brazil prior to the metric system was chaotic. Goods were bought and sold in intricate units of *alqueire, moio,* and *saco* (dry measure), *pipa, almude, canada,* and *medida* (liquid measure), and *covado, vara, pé,* and *braça* (yard goods).[55] In addition to being alien to the measures of Portugal and other European nations, these units commonly differed between major provinces, although going by the same name. More confusingly, they usually had no standard relationship to each other. One of the early jobs of commercial associations was to define such relationships; how many *canadas,* of Rio de Janeiro or of Bahia, for example, in a *pipa* of rum? This decided, it became necessary to relate the varied measurements to the metric system used by many of Brazil's trading partners.

The Brazilian situation made the advantage of the metric system obvious. It was adopted in 1862, allowing ten years to phase out the old measures. As the January 1, 1873 deadline approached, commercial association leaders were ready, but many members and their customers were not. In Pernambuco, in 1869, foodstuffs merchants begged the intervention of the commercial association before the imperial government to delay conversion.[56] Implying the protesters were unprogressive, and even too lazy to learn the new system, the association refused. The Commercial Association of Pará, calling a public meeting in 1871 to promote and explain the metric system, encountered a near-unanimous refusal to cooperate.[57] Shaken, the group stated it would not try again. Difficulties arose even in Rio de Janeiro. In June 1873, the Rio association unsuccessfully begged the Council of Ministers to further delay the date for conversion, which had already been extended. A bill to that effect placed in Parliament at the group's request also failed.[58]

In the meantime, the major commercial associations of Rio de Janeiro, Bahia, and Pernambuco had taken up the task of standardizing exports into kilograms, liters, and meters. The Rio association determined the

55. Gillmer to Department of State, Salvador, Oct. 23, 1854, NA/DS T-331, Vol. 1, unpaginated; Harold B. Johnson, Jr., "A Preliminary Inquiry into Money, Prices, and Wages in Rio de Janeiro, 1763–1823," in *Colonial Roots of Modern Brazil: Papers of the Newberry Library Conference,* ed. Dauril Alden (Berkeley: University of California Press, 1973), pp. 238–239.
56. Minutes, meeting of April 10, 1869, Livro 3 de Atas, AACP, p. 31.
57. Associação Comercial do Pará, *Relatório de 1871,* p. 18.
58. Commercial Association of Rio de Janeiro to President, Council of Ministers, Rio de Janeiro, June 18, 1873, *Relatório de 1873,* Doc. no. 1, unpaginated; ibid., p. 4.

"classic" sixty-kilo bag for coffee and the liter content of a *pipa;* the Pernambuco group apparently set the size of Brazilian cotton and sugar containers.[59] Resistance to the metric system in the cities (although not in the countryside) gradually melted.[60] Most aggressive in promoting the change was the Commercial Association of Pernambuco, which in 1872 arranged a covenant (*convênio*) among Recife merchants to use the metric system and enforced it through committees that supervised commodity purchases.[61] An apprehensive Commercial Association of Pará, calling another public meeting on the metric system in 1874, was relieved to have it accepted without discussion.[62] The conversion, in which commercial associations had played important roles, was a major step toward economic integration with the Atlantic community and an even greater convenience for those who traded.

Introducing the metric system was integral to standardizing Brazilian business practice, as was the regulation of the auxiliary professions of business, promoting business honesty, and formulating uniform, precise rules for the efficient conduct of business. The Commercial Code of 1850, heavily influenced by the Commercial Association of Rio de Janeiro, defined much of the role of the associations. Although not successful in all fields, commercial associations nevertheless were a major force in integrating Brazilian business practice both nationally and with that of its trading partners, thus facilitating the economic development of the nineteenth century.

Filling another vacuum: business services

As with regulation and standardization of business practice, the Brazilian government left to business interest groups the provision of many business services. The groups had the choice of either performing such services or having them unavailable to membership. Conspicuous among them was the provision of statistics. A knowledgeable foreign resident remarked in 1883: "As is known, statistics are not the forte of our government. All statistical tables in Brazil are incomplete and offer a weak base for any type of argumentation."[63] Lack of reliable statistics or, often, any statistics,

---

59. Associação Comercial do Rio de Janeiro, *Relatório de 1872*, p. 7, *Relatório de 1881*, p. 13, and *Relatório de 1884–1885*, pp. 23–24; Minutes, meeting of June 28, 1869, Livro 3 de Atas, AACP, p. 33.

60. Along with a number of other causes of discontent, the imposition of the metric system provoked riots and destruction of records in Alagôas, Pernambuco, Paraíba, and Rio Grande do Norte. Roderick J. Barman, "The Brazilian Peasantry Reexamined: The Implications of the Quebra-Quilo Revolt, 1874–1875," *HAHR*, 57 (Aug. 1977): 401–424.

61. Minutes, meeting of Oct. 5, 1873, Livro 3 de Atas, AACP, p. 106.

62. Associação Comercial do Pará, *Relatório de 1874*, p. 4.

63. Carl von Koseritz, *Imgens do Brasil (1883)*, trans. Afonso Arinos de Melo Franco (São Paulo: Livraria Martins, 1943), pp. 204–205.

seriously handicapped evaluation of Brazil's economic situation. In 1882 the Center for Coffee Agriculture and Commerce, seeking an answer to the coffee crisis, demanded the government publish relevant statistics, and in 1888 the Commercial Association of Rio de Janeiro, responding to complaints from Europe's major entrepôts, sent a committee of directors to plead with the Minister of Agriculture for publication of statistics on Brazil's coffee harvest.[64] Neither action had any effect.

Business interest groups had little choice but to fill the gap. The statutes of all commercial associations listed collection of commercial and industrial statistics as a major objective. Data on volume and value of trade and on ship movement filled much of the space in annual reports. Such information was furnished by customs officials and occasionally by warehouse and railroad employees. It often came at a price, although ideally given gratis as a favor to the group. Collection, thus, was often expensive as well as time-consuming for group clerical staff. Publication of statistical information depended on the availability of clerical manpower and the demands of membership and government and tended to be irregular and varied in content. One money-saving expedient was not to publish statistics but to put them in registers available to members and other consumers. In whatever form, the groups customarily furnished statistical information willingly and without cost to government, companies, and individuals.

The gap in statistical information was enormous. As late as 1881, the Commercial Association of Bahia was virtually that province's only publisher of statistics.[65] The commercial associations of Santos and Maranhão attempted to compile statistical descriptions of their provinces, in the latter case without success because of the noncooperation of local authorities.[66] Located in Brazil's center of economic activity, the Commercial Association of Rio de Janeiro was particularly active in compilation. By 1870 it was keeping figures on the movement of eighty-nine commodities or articles. In 1886, however, it suspended its coffee statistical service because of heavy expense.[67]

Decades of dependence on commercial associations for statistical information led the new Republican regime to make them the seat of the first government statistics gathering bodies. A February 1890 decree established Commercial Statistics Sections (*Seções de Estatística Comercial*), for each state, attached to a local commercial association. The Administrative

---

64. Centro da Lavoura e Comércio do Café, *Representação Submetida ao Poder Legislativo sôbre Algumas das Necessidades da Lavoura e do Comércio* (Rio de Janeiro: Moreira, Maximino, 1882), pp. 26–28; Minutes, meeting of Nov. 3, 1888, Livro de Atas, 1881–1890, AACRJ, pp. 200–201.
65. Prindle to Department of State, Salvador, Nov. 24, 1881, NA/DS T-331, Vol. 4.
66. Minutes, meeting of Aug. 23, 1884, Livro de Atas, 1874–1894, AACS, p. 88; Jerônimo de Viveiros, *História do Comércio do Maranhão, 1612–1895* (São Luís: Associação Comercial do Maranhão, 1954), II: 466.
67. *O Jornal: Edição Comemorativa*, Quarta Seção, p. 6.

Council of each section was composed of the association president and six members chosen by the group, assisted by three or four government employees.[68] Provision of reliable statistics was seen by the decree's author, Rui Barbosa, as a key means of weakening foreign domination of Brazil's export economy.[69] The experiment was not successful. The Commercial Statistics Sections suffered from incompetent personnel, weak funding, noncooperation from government agencies, and perhaps reluctance by the commercial association members directing them, who were not paid.[70] A law of November 1892 abolished the Sections and returned gathering of statistics to the customs houses where, as in the past, the task was clumsily or tardily done.[71] The statistical dearth remained.

By the mid-1890s lack of reliable figures on coffee production in the State of São Paulo, the world's largest producing area, was keenly felt. Coffee was entering its crisis of overproduction. The Minister of Finance had to request from the Commercial Association of São Paulo figures on coffee export and movement and estimates for the 1895 and 1896 harvests.[72] Santos exporters, meanwhile, were concerned about the disturbance to overseas coffee markets from lack of information on harvests. In 1896 they prevailed upon their commercial association to organize a ten-firm committee to gather harvest figures.[73] By 1899, noting that the committees gathering harvest statistics increasingly resented the drain on their time and energy, the Santos association successfully substituted the cooperation of the state's *município* officials.[74] Furnished to various agencies of state and federal government, the Commercial Association of Santos's figures were a blessing to exporters and especially valuable in correcting mistaken estimates that otherwise would have distorted the coffee market.[75] Although the services of commercial associations in furnishing statistics were of necessity irregular, they filled vital lacunae for business and government. Their annual reports remain one of the best sources of statistics for the nineteenth century.

Connected with the provision of statistics was the furnishing of current prices from each of Brazil's commodity markets. Commercial associations, and the Commercial Agricultural Association of Pernambuco, made them

68. Brazil, leis, decretos, etc., *Decretos do Govêrno Provisório*, p. 313.
69. "Exposição ao Chefe do Govêrno Provisório," *Relatório da Associação Comercial da Bahia de 1891*, pp. 53–57.
70. Great Britain, Foreign Office, *Diplomatic and Consular Reports*, no. 1547 (1895): 5; *RMF, 1891*, pp. 79–80; Associação Comercial de Santos, *Relatório de 1891*, pp. 15–19.
71. *RMF, 1894*, p. 141.
72. Minister of Finance to Commercial Association of São Paulo, Rio de Janeiro, March 22, 1895, *Relatório de 1895*, p. 139.
73. Minutes, meeting of Dec. 28, 1896, Livro de Atas, 1894–1904, AACS, p. 25.
74. Minutes, meeting of Nov. 28, 1899, Livro de Atas, 1894–1904, AACS, p. 43.
75. Edward Greene to Charles Edward Johnston, London Manager, Edward Johnston & Co., Santos, July 3, 1899, Personal Copy Book – E. Greene, LABA/UCLL, p. 308; Associação Comercial de Santos, *Relatório de 1900*, p. 10.

available regularly in newspapers or in booklets, with the Commercial Association of Pernambuco for awhile putting out a special version in English.[76] In 1881 the Rio and Santos associations began to furnish daily information to the newly organized New York Coffee Exchange and in 1883 to the important European coffee market at Havre, France, at the cost of the receivers.[77]

Information on economic and political conditions in nations trading with Brazil was vital for the successful conduct of long-range business. Since before the underseas cable such information was likely to be very irregular, several business interest groups hired overseas agents who furnished periodic reports on Europe and the United States gathered from newspapers, journals, and informants.[78] With the establishment of overseas cable connections the need for special arrangements ended. More prosaic but nevertheless important sources of information were the commercial libraries. Establishment of a library useful for business was part of the statutes of all commercial associations. The libraries contained business and trade reference books, newspapers, journals, and publications quoting prices, and often scholarly works on economics and history. The Commercial Association of São Paulo, perhaps typical, in 1895 subscribed to twenty-five Brazilian and fourteen foreign newspapers and journals.[79] Subscription to foreign newspapers and journals was quite expensive, particularly before midcentury, when they had to be purchased and forwarded by an overseas agent. In some cities the commercial association library was a major source of information for educated persons and the only one on economic matters.

Business interest groups offered other varied information services. In the absence of other suitable institutions, commercial associations kept maritime information. Available were not only harbor regulations, charts of local waters, and the location of lighthouses on the Brazilian coast, but information on navigation in European waters. Such a service was easily justified because many ship captains, customarily allowed use of commercial association headquarters, were businessmen as well by being owners or consignees of the cargo they carried. Commercial associations also served as business information exchanges for companies and for government. They furnished without cost information on local companies to those wishing to do business and even to government for tax purposes. In recommending specific local firms or in publicizing the offerings of out-

76. Minutes, meeting of Sept. 17, 1860, Livro 2 de Atas, AACP, p. 129.
77. Associação Comercial do Rio de Janeiro, *Relatório de 1881*, pp. 14–15, and *Relatório de 1882–1883*, pp. 31–32; Commercial Association of Rio de Janeiro to Commercial Association of Santos, Rio de Janeiro, Feb. 18, 1884, *Relatório da Associação Comercial de Santos de 1885*, Anexo no. 4, pp. 19–20.
78. Associação Comercial do Rio de Janeiro, *Relatório de 1872*, pp. 4–5, and *Relatório de 1873*, pp. 7–8; Associação Comercial de Pernambuco, *Relatório de 1858*, p. 10.
79. Associação Comercial de São Paulo, *Relatório de 1895*, pp. 134–135.

side firms, the associations acted in effect as brokers for business arrangements.

Among the information services performed by business interest groups was that of evaluation. The Engineering Club evaluated inventions for their inventors and the products of Brazilian factories for manufacturers, sometimes with painful frankness. For the latter, the Engineering Club charged a small variable fee. Although hardly a part of their stated aims, the Commercial Association of Pernambuco evaluated and financed an invention "to steer balloons," and the Commercial Agricultural Association debated in general assembly backing a device to move ships by air pressure.[80]

A final service for business offered by its interest groups was schooling. Education for business, uncommon in any part of the world in the nineteenth century, was not offered in Brazilian schools. The commercial associations of Rio de Janeiro and Pernambuco, through determined lobbying, were able to put a business curriculum into local public schools in 1846 and 1861, respectively.[81] A Commercial Institute (*Instituto Comercial*), a secondary school state-supported but headed by the President of the Commercial Association of Pernambuco, was inaugurated in Recife in 1891.[82] Business interest groups also financed schools sponsored by voluntary societies, which offered free or low-cost education and compensated somewhat for Brazil's manifestly inadequate public school system. The Commercial Association of Maranhão was the main support of three such schools in backward São Luís, while the Rio association financed not only the business curriculum in one of the city's largest free schools, but also special classes for women, who received little educational attention in nineteenth-century Brazil.[83] The Commercial Association of Bahia had the most direct participation in education, founding in 1846 its own business school for the sons of members and their employees. Considering the state of literacy and learning in Salvador, it was a distinct contribution, although complaints of poor attendance, lack of effort, and bad conduct by students marred its history.[84] Student disorders brought about its closing in 1873.

80. Minutes, meeting of July 30, 1881, Livro 5 de Atas, AACP, p. 43; Minutes, meeting of April 20, 1883, Livro de Atas da ACAP, 1877–1892, AACP, p. 78. There is no information on the outcome of the Commercial Agricultural Association's debate.
81. Barros, *Associação Comercial*, pp. 88–89; Associação Comercial de Pernambuco, *Relatório de 1859*, p. 6; Minutes, meeting of Feb. 8, 1861, Livro 2 de Atas, AACP, p. 135.
82. Associação Comercial de Pernambuco, *Relatório de 1891*, p. 29.
83. Associação Comercial do Maranhão, *Relatório de 1873*, pp. 7–8; Commercial Association of Rio de Janeiro to Liceum of Arts and Professions (*Liceu de Artes e Ofícios*), Rio de Janeiro, Oct. 11, 1881, and Commercial Association of Rio de Janeiro to Liceum of Arts and Professions, Rio de Janeiro, March 11, 1882, *Relatório de 1881*, pp. 23–24, 27–28.
84. Eugene W. Ridings, "The Bahian Commercial Association, 1840–1889: A Pressure Group in an Underdeveloped Area" (Ph.D. Diss., University of Florida, 1970), p. 160; Associação Comercial da Bahia, *Relatório de 1873*, p. 4.

Schooling was a small part of the varied services offered by business interest groups to further the economic integration of Brazil. Other services concerned with information essential for business were provided in the absence of any other source. Increased activity by government and improved communications closed some of the gap by the end of the century, but business interest groups continued to furnish information invaluable to economic development until well into the twentieth century.

Urban integration: facilities and services

The role of business interest groups in urban integration was similar to that in economic integration and impelled by the same sense of urgency. As Brazil's trade expanded, so did its cities. The same traditional prerogatives that gave business interest groups control over harbors extended tacitly to their adjacent waterfront and business areas. The government often was unable to guarantee the convenience, health, and security of these areas, prerequisites for the efficient and safe conduct of business. Again, business interest groups, willing or not, had to fill the gap.

To facilitate conveyance of goods, business interest groups tried to arrange the layout of the urban areas in which their members operated. This was particularly true of Recife, whose commercial district was separated by water from the rest of the city. The Commercial Association and Agricultural Commercial Association of Pernambuco regularly advised government about the design, construction, and location of bridges to Recife's island commercial district and the layout of its streets.[85] The commercial associations of Santos and Bahia also arranged the cutting or extension of streets in their commercial districts.[86] Municipal governments relied heavily on the expertise of business interest groups to resolve problems of urbanization. Most called on was the Engineering Club, which evaluated construction and sanitation, and municipal health regulations for Brazilian cities and in 1887 aided the imperial government in planning the sanitizing of Rio de Janeiro.[87] Other business interest groups intervened when the knowledge of their membership was needed.

85. Associação Comercial de Pernambuco, *Relatório de 1859*, p. 9; Minutes, meeting of Nov. 10, 1862, Livro 2 de Atas, AACP, p. 161; Commercial Association of Pernambuco to Vice-President of Province, Recife, May 29, 1869, *Relatório de 1869*, Anexo no. 11, pp. 1–2; Associação Comercial de Pernambuco, *Relatório de 1881*, p. 20, and *Relatório de 1882*, pp. 6–8; Minutes, meeting of June 12, 1882, Livro de Atas da ACAP, 1877–1892, AACP, p. 62.
86. Minutes, meeting of Sept. 28, 1899, Livro de Atas, 1894–1904, AACS, p. 51; Commercial Association of Bahia to President of Municipal Council, Salvador, Oct. 7, 1896, *Relatório de 1896*, p. 188.
87. *Revista do Clube da Engenharia*, Ano I (1887) and Ano II (1888), passim; Ano I, 3 (March 1887): 36.

The Bahian and Santos associations successfully challenged municipal contracts for sewers and paving as being needlessly expensive.[88] The province of Pará in 1870 asked and received the guidance of its commercial association on paving the streets of Belém.[89] In 1895 the Commercial Association of Santos was called in by the state government to untangle the municipal finances of its entrepôt.[90]

In 1891 that same association exercised the peak of business interest group influence on urban affairs by briefly governing Santos. Following the resignation of Deodoro da Fonseca, first President of the Republic, local Republicans handed rule of the city to the Board of Directors of the Commercial Association of Santos, a body counting a number of his opponents, termed "Historical Republicans." Meeting daily, the Board administered Santos on December 14 and 15 and, when no other authority could be found, from December 18 until December 30, when a regular council was appointed.[91] The situation highlighted public recognition of the administrative skills of business interest group leaders, although the association's political leanings were also important.

No urban problem concerned those leaders more than urban sanitation. The major ports of nineteenth-century Brazil offered a notably dangerous disease environment, including cholera, smallpox, and bubonic plague. Particularly threatening to foreigners was yellow fever, whose mortality in epidemics could surpass fifty percent.[92] In 1879 the Commercial Association of Santos noted that the unhealthiness of its entrepôt was "now proverbial."[93] Most foreigners agreed with a traveler that Rio, "one of the fairest cities in the world is also one of the most fatal to health and even existence."[94] A United States consul remarked: "To no place on earth, perhaps, can be more truthfully applied than to Pará the scriptural quotation, 'In the midst of life we are in death.'"[95]

Ineffectual and sometimes grotesque preventives and cures doubtless contributed to the mortality of yellow fever, whose cause was as yet

88. Commercial Association of Bahia to Governor of State, Salvador, July 30, 1890, *Relatório de 1891*, pp. 144–152; Minutes, meeting of Dec. 24, 1895, Livro de Atas, 1894–1904, AACS, p. 18.

89. Commercial Association of Pará to Comptroller (*Procurador Fiscal*) of Provincial Treasury, Belém, Sept. 30, 1870, *Relatório de 1871*, Anexos, pp. 16–17.

90. Minutes, meeting of July 22, 1895, Livro de Atas, 1894–1904, AACS, pp. 14–15.

91. Associação Comercial de Santos, *Relatório de 1893*, p. 9; João da Costa e Silva Sobrinho, *Santos Noutros Tempos* (São Paulo: Revista dos Tribunais, 1953), p. 255.

92. São Paulo, Governador do Estado, *Mensagens Apresentadas ao Congresso Legislativo de S. Paulo pelos Presidentes do Estado e Vice-Presidentes em Exercício, Desde a Proclamação da República Até ao Ano de 1916* (São Paulo: Diário Oficial, 1916), p. 124.

93. *Relatório de 1879*, p. 14.

94. Frank Vincent, *Around and About South America: Twenty Months of Quest and Query* (5th ed.; New York: D. Appleton, 1895), p. 224.

95. J. Orton Kerbey, *An American Consul in Amazonia* (New York: W. E. Rudge, 1911), p. 142.

unknown in the late nineteenth century. Foreign businessmen in Belém carried bottles of castor oil and swigged from them upon experiencing the slightest discomfort.[96] The remedy of the British consul in Santos for threatened ships' crews was to "serve out from five to ten grains of calomel all around, followed by a strong dose of castor-oil; then cleanse their stomaches by pump and serve out lime-juice and rum. No food whatever! . . . After black vomit, serve out arsenic on the fourth day, with coffee enema!"[97] Observers wondered, only half-jokingly, whether the consul's measures were more threatening to life than the disease itself.

Business interest groups focused on one of the presumed causes of disease: the lack of cleanliness encountered in Brazil's major ports.[98] Unsanitary conditions were often plain. In Salvador, garbage was not collected, human waste was customarily thrown into the gutters of the streets, and alleys served, as a physician delicately put it, "as temples of Cloacina [excretion]."[99] In Santos sewer pipes poured fecal materials into rivulets and drains that traversed the commercial and dock areas, broad-casting an "abominable stench."[100] Not surprisingly, business interest groups first demanded the cleaning of port and business districts. Garbage heaps were removed, standing water drained, sewage lines rerouted, and cemeteries close to congested areas shut down. The groups also formed part of committees to combat recurring epidemics and even rallied city inhabitants for a general cleanup to prevent further outbreaks. Pressure from the groups contributed to notable advances in hygiene by the end of the century, especially in Santos, whose commercial association had aggressively promoted sanitation.[101]

Business interest groups also displayed some ambiguity toward sanitation. While urging improvement, they often opposed government measures against epidemics when such measures halted or slowed trade. They objected to what they considered overzealous inspection of food imports and the prohibition of the entry of ships during epidemics. They heaped protests on Brazil's Foreign Ministry whenever epidemics or rumors of epidemics led the River Plate republics to quarantine commerce with

96. Frank George Carpenter, *South America: Social, Industrial, and Political, a Twenty-Five Thousand Mile Journey in Search of Information* (Akron, Ohio: Saalfield, 1900), p. 575.
97. W. R. Kennedy, *Sporting Sketches in South America* (London: R. H. Porter, 1892), p. 236.
98. For cleanliness, see, for example, London *Times*, Sept. 18, 1858, p. 7; *O Estado de São Paulo* (São Paulo), Aug. 17, 1898, p. 2.
99. Robert Dundas, *Sketches of Brazil, Including New Views on Tropical and European Fever with Remarks on a Premature Decay of the System Incident to Europeans on Their Return from Hot Climates* (London: John Churchill, 1852), p. 202.
100. Costa e Silva Sobrinho, *Santos Noutros Tempos*, p. 400; São Paulo, Governador do Estado, *Mensagens Apresentadas*, p. 62.
101. São Paulo, Governador do Estado, *Mensagens Apresentadas*, p. 87; *O Estado de São Paulo*, Aug. 17, 1898, p. 2.

Brazil.[102] On the other hand, some health regulations were absurdly inconvenient. Vessels coming from regions where cholera had broken out in the 1880s and 1890s were quarantined at Ilha Grande near Rio de Janeiro no matter what their Brazilian destination. Only the Commercial Association of Pará was able to circumvent this by arranging for a quarantine station to be established near Belém.[103]

The Commercial Association of Santos experienced the heavy-handedness of government when bubonic plague broke out in October 1899. Santos was declared quarantined by land and sea, cutting it off from food, and hunger threatened. The association bombarded President Campos Sales with telegrams explaining the danger. He soon authorized Santos to receive food by rail at special rates and later by sea from designated ships.[104] Famine was averted, and eventually the association persuaded Campos Sales to lift the quarantine entirely.[105] When the plague broke out in Rio de Janeiro in May 1900, Santos was quarantined again, although no cases had appeared there. Protesting "energetically and without delay" to the President, the Minister of Interior, and the Governor of the State, the association succeeded in lifting the ban.[106] Santos's experience illustrated why business interest group support of government health measures was often selective.

Fire and police protection, charity and relief

The primitive state of sanitation services in nineteenth-century Brazil paralleled the weakness of other urban institutions. Fire and police protection were also rudimentary or nonexistent in many cities until promoted or strengthened by business interest groups. Foreign members of those groups were familiar with the organization of fire and police services and with standards for their performance. This initiative was not motivated solely by civic spirit. Large-scale fire and crime were most likely to occur in congested waterfront and business districts, with personal loss to membership.

102. Commercial Association of Rio de Janeiro to Foreign Ministry, Rio de Janeiro, Dec. 9, 1872, Commercial Center (*Centro Comercial*), Santa Ana do Livramento to Foreign Ministry, Santa Ana do Livramento, June 7, 1892, and Commercial Center of Rio de Janeiro to Foreign Ministry, Rio de Janeiro, Nov. 10, 1899, AHI, 313, 1, 29.
103. Associação Comercial do Pará, *Relatório de 1893*, p. 3.
104. President of Republic to Commercial Association of Santos, Rio de Janeiro, Oct. 26, 1899, and Minister of Interior to Commercial Association of Santos, Rio de Janeiro, Oct. 29, 1899, *Relatório de 1900*, Anexos no. 27 and 31, unpaginated.
105. Minutes, meeting of Nov. 7, 1899, Livro de Atas da ACAP, 1895–1903, AACP, p. 48; President of Republic to Commercial Association of Santos, Rio de Janeiro, Nov. 29, 1899, *Relatório de 1900*, Anexo no. 43, unpaginated.
106. Associação Comercial de Santos, *Relatório de 1900*, pp. 11–12.

The commercial associations of Amazonas, Pará, and Maranhão promoted the foundation of fire departments in their entrepôts in the last twelve years of the century.[107] The Pernambuco association, aided by local insurance companies, organized a fire department for Recife in 1872.[108] The Bahian association founded Salvador's first modern fire department in 1848, operated it until 1859, and permitted it to remain housed in association headquarters until 1890.[109] That group also demonstrated its concern over fire by organizing within itself Bahia's first two lasting insurance companies in 1841 and 1850–1851.[110] Business interest groups also made sure that police in the port and commercial districts of their city were numerous and efficient, particularly the Commercial Association of Bahia. Since 1816 the police detachment of Salvador's lower city was housed in its headquarters, and from foundation in 1840 until century's end that association donated materials for the detachment's work and kept a close watch over its activities. In 1877 the lower city police detachment was abolished and the association was forced to create its own police unit, using firemen to patrol the streets. Determined lobbying reestablished the lower city force in 1879.[111]

The Commercial Association of Santos was also forced, literally, to take the law into its own hands in 1893. Despite a wave of theft of coffee en route to warehouses, police had not obtained a single conviction. In March, the Santos association organized and armed its own "Commercial Police" (*Polícia Comercial*), funded by local business. It also had the Governor appoint a new Chief of Police and two Assistant Chiefs for Santos, men it recommended, and began to subsidize the Santos police force so that it could be expanded.[112] The Commercial Police did not last long. In June 1893, it was declared illegal by the state Secretary of Justice, whereupon the association angrily discontinued the police subsidy. However, the problem of coffee theft grew. In March 1895, the association organized, with the help of Santos's Chief of Police, and financed a plainclothes "Secret Police," apparently charged with suppressing coffee theft.[113] The Commercial Association of Santos also resumed at roughly this time (its records on the subject are cryptic) subsidizing the regular police, "to keep

107. Associação Comercial do Amazonas, *Documentário Comemorativo do Primeiro Centenário da Associação Comercial do Amazonas, 18 de Junho de 1971* (Manaus: Associação Comercial do Amazonas, 1971), pp. 56–57; Associação Comercial do Pará, *Relatório de 1889*, p. 5; Associação Comercial do Maranhão, *Relatório de 1891*, p. 8.
108. Minutes, meeting of May 20, 1872, LIvro 3 de Atas, AACP, p. 97.
109. Minutes, meeting of Nov. 4, 1848, Livro 1 de Atas, AACB, p. 278; Minutes, meeting of May 25, 1859, Livro 2 de Atas, AACB, p. 143; Governor of State to Commercial Association of Bahia, Salvador, Oct. 14, 1890, *Relatório de 1891*, p. 169.
110. Minutes, meetings of Nov. 22, 1841 and Dec. 23, 1850, Livro 1 de Atas, AACB, pp. 58, 330.
111. Minutes, general assembly of Jan. 23, 1879, Livro 4 de Atas, AACB, p. 331.
112. Associação Comercial de Santos, *Relatório de 1893*, pp. 13, 211–218.
113. Minutes, meeting of March 19, 1895, Livro de Atas, 1894–1904, AACS, pp. 6–7.

good men on the force."[114] It also gave a monthly stipend to the Chief of Police, requiring from him a monthly report on progress against coffee theft.[115] In 1900 it also began to fund a privately organized "Night Guard for Commerce" (*Guarda Noturna Comercial*).[116] In a situation where adequate police protection for commerce was not otherwise available, the Commercial Association of Santos did not hesitate to organize it and to purchase it.

If fire and police services in Brazilian cities were often inadequate, so too were charity and relief. In Luso-Brazilian tradition they were administered by the Church, usually through the lay religious brotherhoods. By the nineteenth century, however, demands for charity and especially relief were beginning to exceed the capabilities of the brotherhoods. For its part, the Brazilian state was as yet inexperienced and ill-equipped for this role. Business interest groups, on the other hand, had the ability to raise and disburse large sums of money, and their members still virtually monopolized the art of efficient and accurate accounting. Group membership also was itself a prime source of charitable funding.

The groups frequently launched charitable drives for the needy families of familiar individuals. In the case of the Commercial Association of Rio de Janeiro, for example, they ranged from the family of a customs house worker who committed suicide in 1840 to that of Minister of War Carlos Machado Bittencourt, killed in an attempt on the life of the President in 1897.[117] Government and even the Church requested much charitable work of business interest groups because of the administrative skills of their membership. The Commercial Association of Bahia, for example, handled three major provincial Paraguayan War patriotic charitable funds and administered the endowment of Salvador's insane asylum, founded by a lay religious brotherhood.[118] The groups helped launch and support many such institutions founded by the Church. A favorite charity of business interest groups was the beggars' asylum. The Pernambuco association founded one for Recife in 1859, with Emperor Pedro II attending the ceremonies, and sustained it financially.[119] In 1870 it boasted that

114. Minutes, meeting of Jan. 15, 1896, Livro de Atas, 1894–1904, AACS, p. 18.
115. Ibid.; Minutes, meetings of Jan. 28, 1896 and Sept. 24, 1898, Livro de Atas, 1894–1904, AACS, pp. 19, 33.
116. Associação Comercial de Santos, *Relatório de 1900*, p. 22.
117. *Jornal do Comércio*, Jan. 23, 1840, p. 2; Associação Comercial do Rio de Janeiro, *Relatório de 1901*, p. 8. Brazil's other commercial associations also collected funds for Machado Bittencourt's family. Associação Comercial da Bahia, *Relatório de 1899*, p. 142; Minutes, meeting of Nov. 16, 1897, Livro 6 de Atas, AACP, p. 138.
118. Ridings, "Bahian Commercial Association," p. 100; Associação Comercial da Bahia, *Relatório de 1869*, pp. 88, 96.
119. Pedro II, Emperor of Brazil, *Viagem a Pernambuco em 1859*, ed. Guilherme Auler (Recife: Arquivo Público Estadual, 1952), p. 155; Associação Comercial de Pernambuco, *Relatório de 1861*, p. 6.

308   *Business interest groups in nineteenth-century Brazil*

since 1859 beggars had disappeared from sight.[120] The Commercial Association of Bahia helped found a beggars' asylum for Salvador in 1877, an institution long headed by its President, Baron Guaí.[121] The sight of beggars offended men steeped in nineteenth-century economic liberalism and was, at any rate, felt to be a poor advertisement for local prosperity.

The most famous charitable institution of a business interest group eventually became a headache and an embarrassment. In 1865, early in the Paraguayan War, the Commercial Association of Rio de Janeiro launched a nationwide drive to build a Home for Disabled Veterans (*Asilo dos Inválidos da Pátria*) and to care for families of the dead, who were not supported by the government.[122] Nearly all directors of the Home for Disabled Veterans Society, which governed the institution, were board members of the Rio association. Since funding was not enough to build the home, which eventually housed more than two thousand disabled veterans, the government provided a building while the Commercial Association purchased the island on which it stood.[123] In 1885, in order to complete needed construction, or so it stated, the Rio group merged itself with the Home for Disabled Veterans Society, acquiring thus the original fund collected for the home. It promised to pay itself all expenses for which the fund had been gathered, except the maintenance of the home.[124]

Military leaders bridled at the takeover by the Commercial Association of Rio de Janeiro of a fund originally contributed by the public. Ministers of War challenged the legality of the union in 1885 and 1895, 1896, and 1897, as did residents of the home in 1900.[125] The challenges failed, but kept the association from legal possession of interest from the fund from 1892 to 1895. Even donating buildings and grounds to found Brazil's Military Academy in 1890 and founding a school for children of the home's veterans in 1899 could not curb military animosity. In the meantime, the press assailed the association for leaving the home in a "state of ruin," and accused it of withholding pensions and other support from veterans.[126] Such accusations, surfacing periodically, continued well into the twentieth century. The quarrel over the administration of the Home

120. *Relatório de 1870*, p. 12.
121. Bahia, Presidente da Província, *Relatório de 1876*, pp. 76–77, and *Relatório de 1877*, p. 48; Baron Guaí to Baron Cotegipe, Salvador, Nov. 5, 1887, ABC, AIHGB, lata 38, doc. 75.
122. Associação Comercial do Rio de Janeiro, *Relatório de 1867*, pp. 5–8; Barros, *Associação Comercial*, p. 100.
123. Sociedade Asilo dos Inválidos da Pátria, *Relatório Apresentado à Assembléia Geral no Dia 15 de Setembro de 1869, pelo seu Presidente o Vereador José Joaquim de Lima e Silva Sobrinho* (Rio de Janeiro: Perseverança, 1869), p. 8; Associação Comercial do Rio de Janeiro, *Relatório de 1867*, p. 13.
124. Associação Comercial do Rio de Janeiro, *Relatório de 1884–1885*, pp. 34–36.
125. Ibid., p. 42; Barros, *Associação Comercial*, pp. 154–155.
126. The association claimed the latter charge was a result of rationalization of pension payments. Associação Comercial do Rio de Janeiro, *Relatório de 1902*, pp. 9, 46.

for Disabled Veterans, fought in newspapers as well as in the courts, contributed greatly to the unpopularity of the Rio group and of commercial associations in general.

It was in the administration of relief where the talents of business interest group members shone most brightly. Relief committees formed by the groups had the complicated task of receiving both public and private contributions and dispensing them in the form of both cash payments and foodstuffs. In lesser emergencies, such as landslides, fires, or the very frequent shipwrecks, business interest groups usually acted privately. In major disasters, such as floods, epidemics, and droughts, they were commissioned by government. Pernambuco's President of Province in 1854 awarded the Commercial Association of Pernambuco the right to style itself "Beneficent" for its work in aiding victims of a major Recife flood.[127] The Pernambuco and Bahian associations played central roles in dispensing relief during cholera epidemics in their provinces at midcentury.[128] The Bahian group also softened the economic impact of the epidemic by obtaining from the imperial government a moratorium on debt payments in its province.[129] The international connections of business interest groups led to relief efforts beyond Brazil. Commercial associations raised funds to help victims of a major fire in Hamburg in 1842 and of a yellow fever epidemic in Buenos Aires in 1871.[130]

Droughts frequently tested the administrative abilities of business interest groups in the Northeast. In the event of hunger the groups could use the far-flung connections of their membership to bring in food from other parts of Brazil and even from as far away as England.[131] They could also manipulate food markets to attenuate scarcity. In severe droughts in the interior of Maranhão in 1878 and of Bahia in 1889 the commercial associations of both provinces arranged the importation of *farinha de mandioca,* staple of the poor, and its sale at cost. Both further lowered its price by arranging special transportation freights.[132] The relief and charitable activities of business interest groups helped to fill a long-lasting gap between Church administration of charity and relief and government assumption of those functions. With the exception of the Home for Disabled Veterans, they also improved the image of the business elite.

127. Minutes, meeting of July 3 and Sept. 25, 1854, Livro 2 de Atas, AACP, pp. 29–30, 38.
128. Minutes, general assembly of Oct. 26, 1855, Livro 2 de Atas, AACB, unpaginated; Minutes, meetings of Feb. 4, 1856 and Feb. 1, 1862, Livro 2 de Atas, AACP, pp. 53–56, 152–153.
129. Minutes, meeting of Dec. 5, 1855, Livro 2 de Atas, AACB, p. 95.
130. Minutes, meeting of July 13, 1842, Livro 1 de Atas, AACB, p. 77; Associação Comercial da Bahia, *Relatório de 1871,* p. 43.
131. Minutes, meeting of July 17, 1889, Livro 5 de Atas, AACB, p. 275.
132. Minutes, meetings of April 17 and May 1, 1889, Livro 5 de Atas, AACB, pp. 254, 256; Associação Comercial do Maranhão, *Relatório de 1879,* pp. 5–6; Commercial Association of Rio de Janeiro to Commercial Association of Maranhão, Rio de Janeiro, May 9, 1878, *Relatório da Associação Comercial do Rio de Janeiro de 1878,* p. 10.

Eventually, business interest groups divested themselves of most of their economic and urban integrating functions. As the Brazilian state grew increasingly capable of handling such services, the groups handed them over willingly. Integrating functions demanded effort, time, and often money. Many, such as registry of businesses, judgment of commercial disputes, and fire protection, were effectively taken over by government agencies during the nineteenth century. Others had to be performed by business interest groups until well into the twentieth century because of government deficiency. As late as 1894 the new Commercial Association of São Paulo was hailed as a source of otherwise unobtainable statistics and economic information.[133] In 1900, the Commercial Association of Ceará had to appeal to all the nation's commercial associations for help in combating a drought, because federal aid was late in arriving.[134]

The economic and urban integrating functions undertaken by business interest groups were among the most vital of their activities and ones in which they enjoyed a remarkable degree of autonomy. The groups were impelled by a combination of corporate tradition, self-interest, and, especially, necessity. Such integrating functions helped fill considerable gaps left by government. They were an invaluable aid to urbanization and a prerequisite to later economic development. They were a prime example of how private agencies can substitute for weak or immature government.

133. *Correio Paulistano* – *Orgão Republicano* (São Paulo), Dec. 21, 1894, p. 1.
134. Commercial Association of Ceará to Commercial Association of Santos, Fortaleza, Sept. 10, 1900, *Relatório da Associação Comercial de Santos de 1900*, Anexo no. 81, unpaginated; Associação Comercial de Pernambuco, *Relatório de 1901*, p. 6; Commercial Association of Amazonas to Commercial Association of Ceará, Manaus, Dec. 20, 1900, in Associação Comercial do Amazonas, *Primeiro Centenário*, p. 56.

12

Business interest groups and the Republic

The coming of the Republic brought major changes in the status and policies of business interest groups and eventually a change in the direction of the nation's economic development. The groups found themselves forced or encouraged to engage in partisan politics more emphatically and openly than before. Several of the older associations found their influence seriously weakened, while others found an opportunity to increase their power. The Center for Coffee Agriculture and Commerce, the Center for Sugar Industry and Commerce, and the Agricultural Industrial Center of Pelotas became inactive during the early years of the Republic, leaving the Commercial Agricultural Association of Pernambuco as Brazil's only factor group and the Engineering Club as its sole industrial group.

The Republic, particularly under its military presidents, expressed to a degree nationalist resentment of foreign domination of the Brazilian economy. This resentment had been fed during the 1880s by disputes between factors and exporters over rubber prices and by the attacks of industrial groups on the export-import economy and those who guided it. Nationalism aside, most business interest groups found the transition to the Republic perturbing. All, save the Engineering Club, were disturbed by the threat to the traditional export-import economy posed by Republican tariff policies. Also with the Republic came revolutionary disorder and civil strife for the first time since the 1840s. The *Encilhamento* brought chronic exchange depreciation and inflation, which contributed to unrest. The political and economic equilibrium of the late Empire had been broken and the response of business interest groups was greater involvement in partisan politics.

During the Empire all business interest groups had openly displayed their adherence to the monarchy and loyalty to the Emperor. This devotion did not stem solely from the natural conservatism of wealthy businessmen or the need for patriotic display. To the older commercial associations, in particular, the Empire and the person of Pedro II represented stability and safety. The Regency Period (1831–1840) and the following decade had been a time of uprisings and disorders, inspired at least partly by republicanism and separatism. Unrest had not only impeded business, but threatened the persons and property of the business elite. In the North and Northeast, Portuguese businessmen had been a target of urban working-class hostility. Revolutionary social upheaval also menaced those areas. Rebels had demanded the expulsion of Portuguese retailers, full manhood suffrage, and in one case even the abolition of slavery – measures that would have shaken the traditional oligarchic social order.[1] In Salvador the class struggle had taken definition along racial lines, with appeals for solidarity among white businessmen against the black and mulatto city masses.[2]

The gradual restoration of order was highlighted by the proclamation of the majority of the fourteen-year-old Pedro II in May 1840, an act that brought the Regency to an end. Soon afterward, Brazil's business elite demonstrated its support for the new regime in concrete fashion. Facing a sudden revenue shortage, the Minister of Finance called Rio de Janeiro's leading merchants together on the first of August to ask for an emergency loan.[3] The meeting, apparently arranged through the Commercial Association, turned out to be unnecessary. Rio's wealthiest merchants, most of whom probably were foreigners, had already learned of the problem and met among themselves, agreeing to offer "all necessary money for state business."[4] Less than a year later, another Minister of Finance took identical action to get emergency funds for the Treasury. In the meantime, Rio business leaders had also contributed heavily to finance suppression of a long-standing separatist rebellion in Rio Grande do Sul.[5] Brazil's business elite was willing to back the new regime with money as well as praise.

The new government's drive to restore order was successful. The Recife-based Praieira Revolution of 1848–1849 was the last major uprising inspired by separatism and republicanism. To commemorate its suppression, the Commercial Association of Pernambuco staged celebratory masses and other acts of thanksgiving, and awarded seven honorary memberships to commanders of loyal troops who had driven the rebels from the business district of Recife.[6] Sentiments of gratitude toward the Empire and Pedro II among the business elite of the Northeast continued strong. The commercial associations of Bahia and Pernambuco entertained the Emperor lavishly on his tour of the Northeast in 1859. The celebration

---

1. Parkinson to Foreign Office, Salvador, April 30, 1831, PRO/FO 13/33, fl. 94; Amaro Quintas, *O Sentido Social da Revolução Praieira* (Rio de Janeiro: Civilização Brasileira, 1967), pp. 16, 27, 124.
2. Private letter, Consul Parkinson to Consul-General Bidwell at Rio de Janeiro, Salvador, July 14, 1831, PRO/FO 13/88, fl. 123; João José Reis, "A Elite Baiana Face aos Movimentos Sociais, Bahia, 1824–1840," *Revista de História*, 54 (Oct.-Dec. 1976): 375–383.
3. *Jornal do Comércio* (Rio de Janeiro), Aug. 3, 1840, p. 3.
4. Ibid., Aug. 13, 1840, p. 3.   5. Ibid., May 1, 1841, p. 3, and April 25, 1841, p. 1.
6. Minutes, meeting of March 1, 1849, Livro 1 de Atas, AACP, p. 171; *Diário de Pernambuco* (Recife), Feb. 6, 1849, p. 1.

staged by the Bahian organization, in fact, was not only excessive but in bad taste. Bahia was just recovering from a drought and a cholera epidemic, and Pedro II was blunt enough to tell its Board of Directors he had rather the entertainment money had been spent on something useful for the province.[7]

If the business elite of nineteenth-century Brazil openly manifested its support for the Empire, the latter reciprocated in honoring the former's representative organizations, the commercial associations. The nine-year-old emperor Pedro II, seated on a specially constructed throne, presided over the inauguration of the the first headquarters of the Commercial Association of Rio de Janeiro in 1834 and was the leading contributor to its construction fund.[8] He also presided over the laying of the cornerstone for a new building in 1875.[9] He never failed to visit local commercial associations on his travels and was a frequent guest, often accompanied by the current president of the Council of Ministers, of the Commercial Association of Rio de Janeiro. Even more heartening to the associations was their unmatched access to the highest levels of government. Their petitions customarily received prompt and serious attention from imperial officials, even if not always acted on favorably. Equally important, the policies of the Imperial Government presented no serious threat to Brazil's traditional export-import economy or to the largely foreign merchant group at its center.

At least two commercial associations looked forward to undiminished, even heightened, influence after the death of Pedro II. The Commercial Association of Rio de Janeiro was on especially good terms with Princess Isabel, heir to the throne. In 1887 she personally promised its leaders government aid in paying for the organization's overly expensive new headquarters (a pledge backed by her prime minister, Baron Cotegipe).[10] In 1889 she accepted a gift of money from the organization.[11] Her consort, Count d'Eu, was an honorary member of the Commercial Association of Bahia, warmly entertained on his visits to Salvador. Pursuing financial security, he undertook numerous business dealings and had made himself a member of the business elite. As a descendant of French royalty deposed in revolutionary upheavals, Count d'Eu was, in the words of a contemporary, "aware, by the experience of his family, of the fragility of all things,

---

7. Pedro II, Emperor of Brazil, *Diário da Viagem ao Norte do Brasil*, ed. Lourenço Luís Lacombe (Salvador: Universidade da Bahia, 1959), p. 144.
8. Heitor Beltrão, "A Ansia de Brasildade: Os Comerciantes e a sua Agremiação Mater," *Mensário do Jornal do Comércio*, 26 (Oct. 1943): 31; *Jornal do Comércio*, Sept. 2, 1834, p. 2.
9. Associação Comercial do Rio de Janeiro, *Relatório da Associação Comercial do Rio de Janeiro no Ano de 1875* (Rio de Janeiro: Apóstolo, 1876), p. 5.
10. Minutes, meetings of Oct. 6 and Nov. 12, 1887, Livro de Atas, 1887–1892, AACRJ, pp. 178, 180.
11. Associação Comercial do Rio de Janeiro, *Relatório de 1902*, p. 45.

and [knew] well that a purse with millions in good securities is an excellent refuge, even better than a good conscience."[12]

Strengthening the support of business interest groups for the Empire was the belief by many foreigners that continued economic stability depended on its survival. Foreign businessmen feared not so much possible revolutionary disorder if the Empire toppled, as an inevitable decline in the value of Brazilian currency. Such a devaluation would lower the profitability of foreign investment, because profits made in declining *mil-reis* would have to be converted into British pounds or other hard currency before repatriation. Foreign investors nodded approval as the restrictive monetary policies of the Conservative Party pushed the *mil-reis* to peak strength in the late 1880s.[13]

Support for the Empire, however, was much weaker in provinces that felt neglected by the central government. Provincial assemblies had little power to correct basic economic problems, while presidents of province, appointed by the Emperor, often were more responsive to the central government than to local demands. Those provinces that felt the Empire unresponsive to their needs but that had the resources to further their own economic development wanted a more decentralized regime. Their business elite members were much more likely to be sympathetic toward Republicanism.

Pará, in the midst of its celebrated rubber boom, but finding the national government unmindful of its problems, was one such province. Such neglect was particularly irritating because the Empire by the 1880s spent in Pará a lower proportion, some one-sixth to one-seventh, of the revenue collected there than in any other province save perhaps São Paulo.[14] The Commercial Association of Pará as early as 1876 characterized its province as "abandoned by the high powers of government."[15] São Paulo also craved to control its own economic destiny. The nation's chief center of Republicanism, by the 1880s it boasted growing industry as well as a rapidly expanding coffee frontier. Not only did it enjoy little of the revenue it produced, but it was badly underrepresented in both Senate and Chamber of Deputies.[16] Santos, its entrepôt, was locked in a struggle with Rio de Janeiro for commercial territory and eager for the harbor

12. Carl von Koseritz, *Imagens do Brasil (1883)*, trans. Afonso Arinos de Melo Franco (São Paulo: Martins, 1943), p. 119.

13. John Gordon to Manager, London and Brazilian Bank at Rio de Janeiro, London, Sept. 13, 1888, Letters, London to Rio, 1885–89, LABA,UCLL, G.2., p. 7.

14. Evaldo Cabral de Melo, *O Norte Agrário e o Império, 1871–1889* (Rio de Janeiro: Nova Fronteira, 1984), p. 253; João Pedro da Veiga Filho, *Estudo Econômico e Financeiro sôbre o Estado de São Paulo* (São Paulo: Diário Oficial, 1896), p. 38; Emília Viotti da Costa, *Da Monarquia à República: Momentos Descisivos* (São Paulo: Ciências Humanas, 1979), p. 314.

15. *Relatório da Comissão da Praça do Comércio do Pará, Apresentado em Assembléia Geral dos Srs. Assinantes em 11 de Janeiro de 1876* (Belém: Comércio do Pará, 1876), p. 3.

16. Viotti da Costa, *Monarquia à República*, pp. 313–314.

modernization and lower railway fares that would enable it to surpass Rio as a coffee exporter. The province's business elite perceived these improvements and others to be blocked by the strong influence of Rio de Janeiro and its two business interest groups in the imperial government.[17] It saw the Empire not only as an obstacle to local development but as a partisan of the province's chief economic rival. Santos was one of the few electoral districts to send a Republican to the Chamber of Deputies. As of 1889 the President of its Commercial Association and several Board members were Republican activists.[18]

São Paulo's suspicion of the Empire heightened during its last administration, that of Liberal Viscount Ouro Preto. A modern historian notes, "Ouro Preto, the 'coming man' of the day, was head of a large group of relatives, business connections, and clients, representing far-ranging congeries of economic interests and regional aspirations, pivoting on Rio."[19] He was a friend of Rio financiers Viscount Figueiredo and Francisco de Paula Mayrink. As a member of the Council of State, he had helped block an attempt of the San [sic] Paulo Railway Company to lower its freight rates.[20] This ruling enabled Rio de Janeiro to preserve its cost advantage over Santos as an outlet for much of the coffee exported from the Province of São Paulo. The near-adulation with which Ouro Preto was regarded by the Commercial Association of Rio de Janeiro was not simply because his policies were felt to benefit overseas trade. He represented a Rio asset in its struggle against its chief commercial rival.

Thus, the attitudes of business interest groups toward the Empire, reflecting those of the business elites they represented, were mixed. The commercial associations of Pará and Santos had more to hope for than to fear from its fall. So did the Engineering Club, desirous to promote industrial development. Other business interest groups had logical reasons to uphold the Empire. The Commercial Association of Rio de Janeiro stood to lose not only matchless access to government, but commercial territory to Santos. The commercial associations of Bahia and Pernambuco, and the latter province's Commercial Agricultural Association, continued to enjoy a national influence by the 1880s quite out of proportion

17. For example, Commercial Association of Santos to Minister of Agriculture, Commerce, and Public Works, Santos, May 2, 1883, *Relatório da Associação Comercial de Santos, Apresentado em Sessão Ordinária da Assembléia Geral em Fevereiro de 1884* (Santos: Diário de Santos, 1884), Anexo no. 5, pp. 25–27; *Diário de Santos*, June 12, 1888, p. 1. During the yellow fever epidemic of 1888–1889, the Conservative cabinet was accused of withholding aid from Santos, by way of reprisal. Francisco Martins dos Santos, *História de Santos, 1532–1936* (São Paulo: Revista dos Tribunaes, 1937), II: 71.
18. Martins dos Santos, *História de Santos*, II: 64–65.
19. R. Frank Colson, "On Expectations-Perspectives on the Crisis of 1889 in Brazil," *JLAS*, 13 (Nov. 1981): 284.
20. The company tried to obtain a ruling that it would no longer have to divide its profits with the government. Ibid., 287–288.

to the fading importance of the regions they represented. Other organizations that logically would favor the Empire would be the commercial associations of Pôrto Alegre, Pelotas, and Rio Grande, which benefited from the special tariff awarded the Province of Rio Grande do Sul. For most commercial associations, the Empire also implied continued good access to government.

But even to supporters of the Empire its future looked uncertain. Observers increasingly doubted it would survive the death of Pedro II. By the late nineteenth century the New World's only surviving monarchy was an anachronism. Neither the pro-clerical Princess Isabel nor her consort was popular. Count d'Eu's eagerness to enrich himself quickly pleased commercial association membership but made him disliked elsewhere. His numerous business ventures and speculations were considered improper and undignified for one of his position.[21] By the late 1880s Pedro II was in his sixties and increasingly beset by serious illnesses. Speaking of the Emperor, an Englishman summed up the feelings of many foreigners in the business elite: " . . . at his death the future of the Empire is far from secure. . . . What is the security of Brazilian stocks? Is the outlook good for investors? The answer . . . is an emphatic *no.*"[22] The exchange rate, like a thermometer, reflected Pedro's state of health. It dipped whenever his condition grew serious, climbing once more when he rallied.[23]

By 1889, furthermore, loyalty to the Empire on the part of the business elite was mitigated by events. Abolition had produced both resentment and economic apprehension. The apparently genuine fear that agricultural ruin would follow the freeing of labor had not had time to subside. The Northeast had long undergone an economic stagnation that the policies of the Empire could not seem to confront, let alone arrest. Its business interest groups frequently complained of governmental favoritism toward the Southeast. Distress in the region was sharpened by increasingly serious shortages of cash and credit from 1887 on.[24] Business leaders knew that

21. Koseritz, *Imagens*, pp. 119, 129–130.
22. Hastings Charles Dent, *A Year in Brazil: With Notes on the Abolition of Slavery, the Finances of the Empire, Religion, Meterology, Natural History, Etc.* (London: Kegan Paul, Trench, 1886), p. 311.
23. John Gordon to Manager, London and Brazilian Bank at Rio de Janeiro, London, May 23, 1888, Letters, London to Rio, 1885–89, LABA, UCLL, G.2., p. 2; Viscount Figueiredo to Francisco Belisário, Rio de Janeiro, May [no day], 1887, Coleção Francisco Belisário, AIHGB, lata 277, doc. 52.
24. On the severity of the cash shortages, see Commercial Association of Bahia to President of Province, Salvador, May 4 and Oct. 5, 1887, Presidência da Província/Govêrno ao Associação Comercial, 1846–1889, AEB; Baron Guaí to Commercial Association of Bahia, Rio de Janeiro, Feb. 15, 1889, *Relatório da Junta Diretora da Associação Comercial da Bahia, Apresentado e Lido em Sessão da Assembléia Geral Ordinária, em 15 de Fevereiro de 1889* (Salvador: Popular, 1889), p. 112; Associação Comercial de Pernambuco, *Relatório da Associação Comercial Beneficente de Pernambuco, Lido em Sessão da Assembléia Geral de 13 de Agôsto de 1888* (Recife: Comércio, 1888), p. 10, and *Relatório de 1889*, pp. 9–12.

the Empire's policy of restricting money supply, followed until late 1888, accentuated the problem. If maintaining a strong currency benefited importers and foreign investors, it tended to hurt the export sector. Lastly, the zealous adherence to the monarchy shown by Negroes and mulattoes following abolition may have lessened the desire of the business elite and other elites to identify with it.[25] Although tradition dictated support of the monarchy, many business interest group members must have contemplated its downfall with mixed emotions.

The coming of the Republic and uncertainty

The overthrow of the Empire on November 15, 1889 was mercifully quick. Business interest groups were not forced, as they would had the struggle been protracted, to take sides. Accepting what had happened, they hastened to climb on the republican bandwagon. Typical was the Commercial Association of Pernambuco, which rushed a telegram to Marshal Deodoro da Fonseca, to "compliment and congratulate the Provisional Government."[26] Only the Commercial Association of Bahia was embarrassed by events. Believing like other members of Salvador's elite that the news of November 15 indicated nothing more than a barracks uprising, the association's Board joined other local leaders and government officials at the palace of the president of province to declare support for the monarchy. Board members signed a telegram to Rio protesting "republican sedition" and were among the most vociferous of those present in pledging loyalty and urging armed resistance.[27] But, like most of Salvador's leaders, they made a quick about-face upon learning of the success of the uprising. When the new Governor visited association headquarters ten days later, the same men who had pledged undying loyalty to the Empire greeted his outline of the new government's program "with great enthusiasm" and ended the meeting with hearty cheers for the Republic.[28]

The initial enthusiasm of the commercial associations of Pará and Santos for the new government was unalloyed. Dominated by factors, the Pará association was cheered not only by a regime more likely to be attentive to the Amazon region, but by the appointment as Provisional Governor of Justo Chermont, a leader in attempts to raise rubber prices. Abandoning political neutrality, it organized a rally for the new governor

25. The most salient and, to the elite, frightening manifestation of Negro loyalty was a secret organization known as the Black Guard, which used violence against Republican activists. Michael R. Trochim, "The Brazilian Black Guard: Racial Conflict in Post-Abolition Brazil," *The Americas*, 44 (Jan. 1988): 285–300.
26. *Relatório de 1890*, p. 5.
27. Afonso Ruy de Souza, *História da Câmera Municipal da Cidade do Salvador* (Salvador: Câmara Municipal do Salvador, 1953), pp. 334–335.
28. Minutes, meeting of November 25, 1889, Livro 5 de Atas, AACB, p. 287.

and later credited the republican regime for an upswing in regional prosperity.[29] The Commercial Association of Santos was virtually a part of the new government. Six of the ten-member Republican governing junta that took control of Santos on November 15 were members of that group, including its President and three other directors.[30] The association hosted Minister of Finance Rui Barbosa on his visit to Santos three months later, offering an elaborate banquet that included turkey *à la Republique* and asparagus *au 15 Novembre*.[31] Rui replied in kind by appointing two association directors to a four-man committee to oversee remodeling of the port of Santos.

Other business interest groups also accepted the Republic with few misgivings, but the harmony did not last. After several months commercial associations noted a subtle but disquieting change in their relations with government. In March 1890, for example, new Governor Manuel Vitorino visited the Salvador customs house and publicly ordered the Chief of Customs to persecute with tenacity all "thieves," that is, merchants who tried to dodge payment of customs duties.[32] No provincial leader under the Empire had the bluntness to air the problem so openly or to describe offending merchants in such terms. Rui Barbosa revealed the new government's attitude toward foreign merchants in a February 1890 circular to commercial associations calling for their cooperation in establishing statistical bureaus. Reliable statistics, he stated with typical verbosity, would aid in ending "the monopoly of exportation of our products, exercised privately by foreign houses in Brazil . . . which exploit the commerce of the fruits of our labor at prices dictated by the arbitrary will of the self-interest of an unbridled speculation."[33] As for importers, the "great profits" extracted by foreign houses with a near-monopoly of trade were a prime cause of the current fall of the exchange rate.[34] Rui knew that his observations would be deeply offensive to the foreigners among commercial association membership, as well as disturbing to all. Foreign dominance of overseas trade was rarely discussed openly at high levels during the Empire, much less with the associations themselves. Apparently deference, even tact, in dealing with business interest groups and the elite they represented were no longer considered essential.

This new attitude of government was to haunt many business interest groups, especially those whose ties to the monarchy had been strongest. In

29. Associação Comercial do Pará, *Relatório de 1890*, p. 3.   30. Santos, *História de Santos*, I: 411.
31. João da Costa e Silva Sobrinho, *Santos Noutros Tempos* (São Paulo: Revista dos Tribunais, 1953), pp. 402–405.
32. *Diário da Bahia* (Salvador), March 27, 1890, p. 1.
33. "Exposição ao Chefe do Govêrno Provisório," in Associação Comercial da Bahia, *Relatório de 1891*, p. 56.
34. Ibid.

November 1894, the Governor of Pernambuco disdainfully returned a petition from the Commercial Association because it was "not properly drawn up." This "unheard-of" gesture provoked deep outrage within the organization.[35] The Commercial Association of Rio de Janeiro found the transition from monarchy to republic particularly painful. In 1891 the government refused to hand over the remainder of a loan to complete the new association headquarters, which the Empire had guaranteed.[36] Construction was not resumed until 1902. Even more distressing to the Rio organization were accusations of improper use of funds intended for its Home for Disabled Veterans (see Chapter 11).

The disfavor of Republican national and state governments toward business interest groups, however, was selective. The experience of commercial associations whose members had shown an early leaning toward republicanism was quite different. Completion of a new headquarters for the Commercial Association of Pará, which it described as a "monumental edifice, without doubt the most grandiose ever planned in this state," was made possible by a generous loan from the state government.[37] An equally generous loan from its state financed a headquarters for the new Commercial Association of São Paulo.[38] And the Commercial Association of Santos received the full support of state and national governments in bringing about the long-awaited modernization of its port. But no business interest group, whatever its background, could continue to count on the favor of government as a matter of course. Indeed, the policies and economic trends of the early Republic seemed to threaten the very basis of the commercial associations and factor groups: Brazil's traditional export-import economy. Following Rui Barbosa's 1890 requirement that import duties be paid in gold, tariff rates climbed during the decade toward protection. Inflation and exchange depreciation, as damaging to the import trade, were chronic from the *Encilhamento* until 1899. The nightmares of importers and foreign investors about currency depreciation in the wake of the Empire's downfall had come true.

Other events under the Republic were equally disconcerting to business interest groups. Revolutionary outbreaks and mob disorder reappeared, inflamed by economic distress. Prices rose faster than wages, with the cost of imported food climbing especially steeply.[39] For the first time in Bra-

35. Associação Comercial de Pernambuco, *Relatório de Abril de 1896*, pp. 35–36.
36. *RMF,1892,*, pp. 34–39.
37. Associação Comercial do Pará, *Relatório de 1896*, p. 4, and *Relatório de 1897*, p. 3.
38. Associação Comercial de São Paulo, *Relatório da Associação Comercial de São Paulo, Ano de 1895* (São Paulo: Industrial, 1896), pp. 84–88.
39. Burke to Department of State, Salvador, March 25, 1891, NA/DS Microfilm Series T-331, Despatches from United States Consuls in Bahia, 1850–1906, unpaginated; Consul-General Townes to Department of State, Rio de Janeiro, May 23, 1895, *USRC*, XLVIII, no. 179 (Aug. 1895): 655–656.

zilian history labor disputes became common. Also disquieting was a recrudescence of anti-Portuguese feeling that threatened the large Portuguese membership in business interest groups. Portuguese shopkeepers were blamed for high food prices and again, as in the 1830s and 1840s, there was sporadic violence against them and calls for the nationalization of retail commerce.[40] Republicans favoring authoritarian nationalism, the so-called *Jacobinos,* accused them of plotting to restore the monarchy and were incensed when Portuguese warships gave asylum to rebels against the Republic in 1894.[41] Finally, the groups were dismayed by the growth of government expenditures. Much stemmed from expansion of the bureaucracy to provide jobs for supporters of the regime.[42] Nor were the new public servants modest in their financial claims: the governor of Bahia arrogated himself a salary more than seven times that of the provincial president under the Empire.[43] For the associations the change was doubly painful. Not only did their membership bear the brunt of taxation, but they had long stressed the need for governmental economy.

Not surprisingly, several commercial associations soon manifested a nostalgia for the Empire. The Commercial Association of Bahia restored the Imperial coat of arms to its main salon, whence it had been torn by a republican mob. The Commercial Association of Rio de Janeiro officially hailed the return of Viscount Ouro Preto from exile in 1891.[44] Many associations marked the death of Pedro II late in 1891 with ostentatious sorrow. The Commercial Association of Rio de Janeiro had itself officially represented at his funeral.[45] The Bahian association closed its doors for eight days and arranged for solemn rites at the Salvador Cathedral. Only the opposition of Salvador municipal authorities prevented the group from staging elaborate public ceremonies honoring the late Emperor.[46] These displays of sympathy for a lost cause may have been sincere, but they were

40. June E. Hahner, "Jacobinos Versus Gallegos: Urban Radicals Versus Portuguese Immigrants in Rio de Janeiro in the 1890s," *Journal of Interamerican Studies and World Affairs,* 18 (May 1976): 128–131.

41. Ibid., 131–132; Luís Edmundo da Costa, *De um Livro de Memórias* (Rio de Janeiro: Imprensa Nacional, 1958), V: 996–999. For the *Jacobinos,* see also June E. Hahner, *Poverty and Politics: The Urban Poor in Brazil, 1870–1920* (Albuquerque: University of New Mexico Press, 1986), pp. 139–155; and Suely Robles Reis de Queiroz, *Os Radicais da República: Jacobinismo – Ideologia e Ação, 1893–1897* (São Paulo: Brasiliense, 1986).

42. Steven Topik, "State Autonomy in Economic Policy: Brazil's Experience, 1822–1930," *Journal of Interamerican Studies and World Affairs,* 26 (Nov. 1984): 468–469; Richard Graham, "Government Expenditures and Political Change in Brazil, 1880–1899: Who Got What," *Journal of Interamerican Studies and World Affairs,* 19 (Aug. 1977): 356, 358.

43. Burke to Department of State, Salvador, Dec. 26, 1889, NA/DS T-331, Vol. 5.

44. Commercial Association of Rio de Janeiro to Viscount Ouro Preto, Rio de Janeiro, Nov. 24, 1892, Coleção Ouro Preto, AIHGB, lata 426, doc. 30.

45. Associação Comercial do Rio de Janeiro, *Relatório de 1901,* Anexos, 1892, p. 3.

46. Associação Comercial da Bahia, *Relatório de 1892,* pp. 236–239; Antônio Moreira Cesar, Chief of Police, to Commercial Association of Bahia, Salvador, Dec. [no day], 1891, *Relatório de 1892,* p. 241.

hardly tactful. They could only contribute to the dislike and suspicion with which republican authorities regarded many commercial associations.

The associations became more reconciled to the Republic after the replacement of military rulers by elected civilian presidents in November 1894. Revolutionary disturbances subsided, the influence of *Jacobinos* in the administration weakened, and the government no longer pursued as aggressively economic nationalism and industrialization.[47] In November 1897, a disgruntled *Jacobino* attempted to assassinate President Prudente de Morais, succeeding only in killing the Minister of War, Marshal Carlos Machado Bittencourt. The commercial associations made conspicuous demonstrations of grief for the Marshal and donated generous sums to his wife and children. They were means of manifesting loyalty to the Republic, gestures doubtless reinforced by relief that the incident virtually ended *Jacobino* influence in the national government.

Neither the restoration of civilian rule nor the eclipse of *Jacobino* influence restricted the tendency of business interest groups toward a more openly partisan political stance. The commercial associations of Santos, Bahia, and Pernambuco, the latter backed by that state's factor-group Commercial Agricultural Association, were particularly active politically in the first decade of the Republic. The four groups dabbled in partisan politics for different reasons and with highly differing outcomes. The latter three hoped to regain power lost with the downfall of the Empire; the former to maintain newly increased influence.

Confronting the Republic in São Paulo, Pernambuco, and Bahia

As noted, the presence of many veteran republicans in the ranks of the Commercial Association of Santos led to the placement of six of its members on the ten-man municipal junta created by the revolution. This influence weakened slightly to three of nine with the appointment of a regular municipal council in February 1890.[48] The association was a stronghold of what were termed "Historical" Republicans – those who had backed the party prior to the revolution and who resented the former supporters of the monarchy now flocking to republicanism for opportunistic reasons. In no other state, however, were the Historical Republicans as numerous or as powerful as in São Paulo.[49]

---

47. Hahner, "Jacobinos Versus Gallegos," 141–145; Queiroz, *Radicais da República,* pp. 31–80; Nícia Vilela Luz, *A Luta pela Industrialização do Brasil* (2d ed.; São Paulo: Alfa Omega, 1975), pp. 180–183.
48. Santos, *História de Santos,* I: 411.
49. Joseph L. Love, *São Paulo in the Brazilian Federation, 1889–1937* (Stanford, Calif.: Stanford University Press, 1980), pp. 110–112, 117.

This worried President Deodoro da Fonseca. To eliminate hostility toward ex-monarchists by São Paulo representatives in Congress, he appointed his own man, Américo Brasiliense, as Governor in March 1891. Among the latter's measures to curb the power of Historical Republicans in the state was the replacement of Santos's Municipal Council by new appointees. None was a member of the Commercial Association. Deodoro soon faced larger problems. Quarreling with his newly seated Congress, he attempted to shut it down by force in November 1891. The reaction was fierce. The Brazilian navy, led by Admiral Custódio de Melo and having the tacit support of Deodoro's Vice-President, Marshal Floriano Peixoto, forced his resignation.

São Paulo's Historical Republicans immediately forced a similar resignation from Américo Brasiliense and turned out the municipal councils that he had appointed. A power vacuum now existed in Santos. Local republicans handed municipal rule to the Commercial Association of Santos on December 14, 1891. Perhaps uneasy in the spotlight, the association the following day turned over authority to a respected member of the former municipal council, only to have this individual resign three days later.[50] There was no alternative but to return control to an administratively competent body loyal to Historical Republicanism, albeit largely foreign. The Board of Directors of the Commercial Association of Santos served as the Municipal Council of the city from December 18 to December 30, when a regular body was appointed.[51] In a literal sense, the incident marks a high point in the municipal power of business interest groups.

Another test of the loyalty of the Commercial Association of Santos to Historical Republicanism soon loomed. In September 1893, Admiral Custódio de Melo and the navy revolted against President Floriano Peixoto, blockading the coast and threatening to bombard Rio de Janeiro into rubble. Resentment over what the Navy felt to be lack of consideration by Floriano fueled the uprising, but the rebels also probably contemplated a restoration of the monarchy. The support of São Paulo leaders was key to Floriano's survival.[52] In Santos a "Civic Guard" was formed to oppose any landing by the rebels. Although Commercial Association records on the subject are cryptic, the organization apparently funded part, if not all, of the two hundred–man force.[53] The collapse of the naval revolt in May of 1894 was followed by the election of a civilian president, part of the price

---

50. Minutes, meeting of Dec. 18, 1891, Livro de Atas, 1874–1894, AACS, pp. 167–168; Costa e Silva Sobrinho, *Santos*, p. 255.
51. Associação Comercial de Santos, *Relatório de 1893*, p. 9.
52. June Hahner, "The Paulistas' Rise to Power: A Civilian Group Ends Military Rule," *HAHR*, 48 (May 1967): 160–161.
53. Minutes, meetings of Oct. 23 and 30, 1893, Livro de Atas, 1874–1894, AACS, pp. 180–181.

exacted by the State of São Paulo for its support of Floriano. The first three civilian presidents of Republican Brazil were natives of São Paulo. After 1894 the Commercial Association of Santos found itself in harmony with both state and nation.

The Commercial Association and Commercial Agricultural Association of Pernambuco found their situation opposite that of the Santos group. Unlike São Paulo, the Republican movement in Pernambuco had been weak, with little following in the Commercial Association or elsewhere. Former adherents of the monarchy effectively disputed the spoils of the Republican victory with the few Historical Republicans.[54] Within months of the take-over, Baron Lucena (Henrique Pereira de Lucena), a veteran Conservative Party leader and friend and principal adviser to Deodoro da Fonseca exercised paramount influence within the state.[55] The Commercial Association of Pernambuco welcomed his control even more when he formed an alliance with José Mariano Carneiro da Cunha, its longtime champion in the Chamber of Deputies. It warmly applauded Lucena's appointment as Governor in July 1890.[56]

This promising situation ended with the downfall of Baron Lucena's patron, Deodoro da Fonseca, in November 1891. It touched off a lengthy period of unrest. An impending armed clash between partisans of Deodoro and of the new President, Floriano Peixoto, threatened public safety and commercial property. Under pressure from banks and leading merchants, the Commercial Association telegraphed Floriano, begging that order be maintained.[57] His assurances that the legal state government would be allowed to stay in power meant little. It was soon overthrown by troops instigated by Pernambuco's Historical Republicans, and Floriano appointed Army Captain Alexandre José Barbosa Lima, a fervid Republican, as Governor in April 1892. Historical Republicans, finding Barbosa Lima surprisingly uncooperative, tried to have him impeached in March 1893. Civil war within the state threatened, as federal troops sympathetic to the Historical Republicans and other enemies of Barbosa Lima faced state police and irregulars loyal to the governor.[58] Commercial property, unprotected by police, was threatened. Pressured by bank directors and leading merchants, the Commercial Association and Commercial Agri-

54. Robert M. Levine, *Pernambuco in the Brazilian Federation, 1889–1937* (Stanford, Calif.: Stanford University Press, 1978), pp. 74–75.
55. Marc J. Hoffnagel, "From Monarchy to Republic in Northeast Brazil: The Case of Pernambuco, 1868–1895" (Ph.D. Diss., Indiana University, 1975), pp. 220–221.
56. Commercial Association of Pernambuco to Baron Lucena, Recife, Aug. 7, 1890, *Relatório de 1890*, pp. 6–7.
57. Minutes, meeting of Nov. 28, 1891, Livro 7 de Atas, AACP, pp. 61–62; *Diário de Pernambuco* (Recife), Nov. 29, 1891, pp. 1–2.
58. *Diário de Pernambuco*, April 18, 1893, p. 1, and April 19, 1893, p. 2; Hoffnagel, "From Monarchy to Republic," pp. 236–238.

cultural Association tried to arrange a truce. The presidents of the two groups met with the Governor and then with his principal opponent, the commander of federal troops, but to no effect.[59] Telegrams to Marshal Floriano and other federal authorities, pleading for a restoration of order, were not even answered.[60]

Barbosa Lima survived the impeachment crisis and the influence of the Commercial Association and Commercial Agricultural Association of Pernambuco reached a nadir. The former's President in 1892–1893, Manuel Gomes de Mattos, was a known enemy of the Governor, whom Recife's young *caixeiros* had demonstrated against during the impeachment struggle.[61] José Mariano, the Commercial Association's legislative paladin, was jailed for plotting against Marshal Floriano. The organization dared not receive him openly after his release in October 1894.[62] Barbosa Lima then and later proved a nationalist of the *Jacobino* stripe.[63] The Commercial Association of Pernambuco and the foreign economic sway it represented were repugnant to him. His disdainful attitude and continuous rejection of its petitions, and the unceasing rise of taxes on commerce led that organization to shut down in protest in June 1895, and the Commercial Agricultural Association the following month. The latter reopened in September, but the Commercial Association only when Barbosa Lima left office in April 1896.

The situation appeared to brighten when control of Pernambuco passed to Francisco de Assis Rosa e Silva, a Federal Deputy and later Vice-President of the nation (1898–1902). Strongly anti-*Jacobino,* the aristocratic Rosa e Silva had been a zealous defender of sugar interests as a Conservative deputy under the Empire. Both groups had not only awarded him honorary membership but hung his portrait in their headquarters.[64] The Commercial Association of Pernambuco decorated its building and greeted him with great ceremony when he visited Recife in 1897.[65]

Pernambuco's business elite soon was disillusioned. Rosa e Silva increased the state's already-high taxes on commerce, even taxing trade within the state. Noted for his ferocity and arbitrary acts against oppo-

59. Minutes, meeting of April 17, 1893, Livro 7 de Atas, AACP, pp. 81–82.
60. Associação Comercial de Pernambuco, *Relatório de 1893,* pp. 26–28, 129–130.
61. Minutes, meeting of April 17, 1893, Livro 7 de Atas, AACP, p. 82; *Diário de Pernambuco,* April 18, 1893, p. 2.
62. Minutes, meeting of Oct. 9, 1894, Livro 7 de Atas, AACP, p. 101.
63. José da Costa Pôrto, *Os Tempos de Rosa e Silva* (Recife: Universidade Federal de Pernambuco), p. 23; Afonso Arinos de Melo Franco, *Rodrigues Alves: Apogeu e Declíneo de Presidencialismo* (São Paulo: Universidade de São Paulo, 1973), I: 390, 394, 397.
64. Minutes, meeting of June 20, 1887, Livro de Atas da Associação Comercial Agrícola de Pernambuco, 1877–1892, AACP, p. 147; Associação Comercial de Pernambuco, *Relatório de 1888,* p. 11.
65. Associação Comercial de Pernambuco, *Relatório de 1897,* p. 7.

nents, he allegedly raised levies on those he felt to be political enemies.[66] His power within Pernambuco left overseas commerce, attacked as "selfish and unpatriotic" by his political party's newspaper, little room to maneuver.[67] In desperation, delegates from the Commercial Association, the Commercial Agricultural Association, and the Agricultural Auxiliary Society of Pernambuco met in July of 1899 to form the Political Center for Farming, Commerce, and Industry (*Centro Político de Lavoura, Comércio e Indústria*). Limited to planters and businessmen, its purpose was to bring down Rosa e Silva.[68] Continued protestations of political neutrality by the Commercial Association fooled no one. The association's President, José da Silva Loyo Junior, and former President, Manuel Gomes de Mattos, led the Political Center's organizers, with Gomes de Mattos serving as its first head.[69] It also used the Commercial Association's headquarters for its meetings. Unable to loosen Rosa e Silva's tight hold on the state, the Political Center for Farming, Commerce, and Industry dissolved itself in frustration in August 1903.[70] The Commercial Association and Commercial Agricultural Association of Pernambuco remained largely exiled from power until enemies in the Federal Government toppled Rosa e Silva in 1911.

The charged political atmosphere of the Republic forced the Commercial Association of Bahia, like its Pernambucan counterpart, into open partisanship. Despite having initially sided with the Empire during the republican uprising, the Bahian group suffered much less damage to its influence. Leadership fell to the cautious Augusto Silvestre de Faria, who followed a policy of conspicuous adhesion to republicanism. He contained the desire of membership for open or even violent demonstrations against increased taxes and missed no opportunity to show support for the Republic. Upon the outbreak of the naval revolt against Floriano Peixoto in September 1893, the association organized a battalion to defend Salvador's lower city against any landing by the rebels.[71] In 1894, it called for all Salvador businesses to close for a day to express sympathy with the French Republic upon the assassination of its President, Sadi Carnot.[72] The death

---

66. Brazil, Congresso, Câmera dos Deputados, *ACD, 1899*, III: 230–231.
67. Associação Comercial de Pernambuco, *Relatório de 1899*, p. 12.
68. Minutes, general assembly of inauguration, July 26, 1899, and general assembly of July 3, 1903, Centro Político de Lavoura, Comércio e Indústria, Livro de Atas, 1899–1903, AACP, unpaginated. A coalition of anti-Rosa e Silva forces, the Republican Concentration (*Concentração Republicana*), which counted among its leaders José Mariano and Baron Lucena, was formed in September 1899. Costa Pôrto, *Rosa e Silva*, pp. 109–110.
69. Meeting of July 11, 1899, Centro Político de Lavoura, Comércio e Indústria, Livro de Atas, 1899–1903, AACP, unpaginated.
70. Minutes, meeting of July 3, 1903, Centro Político de Lavoura, Comércio e Indústria, Livro de Atas, 1899–1903, AACP, unpaginated.
71. Minutes, meeting of Sept. 20, 1893, Livro 6 de Atas, AACB, p. 92.
72. Commercial Association of Bahia to E. Thélene, Consul of France, Salvador, June 27, 1894, *Relatório de 1895*, pp. 72–74.

of Queen Victoria, by contrast, merited only a note of condolence. A key opportunity to display pro-republican sentiments came in 1896 with the hard-fought victory of the Brazilian army at Canudos in the Bahian interior over religious fanatics mistakenly believed to advocate restoration of the monarchy.[73] Hailing "the brilliant victory of Brazilian arms over banditry," the Commercial Association arranged for Salvador's business houses to close in celebration for a total of four days.[74] Such tactics were largely successful in deflecting antimonarchist resentment from the association.

Also pushing the Commercial Association of Bahia into open political activity was an upsurge of violence in the state's interior. Most outbreaks reflected struggles for control of *municípios* by local political bosses and were part of the phenomenon of *coronelismo*, so-called because those bosses bore the National Guard title of colonel.[75] The political conditions of the Old Republic exacerbated the violence of *coronelismo*, whose roots lay deep in the colonial period. The concern of Salvador's business elite to pacify the state's hinterland was by no means solely humanitarian; the area was the heart of its commercial territory and trade had been growing. Telegrams and other petitions flowed from the interior to the Commercial Association of Bahia, begging its intercession with state authorities to restore order. Signed by up to more than six hundred businessmen and landowners, they told of real or threatened murder, arson, looting, or blockage of trade.[76] The association tried to arrange, usually through the governor, the intervention of judicial officials, law enforcement authorities, or in extreme cases, expeditionary forces of state militarized police. In order to have reliable observers and representatives in the larger towns (as well as to aid in ordinary lobbying), it appointed in 1900 local businessmen as association delegates.[77] The vigilance and concern for the politics of the interior demonstrated by the Commercial Association of Bahia diminished little with the new century. Violence associated with *coronelismo* characterized the Bahian hinterland throughout the Old Republic.

73. The basic work on Canudos, a classic of Brazilian letters, is Euclides da Cunha, *Os Sertões* (27th ed.; Rio de Janeiro: Francisco Alves, 1968). A revisionary view is found in Robert M. Levine, "'Mud-Hut Jerusalem': Canudos Revisited," in *The Abolition of Slavery and the Aftermath of Emancipation in Brazil*, ed. Rebecca J. Scott (Durham, N.C.: Duke University Press, 1988), pp. 119–166.
74. Commercial Association of Bahia to Governor of State, Salvador, Oct. 8, 1897, and to Minister of War, Salvador, Oct. 20, 1897, *Relatório de 1898*, pp. 113–116.
75. For Bahian *coronelismo*, see Eul-Soo Pang, *Bahia in the First Brazilian Republic: Coronelismo and Oligarchies, 1889–1934* (Gainesville, Fla.: University of Florida Press, 1979). The standard overall examination is Victor Nunes Leal, *Coronelismo, Enxada e Voto (o Município e o Regime Representativo no Brasil)* (3d ed.; São Paulo: Alfa-Omega, 1976).
76. 653 merchants, planters, and artisans [sic] to Commercial Association of Bahia, Cannavieiras and Belmonte, Bahia, July 23, 1894, *Relatório de 1895*, pp. 83–87.
77. Associação Comercial da Bahia, *Relatório de 1901*, pp. 175–176.

The preservation of order in the interior, and of the group's own influence, required the goodwill of the state administration. Under Silvestre de Faria the association habitually displayed adherence to the governor in power. But in the heated political atmosphere of the Old Republic, such gestures risked offending part of membership. The Commercial Association of Bahia's unflinching support of Governor Luís Vianna (1896–1900) brought about a revolt of its rank-and-file unparalleled elsewhere. Silvestre de Faria and his fellow directors had been assiduous in congratulating the governor at every opportunity, even financing in September 1899 a reception upon his return from what it described as a "brilliantly received" tour of the Brazilian Southeast.[78] Resentment against his administration erupted following allegedly fraudulent Salvador municipal elections in November 1899. Among the unruly anti-Vianna crowd demonstrating in Salvador's Lower City on November 13 were a large number of merchant house *caixeiros*. Police attempting to control the demonstrators were met by stones and, allegedly, pistol shots.[79] The police returned fire, seconded by the rifles of soldiers and a charging troop of cavalry. Two of the crowd, neither connected with commerce, were killed and many *caixeiros* arrested.[80] The merchant houses where demonstrating *caixeiros* had taken refuge were closed down and, in one case, surrounded by troops for days.[81]

Never before had the personnel and property of Brazil's business elite been subject to open government aggression. Salvador's merchant and factor houses closed down in protest, and merchants at a turbulent meeting in Commercial Association headquarters angrily denounced the "inactivity" and "passivity" of its Board of Directors, which had not protested to Luís Vianna.[82] Most businesses remained closed until the last *caixeiros* were released a week later. Those directors who had not already resigned, including Silvestre de Faria, were brusquely turned out at the Commercial Association's annual general assembly in February 1900.[83] Unlike the case in Pernambuco, estrangement from the state administration did not hurt the Commercial Association of Bahia. Rather, its hostility helped topple its adversary. Luís Vianna had already lost the support of the national government and the *coroneis* of the interior; he was replaced as governor by a political enemy early in 1900.[84] Nevertheless, the association was in no mood for forgiveness. Upon Vianna's return to Salvador in September

78. Minutes, meeting of Sept. 18, 1899, Livro 6 de Atas, AACB, p. 353.
79. *Correio de Notícias* (Salvador), Nov. 14, 1899, p. 1, and Nov. 16, 1899, p. 1.
80. *O Treze de Novembro de 1899 na Capital da Bahia (Subsídios Para a História)* (Salvador: Diário da Bahia, 1900), pp. 101–118.
81. *Correio de Notícias*, Nov. 14, 1899, p. 1, and Nov. 22, 1899, p. 1.
82. *Treze de Novembro*, pp. 119–121.
83. Minutes, general assembly of Feb. 14, 1900, Livro 6 de Atas, AACB, pp. 371–373.
84. Pang, *Bahia in the First Republic*, p. 62.

1900, it forbad the ex-Governor to disembark at the quay fronting association headquarters or to pass through the commercial district of the Lower City.[85] Annual symbolic closures of business kept the memory of November 13 fresh for years thereafter.

Business interest groups and the Republic

Business interest groups encountered a new atmosphere under the Republic. Its sharpened political passions forced many into tacit modification of their traditional policy of political neutrality. The influence of the older commercial associations, Rio de Janeiro, Bahia, and especially Pernambuco, weakened, as did that of Brazil's sole remaining factor group, the Commercial Agricultural Association of Pernambuco. Conversely, the power of the commercial associations of Pará and Santos, representing a local business elite originally of stronger republican sympathies, increased.

It was not only the status and influence of the three oldest commercial associations which declined, but that of the associations in general. Much of the fall was due to growing economic nationalism, fed by awareness and resentment of foreign economic domination. Nationalists of *Jacobino* leanings, in particular, saw the commercial associations as prime symbols of the traditional order. The lessening status of the commercial associations was paralleled by legislative blows against the export-import economy, such as Aid for Industry and increasing tariff protection. Conversely, the more nationalistic atmosphere of the Old Republic was propitious for new industrial interest groups, which would begin to emerge around the turn of the century. The first decade of the Republic witnessed a marked decline in the power of the commercial associations and the primacy of the economy that they represented. With that decline, the nation's economic development was pointed in more than one direction.

85. Minutes, meeting of Sept. 26, 1900, Livro 7 de Atas, AACB, pp. 122–123.

13

Conclusion

This study has explored and evaluated the ways in which business interest groups affected Brazilian development in the nineteenth century. In doing so it also has examined the business elite that comprised those groups, both as a key to comprehending group policies and for an understanding of the business elite itself. Business interest groups, unlike abstract concepts of class or sector, are concrete organizations created to influence government, and their actions are usually discernible and readily documented. While business interest groups cannot substitute in historical analysis for such abstractions as the "middle class," their policies can illuminate the true political posture of one of its central elements, the business elite.

Business interest groups, in particular the commercial associations, also provide handy units for study of the background and characteristics of that elite. Fundamental to it was foreignness. Aliens predominated among overseas traders and industrialists and were a sizable minority among factors. That so many businessmen did not become Brazilian when naturalization was easy and convenient indicates that their orientation and sympathies lay abroad. But if foreign predominance serves to explain much of the thrust of commercial association policies, its importance should not be exaggerated. There seems to have been little divergence in opinion between foreign and Brazilian directors or members of the associations on most questions. The interests and necessities of mercantile capitalism appear to have imposed themselves on all. In general, the associations wished to preserve the traditional economy with its strong overseas ties, attached more importance to foreign than to national markets, were more concerned with regional than national prosperity, and had little interest in the nationwide integration of communications. That industrialists, too, were largely non-Brazilian is hardly surprising, because so many of them came to manufacturing by way of importation. Unlike the case with overseas traders and commercial associations, the foreignness of manufacturers was largely irrelevant to the actions of industrial groups.

Alien and Brazilian alike, manufacturers had invested their efforts and fortunes in inward-oriented, that is, industrial, development. The strong alien presence did not lead to business elite disunity. Foreigners themselves were not divided by nationality. Foreign consuls were much more concerned about national rivalry over Brazilian trade than were foreign merchants. Aliens took care to maintain a strong non-Brazilian representation on the boards of commercial associations, but the question of which nationality took the seats seems to have been secondary. Nor, by the time the first lasting business interest groups were formed, was there noticeable rivalry between foreigners and Brazilians engaged in overseas trade. This is in contrast to the experience of some other Latin American nations.[1] Most native merchants held the expatriates, especially British, as models for business methods and even life-style. When rules permitted, they displayed little reluctance to elect foreigners to preside over commercial associations, and there were very few instances in which the boards of directors of business interest groups split along native versus foreign lines. On the other hand, had there been no potential for differences in objectives between natives and foreigners, the latter would not have taken care to maintain their strength on those boards.

From a public relations standpoint, however, foreignness was vulnerability. Commercial associations in particular had to be wary of treading upon nationalist sensibilities. In the last two decades of the century, industrialists and factors used the foreignness of overseas merchants as a weapon against them. Quarrels between overseas merchants and factors, however, were not over the direction of development, but over division of remuneration from the traditional economy.

A second prominent business elite characteristic was diversity of economic interests. It tended to broaden as an individual's fortune increased. Overseas trade or factorage appear to have been the earliest or most basic activities of elite members. Achieving success there, they took their capital and skills into other fields, such as banking, communications, and insurance. Particularly significant was the expansion of importers into manufacturing, often done in anticipation of rising tariffs. Those importers who had not made this move, however, remained collectively the most implacable foes of industrialization. Overseas traders and factors, in any

---

1. Particularly Guatemala and Peru in the decades following independence. Henry Dunn, *Guatemala o las Provincias Unidas de Centro America Durante 1827 y 1828, Siendo Bosquejos e Memorandums Hechos Durante una Residencia de Doce Meses en Aquella República*, tr. Ricardo de León (Guatemala: Tipografía Nacional, 1960), pp. 149, 176; Paul Gootenberg, *Between Silver and Guano: Commercial Policy and the State in Postindependence Peru* (Princeton, N.J.: Princeton University Press, 1989), pp. 21–24, 55–67. For Colombia, a milder case, see Frank Safford, "The Emergence of Economic Liberalism in Colombia," in *Guiding the Invisible Hand: Economic Liberalism and the State in Latin American History*, eds. Joseph L. Love and Nils Jacobsen (New York, Westport, Conn., London: Praeger, 1988), p. 45.

case, can be seen as main entrepreneurial elements in Brazilian development.

The motivation for the actions and attitudes of business elite members was mainly economic and usually logical. It depended on how businessmen perceived their own major economic interest, although this perception was subject to change. As noted, there was much overlapping in economic interests and even origin between factors, overseas merchants, and industrialists, and between them and planters. But it would be quite wrong for that reason to suppose that there was no conflict of interest between these groups. It is naive, for example, to assume that importers and industrialists had no quarrel because most of the latter came from the ranks of the former. Since one favored outward and the other inward-oriented development, their interests were in a sense diametrically opposed. The role of importers in combating state aid for industry was as logical as it was prominent, although many importers eventually found their futures lay with manufacturing and migrated, so to speak, to the enemy camp. On the other hand, having the same basic economic objectives hardly precluded conflict. Exporters and factors were part of the export complex, but their interests clashed regarding division of its profits. Planters and factors shared the same economic policy goals and often the same origin. But open conflicts between them were bitter, if infrequent, and resentment on the part of planters lay just below the surface. Issues such as commodity prices, credit, and reform of mortgage law brought strife among groups in the export sector, strife that was impelled or sharpened by the dwindling of export profits. At the same time, the importance of divisive issues and occasional clashes should not be exaggerated. It may be repeated that there was no lasting conflict, in the sense of a protracted struggle for power, between merchants and planters.

Business interest groups and development

Foreign-dominated, diverse in economic holdings, and usually pursuing well-defined interests, the business elite also enjoyed through its interest groups an access to government scarcely possible today. Among group assets were a near absence of competing interest organizations, prerogatives derived from the centuries-old tradition of Iberian corporatism, governmental weaknesses that required group assistance, leaders who had widespread personal relationships with Brazilian government heads, and a membership that constituted in a sense a bridge for modernizing influences from abroad. The groups pressured a state accustomed to intervening actively in the economy. What was their role in development?

Of all their activities, perhaps most clearly favorable to development was their role in economic and urban integration. Traditional to business interest organizations was the performance of a host of functions that later became the province of government. Such services were particularly relevant because they were at that time beyond the capability of the Brazilian state. Acting with a remarkable degree of autonomy, business interest groups helped integrate the Brazilian economy both nationally and with other nations in the Atlantic trading community. They also helped initiate vital urban services and performed a crucial role in dispensing charity and relief. Next to the Church, business interest groups were the most important surrogates for government in the nineteenth century.

Business interest groups probably made their greatest effort toward development in the area of agriculture. The commercial associations and factor groups were farming's most lasting and articulate voice before government during the nineteenth century. They had some obvious successes in aiding agriculture, such as expanding export markets and improving and maintaining coffee quality. Other triumphs were less clearcut. They standardized the exports of Northeastern Brazil and upgraded their quality, but much of the latter amelioration was only temporary. They brought about piecemeal but not overall improvement in the farming methods of the Northeast. They helped to introduce the *usina,* but initially delayed the modernization of sugar processing by aggressively promoting aid for central mills, impractical and wasteful of tax revenue.

Business interest groups also experienced conspicuous failures in helping agriculture. The groups founded banks, encouraged capitalists to found them, and pushed credit legislation, but in the long run failed to assure ready, cheap credit for all of Brazilian agriculture. Their struggle against export taxation had temporary successes but ultimately had to be abandoned. Certain obstacles beyond their control contributed to failure or lack of clear-cut success. Fiscal necessity first hurt and then killed the drive against export taxation and kept the Brazilian government from establishing solid agricultural credit institutions. Planter conservatism and sloth blunted campaigns to improve the quality of Northeastern export commodities.

Other failures of business interest groups to upgrade agriculture resulted from policies that in retrospect seem wrongheaded. Their anxiety to insure adequate manpower for plantations helped prolong slavery. Their reluctance to help diversify export crops lost an opportunity to enrich and stabilize the export economy. Their neglect of domestic food production missed correcting what has been described as Brazil's most telling economic weakness in the nineteenth century. In such cases the principal obstacles were the attitudes and beliefs of the business interest groups themselves. The lower social status of producers of nontraditional crops may have led to group disinclination to aid exports other than coffee, sugar, and cotton. Encouraging the production of domestic foodstuffs ran counter to vested interests within the groups themselves. Finally, business interest groups, for the most part, could not visualize export production without slavery or the traditional big landholding.

Although not always successful, the extent of business interest group effort on behalf of agriculture should lay to rest any remaining belief in a planter-merchant power struggle. Commercial associations and factor groups not only spoke for agriculture, but tried to establish the concept of planters and businessmen as a unified class. They successfully overcame planter opposition in imposing export inspection and in changing mortgage law, but they considered these to be measures that would benefit landowners in the long run. They dissented from identification with the large landholding only in occasional support for small-farmer immigration and concomitant taxation of rural land. This dissent indicated that business interest group leaders were not entirely immune from the desire of other elements of the urban middle class for a racially whiter Brazil and for a counterweight to the great landowner.

Business interest groups had an equally strong and perhaps more decisive role in Brazilian communications. They helped initiate, and later regulate, the railroad, the river, coastal, and overseas steamer and the telegraph and underseas cable. They pushed modernization of Brazil's ports, but sometimes delayed that modernization by insisting the interests of their members be paramount. But business interest group participation in introducing communications innovations was greatly motivated and ultimately distorted by entrepôt rivalry and regionalism. Only the industrial groups were able to place national interests first.

Entrepôt rivalry and regionalism were most evident in business interest group influence on railway construction. Brazil's rail system generally was disjointed, unprofitable, and a major drain on tax revenues. In their enthusiasm for the railroad, the groups also virtually ignored the building or linkage of roads. Partially because of failure to integrate land communications systems, "Brazil, geographically a subcontinent, was in demographic and economic terms an archipelago."[2] It was not a unified economy but a series of economic regions, each dominated by a single entrepôt and with much stronger ties to overseas markets and suppliers than to each other. Prevailing Brazilian demographic and economic regionalism would change only very slowly. Economists Annibal Villela and Wilson Suzigan note that as late as 1945, "there was still no national market, but only an archipelago of economic regions, precariously linked with one another."[3] The metaphor of the archipelago was long-lasting.

2. Warren Dean, "The Brazilian Economy, 1870–1930," in *The Cambridge History of Latin America, Volume V: c. 1870 to 1930*, ed. Leslie Bethell (Cambridge: Cambridge University Press, 1986), p. 691.
3. *Política do Govêrno e Crescimento da Economia Brasileira, 1889–1945* (Rio de Janeiro: IPEA/INPES, 1975), p. 222.

Business interest groups were central to the struggle for the industrialization of Brazil. It was in a sense a clash of industrial capital, represented by the industrial groups, against mercantile capital, of the commercial associations and factor groups. While trying not to appear openly to oppose industrialization, commercial associations fought tariff protection and other government aid to industry. The prerogative of advising on tariffs or participating in their formulation was their most effective weapon. However, by the 1880s, the antimanufacturing leanings of the associations were being counteracted by the appeals of industrial groups. Despite the brevity of most such groups, they were probably important in convincing educated Brazilians of the desirability of industrialization. By 1900 industrial growth was becoming a serious goal for more and more Brazilians.

By the late 1880s, commercial associations and factor groups were no longer able to slow significantly the increase of tariff protection and other government aid for industry. But by then it had become increasingly difficult for local manufactures to compete with foreign imports, made progressively cheaper by improvements in manufacturing and transportation. The late rise of industrial capitalism also led to a lack of heavy industry and other structural imbalances in manufacturing that were overcome only with difficulty.[4] By thus delaying protection, commercial associations and factor groups probably retarded somewhat Brazilian industrialization.

Linked with the struggle of business interest groups over industrialization was their debate on economic liberalism and their public relations appeals. Unlike the case in, for example, Peru, free trade won control of Brazilian economic policy early, thus its advocates fought a mainly defensive battle.[5] Industrial groups attacked it by appealing for autonomous development and economic independence. Commercial associations and factor groups cited the principles of economic liberalism to oppose aid for industrialization and to justify the traditional economy. But they readily ignored or contradicted those principles when it suited the interests of their membership. Such inconsistency blunted their arguments against state aid for industry. The repeated demands of business interest groups for state intervention and the favorable government response to those demands also show that economic liberalism, despite its intellectual vogue, was for both more a useful ideological tool than a real guide to policy. Brazil's business elite accepted and expected a strong economic role for the state. Historian Charles Jones has postulated for the nineteenth century a worldwide "cosmopolitan bourgeoisie" of overseas merchants

4. See João Manuel Cardoso de Mello, *O Capitalismo Tardio: Contribuição à Revisão Crítica da Formação e do Desenvolvimento da Economia Brasileira* (2d ed.; São Paulo: Brasiliense, 1982).
5. For Peru, see Gootenberg, *Between Silver and Guano.*

bound together by, among other things, the shared ideology of liberalism.[6] But its Brazilian element for the most part ignored liberal political principles and upheld liberal economic ones opportunistically.

The public relations activities of Brazilian business interest groups anticipated by decades those begun by large corporations in the United States at the start of the twentieth century, when the practice of business public relations is considered to have arisen. The business elite of nineteenth-century Brazil labored under the stigmas of traditional low prestige of the business profession in Luso-Brazilian culture and a predominance of foreigners. The commercial associations broadcast images and themes designed to overcome those hindrances. However, the associations only partly succeeded in changing the attitude of the literate Brazilian public. While they were able to raise the prestige of the business profession, mistrust of its overseas trader element and disillusionment with the economy that element represented reached new heights by century's end. The struggle of industrialists and factors, the latter goaded by falling rubber and coffee prices, to defend their economic interests and to obtain government aid helped focus public attention on the foreignness of overseas traders. The Republic and the last decade of the century saw a significant lessening of the prestige of commercial associations and of their power to affect legislation, culminating in the Tariff of 1900. In part it represented a fruition of appeals to the public by industrial groups and the attacks of factors on foreign overseas traders.

The commercial associations had functioned as instruments of foreign influence as well as representatives of overseas trade. Foreign numerical predominance in membership and leadership showed most clearly in association policies on currency and on industrialization, and in contests between overseas merchants and factors. The associations provided a viable means by which foreign traders could use political power to affect the development of their host nations.[7] Association influence on government, although it tended to weaken over time, was both inconspicuous and strong.

The nineteenth-century commercial associations thus provide some modest but interesting illumination of the dependency model. That the political dominance of mercantile capitalism can prove an obstacle to the emergence of an industrial bourgeoisie is a frequent theme among writers in this vein.[8] The policies of the associations and, to a lesser extent, factor

6. This bourgeoise was bound together by business and kinship ties, as well as a shared ideology of radical liberalism and free trade. Charles A. Jones, *International Business in the Nineteenth Century: The Rise and Fall of a Cosmopolitan Bourgeoise* (Brighton, Sussex: Wheatsheaf Books, 1987).

7. As suggested in W. Arthur Lewis, "The Export Stimulus," in *Tropical Development, 1880–1913*, ed. W. Arthur Lewis (Evanston, Ill.: Northwestern University Press, 1970), pp. 40–41.

8. Ian Roxborough, *Theories of Underdevelopment* (Atlantic Highlands, N.J.: Humanities, 1979), p. 68.

groups, indicate this to be true for Brazil. Furthermore, most association members, foreign and native, provide an example of what students of dependency and others who posit an economically dominant-subordinate relationship between developed and underdeveloped nations (often referred to as center and periphery) describe as a collaborating or mediating elite.[9] This is a group whose prosperity or need is interwoven with that of the developed or economically dominant nations and helps provide the local conditions necessary for their continued dominance. Finally, critics of the concept of dependency often have called for precise identification of dependent groups, elites, or classes, and for description of the processes by which external forces exercise their dominance.[10] Although only a small part of this relationship, the commercial associations, representing Brazil's business elite, and their connection to the state may illustrate one such group and process of domination.

If the commercial associations were a vehicle for foreign influence, toward what was that influence aimed? Nothing more sinister than preservation of Brazil's traditional role in the world division of labor. It would be maintained through a policy of free trade and domestic laissez-faire, except where government intervention would aid overseas commerce. Thus foreign influence was eminently conservative in the Brazilian context. Coercion, sometimes assumed to be an element of dependency by critics of the dependency model, was entirely absent. Foreign traders would not have needed to force their goals on their Brazilian peers nor even on most Brazilian government leaders, although this was less true later in the century. Brazil's national symbol, Pedro II, would have found their objectives agreeable.

These influences ensured that the developmental efforts of business interest groups, except for those representing industry, would be aimed toward the traditional economy. However, such efforts encountered two serious obstacles. One was the state's shortage of revenue. Fiscal urgency not only doomed the campaign against export taxation but guaranteed the continuation of provincial import taxes. Increasing national demands for

9. For example, Fernando Henrique Cardoso, "The Consumption of Dependency Theory in the United States," *Latin American Research Review*, 12, no. 3 (1977): 13; John Gallagher and Ronald Robinson, "The Imperialism of Free Trade," *Economic History Review*, 2d Series, 6 (1953): 10; Robin W. Winks, "On Decolonization and Informal Empire," *American Historical Review*, 81 (June 1976): 554–555; Peter Winn, *El Imperio Informal Británico en el Uruguay en el Siglo XIX* (Montevideo: Ediciones de la Banda Oriental, 1975), p. 80.

10. For example, C. Richard Bath and Dilmus D. James, "Dependency Analysis of Latin America: Some Criticisms, Some Suggestions," *Latin American Research Review*, 11, no 3 (1976): 14–15; Philip J. O'Brien, "A Critique of Latin American Theories of Dependency," in *Beyond the Sociology of Development: Economy and Society in Latin America and Africa*, eds. Ivar Oxaal, Tony Barnet, and David Booth (London: Routledge and Kegan Paul, 1975), pp. 23–24; Martin Staniland, *What Is Political Economy? A Study of Social Theory and Underdevelopment* (New Haven, Conn.: Yale University Press, 1985), p. 131.

revenue were as much responsible for raising Brazilian tariffs as were aspirations for industrialization, as illustrated by the establishment in 1900 of a protective tariff by free traders Campos Sales and Murtinho. As noted, business interest groups had themselves to thank for much of their own dilemma. Their unceasing demands for expensive infrastructure improvements, particularly new railroads, contributed much to the financial pinch of nation and provinces. But by refusing to advocate direct taxation, business interest groups shunned the only real remedy for government penury.

The other obstacle was group disunity. The Commercial Association of Rio de Janeiro commonly was more conservative than other associations in monetary policy. It reflected particularly strongly the interests of the Bank of Brazil, as well as of overseas investors and holders of Brazilian debt. The Rio group would support neither plurality of issue nor permanent relief for shortages of cash in other entrepôts. In competition for government aid, commercial associations and factor groups were divided regionally in interest between Northeast and Southeast or, in effect, between sugar and coffee. They also were split between groups representing commodities dominating world markets and groups representing those that were faltering. The opposition of coffee and rubber to sugar interests, for example, impeded any meaningful reduction of export taxes or of provincial import tariffs. Finally, the outcome of contests between business interest groups illustrates the growing hegemony of coffee interests and of the Brazilian Southeast in the second half of the nineteenth century.

How may the role of business interest groups in Brazilian development best be characterized? They operated within a predominantly conservative framework. With the exception of industrial groups, their overriding aim was to preserve and expand the export-import economy inherited from the colonial period. They generally upheld the economic, social, and even governmental patterns existing in the first half of the nineteenth century. They tried to upgrade traditional export commodities, but did little to introduce new ones and nothing to promote self-sufficiency in food. They supported that economy's established base, the large landholding, and, with notable but tardy exceptions, its traditional labor source, slavery. They raged at taxes but, except for the Commercial Association of Pernambuco, would not advocate change in the revenue system. Although spearheading the introduction of modern communications, they made little effort to bridge the regionalism inherited from the colonial period and they continued its parochial outlook. Self-proclaimed bearers of the torch of nineteenth-century liberalism, they were too inconsistent in applying its principles to advance its influence. Although all business interest groups worked for prosperity, only the industrial groups pointed the way toward fundamental change in Brazil.

It is clear that business interest groups played a central role in Brazilian development in the nineteenth century, a participation little appreciated because they tried to keep their influence inconspicuous. How should one ultimately evaluate that role? In some instances the groups slowed or even blocked development. Perhaps their greatest fault was to have missed opportunities. Such errors and inadequacies mainly stemmed from their conservative orientation, from vested interests, and often no doubt from a simple lack of imagination. But it is easy in retrospect to locate failings. The contribution of business interest groups was overwhelmingly positive, and such development as Brazil had achieved by 1900 is inconceivable without them. They were prime channels for modernizing influences. They possessed formidable assets for affecting state policy. They were active in all aspects of development. The role of the business interest groups of the nineteenth century thus was fundamental in laying the basis for the modern Brazilian economy.

Bibliography

Archives and collections

Adam Smith Record Store, the University, Glasgow: Letter Books, John Wylie & Co. Ltd., 1809–1819.

Archives of Norton, Megaw and Company, Ltd., London: Letter Books, London to Rio, 1877–1911; Minutes of General Meetings, 1892–1906.

Arquivo da Associação Comercial da Bahia, Salvador: Livros de Atas, 1840–1903; Registro dos Ofícios, 1840–1850.

Arquivo da Associação Comercial de Pernambuco, Recife: Livros de Atas da Associação Comercial Agrícola de Pernambuco, 1877–1903; Livros de Atas da Associação Comercial de Pernambuco, 1839–1906; Livro de Atas da Assembléia Geral do Centro Político da Lavoura, Comércio e Indústria de Pernambuco, 1899–1903.

Arquivo da Associação Comercial do Rio de Janeiro, Rio de Janeiro: Livros de Atas da Associação Comercial do Rio de Janeiro, 1881–1905; Livro de Atas da Diretoria do Centro Comercial do Rio de Janeiro, 1897–1900; Livro de Atas das Assembléias Gerais do Centro Comercial do Rio de Janeiro, 1897–1905; Ofícios da Associação Comercial do Rio de Janeiro, 1887–1892.

Arquivo da Associação Comercial de Santos: Livros de Atas, 1874–1904.

Arquivo da Associação Comercial de São Paulo: Livro de Atas da Diretoria, 1894–1906.

Arquivo do Centro Industrial do Rio de Janeiro, Rio de Janeiro: Livro de Atas do Centro Industrial do Brasil, 1904–1923; Livro de Atas, Ofícios, Etc. do Imperial Instituto Fluminense de Agricultura, 1860–1862; Livros de Atas da Sociedade Auxiliadora da Indústria Nacional, 1827–1858; Livro do Expediente, Copias, da Sociedade Auxiliadora da Indústria Nacional, 1853–1863; Livro das Propostas Aprovadas e Deliberações da Sociedade Auxiliadora da Indústria Nacional, 1846–1865.

Arquivo do Estado da Bahia, Salvador: Correspondência, Presidência da Província/Govêrno – Associação Comercial, 1828–1889; Correspondência, Presidência da Província/Govêrno – Associação Comercial, 1846–1889.

Arquivo do Estado de Guanabara, Rio de Janeiro.

Arquivo do Estado de São Paulo, São Paulo.

Arquivo Histórico do Itamaraty, Rio de Janeiro.

Arquivo do Instituto Geográfico e Histórico da Bahia, Salvador.

Arquivo do Instituto Histórico e Geográfico Brasileiro, Rio de Janeiro: Arquivo do Barão de Cotegipe; Coleção Francisco Belisário; Coleção Instituto Histórico; Coleção Marquês de Olinda; Coleção Ouro Preto.

Arquivo Nacional, Rio de Janeiro: Seção Histórico; Seção do Poder Executivo.

Arquivo Público Estadual de Pernambuco, Recife: Associação Comercial, 1871 a 1881.

Biblioteca Nacional, Rio de Janeiro: Seção de Manuscritos.

Guildhall Library, London.

Latin American Business Archives, University College, London: British Bank of South America, Letter Books, Packets, Private Letters, and Reports on Firms, Rio de Janeiro and São Paulo to/from London and Santos, 1886–1918; Edward Johnston & Company, Ltd., Letter Books, Santos to London, 1892–1904, Mss. Note Book, Santos, 1892–1904, Private Copy Book, E. Greene; English bank of Rio de Janeiro, Pará Branch to London and Various, 1883–1887; London and Brazilian Bank, Letter books, Packets, and Cable Books, Rio de Janeiro, Pernambuco, and São Paulo to/from London and Various, 1868–1924; London and River Plate Bank, Letter books and Packets, Rio de Janeiro and Pará to/from London and Branches, 1891–1930; Wilson Sons & Company, Ltd., Manager's Letter Book, 1899–1900.

Public Records Office, London: Public Records Office/Foreign Office Microfilm Series 13: Reports from H. M. Consuls in Bahia, 1828–1900.

United States National Archives: Despatches from United States Consuls in Bahia, 1850–1906, Microcopy T-331.

Government documents

Bahia. Diretoria do Serviço de Estatística do Estado. *Anuário Estatístico da Bahia, 1923*. Salvador: Imprensa Oficial do Estado, 1924.

Laws, statutes, etc. *Constituição e Leis do Estado da Bahia, 1892*. Salvador: Diário da Bahia, 1892.

Laws, statutes, etc. *Leis e Resoluções da Assembléia Legislativa da Província da Bahia, Sancionados e Publicados no Ano de 1858 sob Números 704 à 730*. Salvador: Antônio Olavo da França Guerra, 1859.

Presidente da Província. Governador. *Mensagems* [title varies]. 1847–1904.

Secretaria da Agricultura. *Relatórios*. 1896–1897, 1900.

Brazil. Comissão do Comércio Importador. *Anexos ao Parecer da Comissão do Comércio Importador do Rio de Janeiro sôbre as Alterações de Impôstos Feitas pela Lei n. 359 de 30 de Dezembro de 1895*. Rio de Janeiro: Imprensa Nacional, 1896.

Comissão, Exposição Universal, Philadelphia, 1876. *The Empire of Brazil at the Universal Exhibition in 1876 in Philadelphia*. Rio de Janeiro: Imperial Instituto Artístico, 1876.

Comissão de Inquérito Industrial. *Relatório Apresentado a S. Ex, o Sr. Ministro da Fazenda pela Comissão de Inquérito Industrial*. 2 vols. Rio de Janeiro: Tipografia Nacional, 1882.

Congresso. Câmera dos Deputados. *Anais*. 1884–1900.

Congresso. Câmara dos Deputados. *Parecer e Projeto sôbre a Creação de Bancos de Crédito Territorial e Fábricas Centraes de Açúcar Apresentados à Câmera dos Deputados na Sessão de 20 de Julho de 1875, pelas Comissões de Fazenda e Especial Nomeada em 16 de Abril de 1873*. Rio de Janeiro: Tipografia Nacional, 1875.

Congresso. Comissão de Inquérito na Alfândega da Corte. *Relatório da Comissão de Inquérito na Alfândega da Corte sôbre as Censuras e Acusações Feitas à Administração da Mesma Alfândega na Câmera dos Deputados e na Imprensa, em o Ano de 1862*. Rio de Janeiro: Tipografia Nacional, 1862.

Congresso. Comissão Parlamentar de Inquérito. *Informações Apresentadas pela Comissão Parlamentar de Inquérito ao Corpo Legislativo na Terceira Sessão da Décima Oitava Legislatura*. Rio de Janeiro: Tipografia Nacional, 1883.

Congresso. Senado. *Anais*. 1885–1899.

Conselho de Ministros. *Breve Notícia do Estado Financeiro das Províncias, Organizada por Ordem do Barão de Cotegipe, Presidente do Conselho de Ministros*. Rio de Janeiro: Imprensa Nacional, 1887.

Instituto Brasileiro de Geografia e Estatística. *Anuário Estatístico, 1939–1940*. Rio de Janeiro: Imprensa Nacional, 1941.

Laws, statutes, etc. *Código Comercial do Império do Brasil, Anotado . . . pelo Bacharel Salustiano Orlando de Araújo Costa.* 2d ed. Rio de Janeiro: Eduardo & Henrique Laemmert, 1869.

Laws, statutes, etc. *Coleção das Decisões do Govêrno do Império do Brasil de 1868.* Rio de Janeiro: Tipografia Nacional, 1868.

Laws, statutes, etc. *Coleção das Leis.* 1850–1900.

Ministério de Agricultura, Comércio, e Obras Públicas. *Relatórios.* 1861–1892.

Ministério da Fazenda. *Relatórios.* 1852–1900.

Ministério da Fazenda. *Relatório e Projeto de Lei da Comissão Encarregada de Rever e Classificar as Rendas Gerais, Provinciais e Municipais do Império.* Rio de Janeiro: Tipografia Nacional, 1883.

Ministério do Império. *Relatórios.* 1850, 1858.

Ministério da Justiça e Negócios Interiores. Arquivo Nacional. *Registro de Estrangeiros, 1808–1842.* 4 vols. Rio de Janeiro: Arquivo Nacional, 1960–1964.

Ministério de Trabalho, Indústria e Comércio. *Sociedades Mercantis Autorizadas a Funcionar no Brasil, 1808–1946.* Rio de Janeiro: Departamento Nacional de Indústria e Comércio, 1947.

Great Britain. Foreign Office. *Diplomatic and Consular Reports, Annual Series.* Nos. 1–220. London: Harrison and Sons, 1886–1902.

Foreign Office. *Diplomatic and Consular Reports, Miscellaneous Series.* Nos. 45–547. London: Harrison and Sons, 1887–1901.

Pernambuco. Laws, statutes, etc. *Leis Provinciais do Ano de 1883.* Recife: Manuel Figueiroa de Faria e Filhos, 1883.

Presidente da Província. Governador. *Mensagens* [title varies]. 1844–1900.

Secretário da Fazenda. *Relatório Apresentado a S. Exc. o Sr. Dr. Alexandre José Barbosa Lima, Governador do Estado, pelo Dr. Pedro José de Oliveira Pernambuco, Secretário de Estado dos Negócios da Fazenda.* Recife: Manuel Figueiroa de Faria & Filhos, 1895.

São Paulo. Comissão Central de Estatística. *Relatório Apresentado ao Exm. Sr. Presidente da Província de S. Paulo pela Comissão Central de Estatística.* São Paulo: King, 1888.

Governador do Estado. *Mensagens Apresentadas ao Congresso Legislativo de S. Paulo pelos Presidentes do Estado e Vice-Presidentes em Exercício, Desde a Proclamação da República até ao Ano de 1916.* São Paulo: Diário Oficial, 1916.

Presidente da Província. Governador. *Mensagens.* 1870–1905.

Secretaria da Agricultura, Comércio, e Obras Públicas, *Relatório de 1896 Apresentado ao Dr. Manuel Ferraz de Campos Sales, Presidente do Estado pelo Dr. Alvaro Augusto da Costa Carvalho, Secretário dos Negócios da Agricultura, Comércio, e Obras Públicas.* São Paulo: Espíndola, Siqueira, 1897.

Secretaria da Justiça. *Relatório Apresentado ao Presidente do Estado de São Paulo pelo Secretário dos Negócios da Justiça Manuel Pessôa de Siqueira Campos em 31 de Março de 1894.* São Paulo: Espíndola, Siqueira, 1894.

United States. Bureau of Foreign Commerce. "India Rubber," *Special Consular Reports,* 6 (1892): 349–588.

Bureau of Foreign Commerce. *Reports of the Consuls of the United States on the Commerce, Manufactures, etc. of their Consular Districts.* Washington, D.C.: Government Printing Office, 1880–1910.

National Archives. Department of State. *Despatches from United States Consuls in Bahia, 1850–1906.* 6 vols.

Contemporary journals and newspapers

O Auxiliador da Indústria Nacional: Periódico da Sociedade Auxiliadora da Indústria Nacional (Rio de Janeiro). 1833–1896.

Boletim da Sociedade de Medicina e Cirurgia do Rio de Janeiro. 1886–1887.
Correio de Notícias (Salvador).
Correio Paulistano — Orgão Republicano (São Paulo).
O Cruzeiro (Rio de Janeiro).
Diário da Bahia (Salvador).
Diário de Notícias (Rio de Janeiro).
Diário de Pernambuco (Recife).
Diário do Rio de Janeiro.
Diário de Santos.
O Estado de São Paulo.
Gazeta de Notícias (Rio de Janeiro).
Gazeta da Tarde (Rio de Janeiro).
Jornal do Brasil (Rio de Janeiro).
Jornal do Comércio (Rio de Janeiro).
Jornal de Notícias (Salvador).
Jornal do Recife.
A Lavoura (Rio de Janeiro). 1897–1900.
Novedades (Rio de Janeiro).
O País (São Luís).
Revista Agrícola do Imperial Instituto Fluminense de Agricultura (Rio de Janeiro). 1869–1891.
Revista do Clube de Engenharia (Rio de Janeiro). 1887–1888.
Rio Mercantile Journal (Rio de Janeiro).
The Rio News (Rio de Janeiro).
The Times (London).

Books, articles, and unpublished theses

Abranches Moura, João Dunshee de. *Govêrnos e Congressos da República dos Estados Unidos do Brasil*. 2 vols. São Paulo: M. Abranches, 1918.

Transformação do Trabalho: Memória Apresentada à Associação Comercial do Maranhão. São Luís: Pacotilha, 1888.

Aguiar, Pinto de. "História do Banco da Bahia," *Revista da História*, 49 (July–Sept. 1970): 95–110.

Almanach Civil, Político, e Comercial da Cidade da Bahia para o Ano 1845. Salvador: M. A. da Silva Serva, 1844.

Almanak Laemmert, 1844–1904. Rio de Janeiro: Laemmert, 1843–1903.

Almeida, Rómulo. *Traços da História Econômica da Bahia no Ultimo Século e Meio*. Salvador: Instituto de Economia e Finanças da Bahia, 1951.

Amaral, Braz do. *História da Bahia do Império a República*. Salvador: Imprensa Oficial do Estado, 1923.

Amaral, Luís. *História Geral da Agricultura Brasileira*. 3 vols. São Paulo: Editôra Nacional, 1939.

Andrade, Luís Aureliano Gama de. "Dez Anos de Orçamento Imperial, 1867–1877," *Revista Brasileira de Estudos Políticos*, 31 (May 1971): 181–206.

Andrews, C. C. *Brazil: Its Conditions and Prospects*. New York: D. Appleton, 1887.

Araújo Filho, José Ribeiro de. "O Café, Riqueza Paulista," *Boletim Paulista de Geografia*, 23 (July 1956): 78–135.

Associação Comercial Agrícola do Recife [Pernambuco]. *Congresso Agrícola do Recife*. Recife: M. Figueiroa de Faria & Filhos, 1878.

Associação Comercial do Amazonas. *Documentário Comemorativo do Primeiro Centenário da Associação Comercial do Amazonas, 18 de Junho de 1971*. Manaus: Umberto Calderaro, 1971.

Associação Comercial do Amazonas. *Relatório Apresentado 'a Associação Comercial do Amazonas pelo Diretor-Tesoureiro Capitão Honorário do Exército Hannibal Porto.* Rio de Janeiro: Brasil, 1902.

Associação Comercial da Bahia. *Relatórios.* 1863–1904.

"A Associação Comercial Beneficente e as Causas da Decadência Agrícola," *Diário de Pernambuco* (Recife), Jan. 20–26, 1875.

Associação Comercial do Ceará. *Relatórios.* 1867–1872.

Associação Comercial de Desterro. *Estatutos para a Associação Comercial da Cidade do Desterro e sua Comissão Administrativa.* Desterro: Regeneração, 1875.

Associação Comercial de Maceió. *Relatórios.* 1871–1872.

Associação Comercial do Maranhão. "Economia Rural," *Revista Agrícola,* 15, no. 1 (March 1884): 68–77.

Estatutos da Associação Comercial do Maranhão. São Luís: Frias, 1878.

Exposição do Açúcar e Algodão Feita pela Associação Comercial do Maranhão, 1883. São Luís: País, 1883.

Relatórios. 1867–1891.

Associação Comercial do Pará. *Relatórios.* 1868–1899.

Associação Comercial de Pelotas. *Análise 'a Representação que ao Govêrno Imperial Dirigiu à Associação Comercial do Rio Grande Pedindo a Extinção da Mesa de Rendas Alfandegada de Pelotas.* Pelotas: Correio Mercantil, 1880.

A Praça do Comércio da Cidade de Pelotas (Província de S. Pedro do Sul): Representação. Pelotas: Correio Merrcantil, 1880.

Associação Comercial de Pernambuco. *A Associação Comercial Beneficente de Pernambuco.* Recife: Carlos Eduardo Muhlert, 1871.

Descrição dos Festejos Promovidos pela Associação Comercial Beneficente para Receber o Comboio de Café Vindo da Vila do Bonito. Recife: Jornal do Recife, 1876.

Relatórios. 1857–1904.

Associação Comercial do Porto. *Associação Comercial do Porto: Resumo Histórico de sua Atividade desde a Fundação até ao Ano das Comemorações Centenárias.* Porto: Associação Comercial do Porto, 1942.

Associação Comercial de Pôrto Alegre. *Relatórios.* 1870–1873.

Associação Comercial do Rio de Janeiro. *A Associação Comercial do Rio de Janeiro.* Rio de Janeiro: Jornal do Comércio, 1901.

Asilo dos Inválidos da Pátria: Relatório Apresentado à Assembléia Geral no Dia 15 de Setembro de 1869, pelo seu Presidente o Veador José Joaquim de Lima e Silva Sobrinho. Rio de Janeiro: Perseverança, 1869.

Elemento Servil: Primeira Representação da Comissão Especial Nomeada em Assembléia Geral Extraordinária de 2 de Maio de 1884. Rio de Janeiro: J. Villeneuve, 1884.

Estatutos. 1868, 1877, 1883, 1902.

[Comissão da Praça do Comércio do Rio de Janeiro]. *Projeto de Emendas para a Terceira Parte do Código Comercial do Império do Brasil, Oferecido à Assembléia Geral Legislativa.* Rio de Janeiro: J. Villeneuve, 1838.

Projeto de Reforma de Estatutos da Associação Comercial do Rio de Janeiro, Apresentado à Apreciação dos Srs. Sócios, pela sua Diretoria. Rio de Janeiro: Apóstolo, 1875.

"Regulamento para a Praça do Comércio do Rio de Janeiro," in José Vieira Fazenda, *Notas Históricas sôbre a Praça do Comércio e Associação Comercial do Rio de Janeiro.* Rio de Janeiro: Jornal do Comércio, 1915.

Relatórios, 1868–1904.

Relatório da Comissão da Praça do Comércio do Rio de Janeiro, Encarregada da Subscrição International para a Fundação do Asilo dos Inválidos da Pátria. Rio de Janeiro: Perseverança, 1867.

Resposta da Associação Comercial do Rio de Janeiro aos Quesitos da Comissão Parlamentar de Inquérito. Rio de Janeiro: Montenegro, 1883.

Associação Comercial do Rio Grande. *Memorial da Associação Comercial da Cidade do Rio Grande aos Exms. Srs. Deputados à Assembléia Legislativa Provincial pelo Quinto Círculo Eleitoral da Província de S. Pedro do Rio Grande do Sul sôbre o Atual Saldo do Capital Despendido Exclusiviamente no Caes da Mesma Cidade.* Rio Grande: Artista, 1887.

Representação da Associação Comercial do Rio Grande ao Govêrno Imperial Solicitando o Imediato Emprehendimento das Obras da Barra Geral da Província de S. Pedro do Rio Grande do Sul, Segundo o Projeto do Especialista Holandês, Sr. P. Caland. Rio Grande: Artista, 1886.

Representação Dirigida ao Govêrno Imperial pela Associação Comercial da Praça do Rio Grande, Pedindo a Revogação do Decreto N. 7,063 de 21 de Outubro de 1878. Rio Grande: Echo do Sul, 1880.

Associação Comercial de Santos. *A Crise de Transportes no Estado de S. Paulo.* São Paulo: Industrial de São Paulo, 1892.

Relatórios. 1876–1904.

Associação Comercial de São Paulo. *Estatutos da Associação Comercial de São Paulo, Aprovados pela Assembléia Geral dos Sócios em 7 Dezembro de 1894.* São Paulo: Industrial de São Paulo, 1895.

Relatório da Associação Comercial de São Paulo, Ano de 1895. São Paulo: Industrial, 1896.

Representação Dirigida ao Congresso Nacional sôbre as Medidas Financeiras Constantes do Aditivo Apresentado ao Projeto de Orçamento da União pelo Deputado Sr. Francisco Glycério em 26 de Setembro de 1896. São Paulo: Indústrial de São Paulo, 1896.

Associação Comercial de Sergipe. *Associação Comercial de Sergipe, 1872–1972.* Aracaju: Regina, 1972.

Associação Industrial. *Memorial Relativo a uma Exposição de Indústria Nacional em 1888 no Rio de Janeiro, Apresentada a S. Ex. o Sr. Conselheiro Rodrigo Antônio da Silva, DD. Ministro e Secretário de Estado dos Negócios da Agricultura, Comércio e Obras Públicas.* Rio de Janeiro: H. Lombaerts, 1887.

Relatórios. 1882, 1884.

Representação Dirigida ao Exm. Sr. Ministro da Fazenda pela Associação Industrial, Relativamente ao Projeto da Tarifa das Alfândegas, e de Conformidade com os Relatórios dos Representantes de Diversas Indústrias. Rio de Janeiro: Central, 1881.

O Trabalho Nacional e Seus Adversários. Rio de Janeiro: G. Leuzinger & Filhos, 1881.

Auxiliar Comercial do Rio de Janeiro ou Repertório Alfabético de seus Principais Moradores em 1871. Rio de Janeiro: Oliveira Gonçalves & Corrêa, 1871.

Auxilios à Indústria: Representação dos Industriaes ao Congresso Nacional. Rio de Janeiro: Luís Macedo, 1892.

Azevedo, Fernando de. *Canavais e Engenhos na Vida Política do Brasil: Ensaio Sociológico sôbre o Elemento Político na Civilização do Açúcar.* São Paulo: Instituto do Açúcar e do Alcool, 1948.

Azevedo, Manuel Duarte Moreira de. "A Praça do Comércio: Écos de um Passado Glorioso," *Boletim Semanal da Associação Comercial do Rio de Janeiro,* I, no. 2 (Oct. 18, 1935): 9–10, no. 3 (Oct. 25, 1935): 13–15, no. 4 (Nov. 1, 1935): 26, no. 5 (Nov. 8, 1935): 15–16, no. 6 (Nov. 15, 1935): 13–16.

"Sociedades Fundadas no Brasil Desde os Tempos Coloniais até o Começo do Atual Reinado," *Revista do Instituto Histórico e Geográfico Brasileiro,* 48, part 2 (1885): 265–322.

Azevedo, Thales de, and Lins, E. Q. Vieira. *História do Banco da Bahia, 1858–1958.* Rio de Janeiro: J. Olympio, 1969.

Baer, Werner. *Industrialization and Economic Development in Brazil.* Homewood, Ill.: Irwin, 1965.

Baer, Werner, and Villela, Annibal V. "Industrial Growth and Industrialization: Revisions in the Stages of Brazil's Economic Development," *The Journal of Developing Areas,* 7 (Jan. 1973): 217–234.

Ballou, Maturin M. *Equatorial America.* New York: Houghton Mifflin, 1892.

Barbosa, Francisco de Assis. "A Presidência Campos Sales," *Luso-Brazilian Review,* 5 (Summer 1968): 3–26.

Barman, Roderick J. "The Brazilian Peasantry Reexamined: The Implications of the Quebra-Quilo Revolt, 1874–1875," *Hispanic American Historical Review,* 57 (Aug. 1977): 401–424.

Brazil: The Forging of a Nation, 1798–1852. Stanford, Calif.: Stanford University Press, 1988.

"Business and Government in Imperial Brazil: The Experience of Viscount Mauá," *Journal of Latin American Studies,* 13 (Nov. 1981): 239–264.

"The Role of the Law Graduate in the Political Elite of Imperial Brazil," *Journal of Interamerican Studies and World Affairs,* 18 (Nov. 1976): 423–450.

Barros, Eudes. *A Associação Comercial no Império e na República.* 2d ed. revised. Rio de Janeiro: Olímpica, 1975.

"103 Anos de Relatórios na Associação Comercial," *RCP: Revista das Classes Produtoras,* 34, (May 1972): 26–28.

Basadre, Jorge. *Historia da la Cámera de Comercio de Lima.* Lima: Cámera de Comercio de Lima, 1963.

Bastos, Aureliano Cândido Tavares. *Cartas do Solitário.* 3d ed. São Paulo: Editôra Nacional, 1938.

Discursos Parlamentares. Brasilia: Senado Federal, 1977.

Bastos, Humberto. *O Pensamento Industrial no Brasil.* 2d ed. São Paulo: Martins, 1952.

Bath, C. Richard, and James, Dilmus D. "Dependency Analysis of Latin America: Some Criticisms, Some Suggestions," *Latin American Research Review,* 11, no 3 (1976): 3–54.

Bello, José Maria. *A History of Modern Brazil, 1889–1964.* Translated by James L. Taylor. Stanford, Calif.: Stanford University Press, 1966.

Beltrão, Heitor. "A Ansia de Brasildade, os Comerciantes e a sua Agremiação Mater: A Propósito do Cento Nono Aniversário da Associação Comercial do Rio de Janeiro," *Mensário do Jornal do Comércio,* 24 (Oct. 1943): 29–32.

Um Capítulo da História da Praça do Rio de Janeiro: Considerações de Ordem Histórica e Jurídica, 1820–1929. Rio de Janeiro: Imprensa Nacional, 1929.

"O Civismo da Praça num Século de Labor," in Associação Comercial do Rio de Janeiro, *Aspetos Colegidos a Propósito do Centenário da Associação Comercial.* Rio de Janeiro: Associação Comercial do Rio de Janeiro, 1935.

Bendix, Reinhard. *Max Weber: An Intellectual Portrait.* New York: Anchor Books, 1962.

Bethell, Leslie. *The Abolition of the Brazilian Slave Trade: Britain, Brazil and the Slave Trade Question.* Cambridge: Cambridge University Press, 1970.

Bethell, Leslie, and Carvalho, José Murilo de. "Brazil from Independence to the Middle of the Nineteenth Century," in *The Cambridge History of Latin America, Volume III: From Independence to c. 1870.* Edited by Leslie Bethell. Cambridge: Cambridge University Press, 1985.

Bisbee, L. H., and Simonds, J. C. *The Board of Trade and the Produce Exchange: Their History, Methods, and Law.* Chicago: Callaghan, 1884.

Blake, Augusto Vitorino Sacramento. *Dicionário Bibliográfico Brasileiro.* 7 vols. Rio de Janeiro: Imprensa Nacional, 1883–1902.

Borges, Bernardino José. *O Comerciante, ou Completo Manual Instrutivo.* 2d ed. revised. Rio de Janeiro: Eduardo & Henrique Laemmert, 1878.

Boxer, Charles R. *The Portuguese Seaborne Empire, 1415–1825*. New York: Alfred A. Knopf, 1969.

Branner, John Casper. *Cotton in the Empire of Brazil*. Department of Agriculture Special Report no. 8. Washington, D.C.: Government Printing Office, 1885.

"The Cotton Industry in Brazil," *Popular Science Monthly*, 40 (March 1892): 666–674.

British and Latin American Chamber of Commerce. *Commercial Encyclopedia (British and Latin American Chamber of Commerce Sole Official Annual and/or Biennial Organ). Third Sectional Issue: Argentina, Brazil, Chile, Peru, Uruguay. Overseas Supplement, Great Britain*. London: Globe Encyclopedia, 1922.

Brito, João Rodrigues de. *Cartas Econômico-Políticas sôbre a Agricultura e Comércio da Bahia*. Salvador: Imprensa Oficial do Estado, 1924.

Buescu, Mircea. *Brazil: Problemas Econômicas e Experiência Histórica*. Rio de Janeiro: Forense-Universitária, 1985.

Evolução Econômica do Brasil. 2d ed. Rio de Janeiro: APEC, 1974.

Exercícios de História Econômica do Brasil. Rio de Janeiro: APEC, 1968.

História Econômica do Brasil: Pesquisas e Análises. Rio de Janeiro: APEC, 1970.

Bureau of the American Republics. *Brazil*. Bureau of the American Republics Bulletin No. 7, June 1891. Washington, D.C.: Bureau of the American Republics, 1891.

Burke, Ulrick Ralph, and Staples, Jr., Robert. *Business and Pleasure in Brazil*. London: Field and Tuer, 1884.

Burns, E. Bradford. *The Unwritten Alliance: Rio Branco and Brazilian-American Relations*. New York and London: Columbia University Press, 1966.

Bushnell, David, and Macaulay, Neill. *The Emergence of Latin America in the Nineteenth Century*. Oxford: Oxford University Press, 1988.

Callcott, Maria Graham, Lady. *Journal of a Voyage to Brazil and Residence There During the Years 1821, 1822, 1823*. London: Longman, Hurst, Rees, Orme, Brown, and Green, 1824.

Calmon, Francisco Marques de Góes. "Ensaio de Retrospeto sôbre o Comércio e a Vida Econômica e Comercial na Bahia de 1823 a 1900," in *Diário Oficial: Edição Especial do Centenário*, 8 (July 2, 1923): 376–396.

Vida Econômica-Financeira da Bahia: Elementos para a História de 1808 a 1899. Remipressão. Salvador: Fundo de Pesquisas-CPE, 1978.

Calógeras, João Pandiá. *A Política Monetária do Brasil*. São Paulo: Editôra Nacional, 1960.

Cameron, Rondo. *Banking in the Early Stages of Industrialization*. London: Oxford University Press, 1967.

Cano, Wilson. *Raízes da Concentração Industrial em São Paulo*. Rio de Janeiro, São Paulo: DIFEL, 1977.

Canstatt, Oskar. *Brasil: A Terra e a Gente (1871)*. Translated by Eduardo de Lima Castro. Rio de Janeiro: Irmãos Pongetti, 1954.

Cardoso, Eliana A. "Desvalorizações Cambiais, Indústria, e Café: Brasil, 1862–1906," *Revista Brasileira de Economia*, 35, no. 2 (1981): 85–104.

Cardoso, Fernando Henrique. "The Consumption of Dependency Theory in the United States," *Latin American Research Review*, 12, no. 3 (1977): 7–24.

Carone, Edgard. *O Centro Industrial do Rio de Janeiro e a sua Importante Participação na Economia Nacional (1827–1977)*. Rio de Janeiro: Centro Industrial do Rio de Janeiro, 1978.

Movimento Operário no Brasil. São Paulo: DIFEL, 1979.

"Prefácio," in *O Pensamento Industrial no Brasil (1880–1945)*. Edited by Edgard Carone. Rio de Janeiro: Difel, 1977.

A República Velha (Instituições e Classes Sociais). São Paulo: Difusão Européia do Livro, 1970.

Carreira, Liberato de Castro. *História Financeira e Orçamentária do Império do Brasil.* 2 vols. 2d ed. Brasília, Rio de Janeiro: Fundação Casa de Rui Barbosa/MEC, 1980.

O Orçamento do Império desde sua Fundação. Rio de Janeiro: Tipografia Nacional, 1883.

Carvalho, José Murilo de. *A Construção de Ordem: A Elite Política Imperial.* Rio de Janeiro: Campus, 1980.

Teatro de Sombras: A Política Imperial. São Paulo: Vértice/IUPERJ, 1988.

Carvalho, Verediano. *A Praça do Rio, 1890–1891: Série de Artigos do Jornal Fluminense 'O Tempo' com o Pseudonymo Zeferino.* Rio de Janeiro: Laemmert, 1892.

Castro, Agostinho Vitor Borja. "Relatório," in Antônio de Sousa Rego, *Relatório da Segunda Exposição Nacional de 1866.* Rio de Janeiro: Tipografia Nacional, 1869.

Castro, Ana Célia. *As Empresas Estrangeiras no Brasil, 1860–1913.* Rio de Janeiro: Zahar, 1979.

Castro e Almeida, Eduardo de, ed. *Inventário dos Documentos Relativos ao Brasil Existentes no Arquivo da Marinha e Ultramar de Lisboa, Vol. I: Bahia, 1613–1752.* Rio de Janeiro: Biblioteca Nacional, 1913.

Cavalcanti, Amaro. *Resenha Financeira do Ex-Império do Brasil em 1889.* Rio de Janeiro: Imprensa Nacional, 1890.

Centro Comercial do Rio de Janeiro. *Relatório dos Atos da Terceira Direção, Desde 17 de Julho de 1900 a 17 de Julho de 1901.* Porto: Comércio do Porto, 1901.

Centro da Indústria e Comércio de Açúcar. *Crise do Açúcar: Representação e Memorial Apresentado ao Corpo Legislativo da Nação Brasileira pelo Centro da Indústria e Comércio de Açúcar do Rio de Janeiro.* Rio de Janeiro: Imprensa Nacional, 1887.

Centro Industrial do Brasil. *Brazil: Its Natural Riches and Industries (Foreign Edition).* Volume I: Preface – Productive Industry. Paris: Librarie Aillaud, 1910.

Centro Industrial do Brasil [sic]. *Representação ao Sr. Ministro da Fazenda.* Rio de Janeiro: C. Gaspar da Silva, 1890.

Centro da Lavoura e Comércio do Café. *Breve Notícia sôbre a Primeira Exposição de Café do Brasil.* Rio de Janeiro: Moreira, Maximino, 1882.

Representação Submetida ao Poder Legislativo sôbre Algumas das Necessidades da Lavoura e do Comércio. Rio de Janeiro: Moreira, Maximínio, 1882.

Chapman, Stanley. *Merchant Enterprise in Britain: From the Industrial Revolution to World War I.* Cambridge: Cambridge University Press, 1992.

Cochran, Thomas C. *Business in American Life: A History.* New York: McGraw-Hill, 1974.

Coimbra, Creso. *Visão Histórica e Análise Conceitual dos Transportes no Brasil.* Rio de Janeiro: CEDOP do Ministro de Transportes, 1974.

Colson, R. Frank. "The Destruction of a Revolution: Polity, Economy, and Society in Brazil, 1870–1891." 2 vols. Ph.D. Diss., Princeton University, 1979.

"The Failed Reform: Society and the Fiscal Crisis in Late Nineteenth Century Brazil," *Nova Americana,* 5 (1982): 269–294.

"On Expectations-Perspectives on the Crisis of 1889 in Brazil," *Journal of Latin American Studies,* 13 (Nov. 1981): 265–292.

Congresso Agrícola. *Coleção de Documentos.* Rio de Janeiro: Tipografia Nacional, 1878.

Conniff, Michael L. "Voluntary Associations in Rio, 1870–1945: A New Approach to Urban Social Dynamics," *Journal of Interamerican Studies and World Affairs,* 17 (Feb. 1975): 64–81.

Conniff, Michael J., Hendrix, Melvin K., and Nohlgren, Stephen. "Brazil," in *The Urban Development of Latin America, 1750–1920.* Edited by Richard M. Morse. Stanford, Calif.: Center for Latin American Studies, Stanford University, 1971.

Conrad, Robert. *The Destruction of Brazilian Slavery, 1850–1888.* Berkeley: University of California Press, 1972.

"The Planter Class and the Debate over Chinese Immigration ro Brazil, 1850–1893," *International Migration Review,* 9 (Spring 1975): 41–55.

World of Sorrow: The African Slave Trade to Brazil. Baton Rouge and London: Louisiana State University Press, 1986.

Contador, Cláudio, and Haddad, Cláudio. "Produto Real, Moeda e Preços: A Experiência Brasileira no Período 1861–1970," *Revista Brasileira de Estatística*, 36 (July–Sept. 1975): 407–439.

Cortés, Antônio Maria Cardozo. *Homens e Instituições no Rio.* Rio de Janeiro: Instituto Brasileiro de Geografia e Estatística, 1957.

Costa, Emília Viotti da. "Brazil: The Age of Reform, 1870–1889" in *The Cambridge History of Latin America, Volume V: c. 1870–1930.* Edited by Leslie Bethell. Cambridge: Cambridge University Press, 1986.

The Brazilian Empire: Myths and Histories. Chicago: University of Chicago Press, 1985.

Da Monarquia à República: Momentos Decisivos. São Paulo: Ciências Humanas, 1979.

Da Senzala à Colônia. São Paulo: Difusão Européia do Livro, 1966.

Costa, F. A. Pereira da. "Notícia sôbre as Instituições de Crédito Bancário em Pernambuco," in Associação Comercial de Pernambuco, *Relatório da Diretoria da Associação Comercial de Pernambuco, Apresentado na Sessão da Assembléia Geral Ordinária de 10 de Agôsto de 1898.* Recife: Jornal do Recife, 1898.

Costa, Francisco Barreto Picanço da. *Dicionário de Estradas de Ferro.* 2 vols. Rio de Janeiro: H. Lombaerts, 1891–1892.

Estradas de Ferro: Vários Estudos. Rio de Janeiro: Machado, 1887.

Viação Ferrea do Brasil: Descrição Técnica e Estatística de Todas as Nossas Estradas de Ferro. Rio de Janeiro: Machado, 1884.

Costa, Luis Edmundo da. *De um Livro de Memórias.* 5 vols. Rio de Janeiro: Imprensa Nacional, 1958.

O Rio de Janeiro do Meu Tempo. 5 vols. Rio de Janeiro: Imprensa Nacional, 1938.

Costa e Silva Sobrinho, João da. *Santos Noutros Tempos.* São Paulo: Revista dos Tribunais, 1953.

Cruz, Ernesto. *História da Belém.* 2 vols. Belém: Universidade Federal do Pará, 1973.

Curtis, William Eleroy. *Trade and Transportation Between the United States and Spanish America.* Washington, D.C.: Government Printing Office, 1889.

Dean, Warren. *Brazil and the Struggle for Rubber: A Study in Environmental History.* New York: Cambridge University Press, 1987.

"The Brazilian Economy, 1870–1930" in *The Cambridge History of Latin America, Volume V: c. 1870 to 1930.* Edited by Leslie Bethell. Cambridge: Cambridge University Press, 1986.

"A Industrialização Durante a República Velha," in *Estructura de Poder e Economia.* Vol. I of *O Brasil Republicano.* Edited by Boris Fausto. Tomo 3 of *História Geral da Civilização Brasileira.* Edited by Sérgio Buarque de Holanda. São Paulo: Difusão Editorial, 1975.

The Industrialization of São Paulo, 1880–1945. Austin and London: University of Texas Press, 1969.

"Latifundia and Land Policy in Nineteenth-Century Brazil," *Hispanic American Historical Review*, 51 (Nov. 1971): 606–625.

Rio Claro: A Brazilian Plantation System, 1820–1920. Stanford, Calif.: Stanford University Press, 1976.

Deerr, Noel. *The History of Sugar.* 2 vols. London: Chapman and Hall, 1949.

Delfim Netto, Antônio. "Foundations for the Analysis of Brazilian Coffee Problems," in *Essays on Coffee and Economic Development.* Edited by Carlos Manuel Peláez. Rio de Janeiro: Instituto Brasileiro do Café, 1973.

O Problema do Café no Brasil. Rio de Janeiro: Fundação Getúlio Vargas, 1979.

Delson, Roberta M. "Sugar Production for the Nineteenth Century British Market: Rethinking the Roles of Brazil and the British West Indies," in *Crisis and Change in the*

International Sugar Economy, 1860–1914. Edited by Bill Albert and Adrian Graves. Norwich and Edinburgh: ISC Press, 1984.

Denis, Pierre. *Brazil.* Translated by Bernard Miall. London: T. Fisher Unwin, 1911.

Denslow, David. "As Exportações e a Origem do Padrão de Industrialização Regional do Brasil," in *Dimensões do Desenvolvimento Brasileiro.* Edited by Werner Baer, Pedro Pinchas Geiger, and Paulo Roberto Haddad. Rio de Janeiro: Campus, 1978.

——— "As Origens da Desigualdade Regional no Brasil," in *Formação Econômica do Brasil: A Experiência da Industrialização.* Edited by Flávio Rabelo Versiani and José Roberto Mendonça de Barros. São Paulo: Saraiva, 1977.

——— "Sugar Production in Northeastern Brazil and Cuba, 1858–1908." Ph.D. Diss., Yale University, 1974.

Dent, Hastings Charles. *A Year in Brazil: With Notes on the Abolition of Slavery, the Finances of the Empire, Religion, Meterology, Natural History, Etc.* London: Kegan Paul, Trench, 1886.

Deveza, Guilherme. "Política Tributária no Período Imperial," in *Declínio e Queda do Império.* Vol. 4 of *O Brasil Monárquico.* Tomo 2 of *História Geral da Civilização Brasileira.* Edited by Sérgio Buarque de Holanda and Pedro Moacyr Campos. São Paulo: Difusão Européia do Livro, 1971.

Diamanti, Henri. "Nota sôbre a Indústria Açucareira no Brasil [1898]." Translated by Gadiel Perruci. In Perruci, Gadiel. *A República das Usinas: Um Estudo de História Social e Econômica do Nordeste, 1889–1930.* Rio de Janeiro: Paz e Terra, 1978.

Diário de Pernambuco. Livro do Nordeste, Commemorativo do Primeiro Centenário do Diário de Pernambuco, 1825–1925. Recife: Diário de Pernambuco, 1925.

Duncan, Julian Smith. *Public and Private Operation of Railways in Brazil.* New York: Columbia University Press, 1932.

Dundas, Robert. *Sketches of Brazil, Including New Views on Tropical and European Fever with Remarks on a Premature Decay of the System Incident to Europeans on Their Return from Hot Climates.* London: John Churchill, 1852.

Dunn, Henry. *Guatemala o las Provincias Unidas de Centro America Durante 1827 a 1828, Siendo Bosquejos y Memorandums Hechos Durante una Residencia de Doce Meses en Aquella República.* Translated by Ricardo de León. Guatemala: Tipografía Nacional, 1960.

Edward Johnston & Co., Rio de Janeiro. *Um Século de Café.* Rio de Janeiro: Edward Johnston & Co., 1942.

Edwards, Corwin D. "Associações Comerciais Brasileiras," in *A Missão Cooke no Brasil.* Rio de Janeiro: Fundação Getúlio Vargas, 1949.

Edwards, William H. *A Voyage Up the River Amazon, Including a Residence at Pará.* London: John Murray, 1861.

Ehrmann, Henry W., ed. *Interest Groups on Four Continents.* Pittsburgh: University of Pittsburgh Press, 1958.

Eisenberg, Peter L. "Abolishing Slavery: The Process on Pernambuco's Sugar Plantations," *Hispanic American Historical Review,* 52 (Nov. 1972): 580–597.

——— *The Sugar Industry in Pernambuco: Modernization without Change, 1840–1910.* Berkeley: University of California Press, 1974.

El-Kareh, Almir Chaiban. "A Companhia Estrada de Ferro D. Pedro II: Uma Tentativa Capitalista no Brasil Imperial, 1855–1865," in *Ensaios sôbre a Política e a Economia da Província Fluminense no Século XIX.* Edited by Richard Graham. Rio de Janeiro: Arquivo Nacional, 1974.

"Evolução da Cotonicultura Brasileira," *Conjuntura Econômica,* 24 , no. 5 (1970): 41–51.

"Exposição Agrícola: Exposição de Açúcar e Algodão Inagurada no Dia 23 de Dezembro de 1883 no Província de Maranhão por Iniciativa e Esforços da Associação Comercial," *Revista Agrícola,* 15 (March 1884): 48–52.

"Extratos do Relatório do Exm. Sr. Ministro da Agricultura," *Revista Agrícola,* 13 (March 1882): 37–49.

Faoro, Raymundo. *Os Donos do Poder: Formação do Patronato Político Brasileiro.* 2 vols. 2d ed. Pôrto Alegre, São Paulo: Globo/Universidade de São Paulo, 1975.

Faria, Alberto de. *Mauá: Ireneo Evangelista de Souza, Barão e Visconde de Mauá, 1813–1889.* 2d ed. São Paulo: Editôra Nacional, 1933.

Farías, Eduardo Arcila. *El Real Consulado de Caracas.* Caracas: Universidad Central de Venezuela, 1957.

Fausto, Boris. "Brazil: The Political and Social Structure of the First Republic," in *The Cambridge History of Latin America, Volume V: c. 1870 to 1930.* Edited by Leslie Bethell. Cambridge: Cambridge University Press, 1986.

"Expansão do Café e Política Cafeeira," in *Estructura de Poder e Economia.* Vol. 1 of *O Brazil Republicano.* Edited by Boris Fausto. Tomo 3 of *História Geral da Civilização Brasileira.* Edited by Sérgio Buarque de Holanda. São Paulo: Difusão Editorial, 1975.

Fazenda, José Vieira. "Notas Históricas sôbre a Praça do Comércio e Associação Comercial do Rio de Janeiro," *Revista do Instituto Histórico e Geográfico Brasileiro,* 73, Part II (1910): 87–122.

Fendt Júnior, Roberto. "Investimentos Inglêses no Brasil, 1870–1913: Uma Avaliação da Política Brasileira," *Revista Brasileira de Economia,* 31 (July–Sept. 1977): 521–539.

Ferreira, Manuel Jesuino. *A Província da Bahia, Apontamentos.* Rio de Janeiro: Tipografia Nacional, 1875.

Ferreira Neto, Francisco. *150 Anos de Transportes no Brasil: 1822–1972.* Rio de Janeiro: Ministério dos Transportes, 1972.

Fishlow, Albert. "Origins and Consequences of Import-Substitution in Brazil," in *International Economics and Development: Essays in Honor of Raul Prebisch.* Edited by Luiz Eugenio di Marco. New York: Academic Press, 1972.

Fletcher, James C., and Kidder, D. P. *Brazil and the Brazilians.* 8th ed. revised. Boston: Little, Brown and Company, 1868.

Flory, Rae, and Smith, David Grant. "Bahian Merchants and Planters in the Seventeenth and Early Eighteenth Centuries," *Hispanic American Historical Review,* 54 (Nov. 1978): 571–594.

Fonseca, Carlos Pinheiro da. *O Ciclo do Café.* Rio de Janeiro: Departamento Nacional do Café, 1934.

Fonseca, Joaquim Roque. *Cem Anos em Defesa da Economia Nacional, 1834–1934.* Lisbon: Associação Comercial de LIsboa, 1934.

Font, Mauricio A. *Coffee, Contention and Change in the Making of Modern Brazil.* Oxford: Basil Blackwell, 1990.

Fragoso, Arlindo. *Ensino Agrícola: Escola Agrícola da Bahia, Série de Artigos Publicados no "Jornal de Notícias," sôbre a Urgência e Bases de Reforma dêsse Estabelecimento.* Salvador: Dois Mundos, 1893.

Franco, Afonso Arinos de Melo. *Rodrigues Alves: Apogeu e Declíneo de Presidencialismo.* 2 vols. São Paulo: Universidade de São Paulo, 1973.

Franco, Afonso Arinos de Melo, and Pacheco, Cláudio. *História do Banco do Brasil.* 4 vols. Rio de Janeiro: Artenova, 1973.

Franco, Gustavo Henrique Barroso. "A Primeira Década Republicana," in *A Ordem do Progresso: Cem Anos de Política Econômica Republicana, 1889–1989.* Organizador Marcelo Paiva Abreu. Rio de Janeiro: Campus, 1989.

Reforma Monetária e Instabilidade Durante a Transição Republicana. Rio de Janeiro: BNDES, 1983.

Freire, Antônio, ed. *Almanak da Província da Bahia, 1881.* Salvador: João Gonçalves Tourinho, 1881.

Freyre, Gilberto. *Inglêses no Brasil: Aspectos da Influência Britânica sôbre a Vida, A Paisagem, e a Cultura do Brasil.* Rio de Janeiro: José Olympio, 1948.

The Mansions and the Shanties (Sobrados e Mucambos): The Making of Modern Brazil. Translated and edited by Harriet de Onís. New York: Alfred A. Knopf, 1966.

Ordem e Progresso. 2 vols. 2d ed. Rio de Janeiro: José Olympio, 1962

Fritsch, Winston. *External Constraints on Economic Policy in Brazil, 1889–1930.* Houndmills, Basingstoke, Hampshire: Macmillan, 1988.

Furtado, Celso. *The Economic Growth of Brazil: A Survey from Colonial to Modern Times.* Translated by Ricardo W. de Aguiar and Eric Charles Drysdale. Berkeley: University of California Press, 1965.

Gallagher, John, and Robinson, Ronald. "The Imperialism of Free Trade," *Economic History Review,* 2d Series, 6 (1953): 1–15.

Galloway, J. H. "The Sugar Industry of Pernambuco During the Nineteenth Century," *Annals of the Association of American Geographers,* 58 (June 1968): 285–303.

Genovese, Eugene D., and Fox-Genovese, Elizabeth. "The Slave Economies in Political Perspective," *Journal of American History,* 66 (June 1979): 7–23.

Gibbs, John Arthur. *The History of Antony and Dorothea Gibbs and of Their Contemporary Relatives, Including the History of the Origin and Early Years of the House of Antony Gibbs and Sons.* London: Saint Catherine, 1922.

Glade, William. "Latin America and the International Economy, 1870–1914," in *The Cambridge History of Latin America, Volume V: c. 1870 to 1930.* Edited by Leslie Bethell. Cambridge: Cambridge University Press, 1986.

Gnaccarini, José C. "A Economia de Açúcar: Processo de Trabalho e Processo de Acumulação," in *Estructura de Poder e Economia.* Vol. 1 of *O Brazil Republicano.* Edited by Boris Fausto. Tomo 3 of *História Geral da Civilização Brasileira.* Edited by Sérgio Buarque de Holanda. São Paulo: Difusão Editorial, 1975.

Goldsmith, Raymond W. *Brasil, 1850–1984: Desenvolvimento Financeiro sob um Século de Inflação.* São Paulo: Harper & Row do Brasil, 1986.

Gomes, Antônio Osmar. "Associação Comercial da Bahia é a Mais Antiga do Brasil. É a Primaz," *Boletim da Associação Comercial da Bahia,* 45 (Jan. 1954): 2–6.

Gonçalves, Reinaldo and Barros, Amir Coelho. "Tendências dos Termos-de-Troca: A Tese de Prebisch e a Economia Brasileira, 1850–1979," *Pesquisa e Planejamento Econômico,* 12 (April 1982): 109–131.

Gootenberg, Paul. *Between Silver and Guano: Commercial Policy and the State in Postindependence Peru.* Princeton, N.J.: Princeton University Press, 1989.

"The Social Origins of Protectionism and Free Trade in Nineteenth-Century Lima," *Journal of Latin American Studies,* 14 (Nov. 1982): 329–358.

Graham, Richard. "Brazil from the Middle of the Nineteenth Century to the Paraguayan War," in *The Cambridge History of Latin America, Vol. III: From Independence to c. 1870.* Edited by Leslie Bethell. Cambridge: Cambridge University Press, 1985.

Britain and the Onset of Modernization in Brazil, 1850–1914. Cambridge: Cambridge University Press, 1968.

"A British Industry in Brazil: Rio Flour Mills, 1886–1920," *Business History,* 8, no. 1 (1966): 13–38.

"Causes for the Abolition of Negro Slavery in Brazil: An Interpretive Essay," *Hispanic American Historical Review,* 46 (Feb. 1966): 123–127.

"Government Expenditures and Political Change in Brazil, 1880–1899: Who Got What," *Journal of Interamerican Studies and World Affairs,* 19 (Aug. 1977): 339–367.

Landowners and the Overthrow of the Empire," *Luso-Brazilian Review,* 7 (Dec. 1970): 44–56.

Patronage and Politics in Nineteenth-Century Brazil. Stanford, Calif.: Stanford University Press, 1990.

"Sepoys and Imperialists: Techniques of British Power in Nineteenth-Century Brazil," *Inter-American Economic Affairs*, 23, no. 1 (1969): 23–37.

"Slavery and Economic Development: Brazil and the United States' South in the Nineteenth Century," *Comparative Studies in Society and History*, 23 (Oct. 1981): 620–655.

Granziera, Ruy Guilherme. *A Guerra do Paraguay e o Capitalismo no Brasil*. São Paulo: Hucitec, 1979.

Greenhill, Robert. "The Brazilian Coffee Trade," in *Business Imperialism, 1840–1930: An Inquiry Based on British Experience in Latin America*. Edited by D. C. M. Platt. Oxford: Oxford University Press, 1977.

"Merchants and the Latin American Trades: An Introduction," in *Business Imperialism, 1840–1930: An Inquiry Based on British Experience in Latin America*. Edited by D. C. M. Platt. Oxford: Oxford University Press, 1977.

Hahner, June E. "Jacobinos Versus Gallegos: Urban Radicals Versus Portuguese Immigrants in Rio de Janeiro in the 1890s," *Journal of Interamerican Studies and World Affairs* 18 (May 1976): 125–154.

"The Paulistas' Rise to Power: A Civilian Group Ends Military Rule," *Hispanic American Historical Review*, 48 (May 1967): 149–165.

Poverty and Politics: The Urban Poor in Brazil, 1870–1920. Albuquerque: University of New Mexico Press, 1986.

Harlow, Rex F. "Building a Public Relations Definition," *Public Relations Review*, 2 (Winter 1976): 34–42.

Havighurst, Robert J., and Moreira, J. Roberto. *Society and Education in Brazil*. Pittsburgh: University of Pittsburgh Press, 1965.

Heaton, Herbert. "A Merchant Adventurer in Brazil," *Journal of Economic History*, 6 (May 1946): 1–23.

Henshall, Janet D., and Momsen, R. P. *A Geography of Brazilian Development*. London: G. Bell & Sons, 1974.

Herndon, William Lewis. *Exploration of the Valley of the Amazon, Made Under Direction of the Navy Department by William Lewis Herndon and Lardner Gibbon, Part 1*. Washington, D.C.: Robert Armstrong, 1854.

"History of the New York Chamber of Commerce," *Harper's Weekly*, 46 (Nov. 15, 1902): 1720–1722.

Hoffnagel, Marc. J. "From Monarchy to Republic in Northeast Brazil: The Case of Pernambuco, 1868–1895." Ph.D. Diss., University of Indiana, 1975.

Holanda, Sérgio Buarque de. *Do Império à República*. Vol. 5 of Tomo II, *História Geral da Civilização Brasileira*. Edited by Sérgio Buarque de Holanda. São Paulo: Difusão Européia do Livro, 1972

Holloway, Thomas. *The Brazilian Coffee Valorization of 1906: Regional Politics and Economic Dependence*. Madison, Wis.: Department of History, University of Wisconsin, 1975.

Immigrants on the Land: Coffee and Society in São Paulo, 1886–1934. Chapel Hill: University of North Carolina Press, 1980.

Ilersic, Alfred Roman. *Parliament of Commerce: The Story of the Association of British Chambers of Commerce, 1820–1960*. London: Association of British Chambers of Commerce, 1960.

Imperial Instituto Bahiano de Agricultura. "Ensino Profissional Agrícola: Imperial Instituto Bahiano de Agricultura," *Revista Agrícola*, 27 (1886): 193–204.

"Ensino Profissional: Imperial Instituto Bahiano de Agricultura," *Revista Agrícola*, 28 (1887): 151–163.

Instituto Genealógico Brasileiro. *Subsídios Geneológicos. Volume I: Famílias Brasileiras de*

Origem Germânica. São Paulo: Instituto Genealógico Brasileiro and Instituto Hans Staden, 1962.

International Bureau of the American Republics. *Commercial Directory of Brazil.* Washington, D.C.: Government Printing Office, 1891.

[J.R.] *Auxílios à Lavoura.* Rio de Janeiro: C. G. da Silva, 1895.

Jaguaribe, Hélio. *Economic and Political Development: A Theoretical Approach and a Brazilian Case Study.* Cambridge, Mass.: Harvard University Press, 1968.

Javari, Jorge João Dodsworth, Barão de. *Organizações e Programas Ministerais: Regime Parlamentar no Império.* 2d ed. Rio de Janeiro: Estado de Guanabara, 1962.

Johnson, Jr., Harold B. "A Preliminary Inquiry into Money, Prices, and Wages in Rio de Janeiro, 1763–1823," in *Colonial Roots of Modern Brazil: Papers of the Newberry Library Conference.* Edited by Dauril Alden. Berkeley: University of California Press, 1973.

Jones, Charles A. "Commercial Banks and Mortgage Companies," in *Business Imperialism, 1840–1930: An Inquiry Based on British Experience in Latin America.* Edited by D. C. M. Platt. Oxford: Clarendon, 1977.

International Business in the Nineteenth Century: The Rise and Fall of a Cosmopolitan Bourgeoisie. Brighton, Sussex: Wheatsheaf Books, 1987.

O Jornal: Edição Comemorativa do Bi-Centenário do Cafeeiro no Brasil, 1727–1927. São Paulo: Casa Duprat e Casa Mayença, 1927.

Katzman, Martin T. "São Paulo and Its Hinterland: Evolving Relationships and the Rise of an Industrial Power," in *Manchester and São Paulo: Problems of Rapid Urban Growth.* Edited by John D. Wirth and Robert L. Jones. Stanford, Calif.: Stanford University Press, 1978.

Kennedy, John Norman. "Bahian Elites, 1750–1822," *Hispanic American Historical Review,* 53 (Aug. 1973): 415–439.

Kerbey, J. Orton. *An American Consul in Amazonia.* New York: W. E. Rudge, 1911.

Key, V. O. *Politics, Parties, and Pressure Groups.* 4th ed. New York: Thomas Y. Crowell, 1958.

Koseritz, Karl von. *Imagens do Brasil (1883).* Translated by Afonso Arinos de Melo Franco. São Paulo: Martins, 1943.

Kuznesof, Elizabeth Anne. "The Role of the Merchants in the Economic Development of São Paulo, 1765–1850," *Hispanic American Historical Review,* 60 (Nov. 1980): 571–592.

Leal, Victor Nunes. *Coronelismo, Enxada e Voto (o Município e o Regime Representativo no Brasil).* 3d ed. São Paulo: Alfa-Omega, 1976.

Leff, Nathaniel H. "Economic Development and Regional Inequality: Origins of the Brazilian Case," *The Quarterly Journal of Economics,* 86 (May 1972): 243–262.

"Economic Retardation in Nineteenth-Century Brazil," *Economic History Review,* 25 (Aug. 1972): 489–507.

"Long-Term Brazilian Economic Development," *The Journal of Economic History,* 29 (Sept. 1969): 473–493.

Underdevelopment and Development in Brazil. 2 vols. London: George Allen & Unwin, 1982.

Le Riverend, Julio. *Historia Económica de Cuba.* 4th ed. Havana: Instituto Cubano del Libro, 1974.

Lessa, Francisco de Paula Mayrink. *Vida e Obra do Conselheiro Mayrink (Completada por uma Genealogia da Família).* Rio de Janeiro: Pongetti, 1975.

Levi, Darrell. *The Prados of São Paulo, Brazil: An Elite Family and Social Change, 1840–1930.* Athens: University of Georgia Press, 1987.

Levine, Robert M. *Pernambuco in the Brazilian Federation, 1889–1937.* Stanford, Calif.: Stanford University Press, 1978.

354   Bibliography

Levy, Maria Bárbara. "O Encilhamento," in *Economia Brasileira: Uma Visão Histórica.* Edited by Paulo Neuhaus. Rio de Janeiro: Campus, 1980.

História da Bolsa de Valores do Rio de Janeiro. Rio de Janeiro: Instituto Brasileiro de Mercado de Capitais, 1977.

História dos Bancos Comerciais no Brasil (Estudo Preliminar). Rio de Janeiro: IBMEC, 1972.

Lewin, Linda. *Politics and Parentela in Paraíba: A Case Study of Family-Based Oligarchy in Brazil.* Princeton, N.J.: Princeton University Press, 1987.

"Some Historical Implications of Kinship Organization for Family-Based Politics in the Brazilian Northeast," *Comparative Studies in Society and History,* 21 (April 1979): 262–292.

Lewis, Colin M. "Industry in Latin America before 1930," in *The Cambridge History of Latin America. Volume IV: c. 1870 to 1930.* Edited by Leslie Bethell. Cambridge: Cambridge University Press, 1986.

"Railways and Industrialization: Argentina and Brazil, 1870–1929," in *Latin America, Economic Imperialism and the State.* Edited by Christopher Abel and Colin M. Lewis. London & Dover, N.H.: Athlone, 1985.

Lewis, W. Arthur. *The Evolution of the International Economic Order.* Princeton, N.J.: Princeton University Press, 1978.

"The Export Stimulus," in *Tropical Development, 1880–1913.* Edited by W. Arthur Lewis. Evanston, Ill.: Northwestern University Press, 1970.

Growth and Fluctuations, 1870–1913. London: George Allen & Unwin, 1978.

Libby, Douglas Cole. "Proto-Industrialization in a Slave Society: The Case of Minas Gerais," *Journal of Latin American Studies,* 23 (Feb. 1991): 1–35.

Lima, Heitor Ferreira. *História do Pensamento Econômico no Brasil.* São Paulo: Editôra Nacional, 1976.

Lisanti, Luís. "Estudos: Cenário e Personagens," in *Negócios Coloniais (uma Correspondência Comercial do Século XVIII).* Edited by Luís Lisanti. Rio de Janeiro: Ministério da Fazenda, 1973.

"Transações Comerciais: A Demanda," in *Negócios Coloniais (uma Correspondência Comercial no Século XVIII).* Edited by Luís Lisanti. 5 vols. Brasília: Ministério da Fazenda, 1973.

Lloyd, Reginald, et al. *Twentieth Century Impressions of Brazil: Its History, People, Commerce, Industries, and Resources.* London: Lloyd's Greater Britain Publishing Co., 1913.

Lobo, Eulália Maria Lahmeyer. "Evolução dos Preços e do Padrão da Vida no Rio de Janeiro, 1820–1930 – Resultados Preliminares," *Revista Brasileira de Economia,* 25 (Oct.–Dec. 1971): 235–265.

História Político-Administrativa da Agricultura Brasileira, 1808–1889. Rio de Janeiro: Ministério da Agricultura, 1980.

História do Rio de Janeiro (do Capital Comercial ao Capital Industrial e Financeiro). Rio de Janeiro: IBMEC, 1978.

Lobo, Hélio. *Docas de Santos: Suas Origens, Lutas, e Realizações.* Rio de Janeiro: Jornal do Comércio, 1936.

Lopes, Betralda. "O Comércio de Café Através do Pôrto de Santos (1870–1974)," in *O Café: Anais de II Congresso de História de São Paulo.* Edited by Edgard Carone. São Paulo: Coleção da Revista de História, 1975.

Lorenzo-Fernandes, Oscar Soto. *A Evolução da Economia Brasileira.* Rio de Janeiro: Zahar, 1976.

Love, George Thomas. *A Five Years' Residence in Buenos Aires During the Years 1820 to 1825: Containing Remarks on the Country and Inhabitants and a Visit to Colonia del Sacramento.* London: G. Herbert, 1825.

Love, Joseph L. "External Financing and Domestic Politics: The Case of São Paulo, Brazil,

1889–1937," in *Latin American Modernization Problems*. Edited by Robert E. Scott. Urbana, Ill.: University of Illinois Press, 1973.
"Political Participation in Brazil, 1881–1969," *Luso-Brazilian Review,* 7 (Dec. 1970): 3–24.
Rio Grande do Sul and Brazilian Regionalism, 1882–1937. Stanford, Calif.: Stanford University Press, 1971.
São Paulo in the Brazilian Federation, 1889–1937. Stanford, Calif.: Stanford University Press, 1980.
"Structural Change and Conceptual Response in Latin America and Romania, 1860–1950," in *Guiding the Invisible Hand: Economic Liberalism and the State in Latin American History.* Edited by Joseph L. Love and Nils Jacobsen. New York: Praeger, 1988.
Love, Joseph L., and Barickman, Bert J. "Regional Elites," in *Modern Brazil: Elites and Masses in Historical Perspective.* Edited by Michael L. Conniff and Frank D. McCann. Lincoln, Neb.: University of Nebraska Press, 1989.
"Rulers and Owners: A Brazilian Case Study in Comparative Perspective," *Hispanic American Historical Review,* 66 (Nov. 1986): 743–765.
Ludwig, Armin K. *Brazil: A Handbook of Historical Statistics.* Boston: G. K. Hall, 1985.
Lugar, Catherine. "The Merchant Community of Salvador, Bahia, 1780–1830." Ph.D. Diss., State University of New York at Stony Brook, 1980.
"The Portuguese Tobacco Trade and Tobacco Growers of Bahia in the Late Colonial Period," in *Essays Concerning the Socioeconomic History of Brazil and Portuguese India.* Edited by Dauril Alden and Warren Dean. Gainesville, Fla.: University of Florida Press, 1977.
Luz, Nícia Villela. *A Luta pela Industrialização do Brasil (1808 a 1930)* 2d ed. São Paulo: Alfa-Omega, 1975.
"As Tentativas de Industrialização no Brasil," in *Declínio e Queda do Império.* Vol. 4 of *O Brasil Monárquico.* Tomo 2 of *História Geral do Civilização Brasileira.* Edited by Sérgio Buarque de Holanda and Pedro Moacyr Campos. São Paulo: Difusão Européia do Livro, 1971.
Lyra, Heitor. *História de Dom Pedro II, 1825–1891.* 3 vols. São Paulo: Editôra Nacional, 1939.
Macaulay, Neill. *Dom Pedro: The Struggle for Liberty in Brazil and Portugal, 1798–1834.* Durham, N.C.: Duke University Press, 1986.
Macedo, Joaquim Manuel de. *Ano Biográfico Brasileiro.* 3 vols. Rio de Janeiro: Imperial Instituto Artístico, 1876.
Magalhães, Beatriz Ricardina de. "Investimentos Inglêses no Brasil e o Banco Londrino e Brasileiro," *Revista Brasileira de Estudos Políticos,* 49 (July 1979): 233–252.
Magalhães, José Vieira Couto. "Estado Atual da Extração e Comércio da Borracha na Província do Pará," *O Auxiliador da Indústria Nacional,* 6 (June 1865): 219–227.
Malheiro, Agostinho Marques Perdigão. *A Escravidão no Brasil: Ensaio Histórico-Jurídico-Social.* 2 vols. 2d ed. São Paulo: Edições Cultura, 1944.
Mallon, Florencia E. "Economic Liberalism: Where We Are and Where We Need to Go," in *Guiding the Invisible Hand: Economic Liberalism and the State in Latin American History.* Edited by Joseph L. Love and Nils Jacobsen. New York: Praeger, 1988.
Manchester, Alan K. *British Preëminence in Brazil; Its Rise and Decline: A Study in European Expansion.* Chapel Hill, N.C.: University of North Carolina Press, 1933.
Marchant, Anyda. *Viscount Mauá and the Empire of Brazil: A Biography of Irineu Evangelista de Sousa (1813–1889).* Berkeley and Los Angeles: University of California Press, 1965.
Marques, César Augusto. *A Província do Maranhão: Breve Memória Publicada por Ordem do*

Ministério da Agricultura, Comércio, e Obras Públicas. Rio de Janeiro: Tipografia Nacional, 1876.

Martins, José de Souza. "Café e a Gênese da Industrialização em São Paulo." *Contexto,* 3 (July 1977): 1–17.

Empresário e Emprêsa na Biografia do Conde Matarazzo. Rio de Janeiro: Instituto de Ciências Sociais, 1967.

Martins, Luciano. "Formação do Empresariado Industrial no Brasil," *Revista do Empresariado Industrial no Brasil,* 3, no. 1 (1966): 91–138.

Mathews, Franklin. "The Organized Conscience of the Rich," *The World's Work,* 4 (Oct. 1902): 2627–2630.

Matos, Odilon Nogueira de. "Vias de Comunicação," in *Declínio e Queda do Império.* Vol. 4 of *O Brasil Monárquico.* Tomo 2 of *História Geral do Civilização Brasileira.* Edited by Sérgio Buarque de Holanda and Pedro Moacyr Campos. São Paulo: Difusão Européia do Livro, 1971.

Mattoon, Robert H. "Railroads, Coffee, and Big Business in São Paulo, Brazil," *Hispanic American Historical Review,* 57 (May 1977): 273–295.

Mattos, Waldemar. *Palácio da Associação Comercial da Bahia (Antiga Praça do Comércio).* Salvador: Beneditina, 1950.

Mattoso, Kátia M. de Queirós. *Bahia: A Cidade do Salvador e seu Mercado no Século XIX.* São Paulo: Hucitec, 1978.

Mauá, Irineo Evangelista de Souza, Visconde de. *Autobiografia (Exposição aos Credores e ao Público), Seguida de "O Meio Circulante no Brasil".* Edited by Cláudio Ganns. 2d ed. Rio de Janeiro: Zélio Valverde, 1942.

Mawe, John. *Travels in the Interior of Brazil, Particularly in the Gold and Diamond Districts of that Country, by Authority of the Prince Regent of Portugal.* London: Longman, Hurst, Rees, Orme, and Brown, 1812.

Maximilian I, of Mexico. *Recollections of My Life.* Vol. 3. London: R. Bentley, 1868.

Mayo, John. "Before the Nitrate Era: British Commission Houses and the Chilean Economy, 1851–80," *Journal of Latin American Studies,* 11 (Nov. 1979): 283–302.

Mello, João Manuel Cardoso de. *O Capitalismo Tardio: Contribuição à Revisão Crítica da Formação e do Desenvolvimento da Economia Brasileira.* 2d ed. São Paulo: Brasiliense, 1982.

Mello, João Manuel Cardoso de, and Tavares, Maria da Conceição. "The Capitalist Export Economy in Brazil, 1884–1930," in *The Latin American Economies: Growth and the Export Sector, 1880–1930.* Edited by Roberto Cortés Conde and Shane J. Hunt. New York: Holmes & Meier, 1985.

Mello, José Antônio Gonsalves de, ed. *O Diário de Pernambuco e a História Social do Nordeste.* Recife: Diário de Pernambuco, 1975.

Mello, Pedro Carvalho de. "Aspectos Econômicos da Organização do Trabalho da Economia Cafeeira do Rio de Janeiro, 1850–1888," *Revista Brasileira de Economia,* 32 (Jan.–March 1978): 19–67.

Mello, Pedro Carvalho de, and Slenes, Robert W. "Análise Econômica da Escravidão no Brasil," in *Economia Brasileira: Uma Visão Histórica.* Edited by Paulo Neuhaus. Rio de Janeiro: Campus, 1980.

Mello, Zélia Maria Cardoso de. *Metamorfoses da Riqueza: São Paulo, 1845–1895.* São Paulo: Hucitec and Prefeitura do Município de São Paulo, Secretaria Municipal de Cultura, 1985.

Melo, Evaldo Cabral de. *O Norte Agrário e o Império, 1871–1889.* Rio de Janeiro: Nova Fronteira, 1984.

"A Mentalidade Econômica e as Associações Comerciais," *Revista do Direito Comercial,* 40, vol. 10 (1940): 337–340.

Merrick, Thomas W., and Graham, Douglas H. *Population and Economic Development in Brazil: 1800 to the Present*. Baltimore: The Johns Hopkins University Press, 1979.

Milet, Henrique Augusto. *A Lavoura da Cana de Açúcar*. Recife: By the Author, 1881.

Morais, Evaristo de. *A Campanha Abolicionista (1879–1888)*. Rio de Janeiro: Leite Ribeiro, 1924.

Morgan, John. *The Railroad Between the City of Bahia and the River Saint Francisco in the Empire of Brazil: Its Geographic Superiority and Commercial Advantage to Be Derived Therefrom*. London: Smith, Elder & Co., 1853.

Morse, Richard. *From Community to Metropolis: A Biography of São Paulo*. 2d ed. New York: Octagon Books, 1974.

Nabuco, Carolina. *The Life of Joaquim Nabuco*. Translated and edited by Ronald Hilton. New York: Greenwood, 1968.

Nabuco, Joaquim. *Um Estadista do Império: Nabuco de Araújo, sua Vida, suas Opiões, sua Época*. 2 vols. São Paulo: Editôra Nacional, 1936.

Needell, Jeffrey. "The Origins of the Carioca Belle Epoque: The Emergence of the Elite Culture and Society in Turn-of-the-Century Rio de Janeiro." Ph.D. Diss., Stanford University, 1982.

"The *Revolta Contra Vacina* of 1904: The Revolt Against 'Modernization' in *Belle Époque* Rio de Janeiro," *Hispanic American Historical Review*, 65 (May 1987): 233–269.

A Tropical Belle Epoque: Elite Culture and Society in Turn-of-the-Century Rio de Janeiro. Cambridge: Cambridge University Press, 1987.

Newton, Ronald C. "On 'Functional Groups,' 'Fragmentation,' and 'Pluralism' in Spanish American Political Society," *Hispanic American Historical Review*, 50 (Feb. 1970): 1–29.

"Natural Corporatism and the Passing of Populism in Spanish America," in *The New Corporatism: Social-Political Structures in the Iberian World*. Edited by Frederick B. Pike and Thomas Stritch. Notre Dame, Ind.: University of Notre Dame Press, 1974.

Nicol, Robert N. V. C. "A Agricultura e a Industrialização no Brasil (1850–1930)." Tese de Doutorado, Universidade de São Paulo, 1974.

North, Douglass. "Ocean Freights and Economic Development, 1750–1913," *Journal of Economic History*, 18 (Dec. 1958): 537–555.

O'Brien, Philip J. "A Critique of Latin American Theories of Dependency," in *Beyond the Sociology of Development: Economy and Society in Latin America and Africa*. Edited by Ivar Oxaal, Tony Barnet, and David Booth. London: Routledge and Kegan Paul, 1975.

Ornstein, Norman J., and Elder, Shirley. *Interest Groups, Lobbying, and Policymaking*. Washington, D.C.: Congressional Quarterly, 1978.

Pan American Union. *Brazil*. Washington, D.C.: Pan American Union, 1891.

Pang, Eul-Soo. *Bahia in the First Brazilian Republic: Coronelismo and Oligarchies, 1889–1934*. Gainesville, Fla.: University of Florida Press, 1979.

In Pursuit of Honor: The Noblemen of the Southern Cross in the Nineteenth Century in Brazil. Tuscaloosa, Ala.: University of Alabama Press, 1988.

"Modernizaton and Slavocracy in Nineteenth-Century Brazil," *The Journal of Interdisciplinary History*, 9 (Spring 1979): 667–688.

Pang, Eul-Soo, and Seckinger, Ron. "The Mandarins of Imperial Brazil," *Comparative Studies in Society and History*, 14 (March 1972): 215–244.

Pang, Laura Jarnagin. "The State and Agricultural Clubs of Imperial Brazil, 1860–1889." Ph.D. Diss., Vanderbilt University, 1981.

Particular Contrato de Sociedade em Comandita para o Estabelecimento de uma Fábrica Central de Açúcar no Município de Santo Amaro em Ponto Fixado de Acordo com o Govêrno pela Sistema Adotada nas Colônias Francêzas de Martinica e Guadeloupe. Salvador: J. G. Tourinho, 1875.

358   *Bibliography*

Pedro II, Emperor of Brazil. *Diário da Viagem ao Norte do Brasil.* Edited by Lourenço Luiz Lacombe. Salvador: Universidade da Bahia, 1959.
Viagem a Pernambuco em 1859. Edited by Guilherme Auler. Recife: Arquivo Público Estadual, 1952.
Peláez, Carlos Manuel. "Uma Análise Econômica da História do Café Brasileiro," in *Economia Brasileira: Uma Visão Histórica.* Edited by Paulo Neuhaus. Rio de Janeiro: Campus, 1980.
"As Conseqüências Econômicas da Ortodoxia Monetária, Fiscal e Cambial no Brasil de 1889 a 1945," *Revista Brasileira de Economia,* 25 (July–Sept. 1971): 5–82.
"The Establishment of Banking Institutions in a Backward Economy," *Business History Review,* 49 (Winter 1975): 446–472.
História Econômica do Brasil: Um Elo Entre a Teoria e a Realidade Econômica. São Paulo: Atlas, 1979.
"The Theory and Reality of Imperialism in the Coffee Economy of Ninteenth Century Brazil," *Economic History Review,* Second Series. 29 (May 1976): 276–290.
Peláez, Carlos Manuel, and Suzigan, Wilson. *História Monetária do Brasil.* Rio de Janeiro: IPES, Instituto de Pesquisas, 1976.
Pereira, Luís Carlos Bresser. "Origens Étnicas e Sociais do Empresário Paulista," *Revista de Administração de Emprêsas,* 4 (June 1964): 83–106.
Pereira, Manuel Vitorino. *Idéias Políticas de Manuel Vitorino: Introdução, Notas Bibliográficas, Cronologia, e Textos Selecionados.* Edited and Organized by Luís Henrique Dias Tavares. Rio de Janeiro: Senado Federal/Fundação Casa de Rui Barbosa/MEC, 1981.
Pereira, Virgílio de Sa. "Os Códigos Criminal, de Processo e Comercial; Formação de Nosso Direito Civil; A Reforma Judiciária de 1871," in *Tomo Especial Consagrado ao Primeiro Congresso de História Nacional: Revista do Instituto Histórico e Geográfico Brasileiro.* Volume IV. Rio de Janeiro: Imprensa Nacional, 1916.
Perruci, Gadiel. *A República das Usinas: Um Estudo de História Social e Econômica do Nordeste, 1889–1930.* Rio de Janeiro: Paz e Terra, 1978.
Pimenta, Altino Rodrigues, ed. *Almanaque Administrativo, Comercial, e Industrial da Província da Bahia para o Ano de 1873.* Salvador: Oliveira Mendes, 1872.
Pincus, Jonathan J. *Pressure Groups and Politics in Antebellum Tariffs.* New York: Columbia University Press, 1977.
Pinho, Joaquim Wanderley de Araújo. "A Cultura do Cacaoeiro na Bahia," in *Diário Oficial: Edição Especial do Centenário,* 8 (July 2, 1923): 233–236.
Pinho, José Wanderley de Araújo. *Cotegipe e seu Tempo.* São Paulo: Editôra Nacional, 1937.
História de um Engenho do Recôncavo: Matoim-Novo Caboto-Freguezia, 1553–1944. Rio de Janeiro: Zélio Valverde, 1946.
Salões e Damas do Segundo Reinado. São Paulo: Martins, 1945.
Pinho, Pericles Madureira de. *Luiz Tarqüínio: Pioneiro da Justiça Social no Brasil.* Salvador: Vitória, 1944.
Pinto, Estevão. *A Associação Comercial de Pernambuco.* Recife: Jornal do Comércio, 1940.
Pinto Junior, Joaquim Antônio. *Santos e São Vicente de 1868 a 1876.* Rio de Janeiro: D. L. dos Santos, 1877.
Platt, D. C. M. "Economic Imperialism and the Businessman: Britain and Latin America Before 1914," in *Studies in the Theory of Imperialism.* Edited by Roger Owen and Bob Sutcliffe. London: Longman, 1972.
Latin America and British Trade, 1806–1914. New York: Barnes & Noble, 1972.
"Problems in the Interpretation of Foreign Trade Statistics Before 1914," *Journal of Latin American Studies,* 3, no. 2 (1971): 119–130.
Poliano, Luís Márquez. *A Sociedade Nacional de Agricultura: Resumo Histórico.* Rio de Janeiro: Gráfica Econômica, 1942.

Pontes, Carlos. *Tavares Bastos (Aureliano Cândido), 1839–1875*. São Paulo: Editôra Nacional, 1939.

Pôrto, José da Costa. *Os Tempos da República Velha*. Recife: Govêrno de Pernambuco, Secretaria de Turismo, Cultura, e Esportes, 1986.

Os Tempos de Rosa e Silva. Recife: Universidade Federal de Pernambuco, 1970.

Prado, J. F. de Almeida. *Dom João VI e o Início da Classe Dirigente do Brasil, 1815–1889*. São Paulo: Editôra Nacional, 1968.

Przewodowski, André. "Comunicação Entre a Cidade da Bahia e a Vila de Juazeiro," *Revista do Instituto Histórico e Geográfico Brasileiro*, 10 (1848): 374–385.

Pujol, Alfredo. "Consultas e Pareceres: LXXXVI, Associações Comerciais," *Revista de Comércio e Indústria: Publicação Mensal do Centro do Comércio e Indústria de São Paulo*, 3 (Jan.–Dec. 1917): 388–389.

Queiroz, Suely Robles Reis de. *Os Radicais da República: Jacobinismo – Ideologia e Ação, 1893–1897*. São Paulo: Brasiliense, 1986.

Quintas, Amaro. *O Sentido Social da Revolução Praieira*. Rio de Janeiro: Civilização Brasileira, 1967.

Raffard, Henri. *O Centro da Indústria e Comércio de Açúcar no Rio de Janeiro*. Rio de Janeiro: Brasil, 1892.

Randall, Laura. *A Comparative Economic History of Latin America, 1500–1914. Vol. 3: Brazil*. Ann Arbor, Mich.: University Microfilms International, 1977.

Raucher, Alan. *Public Relations and Business, 1900–1929*. Baltimore, Md.: The Johns Hopkins University Press, 1968.

Reber, Vera Blinn. *British Mercantile Houses in Buenos Aires, 1810–1880*. Cambridge, Mass.: Harvard University Press, 1979.

Reis, Antônio Alexandre Borges dos, ed. *Almanak do Estado da Bahia: Administrativo, Indicador, Noticioso, Comercial, Literário, 1898–1909*. 8 vols. Salvador: Reis, 1898–1909.

Reis, Jaime. "Abolition and the Economics of Slavery in Northeastern Brazil," *Boletín de Estudios Latinoamericanos y del Caribe*, 17 (Dec. 1974): 3–20.

"From Bangüê to Usina: Pernambuco, 1850–1920," in *Land and Labour in Latin America*. Edited by Kenneth Duncan and Ian Rutledge. Cambridge: Cambridge University Press, 1977.

Reis, João José. "A Elite Baiana Face aos Movimentos Sociais: Bahia, 1824–1840," *Revista de História*, 54 (Oct.–Dec. 1976): 341–384.

Relatório da Comissão Encarregada pelo Govêrno Imperial, por Avisos do l de Outubro e 28 de Dezembro de 1864 de Proceder a um Inquérito sôbre as Causas Principais e Acidentais da Crise do Mês de Setembro de 1864. Rio de Janeiro: Tipografia Nacional, 1865.

Resor, Randolph R. "Rubber in Brazil: Dominance and Collapse, 1876–1945," *Business History Review*, 51 (Autumn 1977): 341–366.

Rheingantz, Carlos G. *Titulares do Império*. Rio de Janeiro: Imprensa Nacional, 1960.

Ridings, Eugene W. "The Bahian Commercial Association, 1840–1889: A Pressure Group in an Underdeveloped Area." Ph.D. Diss., University of Florida, 1970.

"The Business Elite and the Economic and Urban Integration of Brazil," *SECOLAS Annals: Journal of the Southeastern Council of Latin American Studies*, 12 (March 1981): 14–26.

Business Interest Groups and Communications: The Brazilian Experience in the Nineteenth Century, *Luso-Brazilian Review*, 20 (Winter 1983): 241–257.

"Business, Nationality, and Dependency in Late Nineteenth Century Brazil," *Journal of Latin American Studies*, 14 (May 1982): 55–96.

"Class Sector Unity in an Export Economy: The Case of Nineteenth-Century Brazil," *Hispanic American Historical Review*, 58 (Aug. 1978): 432–450.

"Elite Conflict and Cooperation in the Brazilian Empire: The Case of Bahia's Business-men and Planters," *Luso-Brazilian Review,* 12 (Summer 1975): 80–99.

"The Foreign Connection: A Look at the Business Elite of Rio de Janeiro in the Nineteenth Century," *New Scholar,* 7 1/2 (1979): 167–181.

"Interest Groups and Development: The Case of Brazil in the Nineteenth Century," *Journal of Latin American Studies,* 9 (Nov. 1977): 225–250.

Rios, José Arthur. "A Tradição Mercantilista na Formação Brasileira," *Revista Brasileira da Economia,* 26 (July–Sept. 1972): 255–272.

Rippy, J. Fred. *British Investments in Latin America, 1822–1949: A Case Study in the Operations of Private Enterprise in Retarded Regions.* 2d ed. Hamden, Conn.: Archon Books, 1966.

Rodrigues, Jorge Martins. "A Rivaldade Comercial de Inglêses e Norteamericanos no Brasil do Século XIX," *Revista de História da Economia Brasileira,* 1 (June 1953): 73–82.

Rostow, W. W. *The Stages of Economic Growth: A Non-Communist Manifesto.* 2d ed. Cambridge: Cambridge University Press, 1971.

Roxborough, Ian. *Theories of Underdevelopment.* Atlantic Highlands, N.J.: Humanities, 1979.

Russell-Wood, A. J. R. *Fidalgos and Philanthropists: The Santa Casa da Misericórdia of Bahia, 1550–1755.* London: Macmillan, 1968.

Sabine, Lorenzo. "The Origin of Boards of Trade," *The Banker's Magazine and Statistical Register,* 13 (March 1859): 678–692.

Safford, Frank. "The Emergence of Economic Liberalism in Colombia," in *Guiding the Invisible Hand: Economic Liberalism and the State in Latin American History.* Edited by Joseph L. Love and Nils Jacobsen. New York, Westport, Conn., London: Praeger, 1988.

Santa Ana, Moacir Medeiros de. *Uma Associação Centenária.* Maceió: Arquivo Público de Alagôas, 1966.

Contribuição à História do Açúcar em Alagôas. Recife: Instituto do Açúcar e do Alcool, 1970.

Santos, Francisco Martins dos. *História de Santos, 1532–1936.* 2 vols. São Paulo: Revista dos Tribunaes, 1937.

Santos, Roberto. *História Econômica de Amazônia, 1800–1920.* São Paulo: T. A. Queiroz, 1980.

Santos Filho, Lycurgo. *Uma Comunidade Rural do Brasil Antigo (Aspectos da Vida Patriarchal no Sertão da Bahia nos Séculos XVIII e XIX).* São Paulo: Editôra Nacional, 1956.

Schmitter, Philippe C. *Interest Conflict and Political Change in Brazil.* Stanford, Calif.: Stanford University Press, 1971.

Schriftgiesser, Karl. *The Lobbyists: The Art and Business of Influencing Lawmakers.* Boston: Little, Brown and Company, 1951.

Schwartz, Stuart B. "Free Labor in a Slave Economy: The *Lavradores de Cana* of Colonial Bahia," in *The Colonial Roots of Modern Brazil: Papers of the Newberry Library Conference.* Edited by Dauril Alden. Berkeley: University of California Press, 1973.

Sovereignty and Society in Colonial Brazil: The High Court of Bahia and Its Judges, 1609–1751. Berkeley: University of California Press, 1973.

Sugar Plantations in the Formation of Brazilian Society: Bahia, 1550–1835. Cambridge: Cambridge University Press, 1985.

Shafer, Robert Jones. *Economic Societies in the Spanish World, 1763–1821.* Syracuse, N.Y.: Syracuse University Press, 1958.

Silva, H. Schlitter. "Tendências e Caraterísticas Gerais do Comércio Exterior no Século XIX," *Revista de História da Economia Brasileira,* I (June 1953): 5–21.

Silva, Inocêncio Francisco da. *Dicionário Bibliográfico Português. Estudos de Inocêncio Francisco da Silva, Aplicáveis a Portugal e ao Brasil.* 23 vols. Coimbra: Biblioteca da Universidade; Lisbon: Imprensa Nacional, 1858–1958.

Silva, Miguel Antônio da. "Agricultura Nacional: Congresso Agrícola do Rio de Janeiro, Congresso Agrícola de Pernambuco," *Revista Agrícola,* 10 (March 1879): 3–8.

"Agricultura Nacional: Estudos Agrícolas," *Revista Agrícola,* 8 (Dec. 1877): 140–143.

"Agricultura Nacional: Estudos Agrícolas," *Revista Agrícola,* 9 (March 1878): 15–20.

Silva, Moacir Fecury Fereira da. "O Desenvolvimento Comercial do Pará no Período da Borracha (1870–1914)." Master's Thesis, Universidad Federal Fluminense, Instituto de Ciências Humanas e Filosofia, 1978.

Silva, Sérgio. *Expansão Cafeeira e Origens da Indústria no Brasil.* São Paulo: Alfa Omega, 1976.

Simonsen, Roberto. *Evolução Industrial do Brasil e Outros Estudos.* Edited by Edgard Carone. São Paulo: Editôra Nacional e Universidade de São Paulo, 1973.

História Econômica do Brasil, 1500–1820. 2 vols. São Paulo: Editôra Nacional, 1937.

Singer, Paul. *Desenvolvimento Econômico e Evolução Urbana (Análise da Evolução Econômica de São Paulo, Blumenau, Pôrto Alegre, Belo Horizonte e Recife).* 2d ed. São Paulo: Editôra Nacional, 1977.

Sintoni, Evaldo. "A Indústria de Aniagem e o Café (1897–1899)," in *O Café: Anais do Segundo Congresso de História de São Paulo.* Edited by Edgard Carone. São Paulo: Revista de História, 1975.

Smith, Robert Sidney "The Institution of the Consulado in New Spain," *Hispanic American Historical Review,* 24 (Feb. 1944): 61–83.

"A Research Report on Consulado History," *Journal of Interamerican Studies,* 3 (Jan. 1961): 41–52.

The Spanish Guild Merchant: A History of the Consulado, 1250–1700. Durham, N.C.: Duke University Press, 1940.

Smith, T. Lynn. *Brazil: People and Institutions.* Rev. ed. Baton Rouge: Louisiana State University Press, 1963.

Soares, Sebastião Ferreira. *Elementos de Estatística.* Vol. 1. Rio de Janeiro: J. Villeneuve, 1865.

Notas Estatísticas sôbre a Produção Agrícola e Carestia dos Gêneros Alimentícios no Império do Brasil. Rio de Janeiro: J. Villeneuve, 1860.

Sociedade Asilo dos Inválidos da Pátria. *Relatório Apresentado à Assembléia Geral no Dia 15 de Setembro de 1869, pelo Seu Presidente o Vereador José Joaquim de Lima e Silva Sobrinho.* Rio de Janeiro: Perseverança, 1869.

Sociedade Auxiliadora da Agricultura de Pernambuco. *Estatutos da Sociedade Auxiliadora da Agricultura de Pernambuco.* Recife: Manuel Figueirôa de Faria & Filhos, 1875.

Relatório Anual Apresentado na Sessão de 4 de Julho de 1878 da Assembléia Geral, pelo Gerente Inácio de Barros Barreto em Ata da Mesma Sessão. Recife: Jornal do Recife, 1878.

Trabalhos do Congresso Agrícola do Recife em Outubro de 1878. Recife: Manuel Figueirôa de Faria e Filhos, 1879.

Sociedade Auxiliadora da Indústria Nacional. *Estatutos.* 1828, 1831, 1857, 1869, 1891.

Numeros 5, 6 e 7, Maio, Junho e Julho de 1877: Sessão do Concelho Administrativo da Sociedade Auxilidora da Indústria Nacional em 21 de Junho de 1876. Rio de Janeiro: Sociedade Auxiliadora da Indústria Nacional, 1877.

Relação dos Sócios. 1866, 1877.

Sociedade Internacional de Imigração. *Sociedade Internacional de Imigração, Relatório Anual da Diretoria . . . Numero 1.* Rio de Janeiro: J. Villeneuve, 1867.

Sociedade Nacional de Agricultura. *Representação da Sociedade Nacional de Agricultura ao Congresso Federal.* Rio de Janeiro: Casa Mont' Alverne, 1899.

Sociedade Nacional de Agricultura: Histórico dos Trabalhos da Sociedade Durante o Ano de 1899. Rio de Janeiro: Imprensa Nacional, 1900.

Sociedade Reunião dos Expositores da Indústria Brasileira. *Relatórios.* 1875–1877.

Sociedade Reunião Comercial dos Varegistas. *Relatórios.* 1881, 1897.

Sodré, Nelson Werneck. *Formação Histórica do Brasil.* 4th ed. São Paulo: Brasiliense, 1967.

Sojo, José Raimundo. *El Comercio en la Historia de Colombia.* Bogotá: Cámera de Comercio de Bogotá, 1970.

Souza, Afonso Ruy de. *História da Câmera Municipal da Cidade do Salvador.* Salvador: Câmera Municipal do Salvador, 1953.

Sousa, José Bonifácio de. *Associação Comercial do Ceará: Memória Histórica, 1868–1968.* Fortaleza: Associação Comercial do Ceará, 1969.

Spínola, Celso. "Pôrtos do Estado da Bahia," in *Diário Oficial: Edição Especial do Centenário,* VIII (July 2, 1923): 165–170.

Staniland, Martin. *What Is Political Economy? A Study of Social Theory and Underdevelopment.* New Haven, Conn.: Yale University Press, 1985.

Stein, Stanley J. *The Brazilian Cotton Manufacture: Textile Enterprise in an Underdeveloped Area, 1850–1950.* Cambridge, Mass.: Harvard University Press, 1957.

Vassouras: A Brazilian Coffee County, 1850–1900. Cambridge, Mass.: Harvard University Press, 1957.

Stein, Stanley J., and Stein, Barbara H. *The Colonial Heritage of Latin America: Essays on Economic Development in Perspective.* New York: Oxford University Press, 1970.

Stone, Irving. "British Long-Term Investment in Latin America, 1865–1913," *Business History Review,* 42 (Autumn 1968): 311–339.

Sturges, Kenneth. *American Chambers of Commerce.* New York: Moffat Bard, 1915.

Suzigan, Wilson. *Indústria Brasileira: Origem e Desenvolvimento.* São Paulo: Brasiliense, 1986.

"Investimento na Indústria de Transformação no Brasil, 1869–1939: Uma Visão Geral," *Pesquisa e Planejamento Econômico,* 15 (Aug. 1985): 369–399.

Swartz, W. R. "Codification in Latin America: The Brazilian Commercial Code of 1850," *Texas International Law Journal,* 10 (1975): 347–356.

Sweigart, Joseph E. "Financing and Marketing Brazilian Export Agriculture: The Coffee Factors of Rio de Janeiro, 1850–1888." Ph.D. Diss., University of Texas, 1980.

Tannuri, Luiz Antônio. *O Encilhamento.* São Paulo: Hucitec/Fundação de Desenvolvimento da UNICAMP, 1981.

Taunay, Afonso de Escragnolle. *História do Café no Brasil.* 15 vols. Rio de Janeiro: Departamento Nacional do Café, 1939–1943.

Tavares, Luís Henrique Dias. *Comércio Proibido de Escravos.* São Paulo: Atica, 1988.

Tedlow, Richard S. *Keeping the Corporate Image: Public Relations and Business, 1900–1950.* Greenwich, Conn.: JAI Press, 1979.

Tischendorf, Alfred. "The Recife and San Francisco Railway Company, 1854–1860," *Inter-American Economic Affairs,* 13 (Spring 1960): 87–94.

Topik, Steven. "The Evolution of the Economic Role of the Brazilian State, 1889–1930," *Journal of Latin American Studies,* 11 (Nov. 1979): 325–342.

"Francisco de Paula Mayrink of Brazil: A Bourgeois Aristocrat," in *The Human Tradition in Latin America: The Nineteenth Century.* Edited by Judith Ewell and William H. Beezley. Wilmington, Del.: Scholarly Resources, 1987.

"The Old Republic," in *Modern Brazil: Elites and Masses in Historical Perspective.* Edited by Michael L. Conniff and Frank D. McCann. Lincoln, Neb.: University of Nebraska Press, 1989.

The Political Economy of the Brazilian State, 1889–1930. Austin: University of Texas Press, 1987.

"State Autonomy in Economic Policy: Brazil's Experience, 1822–1930," *Journal of Interamerican Studies and World Affairs*, 26 (Nov. 1984): 449–476.

"The State's Contribution to the Development of Brazil's Internal Economy, 1850–1930," *Hispanic American Historical Review*, 65 (May 1985): 203–228.

Toplin, Robert Brent. *The Abolition of Slavery in Brazil*. New York: Athneum, 1975.

Tôrres, João Camillo de Oliveira. *Os Construtores do Império*. São Paulo: Editôra Nacional, 1968.

"Paraná e a Conciliação," *Revista Brasileira de Estudos Políticos*, 1 (Dec. 1956): 94–100.

O Presidencialismo no Brasil. Rio de Janeiro: O Cruzeiro, 1962.

Tourinho, J. Caetano. "Associação Comercial da Bahia: Apontamentos para sua História, sua Fundação, seu Desenvolvimento," *Jornal de Notícias* (Salvador), July 15, 1911.

O Treze de Novembro de 1899 na Capital da Bahia (Subsídios Para a História). Salvador: Diário da Bahia, 1900.

Trochim, Michael. "The Brazilian Black Guard: Racial Conflict in Post-Abolition Brazil," *The Americas*, 44 (Jan. 1988): 285–300.

"Retreat from Reform: The Fall of the Brazilian Empire, 1888–1889." Ph.D. Diss., University of Illinois at Chicago Circle, 1983.

Truman, David. *The Governmental Process: Political Interests and Public Opinion*. New York: Alfred A. Knopf, 1962.

Uricoechea, Fernando. *O Minotauro Imperial: A Burocratização do Estado Patrimonial Brasileiro no Século XIX*. Rio de Janeiro, São Paulo: DIFEL, 1978.

Valverde, M. S. L. *Subsídio para a História da Associação Comercial da Bahia*. Salvador: Duas Américas, 1917.

Van Delden Laërne, C. F. *Brazil and Java: Report on Coffee Culture in America, Asia, and Africa*. London: W. H. Allen, 1885.

Veiga Filho, João Pedro da. *Estudo Econômico e Financeiro sôbre o Estado de São Paulo*. São Paulo: Diário Oficial, 1896.

Velho Sobrinho, João Francisco. *Dicionário Bio-Bibliográfico Brasileiro*. Rio de Janeiro: Irmãos Pongetti, 1937.

Versiani, Flávio Rabelo. "Industrial Investment in an 'Export' Economy: The Brazilian Experience Before 1914," *Journal of Development Economics*, (Sept. 1980): 307–327.

Versiani, Flávio Rabelo, and Versiani, Maria Teresa R. O. "A Industrialização Brasileira Antes de 1930: Uma Contribuição," in *Formação Econômica do Brasil: A Experiência da Industrialização*. Edited by Flávio Versiani and José Roberto Mendonça de Barros. São Paulo: Saraiva, 1977.

Viana Filho, Luís. *A Vida de Rui Barbosa*. 7th ed. revised. São Paulo: Martins, 1965.

Vianna, Hélio. *Vultos do Império*. São Paulo: Editôra Nacional, 1968.

Victorino, Carlos. *Santos: Reminiscências (1875–1898)*. São Paulo: By the Author, 1904.

Vieira, Dorival Teixeira. *Evolução do Sistema Monetário Brasileiro*. São Paulo: Universidade de São Paulo, 1962.

Villela, Anibal Villanova, and Suzigan, Wilson. *Política do Govêrno e Crescimento da Economia Brasileira, 1889–1945*. Rio de Janeiro: IPEA/INPES, 1975.

Vincent, Frank. *Around and About South America: Twenty Months of Quest and Query*. 5th ed. New York: D. Appleton, 1895.

Viola, Jorge Navarro. *El Club de Residentes Estranjeros: Breve Reseña Histórica en Homenaje a sus Fundadores*. Buenos Aires: Coni, 1941.

Viveiros, Jerônimo de. *História do Comércio do Maranhão, 1612–1895*. 2 vols. São Luís: Associação Comercial do Maranhão, 1954.

Von der Weid, Elizabeth, et al. *Apontamentos para a História do Centro Industrial do Rio de Janeiro: Edição Comemorativa do Sesquicentenário do Centro Industrial do Rio de Janeiro*. Rio de Janeiro: Centro Industrial do Rio de Janeiro, 1977.

Von Spix, Johann B., and von Martius, Karl F. P. *Travels in Brazil in the Years 1817–1820, Undertaken by Command of His Majesty the King of Bavaria.* Vol. 1. London: Longman Hurst, Rees, Orme, Brown, and Green, 1824.

Weinstein, Barbara. *The Amazon Rubber Boom, 1850–1920.* Stanford, Calif.: Stanford University Press, 1983.

Wells, James W. *Exploring and Traveling Three Thousand Miles Through Brazil from Rio de Janeiro to Maranhão.* 2 vols. London: Low, Searle, and Rivington, 1886.

Wetherell, James. *Stray Notes from Bahia.* Liverpool: Webb and Hunt, 1860.

Wheatley, Richard. "The New York Chamber of Commerce," *Harper's Magazine,* 83 (Sept. 1891): 502–517.

Wiarda, Howard J. "Corporatism and Development in the Iberic-Latin World: Persistent Strains and New Variations," in *The New Corporatism: Social-Political Structures in the Iberian World.* Edited by Frederick B. Pike and Thomas Stritch. Notre Dame, Ind.: University of Notre Dame Press, 1974.

Wildberger, Arnold. *Os Presidentes da Província da Bahia, Efetivos e Interinos, 1824–1889.* Salvador: Beneditina, 1949.

Wileman, J. P. *Brazilian Exchange: The Study of an Incontrovertible Currency* [1896]. Reprint edition. New York: Greenwood Press, 1969.

——— ed. *The Brazilian Year Book.* 2 vols. New York: G. R. Fairbanks, 1908–1909.

Winks, Robin W. "On Decolonization and Informal Empire," *American Historical Review,* 81 (June 1976): 540–556.

Winn, Peter. *El Imperio Informal Británico en el Uruguay en el Siglo XIX.* Montevideo: Ediciones de la Banda Oriental, 1975.

Wolf, Howard, and Wolf, Ralph. *Rubber: A Story of Glory and Greed.* New York: Covici, Friede, 1936.

Woodward, Ralph Lee. *Class Privilege and Economic Development: The Consulado de Comercio of Guatemala, 1793–1871.* Chapel Hill: University of North Carolina Press, 1966.

Wootton, Graham. *Interest Groups.* Englewood Cliffs, N.J.: Prentice Hall, 1970.

——— *Interest Groups: Policy and Politics in America.* Englewood Cliffs, N.J.: Prentice-Hall, 1985.

——— *Pressure Groups in Britain, 1720–1970: An Essay in Interpretation with Original Documents.* London: Allen Lane, 1975.

Wright, Antônia Fernanda Pacca de Almeida. *Desafio Americano à Preponderância Britânica no Brasil, 1808–1850.* Rio de Janeiro: Imprensa Nacional, 1972.

Wright, George Henry. *Chronicles of the Birmingham Chamber of Commerce, A.D. 1813–1913, and of the Birmingham Commercial Society, A.D. 1783–1812.* Birmingham: Birmingham Chamber of Commerce, 1913.

Wright, Walter. *A Few Facts About Brazil, by a Twenty Years' Resident in That Country.* Birmingham: Cornish Brothers, 1892.

Zisk, Betty H. "Interest Groups and the Political Process," in *American Political Interest Groups: Readings in Theory and Research.* Edited by Betty H. Zisk. Belmont, Calif.: Wadsworth, 1969.

Index

abolition of slavery: abolitionist movement, 159–60; effects by province, 167–8; reaction by business interest groups, 168–9; rural credit, effect on, 150

Abrantes, Miguel Calmon du Pin e Almeida, Marquis, 23

Agricultural, Commercial, and Industrial Society of Bahia, 23–5

Agricultural Congress of Rio de Janeiro in 1884, 162

agricultural credit: 132–3, 144–52; factors as source, 94–5; reasons for lack of, 144–6; reform of legislation, 149–50; see also crop collateral

Agricultural Industrial Center: and annulment of binding labor contracts, 167; and commercial associations, 219; dates of activity, 55; history, 219–20; rural land tax advocacy, 219; Special Tariff for Rio Grande do Sul, 219–20

agricultural interest groups, 55–7; reasons for scarcity of, 57; see also agricultural societies and clubs

agricultural societies and clubs, 56, 161, 162

agriculture: business interest group impact on, 120–1; and business interest groups, 4, 332–3; commercial association concern for, 93–4; commercial associations as spokesmen for, 93–4; innovations, 9, 97–8; technological backwardness, 96–8, 332; see also planters

Agriculture Auxiliary Society of Pernambuco: and central sugar mills, 108; coffee growing in province, promotion of, 117; legislation protecting borrowers, 146; low exchange rate advocacy, 141; membership and aims, 56–7; mortgage bank, 135; Political Center for Farming, Commerce, and Industry, 325; proslavery congress organizer, 163

Agriculture Club of Campinas, São Paulo, 56

Agriculture and Commerce Club, 160

Aid to Agriculture bill, 150–1

Aid to Industry bill, 223–4

Alagôas (province and state), 103–4, 222; see also Commercial Association of Maceió

Amazonas (province and state), 197, 198–9, 247; see also Commercial Association of Amazonas

Amazon Navigation and Commerce Company, 247–8

Amazon region, 118–19, 128–31, 247–8

Amazon Steam Navigation Company, 248–9

annual reports, 46–7, 71, 299

Araújo, José Antônio de, 277

Arcos, count dos , 18

arson, 291

Auxiliary Society for National Industry: activities, 55; applications for patents evaluation, 58; Brazil's foremost learned society, 24; as supporter of industrialization, 214–15; tariff debate of 1877, 215

aviadores: and Commercial Association of Pará, 128, 130–1; conflict against exporters, 89, 128–31; importance in Amazon, 128–9; see also factors

Bahia (province and state): cacao, 118; coffee, 114, 116, 118; and Commercial Association of Bahia, 75; *coronelismo*, 326; cotton, 104; counterfeiting, 291–2; European goods in, 202–3; federalism in, 23–4; immigration, public support for, 171, 172; industrialization, 203, 204, 208–9; industrialization, provincial aid for, 207–8; provincial export tax rates, 198; provincial tariffs, 186–90; public debt, 189–90; Republic, early years of, 325–8; rural credit lacking, 144; slavery, transition from, 167; statistics, lack of, 298; tobacco, 117–8; traveling salesmen, tax on, 294–5; *usina*, 109; see also Commercial Association of Bahia

Bahian Immigration Society, 172

Bahian Navigation Company, 31

365